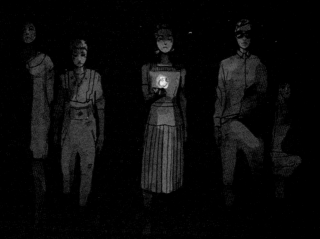

MISS PEREGRINE'S
HOME FOR
PECULIAR CHILDREN

— THE GRAPHIC NOVEL —

STORY BY RANSOM RIGGS   ART BY CASSANDRA JEAN

Yen
Press

MISS PEREGRINE'S HOME FOR PECULIAR CHILDREN:
THE GRAPHIC NOVEL

Adaption and Illustration: Cassandra Jean
Lettering: JuYoun Lee & Stephanie Lee

Yen Press
1290 Avenue of the Americas
New York, NY 10104

www.YenPress.com

Yen Press is an imprint of Yen Press, LLC.
The Yen Press name and logo are trademarks of Yen Press, LLC.
First Edition: October 2013

ISBN: 978-0-316-24528-9

10 9 8 7 6 5 4

WOR

Printed in the United States of America

GROWING UP, GRANDPA PORTMAN WAS THE MOST FASCINATING PERSON I KNEW, AND I BEGGED HIM TO REGALE ME WITH STORIES WHENEVER I SAW HIM.

HE HAD LIVED IN AN ORPHANAGE, FOUGHT IN WARS, CROSSED OCEANS BY STEAMSHIP AND DESERTS ON HORSEBACK, PERFORMED IN CIRCUSES, KNEW EVERYTHING ABOUT GUNS AND SELF-DEFENSE AND SURVIVING IN THE WILDERNESS.

THE TALLEST TALES WERE ALWAYS ABOUT HIS CHILDHOOD, LIKE HOW HE WAS BORN IN POLAND BUT AT TWELVE HAD BEEN SHIPPED OFF TO A CHILDREN'S HOME IN WALES BECAUSE THE MONSTERS WERE AFTER HIM. IT WAS AN ENCHANTED PLACE, HE SAID, DESIGNED TO KEEP KIDS SAFE FROM THE MONSTERS, ON AN ISLAND WHERE THE SUN SHINED EVERY DAY AND NOBODY EVER GOT SICK OR DIED. EVERYONE LIVED TOGETHER IN A BIG HOUSE THAT WAS PROTECTED BY A WISE OLD BIRD.

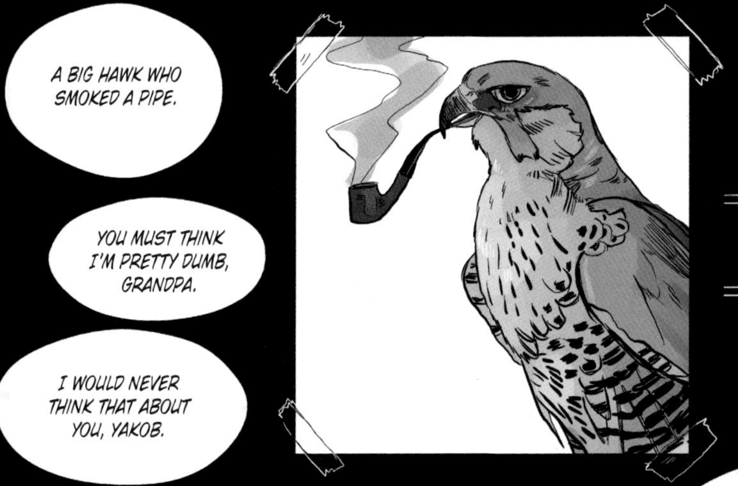
A BIG HAWK WHO SMOKED A PIPE.
YOU MUST THINK I'M PRETTY DUMB, GRANDPA.
I WOULD NEVER THINK THAT ABOUT YOU, YAKOB.

CHAPTER ONE

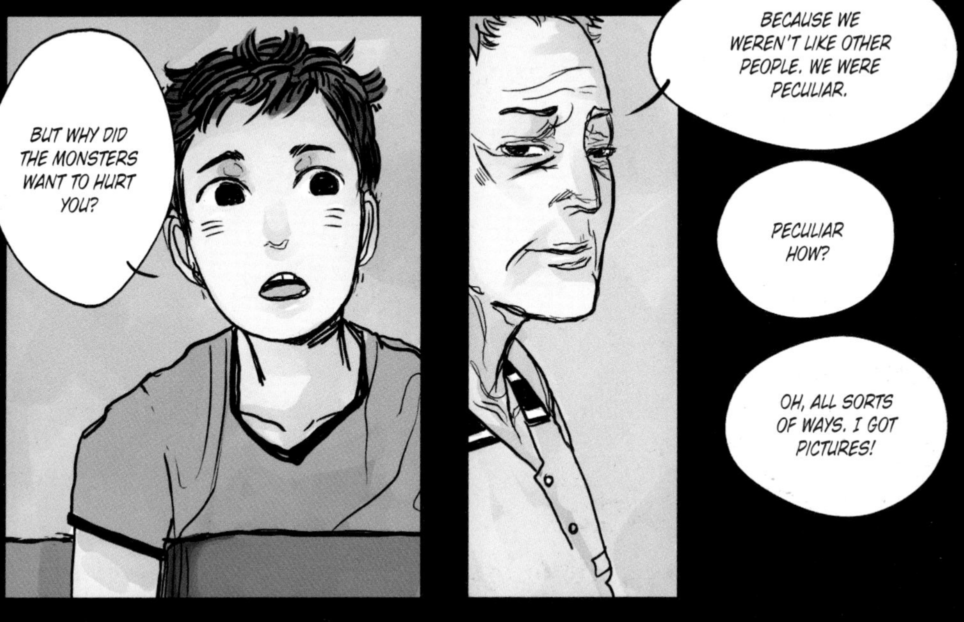
BUT WHY DID THE MONSTERS WANT TO HURT YOU?
BECAUSE WE WEREN'T LIKE OTHER PEOPLE. WE WERE PECULIAR.
PECULIAR HOW?
OH, ALL SORTS OF WAYS. I GOT PICTURES!

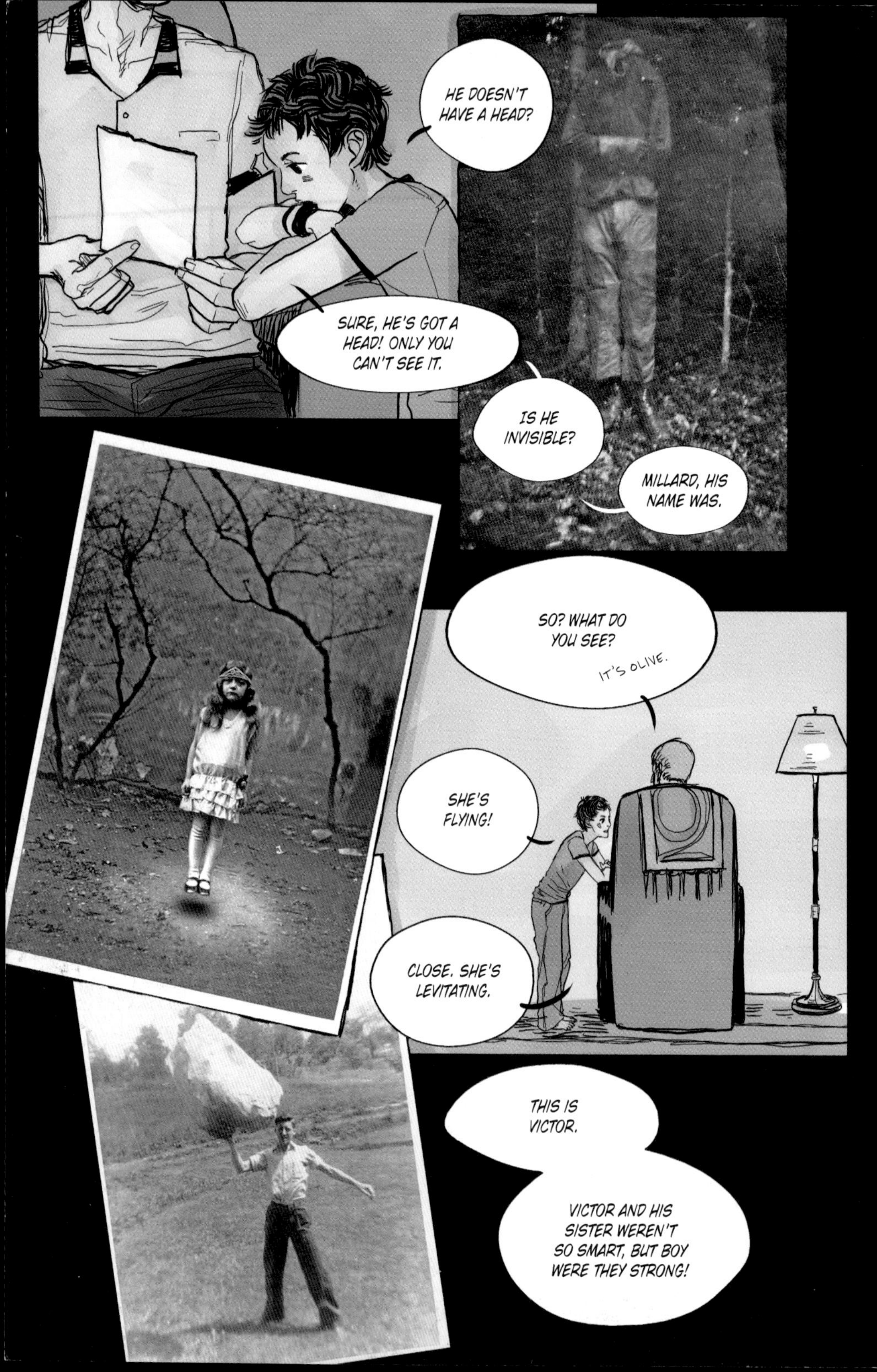
HE DOESN'T HAVE A HEAD?
SURE, HE'S GOT A HEAD! ONLY YOU CAN'T SEE IT.
IS HE INVISIBLE?
MILLARD, HIS NAME WAS.
SO? WHAT DO YOU SEE?
IT'S OLIVE.
SHE'S FLYING!
CLOSE. SHE'S LEVITATING.
THIS IS VICTOR.
VICTOR AND HIS SISTER WEREN'T SO SMART, BUT BOY WERE THEY STRONG!

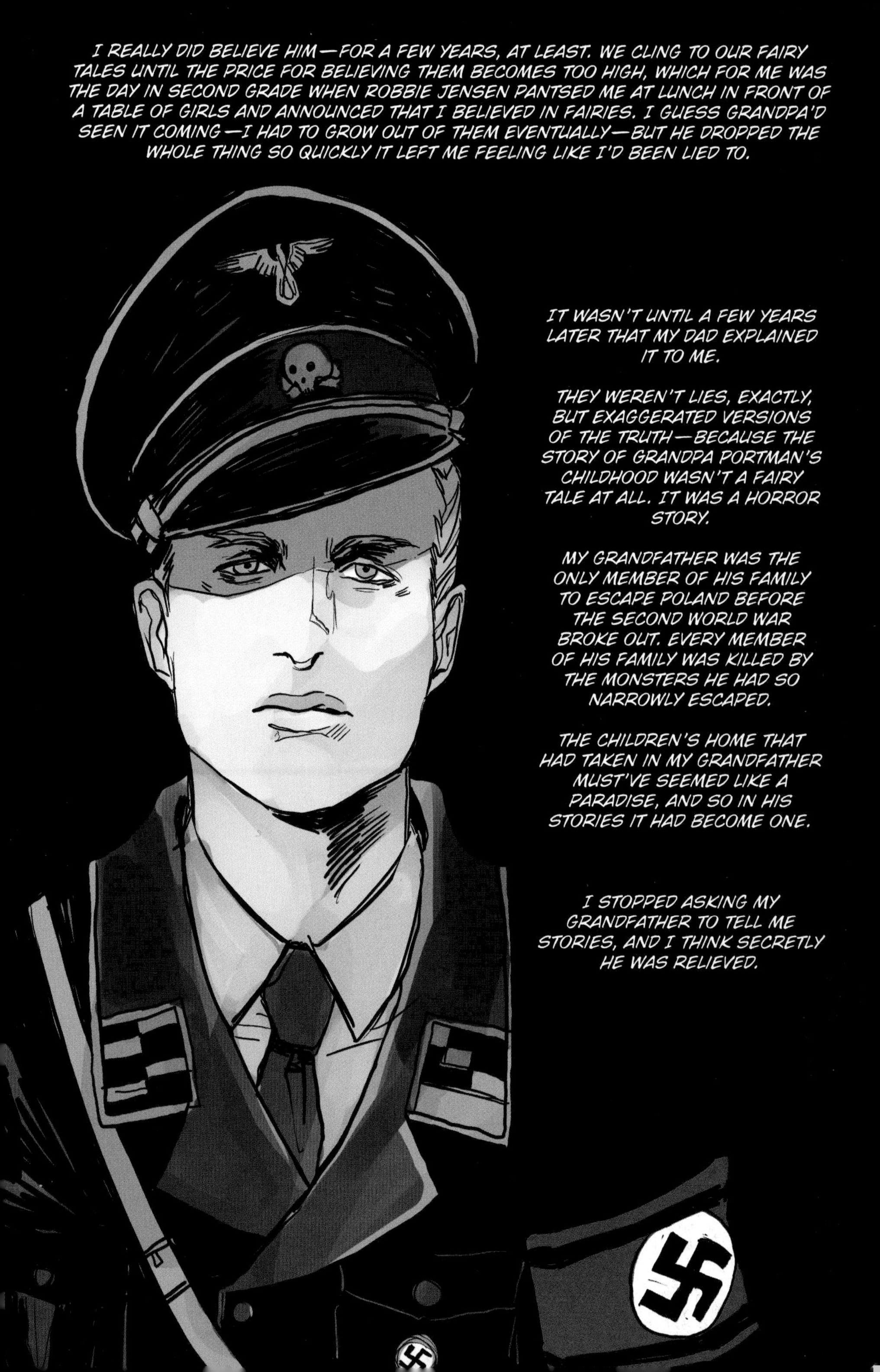
I REALLY DID BELIEVE HIM—FOR A FEW YEARS, AT LEAST. WE CLING TO OUR FAIRY TALES UNTIL THE PRICE FOR BELIEVING THEM BECOMES TOO HIGH, WHICH FOR ME WAS THE DAY IN SECOND GRADE WHEN ROBBIE JENSEN PANTSED ME AT LUNCH IN FRONT OF A TABLE OF GIRLS AND ANNOUNCED THAT I BELIEVED IN FAIRIES. I GUESS GRANDPA'D SEEN IT COMING—I HAD TO GROW OUT OF THEM EVENTUALLY—BUT HE DROPPED THE WHOLE THING SO QUICKLY IT LEFT ME FEELING LIKE I'D BEEN LIED TO.
IT WASN'T UNTIL A FEW YEARS LATER THAT MY DAD EXPLAINED IT TO ME.
THEY WEREN'T LIES, EXACTLY, BUT EXAGGERATED VERSIONS OF THE TRUTH—BECAUSE THE STORY OF GRANDPA PORTMAN'S CHILDHOOD WASN'T A FAIRY TALE AT ALL. IT WAS A HORROR STORY.
MY GRANDFATHER WAS THE ONLY MEMBER OF HIS FAMILY TO ESCAPE POLAND BEFORE THE SECOND WORLD WAR BROKE OUT. EVERY MEMBER OF HIS FAMILY WAS KILLED BY THE MONSTERS HE HAD SO NARROWLY ESCAPED.
THE CHILDREN'S HOME THAT HAD TAKEN IN MY GRANDFATHER MUST'VE SEEMED LIKE A PARADISE, AND SO IN HIS STORIES IT HAD BECOME ONE.
I STOPPED ASKING MY GRANDFATHER TO TELL ME STORIES, AND I THINK SECRETLY HE WAS RELIEVED.

I FELT ASHAMED FOR HAVING BEEN JEALOUS OF HIS LIFE, AND TRIED TO FEEL LUCKY FOR THE SAFE AND UNEXTRAORDINARY ONE THAT I HAD DONE NOTHING TO DESERVE. THEN, WHEN I WAS FIFTEEN, AN EXTRAORDINARY AND TERRIBLE THING HAPPENED, AND THERE WAS ONLY

BEFORE AND AFTER.

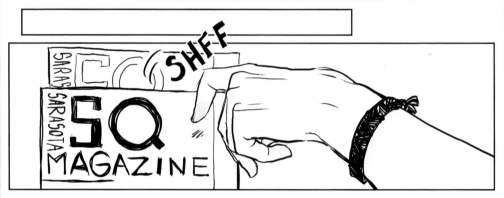

SHFF

SARASOTA

SARASOTA

5Q
MAGAZINE

I HATE THIS JOB...

CARS

5Q MAGAZINE

FLORIDA

Poise ♥

MAYBE IF I MISSHELVE ALL OF THESE, THEY'LL FINALLY FIRE ME.

SMART ✚ AID

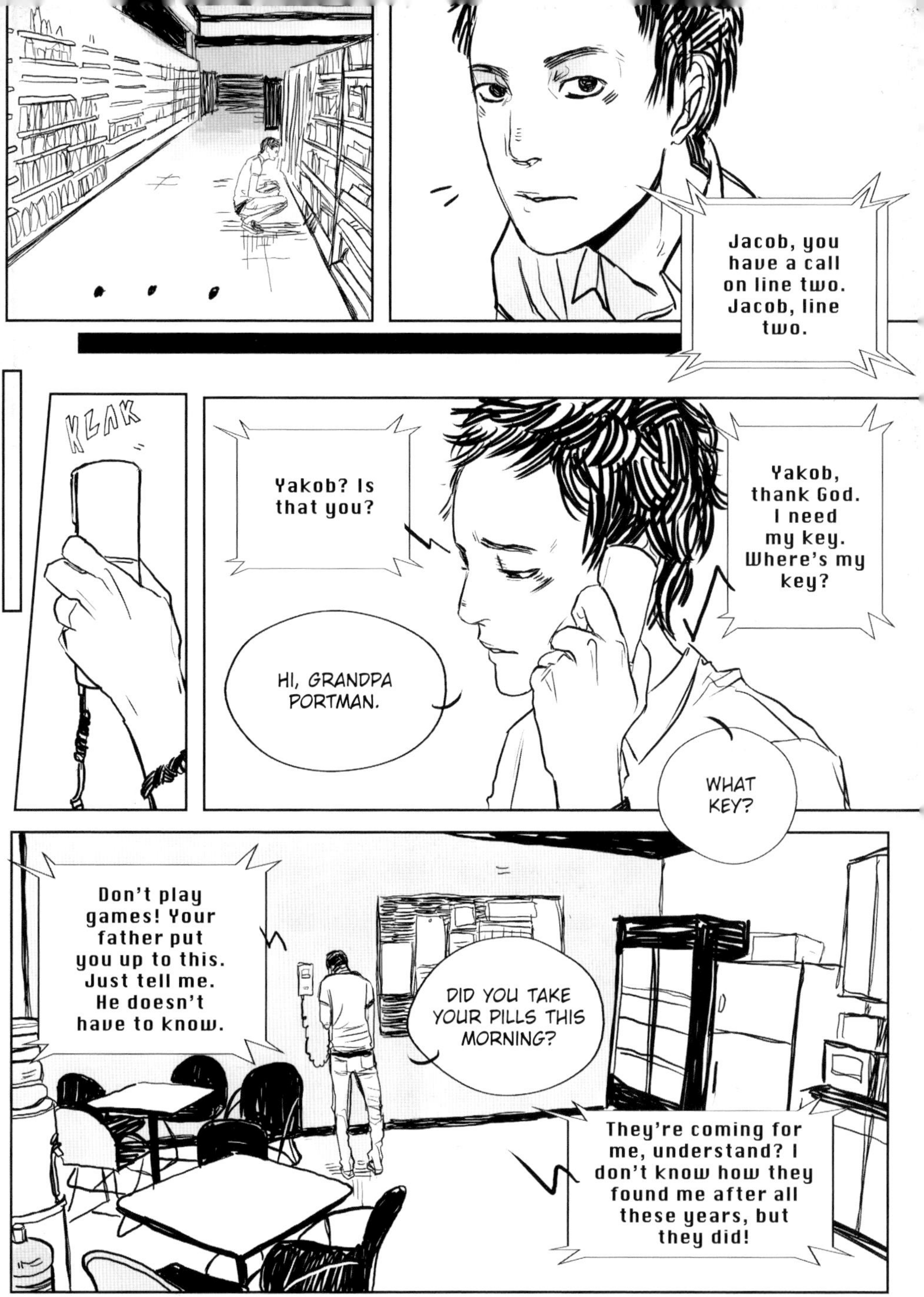
Jacob, you have a call on line two. Jacob, line two.
KLAK
Yakob? Is that you?
Yakob, thank God. I need my key. Where's my key?
HI, GRANDPA PORTMAN.
WHAT KEY?
Don't play games! Your father put you up to this. Just tell me. He doesn't have to know.
DID YOU TAKE YOUR PILLS THIS MORNING?
They're coming for me, understand? I don't know how they found me after all these years, but they did!

IT WASN'T THE FIRST TIME I'D HEARD HIM TALK LIKE THIS. MY GRANDFATHER WAS GETTING OLD, AND FRANKLY HE WAS STARTING TO LOSE IT. THE FANTASTIC STORIES HE'D INVENTED ABOUT HIS LIFE DURING THE WAR—THE MONSTERS, THE ENCHANTED ISLAND—HAD BECOME COMPLETELY, OPPRESSIVELY REAL TO HIM.

BANG

You stay away, hear me? I'll be fine— cut out their tongues and stab them in the eyes, that's all you gotta do! If I could just find that goddamned KEY!

SCUFF

GRANDPA—

:KLIK:

I'D BETTER STOP BY AND MAKE SURE HE'S OKAY...

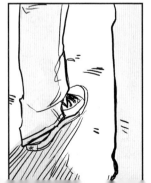

THE KEY HE WAS TALKING ABOUT OPENED A GIANT LOCKER FULL OF GUNS AND KNIVES. IF THIS KEEPS UP, DAD IS GOING TO PUT HIM IN A HOME...

WHO AM I KIDDING? DAD HAS ALREADY DECIDED. BUT WHY? I CAN HANDLE GRANDPA...

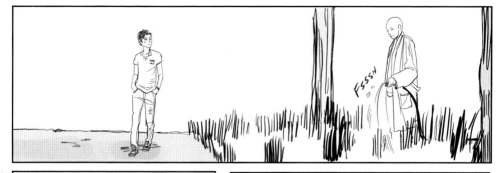

··· HE'S BLIND?

GRANDPA?

?!

CREEK

WHAT HAPPENED?

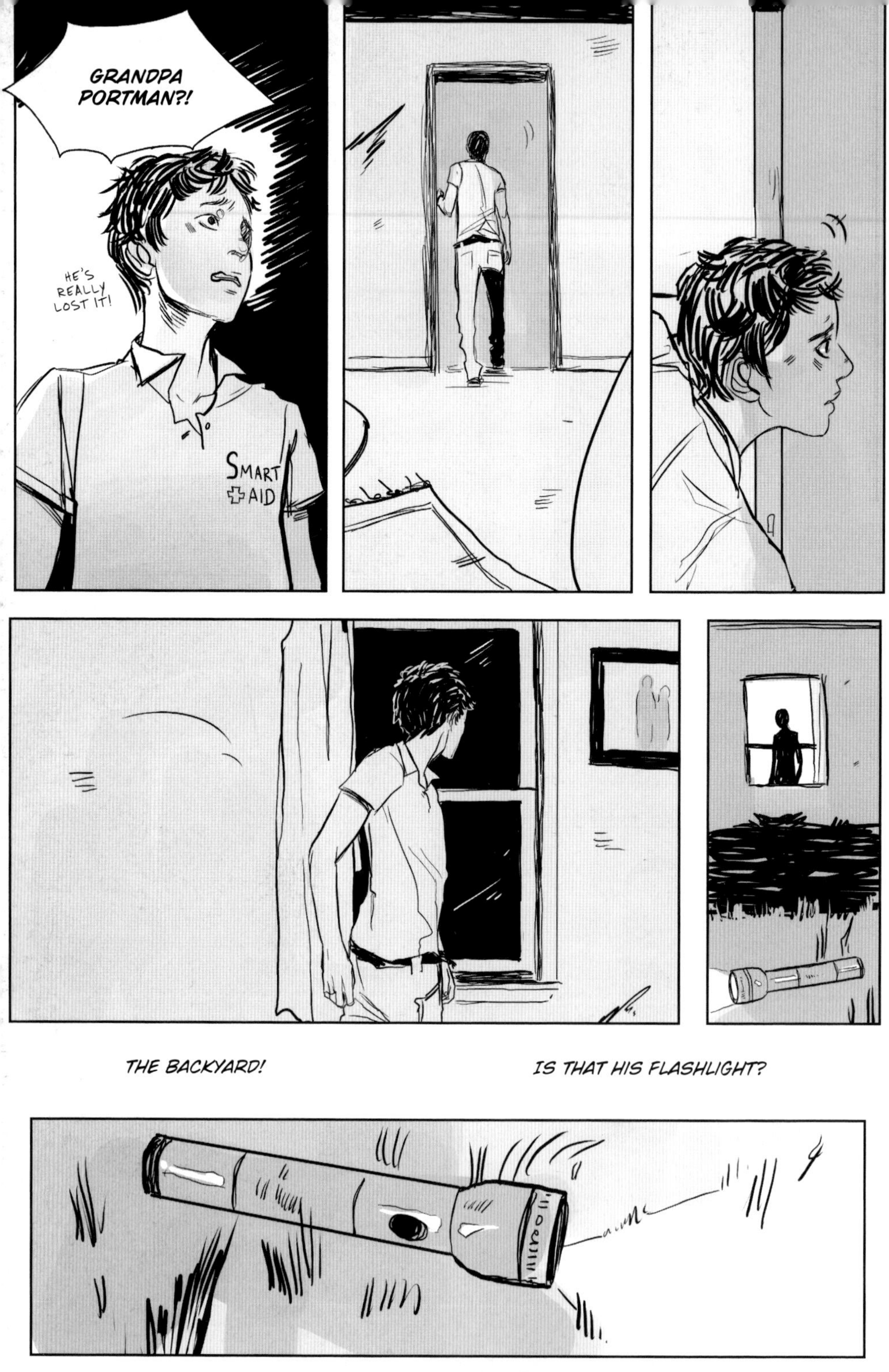
GRANDPA PORTMAN?!
HE'S REALLY LOST IT!
SMART AID
THE BACKYARD!
IS THAT HIS FLASHLIGHT?

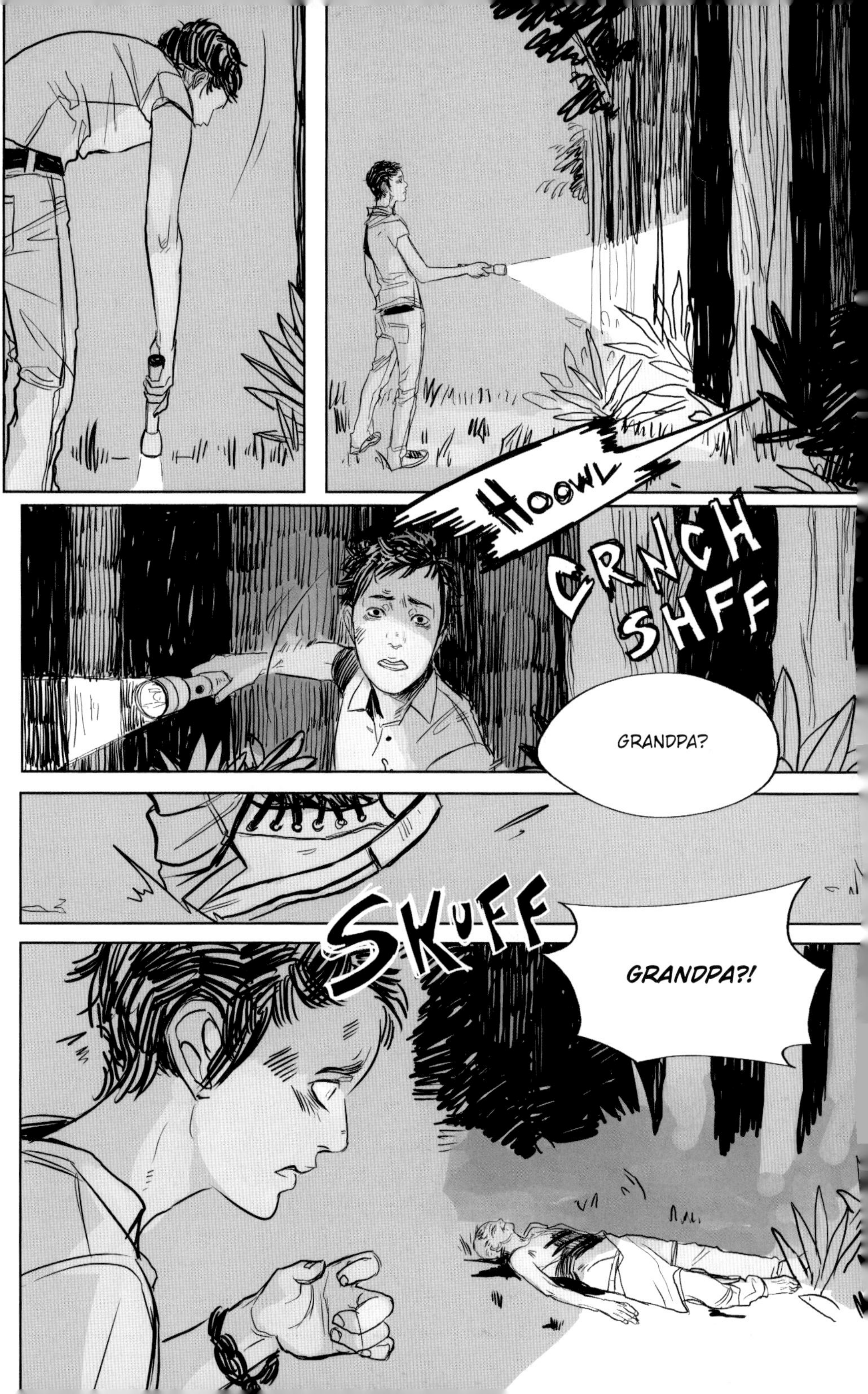
HOOWL
CRNCH
SHFF
GRANDPA?
SKUFF
GRANDPA?!

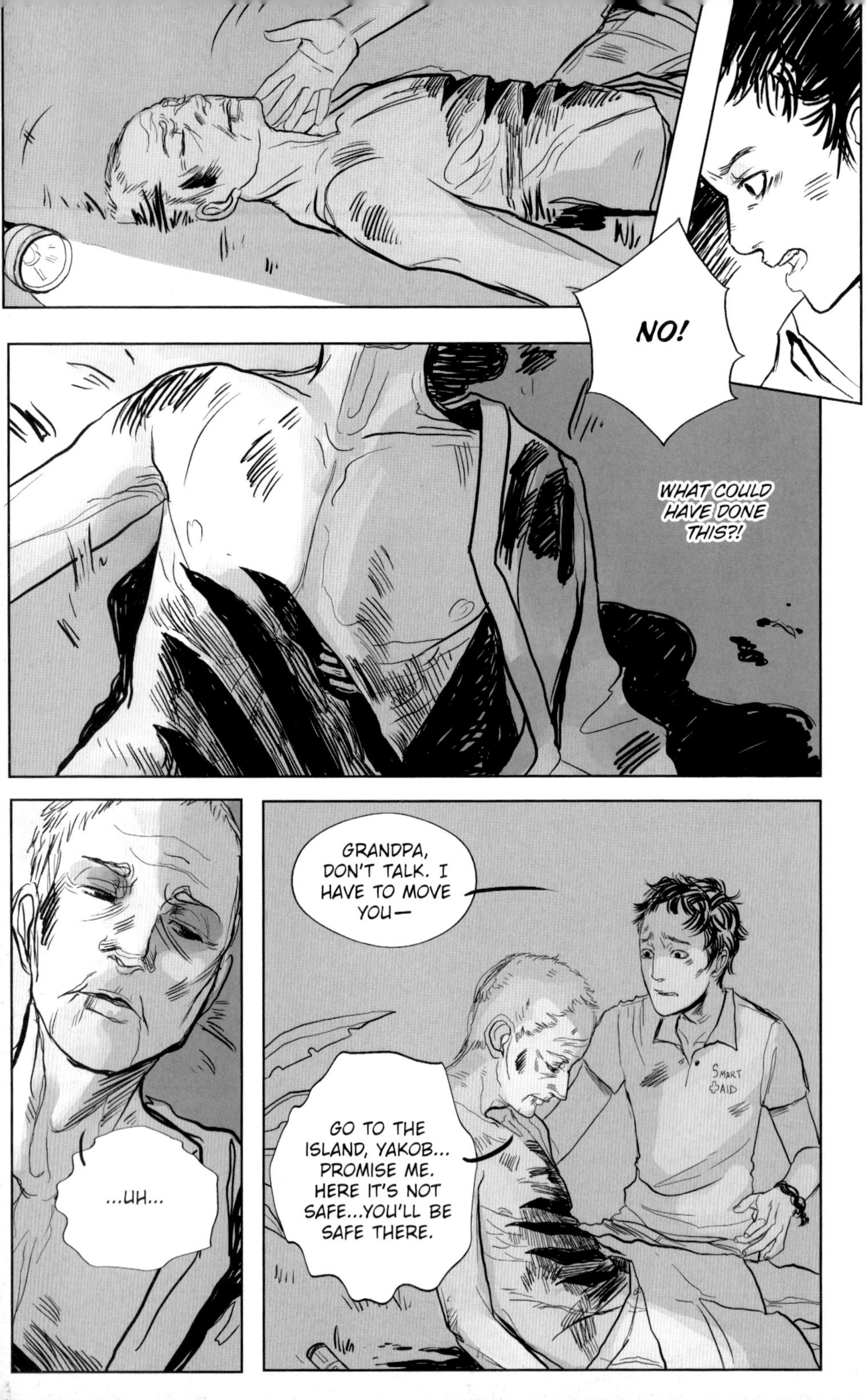
NO!
WHAT COULD HAVE DONE THIS?!
...UH...
GRANDPA, DON'T TALK. I HAVE TO MOVE YOU—
SMART AID
GO TO THE ISLAND, YAKOB... PROMISE ME. HERE IT'S NOT SAFE...YOU'LL BE SAFE THERE.

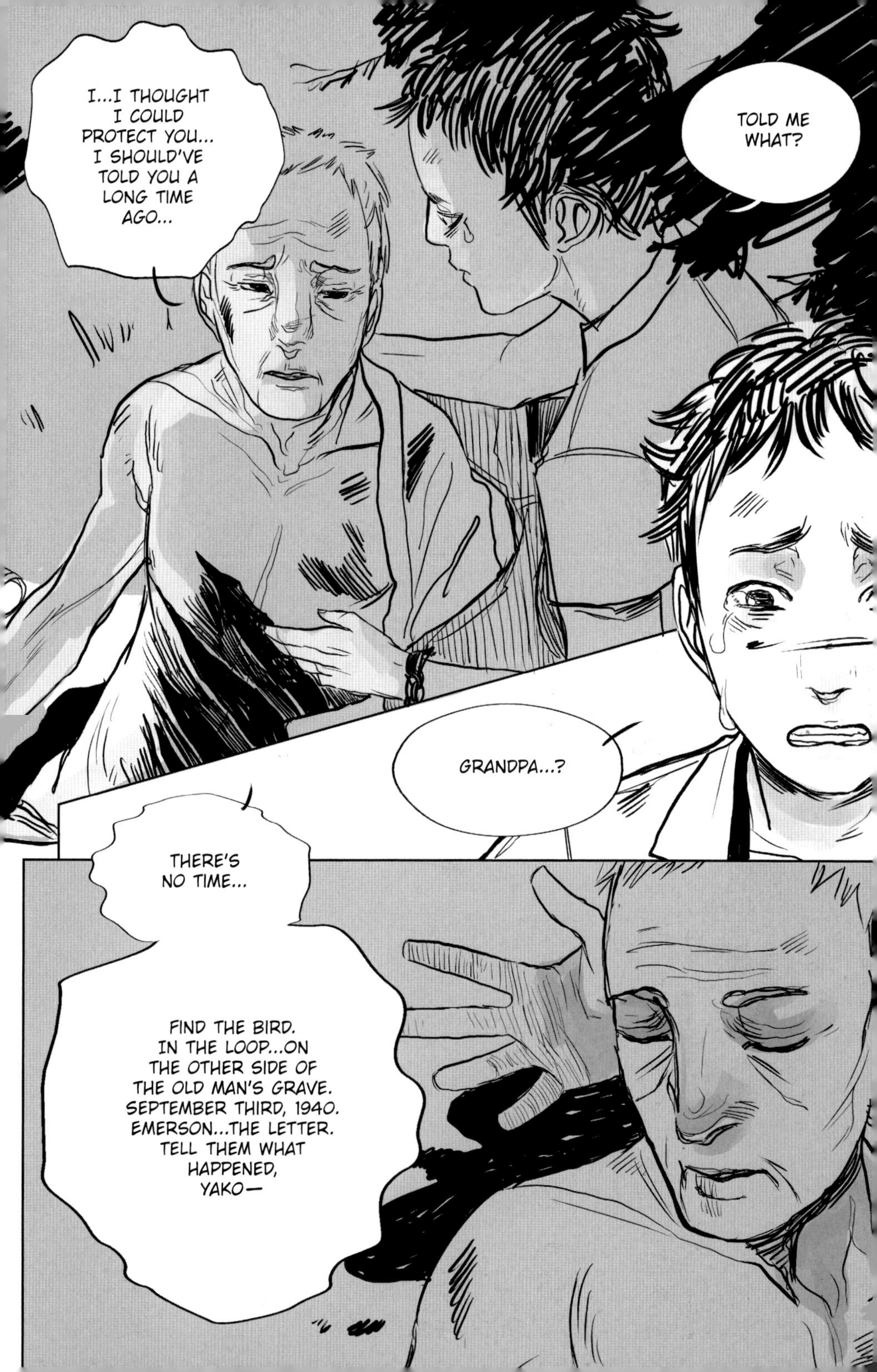
I...I THOUGHT I COULD PROTECT YOU... I SHOULD'VE TOLD YOU A LONG TIME AGO...
TOLD ME WHAT?
GRANDPA...?
THERE'S NO TIME...
FIND THE BIRD. IN THE LOOP...ON THE OTHER SIDE OF THE OLD MAN'S GRAVE. SEPTEMBER THIRD, 1940. EMERSON...THE LETTER. TELL THEM WHAT HAPPENED, YAKO—

TREMBLE

GRANDPA...

SNUFF

I LOVE YOU.

GRRR JOLT

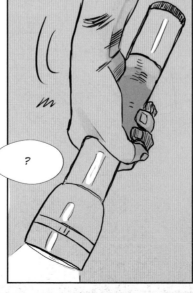

?

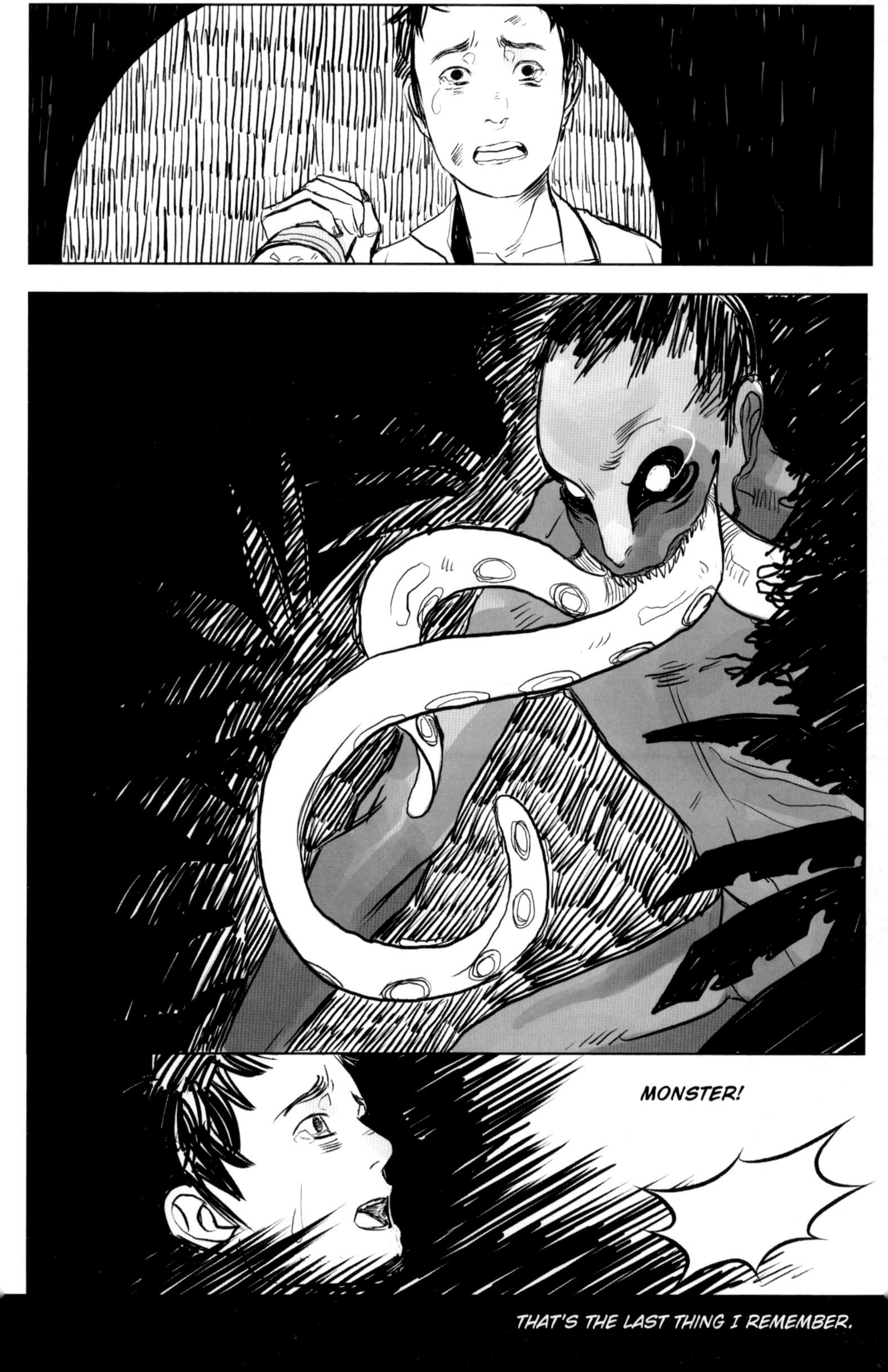
MONSTER!
THAT'S THE LAST THING I REMEMBER.

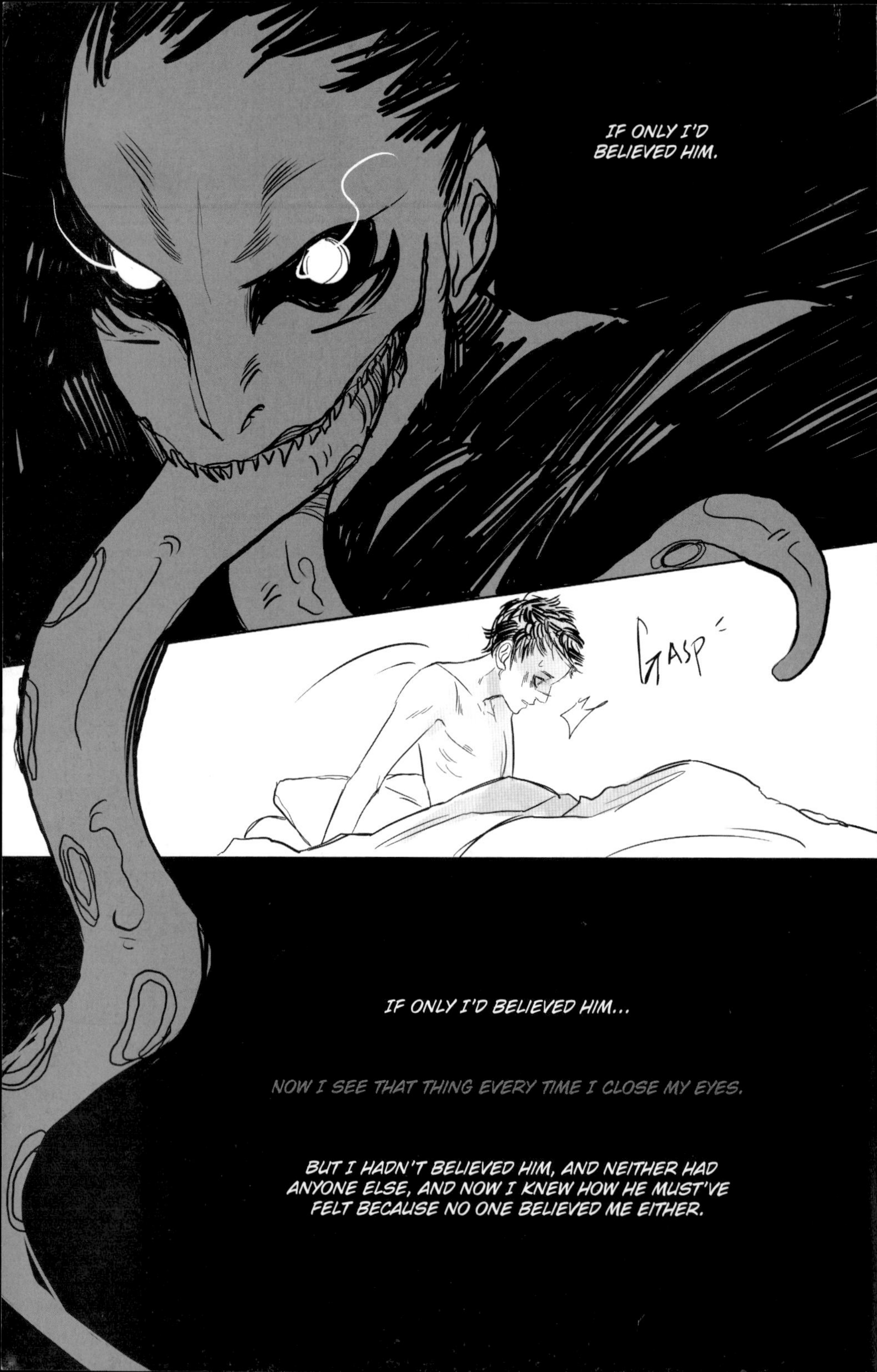
IF ONLY I'D BELIEVED HIM.
GASP
IF ONLY I'D BELIEVED HIM...
NOW I SEE THAT THING EVERY TIME I CLOSE MY EYES.
BUT I HADN'T BELIEVED HIM, AND NEITHER HAD ANYONE ELSE, AND NOW I KNEW HOW HE MUST'VE FELT BECAUSE NO ONE BELIEVED ME EITHER.

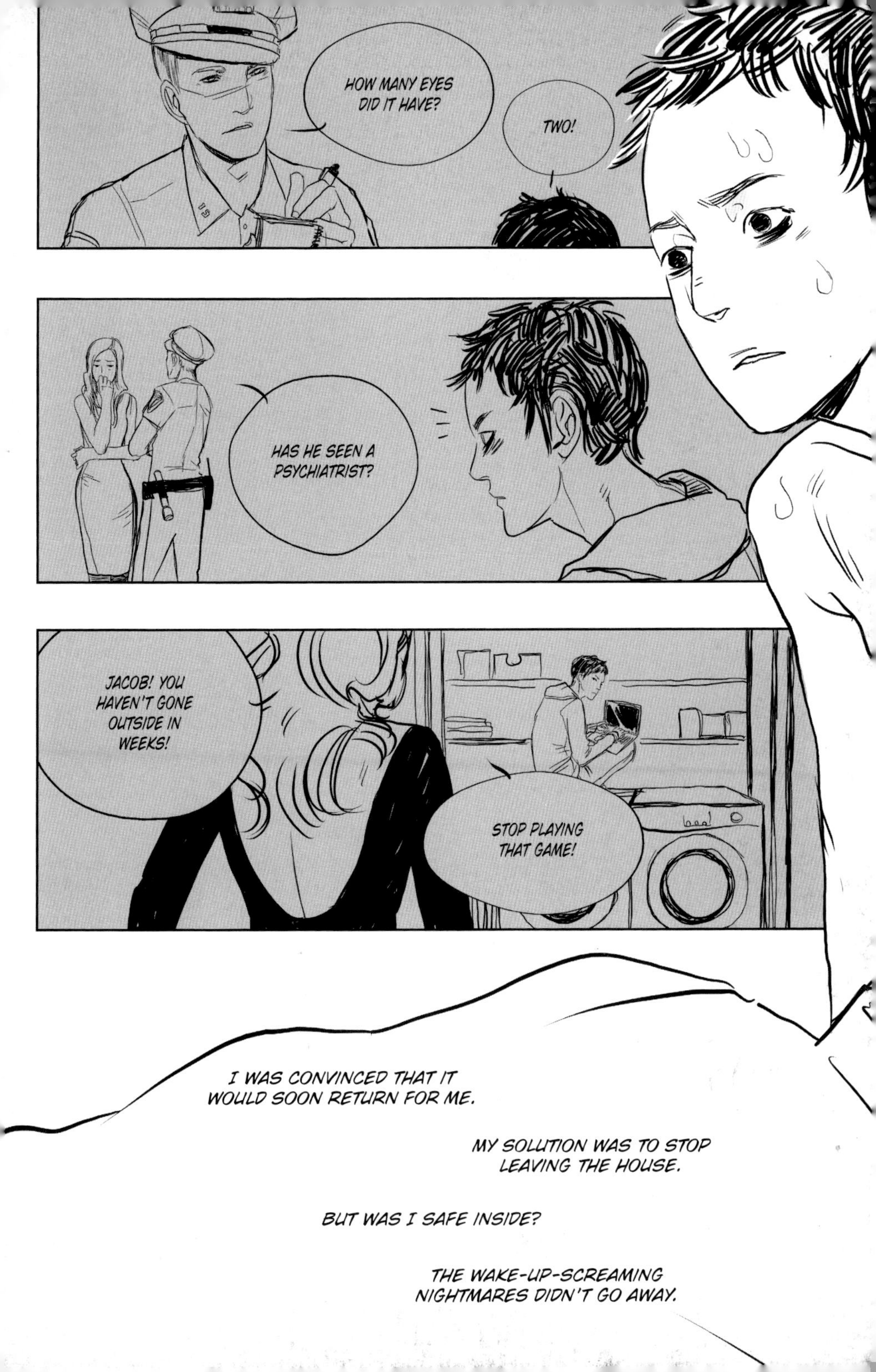
HOW MANY EYES DID IT HAVE?
TWO!
HAS HE SEEN A PSYCHIATRIST?
JACOB! YOU HAVEN'T GONE OUTSIDE IN WEEKS!
STOP PLAYING THAT GAME!
I WAS CONVINCED THAT IT WOULD SOON RETURN FOR ME.
MY SOLUTION WAS TO STOP LEAVING THE HOUSE.
BUT WAS I SAFE INSIDE?
THE WAKE-UP-SCREAMING NIGHTMARES DIDN'T GO AWAY.

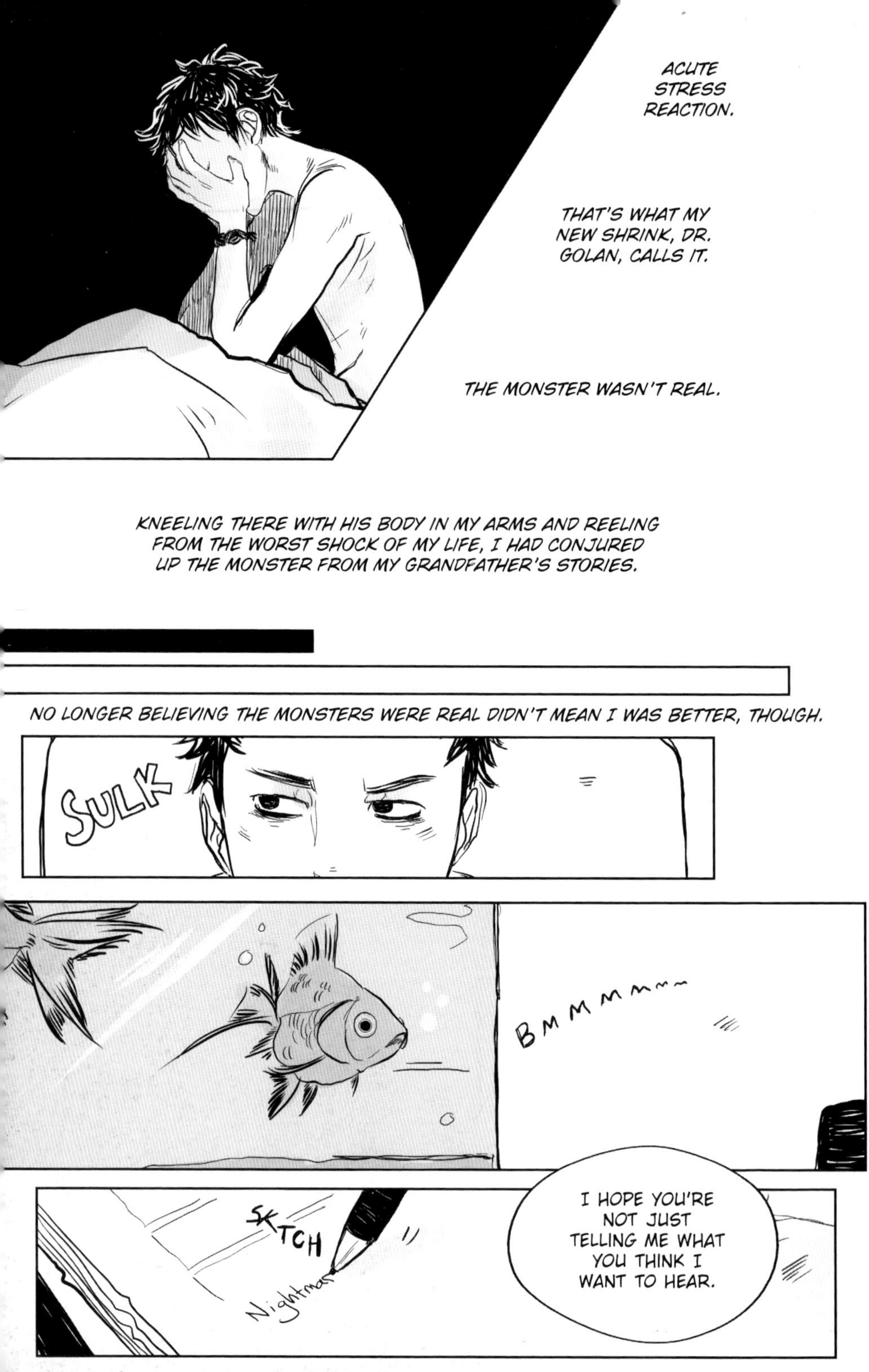
ACUTE STRESS REACTION.
THAT'S WHAT MY NEW SHRINK, DR. GOLAN, CALLS IT.
THE MONSTER WASN'T REAL.
KNEELING THERE WITH HIS BODY IN MY ARMS AND REELING FROM THE WORST SHOCK OF MY LIFE, I HAD CONJURED UP THE MONSTER FROM MY GRANDFATHER'S STORIES.
NO LONGER BELIEVING THE MONSTERS WERE REAL DIDN'T MEAN I WAS BETTER, THOUGH.
SULK
BMMMMM~~
SKTCH
I HOPE YOU'RE NOT JUST TELLING ME WHAT YOU THINK I WANT TO HEAR.

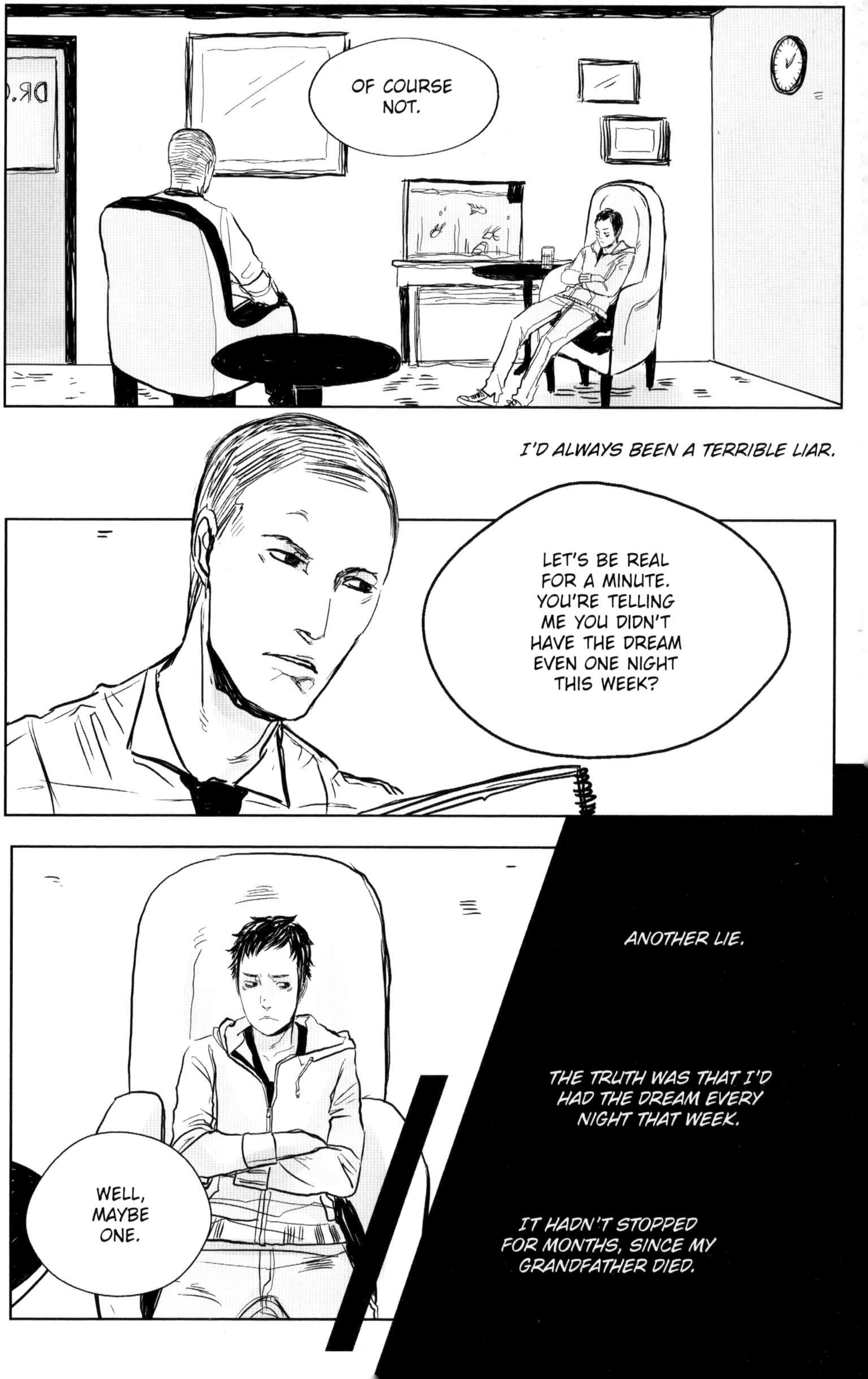
OF COURSE NOT.
I'D ALWAYS BEEN A TERRIBLE LIAR.
LET'S BE REAL FOR A MINUTE. YOU'RE TELLING ME YOU DIDN'T HAVE THE DREAM EVEN ONE NIGHT THIS WEEK?
WELL, MAYBE ONE.
ANOTHER LIE.
THE TRUTH WAS THAT I'D HAD THE DREAM EVERY NIGHT THAT WEEK.
IT HADN'T STOPPED FOR MONTHS, SINCE MY GRANDFATHER DIED.

SHLLP
SHHLLP
SHHHLP
FIND THE BIRD, FIND THE LOOP!
YAKOB VAI DON'T YOU UNDERSTAND YOU GODDAMNED STUPID YUTZI—
CRASH
HIS LAST WORDS.

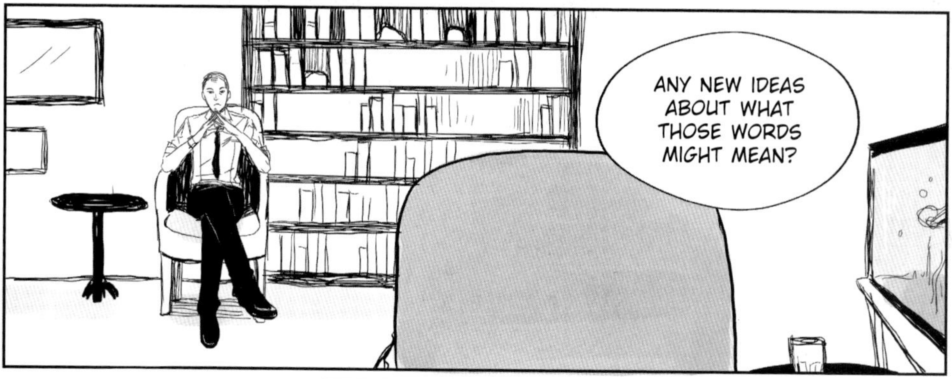
ANY NEW IDEAS ABOUT WHAT THOSE WORDS MIGHT MEAN?

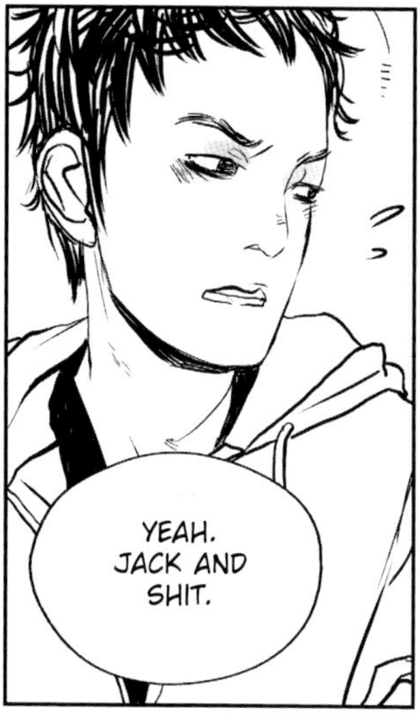
YEAH. JACK AND SHIT.

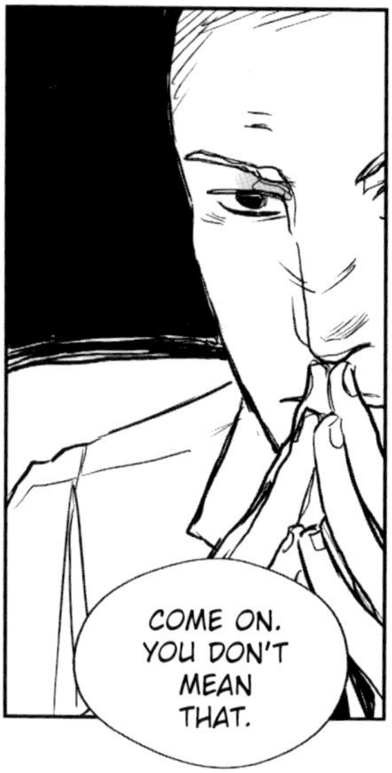
COME ON. YOU DON'T MEAN THAT.

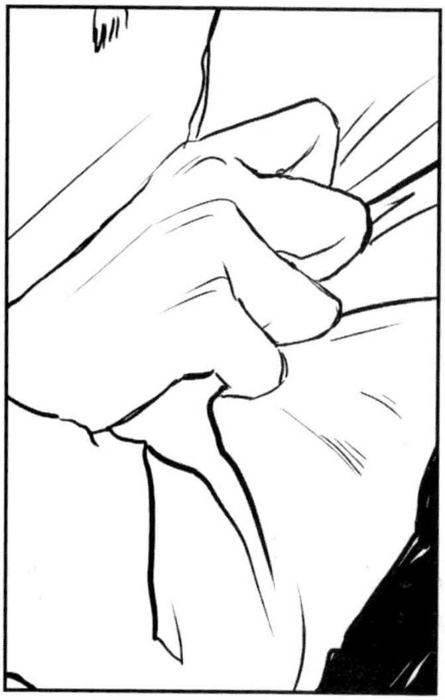

I WANTED TO ACT LIKE I DIDN'T CARE ABOUT THE LAST WORDS, BUT I DID.

DR. GOLAN WAS CONVINCED THAT UNDERSTANDING THEM MIGHT HELP PURGE MY AWFUL DREAMS.

SO I TRIED.

THE ISLAND MADE SENSE, BUT I WAS LOST WITH THE LOOP AND THE GRAVE AND THE LETTER...

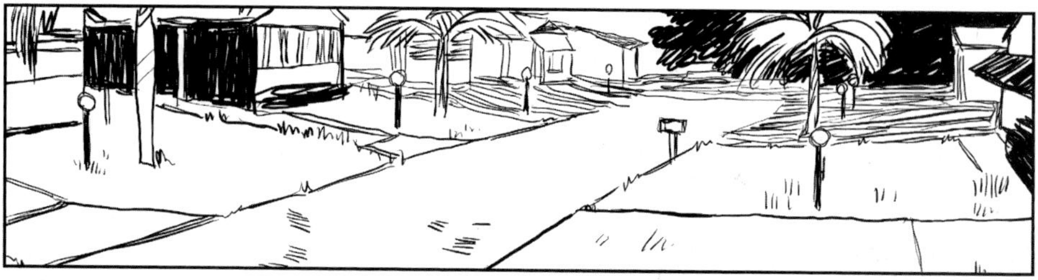

ON THE ADVICE OF DR. GOLAN, I FINALLY CONFRONTED THE SCENE OF MY TRAUMA, WONDERING IF THERE WERE ANY CLUES.

KLIK

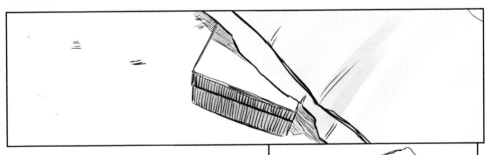

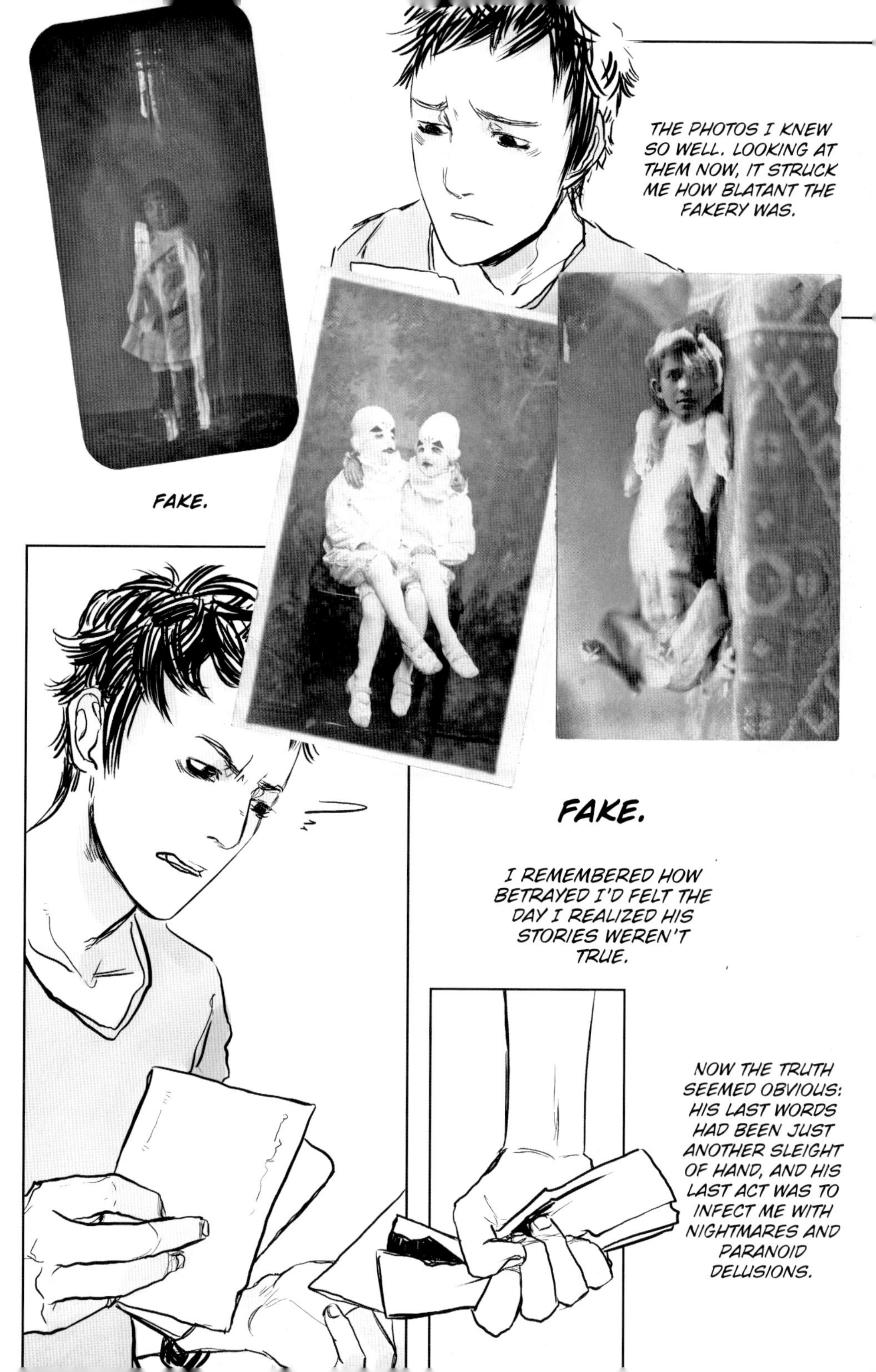
THE PHOTOS I KNEW SO WELL. LOOKING AT THEM NOW, IT STRUCK ME HOW BLATANT THE FAKERY WAS.
FAKE.
FAKE.
I REMEMBERED HOW BETRAYED I'D FELT THE DAY I REALIZED HIS STORIES WEREN'T TRUE.
NOW THE TRUTH SEEMED OBVIOUS: HIS LAST WORDS HAD BEEN JUST ANOTHER SLEIGHT OF HAND, AND HIS LAST ACT WAS TO INFECT ME WITH NIGHTMARES AND PARANOID DELUSIONS.

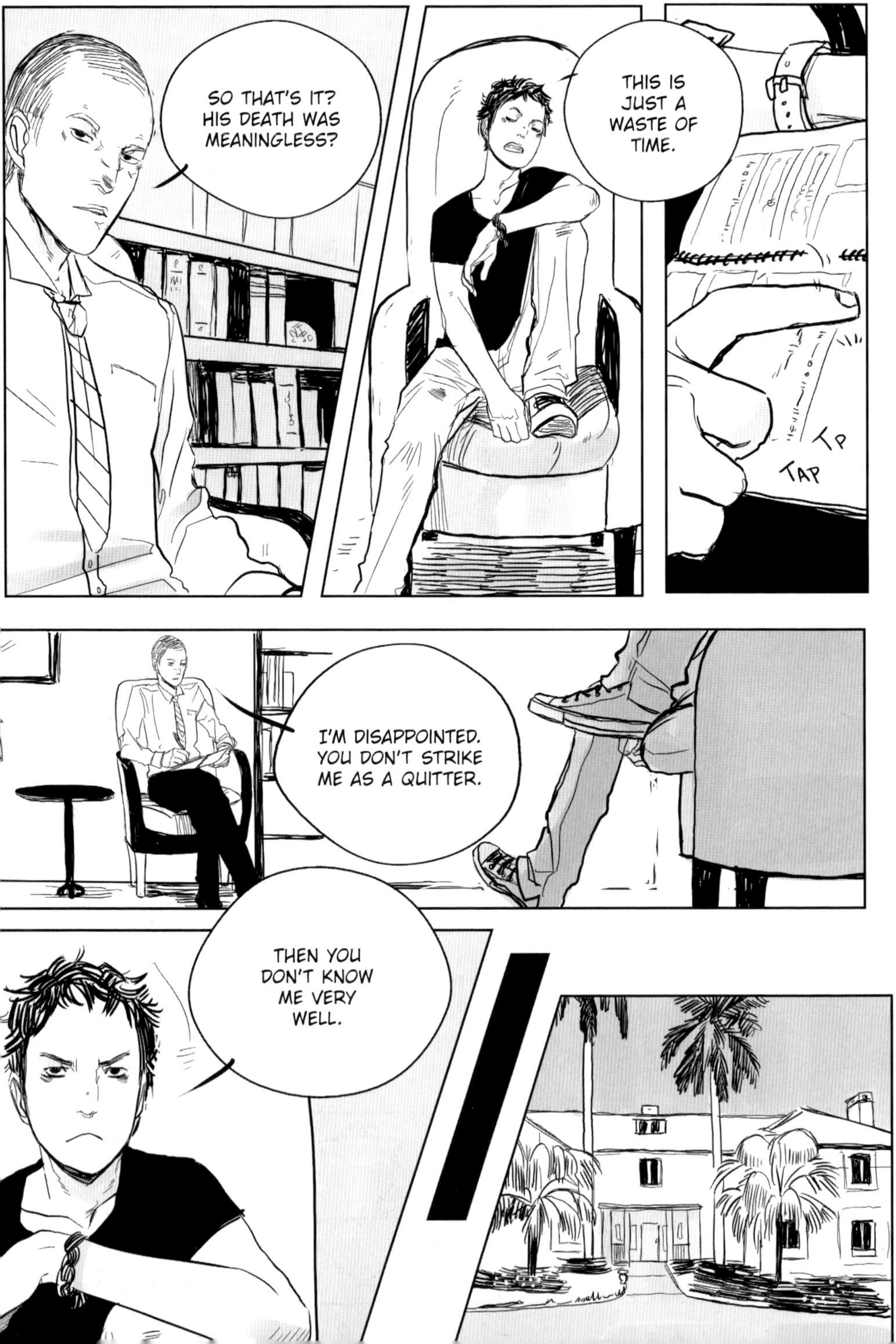
SO THAT'S IT? HIS DEATH WAS MEANINGLESS?
THIS IS JUST A WASTE OF TIME.
TAP
TP
I'M DISAPPOINTED. YOU DON'T STRIKE ME AS A QUITTER.
THEN YOU DON'T KNOW ME VERY WELL.

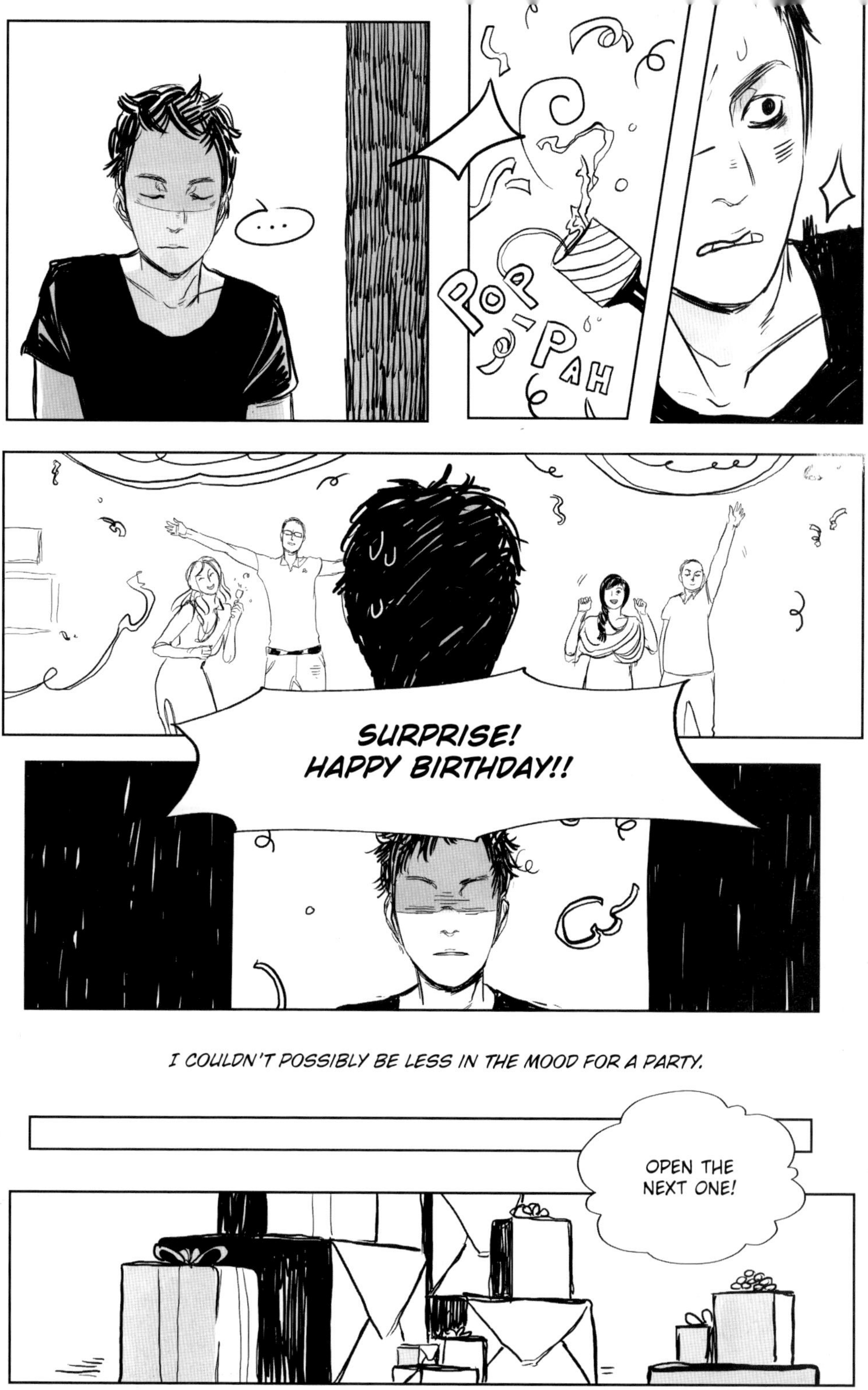
...
POP-PAH
SURPRISE! HAPPY BIRTHDAY!!
I COULDN'T POSSIBLY BE LESS IN THE MOOD FOR A PARTY.
OPEN THE NEXT ONE!

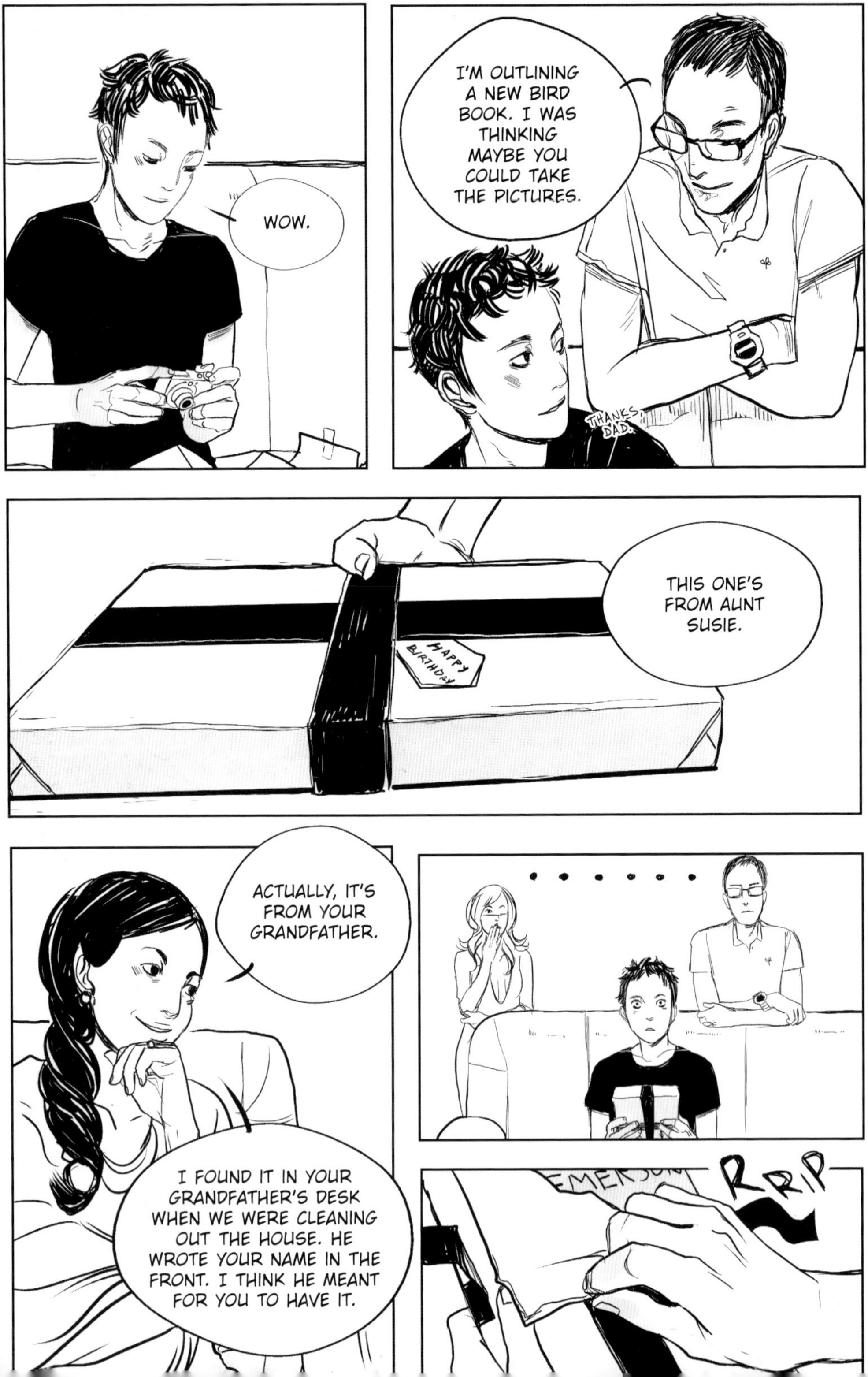
WOW.
I'M OUTLINING A NEW BIRD BOOK. I WAS THINKING MAYBE YOU COULD TAKE THE PICTURES.
THANKS, DAD.
HAPPY BIRTHDAY
THIS ONE'S FROM AUNT SUSIE.
ACTUALLY, IT'S FROM YOUR GRANDFATHER.
I FOUND IT IN YOUR GRANDFATHER'S DESK WHEN WE WERE CLEANING OUT THE HOUSE. HE WROTE YOUR NAME IN THE FRONT. I THINK HE MEANT FOR YOU TO HAVE IT.
......
RRIP

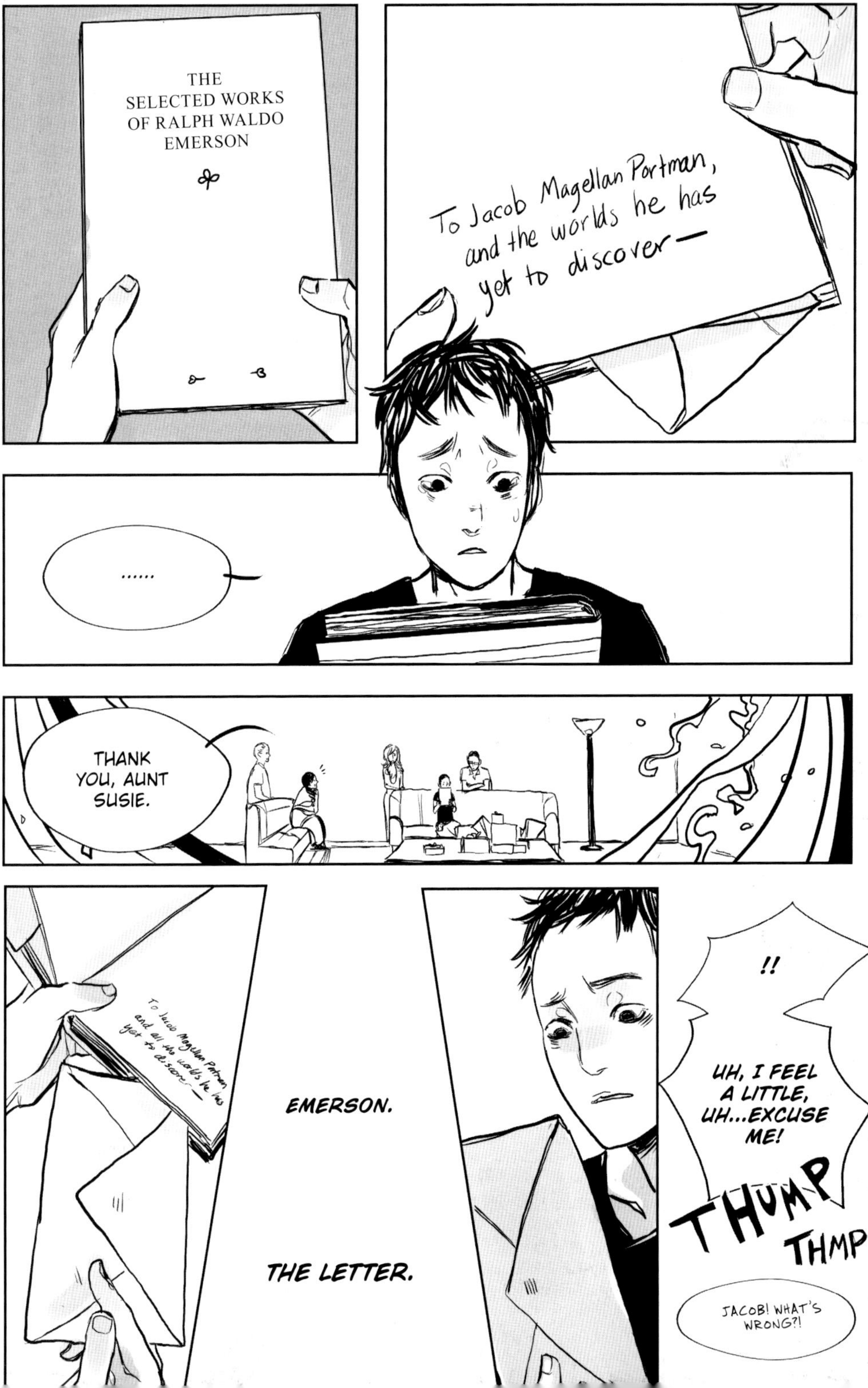
THE SELECTED WORKS OF RALPH WALDO EMERSON
To Jacob Magellan Portman, and the worlds he has yet to discover—
......
THANK YOU, AUNT SUSIE.
To Jacob Magellan Portman and all the worlds he has yet to discover—
EMERSON.
THE LETTER.
!!
UH, I FEEL A LITTLE, UH...EXCUSE ME!
THUMP
THMP
JACOB! WHAT'S WRONG?!

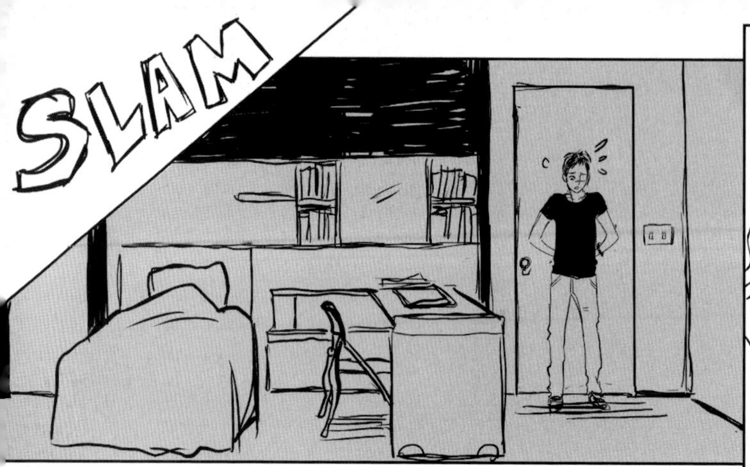
SLAM

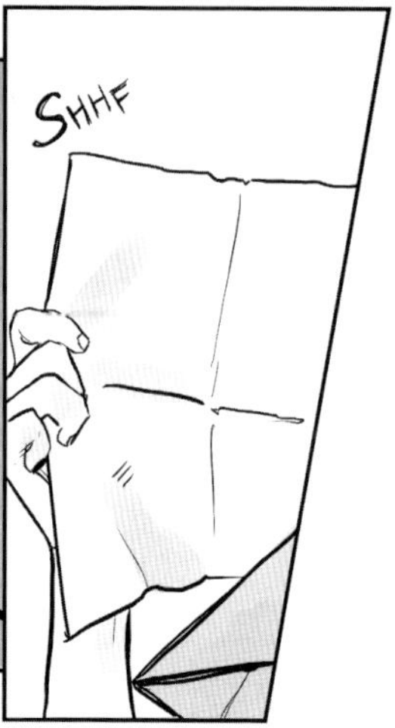
SHHF

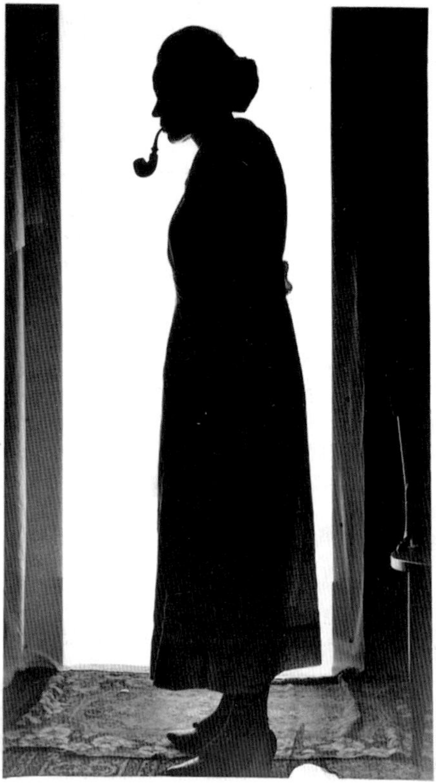

Dearest Abe,

I hope this note finds you safe & in the best of health. It's been such a long time since we last received word from you! But I write not to admonish, only to let you know that we still think of you often & pray for your well-being. Our brave, handsome Abe!

As for life on the island, little has changed. But quiet & orderly is the way we prefer things! I wonder if we would recognize you after so many years, though I'm certain you'd recognize us— those few who remain, that is. It would mean a great deal to have a recent picture of you, if you've one to send. I've included a positively ancient snap of myself.

E misses you terribly. Won't you write to her?

With respect & admiration,

Headmistress Alma LeFay Peregrine

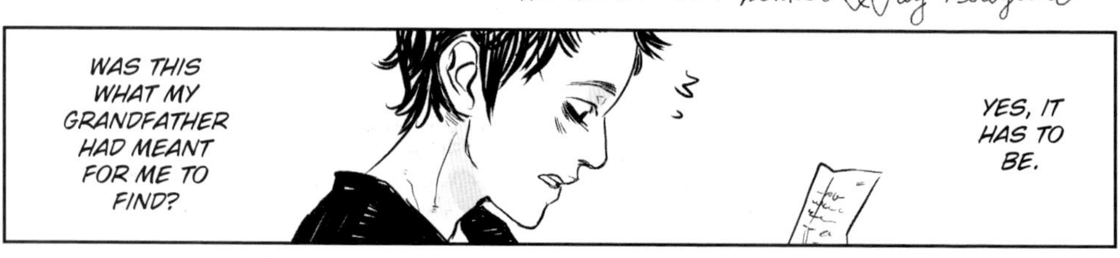
WAS THIS WHAT MY GRANDFATHER HAD MEANT FOR ME TO FIND?
YES, IT HAS TO BE.

NINE MONTHS AGO HE'D TOLD ME TO "FIND THE BIRD."

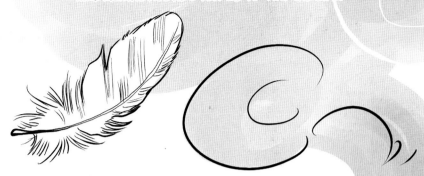

NINE YEARS AGO HE HAD SWORN THAT THE CHILDREN'S HOME WHERE HE'D LIVED WAS PROTECTED BY ONE—BY "A BIRD WHO SMOKED A PIPE."

THE HEADMISTRESS IN THE PICTURE WAS SMOKING A PIPE, AND HER NAME WAS PEREGRINE, A KIND OF HAWK.

MAYBE SHE WAS STILL ON THE ISLAND, AFTER ALL THESE YEARS.

MY GRANDFATHER WANTED ME TO GO TO THE ISLAND AND FIND THIS WOMAN. IF ANYONE KNEW THE SECRETS OF HIS CHILDHOOD, IT WOULD BE HER.

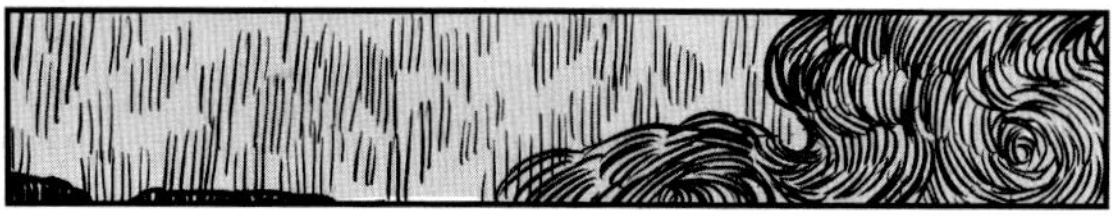

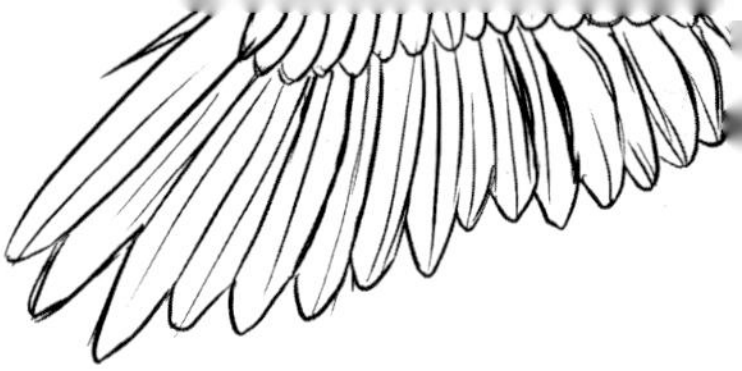

CONVINCING MY PARENTS TO LET ME SPEND PART OF MY SUMMER ON A TINY ISLAND OFF THE COAST OF WALES WAS NO EASY TASK. I CERTAINLY WASN'T GOING TO TELL MY PARENTS ABOUT GRANDPA'S LAST WORDS OR THE LETTER OR THE PHOTO. BUT WHEN MY DAD LEARNED THAT CAIRNHOLM ISLAND IS A SUPER-IMPORTANT BIRD HABITAT AND DR. GOLAN SHOCKED US ALL BY NOT ONLY SIGNING OFF ON THE IDEA BUT ALSO ENCOURAGING MY PARENTS TO LET ME GO, THINGS FELL INTO PLACE WITH ASTONISHING SPEED.

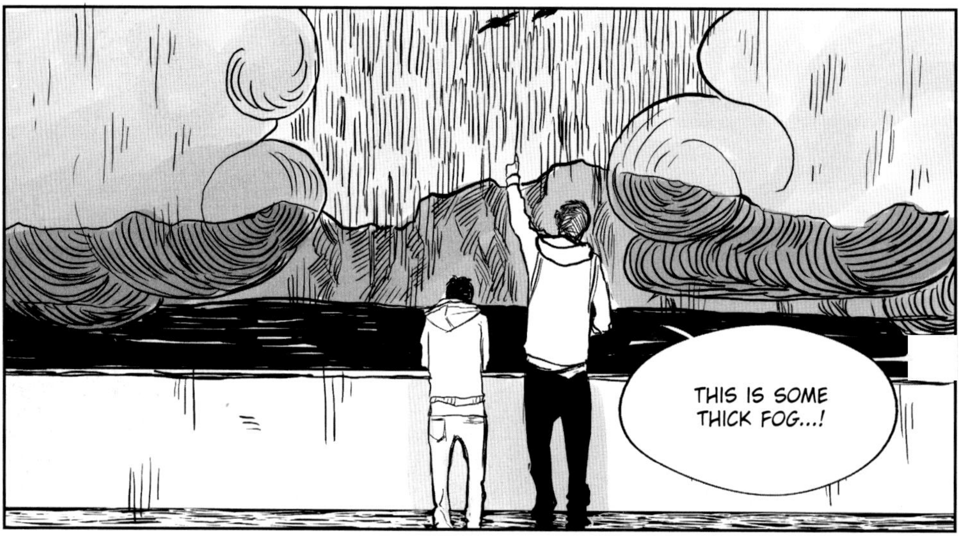
THIS IS SOME THICK FOG...!

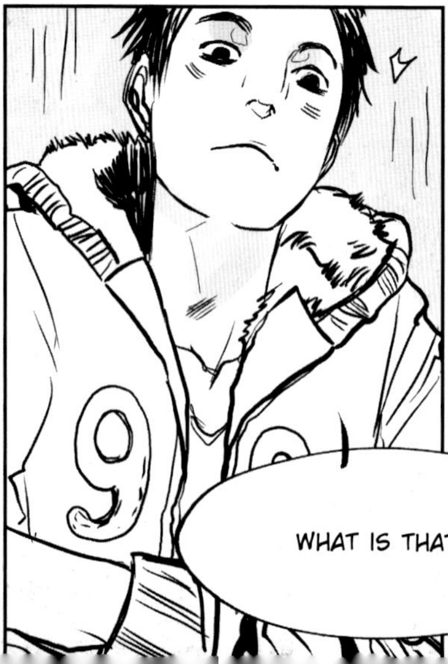
WHAT IS THAT?

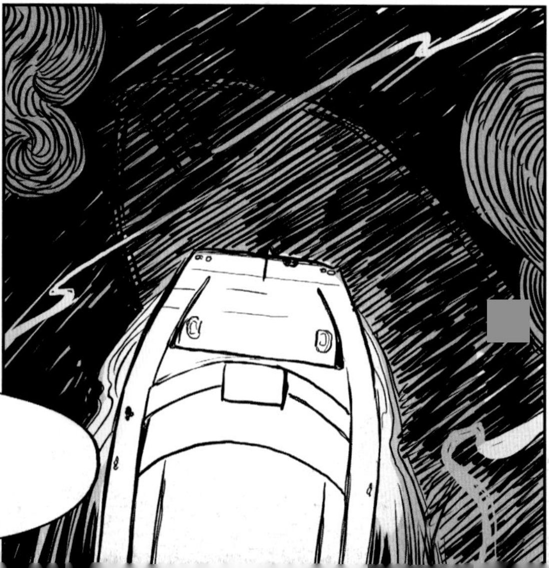

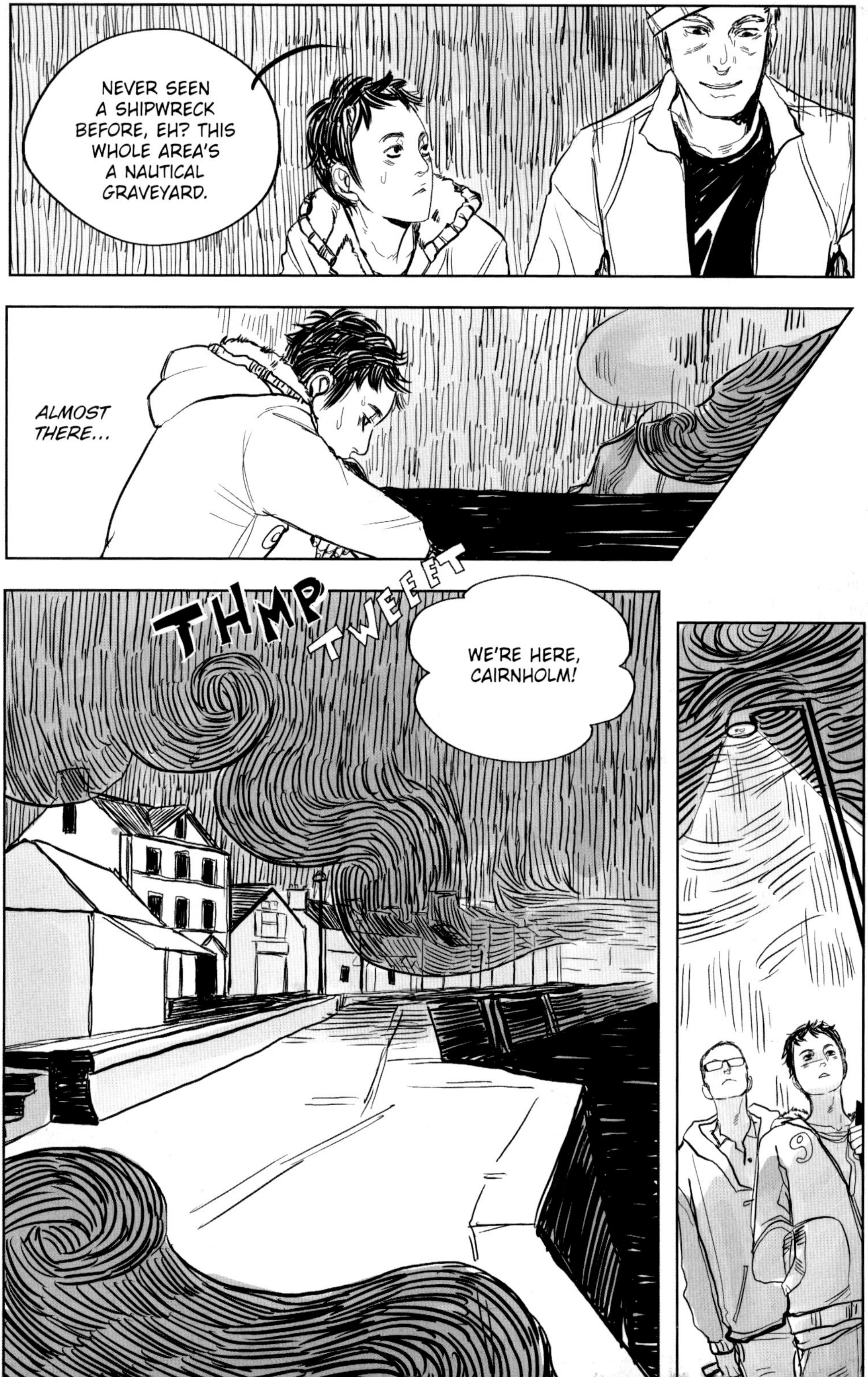
NEVER SEEN A SHIPWRECK BEFORE, EH? THIS WHOLE AREA'S A NAUTICAL GRAVEYARD.
ALMOST THERE...
THMP
TWEEET
WE'RE HERE, CAIRNHOLM!

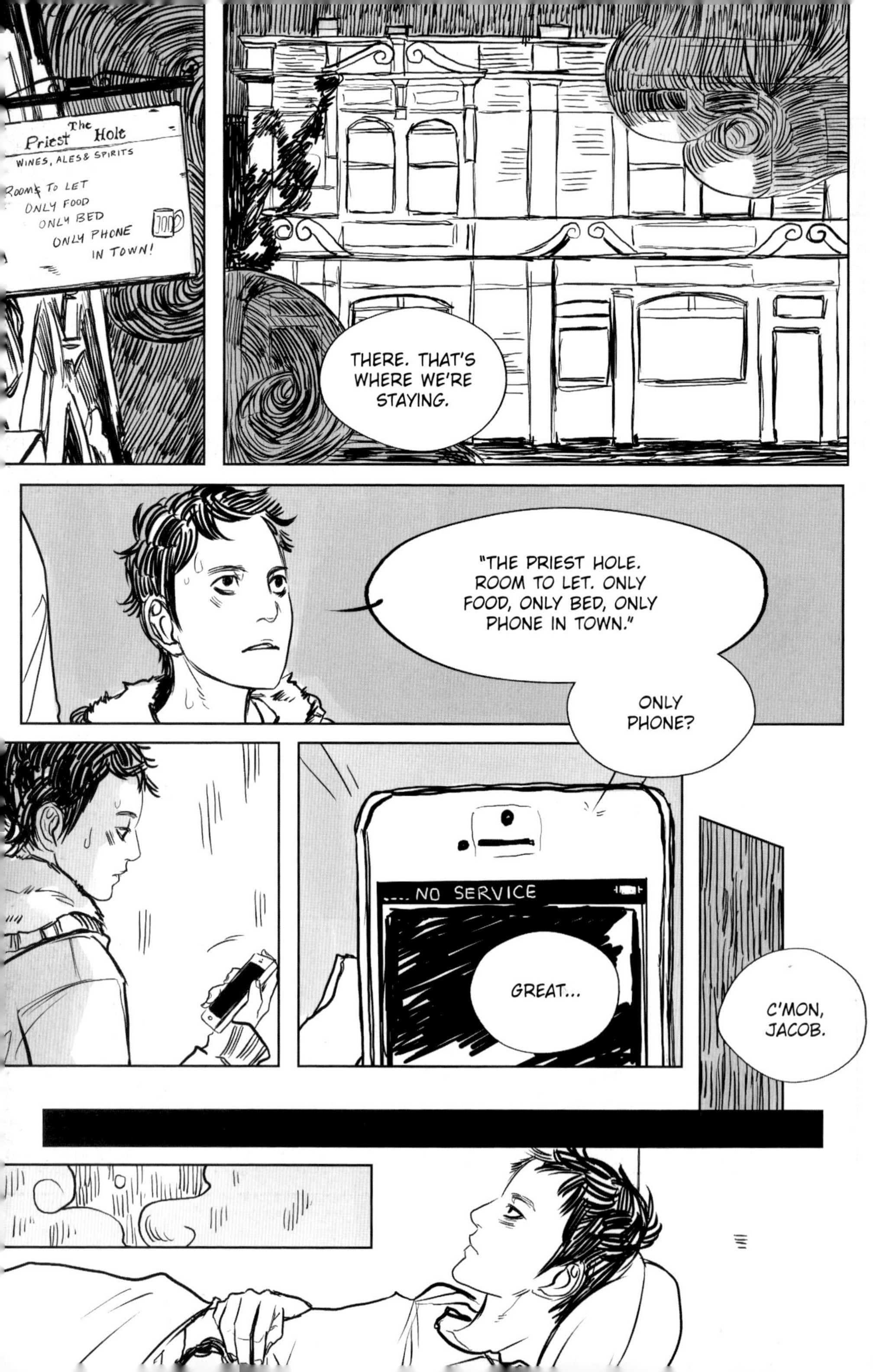
The Priest Hole
WINES, ALES & SPIRITS
ROOMS TO LET
ONLY FOOD
ONLY BED
ONLY PHONE
IN TOWN!
THERE. THAT'S WHERE WE'RE STAYING.
"THE PRIEST HOLE. ROOM TO LET. ONLY FOOD, ONLY BED, ONLY PHONE IN TOWN."
ONLY PHONE?
.... NO SERVICE
GREAT...
C'MON, JACOB.

FOR THE FIRST TIME IN MONTHS, I FELL INTO A DEEP, NIGHTMARE-FREE SLUMBER.

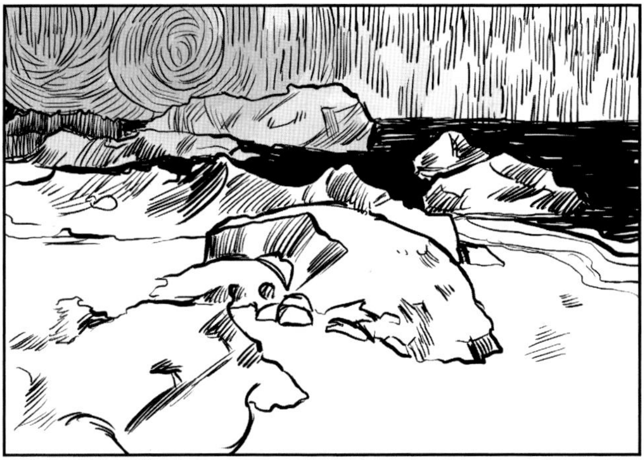

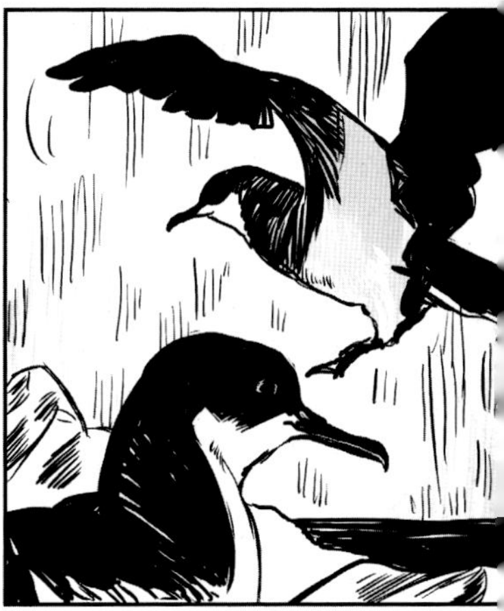

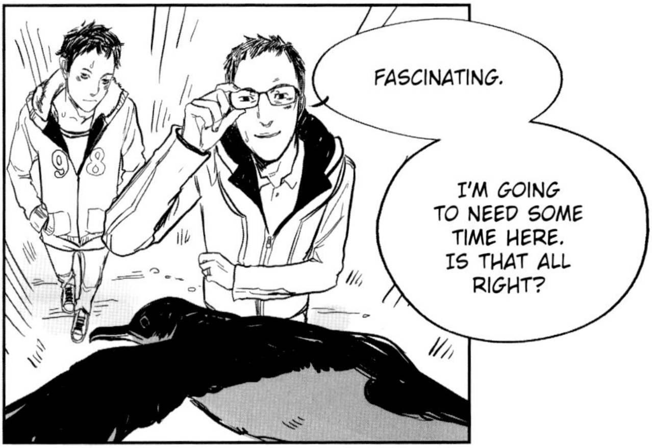
FASCINATING.
I'M GOING TO NEED SOME TIME HERE. IS THAT ALL RIGHT?

I'D SEEN THIS LOOK ON HIS FACE BEFORE, AND I KNEW EXACTLY WHAT "SOME TIME" MEANT: HOURS AND HOURS.

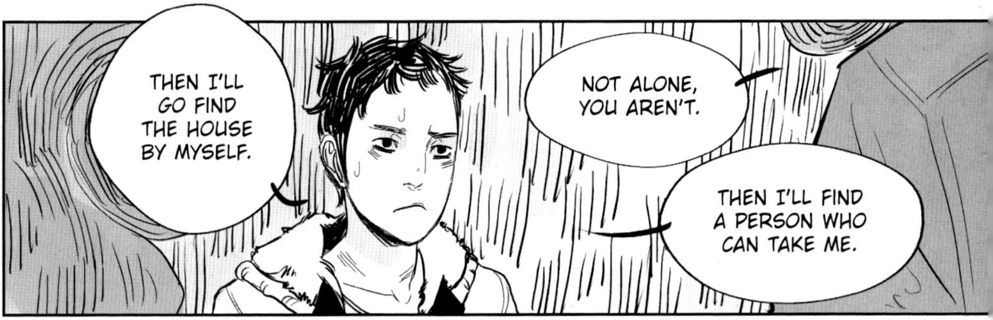
THEN I'LL GO FIND THE HOUSE BY MYSELF.
NOT ALONE, YOU AREN'T.
THEN I'LL FIND A PERSON WHO CAN TAKE ME.

...OKAY.

I WENT INTO THE NEAREST SHOP.

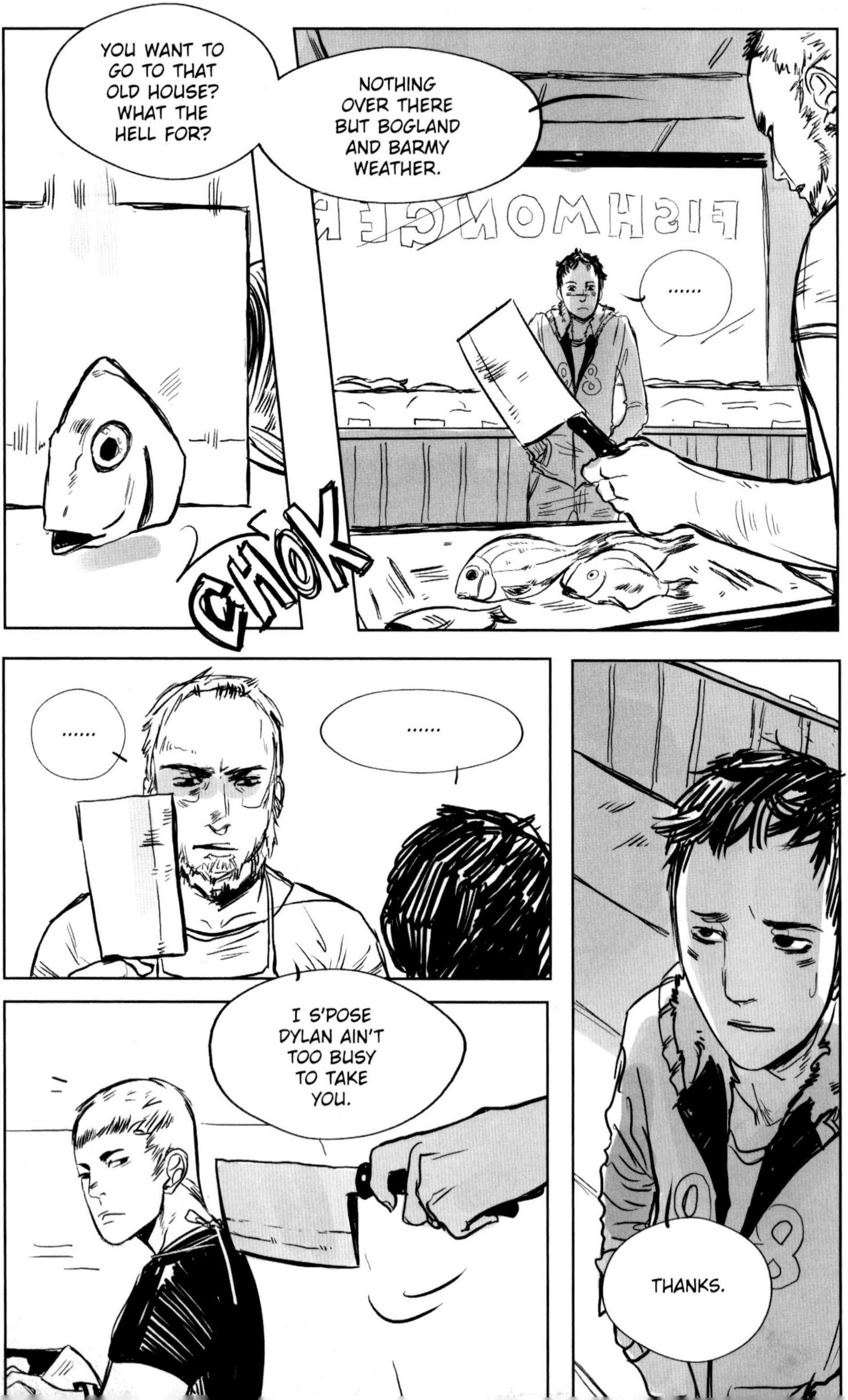
YOU WANT TO GO TO THAT OLD HOUSE? WHAT THE HELL FOR?
NOTHING OVER THERE BUT BOGLAND AND BARMY WEATHER.
CHOK
FISHMONGER
......
......
......
I S'POSE DYLAN AIN'T TOO BUSY TO TAKE YOU.
THANKS.

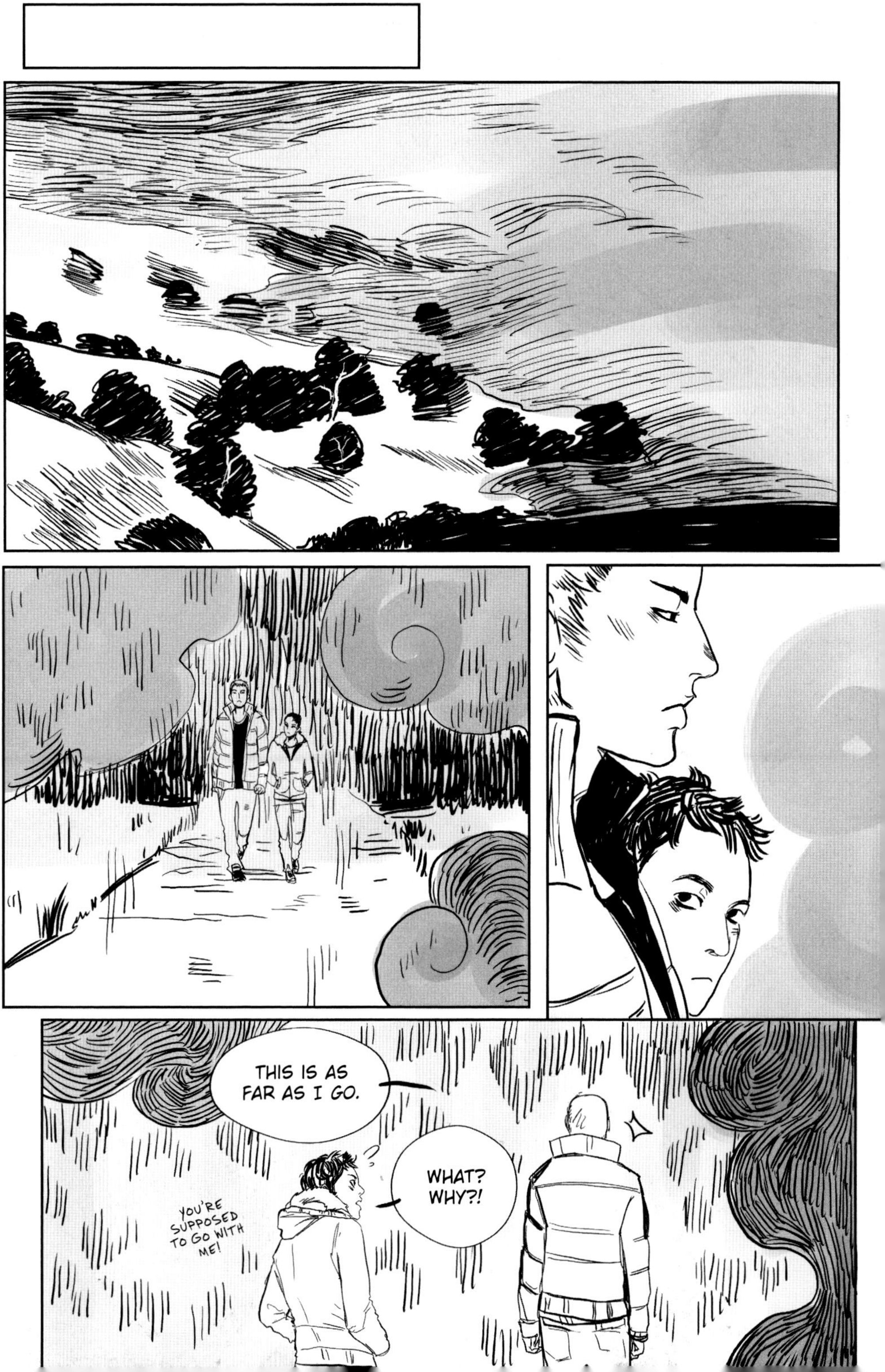
THIS IS AS FAR AS I GO.
WHAT? WHY?!
YOU'RE SUPPOSED TO GO WITH ME!

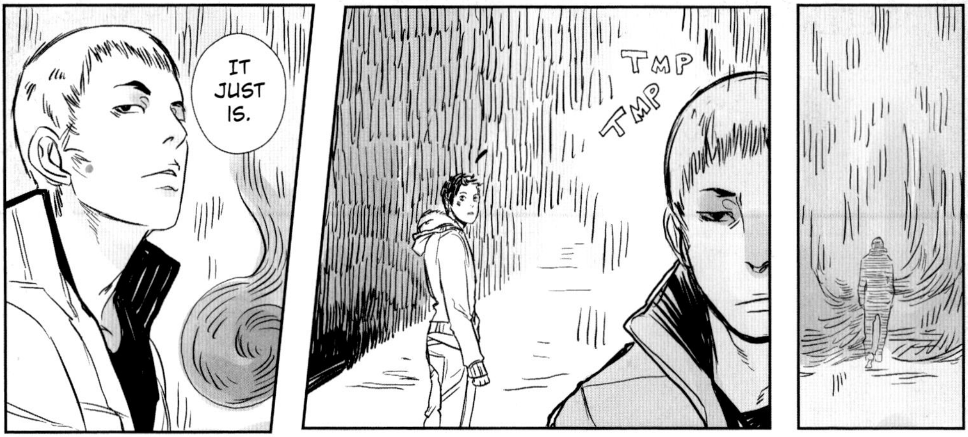
IT JUST IS.
TMP
TMP

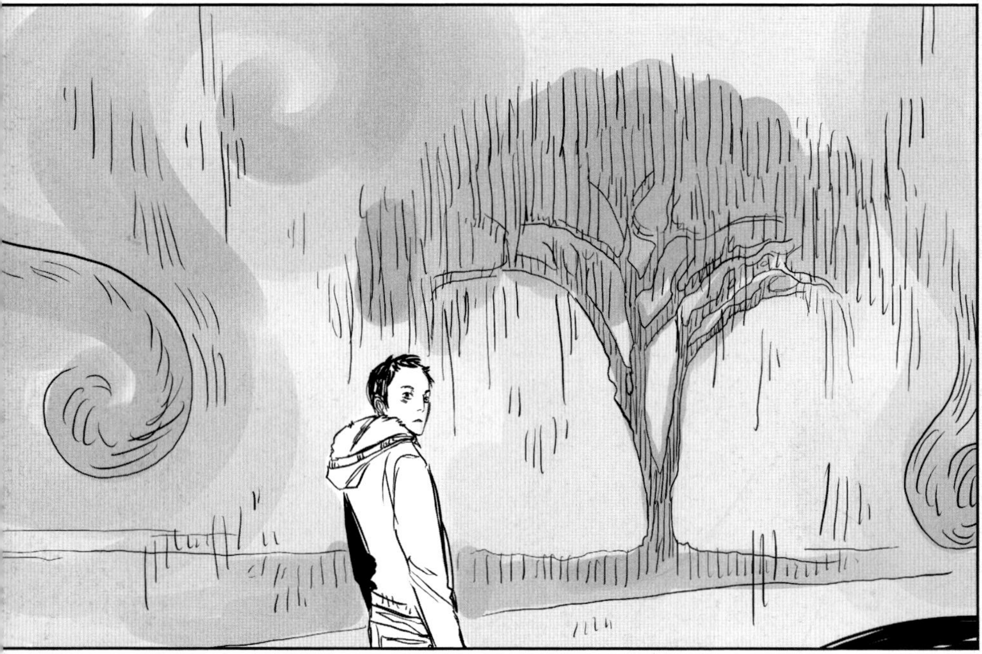

WELL, I COULD TUCK TAIL AND GO BACK TO TOWN...

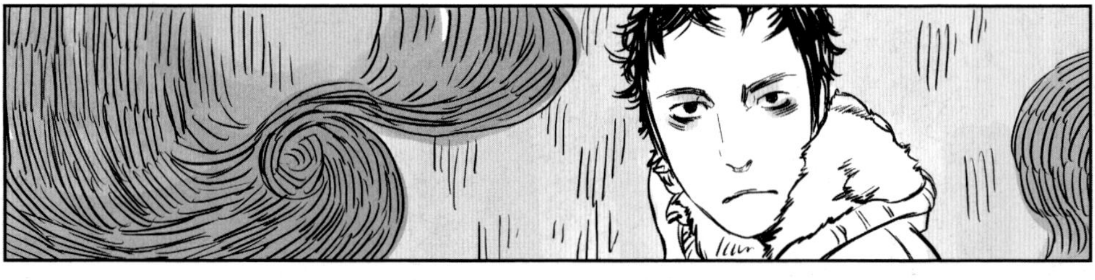

...OR GO AHEAD ALONE AND LIE TO DAD ABOUT IT.

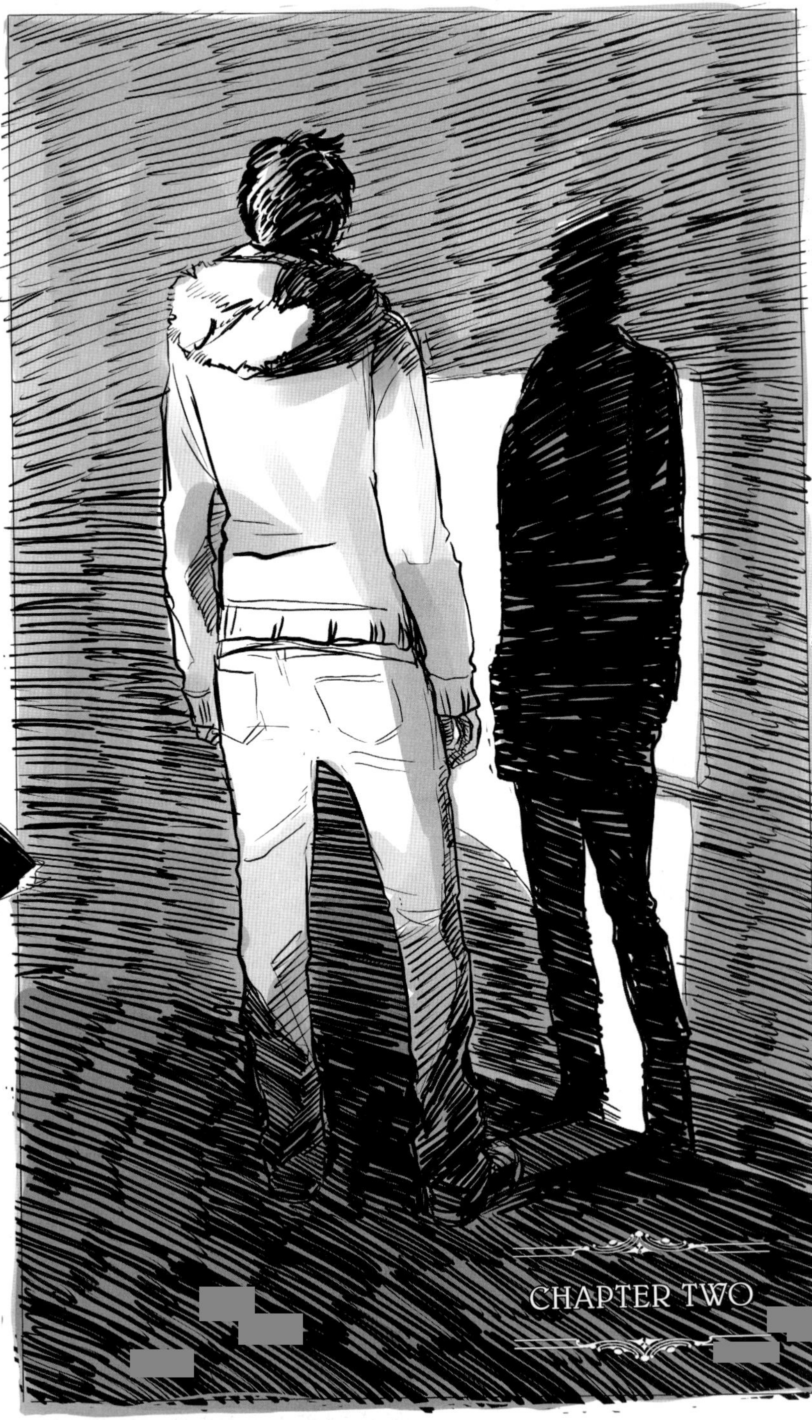
CHAPTER TWO

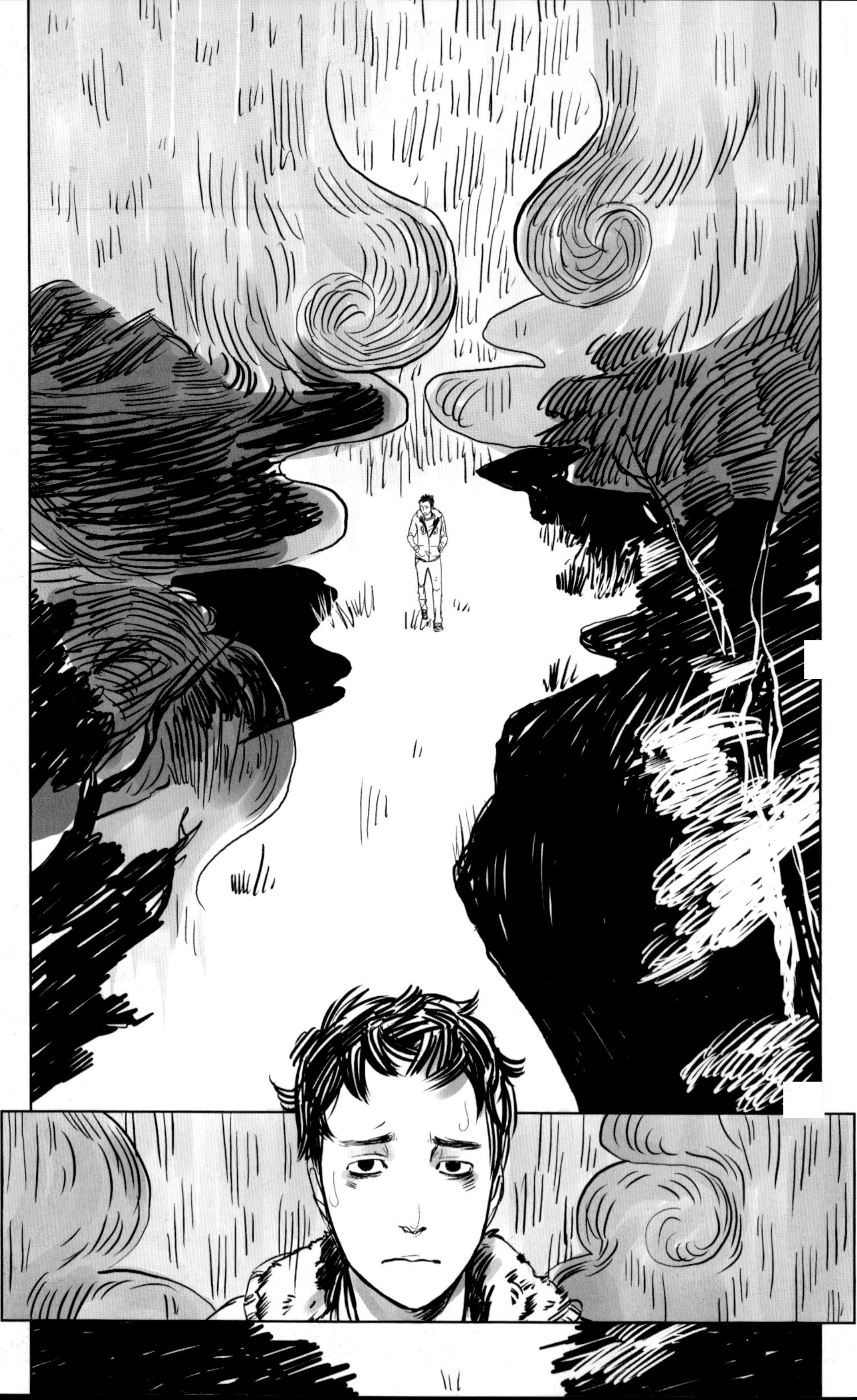

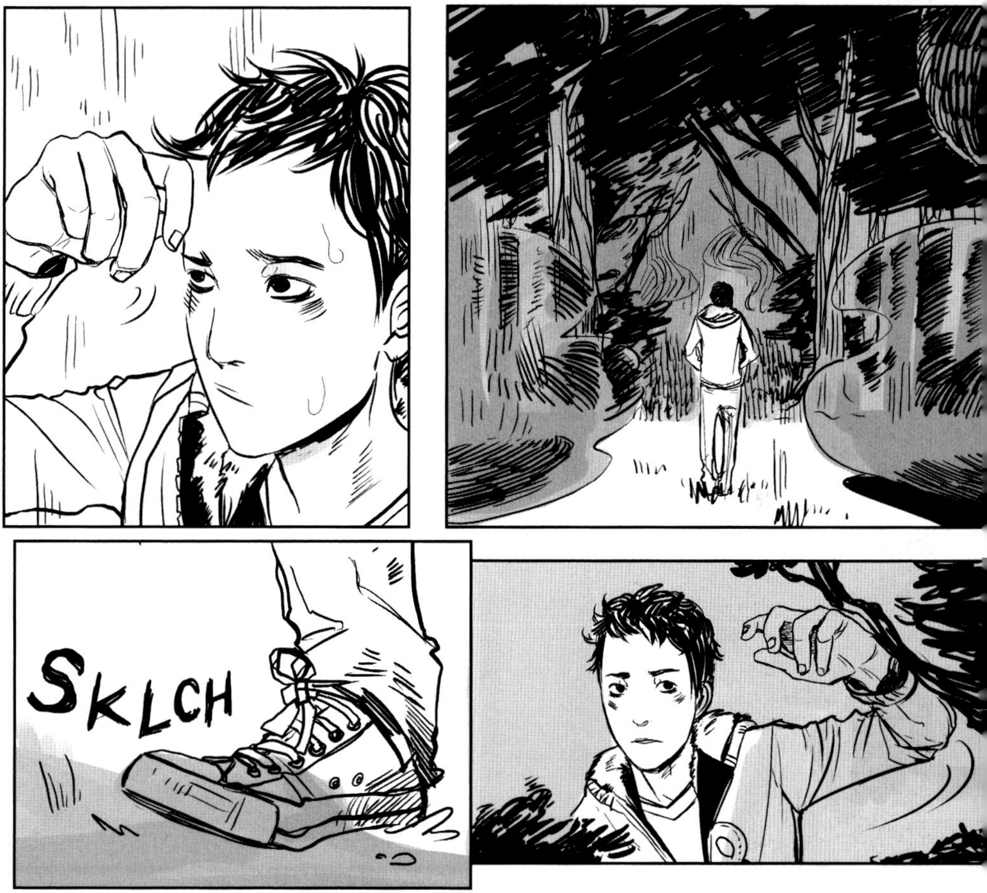
SKLCH

I WONDER HOW AN ELDERLY PERSON LIKE MISS PEREGRINE COULD EVER NEGOTIATE SUCH AN OBSTACLE COURSE. SHE MUST GET DELIVERIES.

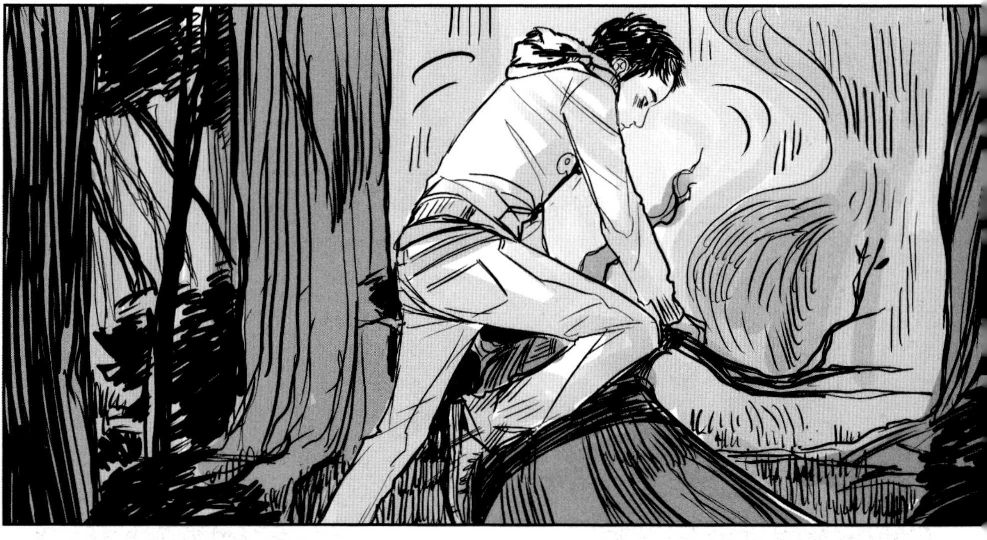

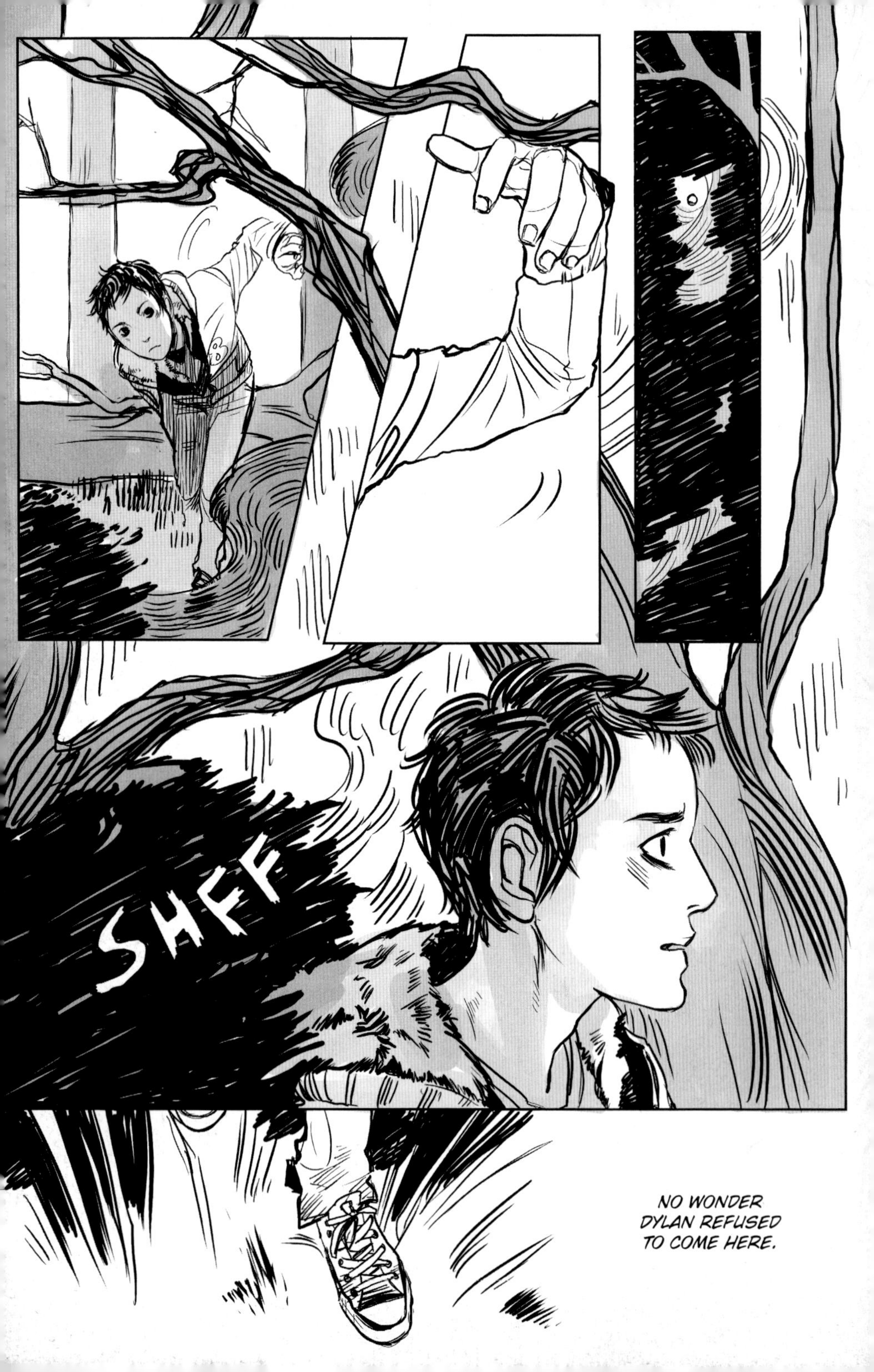
SHFF
NO WONDER DYLAN REFUSED TO COME HERE.

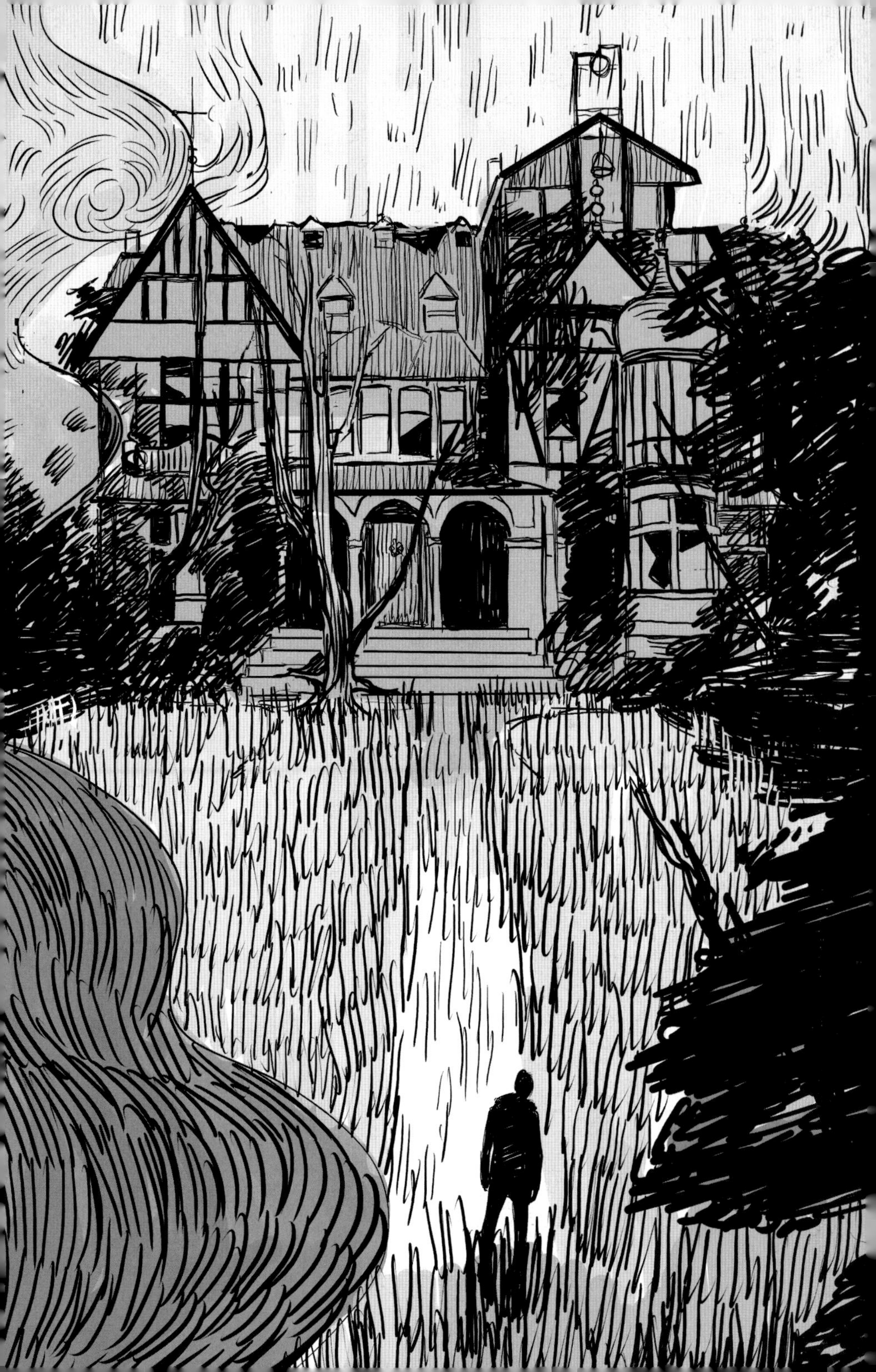

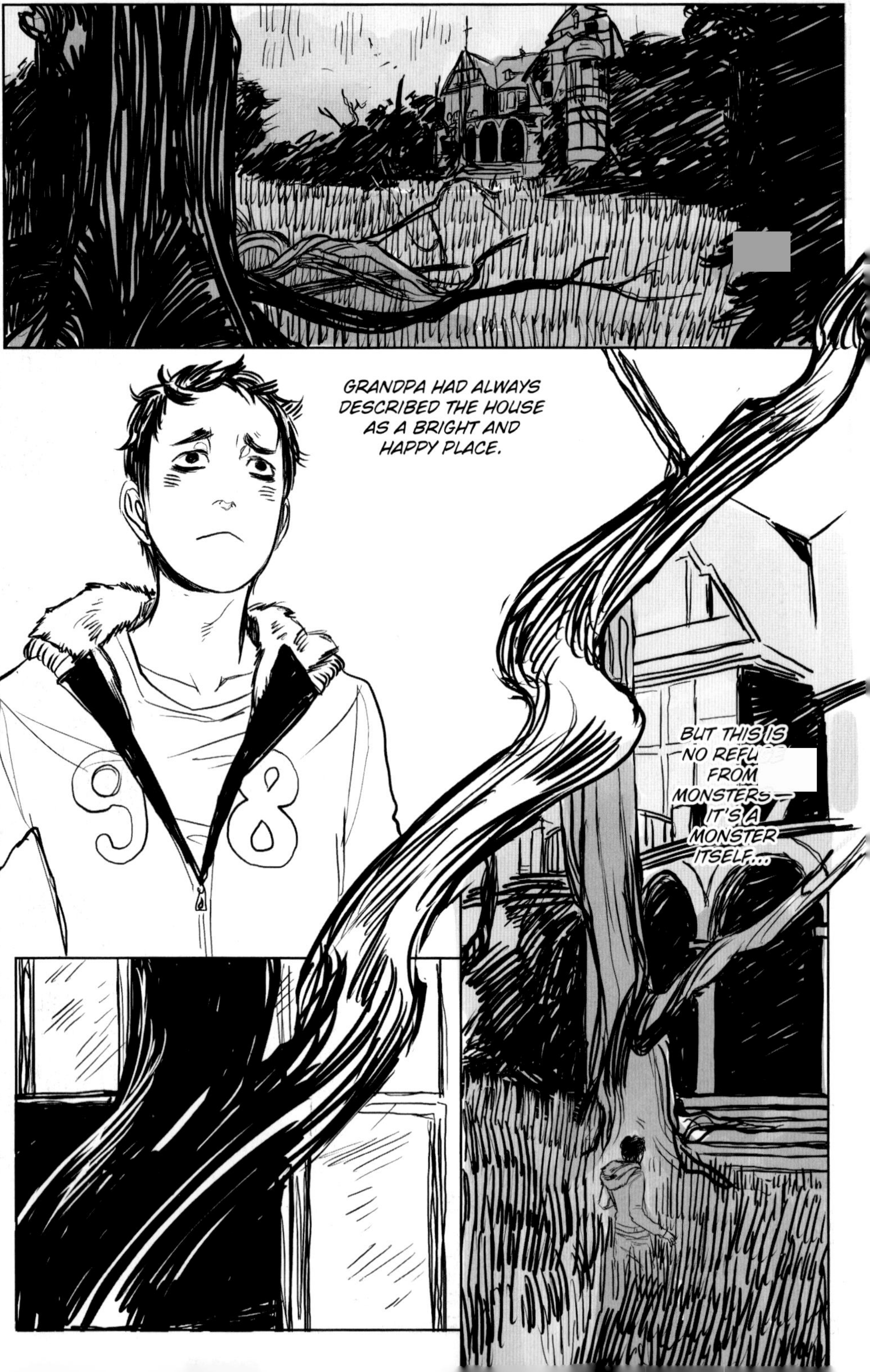
GRANDPA HAD ALWAYS DESCRIBED THE HOUSE AS A BRIGHT AND HAPPY PLACE.
BUT THIS IS NO REFU FROM MONSTERS— IT'S A MONSTER ITSELF...

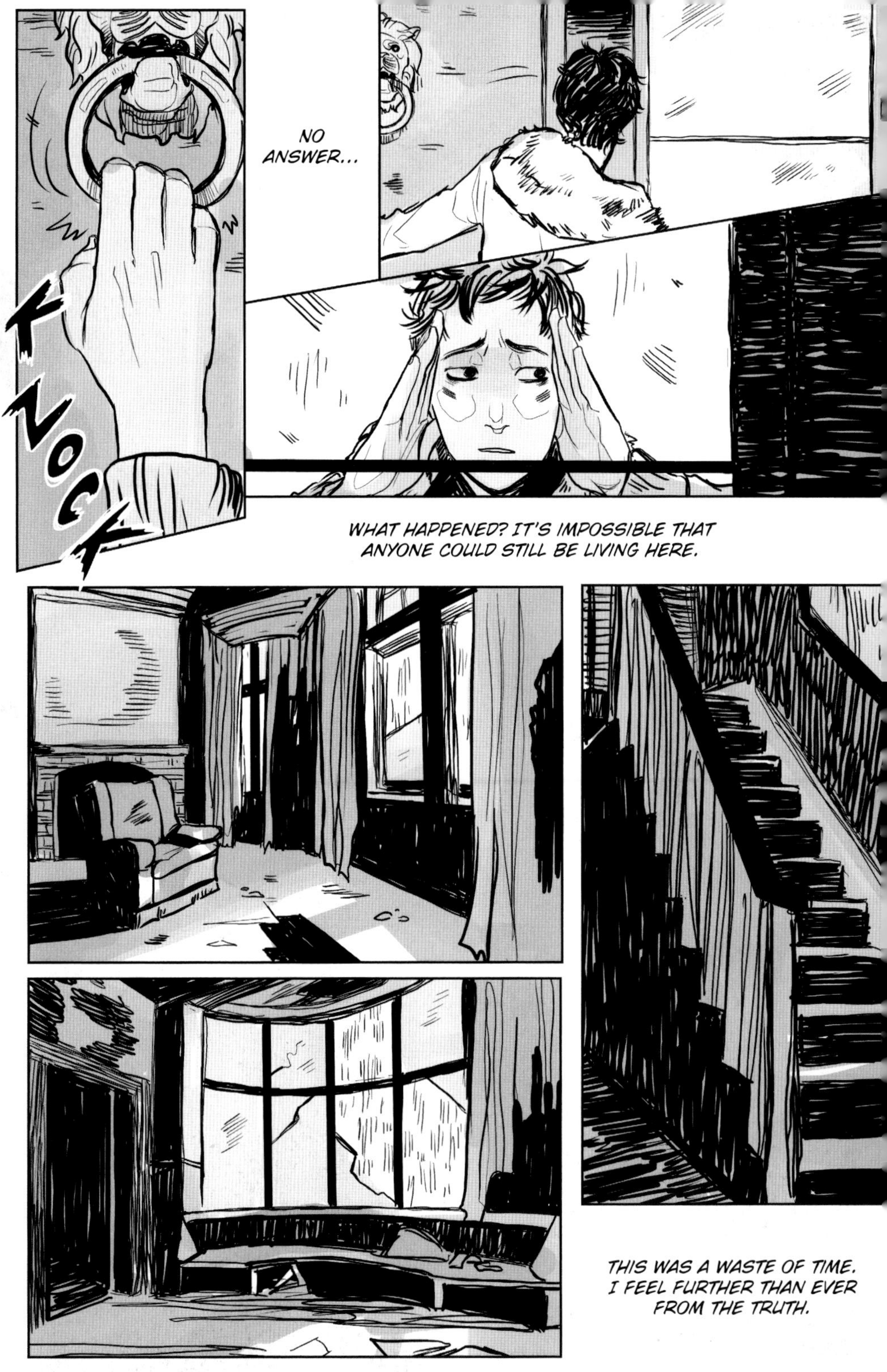
KNOCK
NO ANSWER...
WHAT HAPPENED? IT'S IMPOSSIBLE THAT ANYONE COULD STILL BE LIVING HERE.
THIS WAS A WASTE OF TIME. I FEEL FURTHER THAN EVER FROM THE TRUTH.

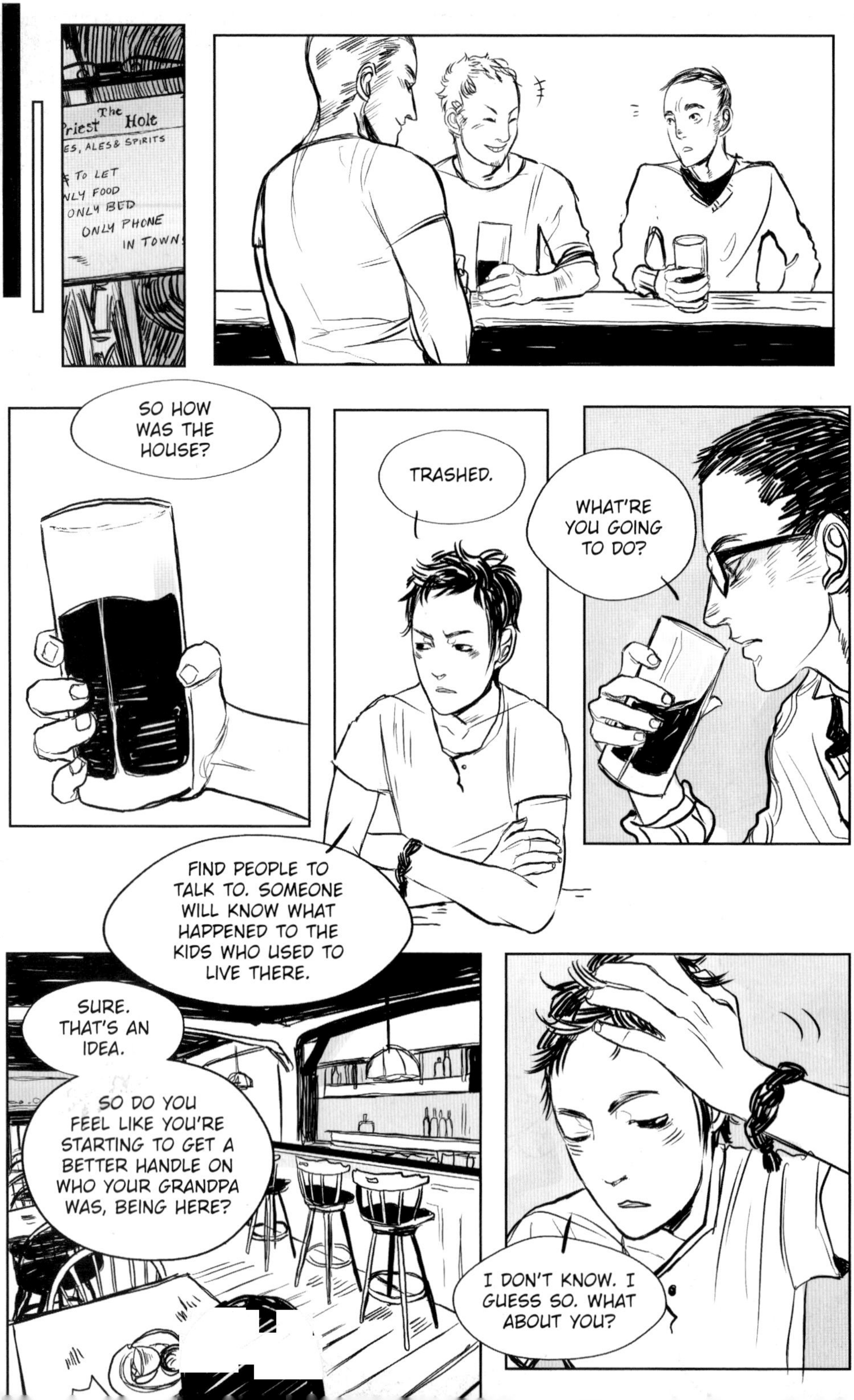

The Priest Hole
ALES & SPIRITS
TO LET
ONLY BED
ONLY PHONE
IN TOWN
SO HOW WAS THE HOUSE?
TRASHED.
WHAT'RE YOU GOING TO DO?
FIND PEOPLE TO TALK TO. SOMEONE WILL KNOW WHAT HAPPENED TO THE KIDS WHO USED TO LIVE THERE.
SURE. THAT'S AN IDEA.
SO DO YOU FEEL LIKE YOU'RE STARTING TO GET A BETTER HANDLE ON WHO YOUR GRANDPA WAS, BEING HERE?
I DON'T KNOW. I GUESS SO. WHAT ABOUT YOU?

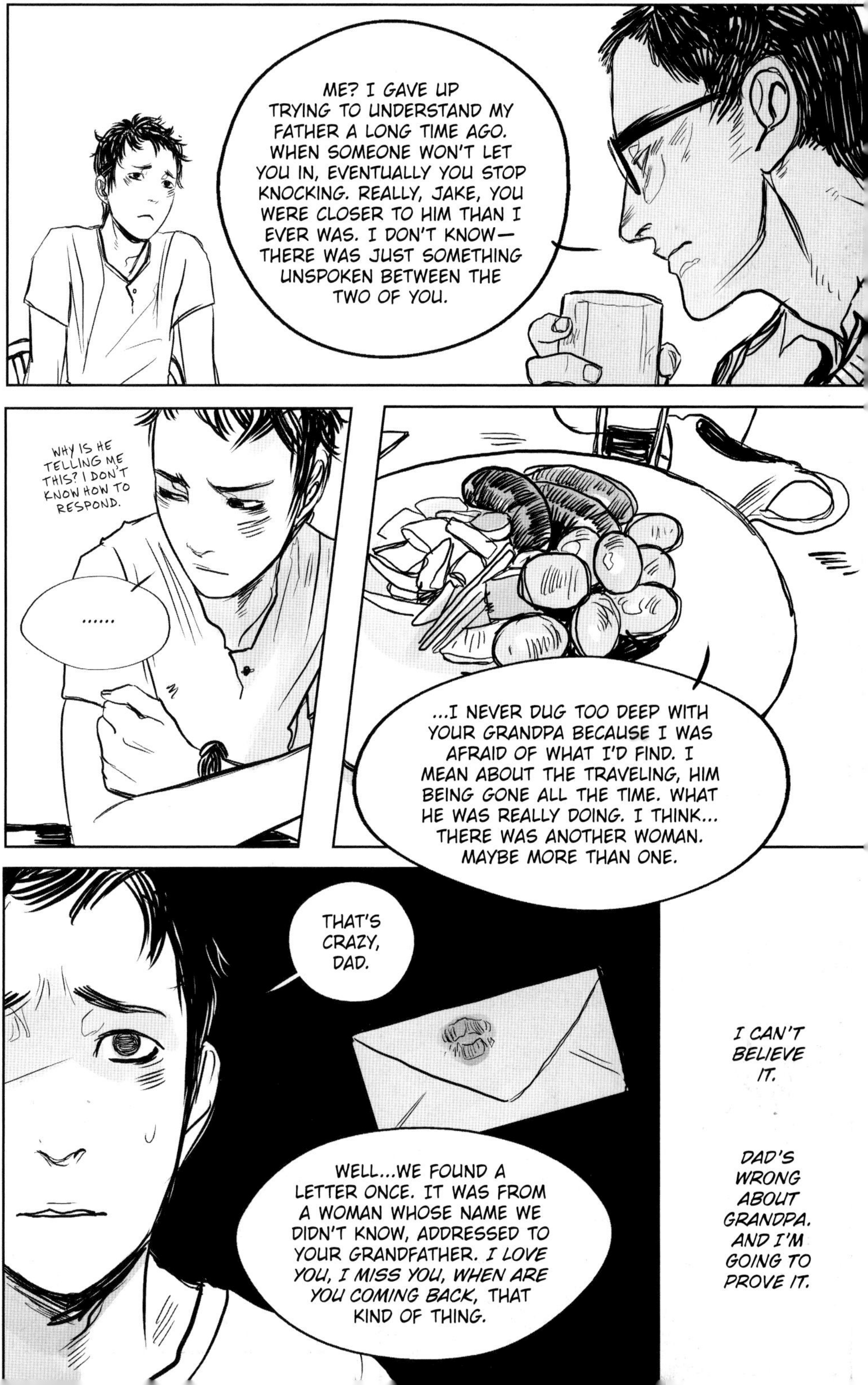
ME? I GAVE UP TRYING TO UNDERSTAND MY FATHER A LONG TIME AGO. WHEN SOMEONE WON'T LET YOU IN, EVENTUALLY YOU STOP KNOCKING. REALLY, JAKE, YOU WERE CLOSER TO HIM THAN I EVER WAS. I DON'T KNOW— THERE WAS JUST SOMETHING UNSPOKEN BETWEEN THE TWO OF YOU.
WHY IS HE TELLING ME THIS? I DON'T KNOW HOW TO RESPOND.
......
...I NEVER DUG TOO DEEP WITH YOUR GRANDPA BECAUSE I WAS AFRAID OF WHAT I'D FIND. I MEAN ABOUT THE TRAVELING, HIM BEING GONE ALL THE TIME. WHAT HE WAS REALLY DOING. I THINK... THERE WAS ANOTHER WOMAN. MAYBE MORE THAN ONE.
THAT'S CRAZY, DAD.
WELL...WE FOUND A LETTER ONCE. IT WAS FROM A WOMAN WHOSE NAME WE DIDN'T KNOW, ADDRESSED TO YOUR GRANDFATHER. *I LOVE YOU, I MISS YOU, WHEN ARE YOU COMING BACK*, THAT KIND OF THING.
I CAN'T BELIEVE IT.
DAD'S WRONG ABOUT GRANDPA. AND I'M GOING TO PROVE IT.

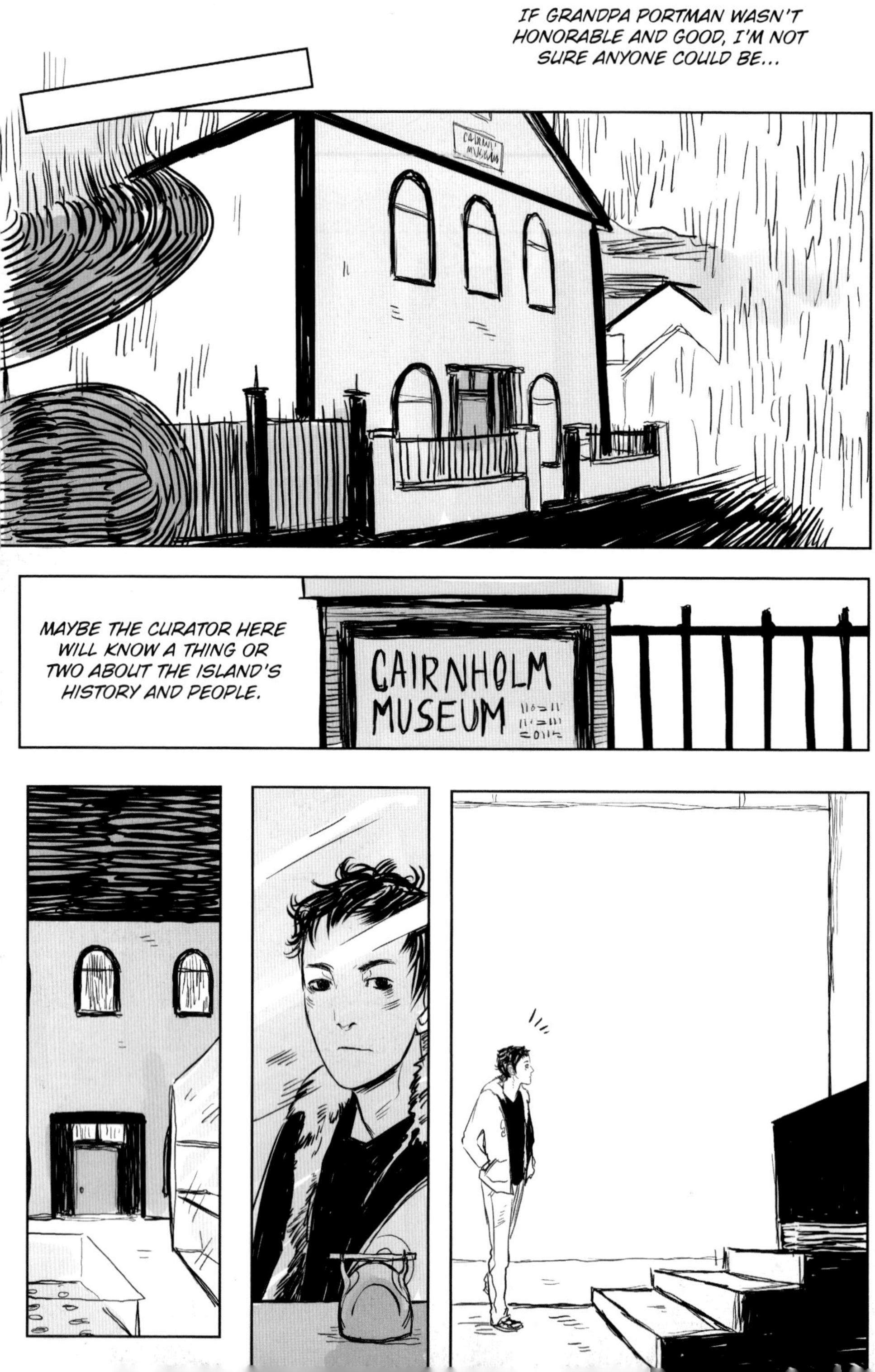
IF GRANDPA PORTMAN WASN'T HONORABLE AND GOOD, I'M NOT SURE ANYONE COULD BE...
MAYBE THE CURATOR HERE WILL KNOW A THING OR TWO ABOUT THE ISLAND'S HISTORY AND PEOPLE.
CAIRNHOLM MUSEUM

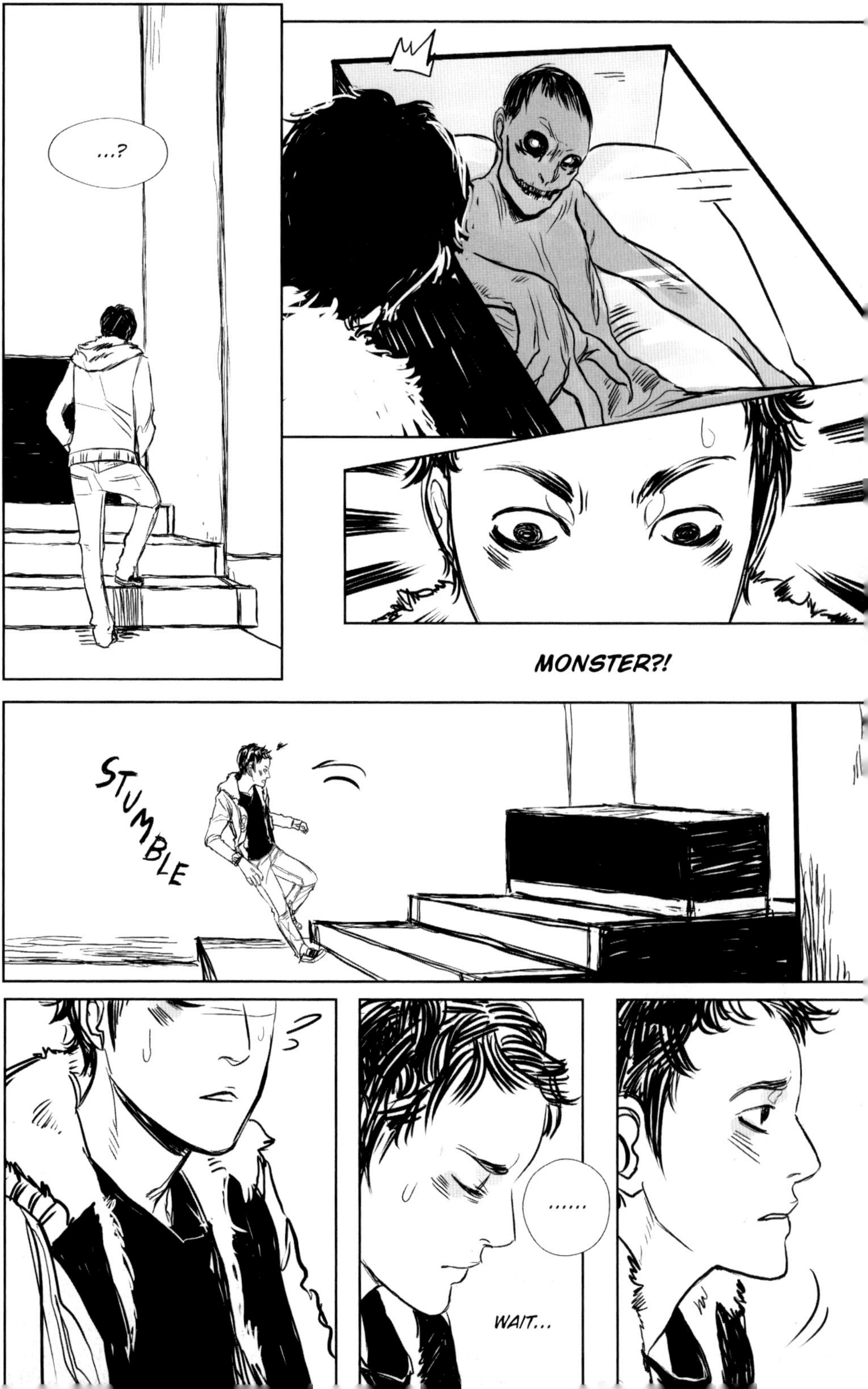
...?
MONSTER?!
STUMBLE
......
WAIT...

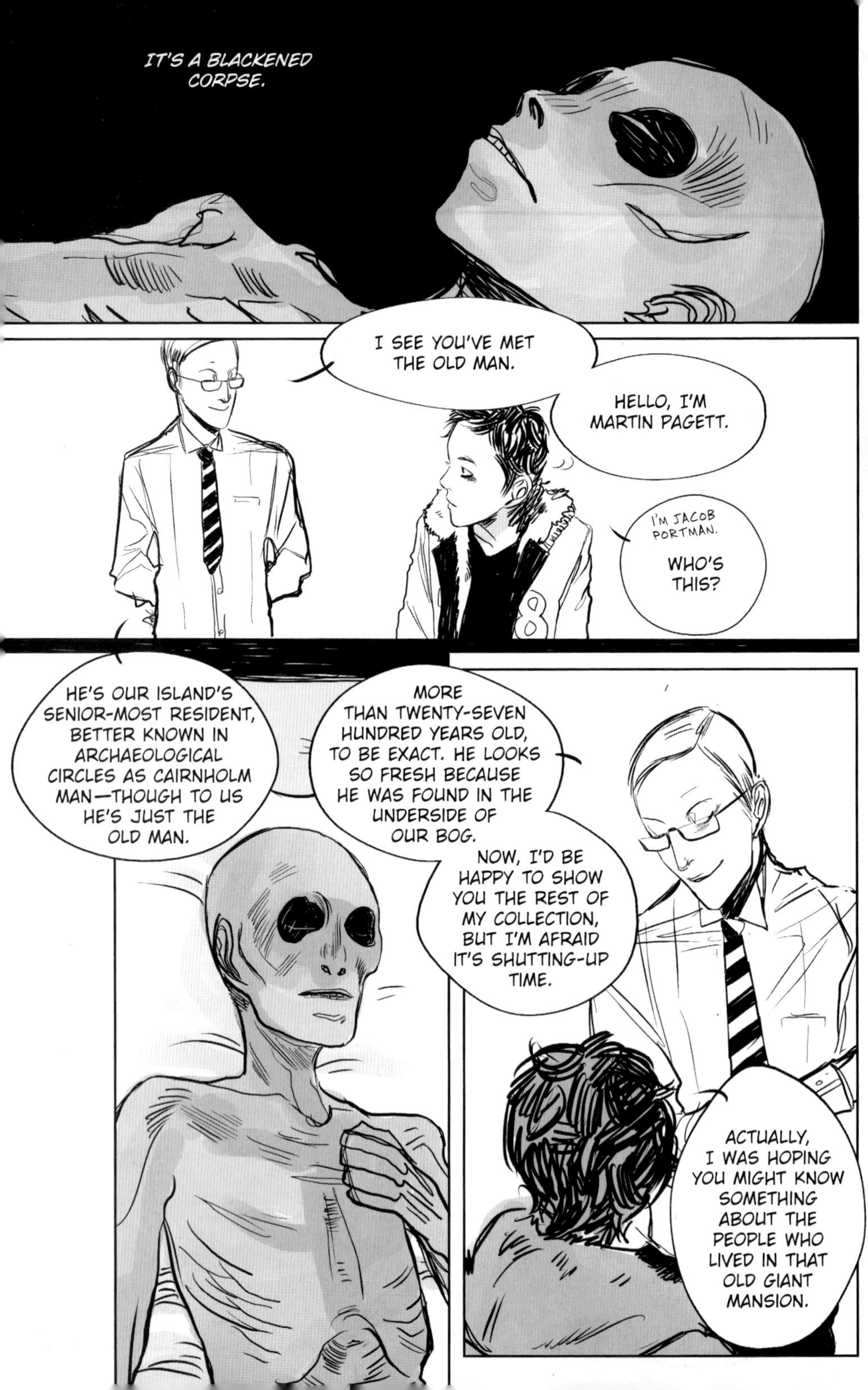
IT'S A BLACKENED CORPSE.
I SEE YOU'VE MET THE OLD MAN.
HELLO, I'M MARTIN PAGETT.
I'M JACOB PORTMAN.
WHO'S THIS?
HE'S OUR ISLAND'S SENIOR-MOST RESIDENT, BETTER KNOWN IN ARCHAEOLOGICAL CIRCLES AS CAIRNHOLM MAN—THOUGH TO US HE'S JUST THE OLD MAN.
MORE THAN TWENTY-SEVEN HUNDRED YEARS OLD, TO BE EXACT. HE LOOKS SO FRESH BECAUSE HE WAS FOUND IN THE UNDERSIDE OF OUR BOG.
NOW, I'D BE HAPPY TO SHOW YOU THE REST OF MY COLLECTION, BUT I'M AFRAID IT'S SHUTTING-UP TIME.
ACTUALLY, I WAS HOPING YOU MIGHT KNOW SOMETHING ABOUT THE PEOPLE WHO LIVED IN THAT OLD GIANT MANSION.

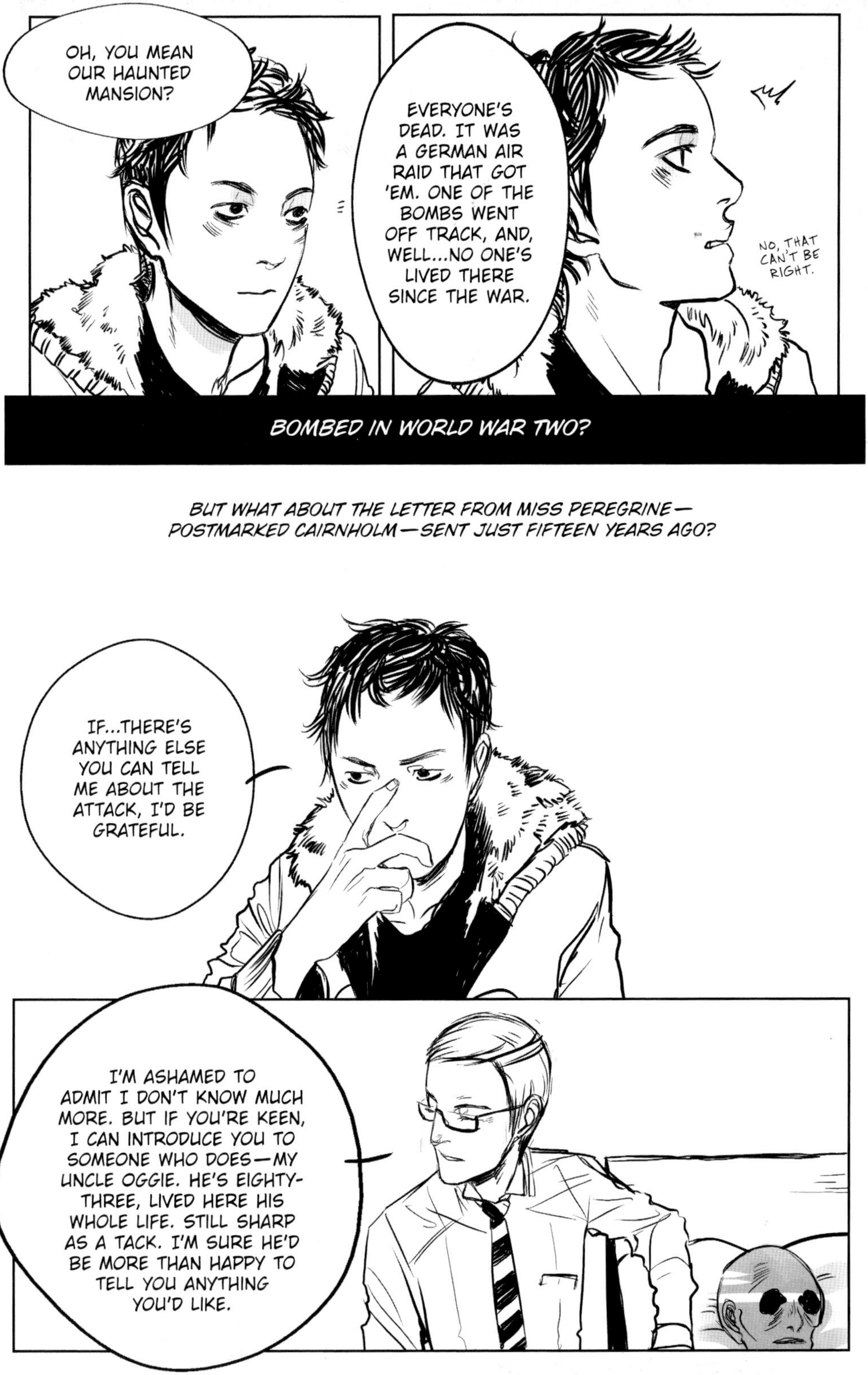
OH, YOU MEAN OUR HAUNTED MANSION?
EVERYONE'S DEAD. IT WAS A GERMAN AIR RAID THAT GOT 'EM. ONE OF THE BOMBS WENT OFF TRACK, AND, WELL...NO ONE'S LIVED THERE SINCE THE WAR.
NO, THAT CAN'T BE RIGHT.
BOMBED IN WORLD WAR TWO?
BUT WHAT ABOUT THE LETTER FROM MISS PEREGRINE—POSTMARKED CAIRNHOLM—SENT JUST FIFTEEN YEARS AGO?
IF...THERE'S ANYTHING ELSE YOU CAN TELL ME ABOUT THE ATTACK, I'D BE GRATEFUL.
I'M ASHAMED TO ADMIT I DON'T KNOW MUCH MORE. BUT IF YOU'RE KEEN, I CAN INTRODUCE YOU TO SOMEONE WHO DOES—MY UNCLE OGGIE. HE'S EIGHTY-THREE, LIVED HERE HIS WHOLE LIFE. STILL SHARP AS A TACK. I'M SURE HE'D BE MORE THAN HAPPY TO TELL YOU ANYTHING YOU'D LIKE.

[redacted]

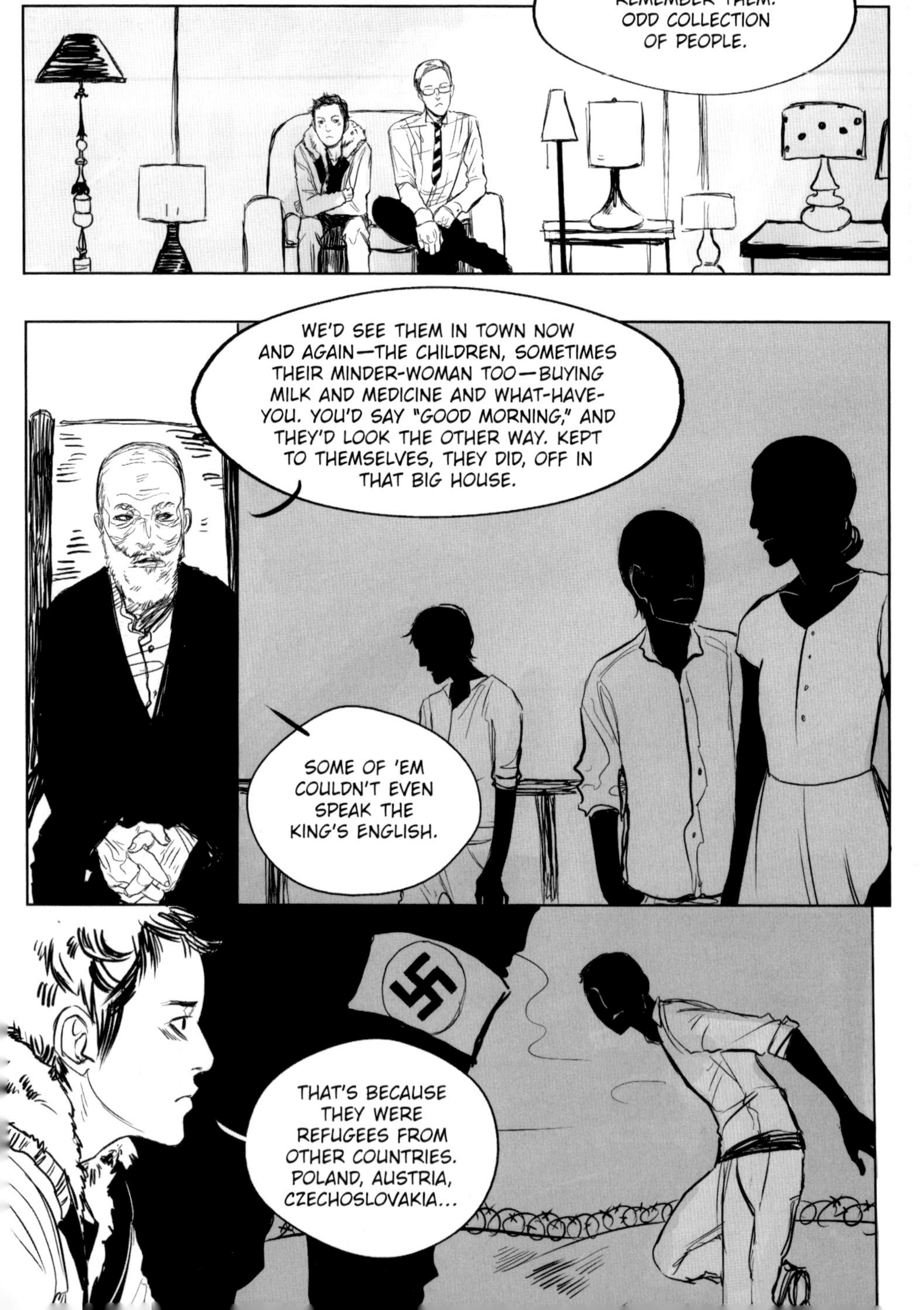
SURE, I REMEMBER THEM. ODD COLLECTION OF PEOPLE.
WE'D SEE THEM IN TOWN NOW AND AGAIN—THE CHILDREN, SOMETIMES THEIR MINDER-WOMAN TOO—BUYING MILK AND MEDICINE AND WHAT-HAVE-YOU. YOU'D SAY "GOOD MORNING," AND THEY'D LOOK THE OTHER WAY. KEPT TO THEMSELVES, THEY DID, OFF IN THAT BIG HOUSE.
SOME OF 'EM COULDN'T EVEN SPEAK THE KING'S ENGLISH.
THAT'S BECAUSE THEY WERE REFUGEES FROM OTHER COUNTRIES. POLAND, AUSTRIA, CZECHOSLOVAKIA...

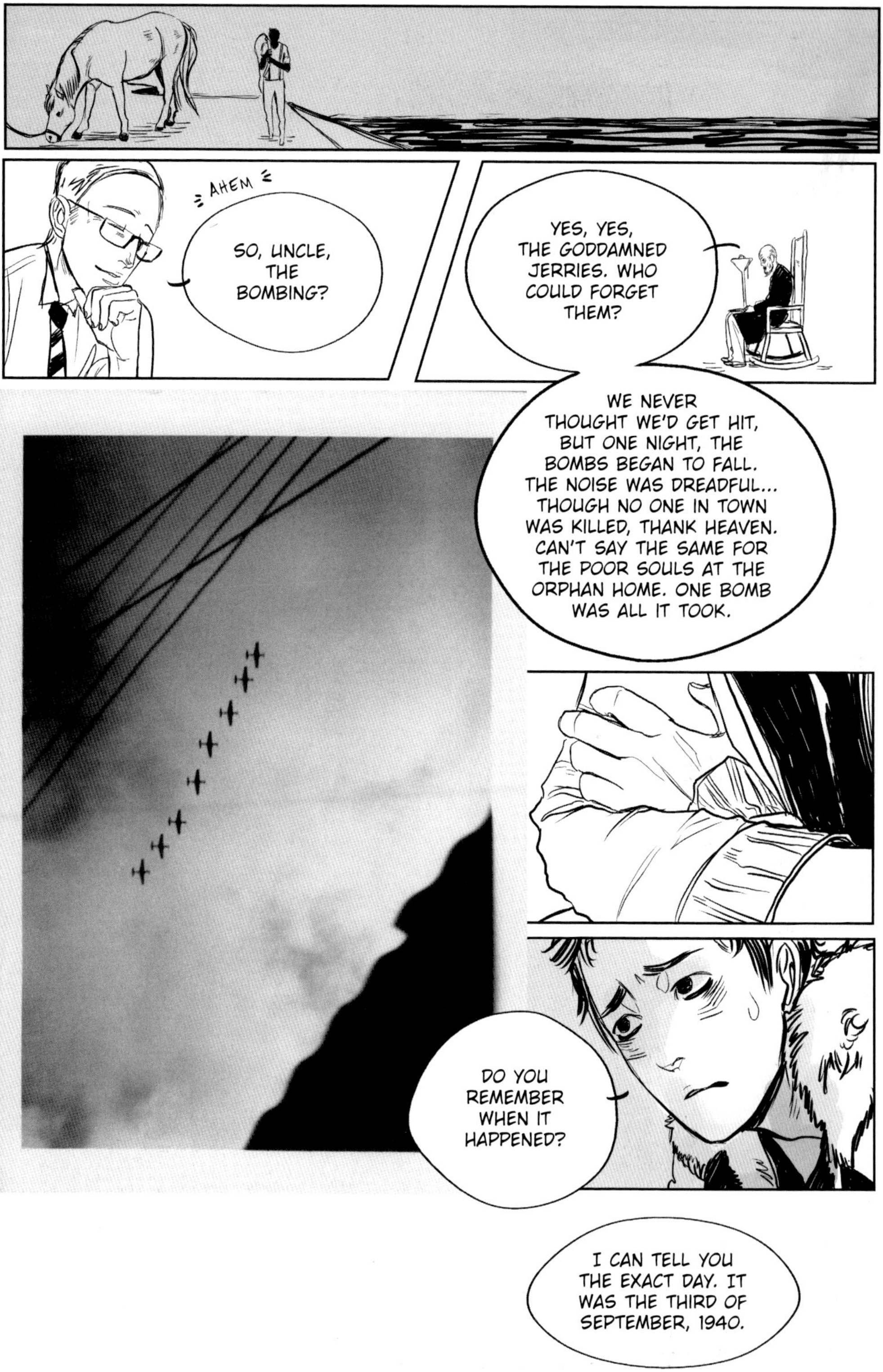
AHEM
SO, UNCLE, THE BOMBING?
YES, YES, THE GODDAMNED JERRIES. WHO COULD FORGET THEM?
WE NEVER THOUGHT WE'D GET HIT, BUT ONE NIGHT, THE BOMBS BEGAN TO FALL. THE NOISE WAS DREADFUL... THOUGH NO ONE IN TOWN WAS KILLED, THANK HEAVEN. CAN'T SAY THE SAME FOR THE POOR SOULS AT THE ORPHAN HOME. ONE BOMB WAS ALL IT TOOK.
DO YOU REMEMBER WHEN IT HAPPENED?
I CAN TELL YOU THE EXACT DAY. IT WAS THE THIRD OF SEPTEMBER, 1940.

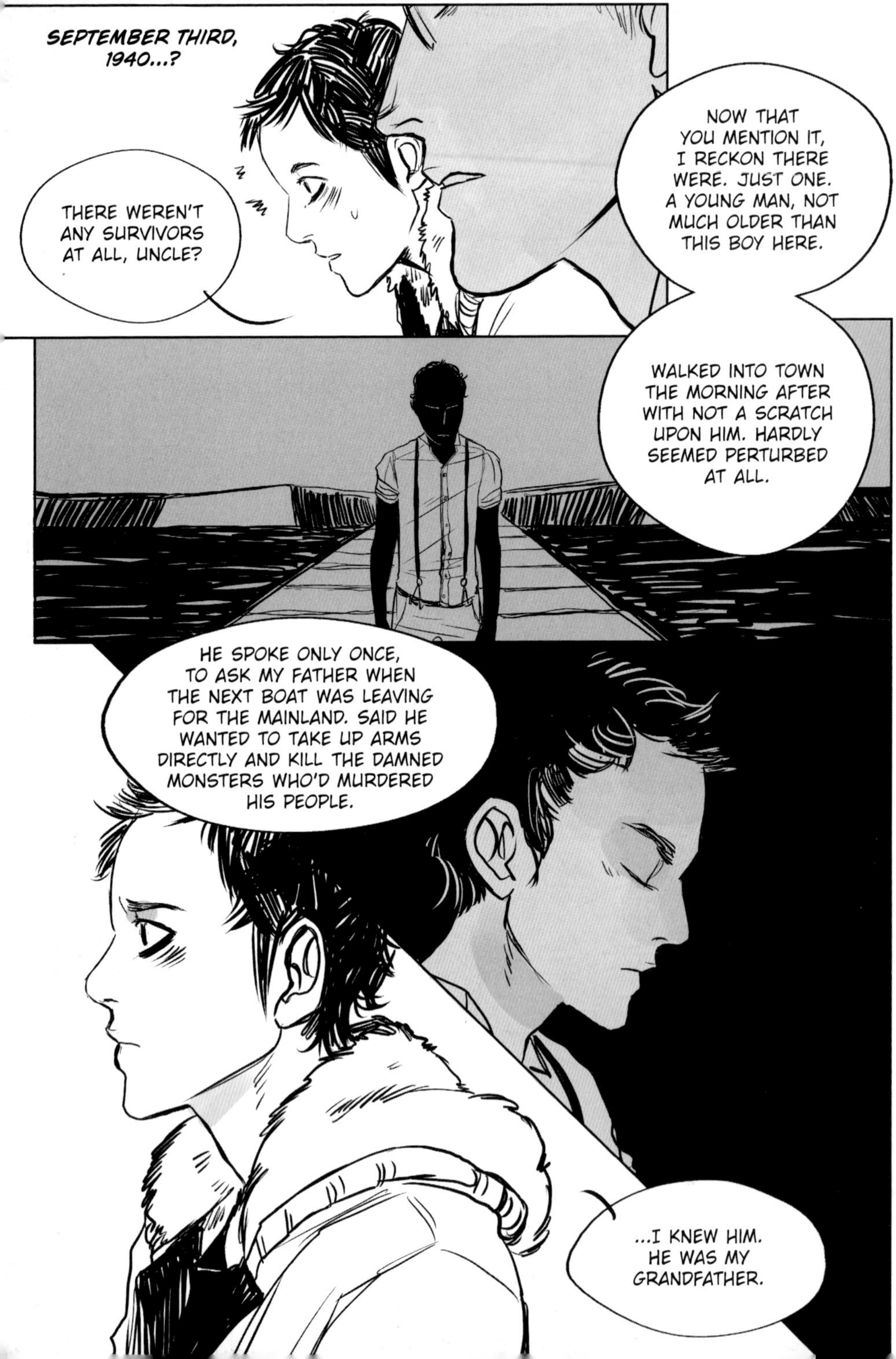
SEPTEMBER THIRD, 1940...?
THERE WEREN'T ANY SURVIVORS AT ALL, UNCLE?
NOW THAT YOU MENTION IT, I RECKON THERE WERE. JUST ONE. A YOUNG MAN, NOT MUCH OLDER THAN THIS BOY HERE.
WALKED INTO TOWN THE MORNING AFTER WITH NOT A SCRATCH UPON HIM. HARDLY SEEMED PERTURBED AT ALL.
HE SPOKE ONLY ONCE, TO ASK MY FATHER WHEN THE NEXT BOAT WAS LEAVING FOR THE MAINLAND. SAID HE WANTED TO TAKE UP ARMS DIRECTLY AND KILL THE DAMNED MONSTERS WHO'D MURDERED HIS PEOPLE.
...I KNEW HIM. HE WAS MY GRANDFATHER.

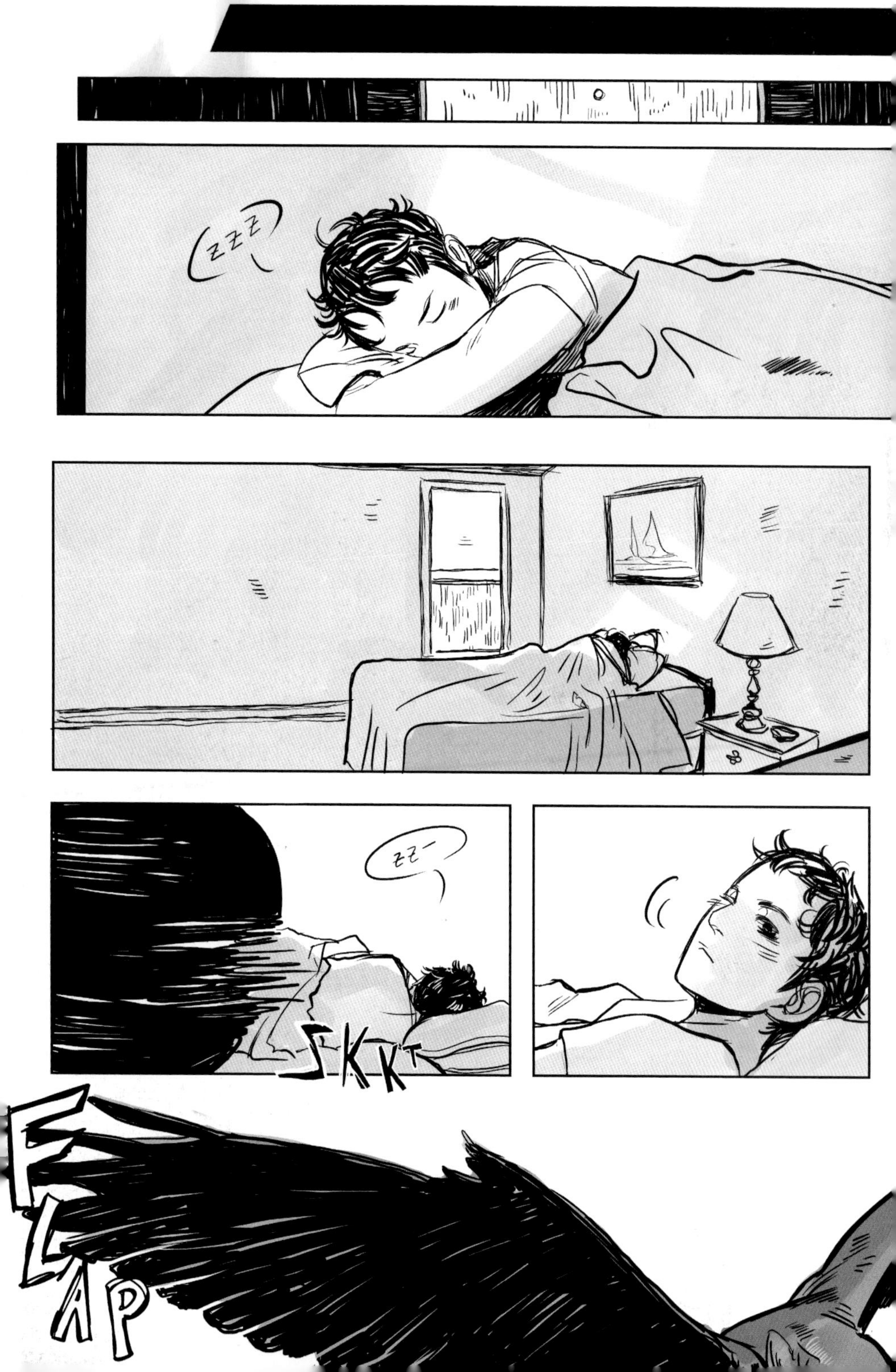
ZZZ
ZZ–
SKKT
FLAP

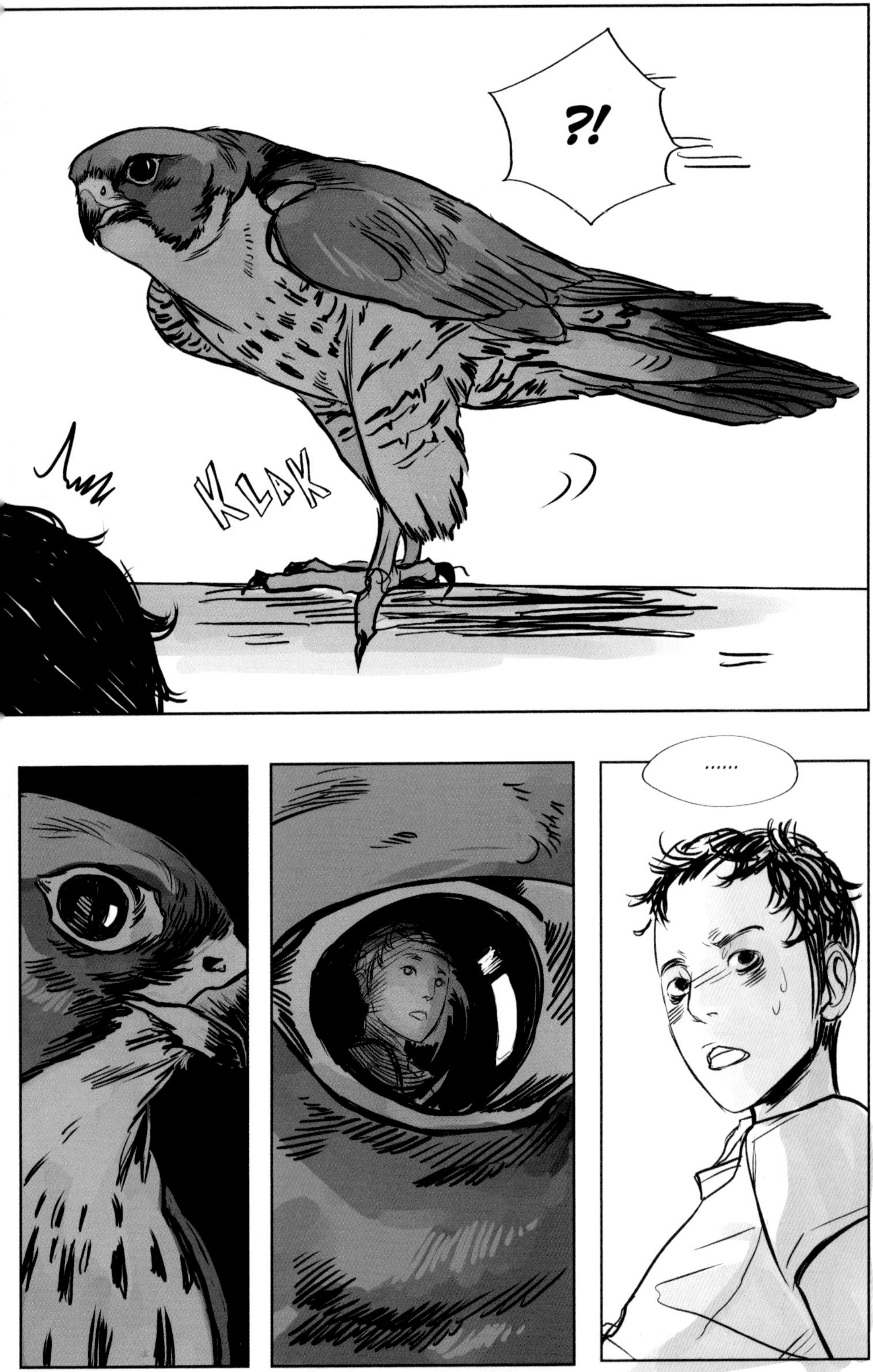
?!
KLAK
......

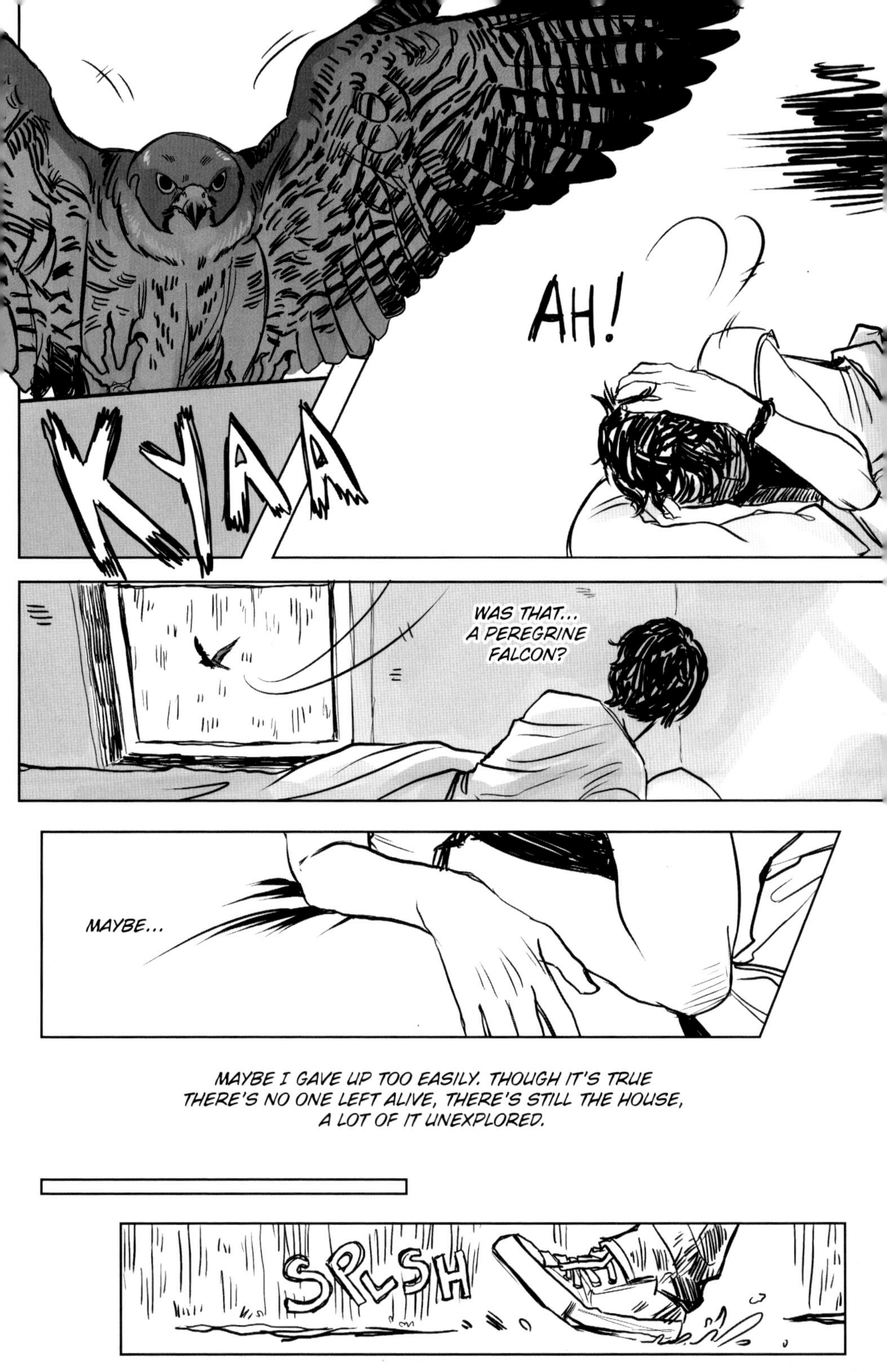
KYAA
AH!
WAS THAT... A PEREGRINE FALCON?
MAYBE...
MAYBE I GAVE UP TOO EASILY. THOUGH IT'S TRUE THERE'S NO ONE LEFT ALIVE, THERE'S STILL THE HOUSE, A LOT OF IT UNEXPLORED.
SPLSH

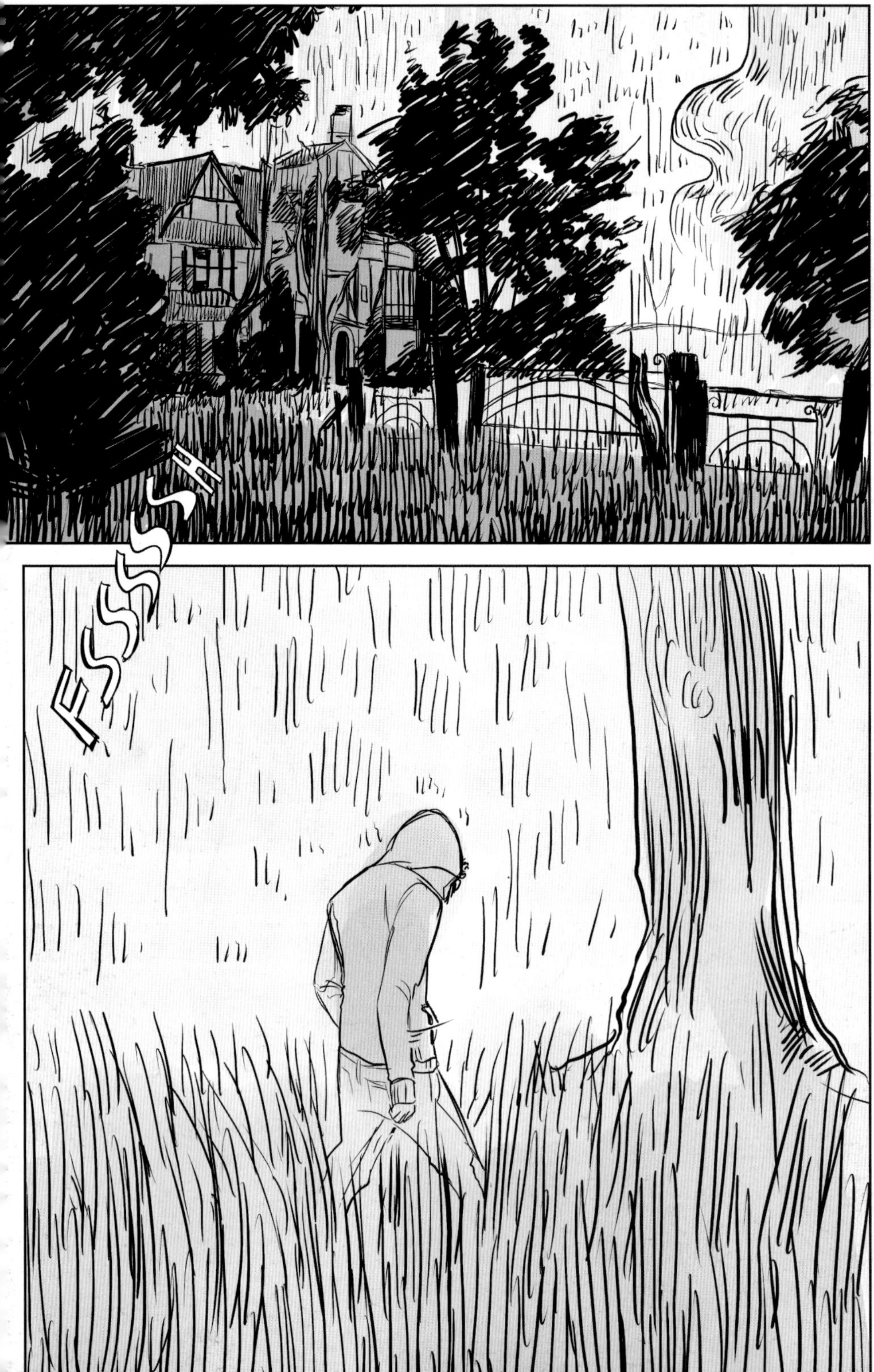
FSSSSSH

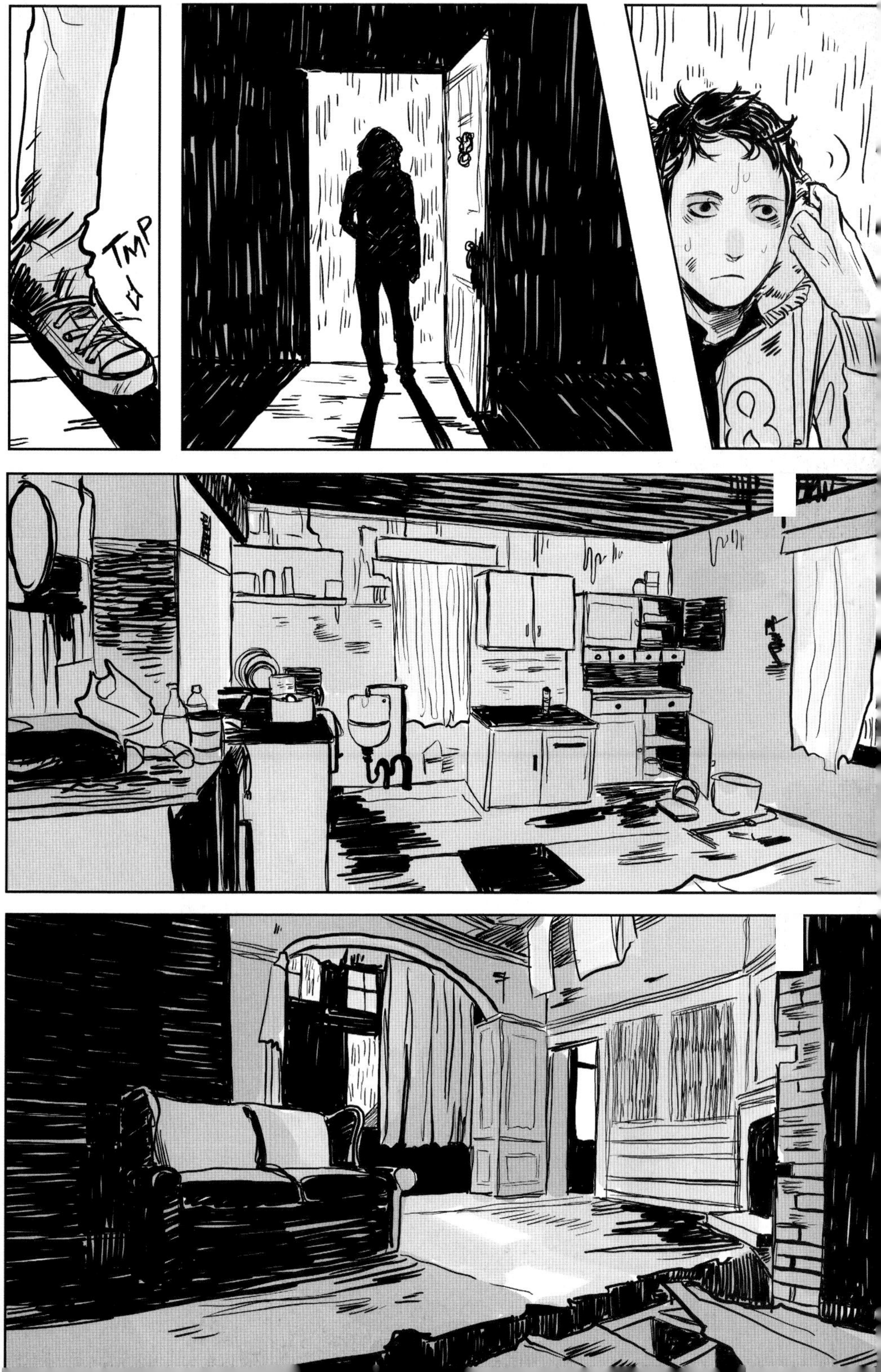
TMP

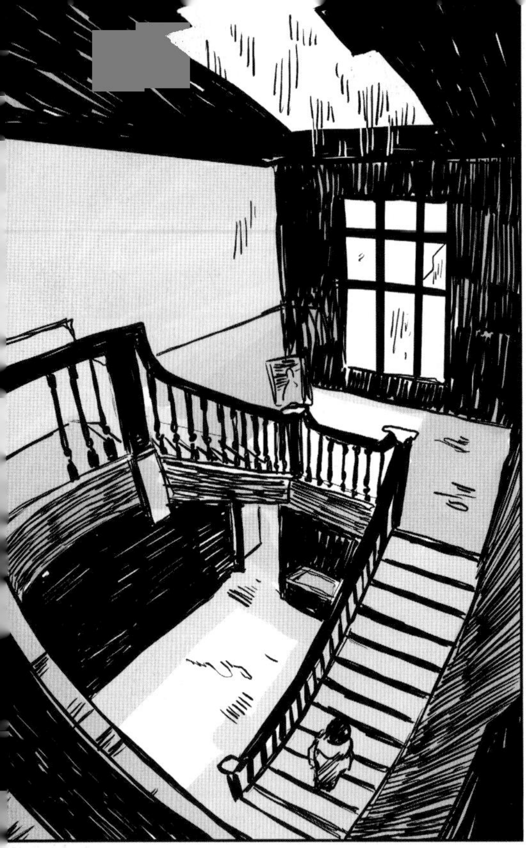

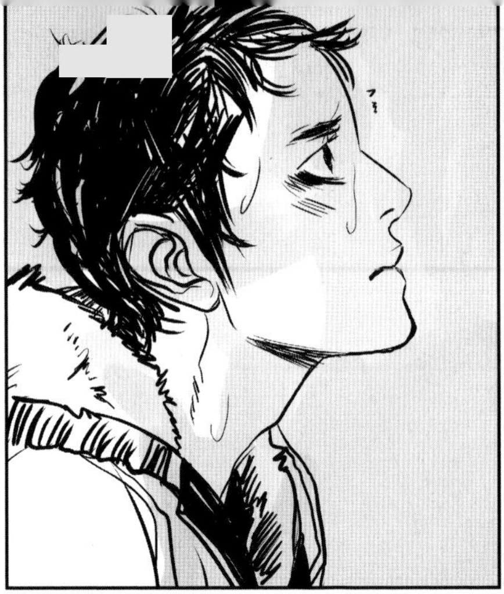

WISH I HAD A FLASHLIGHT...

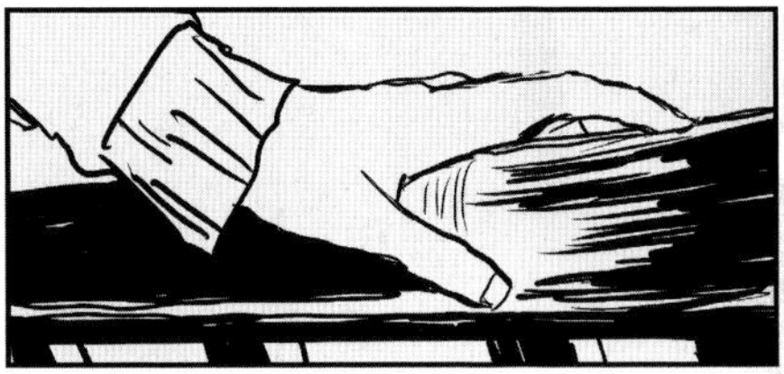

IT LOOKS LIKE THE UPSTAIRS ISN'T AS BOMBED OUT.

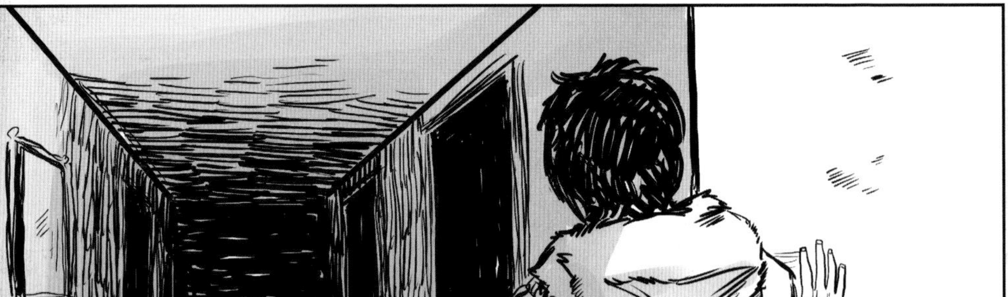

ALL THE BEDROOMS...THEY'RE IN SURPRISINGLY GOOD SHAPE.

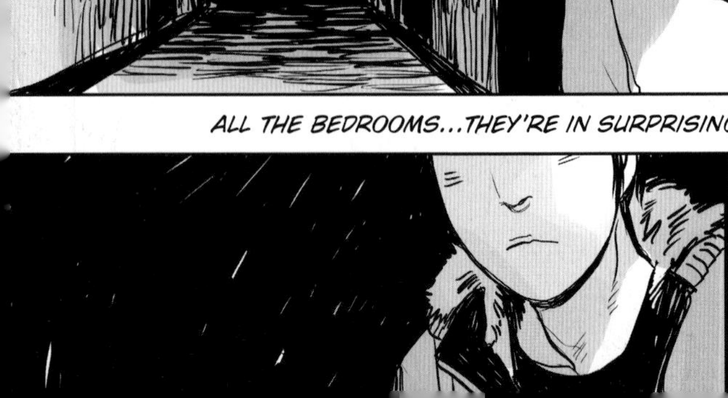

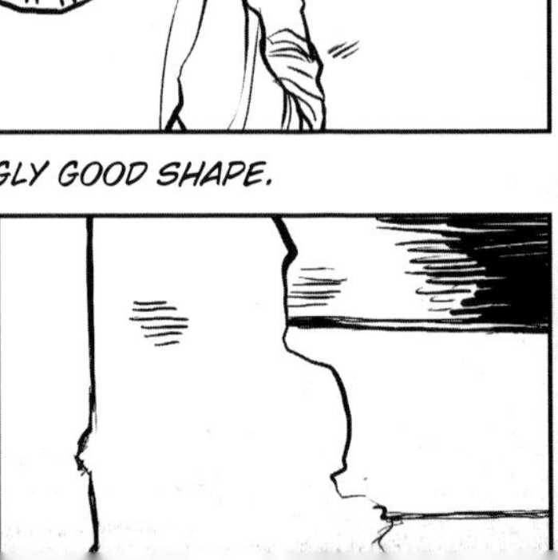

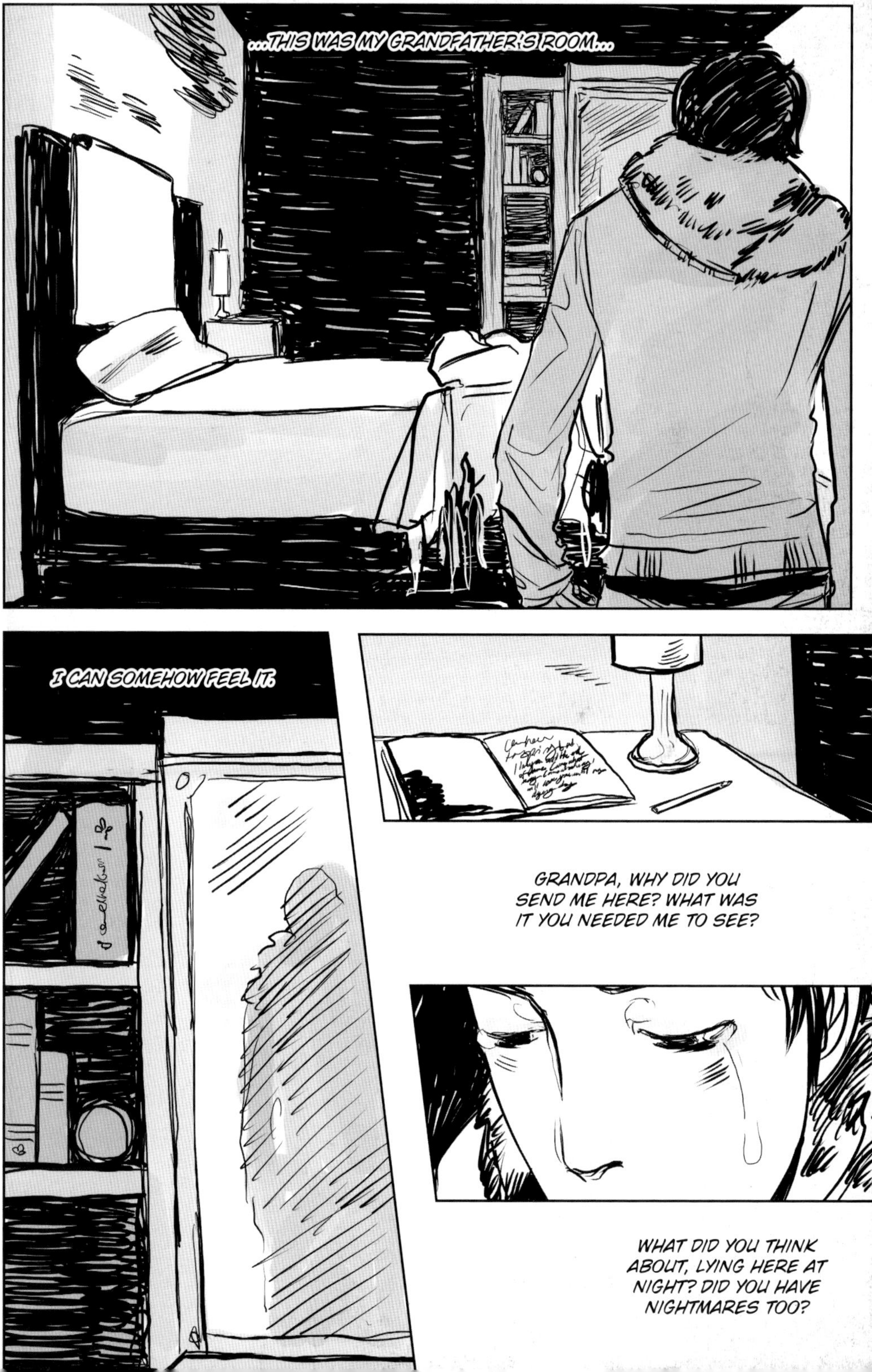
...THIS WAS MY GRANDFATHER'S ROOM...
I CAN SOMEHOW FEEL IT.
GRANDPA, WHY DID YOU SEND ME HERE? WHAT WAS IT YOU NEEDED ME TO SEE?
WHAT DID YOU THINK ABOUT, LYING HERE AT NIGHT? DID YOU HAVE NIGHTMARES TOO?

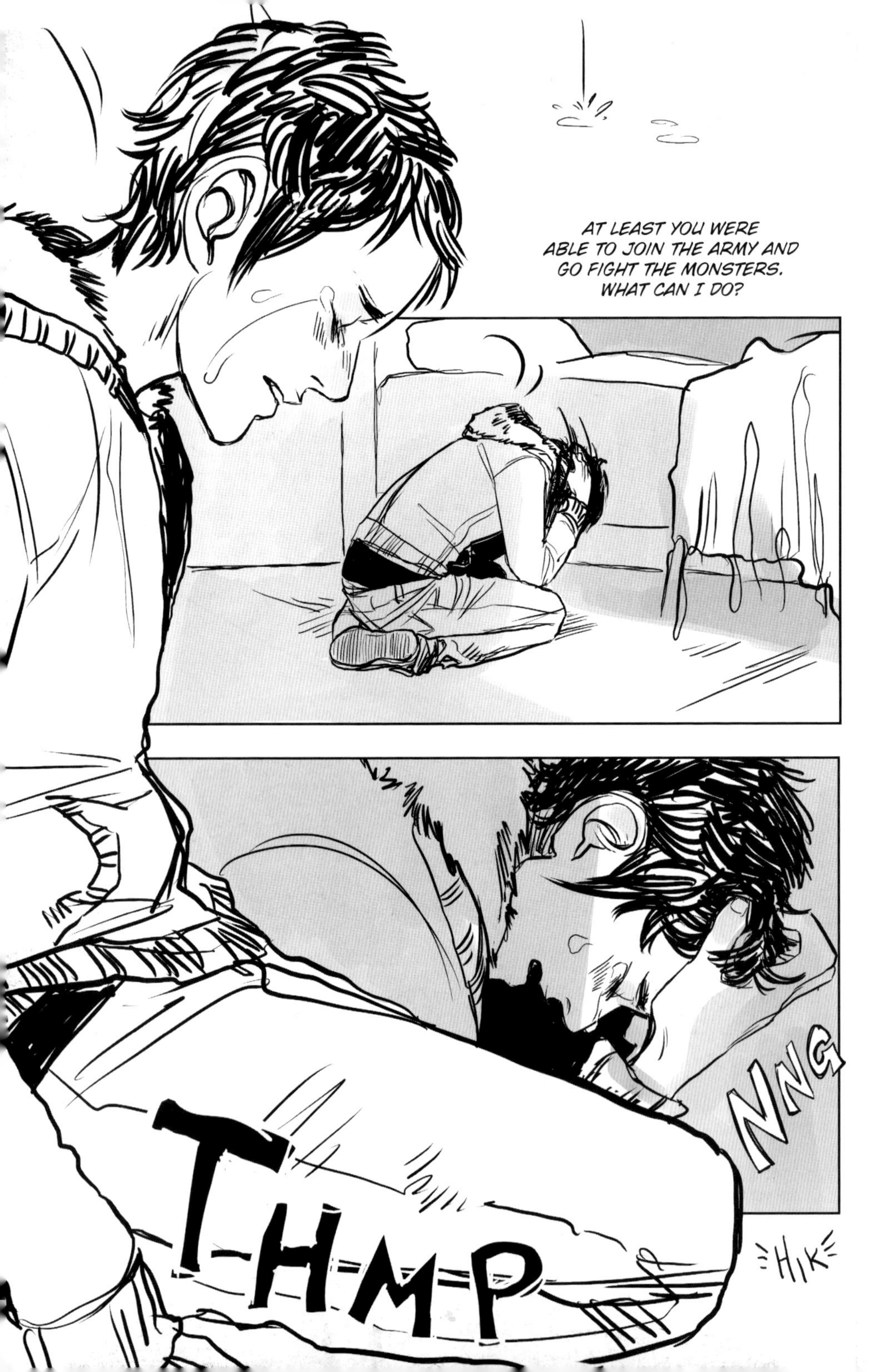
AT LEAST YOU WERE ABLE TO JOIN THE ARMY AND GO FIGHT THE MONSTERS. WHAT CAN I DO?
NNG
THMP
HIK

siiiig

SNIFF

WAS THAT
THERE THE
WHOLE
TIME?

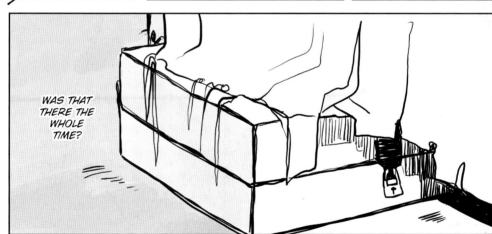

IT'S LOCKED.
YOU DON'T LOCK
AN EMPTY TRUNK.

AND IT'S JUST
BEGGING TO
BE OPENED.

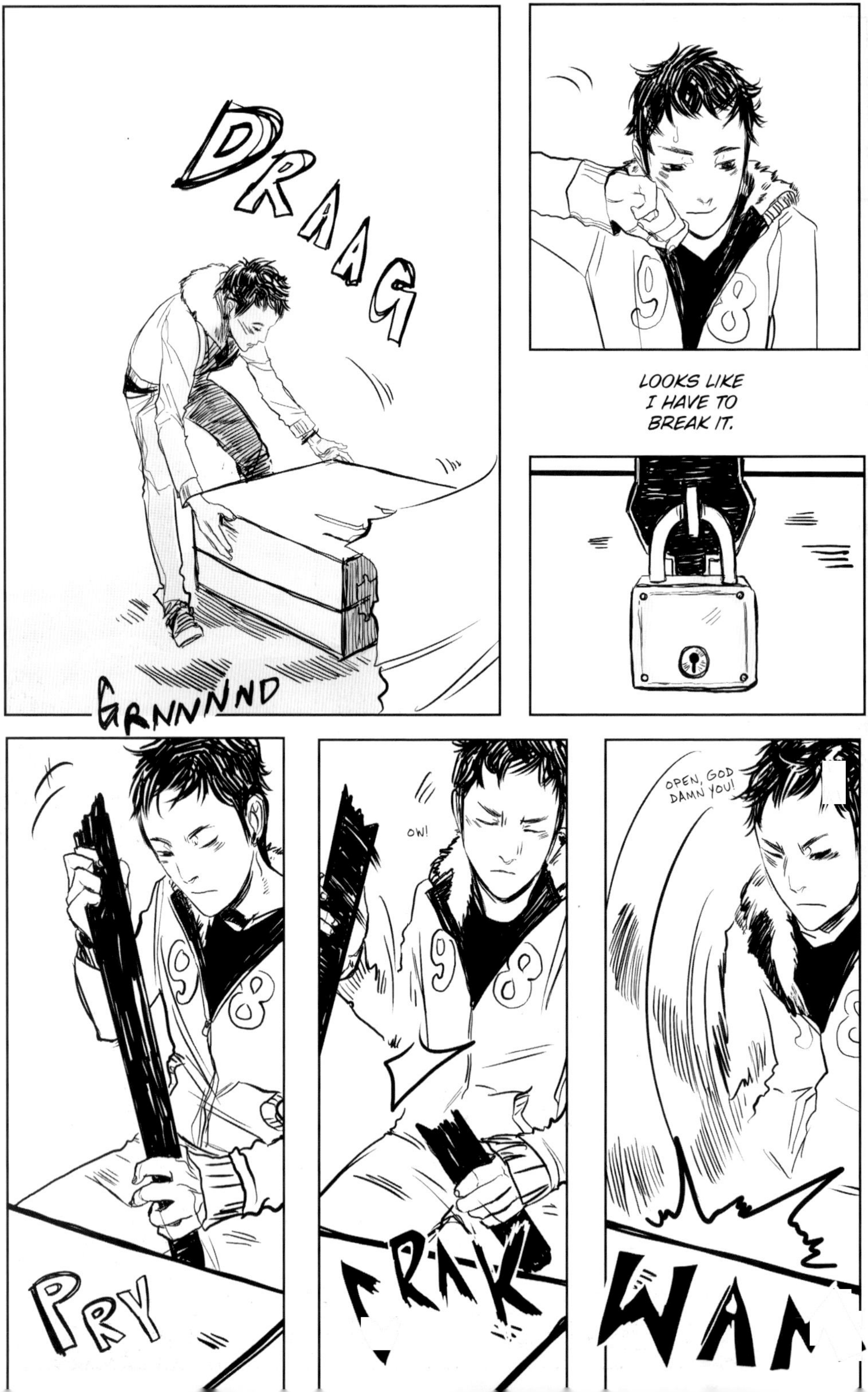
DRAAG
GRNNNND
LOOKS LIKE I HAVE TO BREAK IT.
PRY
OW!
RA-K
OPEN, GOD DAMN YOU!
WAM

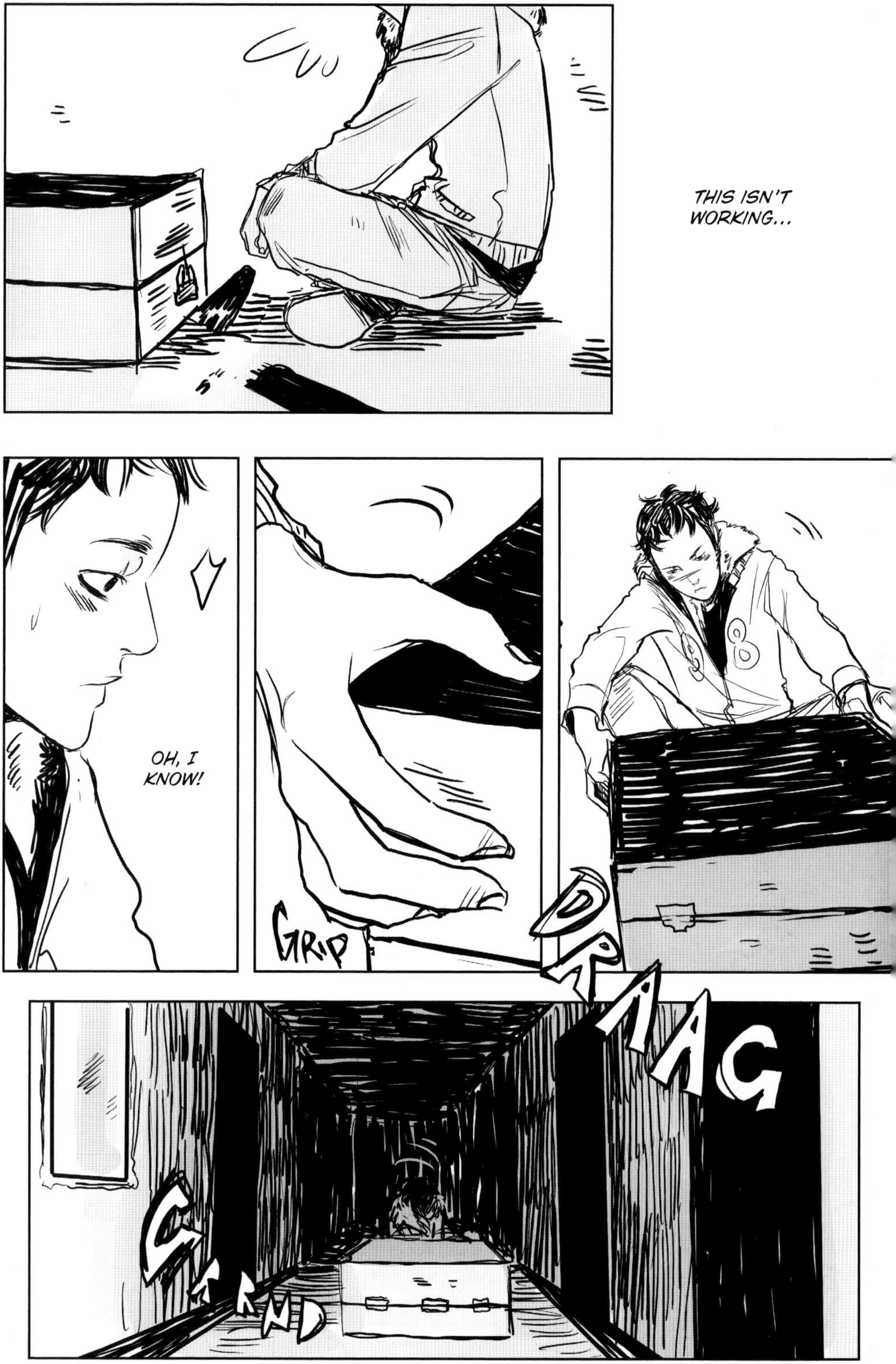

THIS ISN'T WORKING...
OH, I KNOW!
GRIP
DRAAG

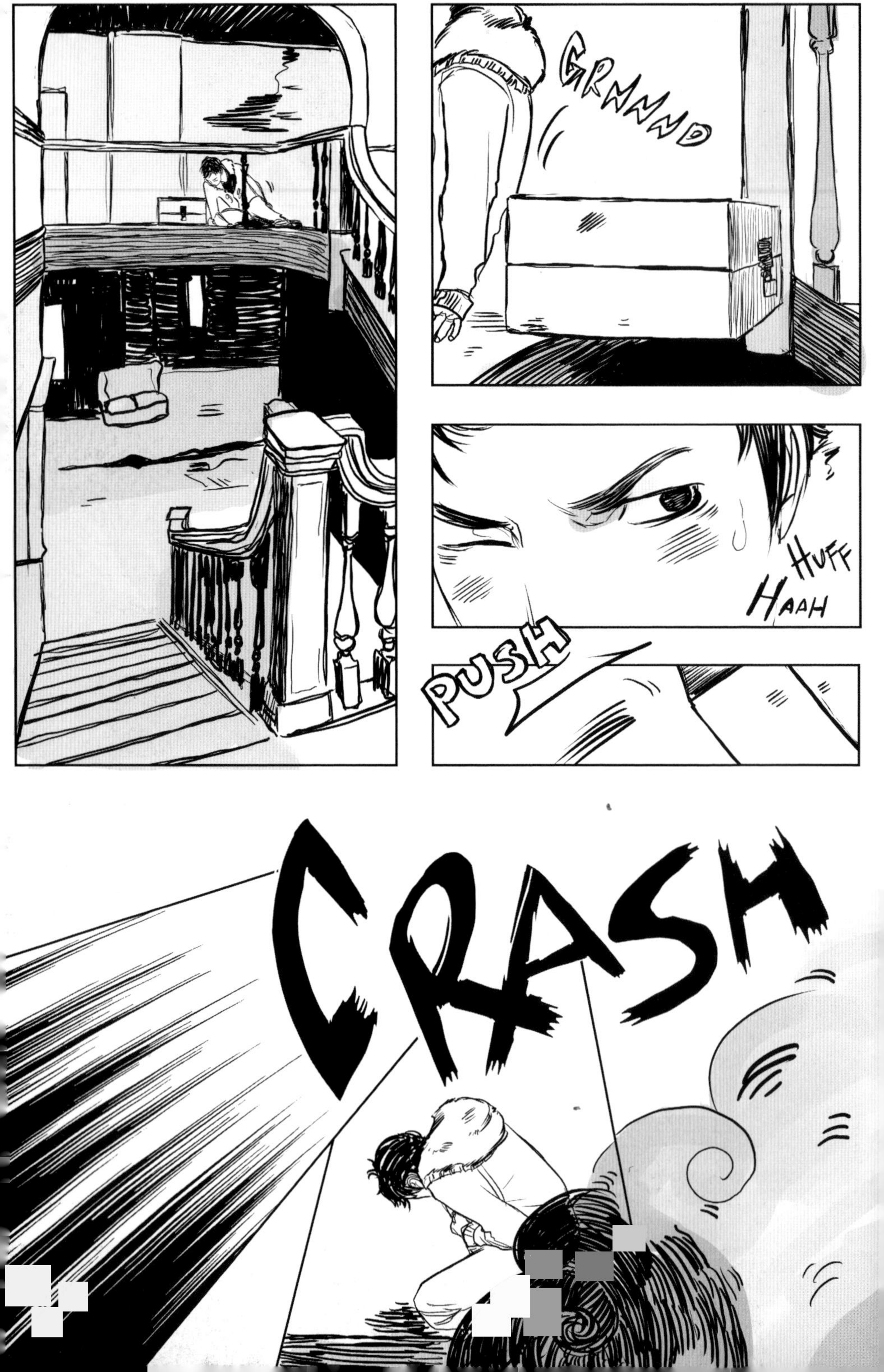
GRNNND
HUFF
HAAH
PUSH
CRASH

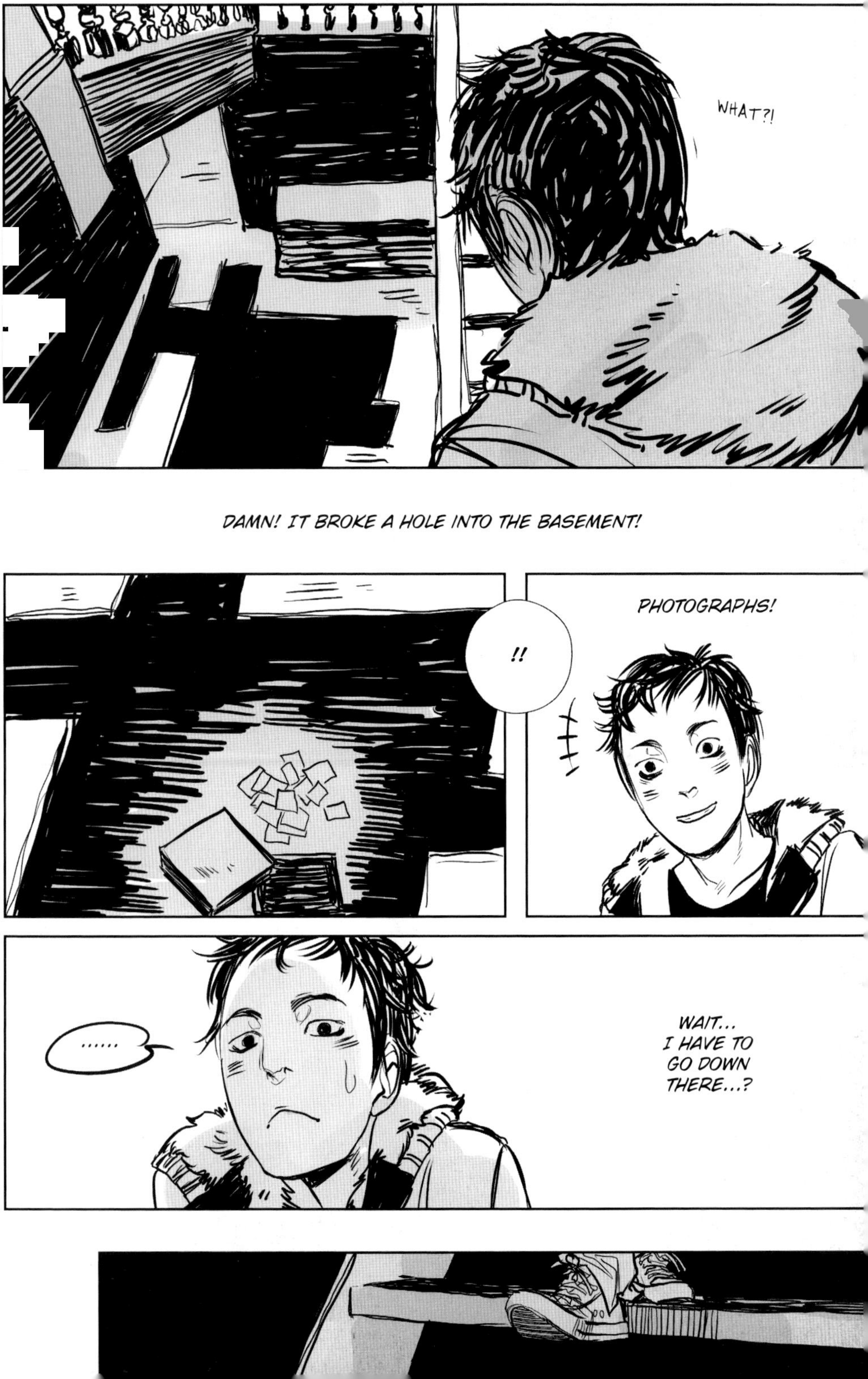
WHAT?!
DAMN! IT BROKE A HOLE INTO THE BASEMENT!
!!
PHOTOGRAPHS!
......
WAIT... I HAVE TO GO DOWN THERE...?

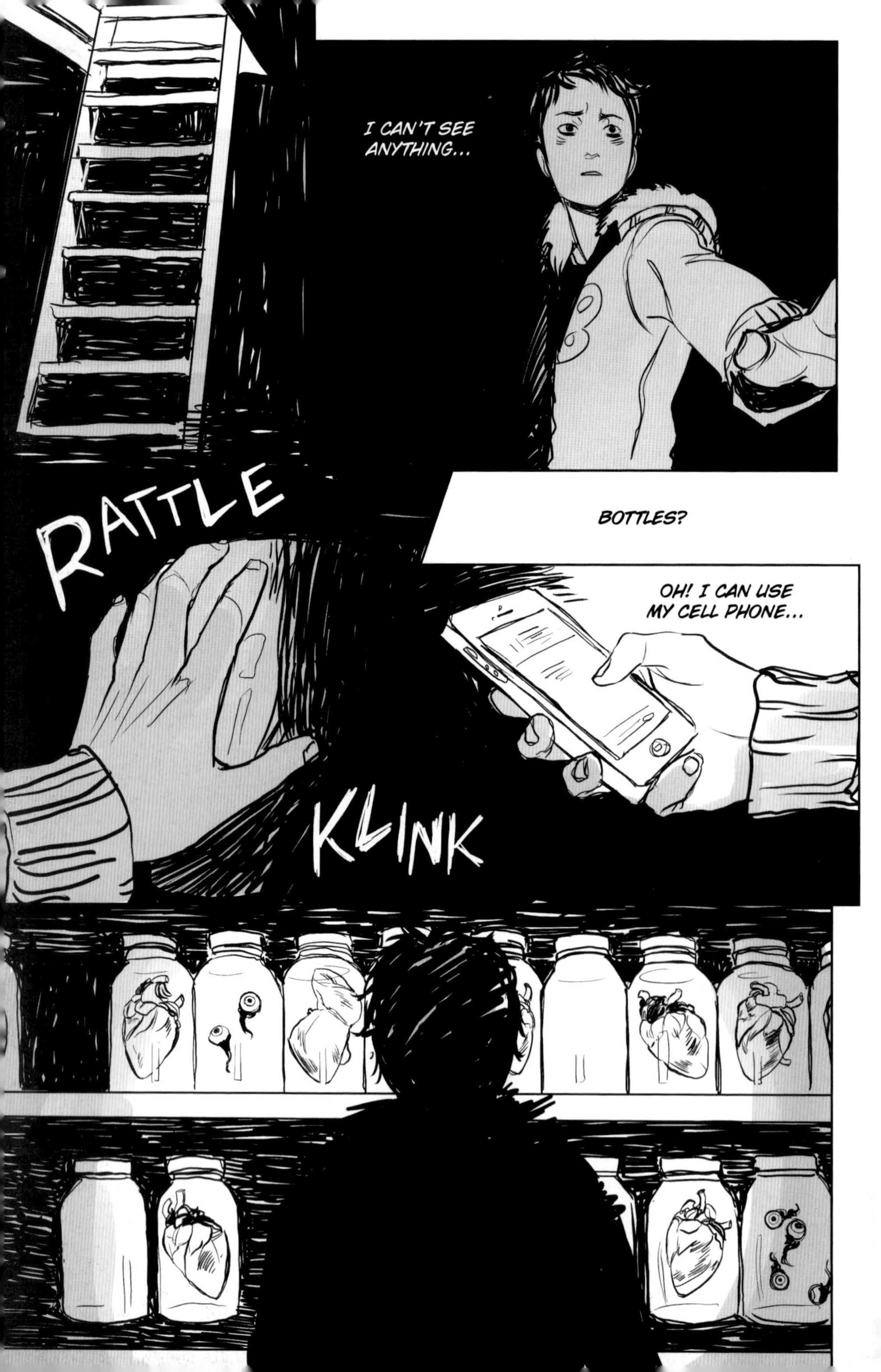
I CAN'T SEE ANYTHING...
RATTLE
BOTTLES?
OH! I CAN USE MY CELL PHONE...
KLINK

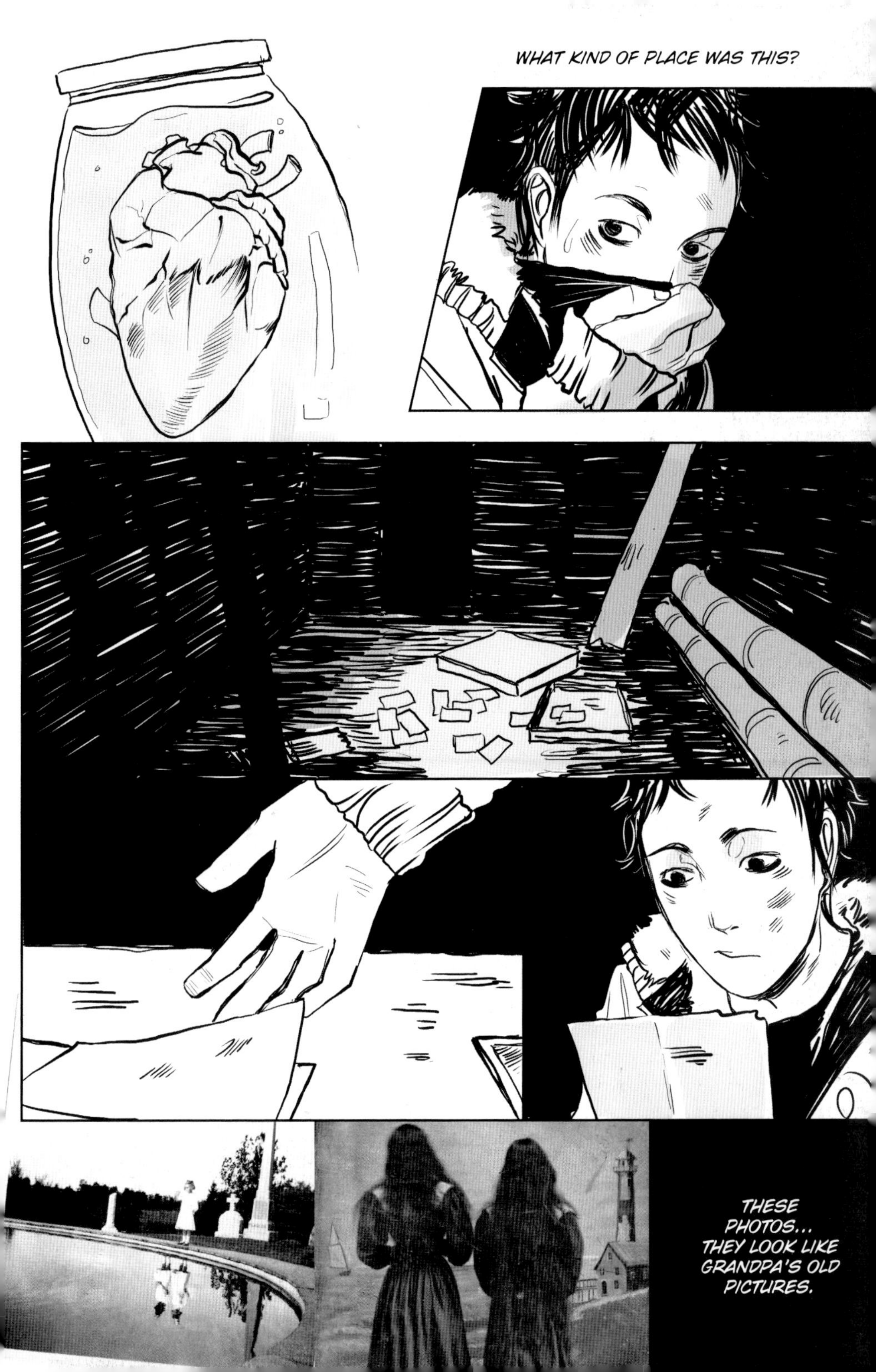
WHAT KIND OF PLACE WAS THIS?
THESE PHOTOS... THEY LOOK LIKE GRANDPA'S OLD PICTURES.

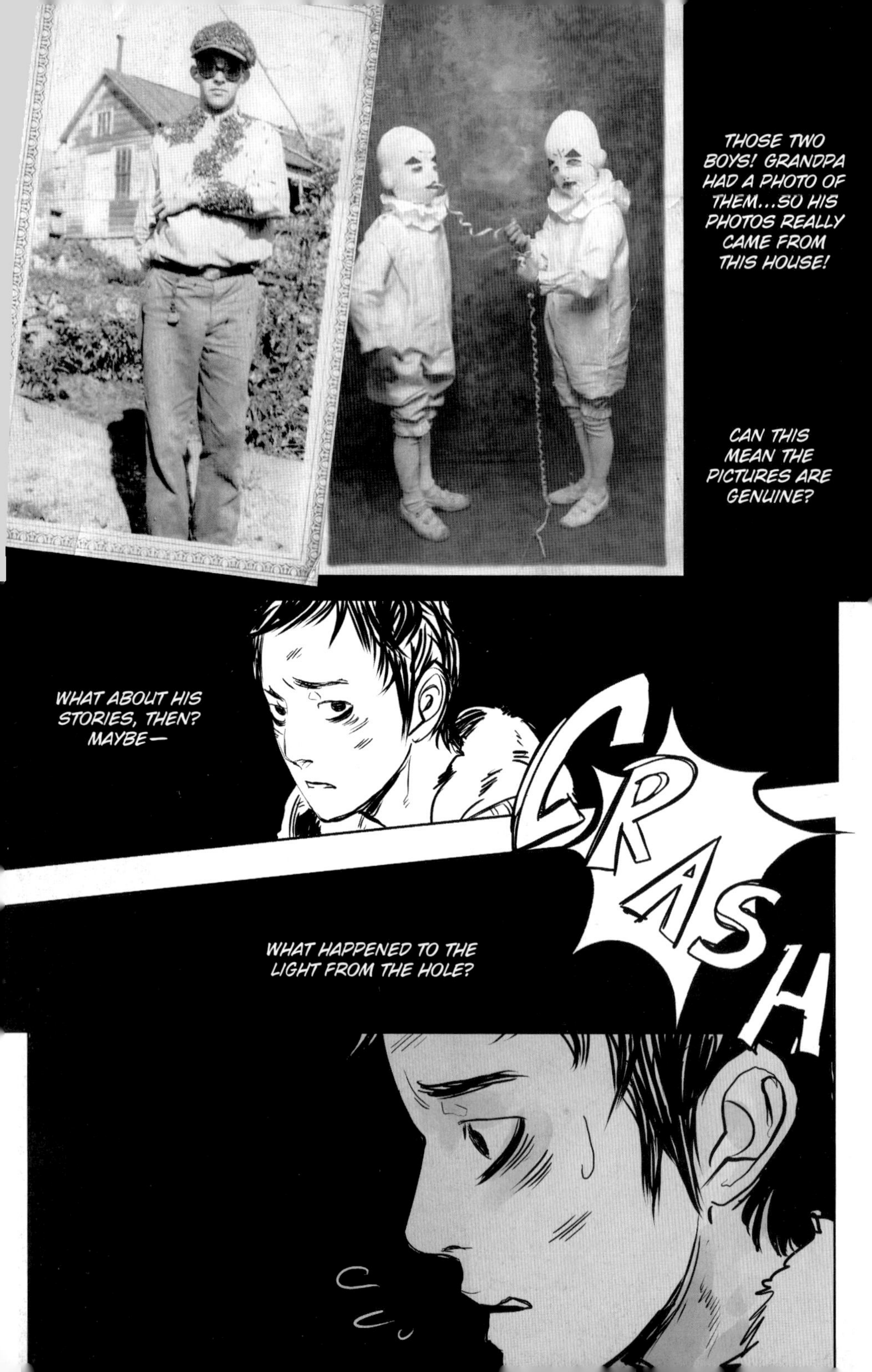
THOSE TWO BOYS! GRANDPA HAD A PHOTO OF THEM...SO HIS PHOTOS REALLY CAME FROM THIS HOUSE!
CAN THIS MEAN THE PICTURES ARE GENUINE?
WHAT ABOUT HIS STORIES, THEN? MAYBE—
CRASH
WHAT HAPPENED TO THE LIGHT FROM THE HOLE?

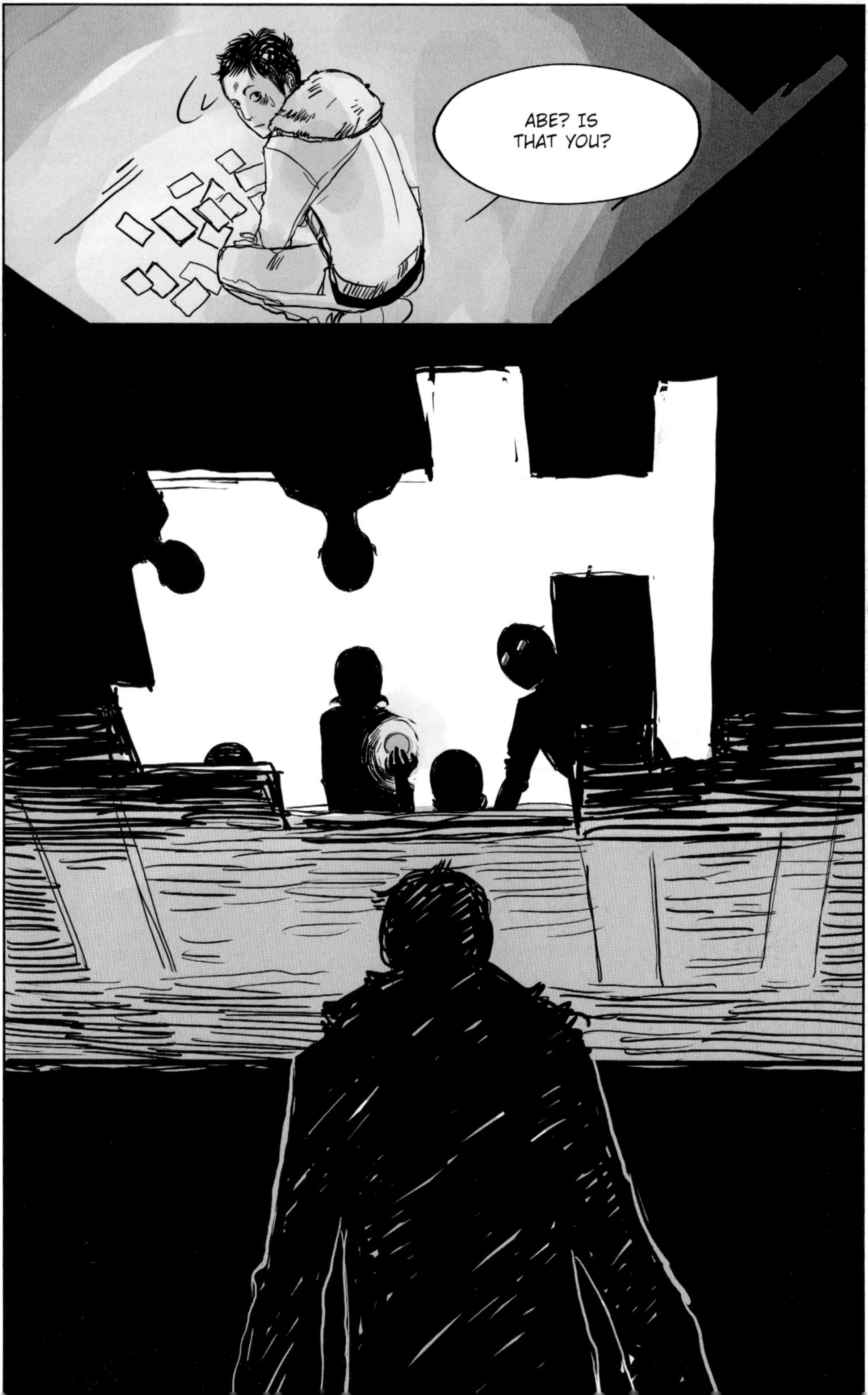
ABE? IS THAT YOU?

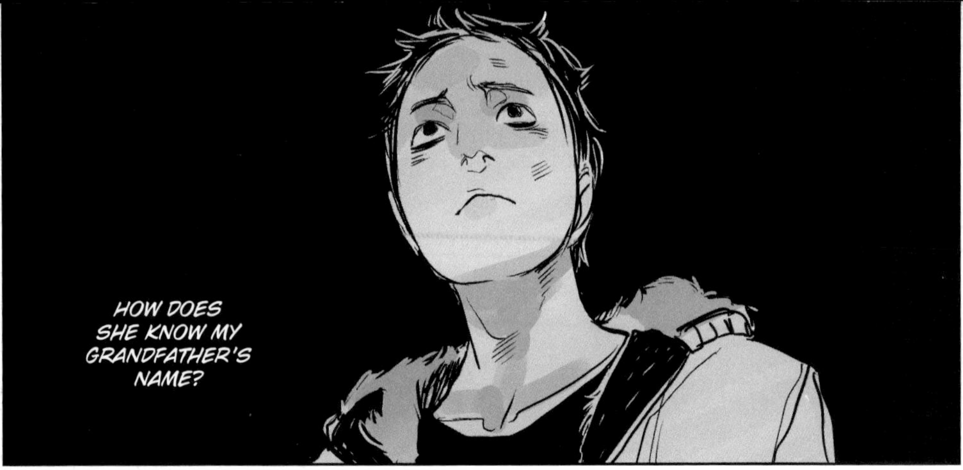
HOW DOES SHE KNOW MY GRANDFATHER'S NAME?

WAIT, I KNOW THEM!

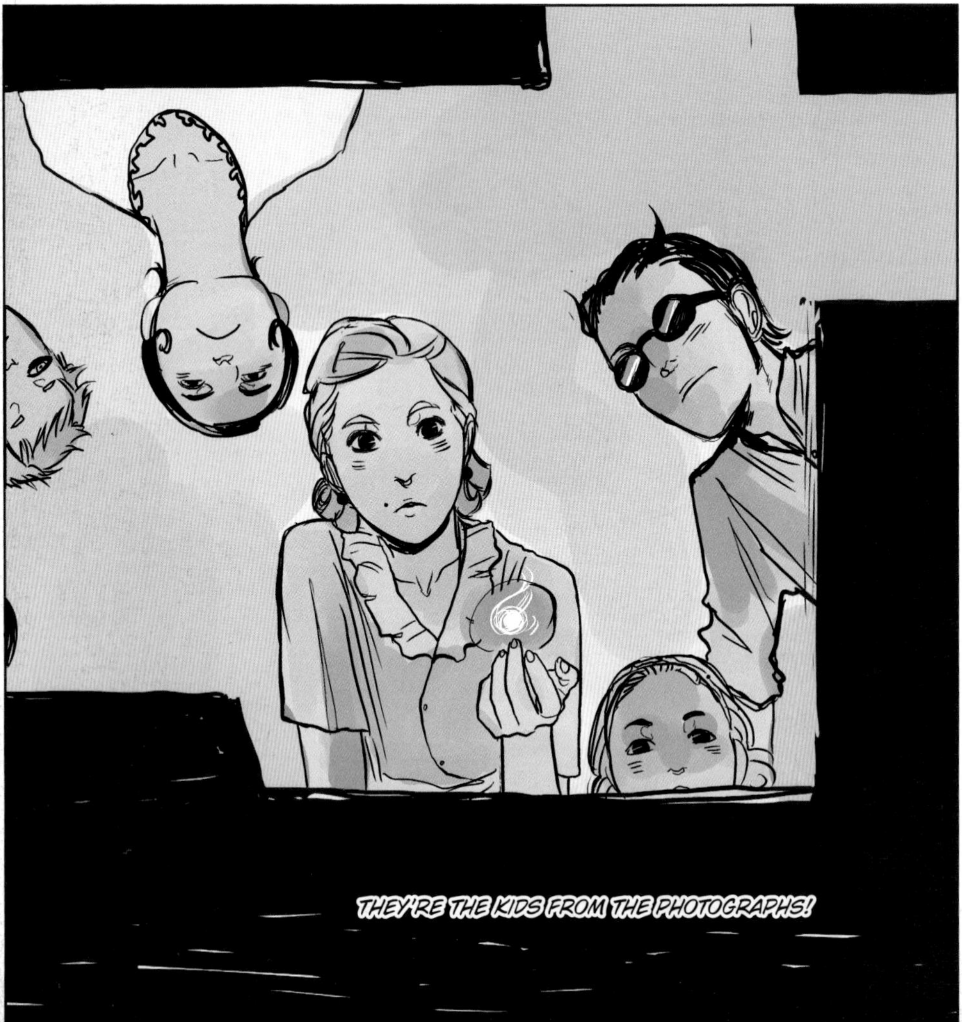
THEY'RE THE KIDS FROM THE PHOTOGRAPHS!

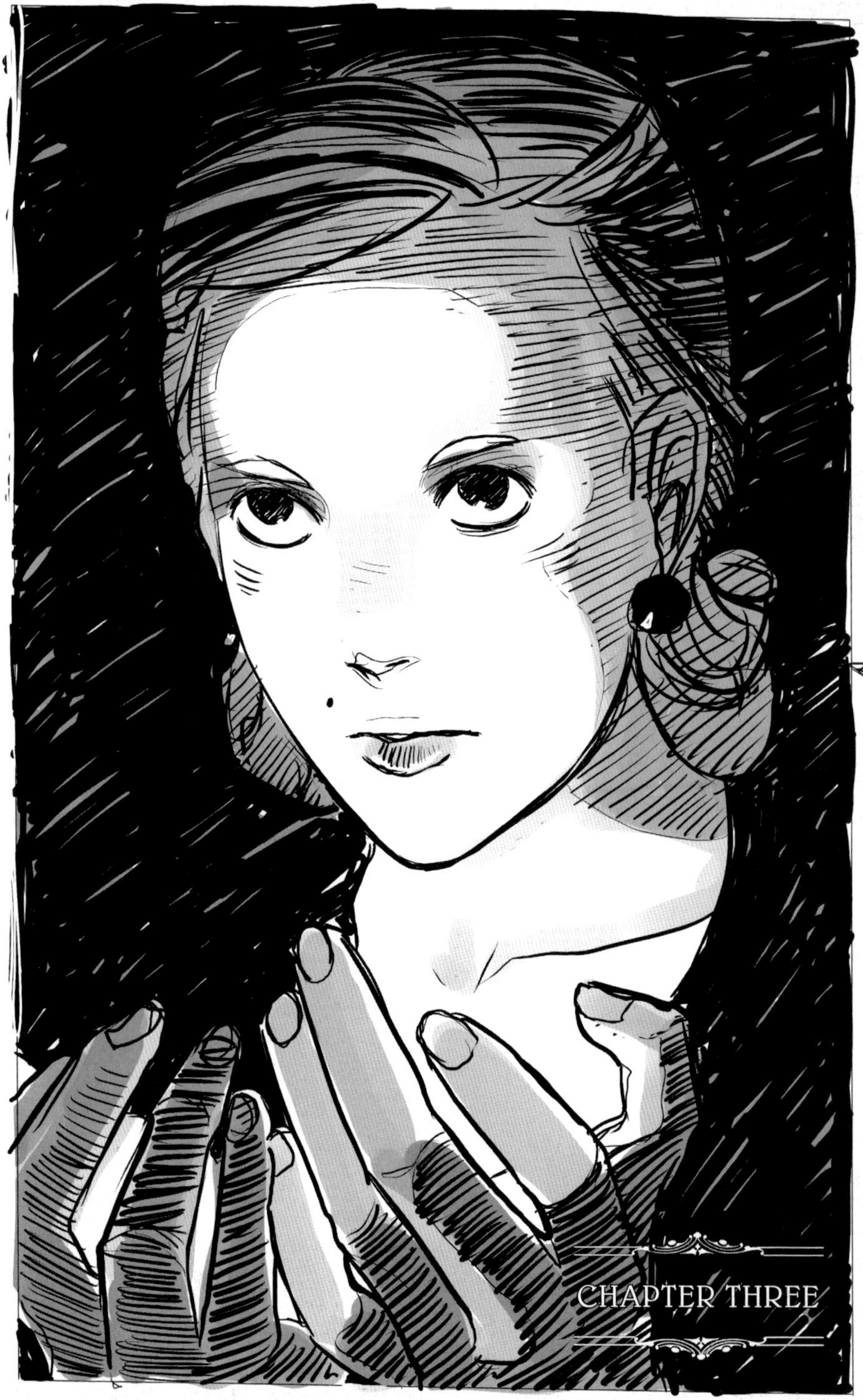
CHAPTER THREE

I FOUND THEM.

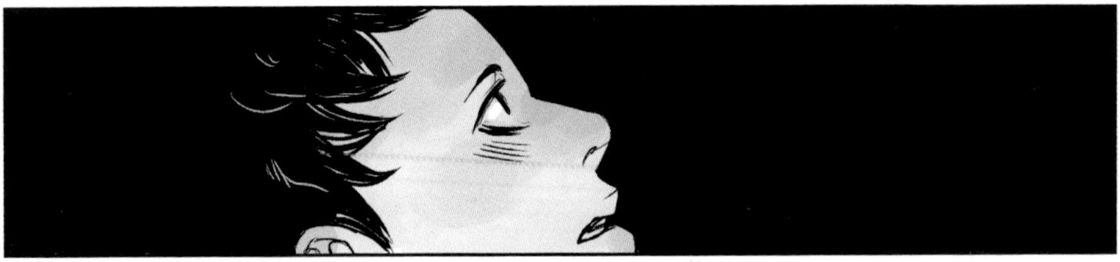

THEIR FACES...

THEIR CLOTHES...

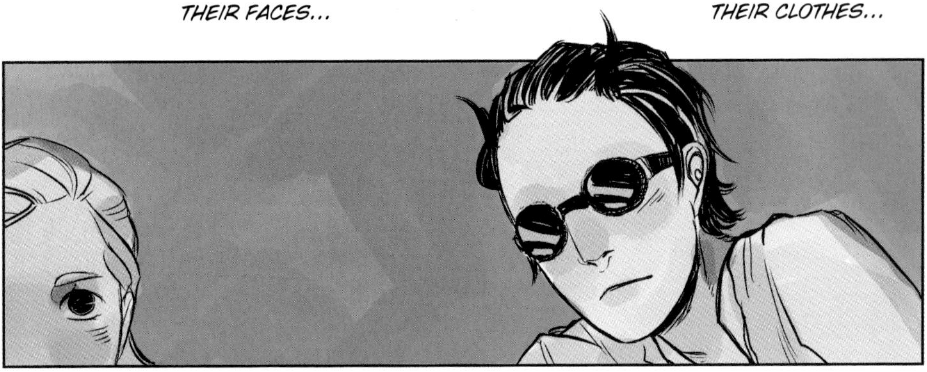

THEY'RE EXACTLY AS I REMEMBER...

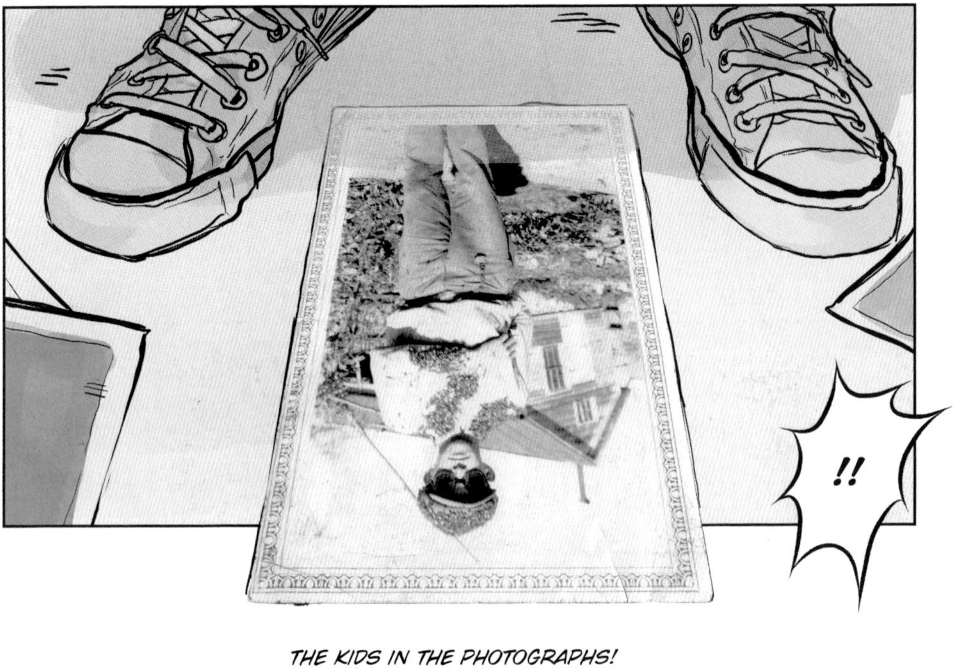
!!

THE KIDS IN THE PHOTOGRAPHS!

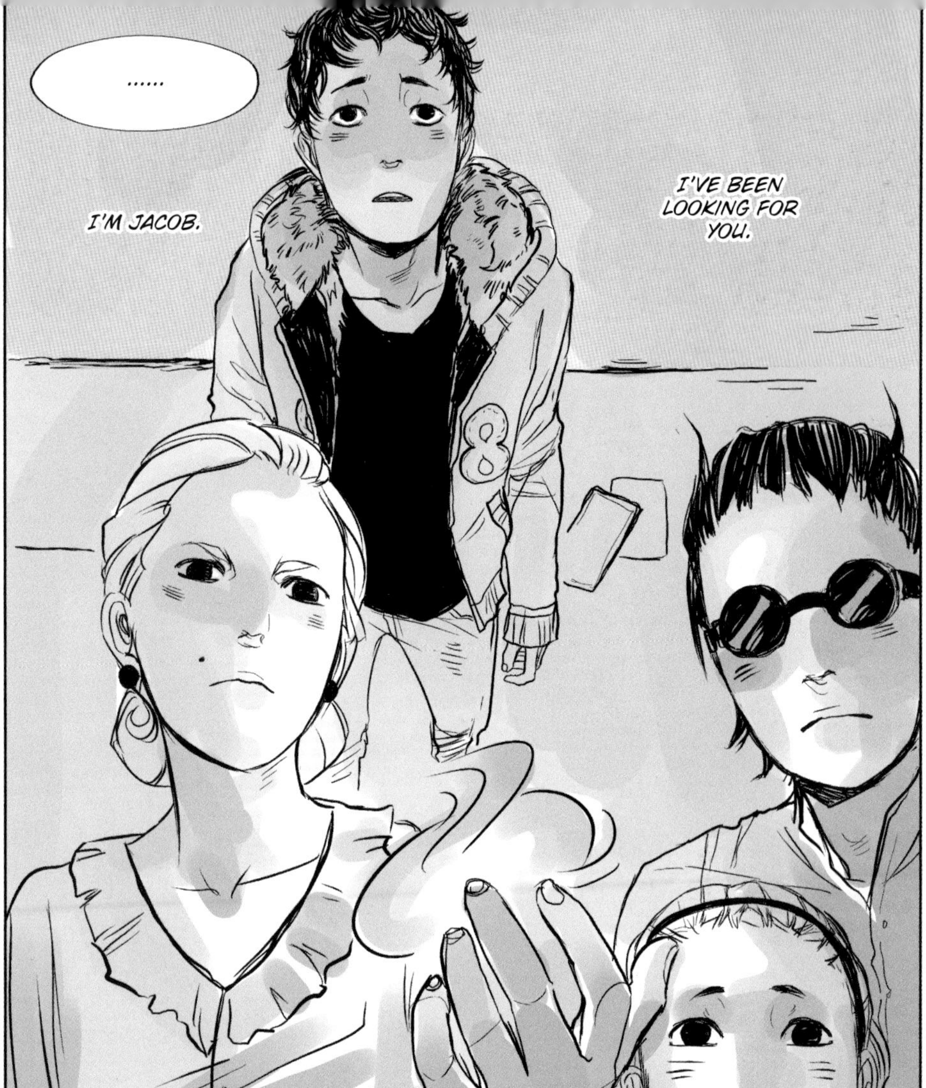
......
I'M JACOB.
I'VE BEEN LOOKING FOR YOU.
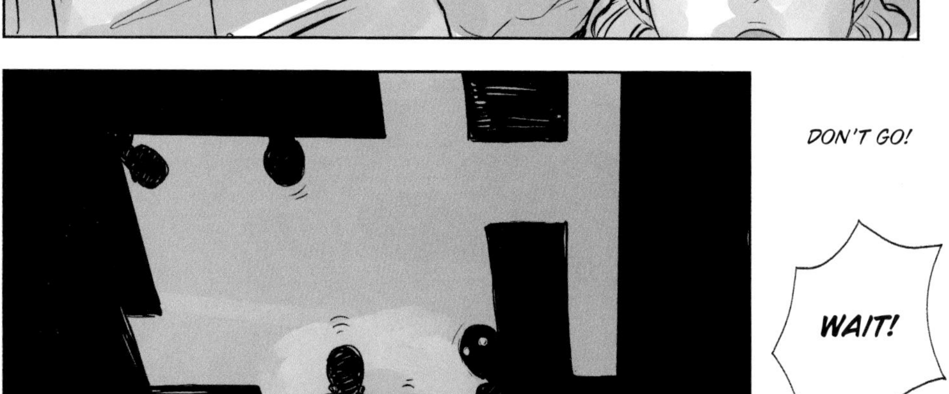
DON'T GO!
WAIT!

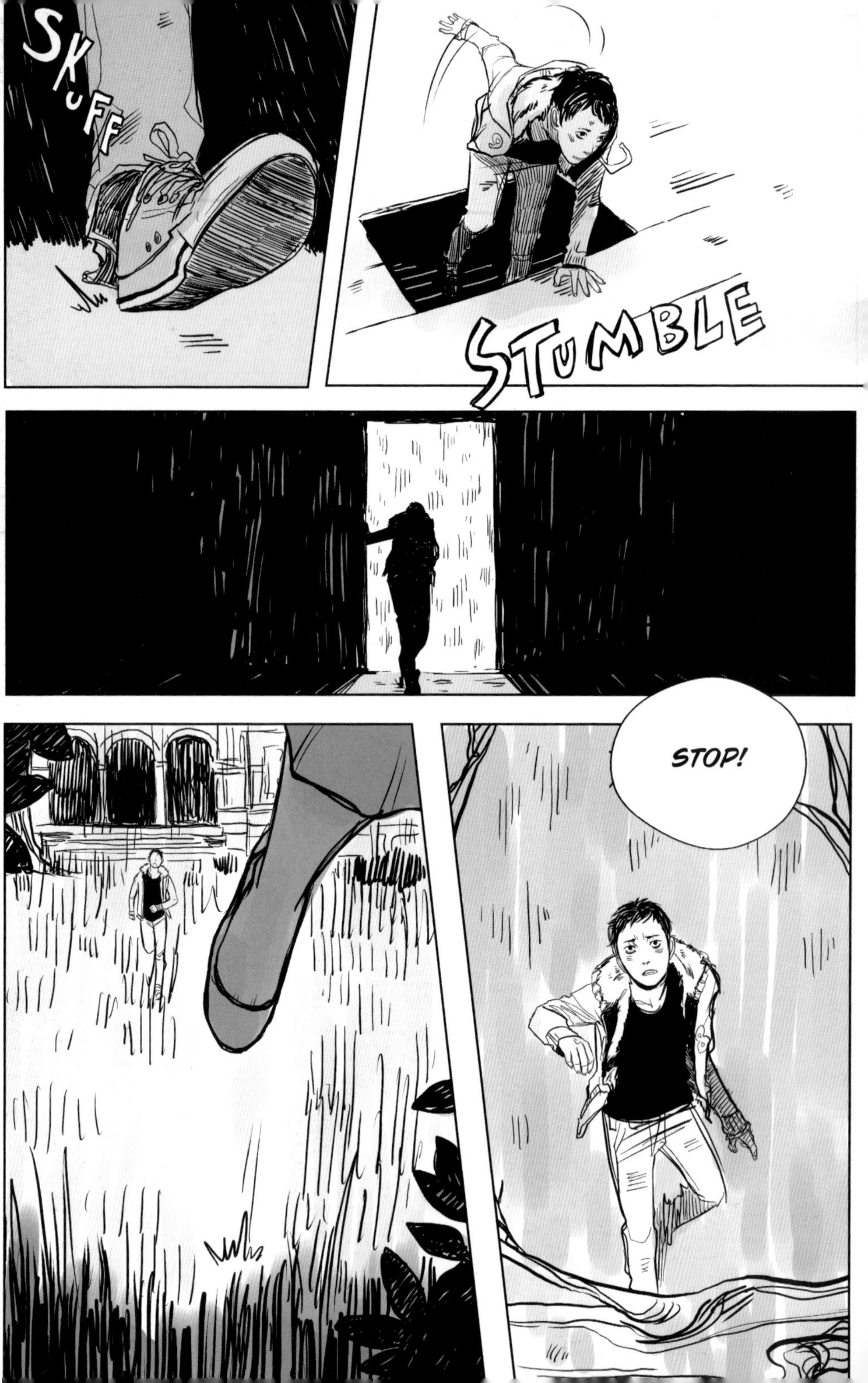
SKUFF
STUMBLE
STOP!

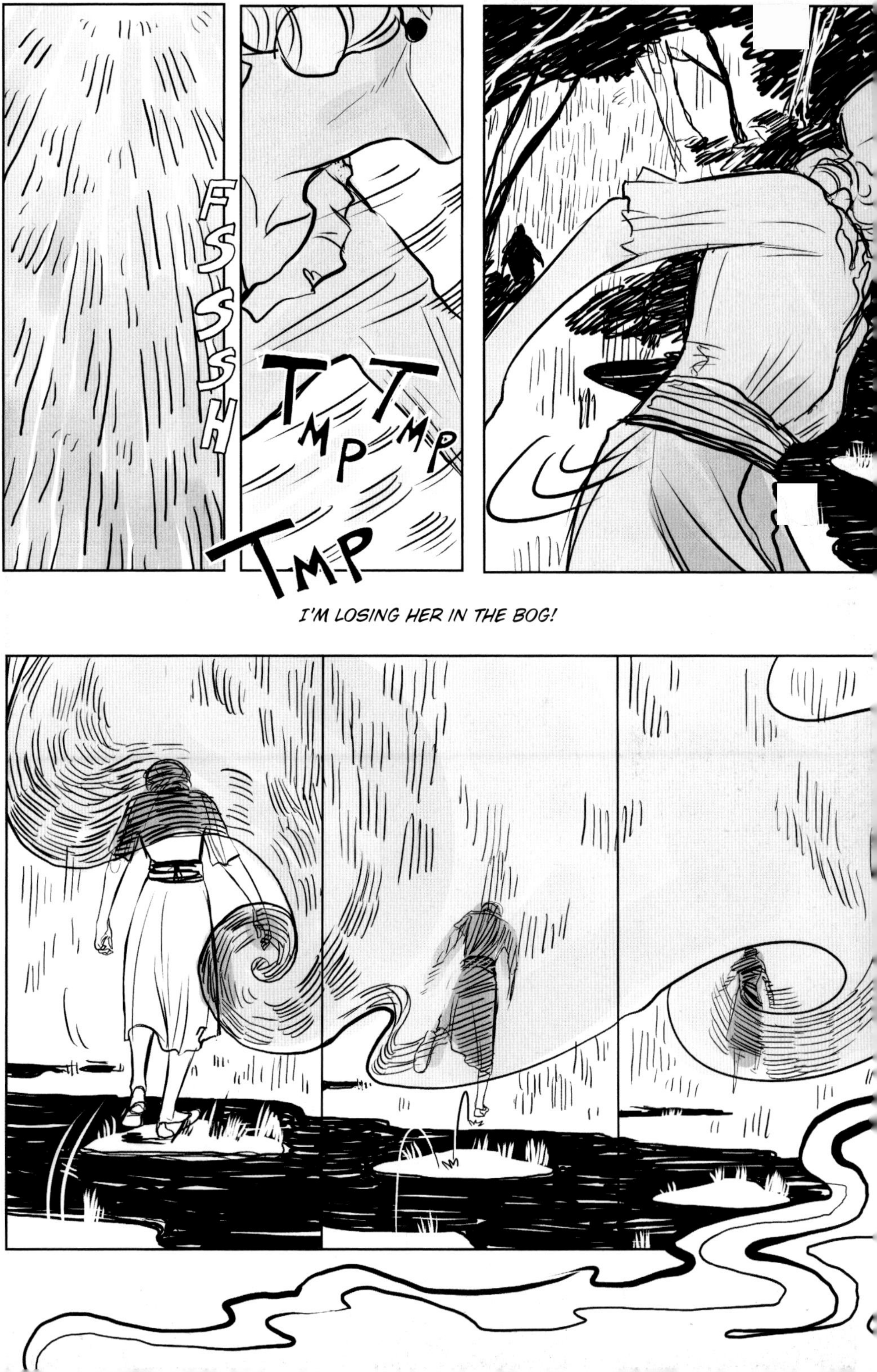
FSSSH
TMP TMP
TMP
I'M LOSING HER IN THE BOG!

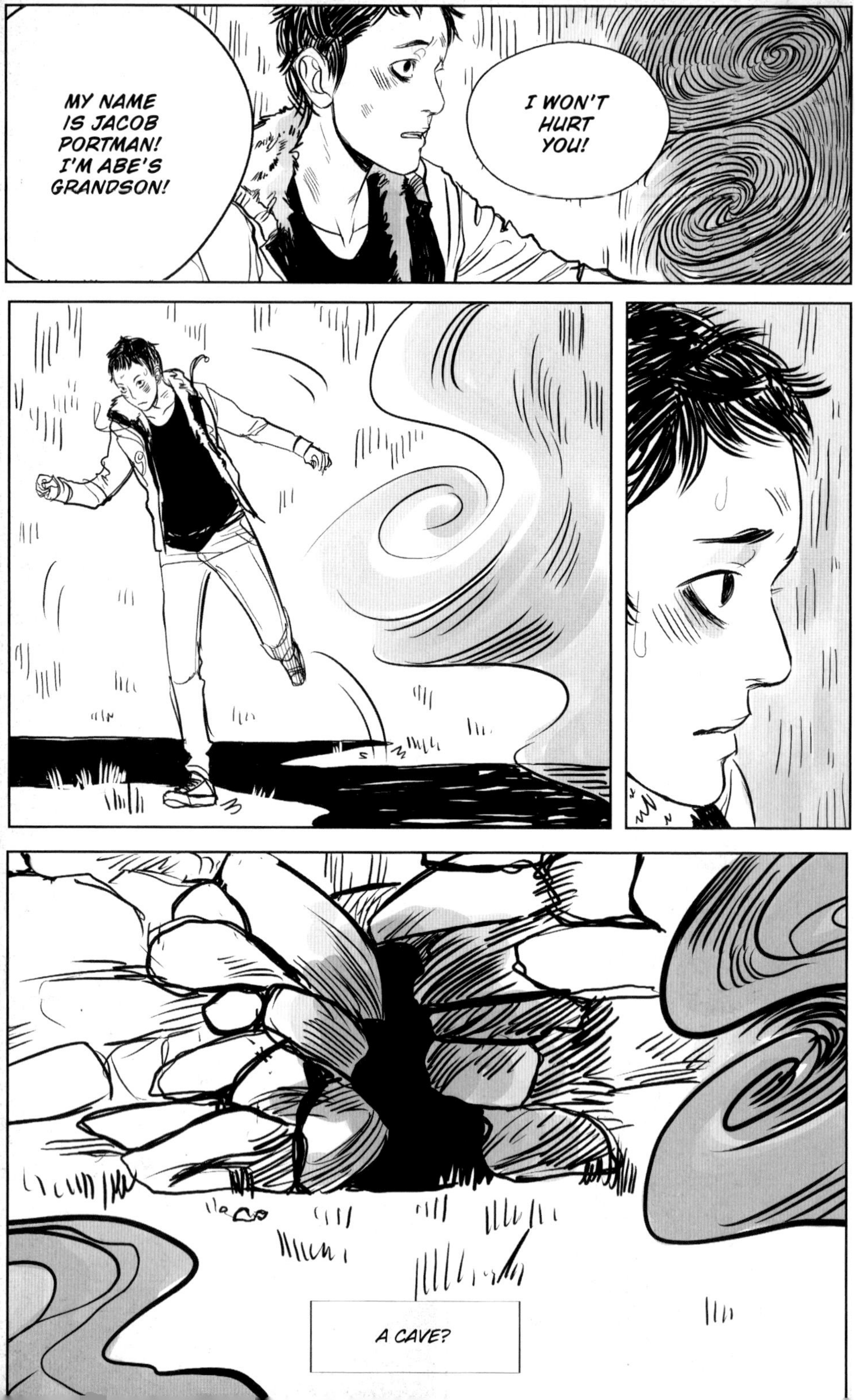
MY NAME IS JACOB PORTMAN! I'M ABE'S GRANDSON!
I WON'T HURT YOU!
A CAVE?

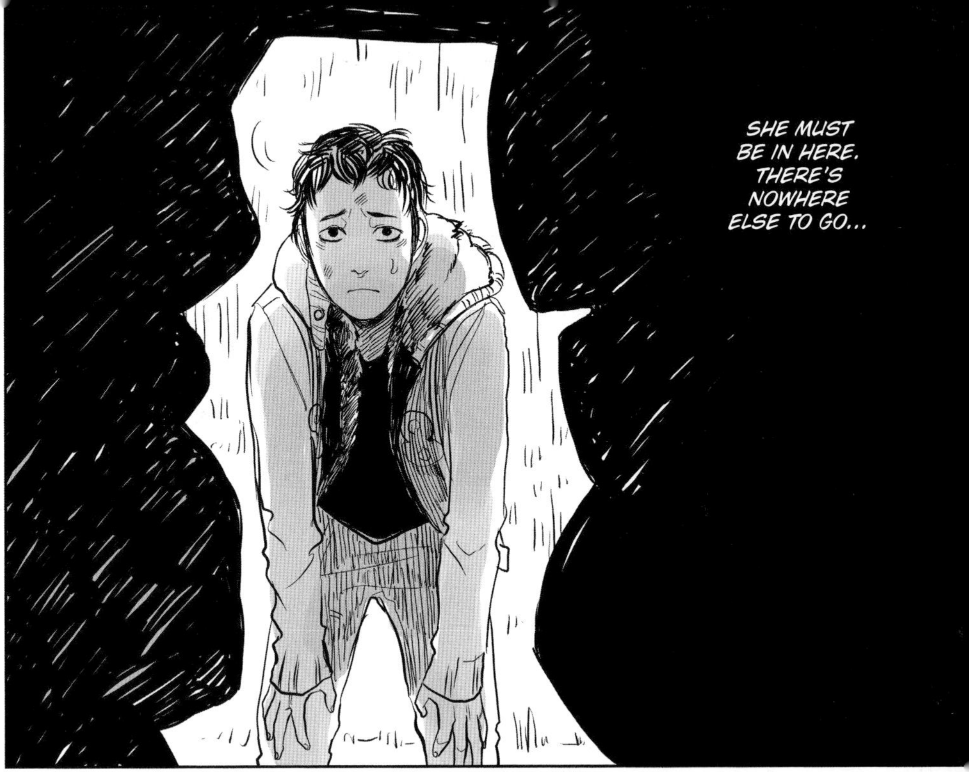
SHE MUST
BE IN HERE.
THERE'S
NOWHERE
ELSE TO GO...

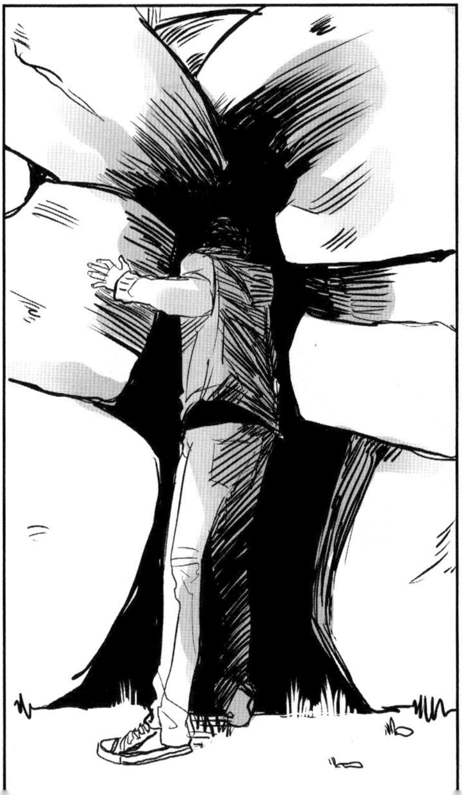

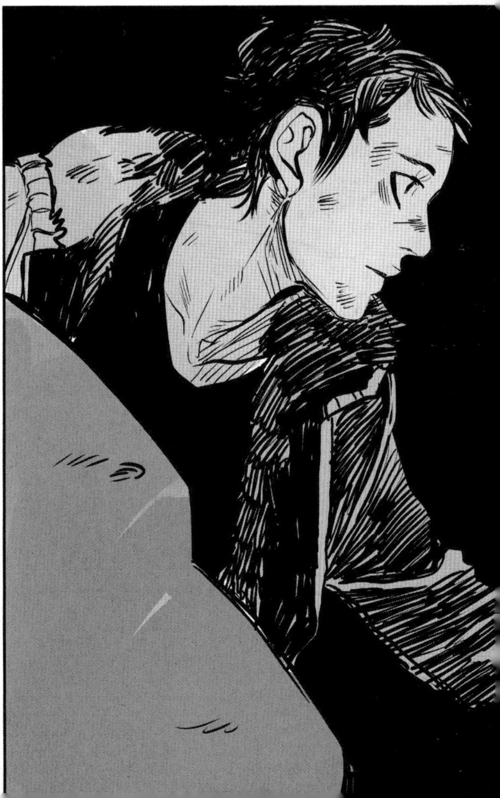

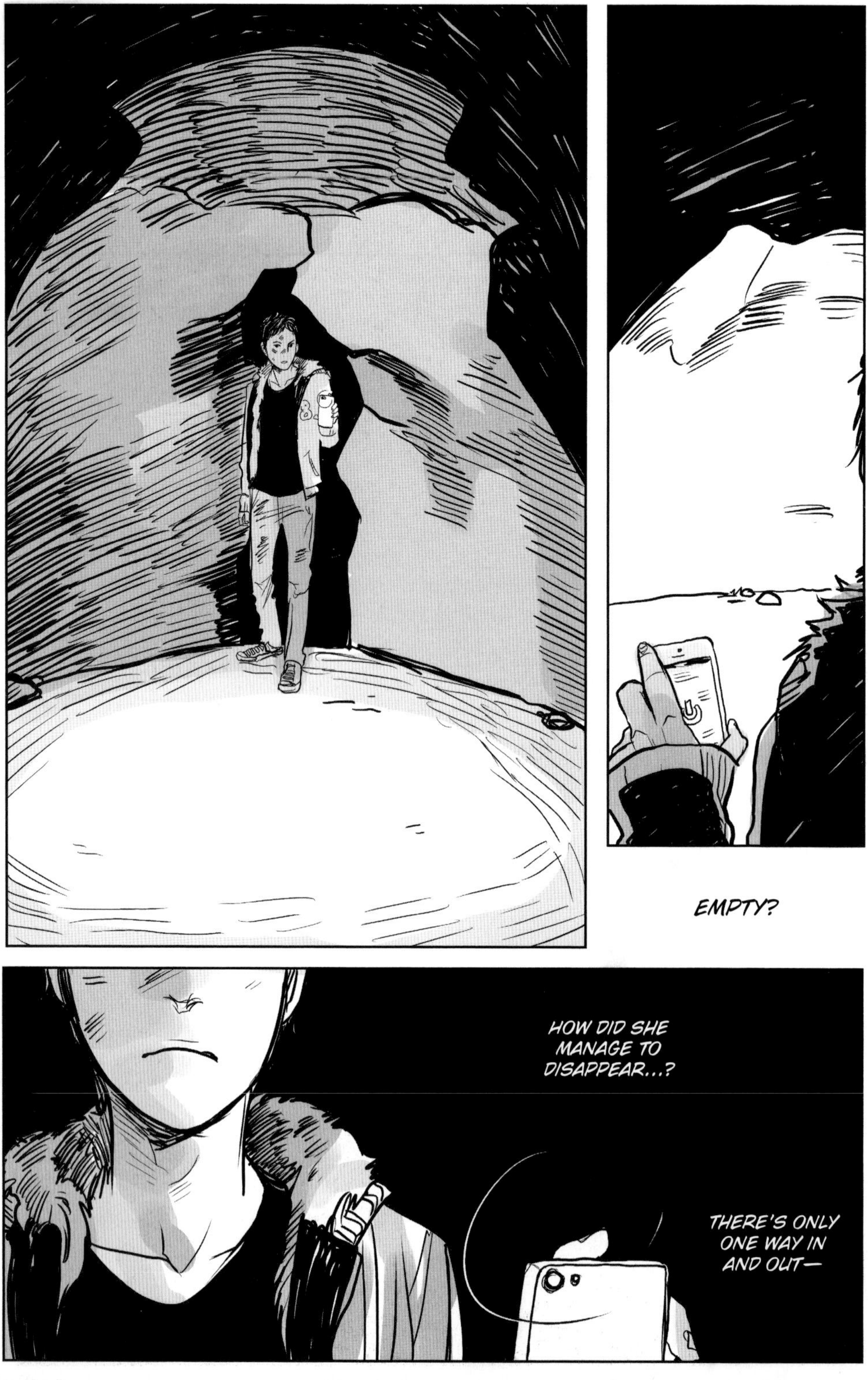
EMPTY?
HOW DID SHE MANAGE TO DISAPPEAR...?
THERE'S ONLY ONE WAY IN AND OUT—

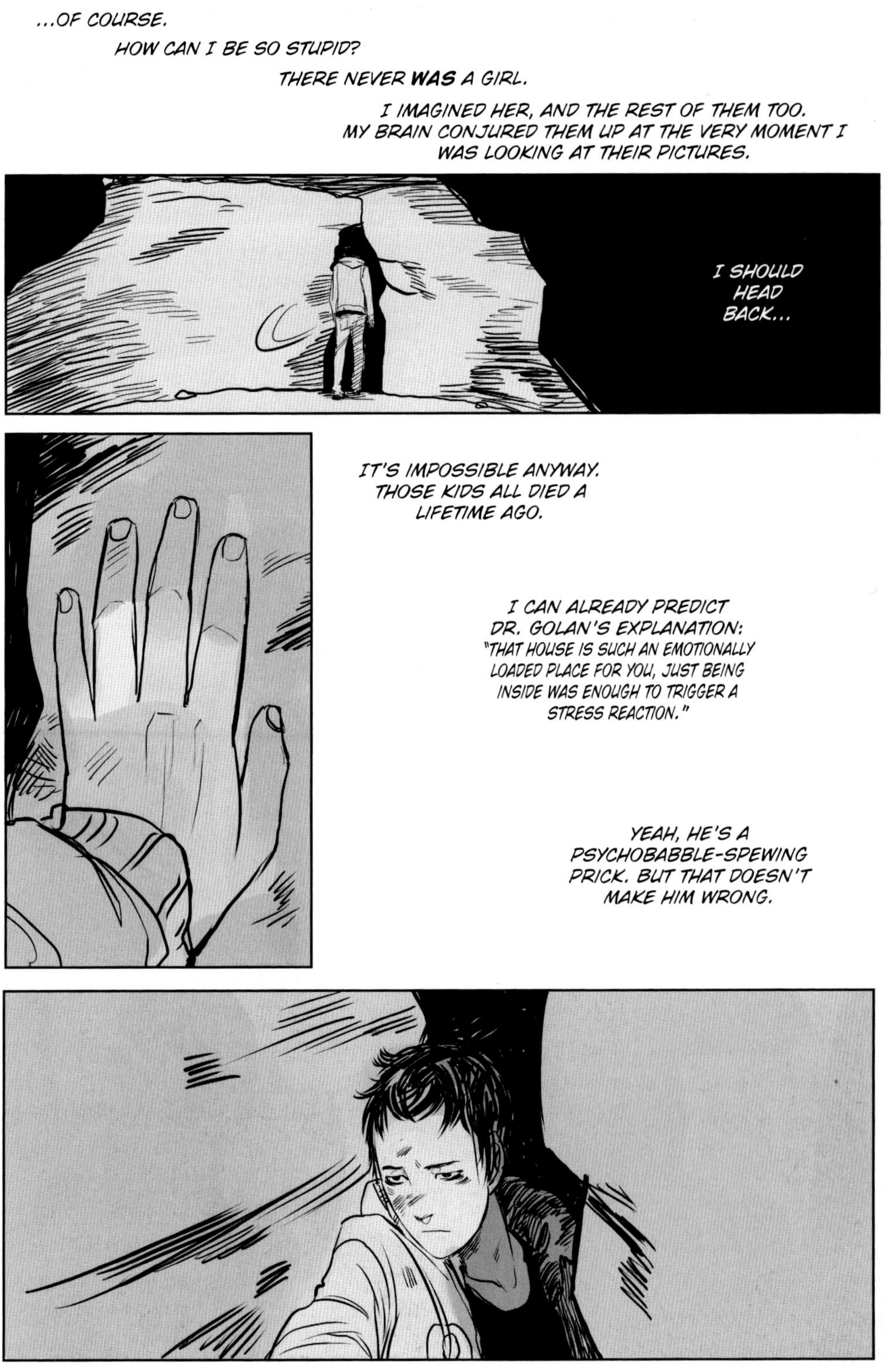
...OF COURSE.
HOW CAN I BE SO STUPID?
THERE NEVER **WAS** A GIRL.
I IMAGINED HER, AND THE REST OF THEM TOO. MY BRAIN CONJURED THEM UP AT THE VERY MOMENT I WAS LOOKING AT THEIR PICTURES.
I SHOULD HEAD BACK...
IT'S IMPOSSIBLE ANYWAY. THOSE KIDS ALL DIED A LIFETIME AGO.
I CAN ALREADY PREDICT DR. GOLAN'S EXPLANATION: "THAT HOUSE IS SUCH AN EMOTIONALLY LOADED PLACE FOR YOU, JUST BEING INSIDE WAS ENOUGH TO TRIGGER A STRESS REACTION."
YEAH, HE'S A PSYCHOBABBLE-SPEWING PRICK. BUT THAT DOESN'T MAKE HIM WRONG.

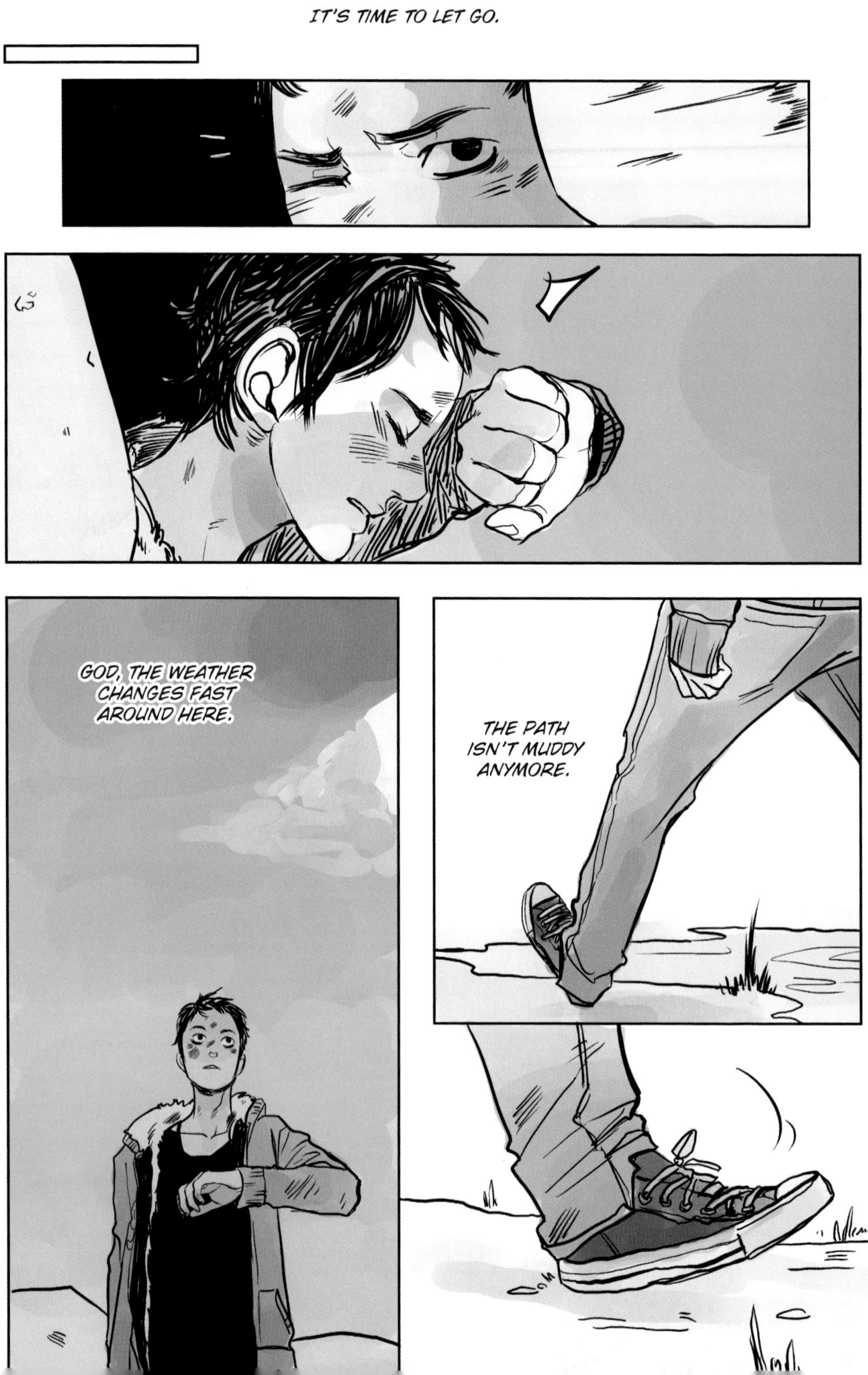
IT'S TIME TO LET GO.
GOD, THE WEATHER CHANGES FAST AROUND HERE.
THE PATH ISN'T MUDDY ANYMORE.

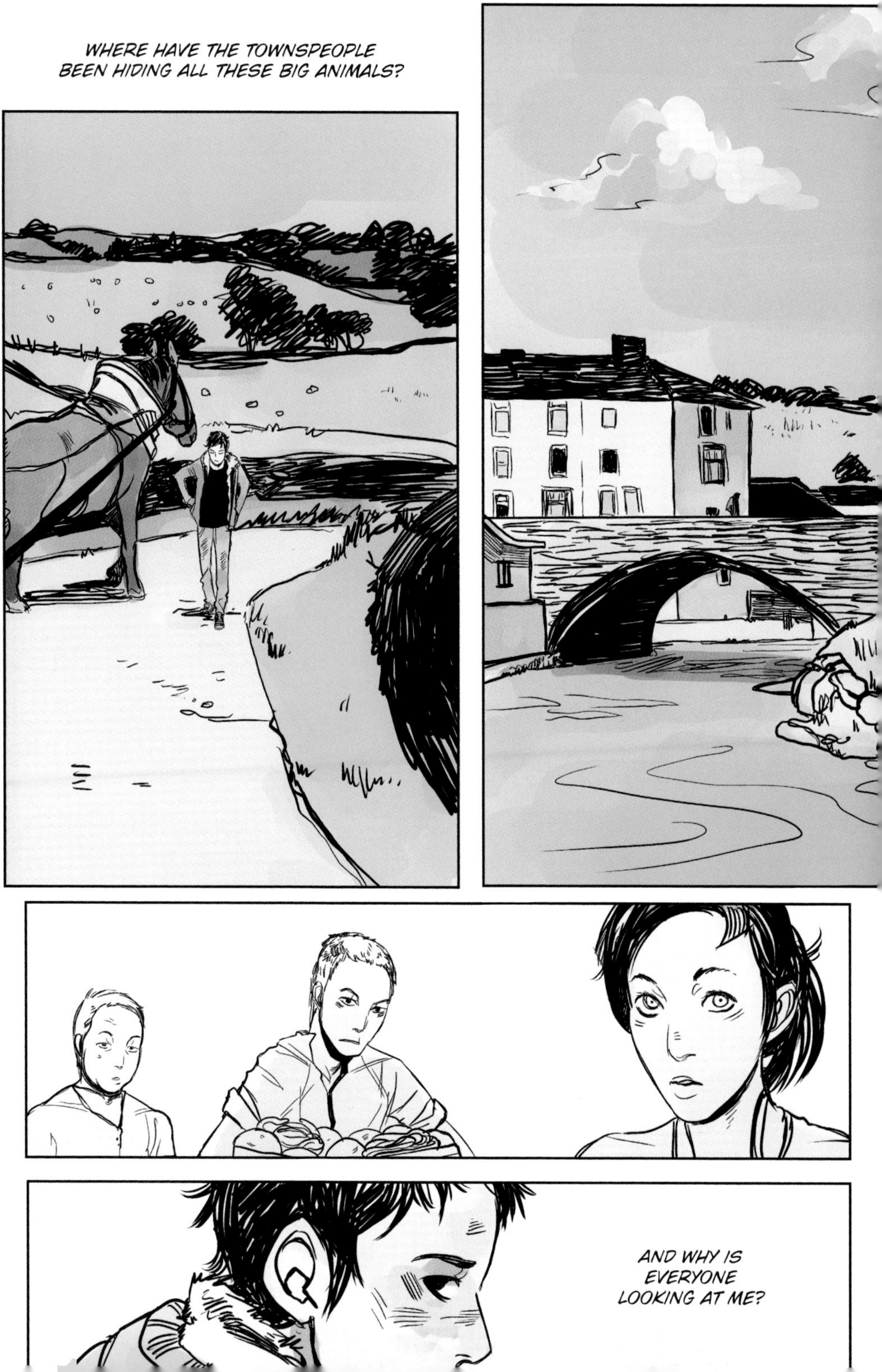
WHERE HAVE THE TOWNSPEOPLE BEEN HIDING ALL THESE BIG ANIMALS?
AND WHY IS EVERYONE LOOKING AT ME?

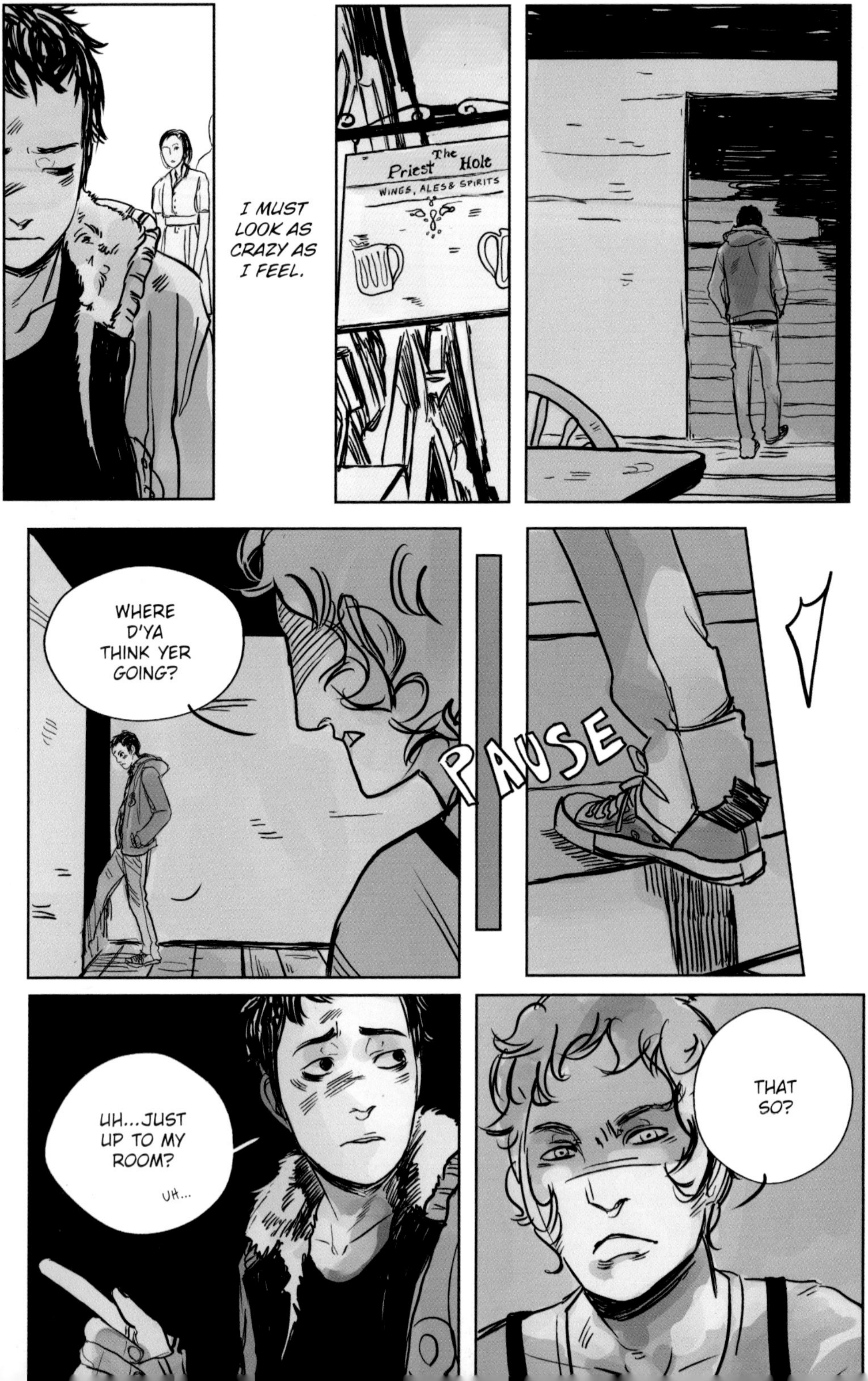
I MUST LOOK AS CRAZY AS I FEEL.
The Priest Holt
WINGS, ALES & SPIRITS
WHERE D'YA THINK YER GOING?
PAUSE
UH...JUST UP TO MY ROOM?
UH...
THAT SO?

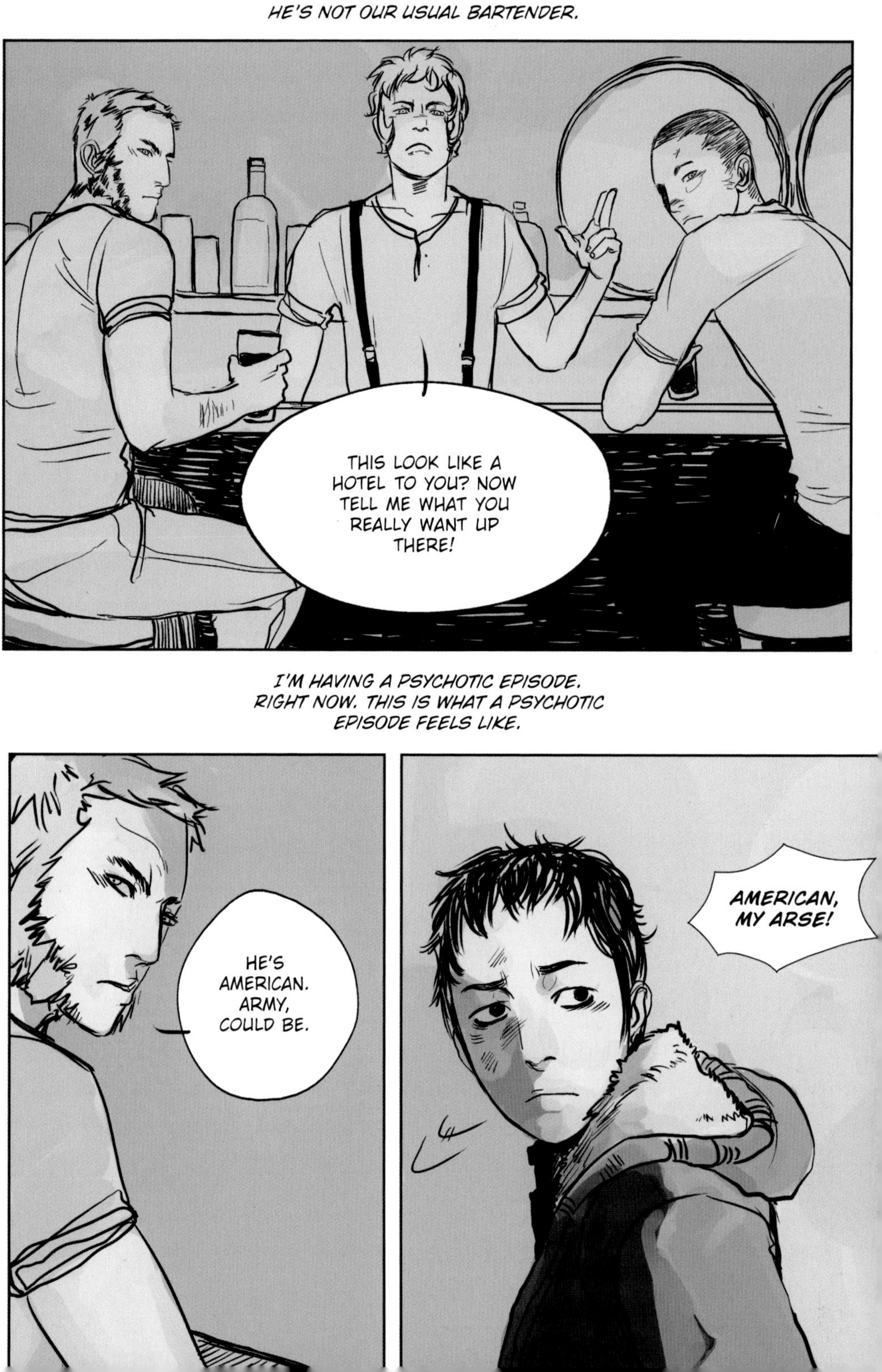
HE'S NOT OUR USUAL BARTENDER.
THIS LOOK LIKE A HOTEL TO YOU? NOW TELL ME WHAT YOU REALLY WANT UP THERE!
I'M HAVING A PSYCHOTIC EPISODE. RIGHT NOW. THIS IS WHAT A PSYCHOTIC EPISODE FEELS LIKE.
HE'S AMERICAN. ARMY, COULD BE.
AMERICAN, MY ARSE!

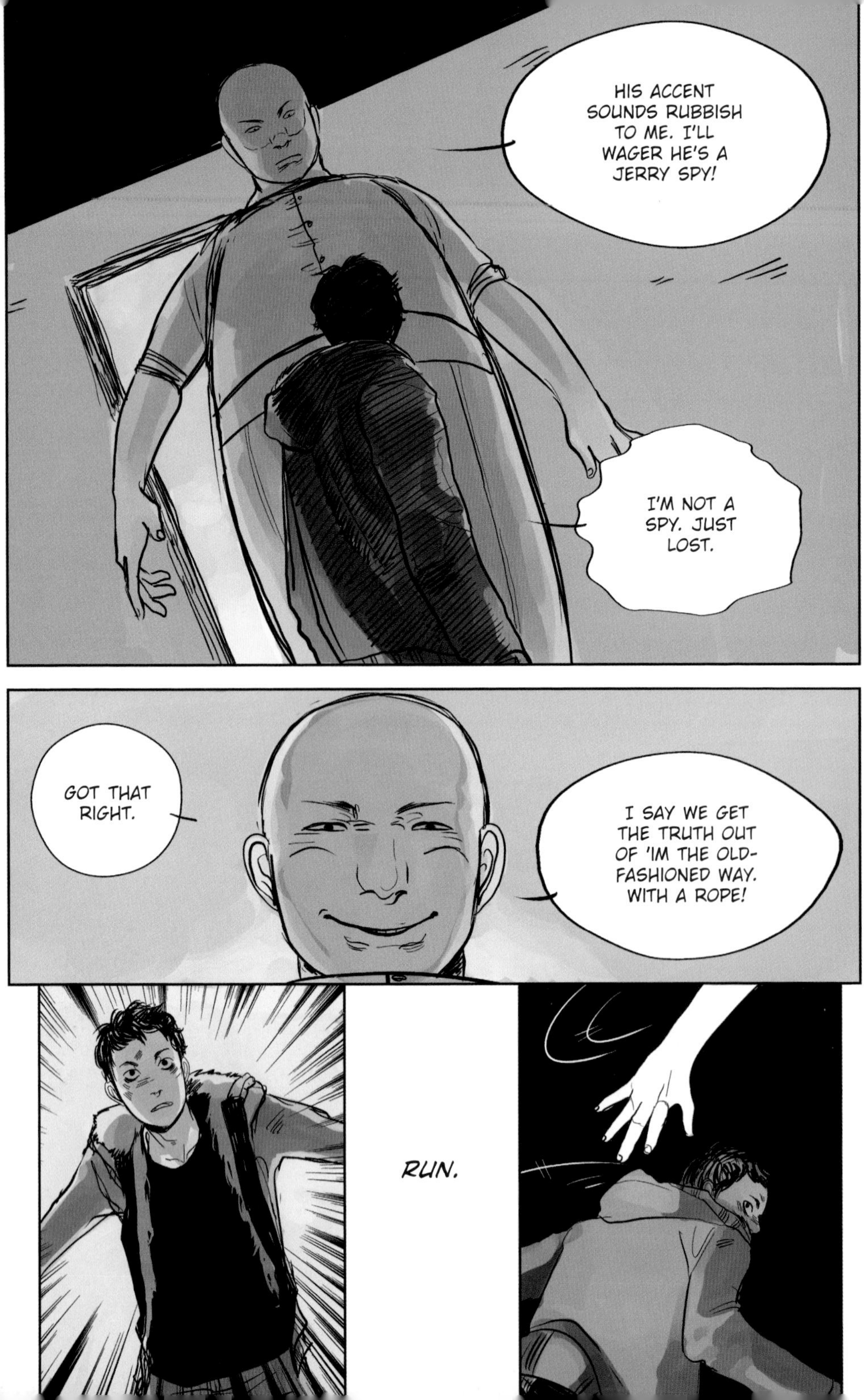
HIS ACCENT SOUNDS RUBBISH TO ME. I'LL WAGER HE'S A JERRY SPY!
I'M NOT A SPY. JUST LOST.
GOT THAT RIGHT.
I SAY WE GET THE TRUTH OUT OF 'IM THE OLD-FASHIONED WAY. WITH A ROPE!
RUN.

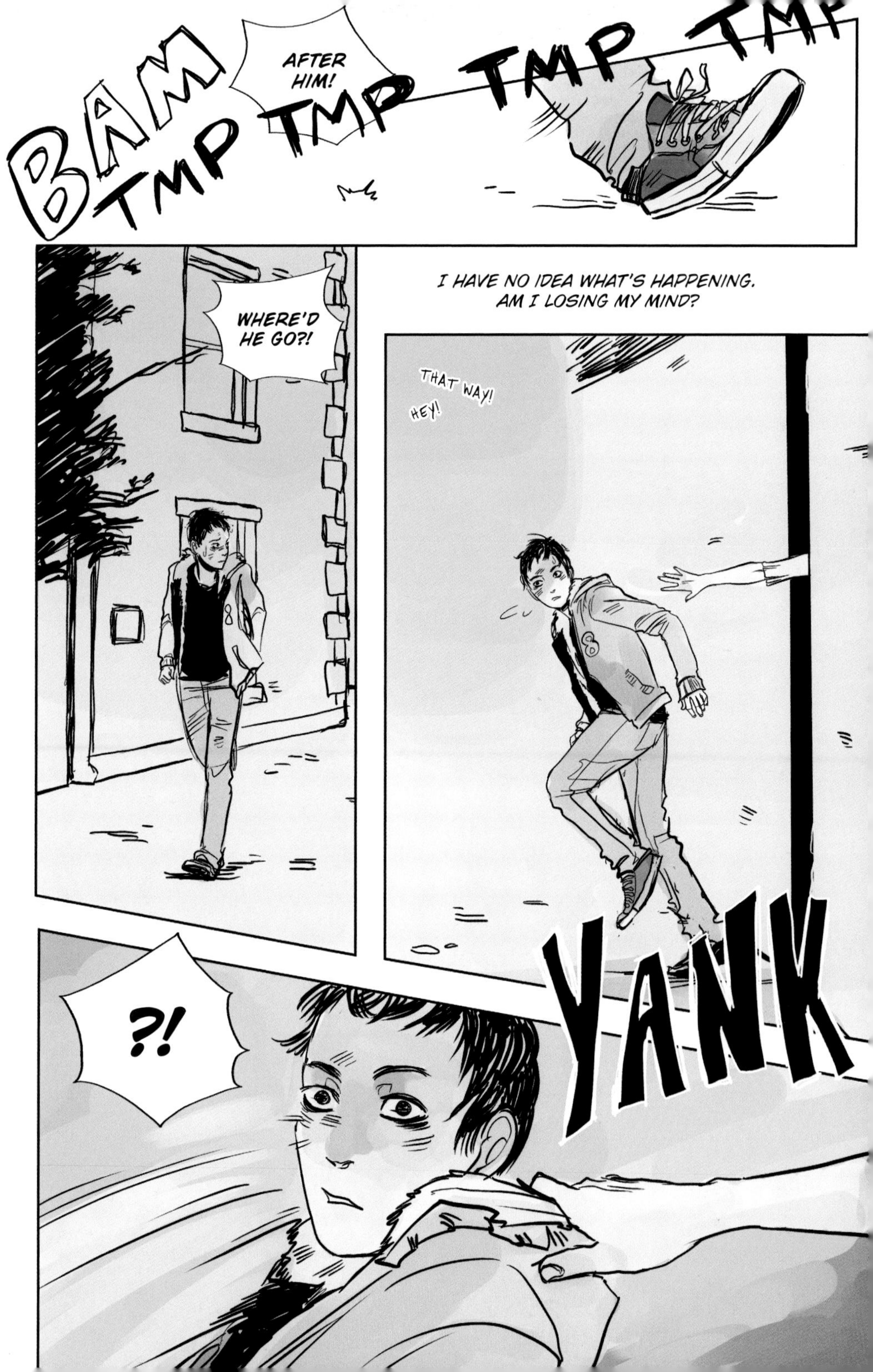

BAM
TMP TMP TMP TMP TMP
AFTER HIM!
WHERE'D HE GO?!
I HAVE NO IDEA WHAT'S HAPPENING. AM I LOSING MY MIND?
THAT WAY!
HEY!
?!
YANK

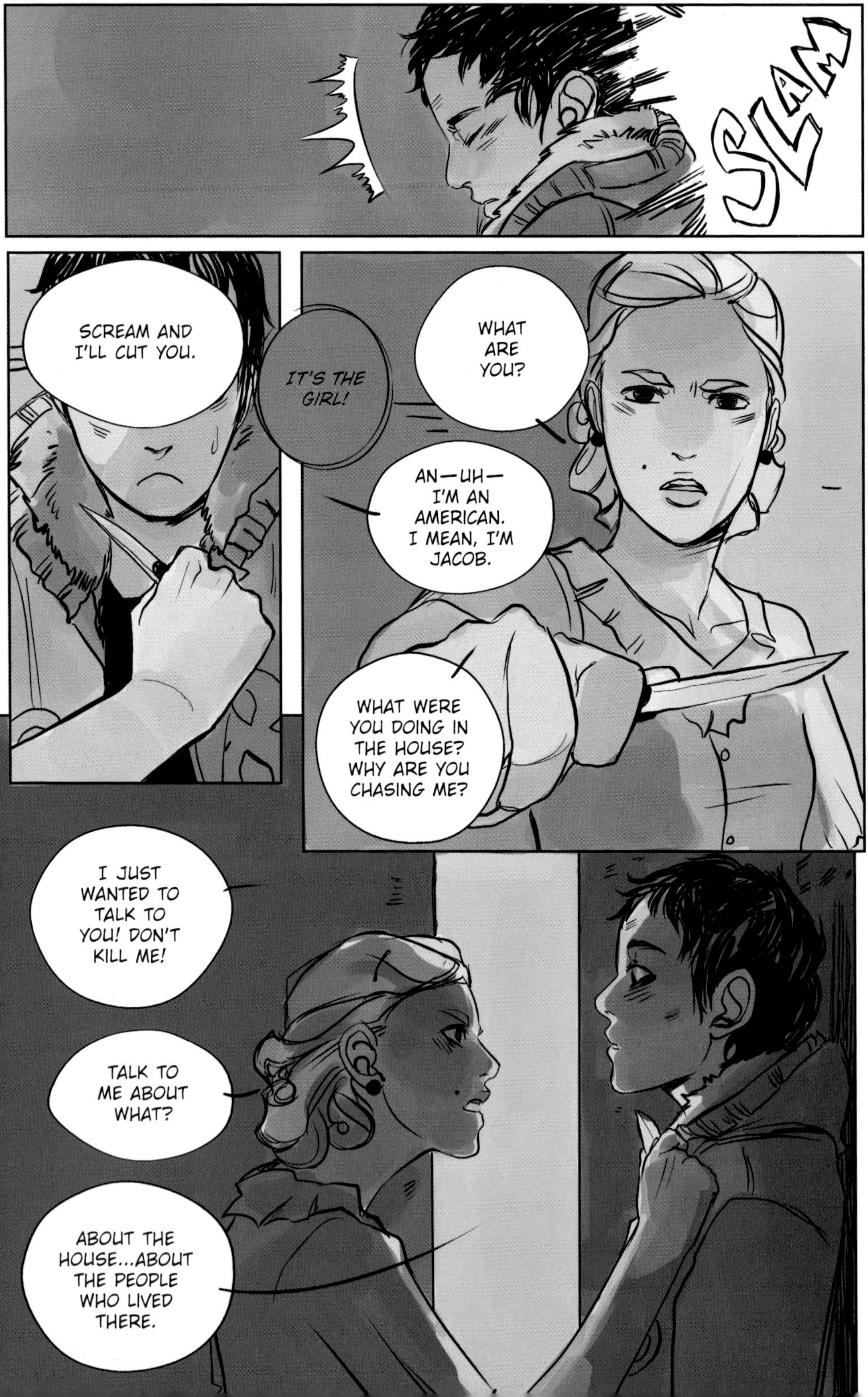
SLAM
SCREAM AND I'LL CUT YOU.
IT'S THE GIRL!
WHAT ARE YOU?
AN—UH— I'M AN AMERICAN. I MEAN, I'M JACOB.
WHAT WERE YOU DOING IN THE HOUSE? WHY ARE YOU CHASING ME?
I JUST WANTED TO TALK TO YOU! DON'T KILL ME!
TALK TO ME ABOUT WHAT?
ABOUT THE HOUSE...ABOUT THE PEOPLE WHO LIVED THERE.

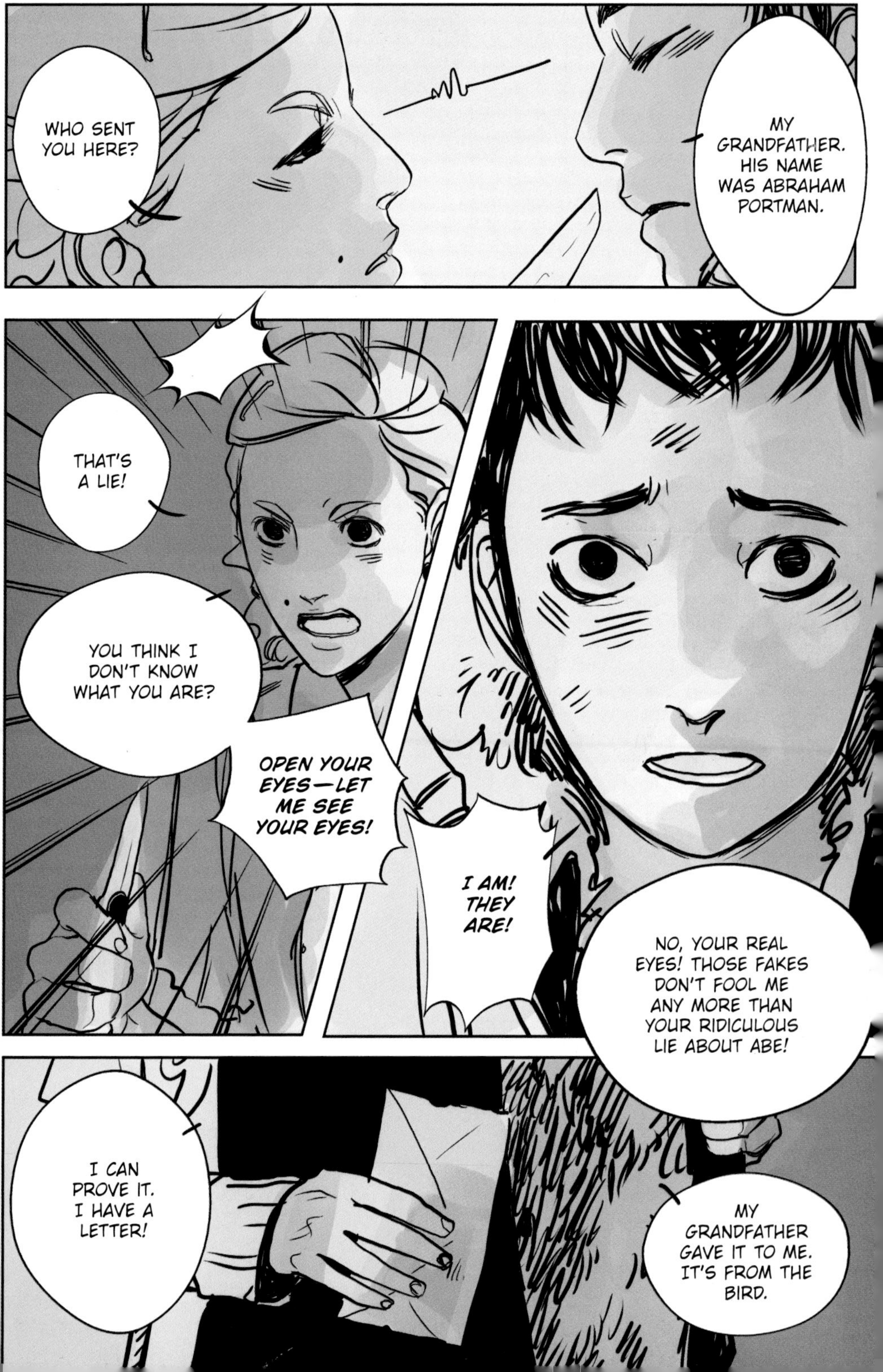
WHO SENT YOU HERE?
MY GRANDFATHER. HIS NAME WAS ABRAHAM PORTMAN.
THAT'S A LIE!
YOU THINK I DON'T KNOW WHAT YOU ARE?
OPEN YOUR EYES—LET ME SEE YOUR EYES!
I AM! THEY ARE!
NO, YOUR REAL EYES! THOSE FAKES DON'T FOOL ME ANY MORE THAN YOUR RIDICULOUS LIE ABOUT ABE!
I CAN PROVE IT. I HAVE A LETTER!
MY GRANDFATHER GAVE IT TO ME. IT'S FROM THE BIRD.

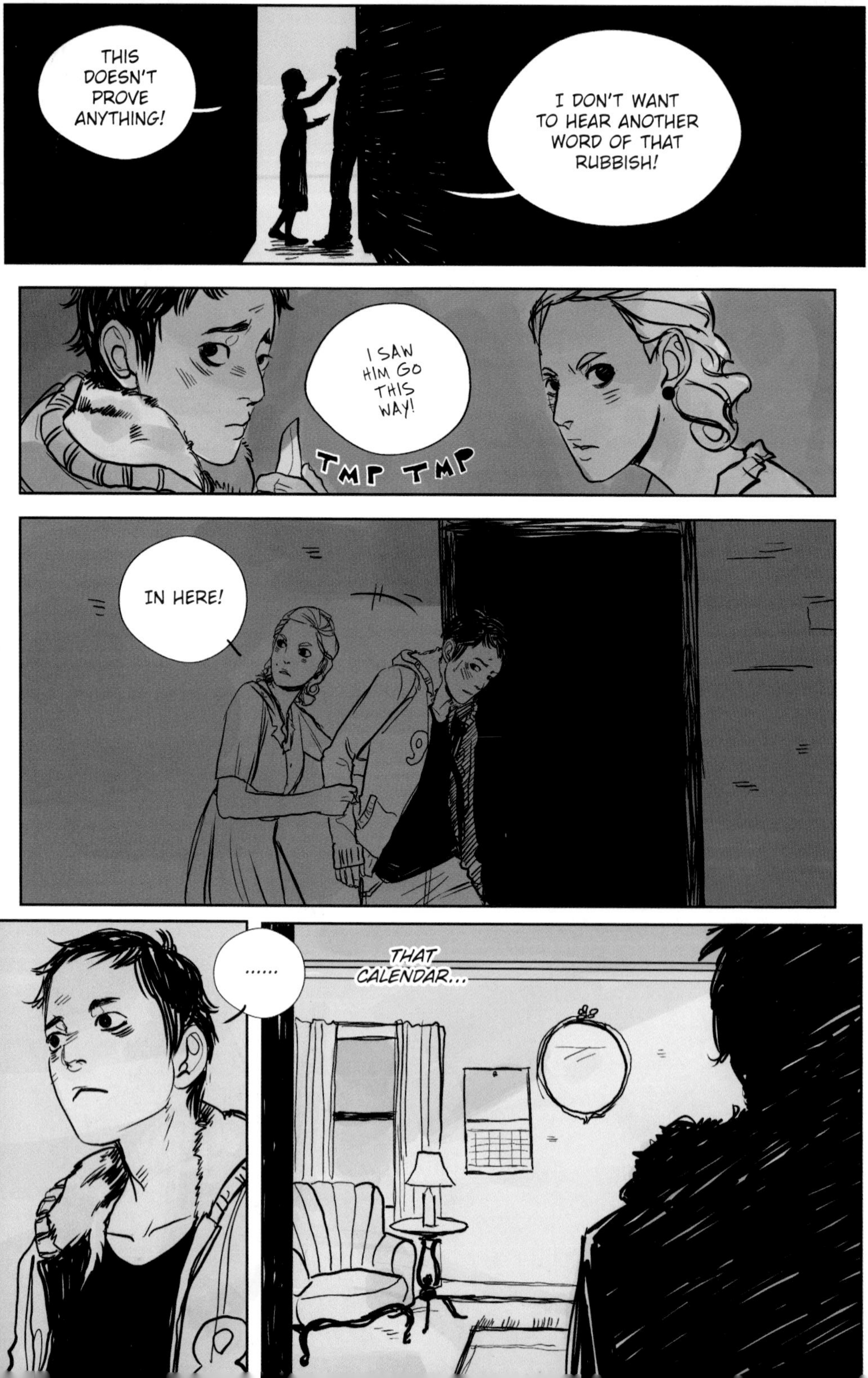

THIS DOESN'T PROVE ANYTHING!
I DON'T WANT TO HEAR ANOTHER WORD OF THAT RUBBISH!
I SAW HIM GO THIS WAY!
TMP TMP
IN HERE!
......
THAT CALENDAR...

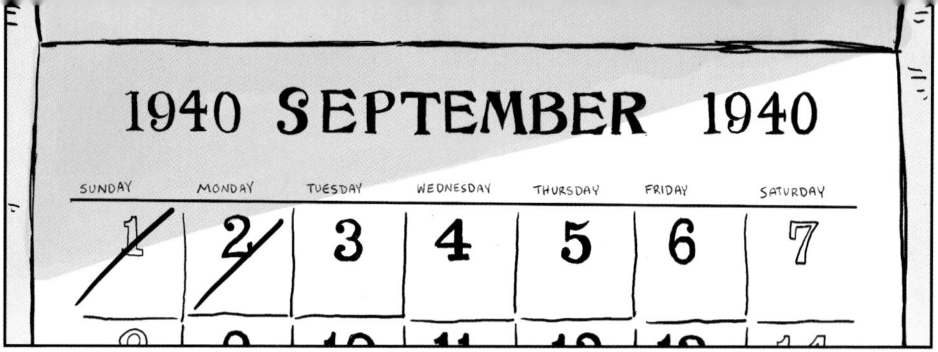
1940 SEPTEMBER 1940
SUNDAY MONDAY TUESDAY WEDNESDAY THURSDAY FRIDAY SATURDAY
1 2 3 4 5 6 7

SEPTEMBER 3, 1940.

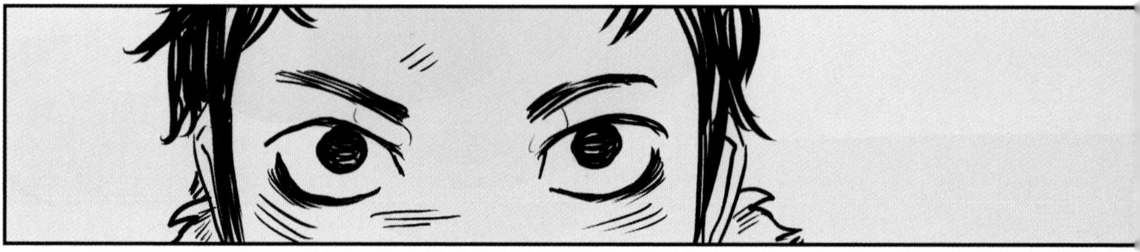

"ON THE OTHER SIDE OF THE OLD MAN'S GRAVE."

MY GRANDFATHER WAS LITERAL MINDED, NOT A MAN WHO TRADED IN METAPHOR OR SUGGESTION. HE'D GIVEN ME STRAIGHTFORWARD DIRECTIONS THAT HE SIMPLY HADN'T HAD TIME TO EXPLAIN.

"THE OLD MAN" WAS WHAT THE LOCALS CALLED THE BOG BOY, AND HIS GRAVE WAS THE CAVE. AND I WENT INSIDE IT AND CAME OUT SOMEPLACE ELSE...

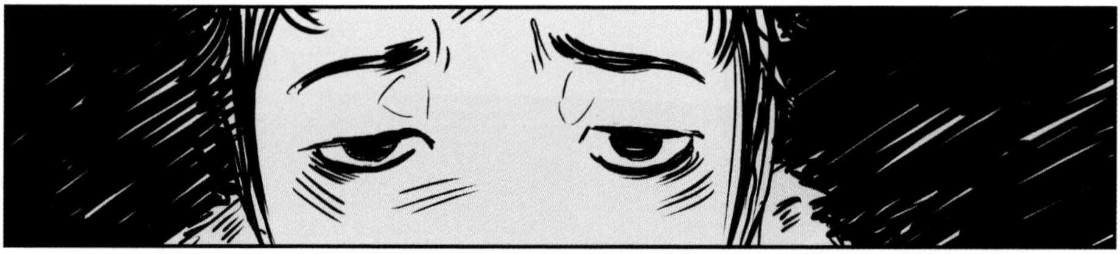

SEPTEMBER 3, 1940.

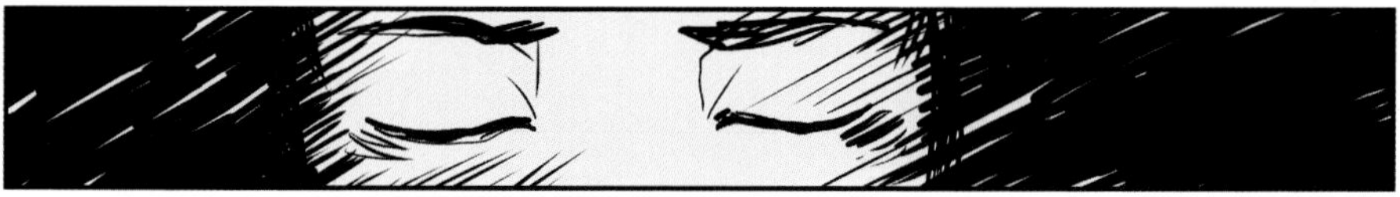

THE ROOM IS TURNING UPSIDE DOWN...

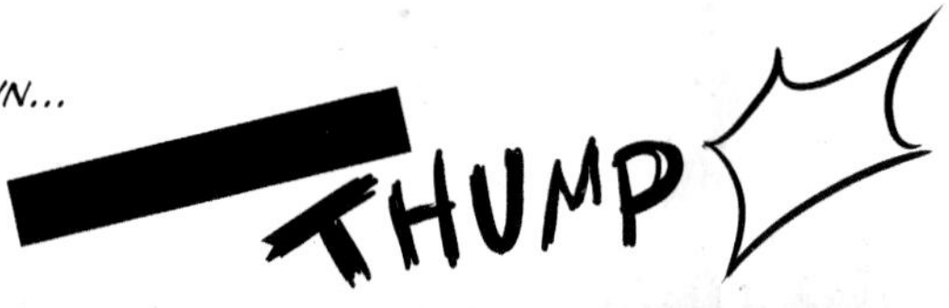
THUMP

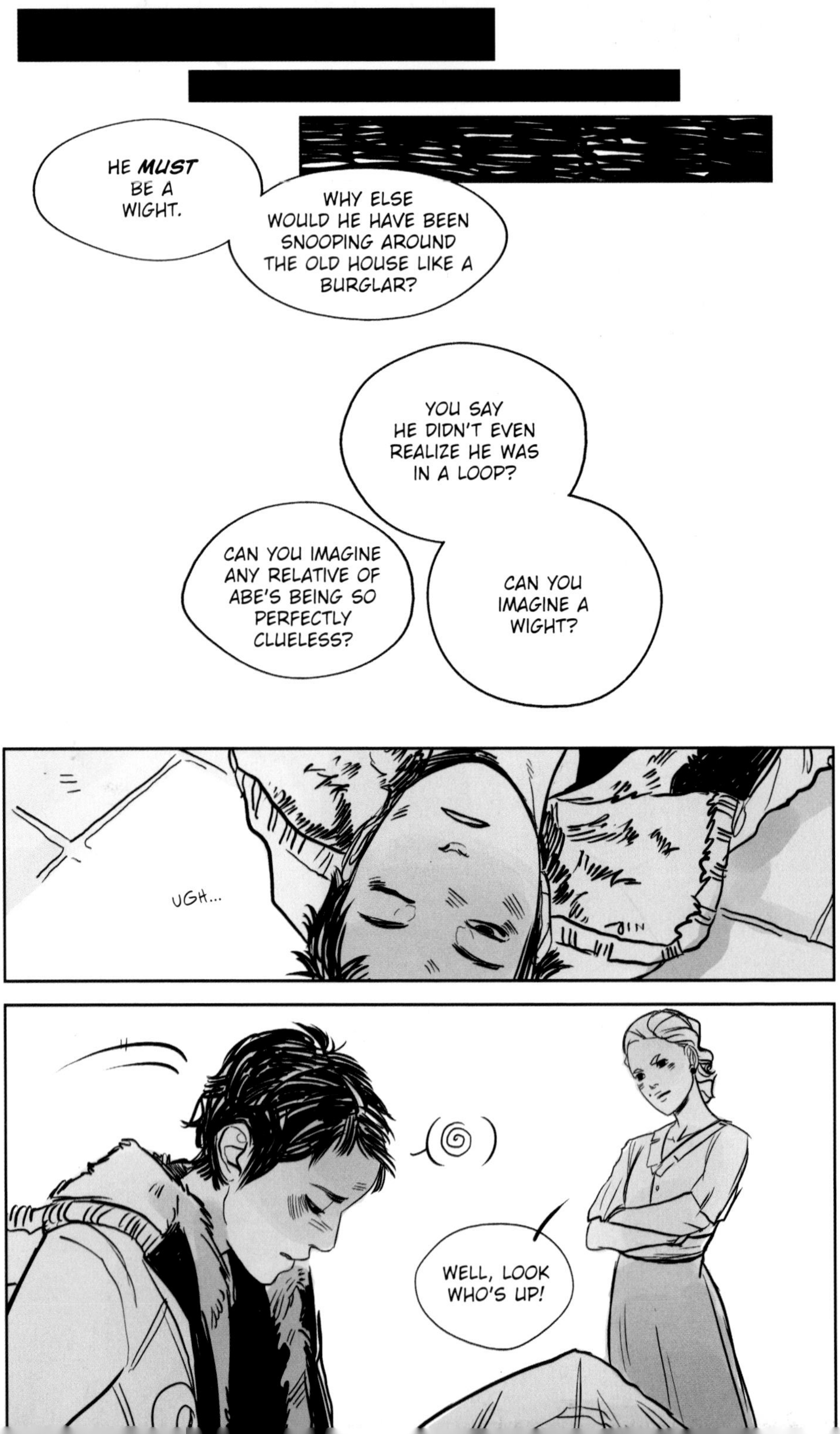
HE MUST BE A WIGHT.
WHY ELSE WOULD HE HAVE BEEN SNOOPING AROUND THE OLD HOUSE LIKE A BURGLAR?
YOU SAY HE DIDN'T EVEN REALIZE HE WAS IN A LOOP?
CAN YOU IMAGINE ANY RELATIVE OF ABE'S BEING SO PERFECTLY CLUELESS?
CAN YOU IMAGINE A WIGHT?
UGH...
WELL, LOOK WHO'S UP!

?

HAVE SOME WATER. CAN'T HAVE YOU DYING BEFORE WE GET YOU BACK TO THE HEADMISTRESS, NOW CAN WE?

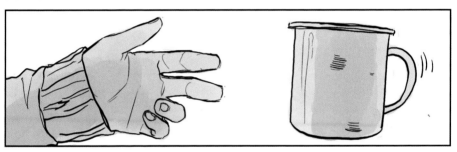

YOU'RE INVISIBLE.

INDEED.

MILLARD NULLINGS, AT YOUR SERVICE.

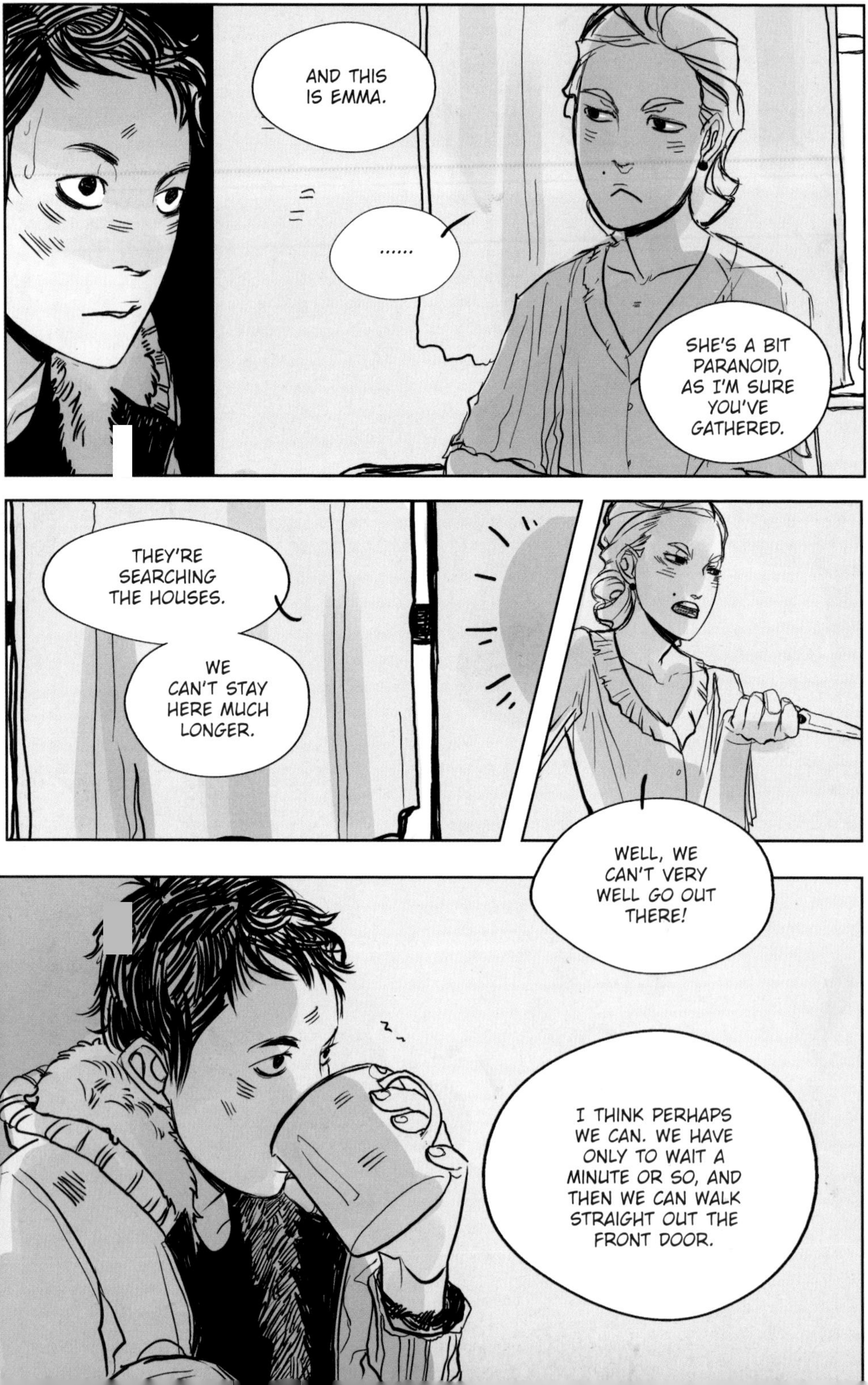
AND THIS IS EMMA.
......
SHE'S A BIT PARANOID, AS I'M SURE YOU'VE GATHERED.
THEY'RE SEARCHING THE HOUSES.
WE CAN'T STAY HERE MUCH LONGER.
WELL, WE CAN'T VERY WELL GO OUT THERE!
I THINK PERHAPS WE CAN. WE HAVE ONLY TO WAIT A MINUTE OR SO, AND THEN WE CAN WALK STRAIGHT OUT THE FRONT DOOR.

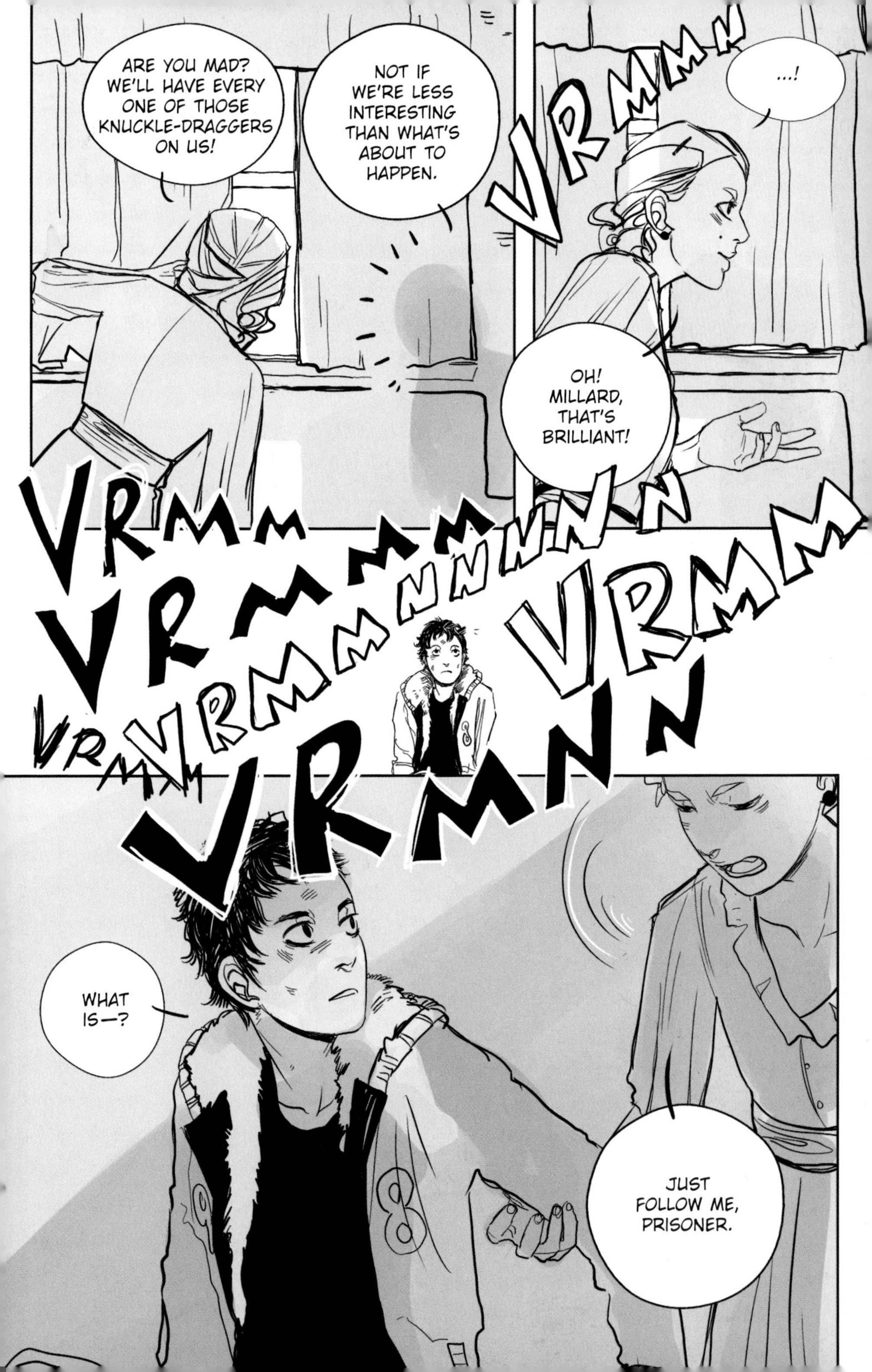
ARE YOU MAD? WE'LL HAVE EVERY ONE OF THOSE KNUCKLE-DRAGGERS ON US!
NOT IF WE'RE LESS INTERESTING THAN WHAT'S ABOUT TO HAPPEN.
VRMMN
...!
OH! MILLARD, THAT'S BRILLIANT!
VRMMMMNNNN
VRMMMMNNNN
VRMM
VRMM
VRMNN
WHAT IS—?
JUST FOLLOW ME, PRISONER.

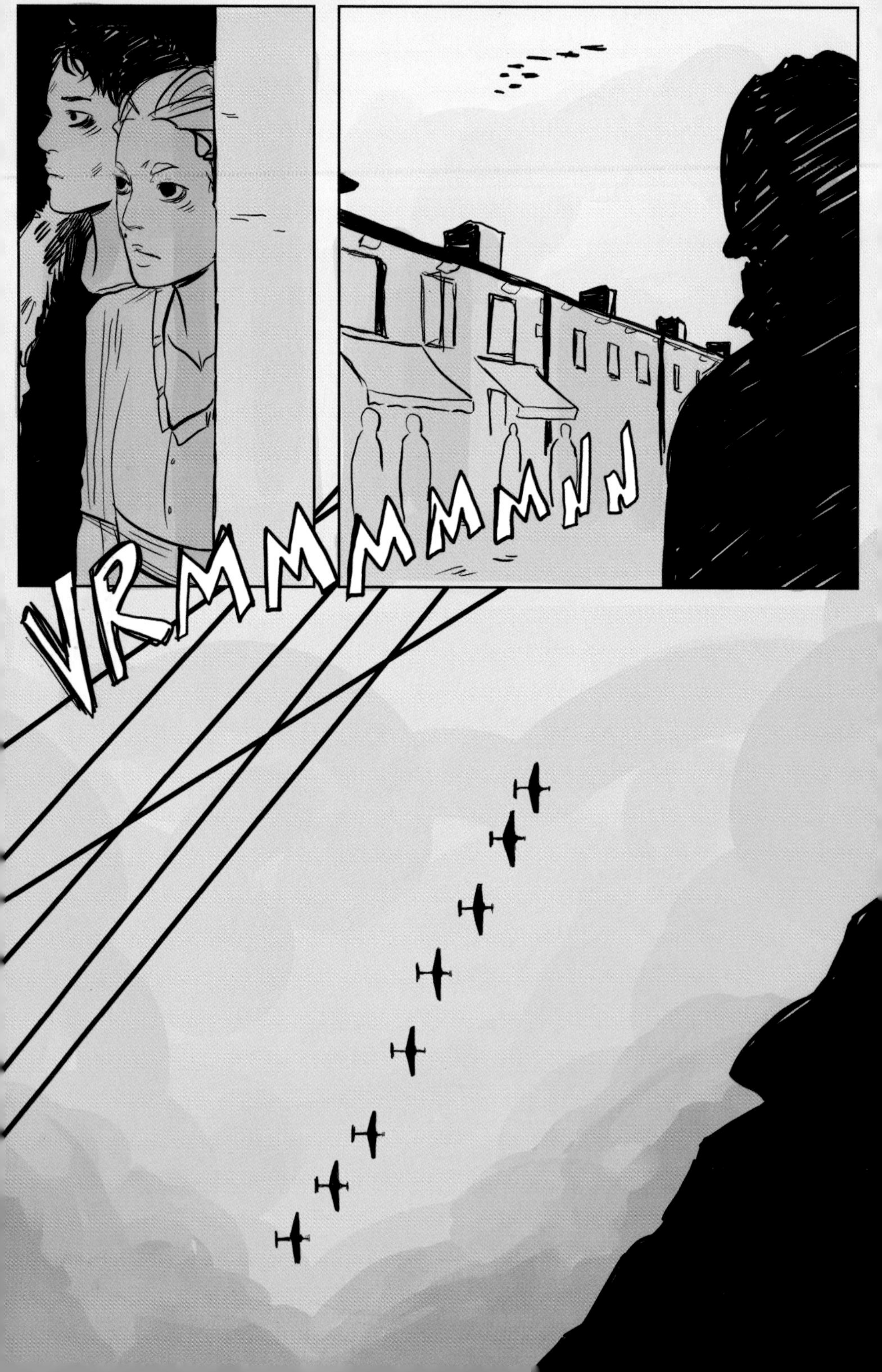
VRMMMMMMMNN

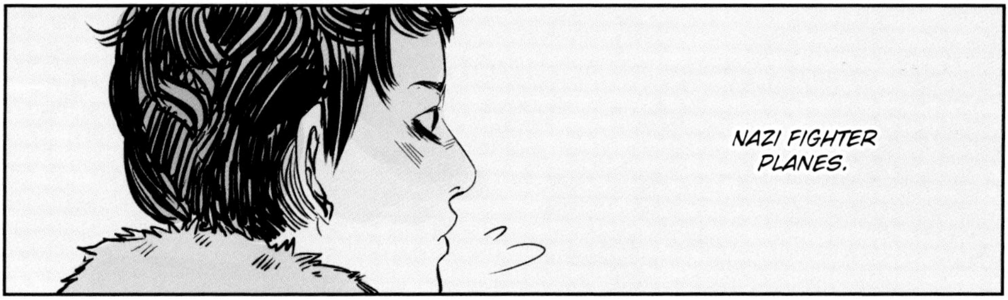
NAZI FIGHTER
PLANES.

ANY MINUTE NOW, I'M GOING TO WAKE UP.

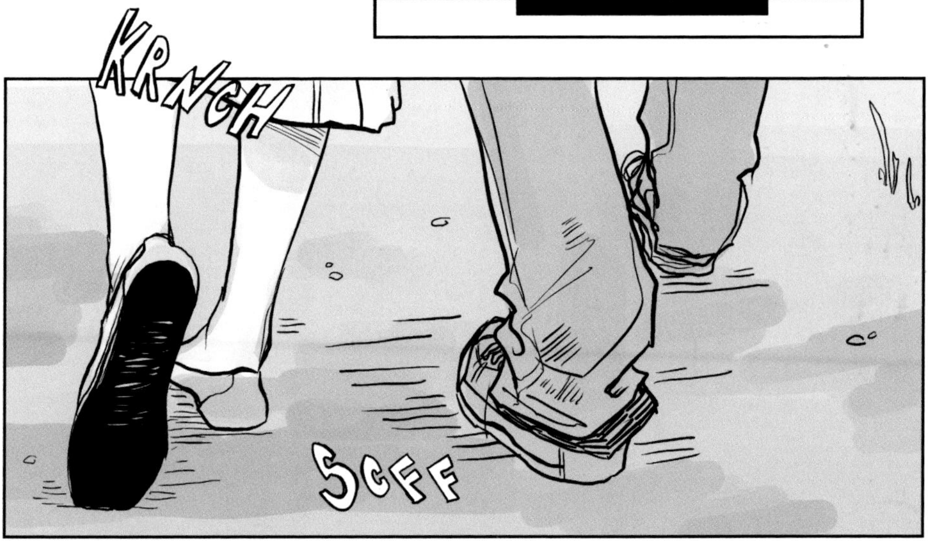
KRNCH
SCFF

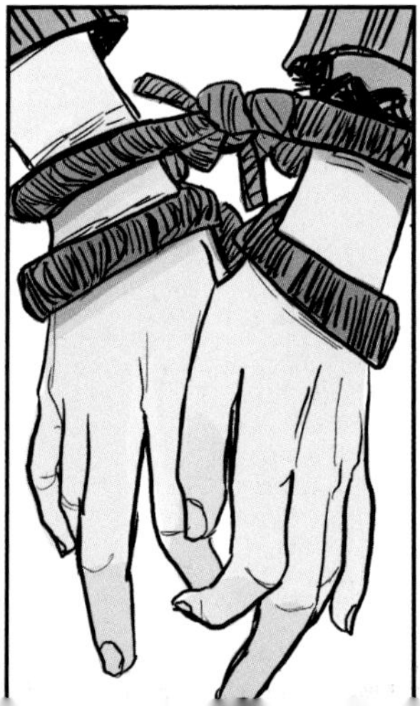

BUT I'M NOT WAKING UP...

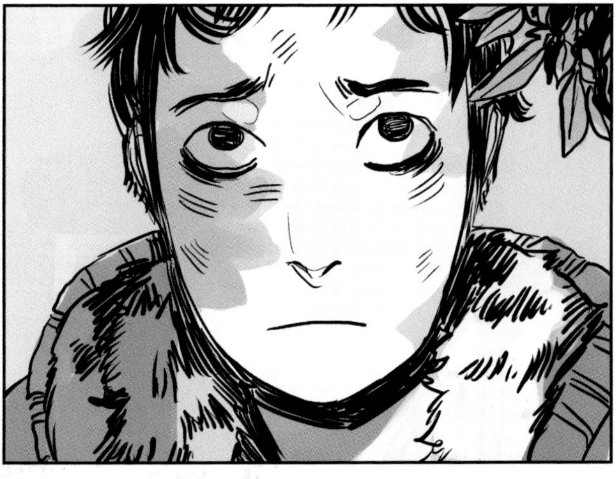

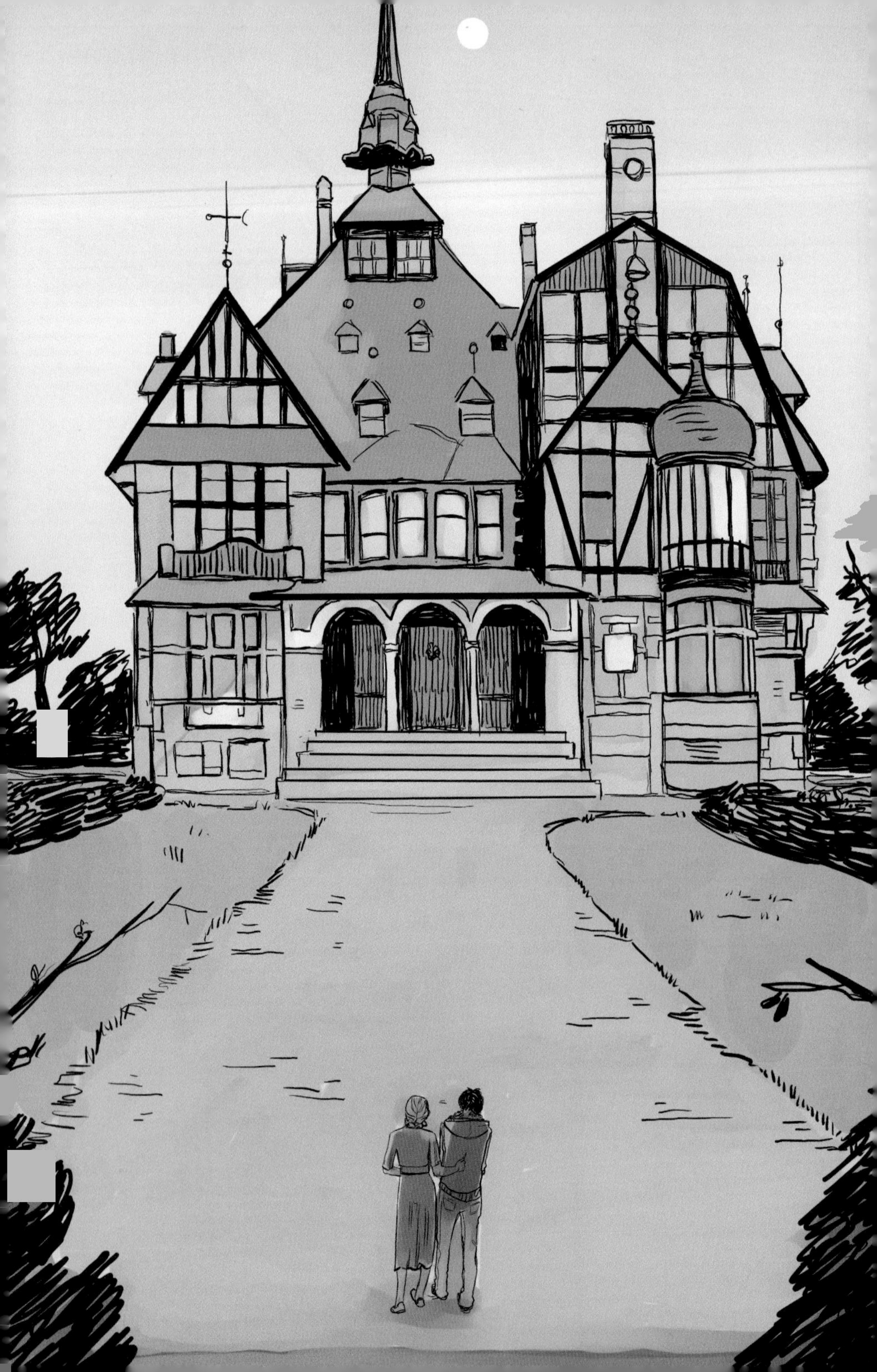

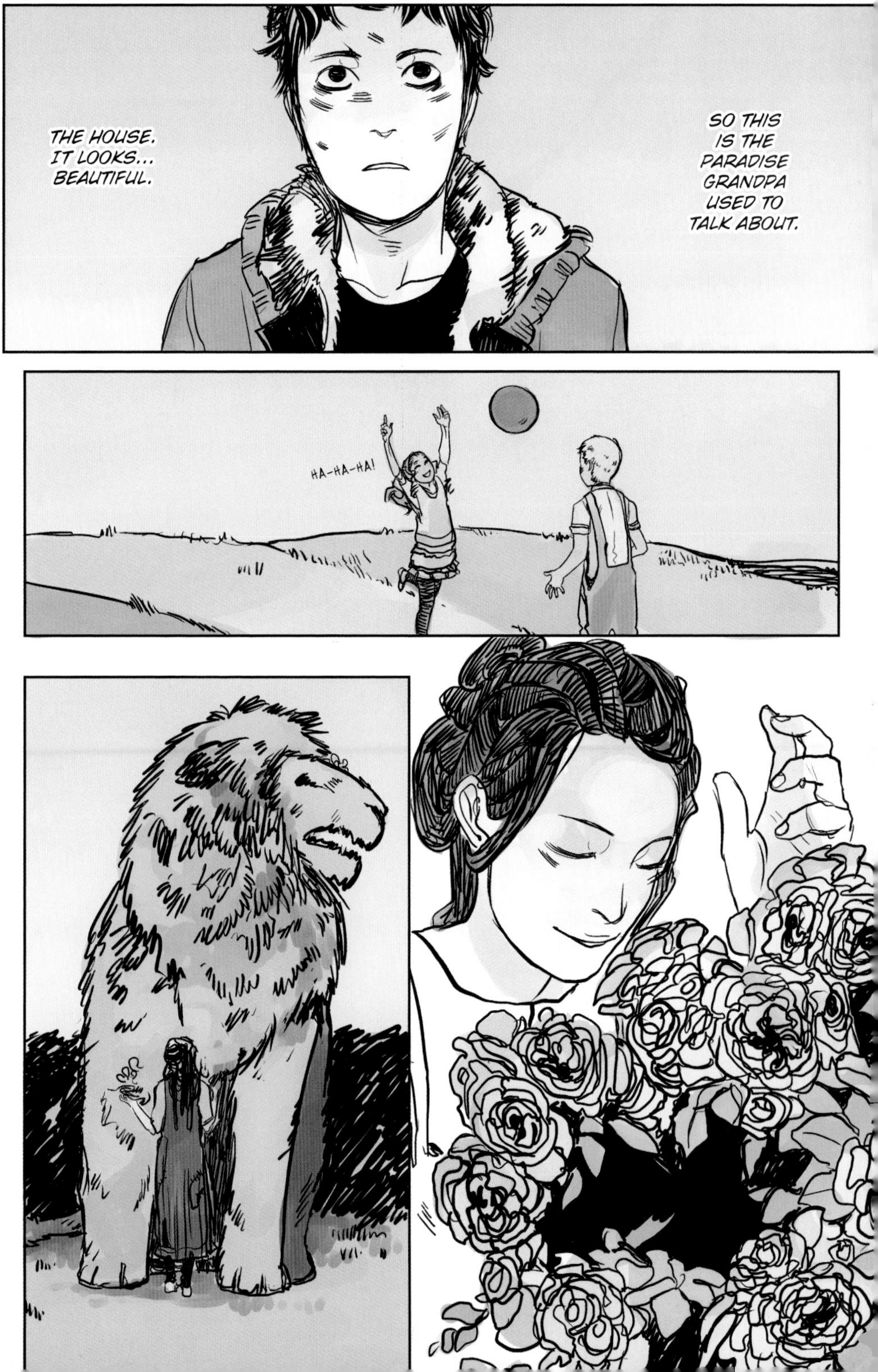
THE HOUSE. IT LOOKS... BEAUTIFUL.
SO THIS IS THE PARADISE GRANDPA USED TO TALK ABOUT.
HA-HA-HA!

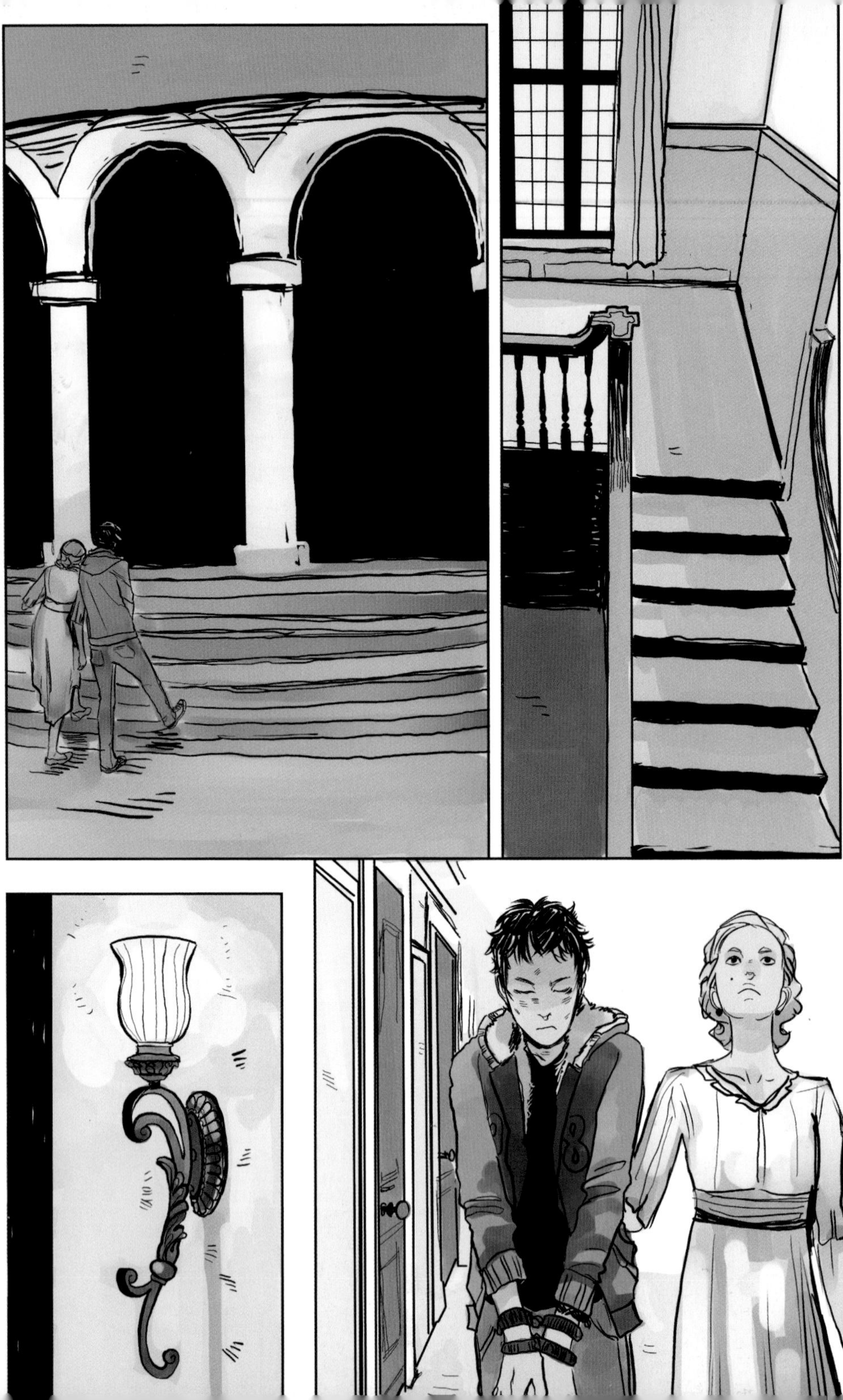

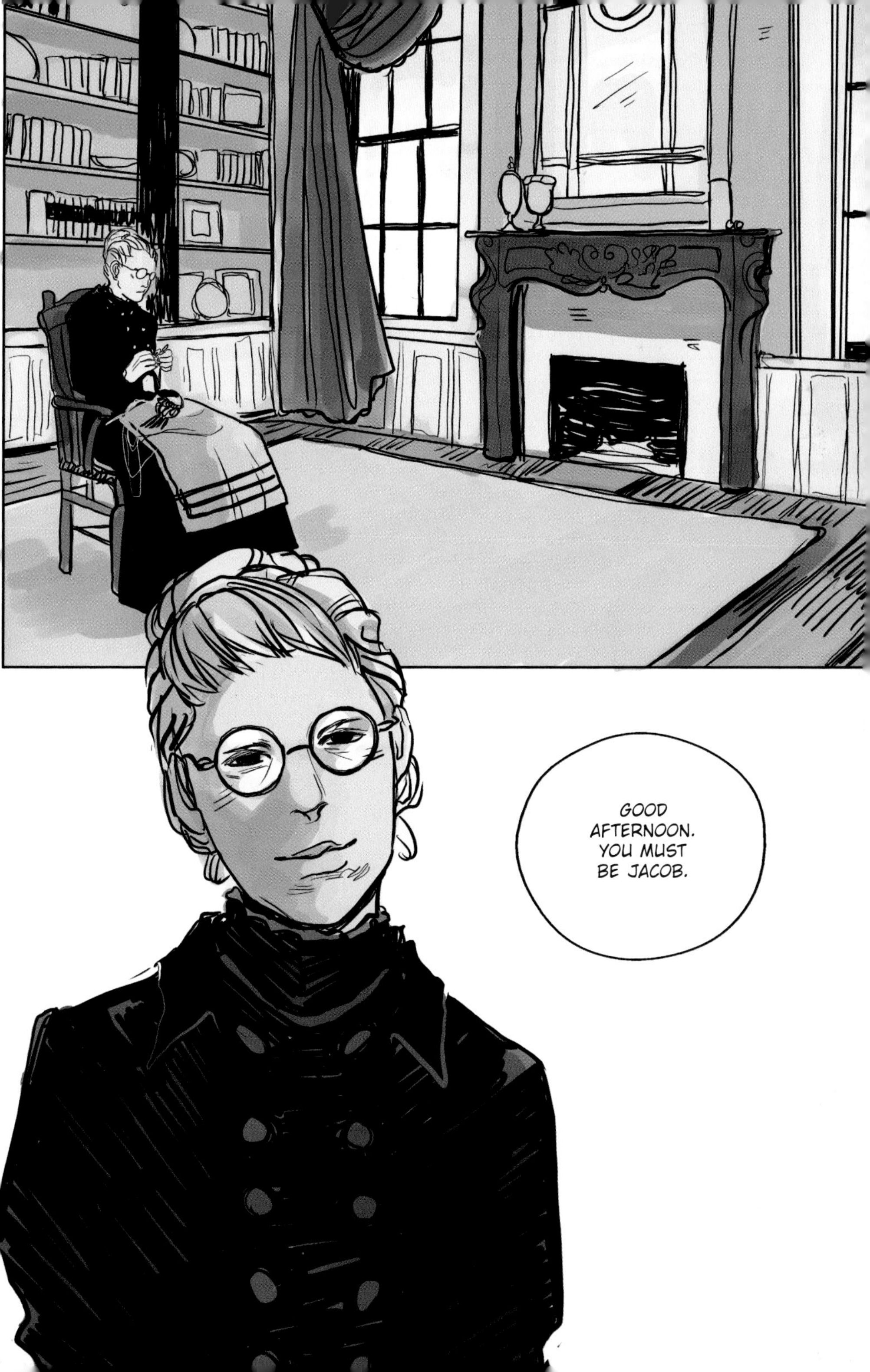
GOOD AFTERNOON. YOU MUST BE JACOB.

CHAPTER FOUR

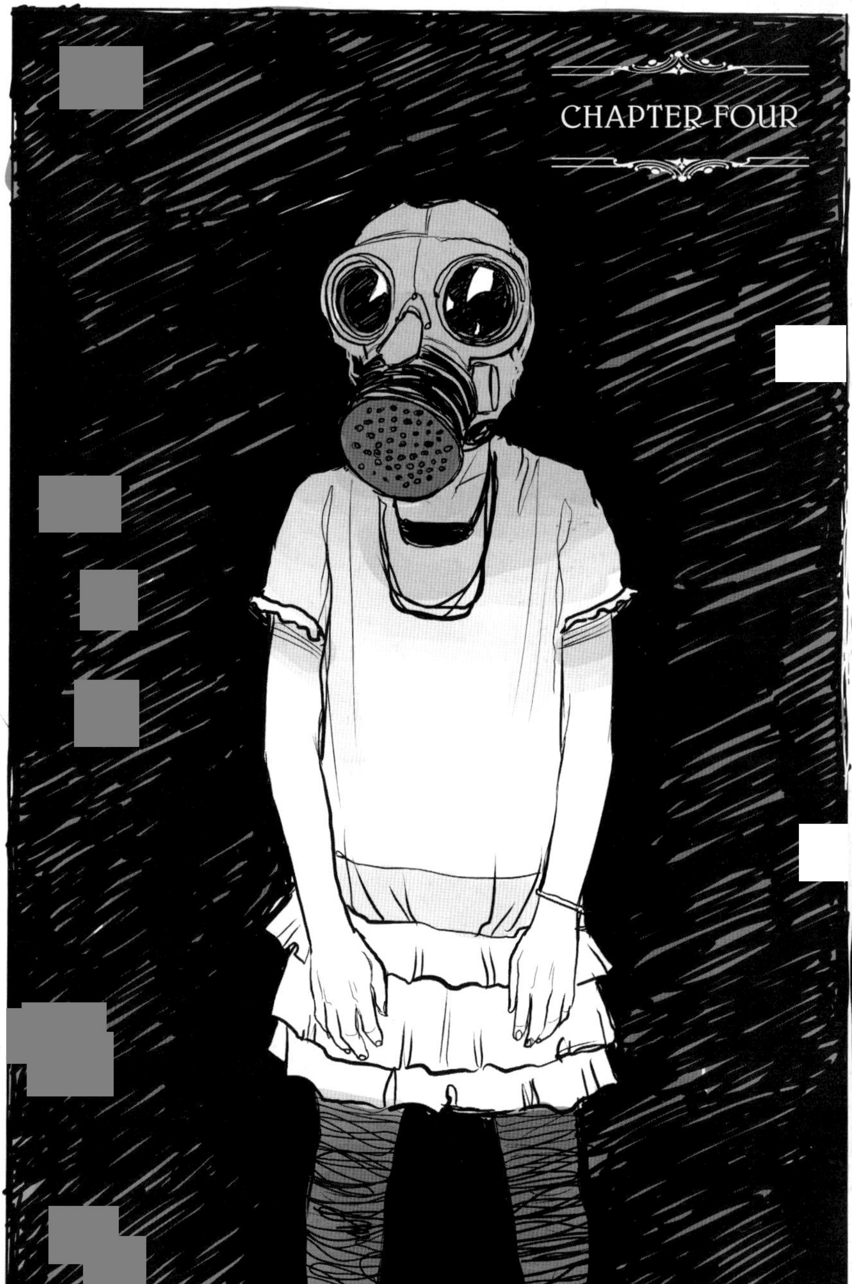

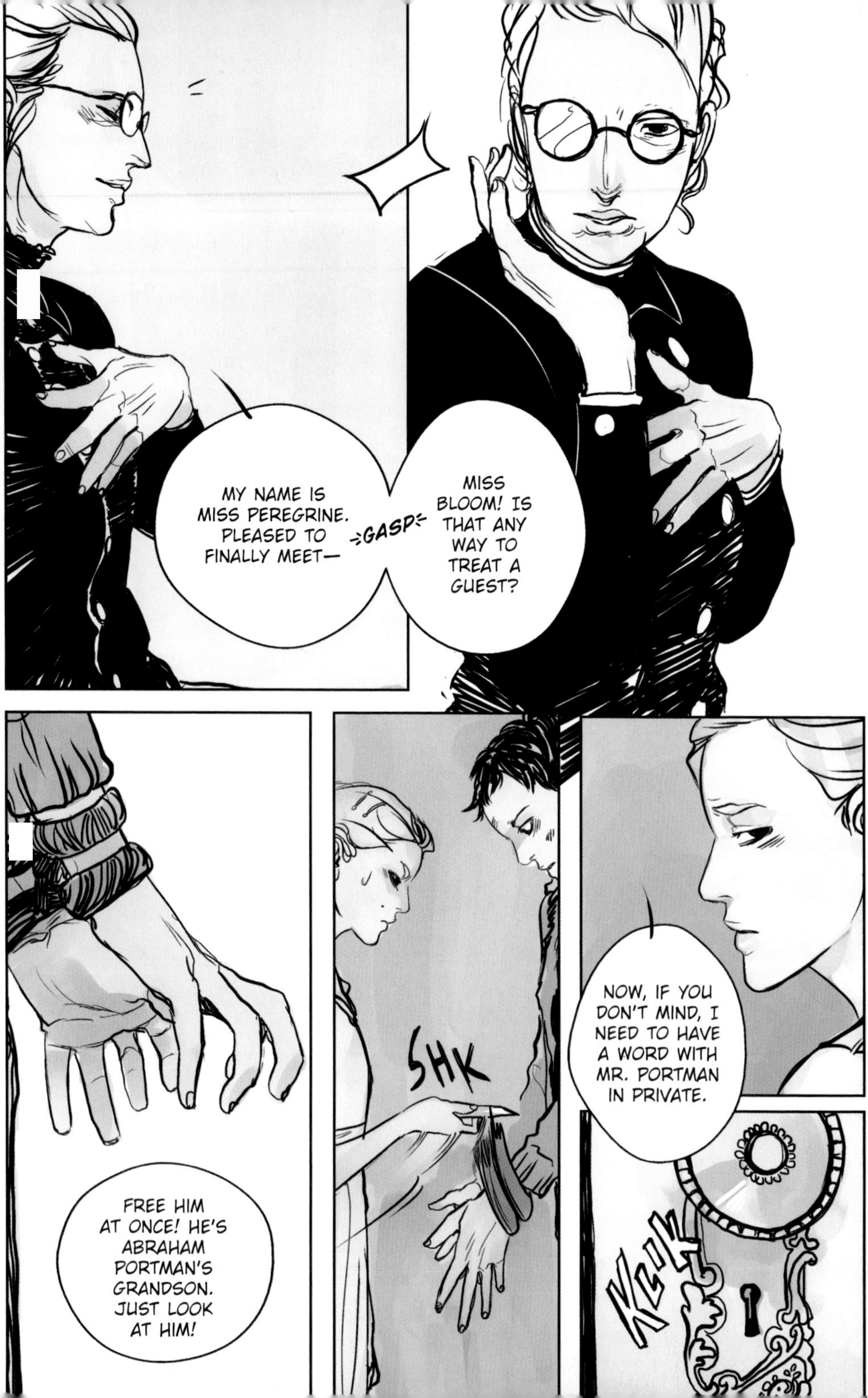
MY NAME IS MISS PEREGRINE. PLEASED TO FINALLY MEET—
GASP
MISS BLOOM! IS THAT ANY WAY TO TREAT A GUEST?
FREE HIM AT ONCE! HE'S ABRAHAM PORTMAN'S GRANDSON. JUST LOOK AT HIM!
SHK
NOW, IF YOU DON'T MIND, I NEED TO HAVE A WORD WITH MR. PORTMAN IN PRIVATE.
KCLIK

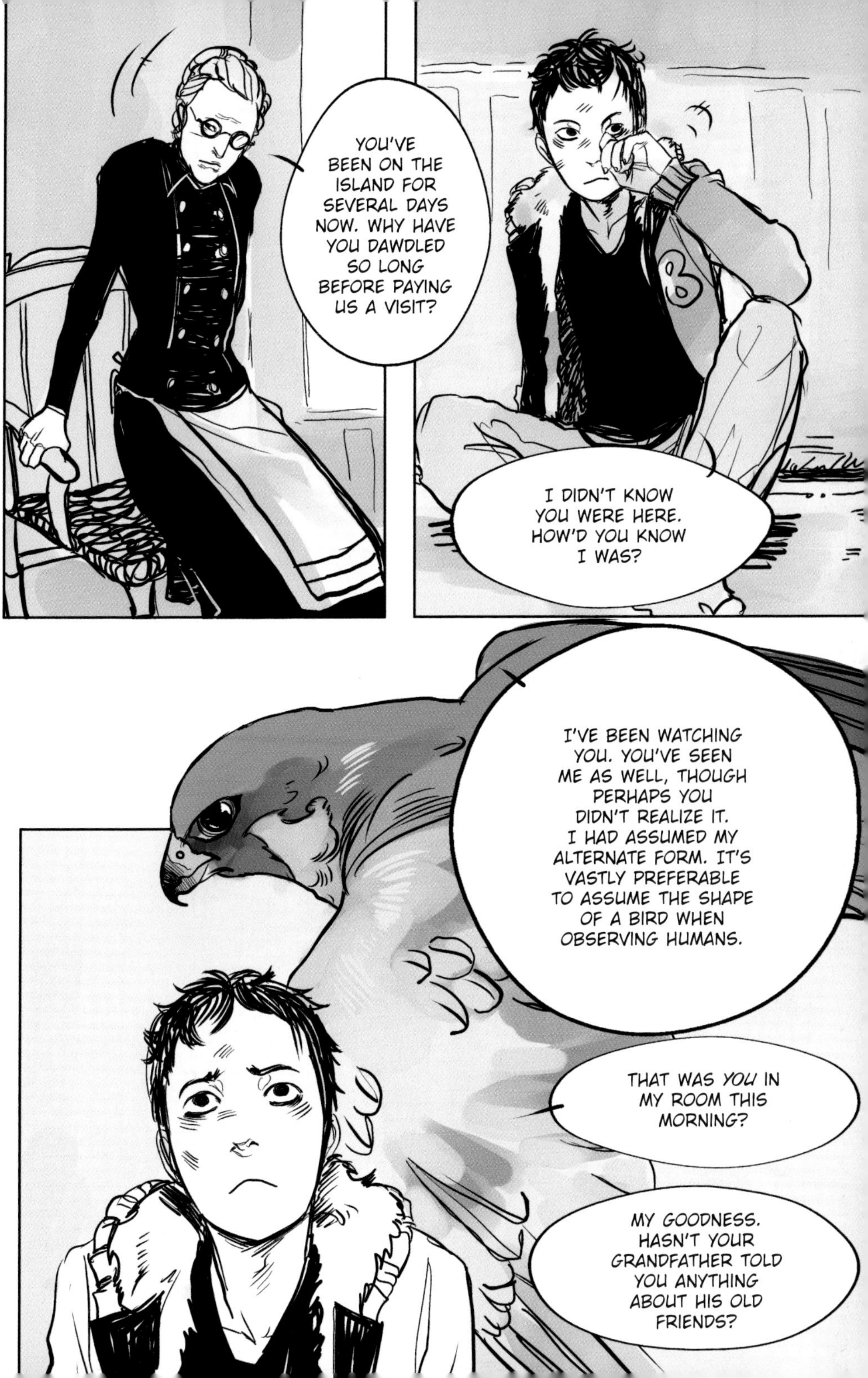
YOU'VE BEEN ON THE ISLAND FOR SEVERAL DAYS NOW. WHY HAVE YOU DAWDLED SO LONG BEFORE PAYING US A VISIT?
I DIDN'T KNOW YOU WERE HERE. HOW'D YOU KNOW I WAS?
I'VE BEEN WATCHING YOU. YOU'VE SEEN ME AS WELL, THOUGH PERHAPS YOU DIDN'T REALIZE IT. I HAD ASSUMED MY ALTERNATE FORM. IT'S VASTLY PREFERABLE TO ASSUME THE SHAPE OF A BIRD WHEN OBSERVING HUMANS.
THAT WAS *YOU* IN MY ROOM THIS MORNING?
MY GOODNESS. HASN'T YOUR GRANDFATHER TOLD YOU ANYTHING ABOUT HIS OLD FRIENDS?

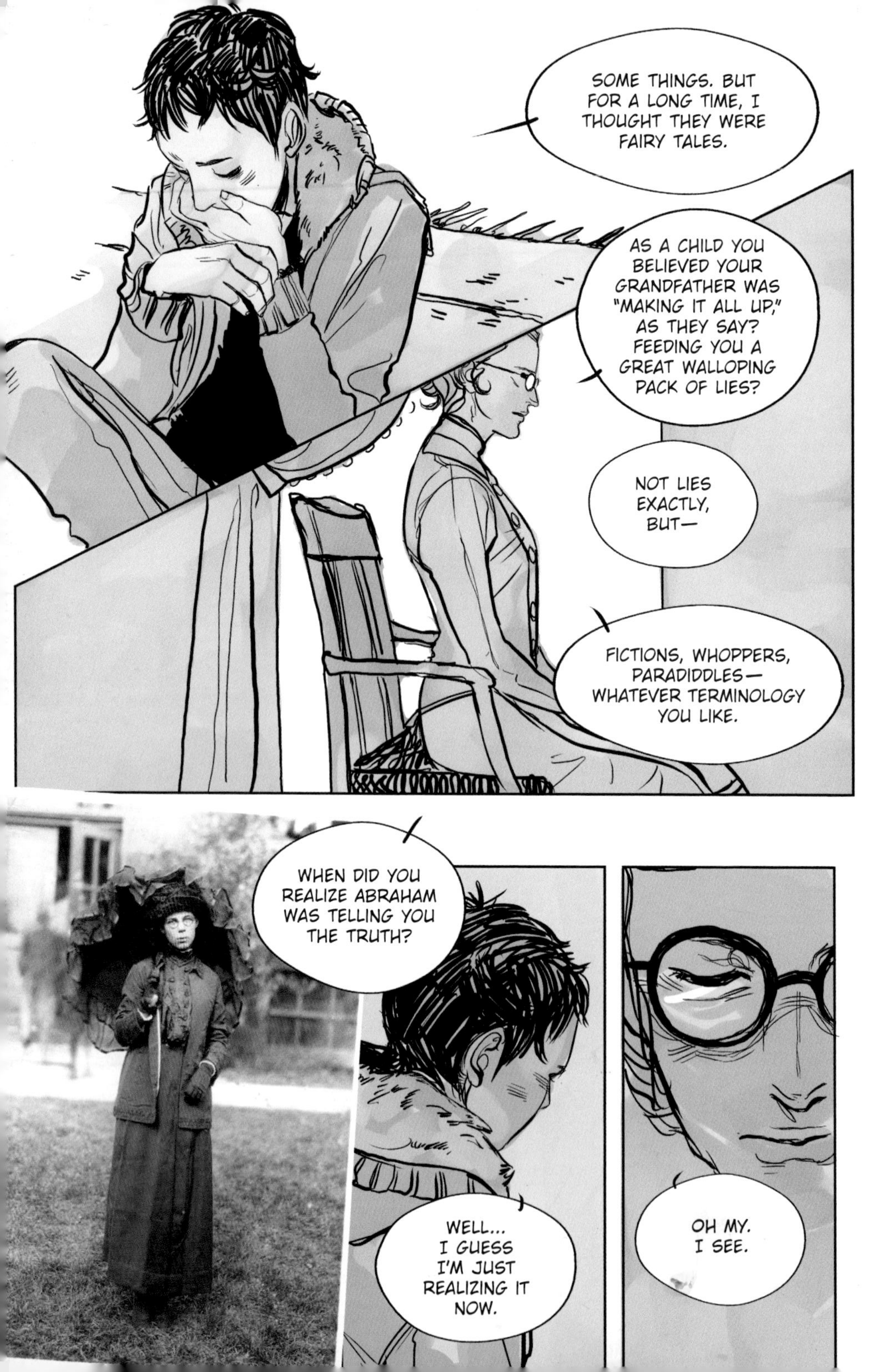
SOME THINGS. BUT FOR A LONG TIME, I THOUGHT THEY WERE FAIRY TALES.
AS A CHILD YOU BELIEVED YOUR GRANDFATHER WAS "MAKING IT ALL UP," AS THEY SAY? FEEDING YOU A GREAT WALLOPING PACK OF LIES?
NOT LIES EXACTLY, BUT—
FICTIONS, WHOPPERS, PARADIDDLES— WHATEVER TERMINOLOGY YOU LIKE.
WHEN DID YOU REALIZE ABRAHAM WAS TELLING YOU THE TRUTH?
WELL... I GUESS I'M JUST REALIZING IT NOW.
OH MY. I SEE.

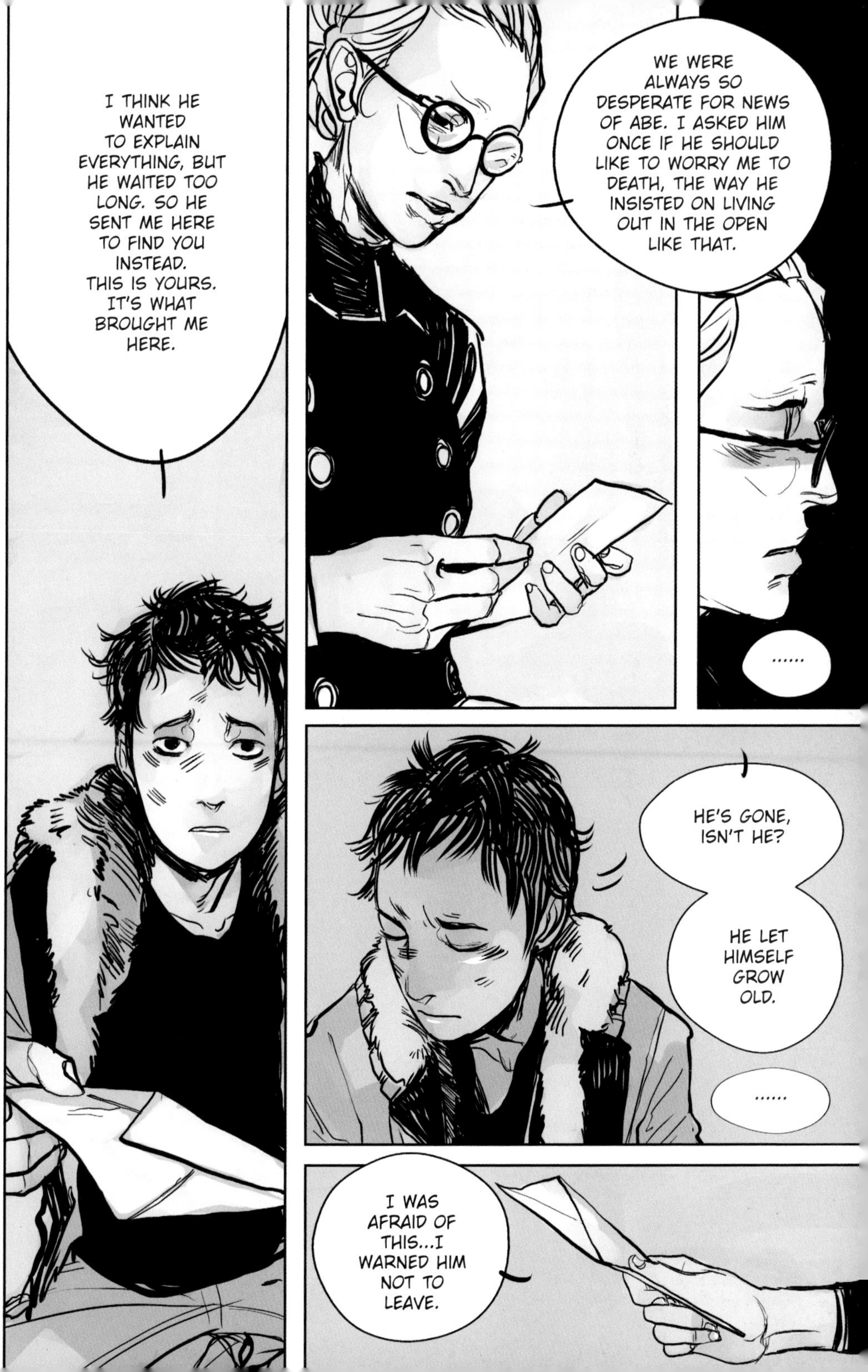
I THINK HE WANTED TO EXPLAIN EVERYTHING, BUT HE WAITED TOO LONG. SO HE SENT ME HERE TO FIND YOU INSTEAD. THIS IS YOURS. IT'S WHAT BROUGHT ME HERE.
WE WERE ALWAYS SO DESPERATE FOR NEWS OF ABE. I ASKED HIM ONCE IF HE SHOULD LIKE TO WORRY ME TO DEATH, THE WAY HE INSISTED ON LIVING OUT IN THE OPEN LIKE THAT.
......
HE'S GONE, ISN'T HE?
HE LET HIMSELF GROW OLD.
......
I WAS AFRAID OF THIS...I WARNED HIM NOT TO LEAVE.

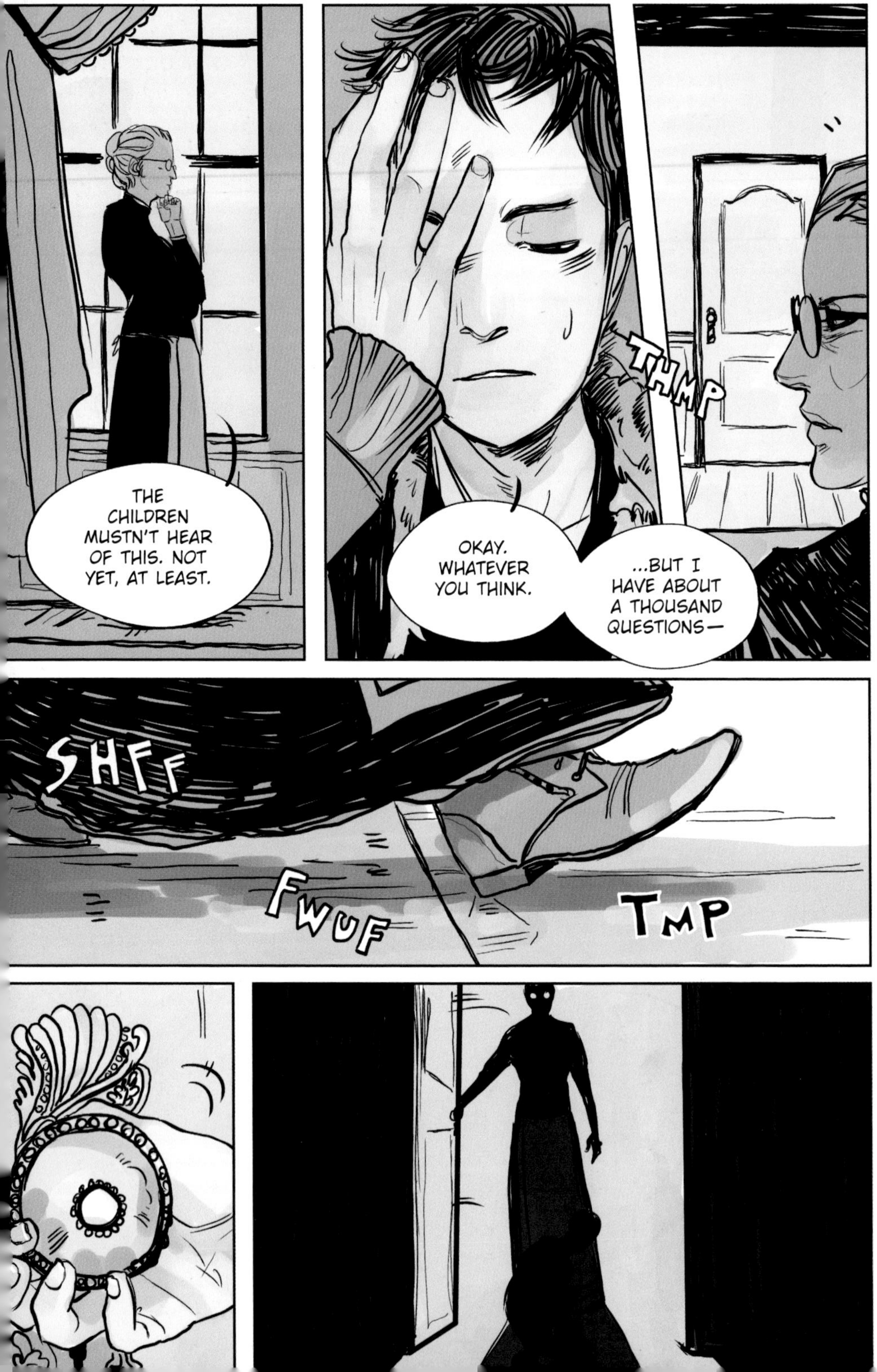
THE CHILDREN MUSTN'T HEAR OF THIS. NOT YET, AT LEAST.
OKAY. WHATEVER YOU THINK.
THMP
...BUT I HAVE ABOUT A THOUSAND QUESTIONS—
SHFF
FWUF
TMP

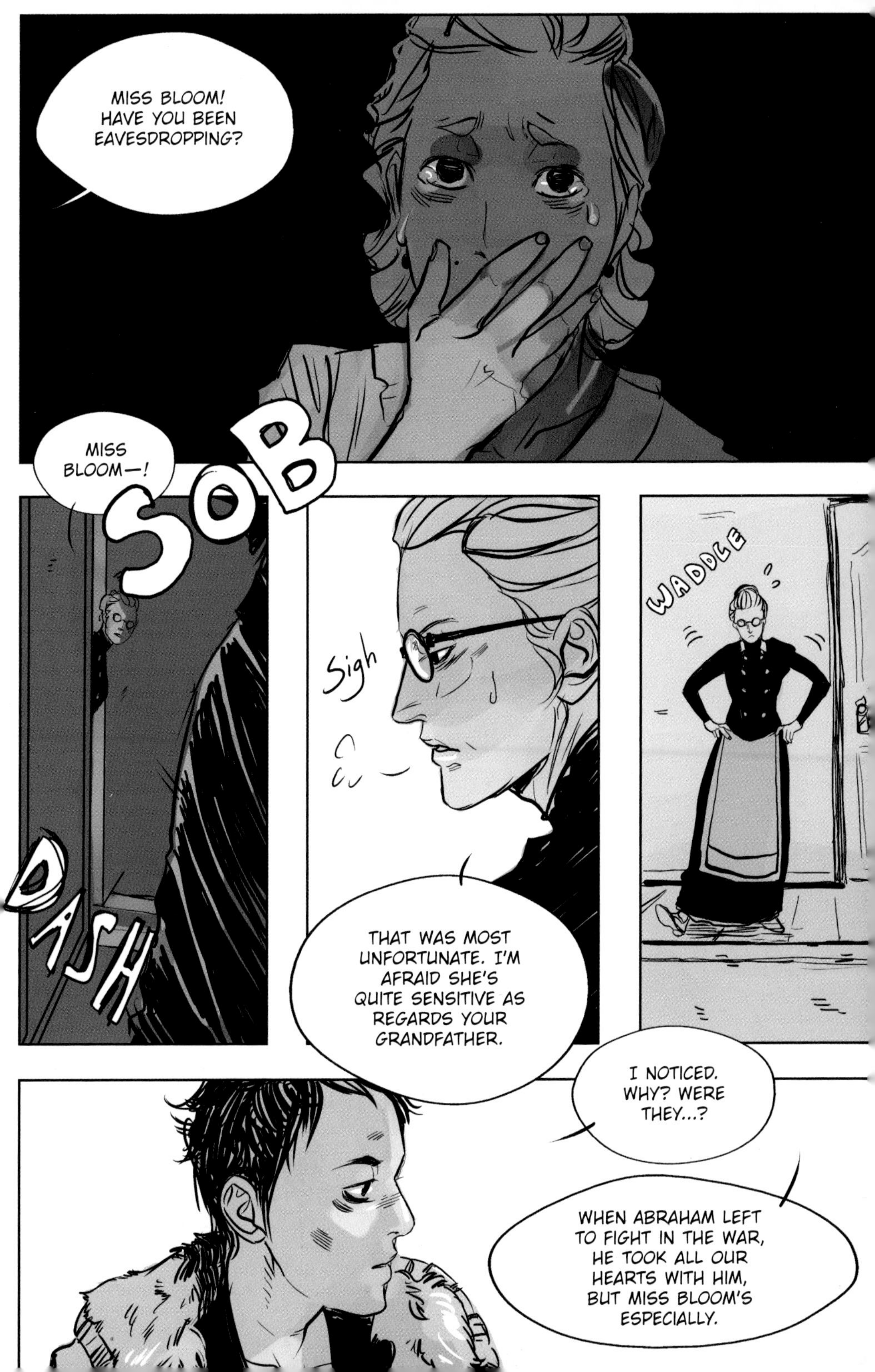
MISS BLOOM! HAVE YOU BEEN EAVESDROPPING?
MISS BLOOM—!
SOB
DASH
Sigh
THAT WAS MOST UNFORTUNATE. I'M AFRAID SHE'S QUITE SENSITIVE AS REGARDS YOUR GRANDFATHER.
WADDLE
I NOTICED. WHY? WERE THEY...?
WHEN ABRAHAM LEFT TO FIGHT IN THE WAR, HE TOOK ALL OUR HEARTS WITH HIM, BUT MISS BLOOM'S ESPECIALLY.

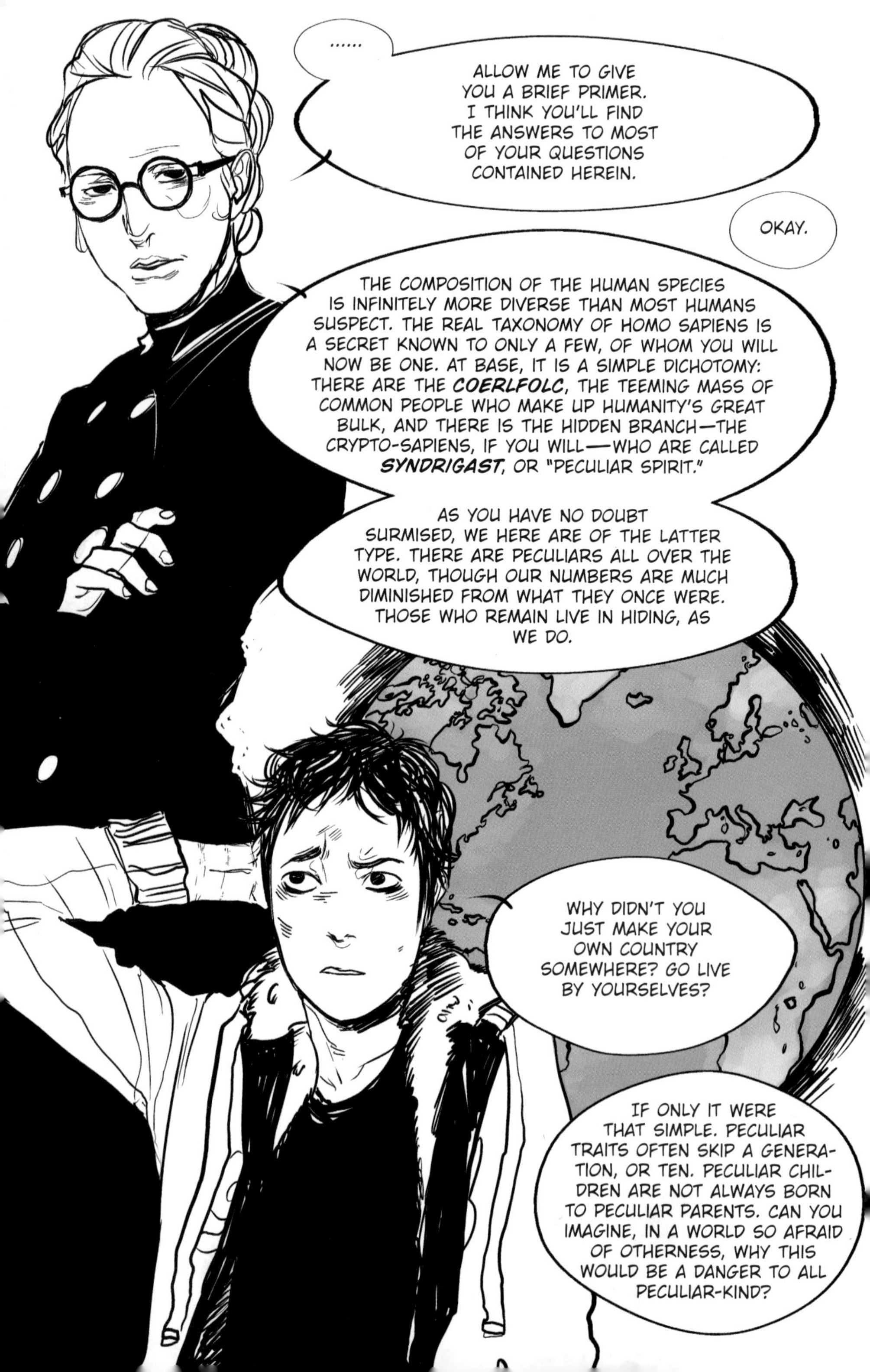
......
ALLOW ME TO GIVE YOU A BRIEF PRIMER. I THINK YOU'LL FIND THE ANSWERS TO MOST OF YOUR QUESTIONS CONTAINED HEREIN.
OKAY.
THE COMPOSITION OF THE HUMAN SPECIES IS INFINITELY MORE DIVERSE THAN MOST HUMANS SUSPECT. THE REAL TAXONOMY OF HOMO SAPIENS IS A SECRET KNOWN TO ONLY A FEW, OF WHOM YOU WILL NOW BE ONE. AT BASE, IT IS A SIMPLE DICHOTOMY: THERE ARE THE ***COERLFOLC***, THE TEEMING MASS OF COMMON PEOPLE WHO MAKE UP HUMANITY'S GREAT BULK, AND THERE IS THE HIDDEN BRANCH—THE CRYPTO-SAPIENS, IF YOU WILL—WHO ARE CALLED ***SYNDRIGAST***, OR "PECULIAR SPIRIT."
AS YOU HAVE NO DOUBT SURMISED, WE HERE ARE OF THE LATTER TYPE. THERE ARE PECULIARS ALL OVER THE WORLD, THOUGH OUR NUMBERS ARE MUCH DIMINISHED FROM WHAT THEY ONCE WERE. THOSE WHO REMAIN LIVE IN HIDING, AS WE DO.
WHY DIDN'T YOU JUST MAKE YOUR OWN COUNTRY SOMEWHERE? GO LIVE BY YOURSELVES?
IF ONLY IT WERE THAT SIMPLE. PECULIAR TRAITS OFTEN SKIP A GENERATION, OR TEN. PECULIAR CHILDREN ARE NOT ALWAYS BORN TO PECULIAR PARENTS. CAN YOU IMAGINE, IN A WORLD SO AFRAID OF OTHERNESS, WHY THIS WOULD BE A DANGER TO ALL PECULIAR-KIND?

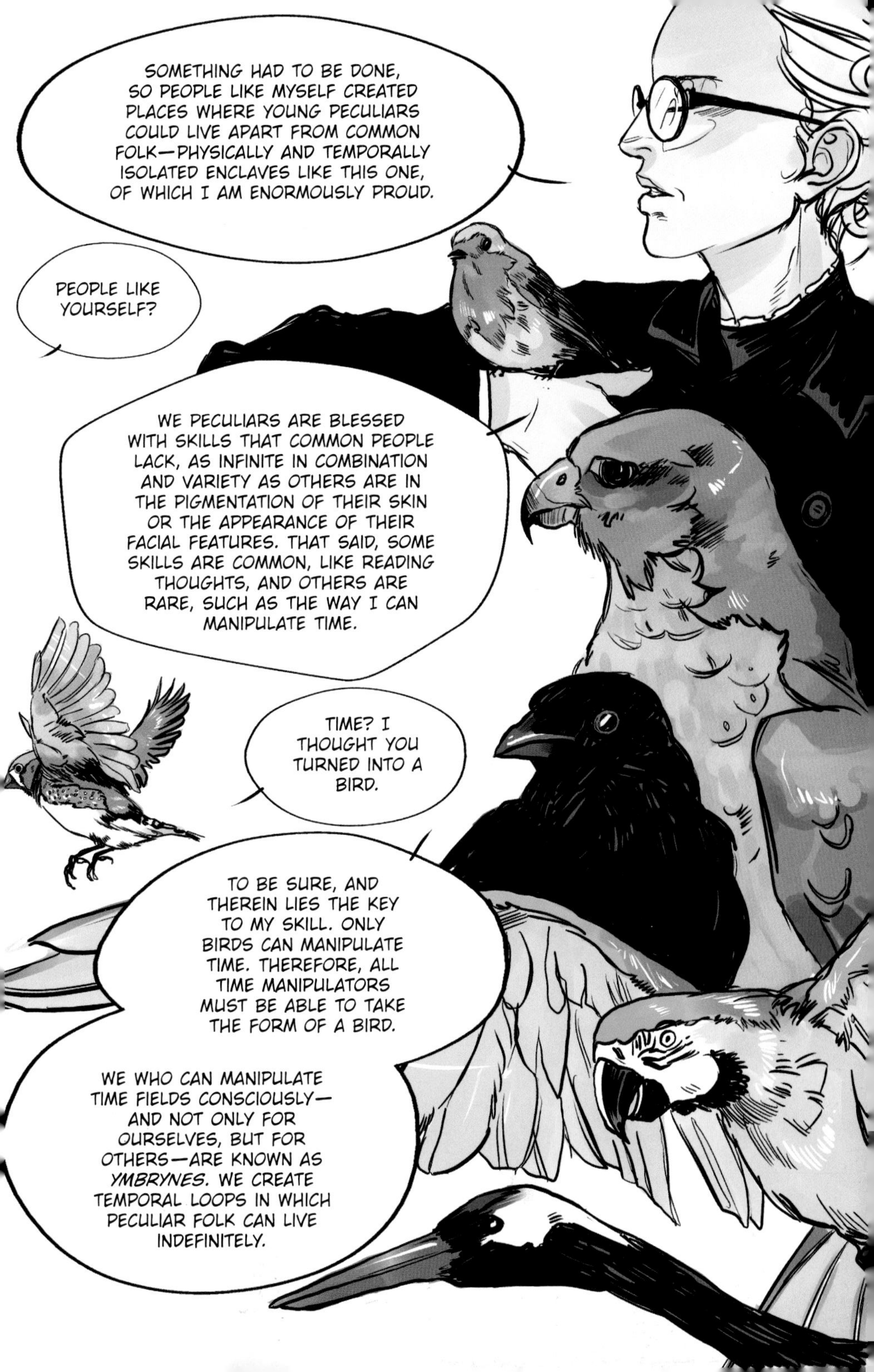
SOMETHING HAD TO BE DONE, SO PEOPLE LIKE MYSELF CREATED PLACES WHERE YOUNG PECULIARS COULD LIVE APART FROM COMMON FOLK—PHYSICALLY AND TEMPORALLY ISOLATED ENCLAVES LIKE THIS ONE, OF WHICH I AM ENORMOUSLY PROUD.
PEOPLE LIKE YOURSELF?
WE PECULIARS ARE BLESSED WITH SKILLS THAT COMMON PEOPLE LACK, AS INFINITE IN COMBINATION AND VARIETY AS OTHERS ARE IN THE PIGMENTATION OF THEIR SKIN OR THE APPEARANCE OF THEIR FACIAL FEATURES. THAT SAID, SOME SKILLS ARE COMMON, LIKE READING THOUGHTS, AND OTHERS ARE RARE, SUCH AS THE WAY I CAN MANIPULATE TIME.
TIME? I THOUGHT YOU TURNED INTO A BIRD.
TO BE SURE, AND THEREIN LIES THE KEY TO MY SKILL. ONLY BIRDS CAN MANIPULATE TIME. THEREFORE, ALL TIME MANIPULATORS MUST BE ABLE TO TAKE THE FORM OF A BIRD.
WE WHO CAN MANIPULATE TIME FIELDS CONSCIOUSLY—AND NOT ONLY FOR OURSELVES, BUT FOR OTHERS—ARE KNOWN AS *YMBRYNES*. WE CREATE TEMPORAL LOOPS IN WHICH PECULIAR FOLK CAN LIVE INDEFINITELY.

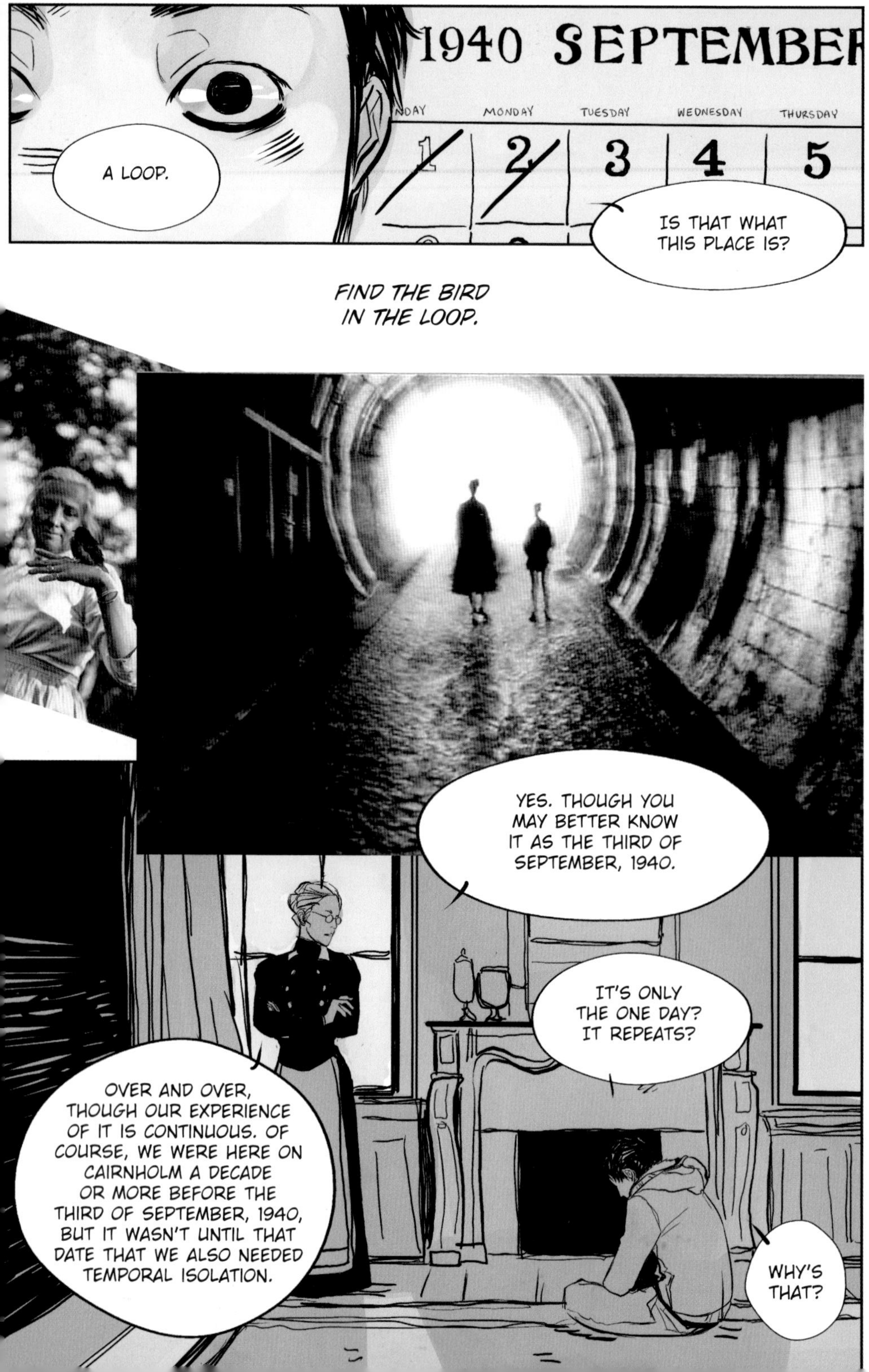
A LOOP.
1940 SEPTEMBER
NDAY MONDAY TUESDAY WEDNESDAY THURSDAY
1 2 3 4 5
IS THAT WHAT THIS PLACE IS?
FIND THE BIRD IN THE LOOP.
YES. THOUGH YOU MAY BETTER KNOW IT AS THE THIRD OF SEPTEMBER, 1940.
IT'S ONLY THE ONE DAY? IT REPEATS?
OVER AND OVER, THOUGH OUR EXPERIENCE OF IT IS CONTINUOUS. OF COURSE, WE WERE HERE ON CAIRNHOLM A DECADE OR MORE BEFORE THE THIRD OF SEPTEMBER, 1940, BUT IT WASN'T UNTIL THAT DATE THAT WE ALSO NEEDED TEMPORAL ISOLATION.
WHY'S THAT?

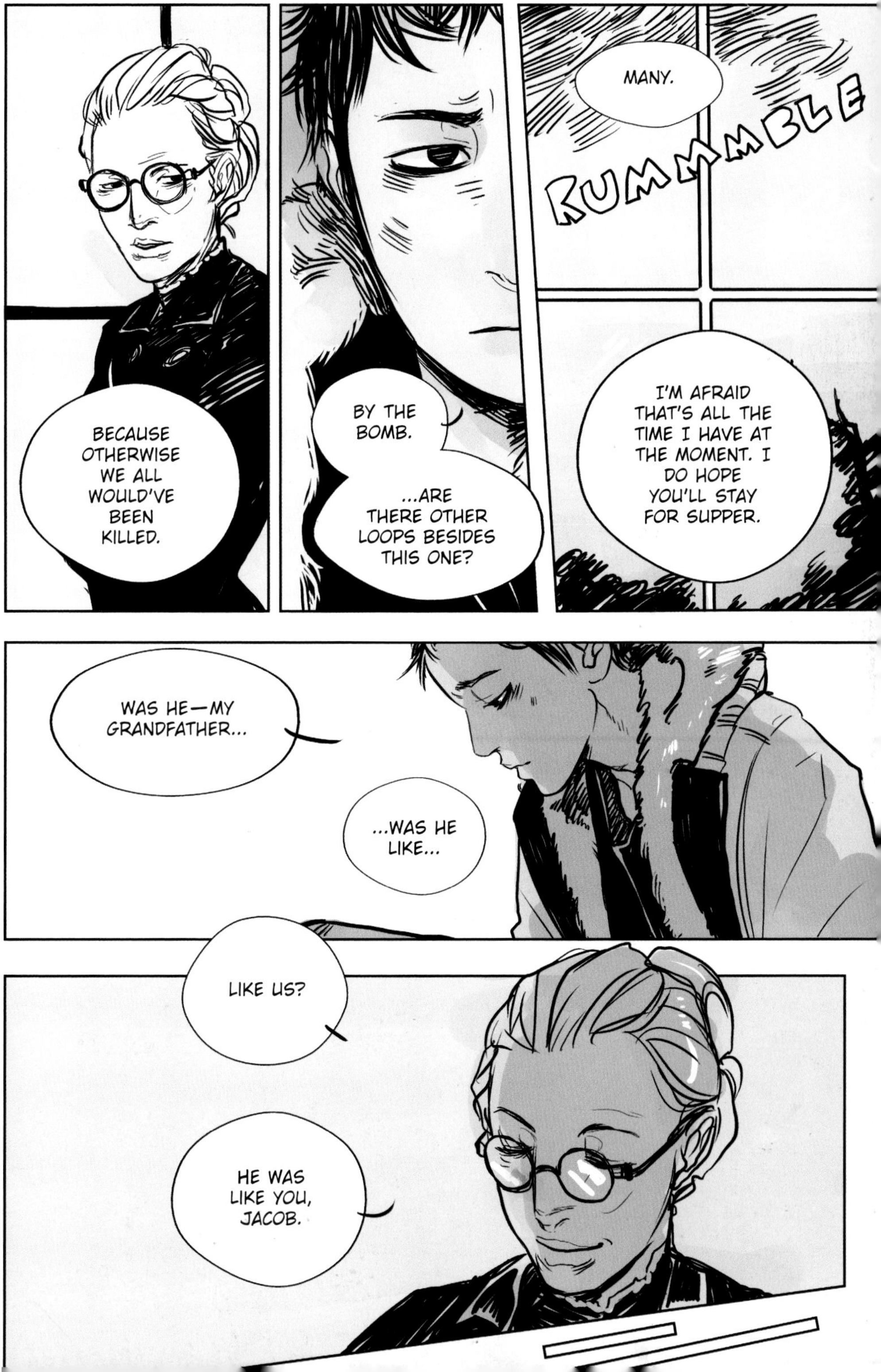
BECAUSE OTHERWISE WE ALL WOULD'VE BEEN KILLED.
BY THE BOMB.
...ARE THERE OTHER LOOPS BESIDES THIS ONE?
MANY.
RUMMMBLE
I'M AFRAID THAT'S ALL THE TIME I HAVE AT THE MOMENT. I DO HOPE YOU'LL STAY FOR SUPPER.
WAS HE—MY GRANDFATHER...
...WAS HE LIKE...
LIKE US?
HE WAS LIKE YOU, JACOB.

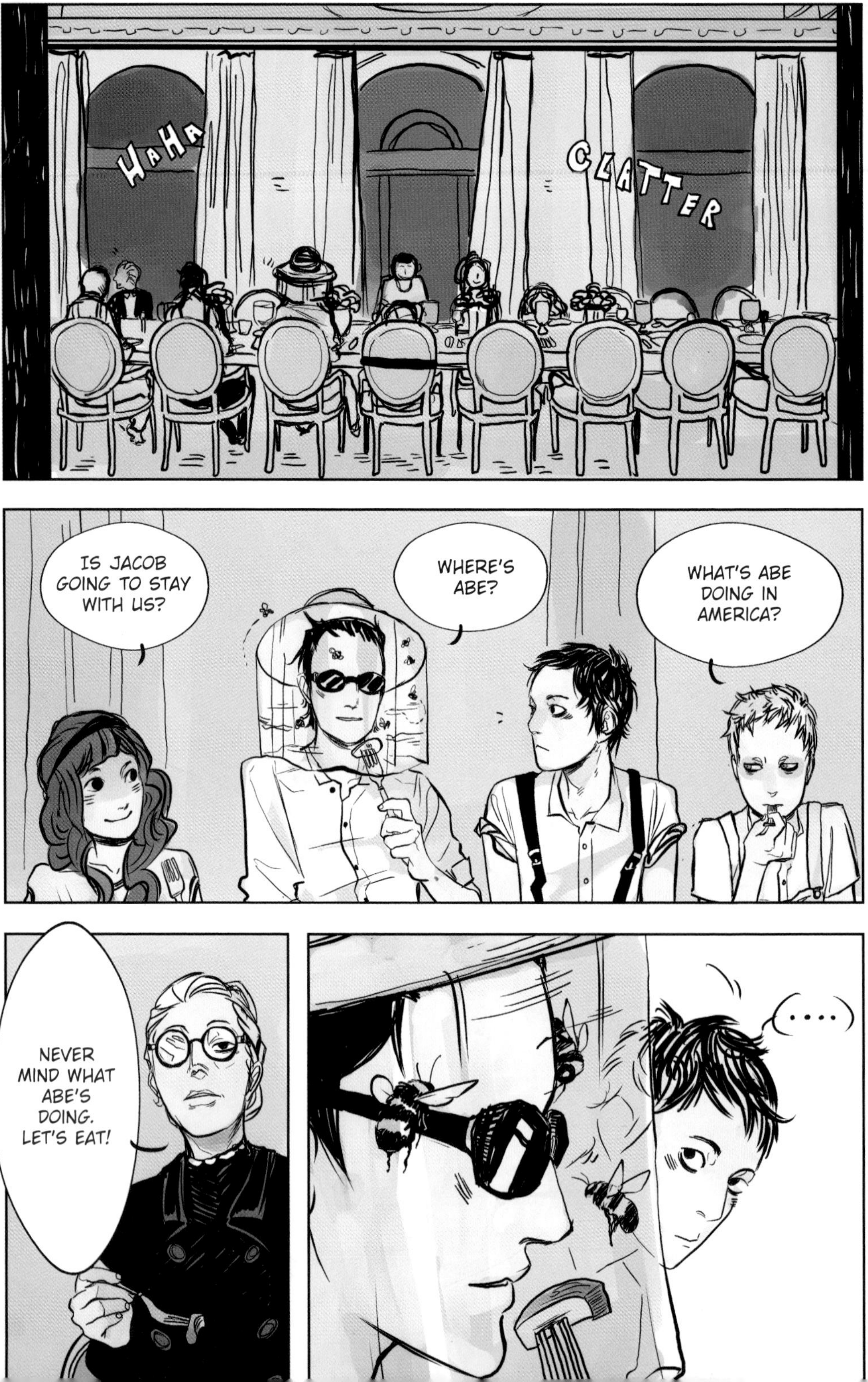
HAHA
CLATTER
IS JACOB GOING TO STAY WITH US?
WHERE'S ABE?
WHAT'S ABE DOING IN AMERICA?
NEVER MIND WHAT ABE'S DOING. LET'S EAT!
(....)

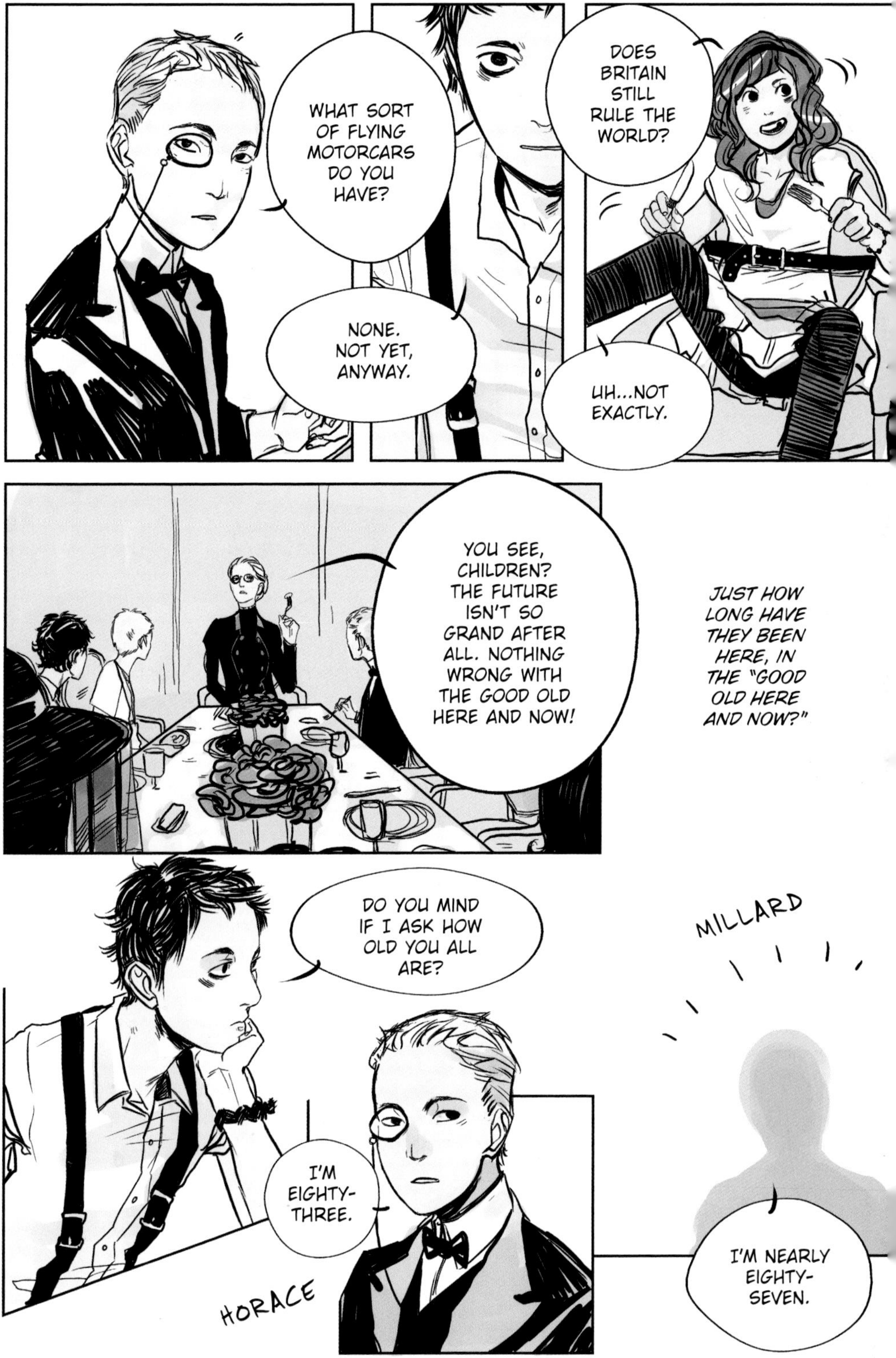
WHAT SORT OF FLYING MOTORCARS DO YOU HAVE?
NONE. NOT YET, ANYWAY.
DOES BRITAIN STILL RULE THE WORLD?
UH...NOT EXACTLY.
YOU SEE, CHILDREN? THE FUTURE ISN'T SO GRAND AFTER ALL. NOTHING WRONG WITH THE GOOD OLD HERE AND NOW!
JUST HOW LONG HAVE THEY BEEN HERE, IN THE "GOOD OLD HERE AND NOW?"
DO YOU MIND IF I ASK HOW OLD YOU ALL ARE?
MILLARD
I'M EIGHTY-THREE.
HORACE
I'M NEARLY EIGHTY-SEVEN.

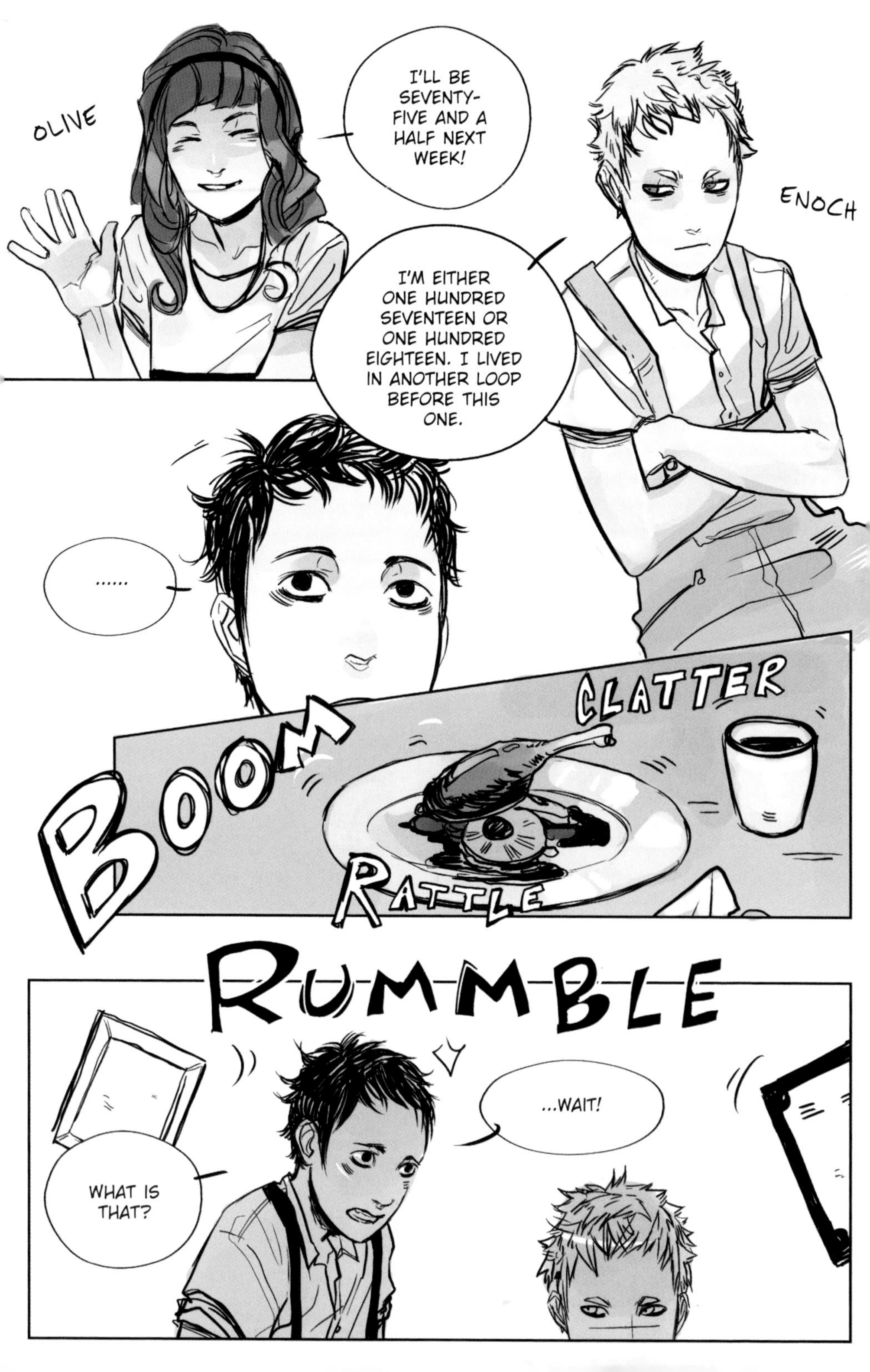
OLIVE
I'LL BE SEVENTY-FIVE AND A HALF NEXT WEEK!
ENOCH
I'M EITHER ONE HUNDRED SEVENTEEN OR ONE HUNDRED EIGHTEEN. I LIVED IN ANOTHER LOOP BEFORE THIS ONE.
......
CLATTER
BOOM
RATTLE
RUMMBLE
WHAT IS THAT?
...WAIT!

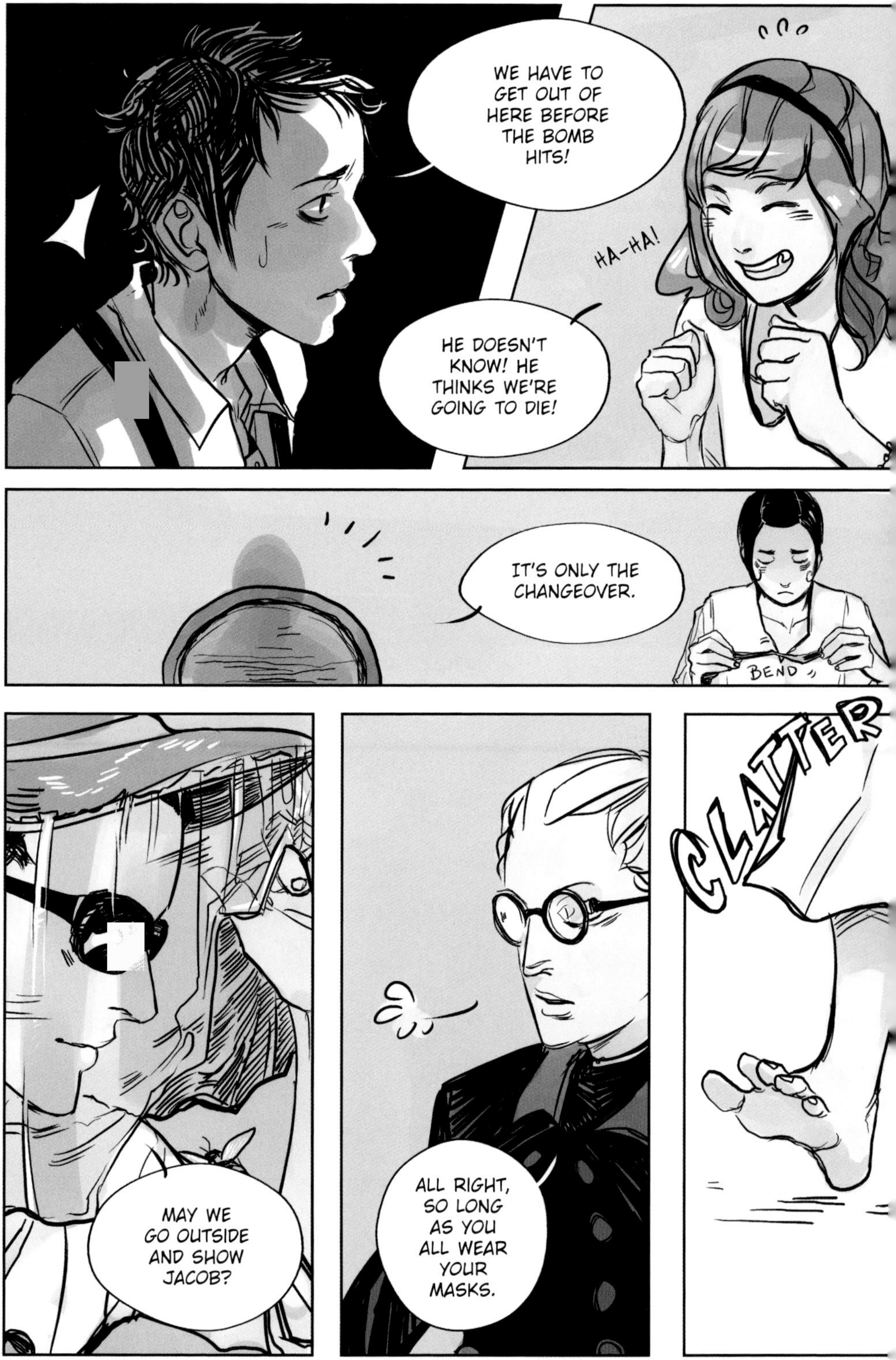
WE HAVE TO GET OUT OF HERE BEFORE THE BOMB HITS!
HA-HA!
HE DOESN'T KNOW! HE THINKS WE'RE GOING TO DIE!
IT'S ONLY THE CHANGEOVER.
BEND
MAY WE GO OUTSIDE AND SHOW JACOB?
ALL RIGHT, SO LONG AS YOU ALL WEAR YOUR MASKS.
CLATTER

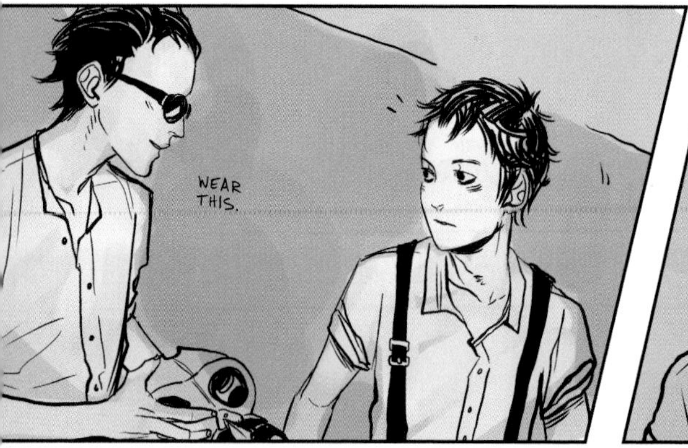
WEAR THIS.
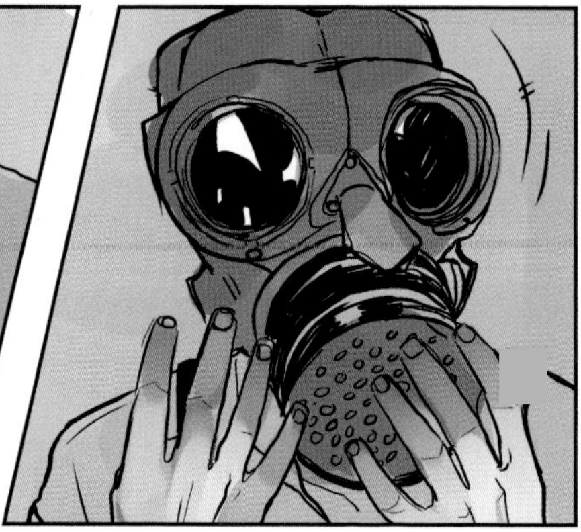
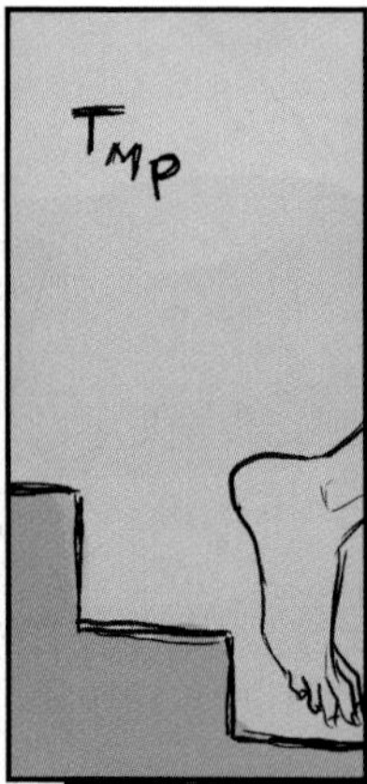
TMP
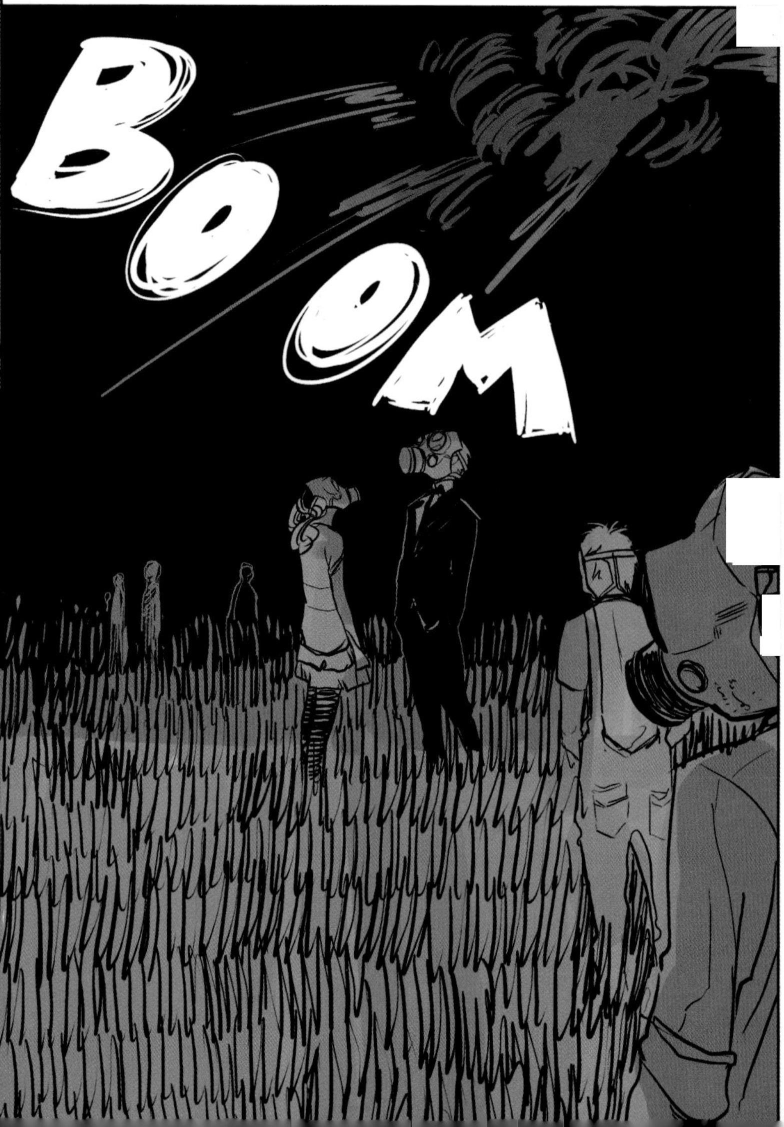
BOOM

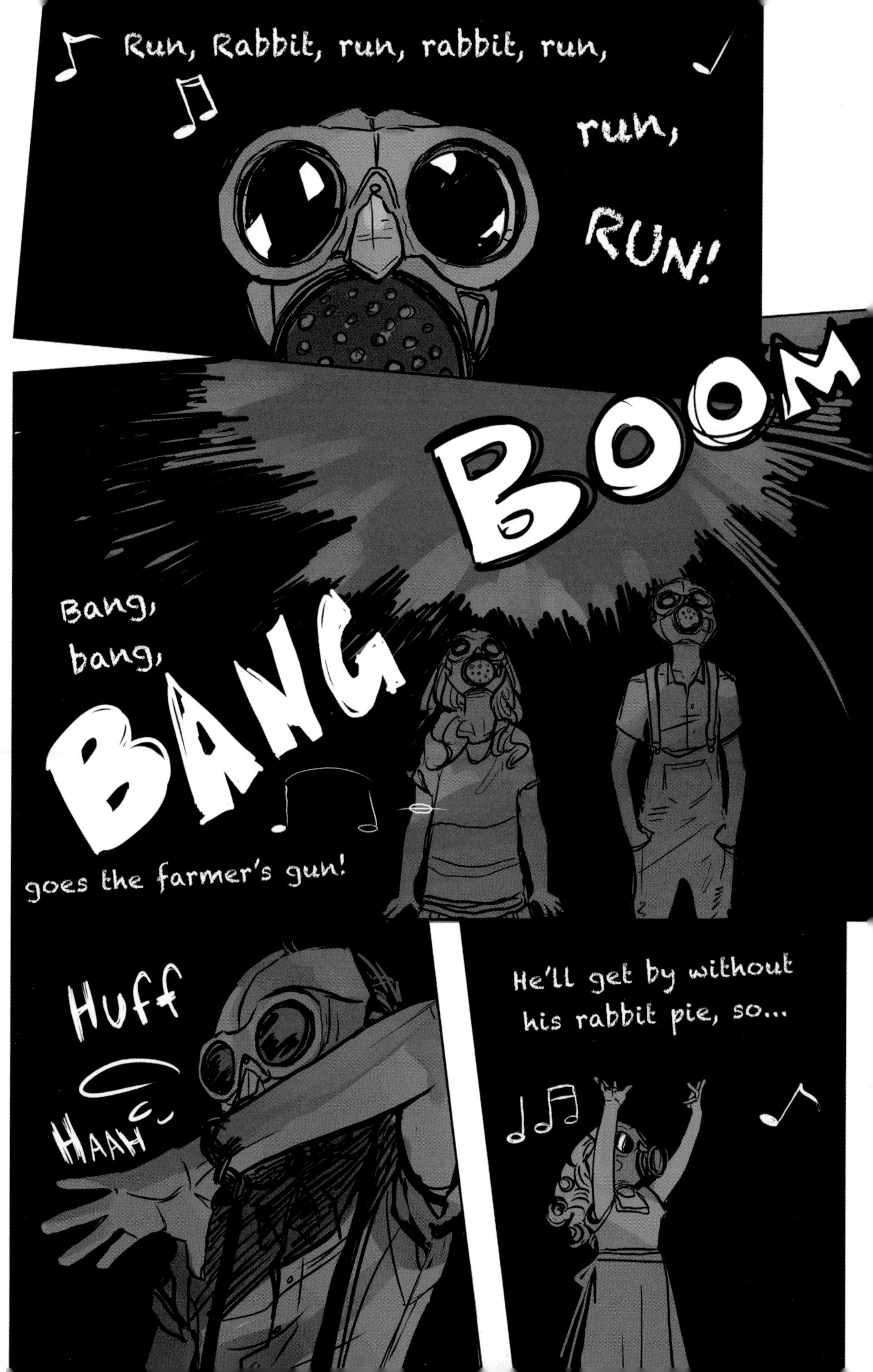
Run, Rabbit, run, rabbit, run,
run,
RUN!
BOOM
Bang,
bang,
BANG
goes the farmer's gun!
Huff
HAAH
He'll get by without
his rabbit pie, so...

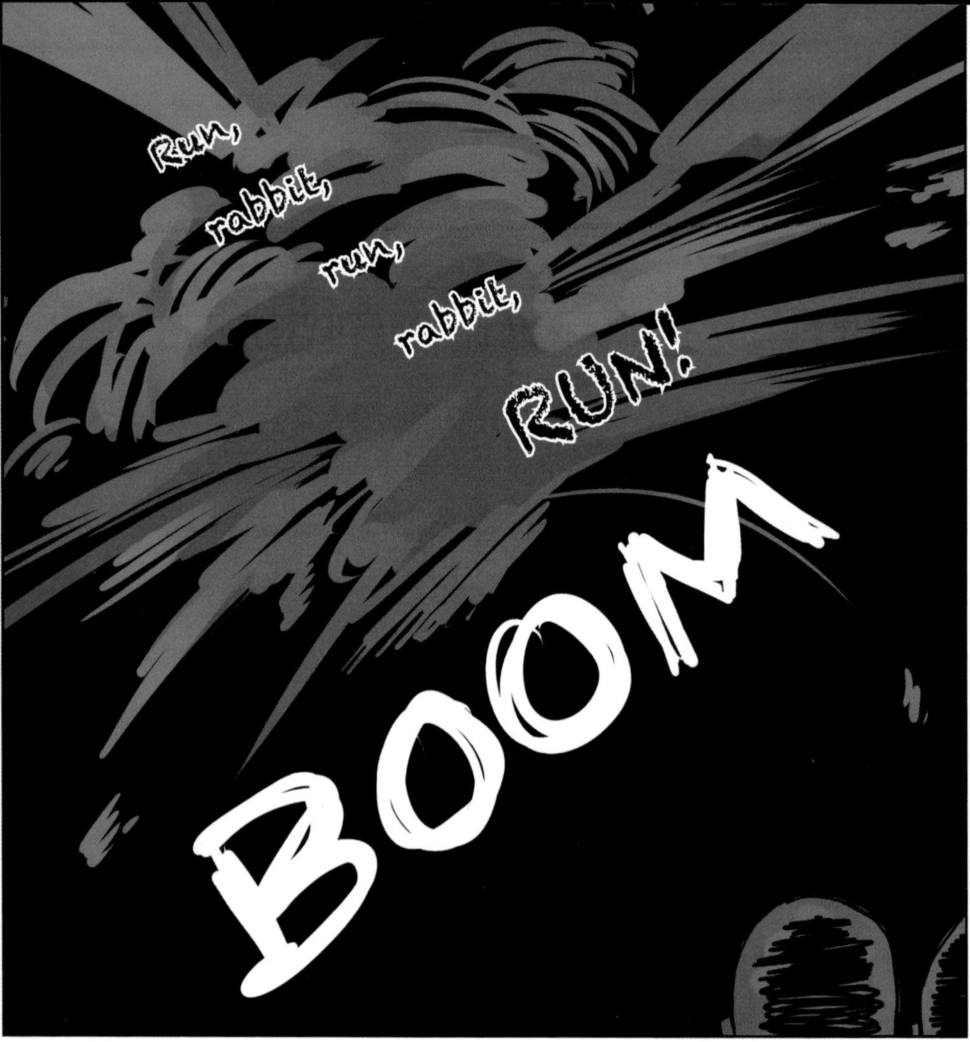
Run,
rabbit,
run,
rabbit,
RUN!
BOOM
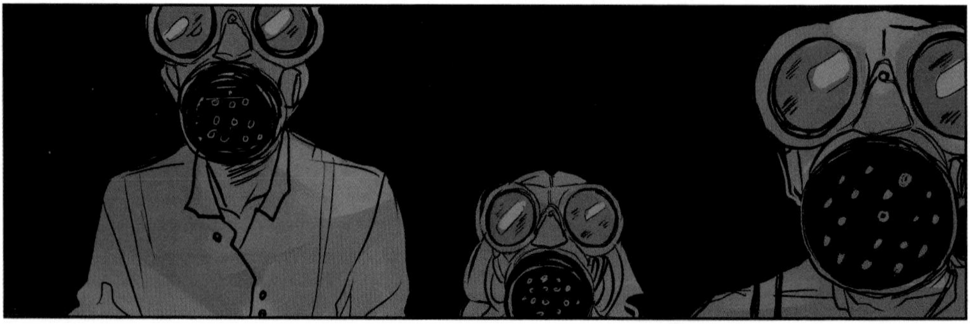
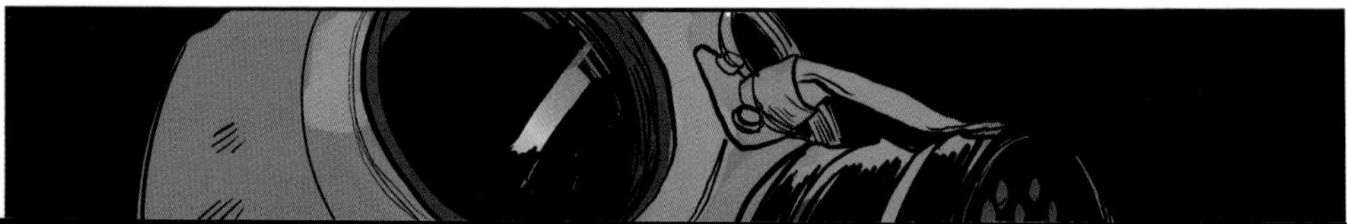

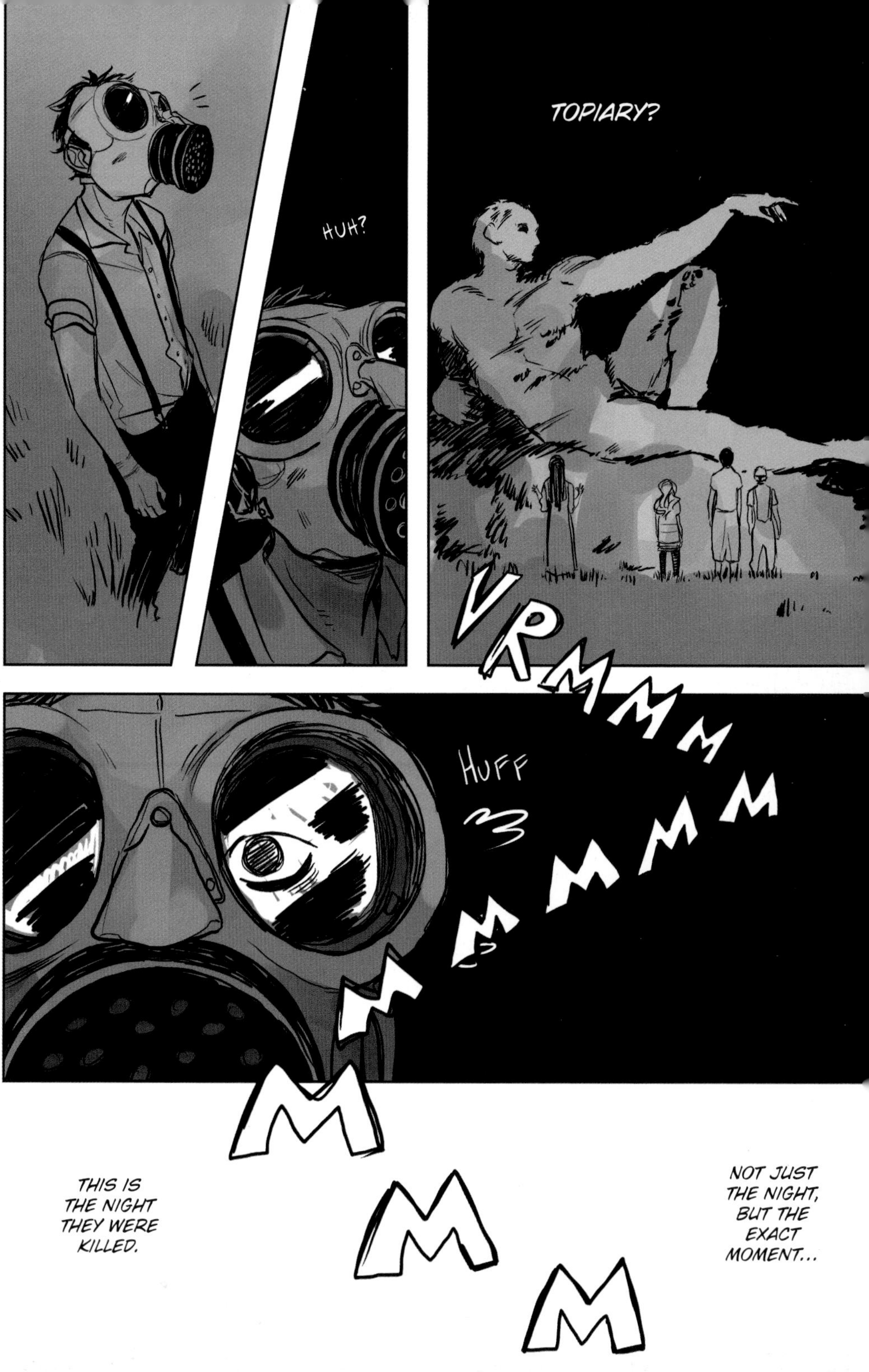
HUH?
TOPIARY?
VRMMMMMMMMMMMMM
HUFF
THIS IS THE NIGHT THEY WERE KILLED.
NOT JUST THE NIGHT, BUT THE EXACT MOMENT...

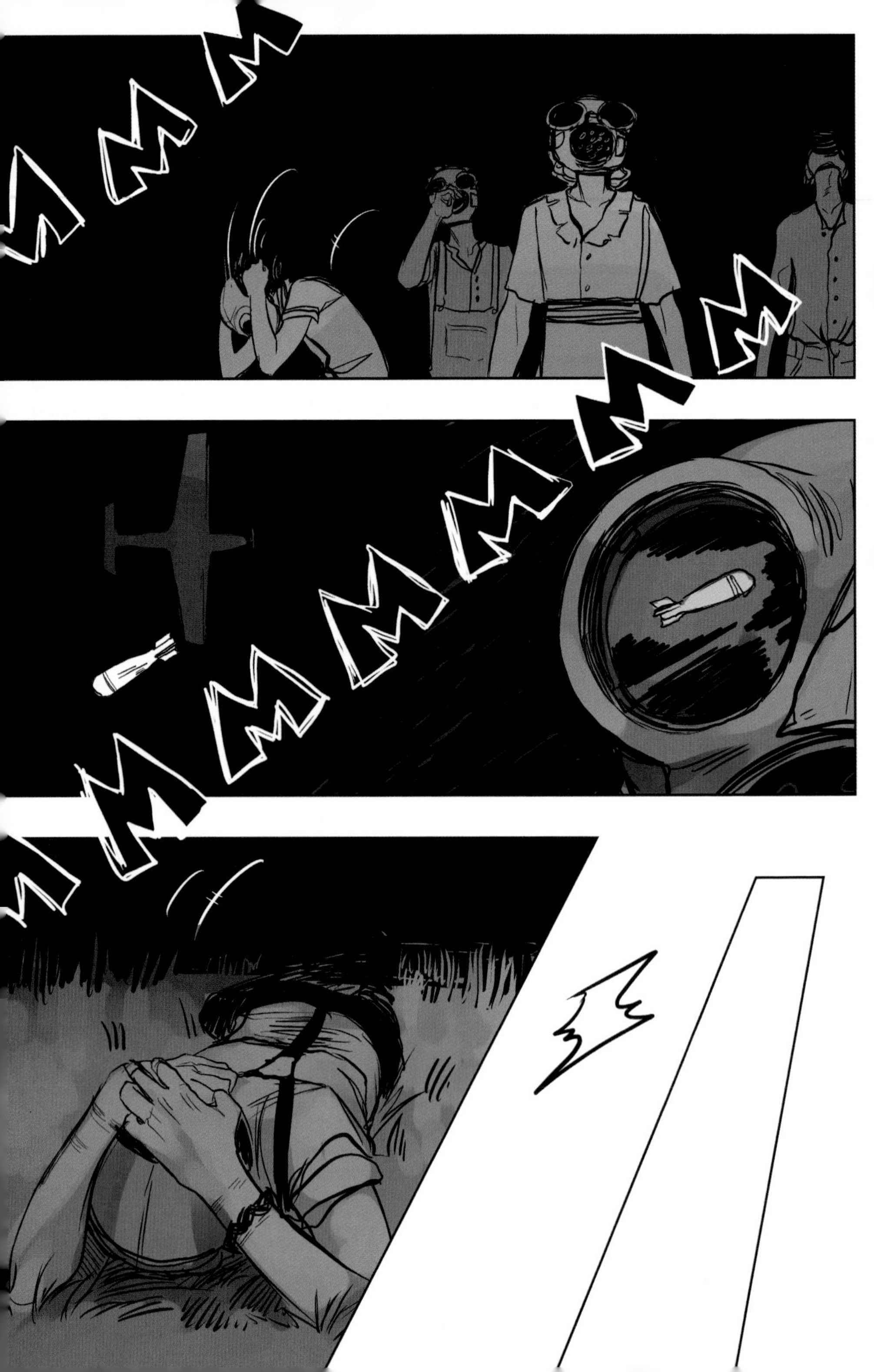
MMMM
M
MMMMMMM
MM

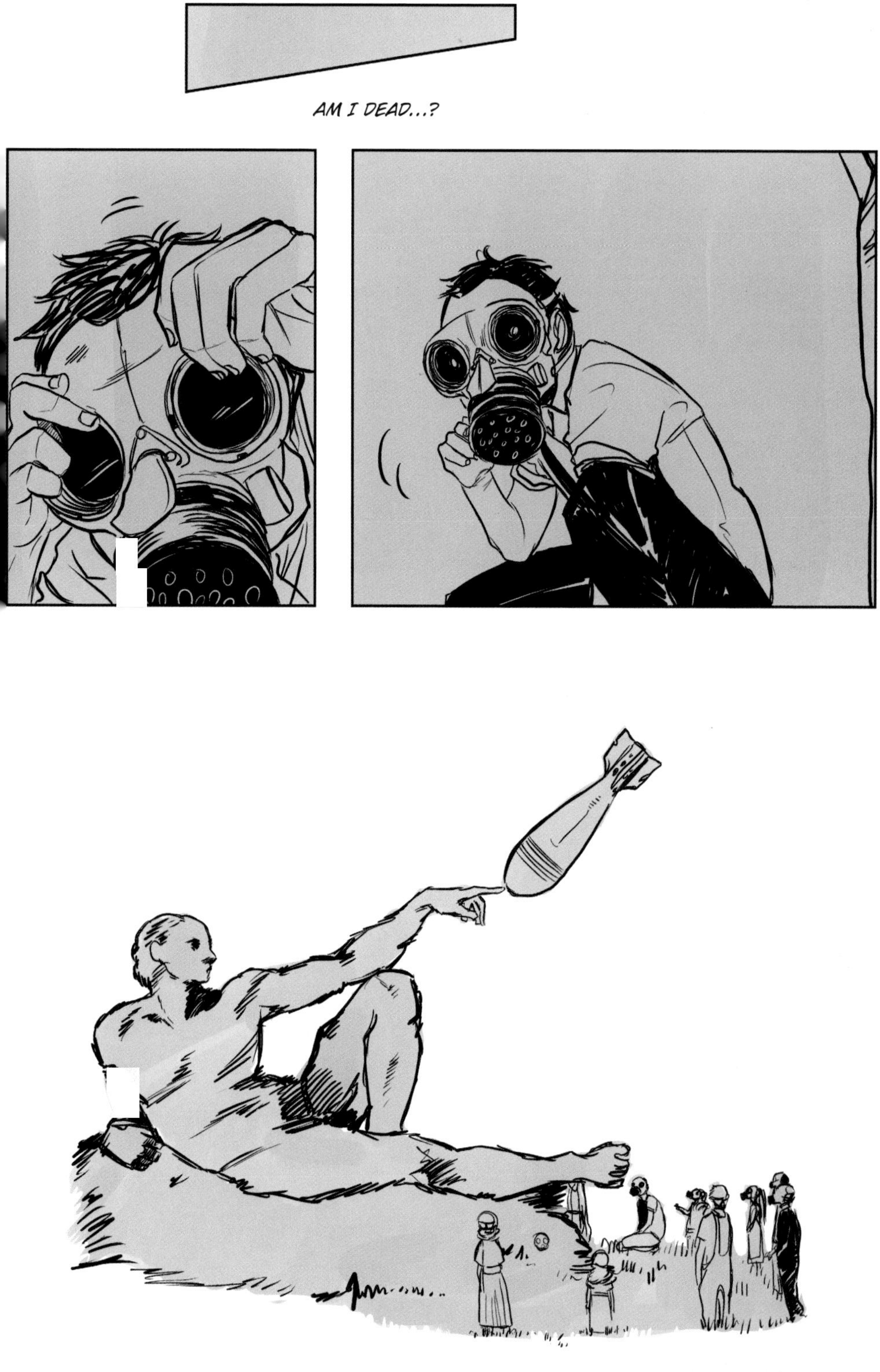
AM I DEAD...?

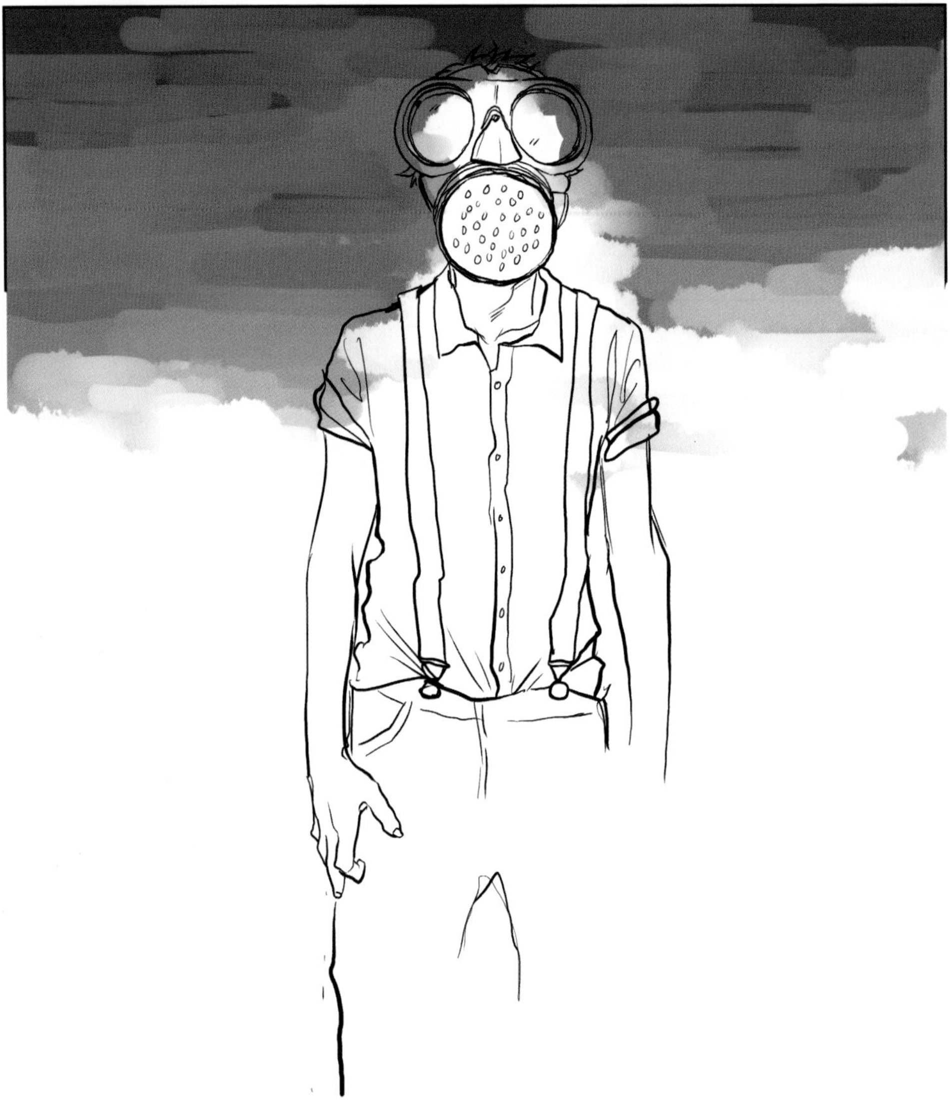

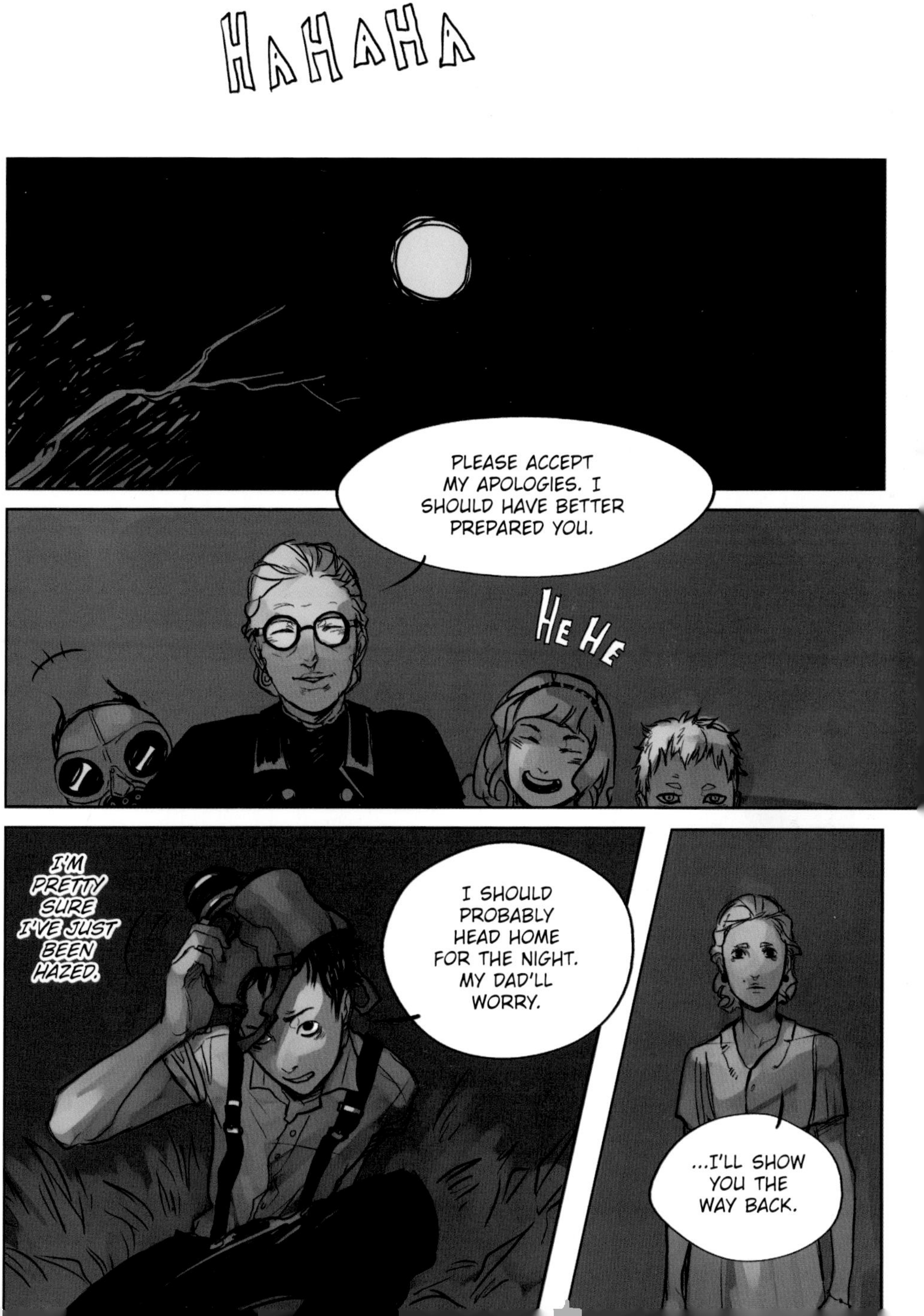
HAHAHA
PLEASE ACCEPT MY APOLOGIES. I SHOULD HAVE BETTER PREPARED YOU.
HE HE
I'M PRETTY SURE I'VE JUST BEEN HAZED.
I SHOULD PROBABLY HEAD HOME FOR THE NIGHT. MY DAD'LL WORRY.
...I'LL SHOW YOU THE WAY BACK.

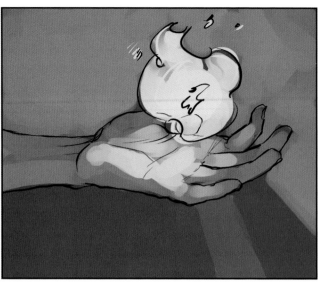

THAT'S REALLY COOL.

IT ISN'T COOL AT ALL.

QUITE HOT, ACTUALLY!

I DIDN'T MEAN—

THIS IS AWKWARD.

IS SHE EVEN OKAY WITH ME HERE?

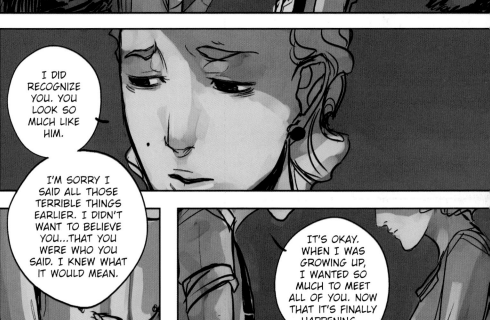

I DID RECOGNIZE YOU. YOU LOOK SO MUCH LIKE HIM.

I'M SORRY I SAID ALL THOSE TERRIBLE THINGS EARLIER. I DIDN'T WANT TO BELIEVE YOU...THAT YOU WERE WHO YOU SAID. I KNEW WHAT IT WOULD MEAN.

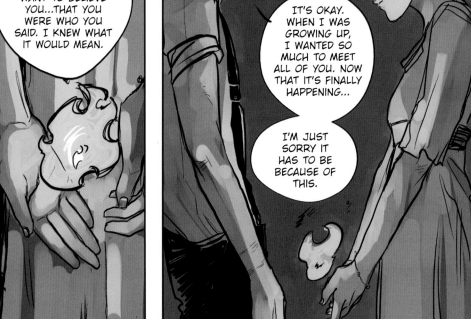

IT'S OKAY. WHEN I WAS GROWING UP, I WANTED SO MUCH TO MEET ALL OF YOU. NOW THAT IT'S FINALLY HAPPENING...

I'M JUST SORRY IT HAS TO BE BECAUSE OF THIS.

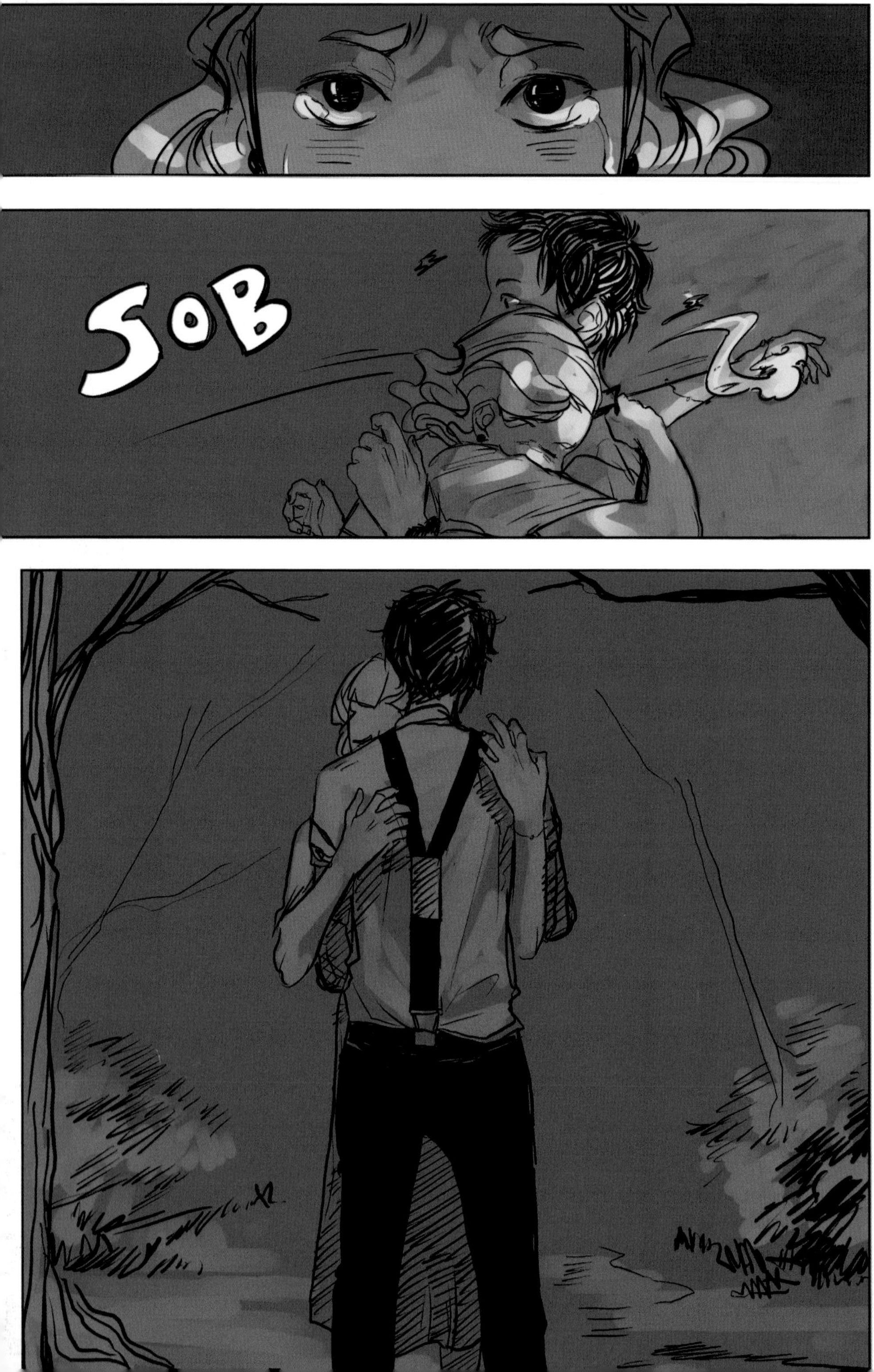
SOB

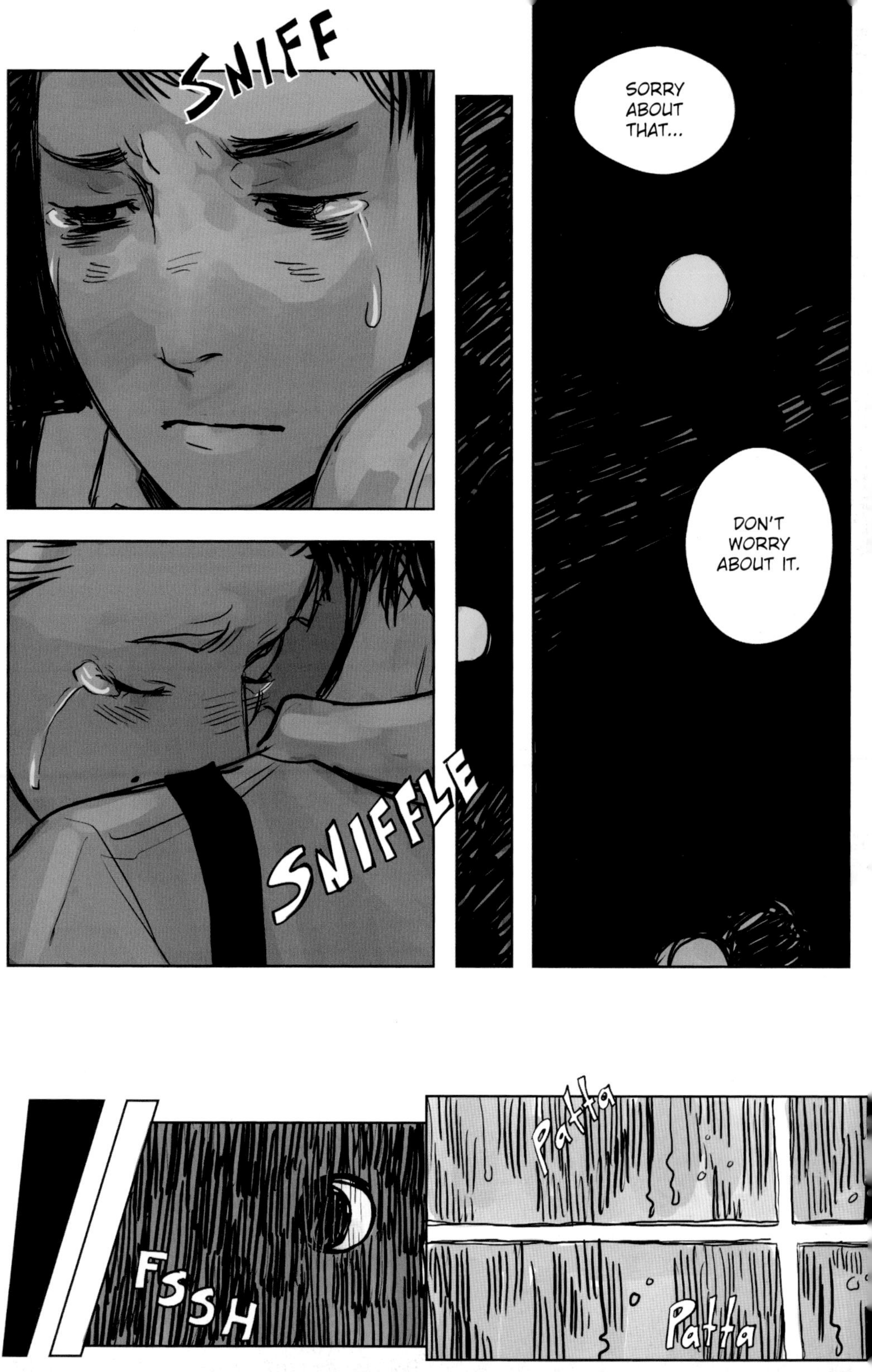
SNIFF
SNIFFLE
SORRY ABOUT THAT...
DON'T WORRY ABOUT IT.
FSSH
Patta
Patta

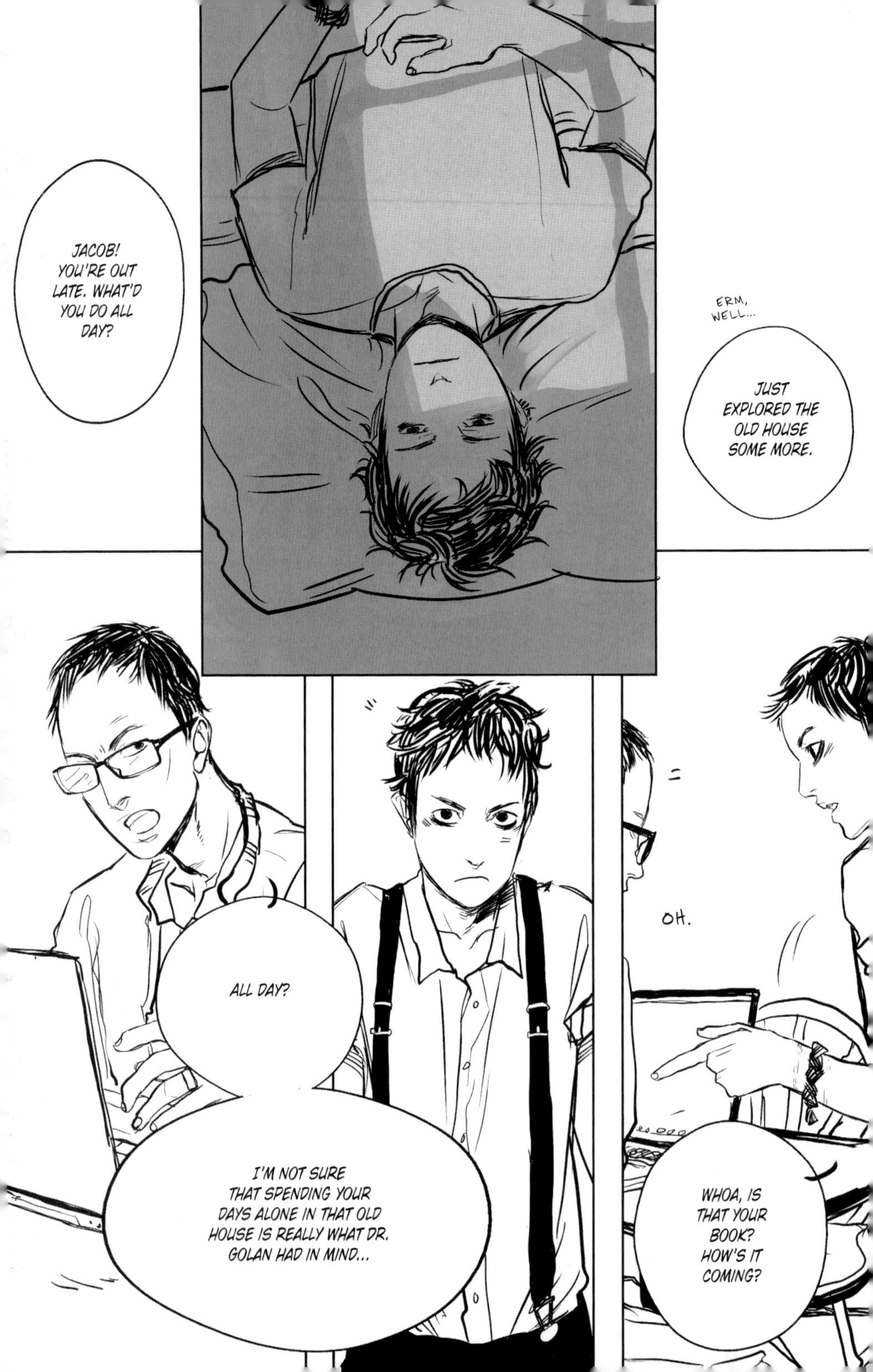
JACOB! YOU'RE OUT LATE. WHAT'D YOU DO ALL DAY?
ERM, WELL...
JUST EXPLORED THE OLD HOUSE SOME MORE.
ALL DAY?
I'M NOT SURE THAT SPENDING YOUR DAYS ALONE IN THAT OLD HOUSE IS REALLY WHAT DR. GOLAN HAD IN MIND...
OH.
WHOA, IS THAT YOUR BOOK? HOW'S IT COMING?

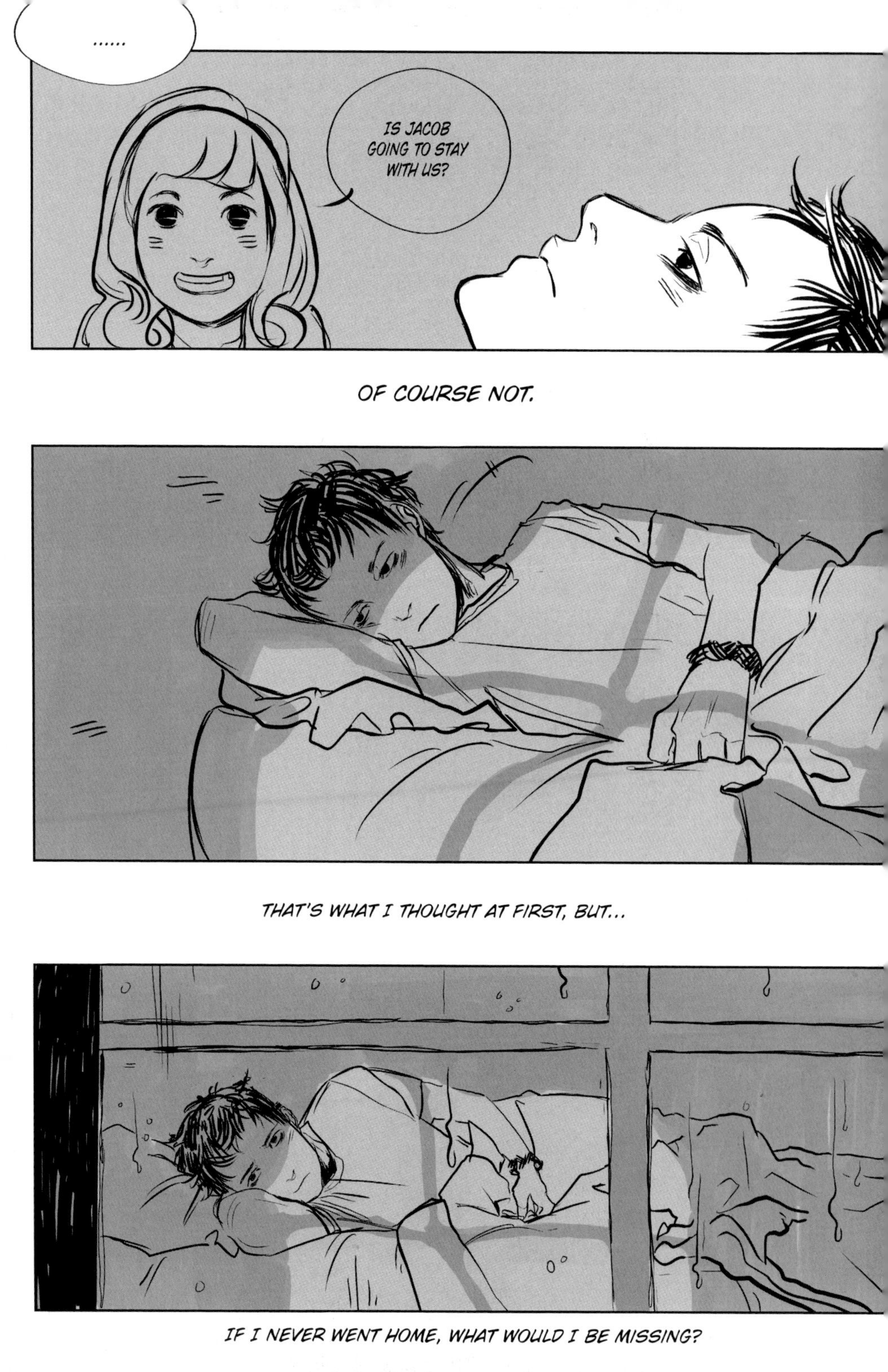
......
IS JACOB GOING TO STAY WITH US?
OF COURSE NOT.
THAT'S WHAT I THOUGHT AT FIRST, BUT...
IF I NEVER WENT HOME, WHAT WOULD I BE MISSING?

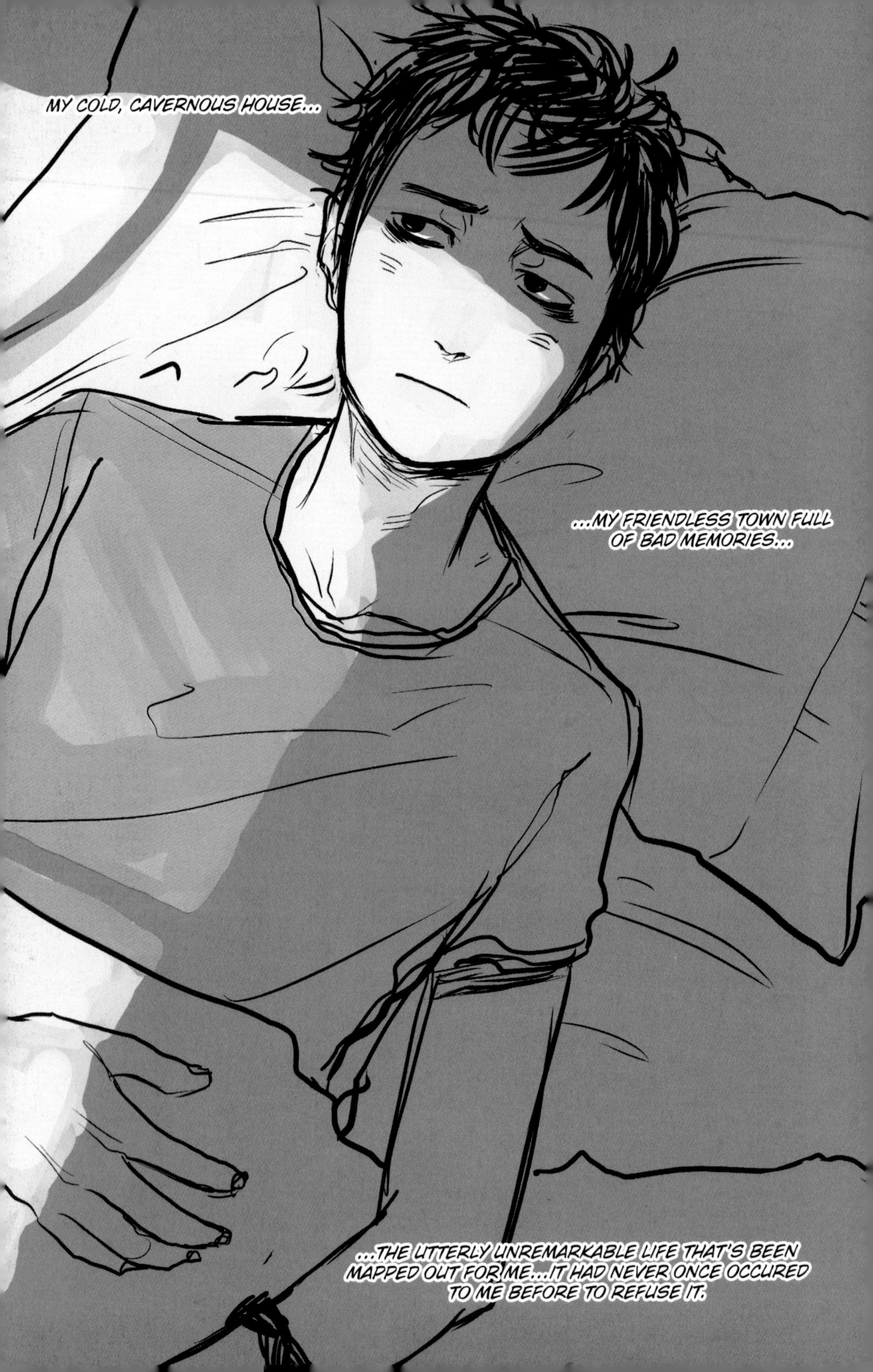
MY COLD, CAVERNOUS HOUSE...
...MY FRIENDLESS TOWN FULL OF BAD MEMORIES...
...THE UTTERLY UNREMARKABLE LIFE THAT'S BEEN MAPPED OUT FOR ME...IT HAD NEVER ONCE OCCURED TO ME BEFORE TO REFUSE IT.

CHAPTER FIVE

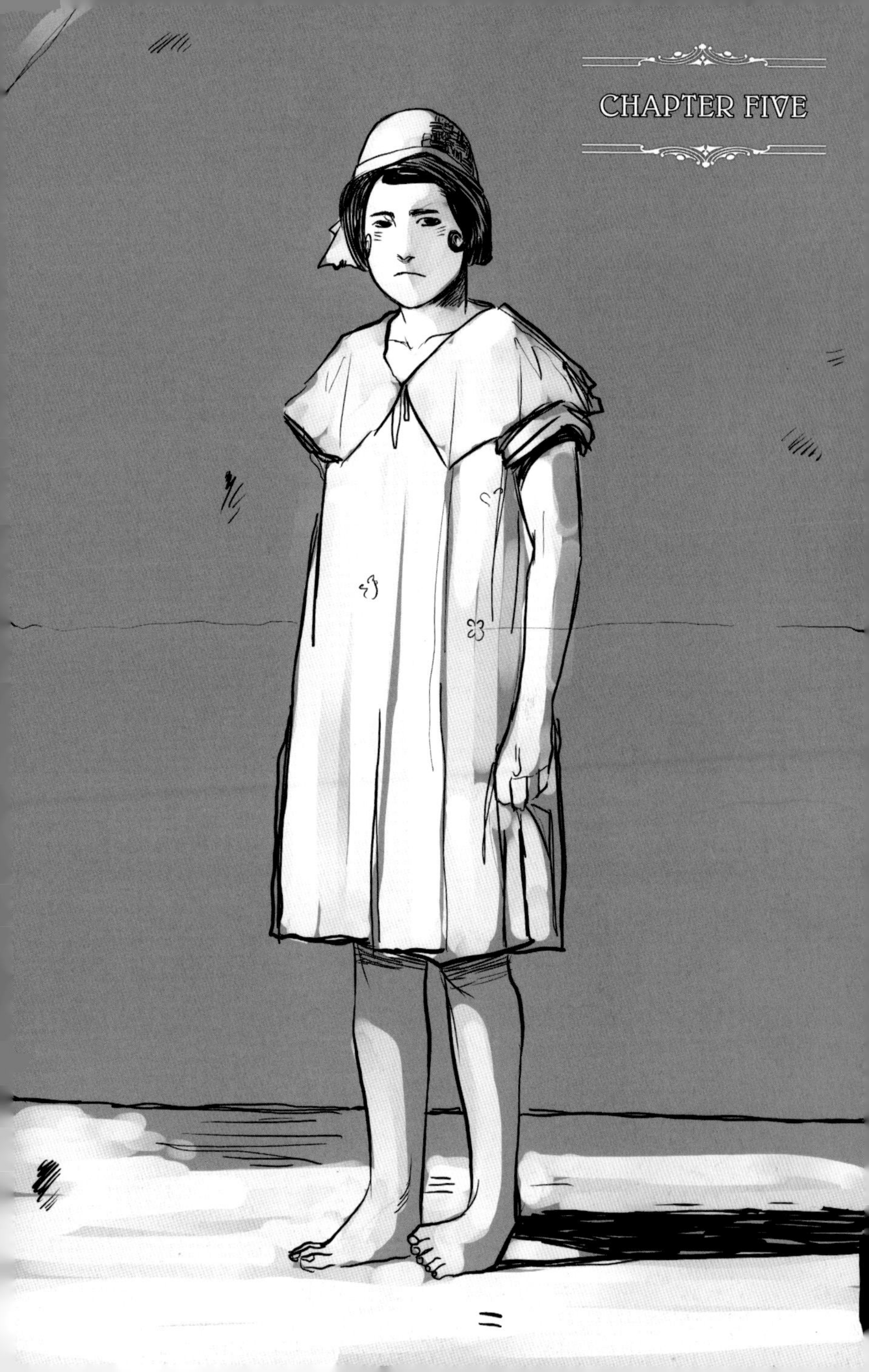

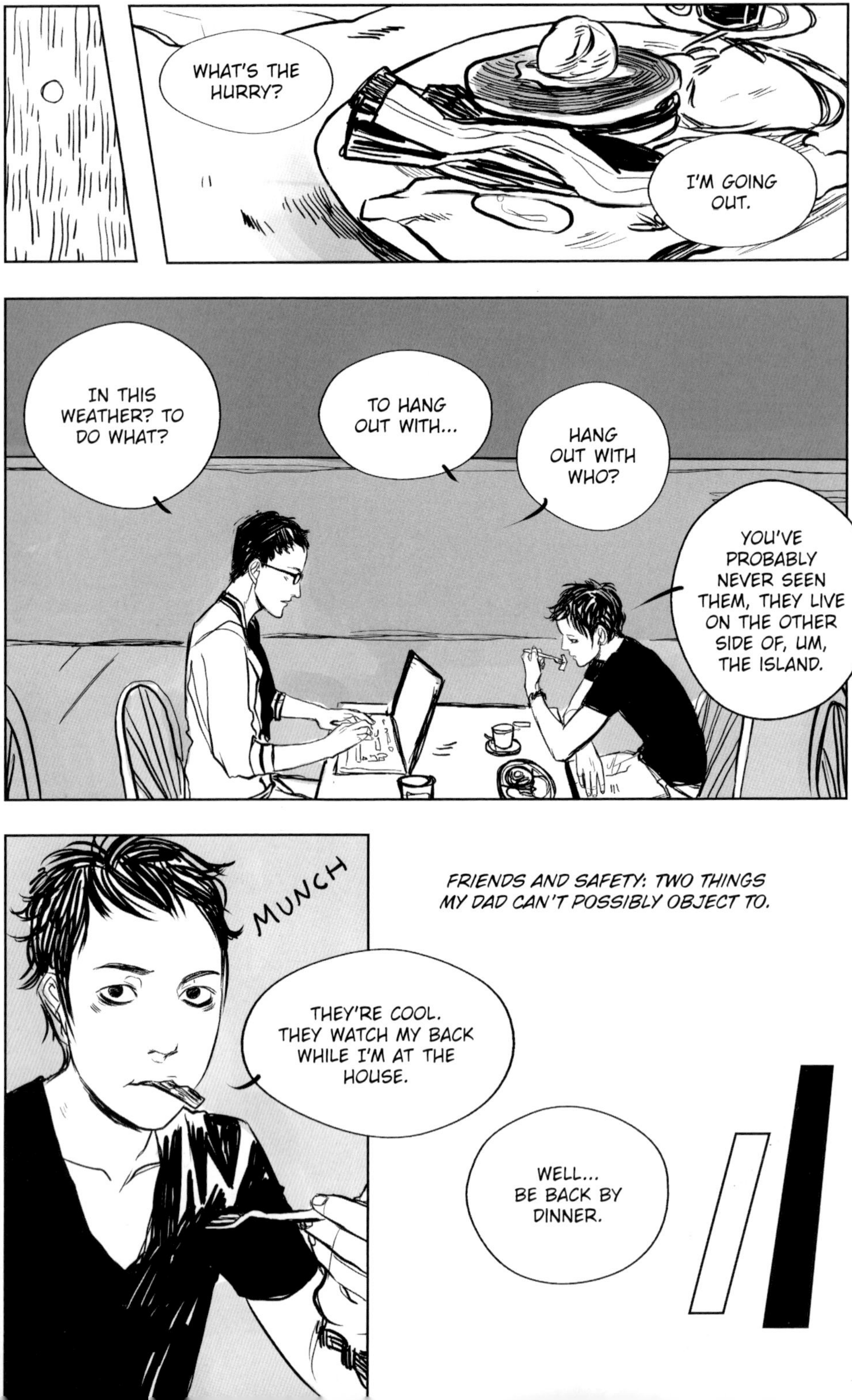
WHAT'S THE HURRY?
I'M GOING OUT.
IN THIS WEATHER? TO DO WHAT?
TO HANG OUT WITH...
HANG OUT WITH WHO?
YOU'VE PROBABLY NEVER SEEN THEM, THEY LIVE ON THE OTHER SIDE OF, UM, THE ISLAND.
MUNCH
FRIENDS AND SAFETY: TWO THINGS MY DAD CAN'T POSSIBLY OBJECT TO.
THEY'RE COOL. THEY WATCH MY BACK WHILE I'M AT THE HOUSE.
WELL... BE BACK BY DINNER.

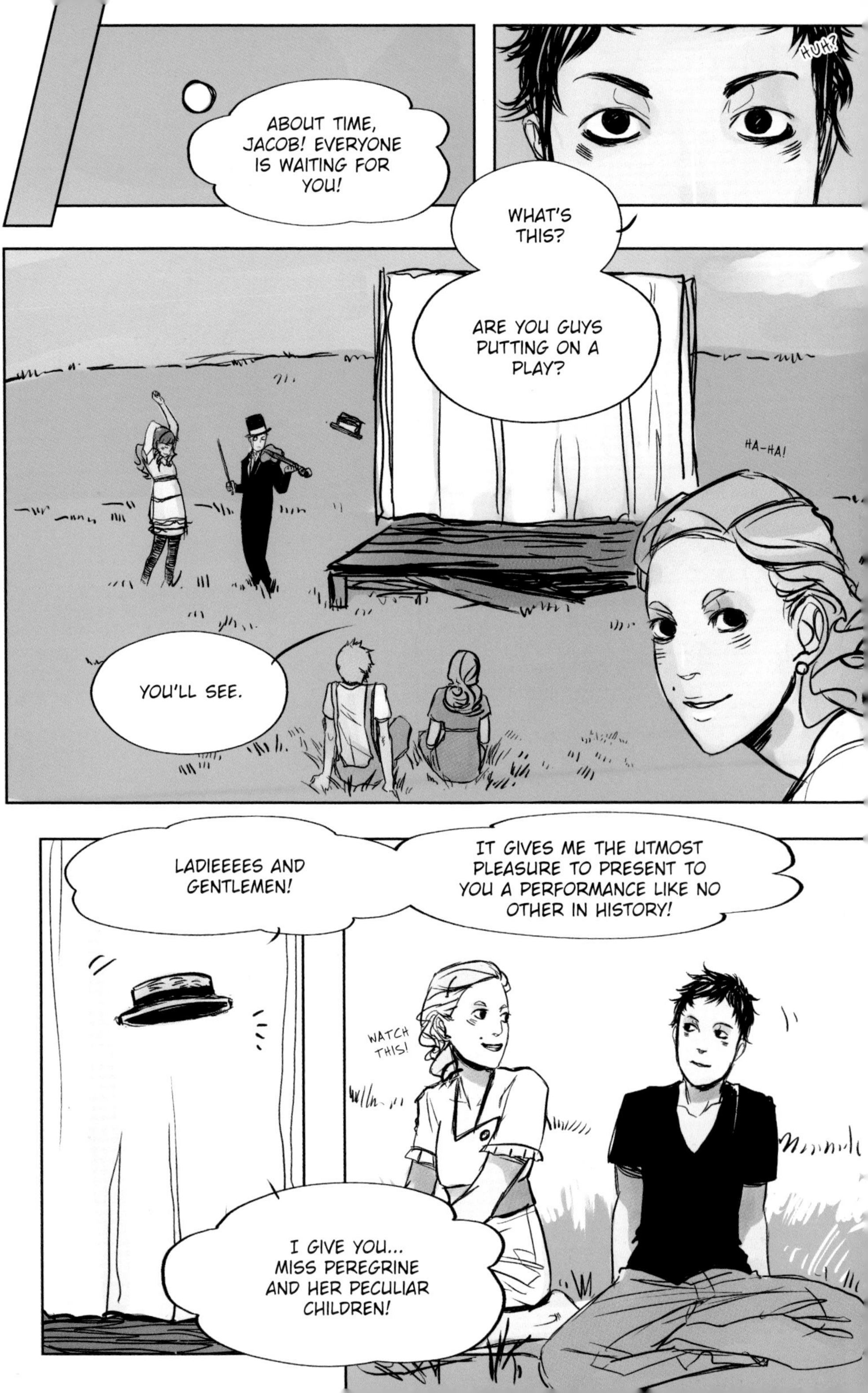
ABOUT TIME, JACOB! EVERYONE IS WAITING FOR YOU!
HUH?
WHAT'S THIS?
ARE YOU GUYS PUTTING ON A PLAY?
HA-HA!
YOU'LL SEE.
LADIEEEES AND GENTLEMEN!
IT GIVES ME THE UTMOST PLEASURE TO PRESENT TO YOU A PERFORMANCE LIKE NO OTHER IN HISTORY!
WATCH THIS!
I GIVE YOU... MISS PEREGRINE AND HER PECULIAR CHILDREN!

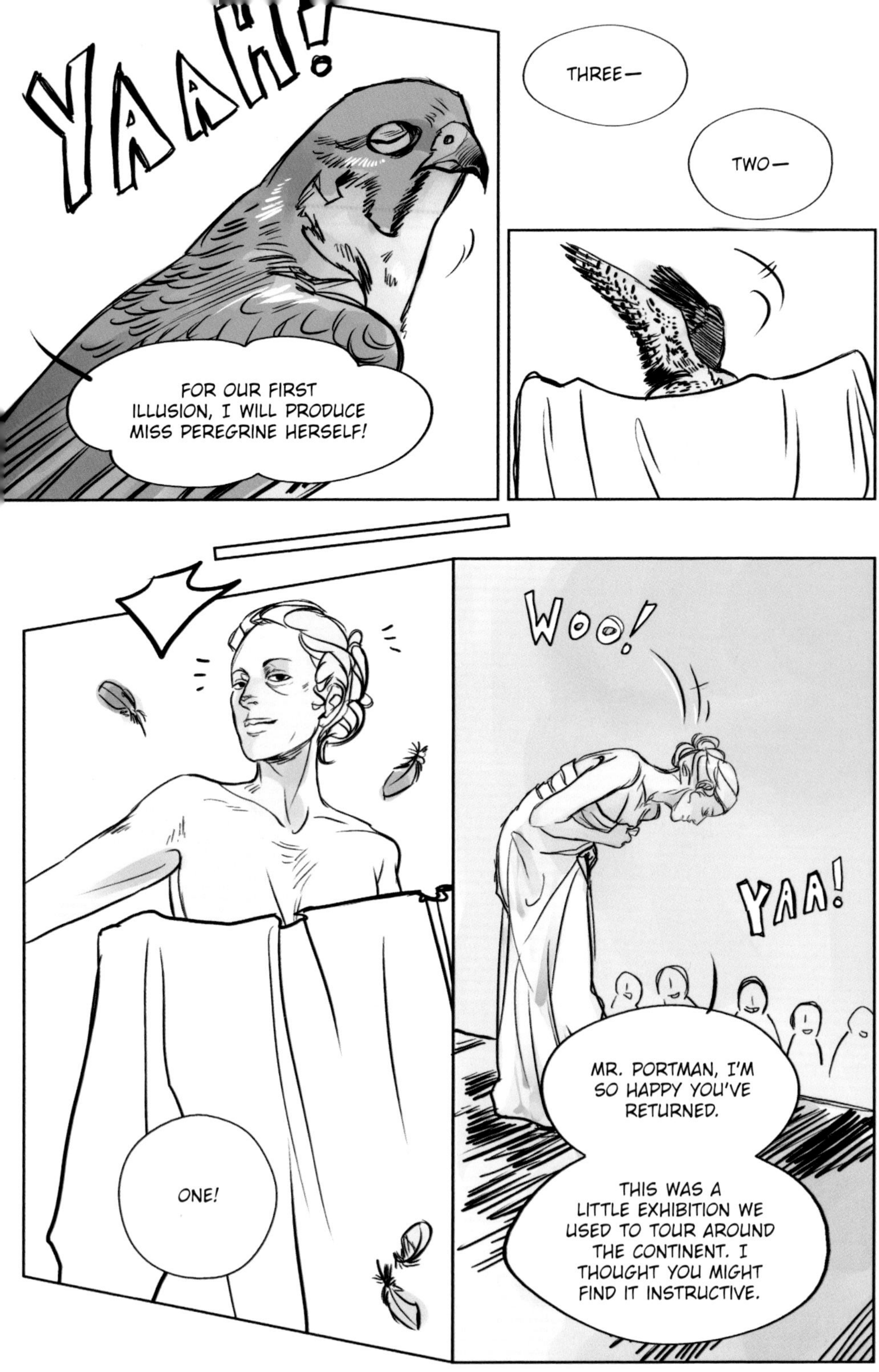
YAAH!
FOR OUR FIRST ILLUSION, I WILL PRODUCE MISS PEREGRINE HERSELF!
THREE—
TWO—
ONE!
WOO!
YAA!
MR. PORTMAN, I'M SO HAPPY YOU'VE RETURNED.
THIS WAS A LITTLE EXHIBITION WE USED TO TOUR AROUND THE CONTINENT. I THOUGHT YOU MIGHT FIND IT INSTRUCTIVE.

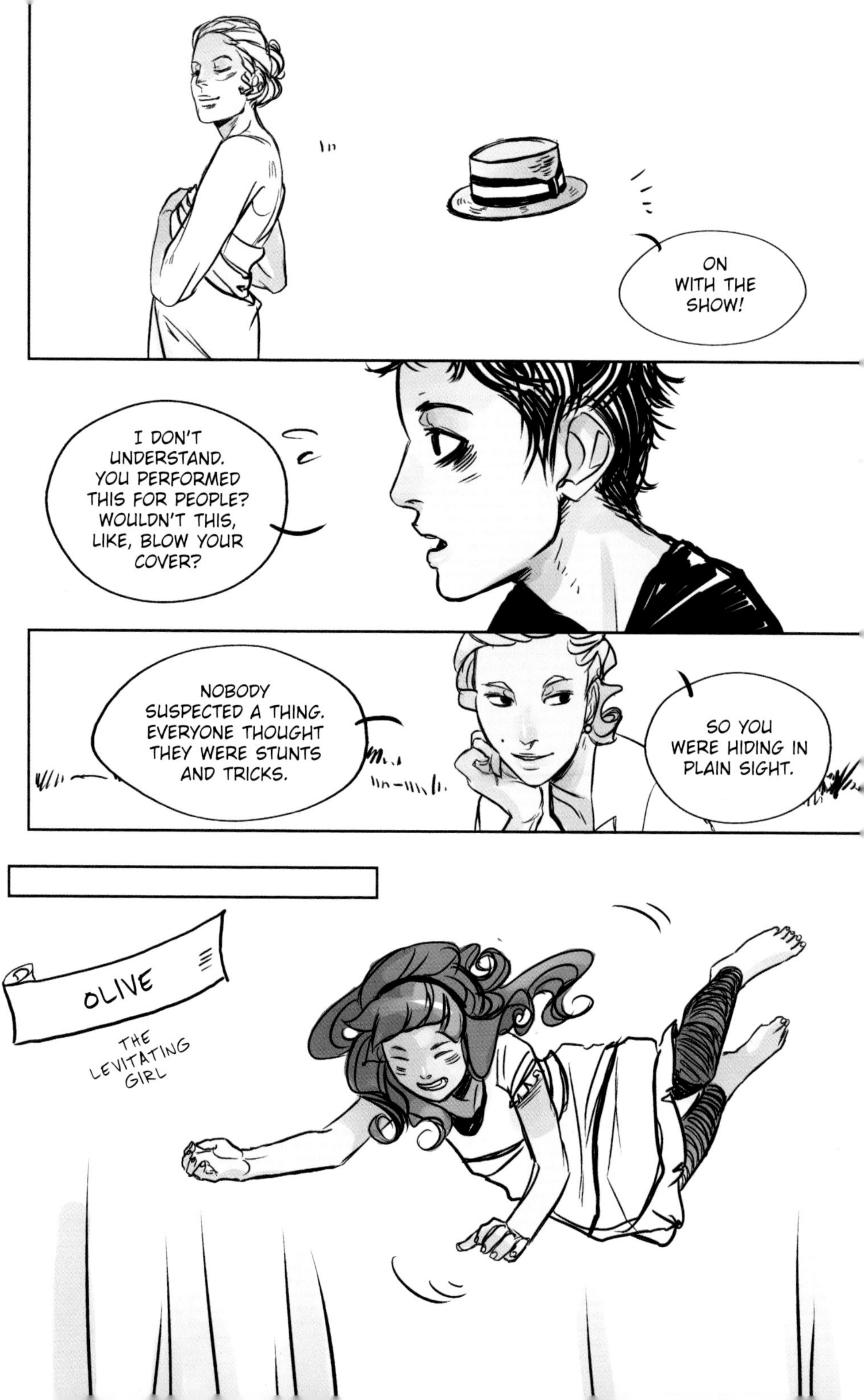
ON WITH THE SHOW!
I DON'T UNDERSTAND. YOU PERFORMED THIS FOR PEOPLE? WOULDN'T THIS, LIKE, BLOW YOUR COVER?
NOBODY SUSPECTED A THING. EVERYONE THOUGHT THEY WERE STUNTS AND TRICKS.
SO YOU WERE HIDING IN PLAIN SIGHT.
OLIVE
THE LEVITATING GIRL

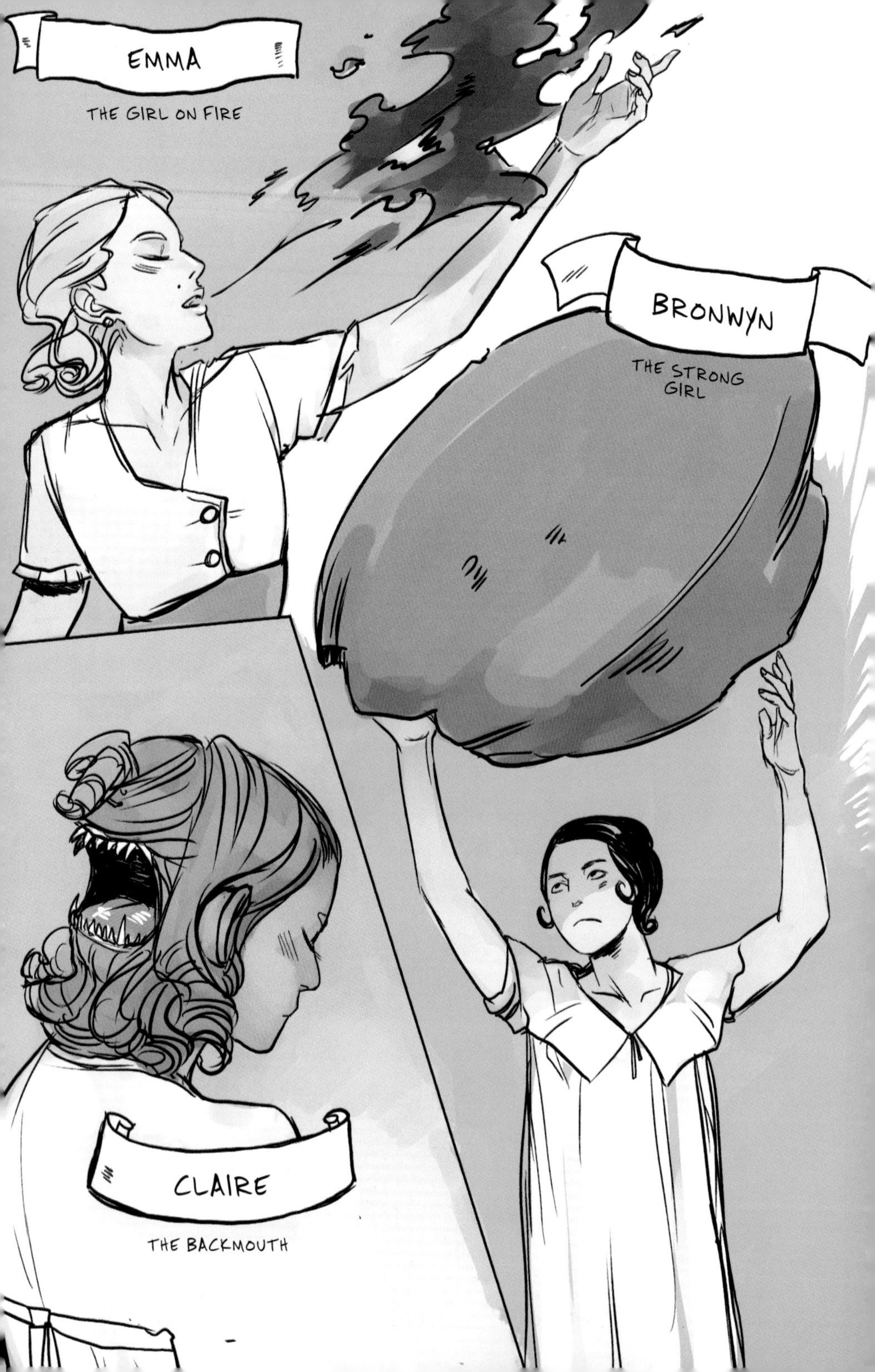
EMMA
THE GIRL ON FIRE
BRONWYN
THE STRONG GIRL
CLAIRE
THE BACKMOUTH

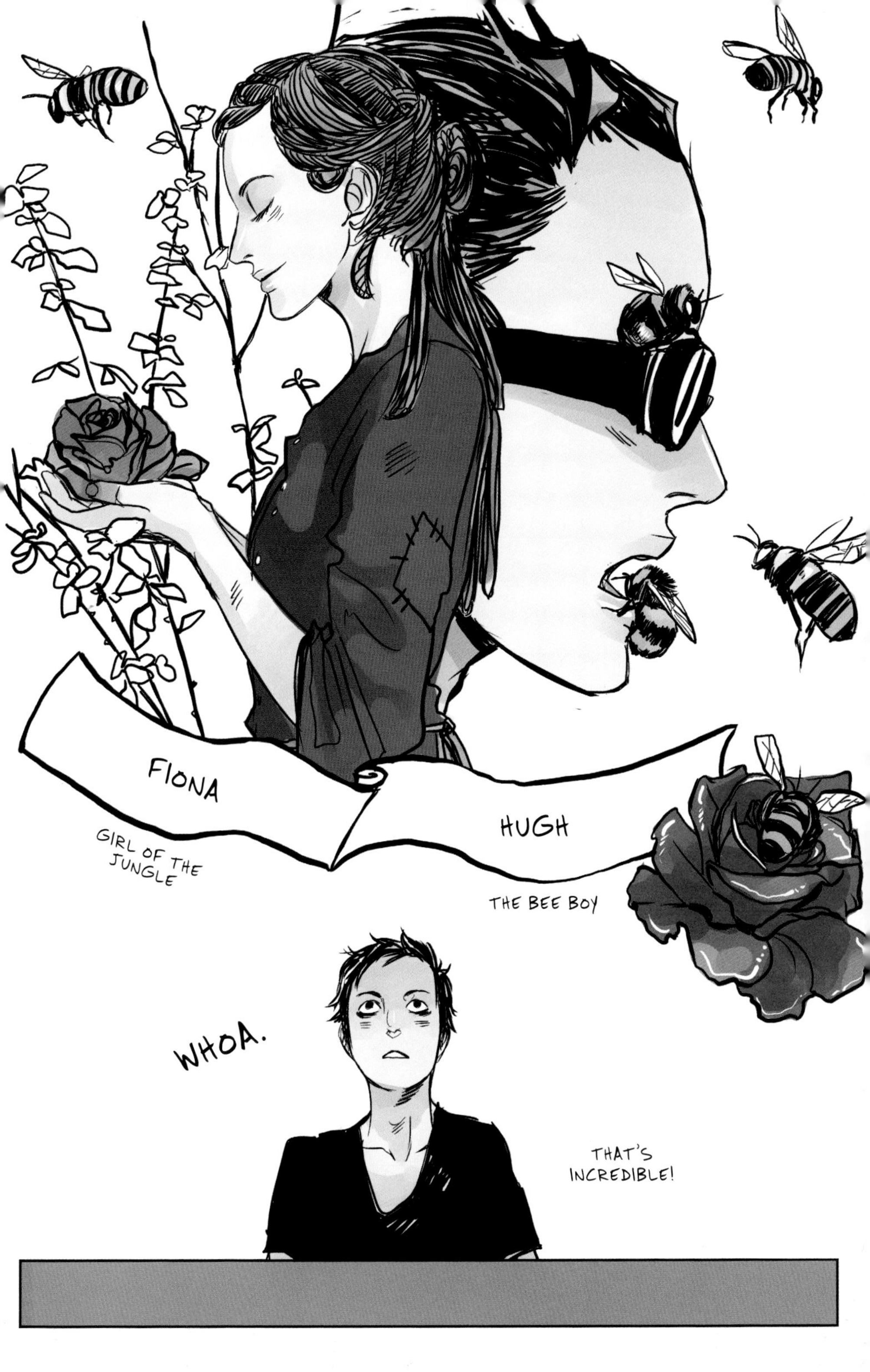
FIONA
GIRL OF THE JUNGLE
HUGH
THE BEE BOY
WHOA.
THAT'S INCREDIBLE!

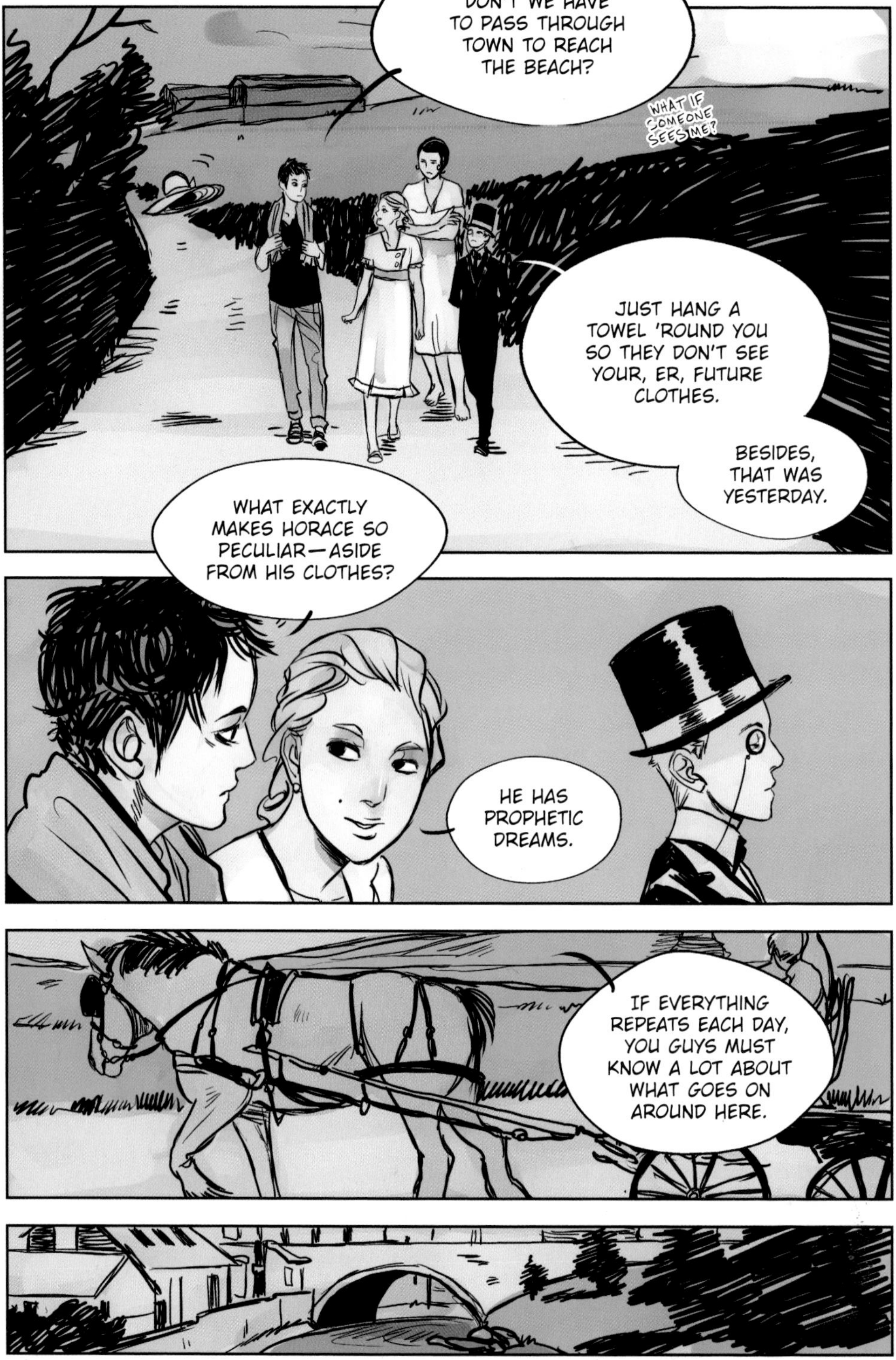
DON'T WE HAVE TO PASS THROUGH TOWN TO REACH THE BEACH?
WHAT IF SOMEONE SEES ME?
JUST HANG A TOWEL 'ROUND YOU SO THEY DON'T SEE YOUR, ER, FUTURE CLOTHES.
BESIDES, THAT WAS YESTERDAY.
WHAT EXACTLY MAKES HORACE SO PECULIAR—ASIDE FROM HIS CLOTHES?
HE HAS PROPHETIC DREAMS.
IF EVERYTHING REPEATS EACH DAY, YOU GUYS MUST KNOW A LOT ABOUT WHAT GOES ON AROUND HERE.

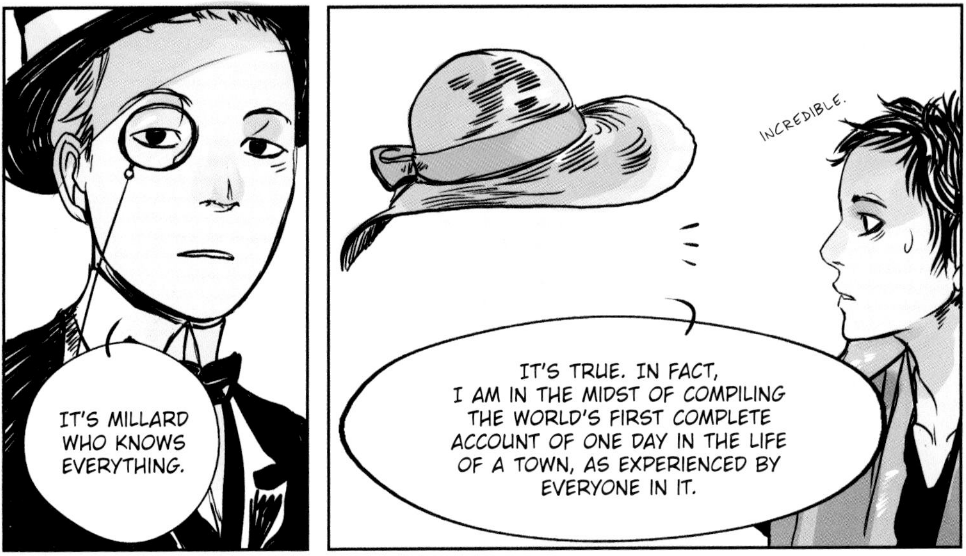
IT'S MILLARD WHO KNOWS EVERYTHING.
INCREDIBLE.
IT'S TRUE. IN FACT, I AM IN THE MIDST OF COMPILING THE WORLD'S FIRST COMPLETE ACCOUNT OF ONE DAY IN THE LIFE OF A TOWN, AS EXPERIENCED BY EVERYONE IN IT.

WE GOT TO TALKING.

THEY HAD A MILLION QUESTIONS FOR ME.

WHAT WAS MY WORLD LIKE?
WHAT DID PEOPLE EAT, DRINK, WEAR?
WHEN WOULD SICKNESS AND DEATH BE OVERCOME BY SCIENCE?

THEY LIVED IN SPLENDOR, BUT WERE STARVING FOR NEW STORIES.

IT WAS MY TIME'S TECHNOLOGY THAT AMAZED THEM MOST.
AIR-CONDITIONING.

TELEVISIONS.

CELL PHONES.

COMPUTERS.

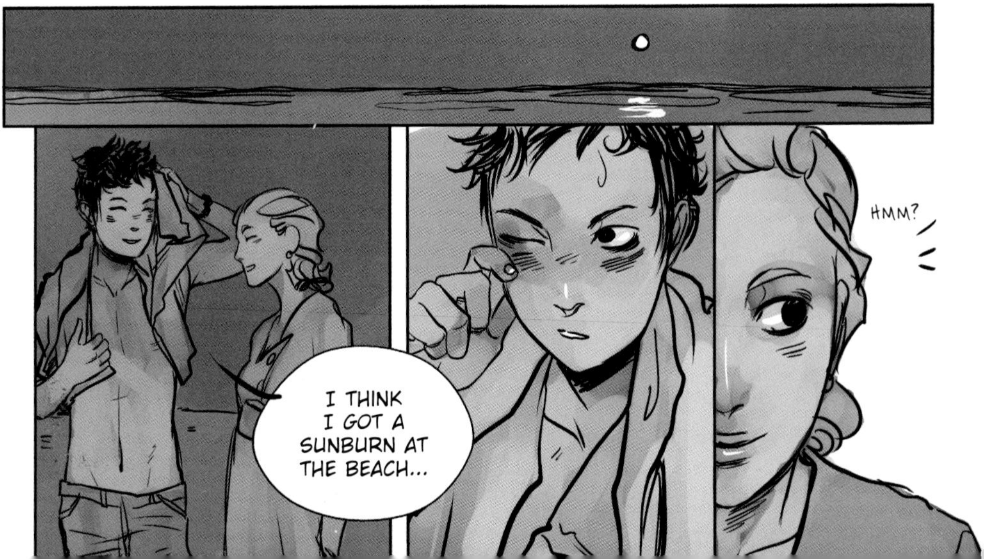
I THINK I GOT A SUNBURN AT THE BEACH...
HMM?

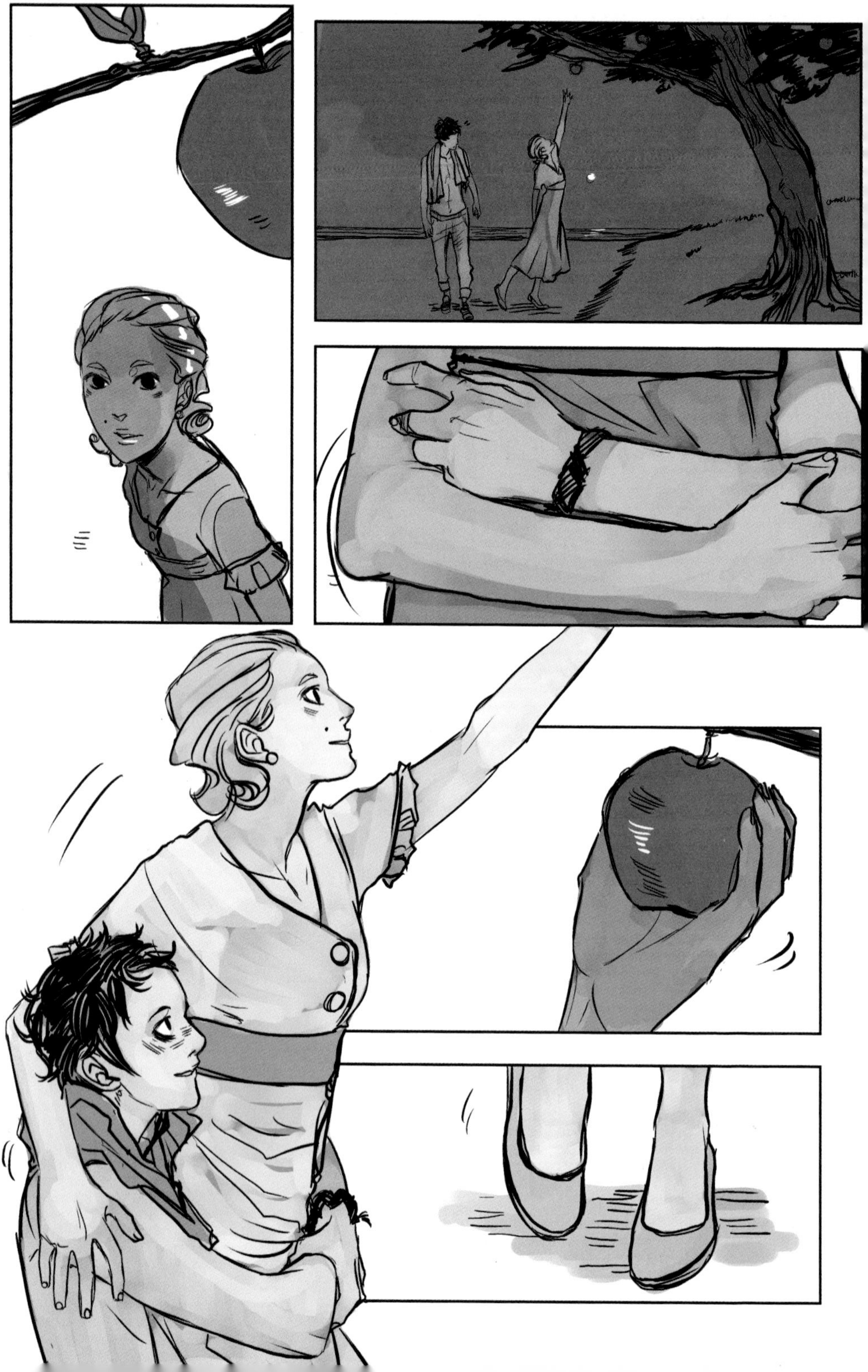

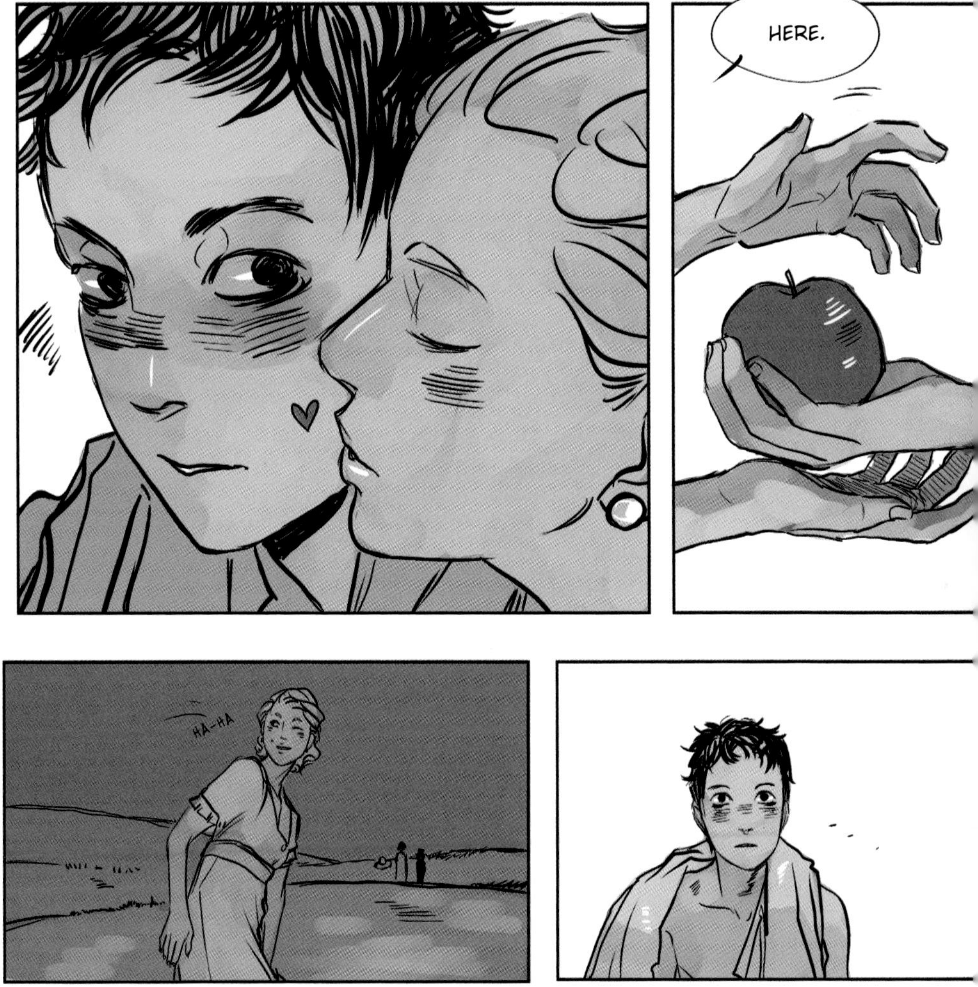
HERE.
HA-HA

[redacted]

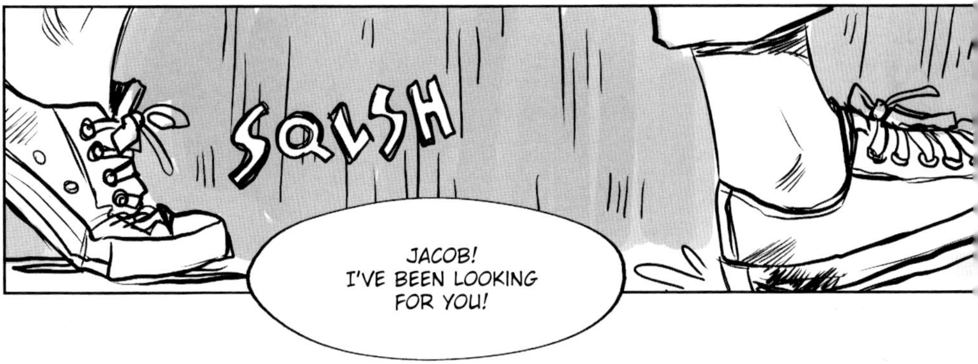
SQLSH
JACOB!
I'VE BEEN LOOKING
FOR YOU!

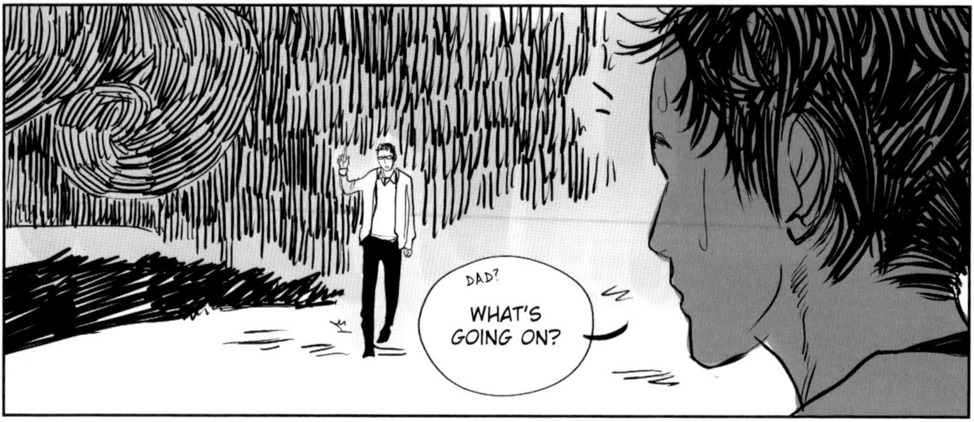
DAD? WHAT'S GOING ON?

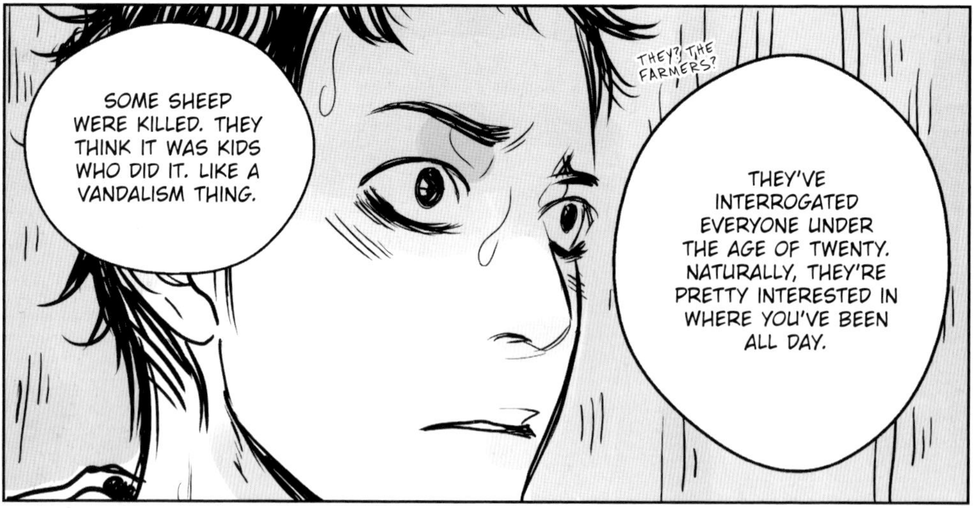
SOME SHEEP WERE KILLED. THEY THINK IT WAS KIDS WHO DID IT. LIKE A VANDALISM THING.
THEY? THE FARMERS?
THEY'VE INTERROGATED EVERYONE UNDER THE AGE OF TWENTY. NATURALLY, THEY'RE PRETTY INTERESTED IN WHERE YOU'VE BEEN ALL DAY.

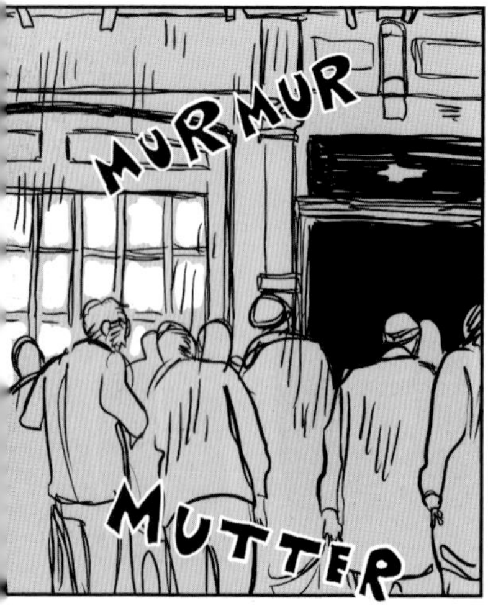
MURMUR
MUTTER

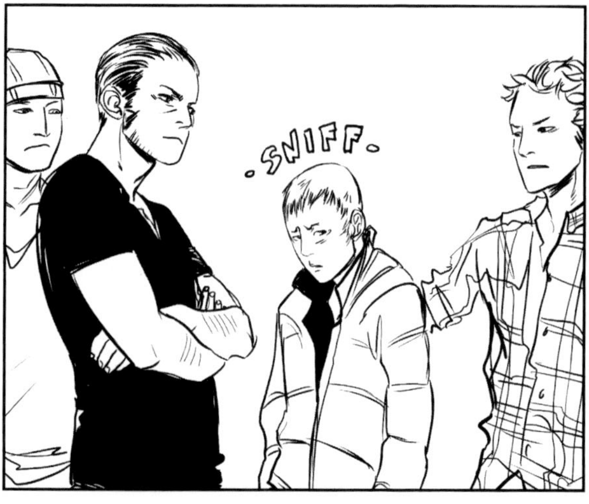
SNIFF

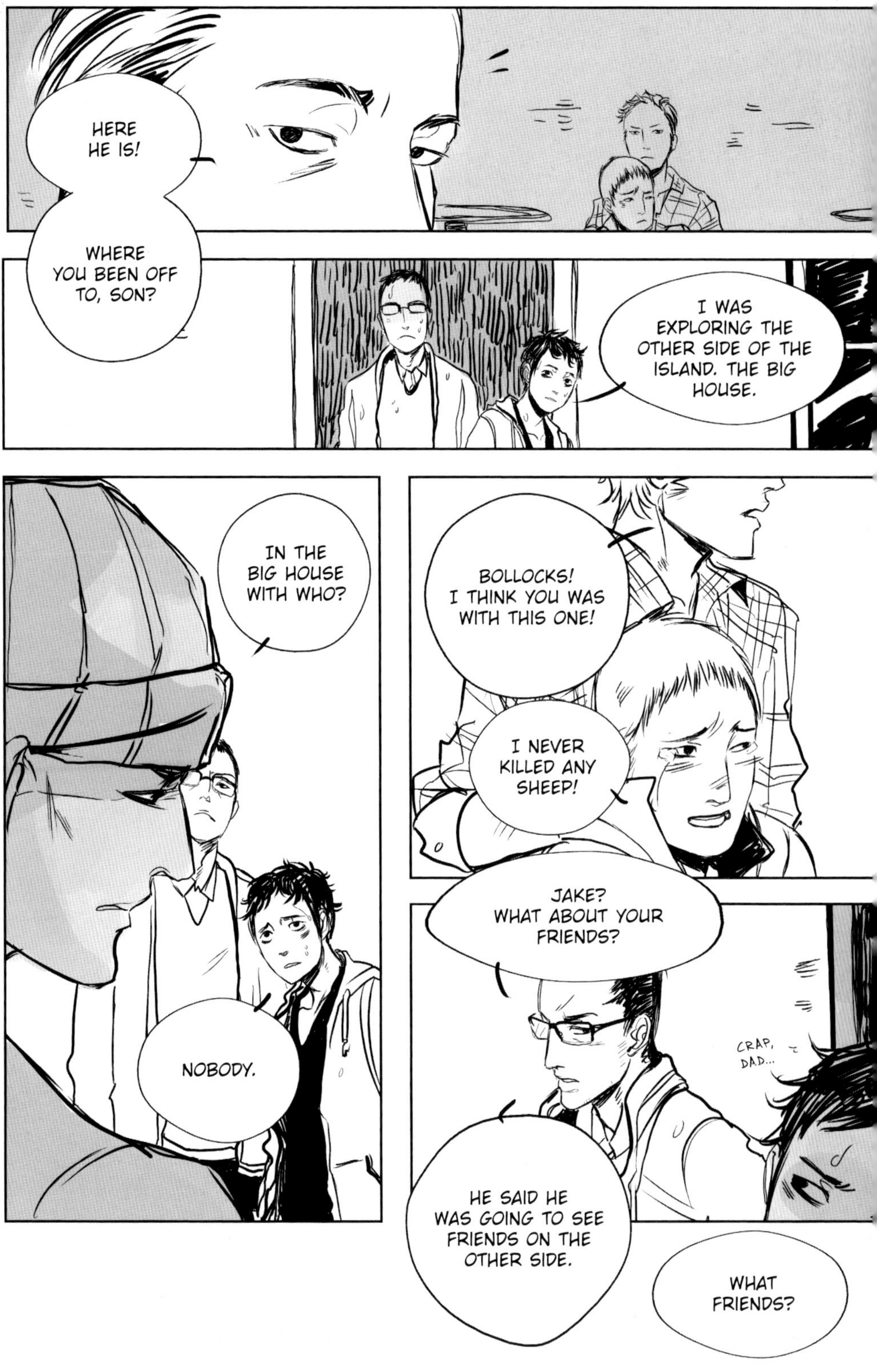
HERE HE IS!
WHERE YOU BEEN OFF TO, SON?
I WAS EXPLORING THE OTHER SIDE OF THE ISLAND. THE BIG HOUSE.
IN THE BIG HOUSE WITH WHO?
NOBODY.
BOLLOCKS! I THINK YOU WAS WITH THIS ONE!
I NEVER KILLED ANY SHEEP!
JAKE? WHAT ABOUT YOUR FRIENDS?
CRAP, DAD...
HE SAID HE WAS GOING TO SEE FRIENDS ON THE OTHER SIDE.
WHAT FRIENDS?

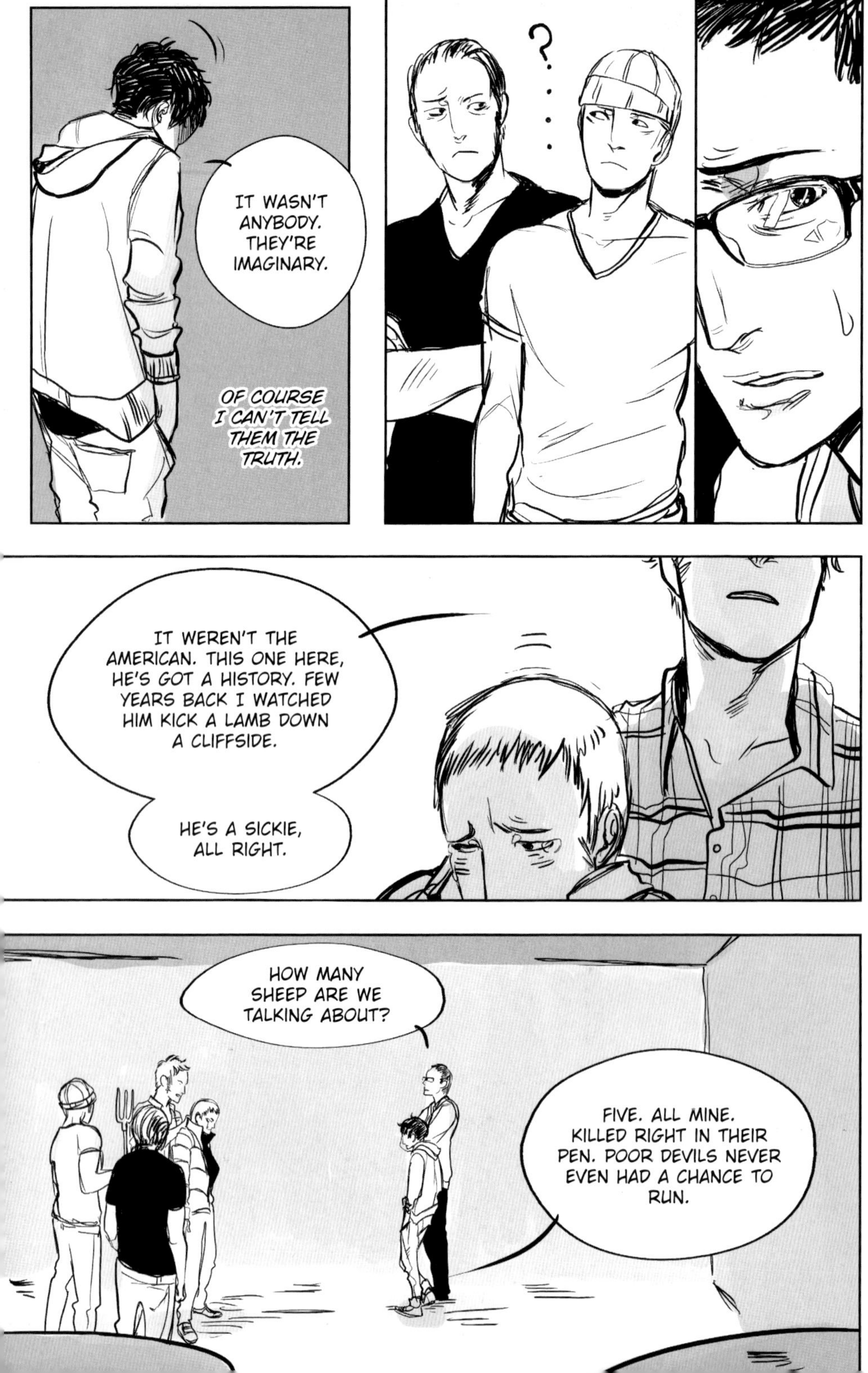
IT WASN'T ANYBODY. THEY'RE IMAGINARY.
OF COURSE I CAN'T TELL THEM THE TRUTH.
?
IT WEREN'T THE AMERICAN. THIS ONE HERE, HE'S GOT A HISTORY. FEW YEARS BACK I WATCHED HIM KICK A LAMB DOWN A CLIFFSIDE.
HE'S A SICKIE, ALL RIGHT.
HOW MANY SHEEP ARE WE TALKING ABOUT?
FIVE. ALL MINE. KILLED RIGHT IN THEIR PEN. POOR DEVILS NEVER EVEN HAD A CHANCE TO RUN.

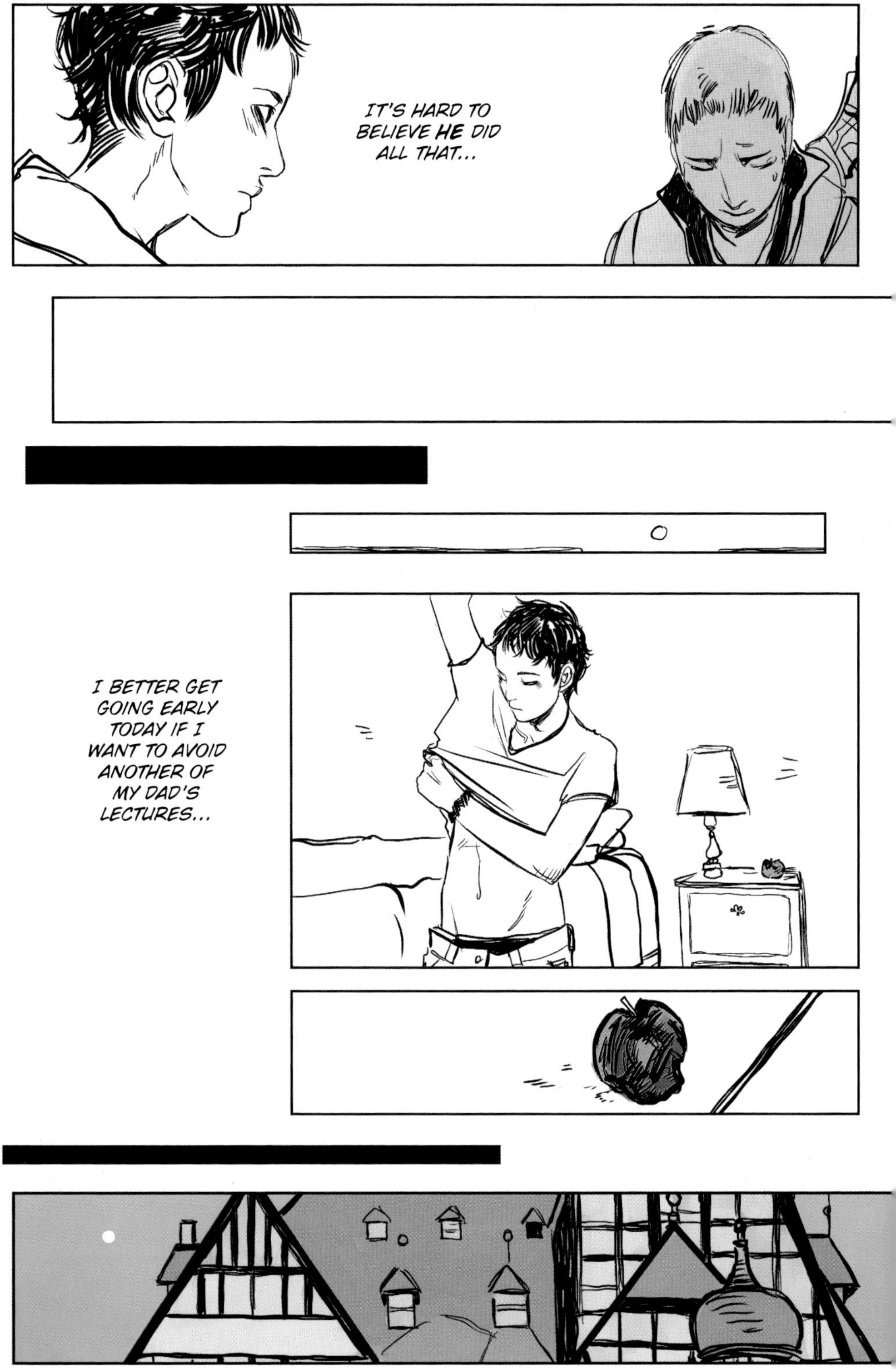
IT'S HARD TO BELIEVE **HE** DID ALL THAT...
I BETTER GET GOING EARLY TODAY IF I WANT TO AVOID ANOTHER OF MY DAD'S LECTURES...

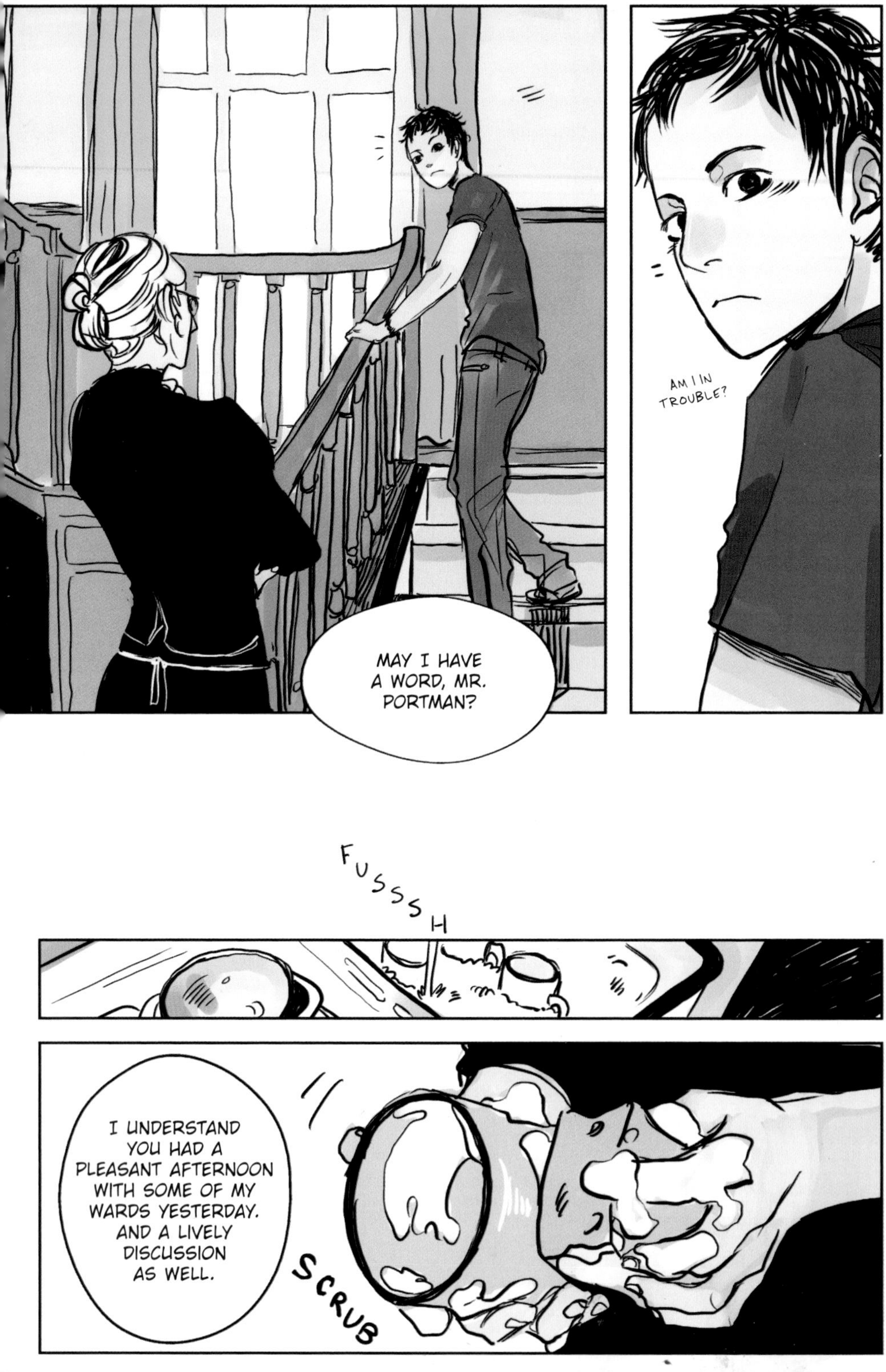
MAY I HAVE A WORD, MR. PORTMAN?
AM I IN TROUBLE?
FUSSSSH
I UNDERSTAND YOU HAD A PLEASANT AFTERNOON WITH SOME OF MY WARDS YESTERDAY. AND A LIVELY DISCUSSION AS WELL.
SCRUB

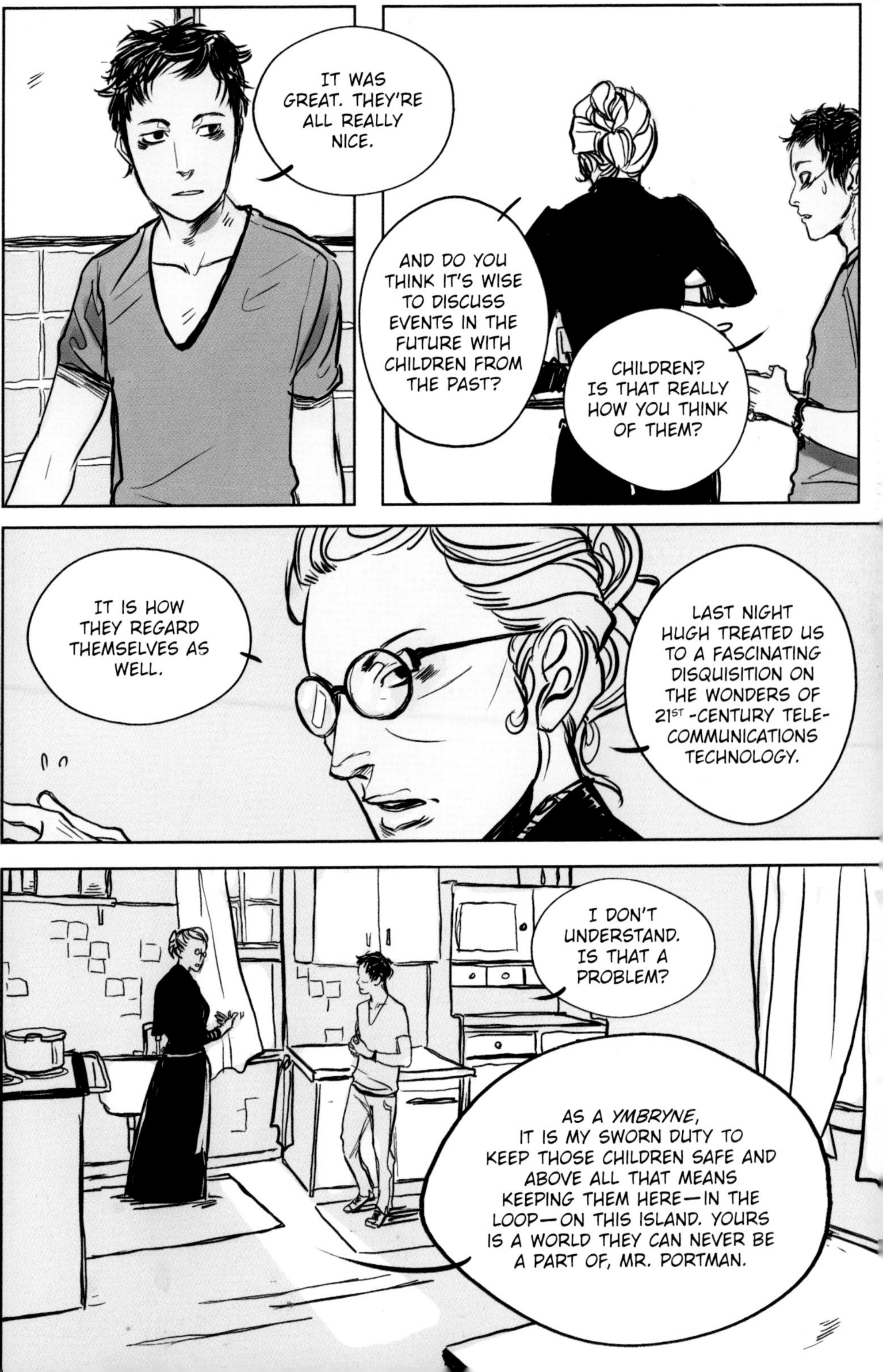
IT WAS GREAT. THEY'RE ALL REALLY NICE.
AND DO YOU THINK IT'S WISE TO DISCUSS EVENTS IN THE FUTURE WITH CHILDREN FROM THE PAST?
CHILDREN? IS THAT REALLY HOW YOU THINK OF THEM?
IT IS HOW THEY REGARD THEMSELVES AS WELL.
LAST NIGHT HUGH TREATED US TO A FASCINATING DISQUISITION ON THE WONDERS OF 21ST-CENTURY TELECOMMUNICATIONS TECHNOLOGY.
I DON'T UNDERSTAND. IS THAT A PROBLEM?
AS A *YMBRYNE*, IT IS MY SWORN DUTY TO KEEP THOSE CHILDREN SAFE AND ABOVE ALL THAT MEANS KEEPING THEM HERE—IN THE LOOP—ON THIS ISLAND. YOURS IS A WORLD THEY CAN NEVER BE A PART OF, MR. PORTMAN.

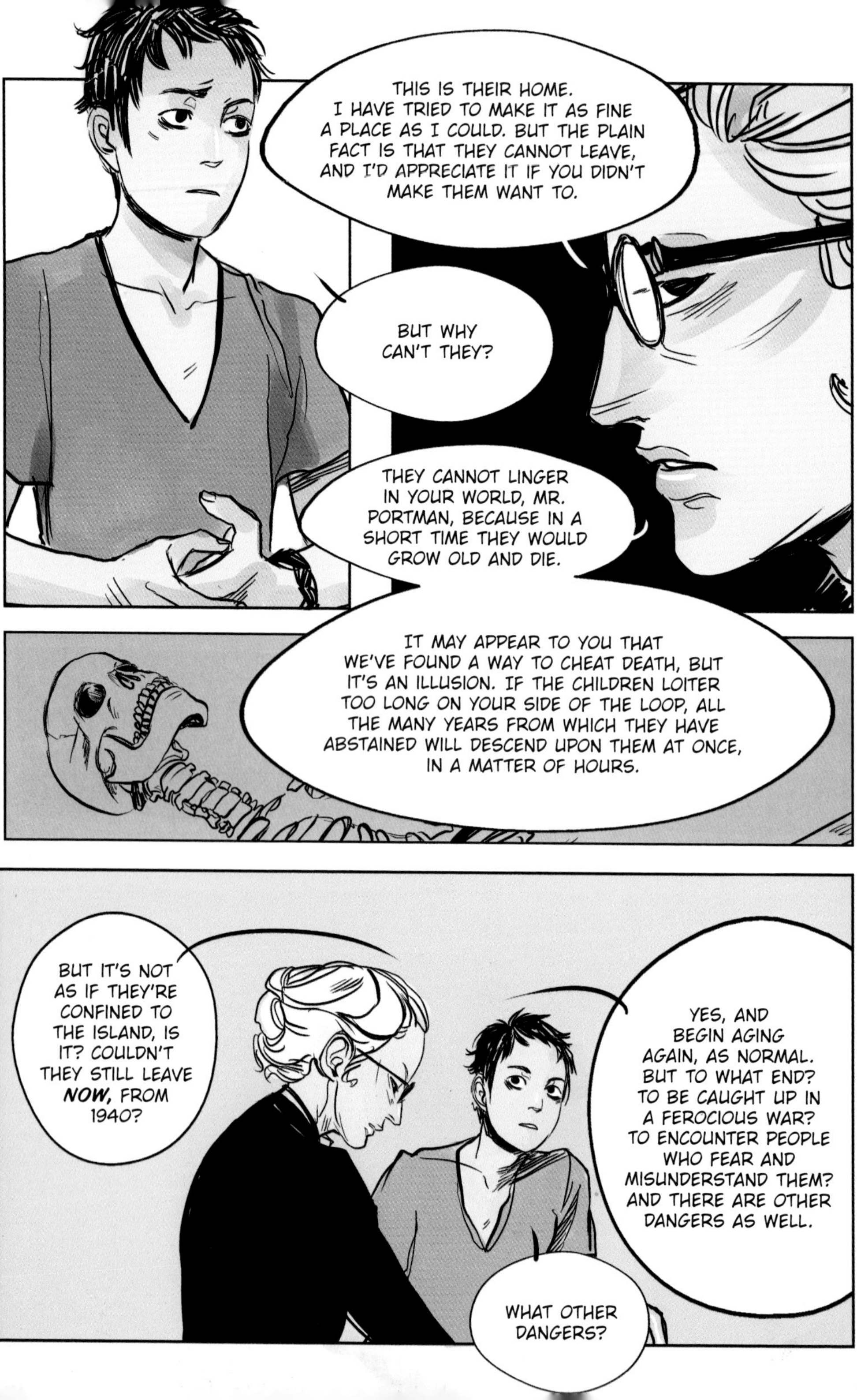
THIS IS THEIR HOME. I HAVE TRIED TO MAKE IT AS FINE A PLACE AS I COULD. BUT THE PLAIN FACT IS THAT THEY CANNOT LEAVE, AND I'D APPRECIATE IT IF YOU DIDN'T MAKE THEM WANT TO.
BUT WHY CAN'T THEY?
THEY CANNOT LINGER IN YOUR WORLD, MR. PORTMAN, BECAUSE IN A SHORT TIME THEY WOULD GROW OLD AND DIE.
IT MAY APPEAR TO YOU THAT WE'VE FOUND A WAY TO CHEAT DEATH, BUT IT'S AN ILLUSION. IF THE CHILDREN LOITER TOO LONG ON YOUR SIDE OF THE LOOP, ALL THE MANY YEARS FROM WHICH THEY HAVE ABSTAINED WILL DESCEND UPON THEM AT ONCE, IN A MATTER OF HOURS.
BUT IT'S NOT AS IF THEY'RE CONFINED TO THE ISLAND, IS IT? COULDN'T THEY STILL LEAVE ***NOW,*** FROM 1940?
YES, AND BEGIN AGING AGAIN, AS NORMAL. BUT TO WHAT END? TO BE CAUGHT UP IN A FEROCIOUS WAR? TO ENCOUNTER PEOPLE WHO FEAR AND MISUNDERSTAND THEM? AND THERE ARE OTHER DANGERS AS WELL.
WHAT OTHER DANGERS?

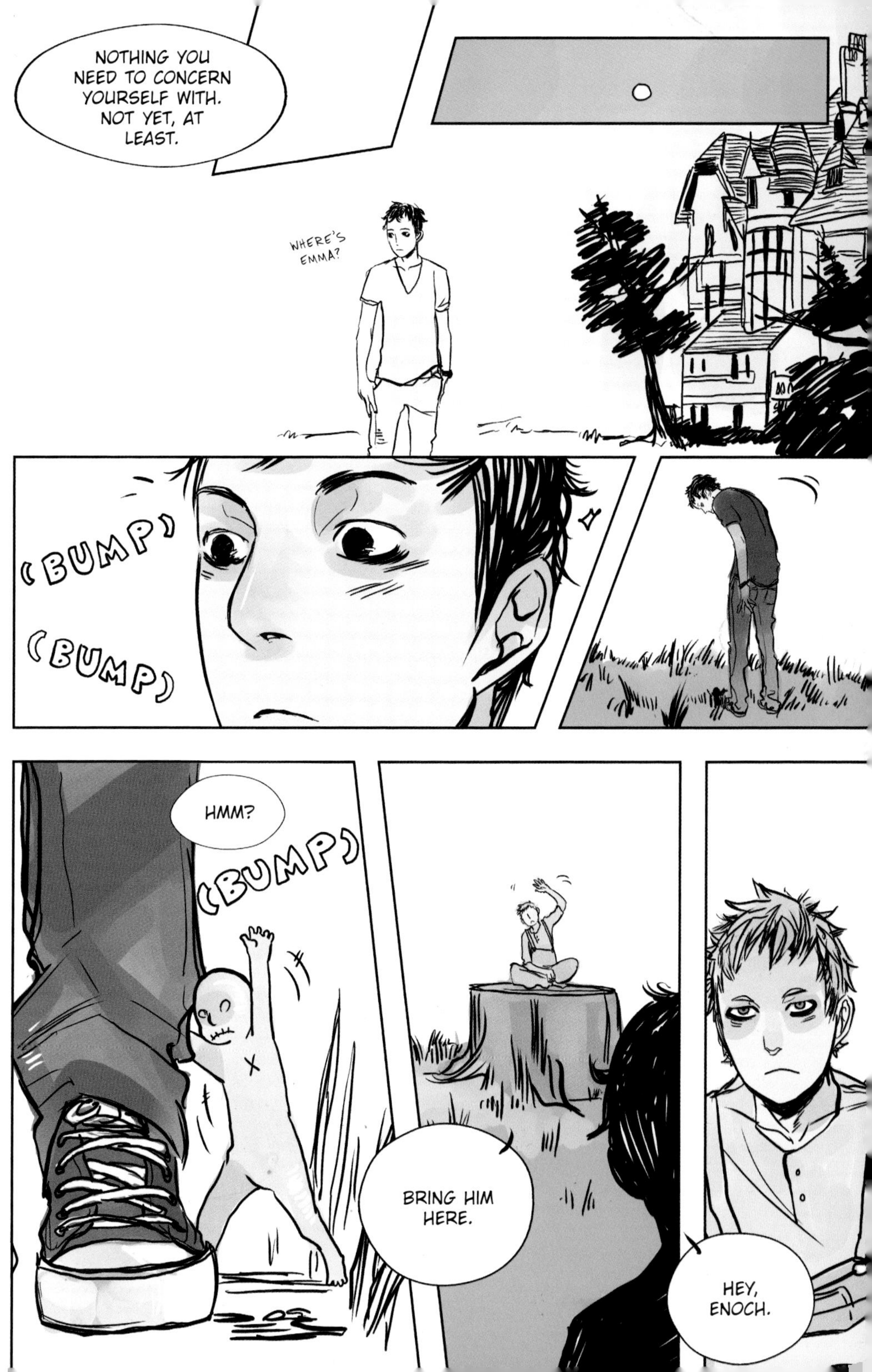
NOTHING YOU NEED TO CONCERN YOURSELF WITH. NOT YET, AT LEAST.
WHERE'S EMMA?
(BUMP)
(BUMP)
HMM?
(BUMP)
BRING HIM HERE.
HEY, ENOCH.

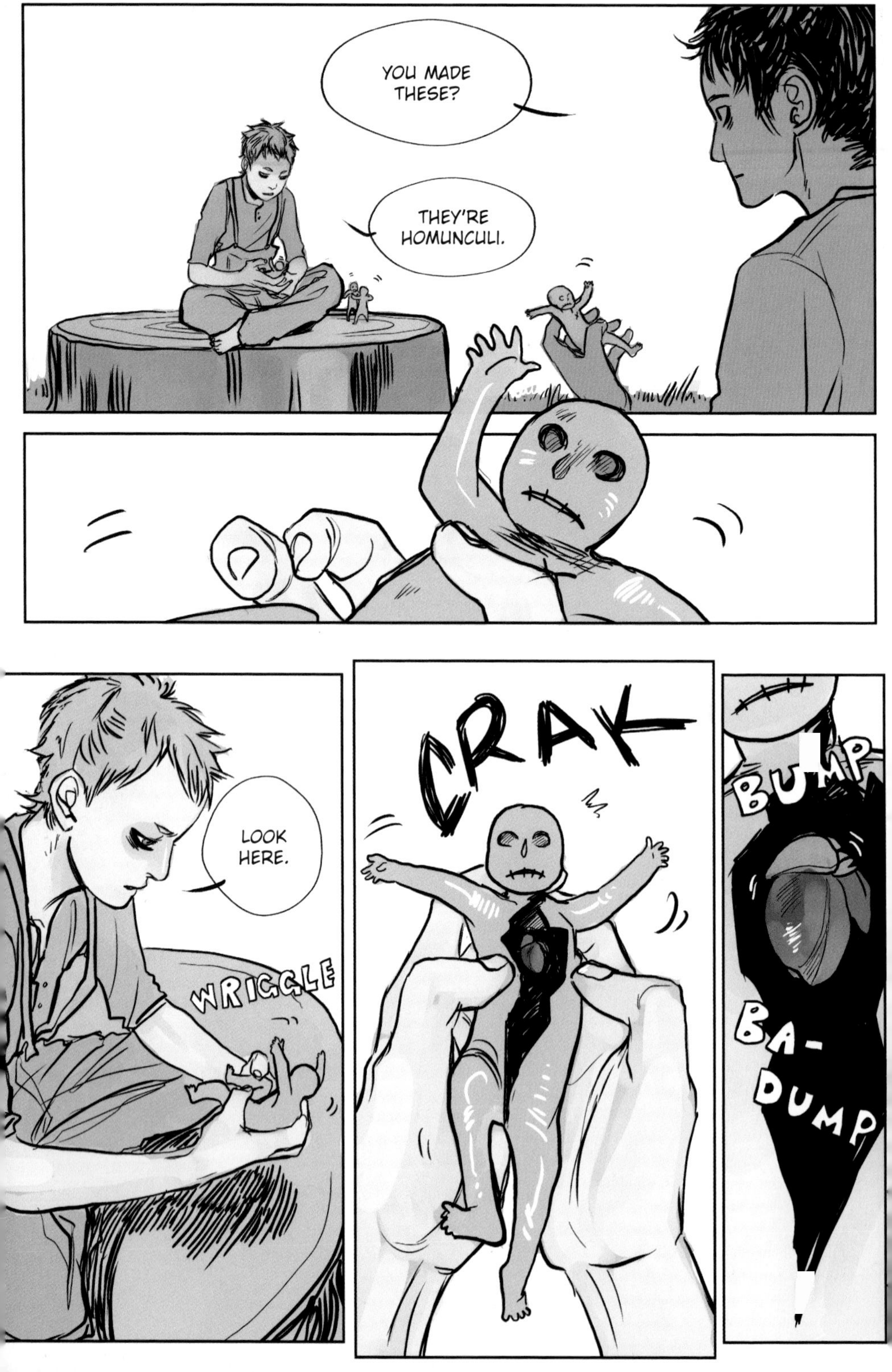
YOU MADE THESE?
THEY'RE HOMUNCULI.
LOOK HERE.
WRIGGLE
CRAK
BUMP
BA-DUMP

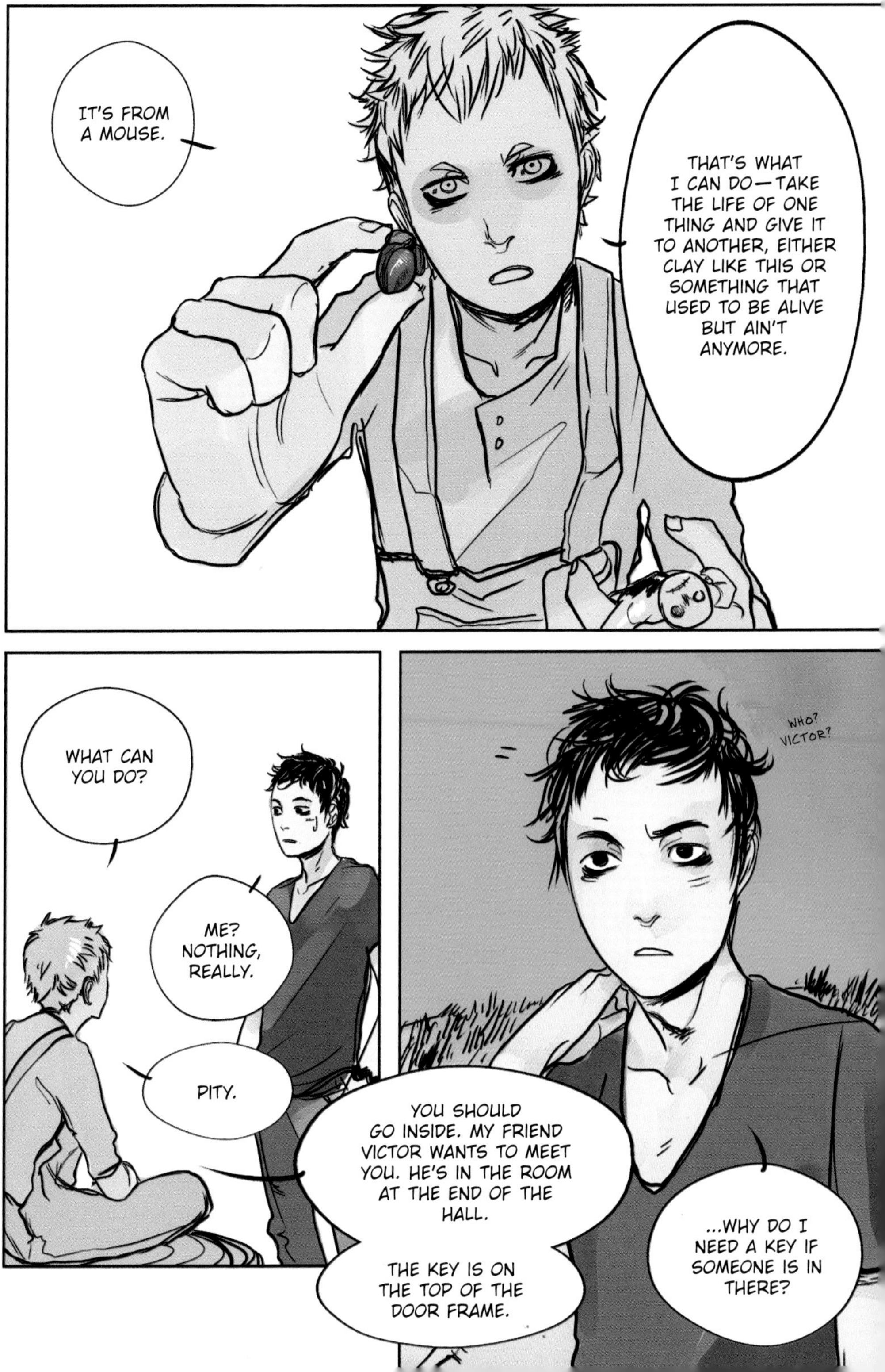
IT'S FROM A MOUSE.
THAT'S WHAT I CAN DO—TAKE THE LIFE OF ONE THING AND GIVE IT TO ANOTHER, EITHER CLAY LIKE THIS OR SOMETHING THAT USED TO BE ALIVE BUT AIN'T ANYMORE.
WHAT CAN YOU DO?
ME? NOTHING, REALLY.
PITY.
YOU SHOULD GO INSIDE. MY FRIEND VICTOR WANTS TO MEET YOU. HE'S IN THE ROOM AT THE END OF THE HALL.
THE KEY IS ON THE TOP OF THE DOOR FRAME.
WHO? VICTOR?
...WHY DO I NEED A KEY IF SOMEONE IS IN THERE?

CREEAK

VICTOR...?

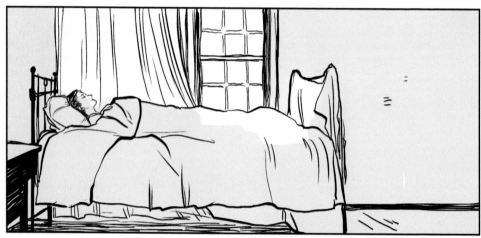

HELLO?
ARE YOU
AWAKE?

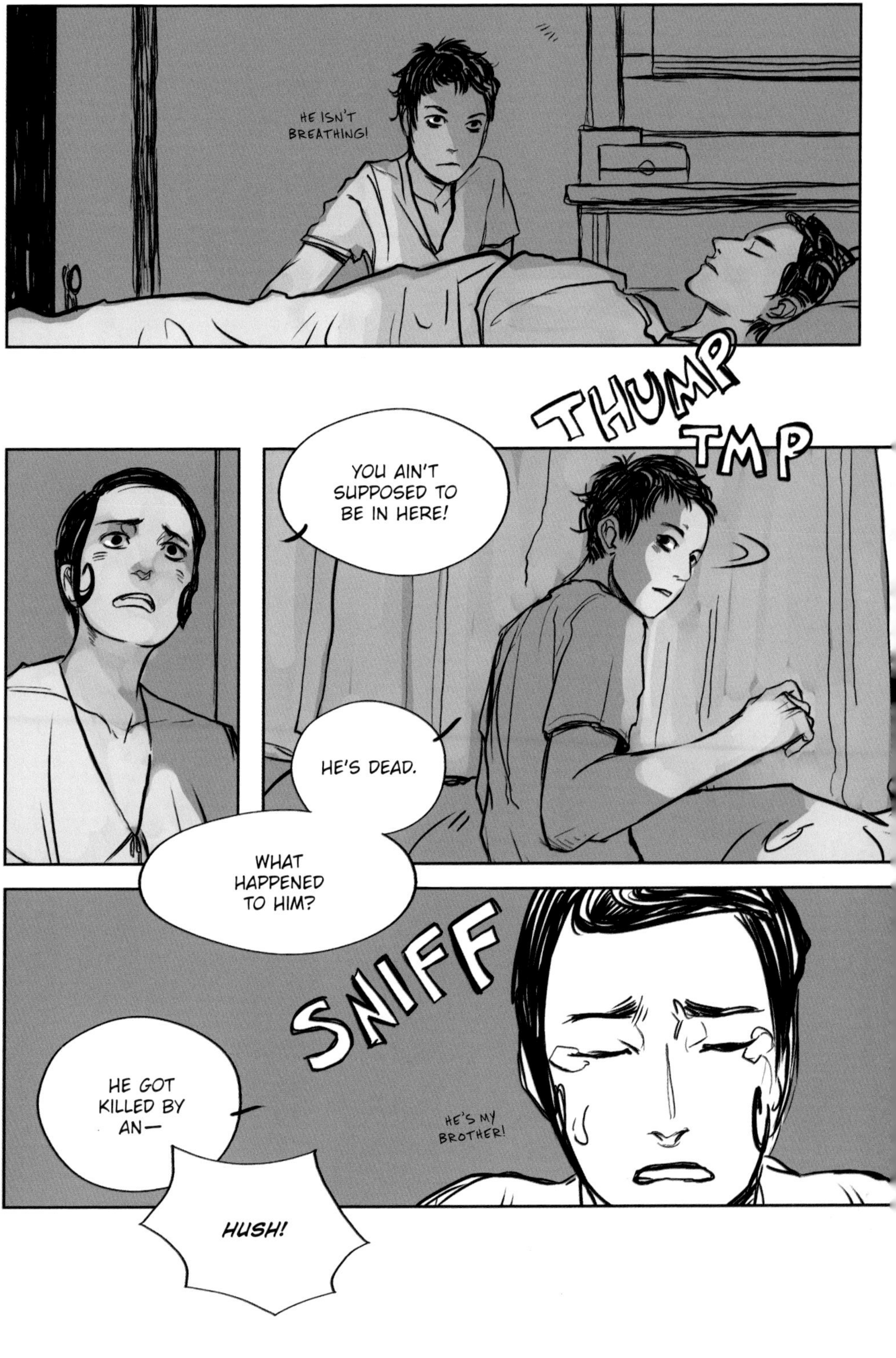
HE ISN'T BREATHING!
THUMP TMP
YOU AIN'T SUPPOSED TO BE IN HERE!
HE'S DEAD.
WHAT HAPPENED TO HIM?
SNIFF
HE GOT KILLED BY AN—
HUSH!
HE'S MY BROTHER!

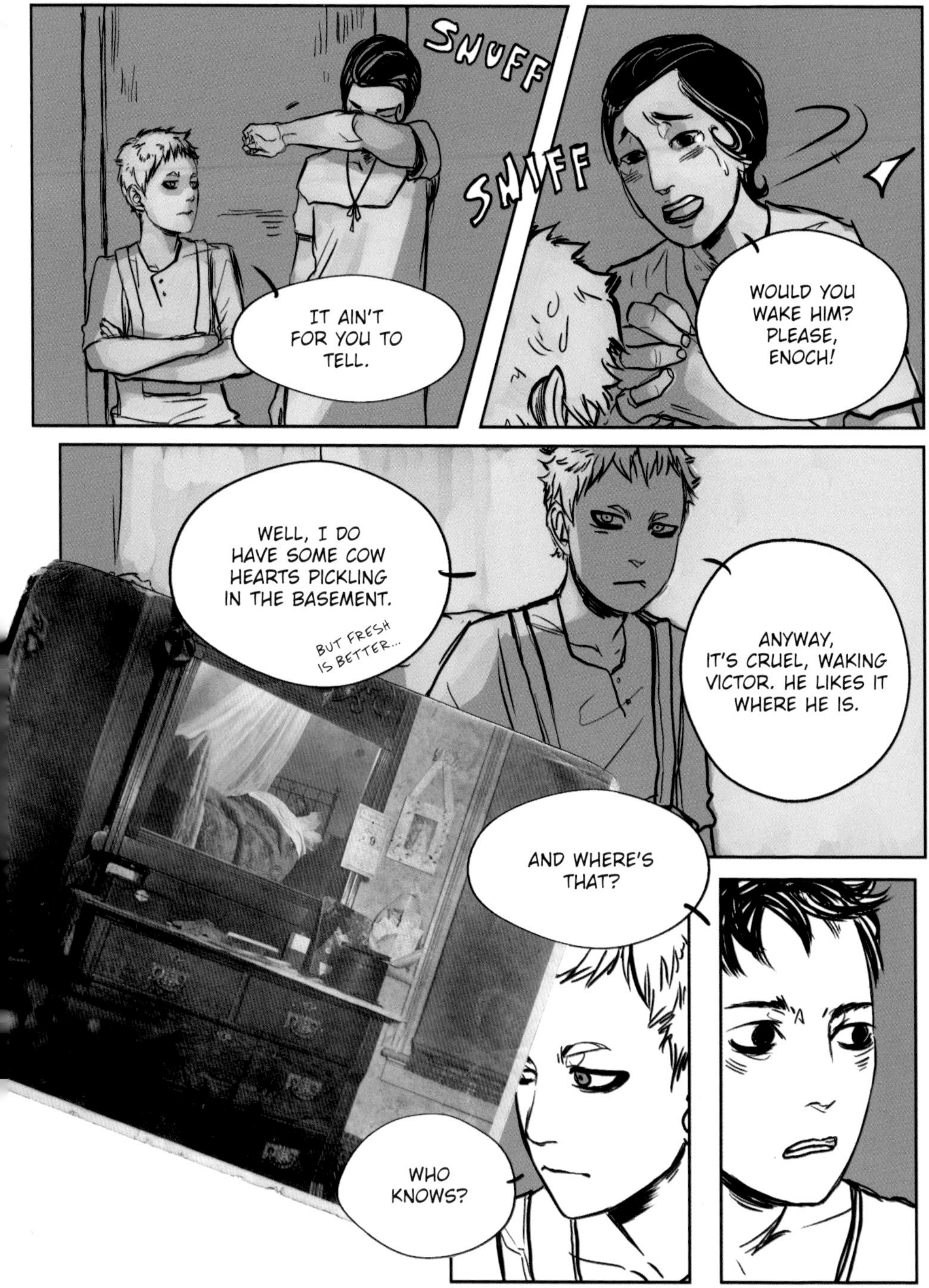
SNUFF
IT AIN'T FOR YOU TO TELL.
SNIFF
WOULD YOU WAKE HIM? PLEASE, ENOCH!
WELL, I DO HAVE SOME COW HEARTS PICKLING IN THE BASEMENT.
BUT FRESH IS BETTER...
ANYWAY, IT'S CRUEL, WAKING VICTOR. HE LIKES IT WHERE HE IS.
AND WHERE'S THAT?
WHO KNOWS?

WHY SEND ME UP HERE, THEN?

WHAT HAPPENED TO YOU, VICTOR?

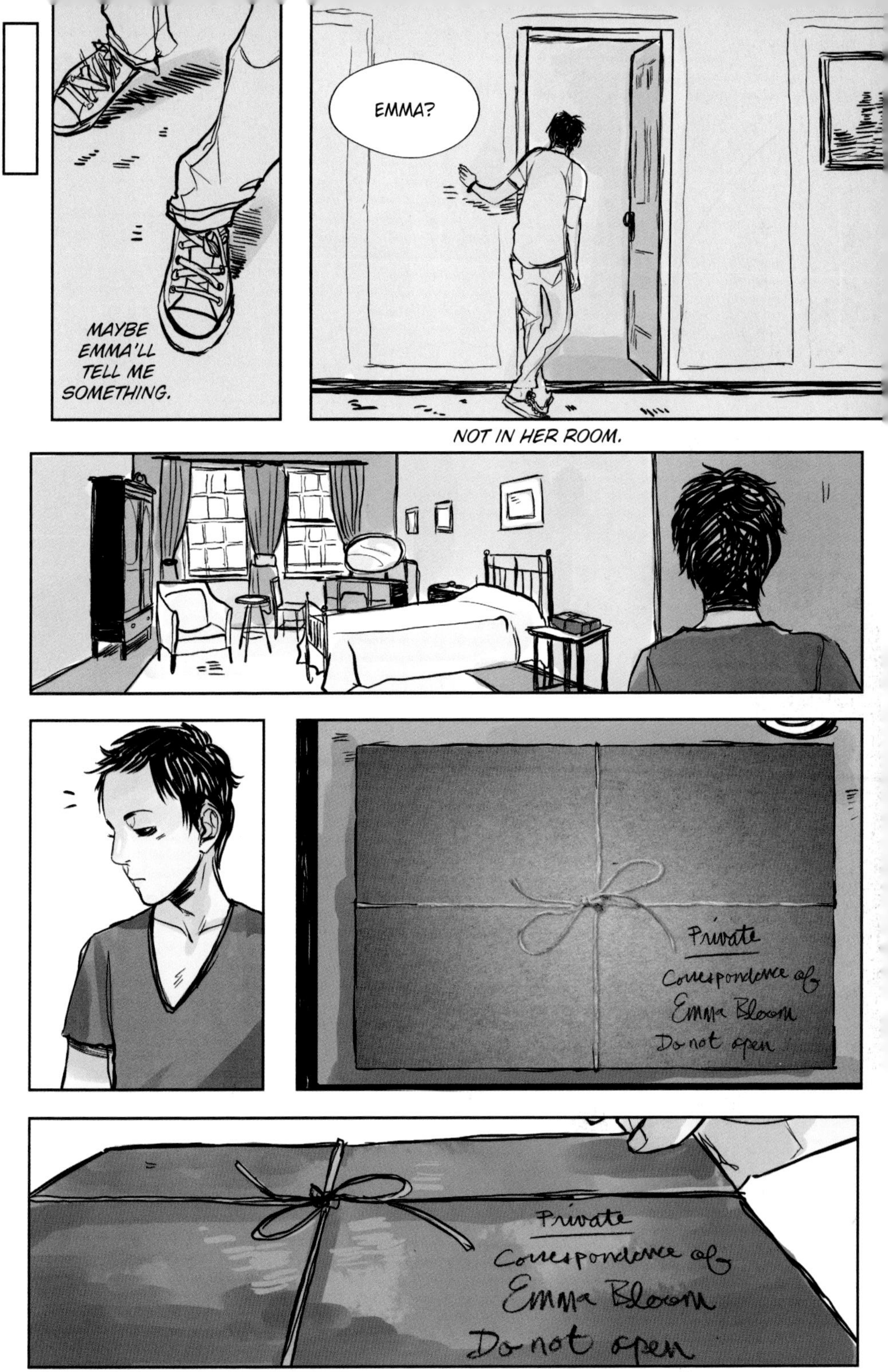
MAYBE EMMA'LL TELL ME SOMETHING.
EMMA?
NOT IN HER ROOM.
Private
Correspondence of
Emma Bloom
Do not open
Private
Correspondence of
Emma Bloom
Do not open

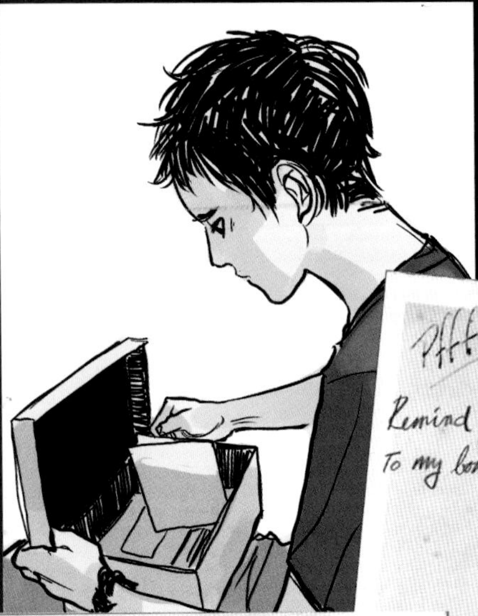

HUNDREDS OF LETTERS, ALL FROM MY GRANDFATHER.

BUT IT LOOKS LIKE HE STARTED WRITING TO EMMA LESS AND LESS...

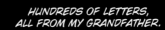

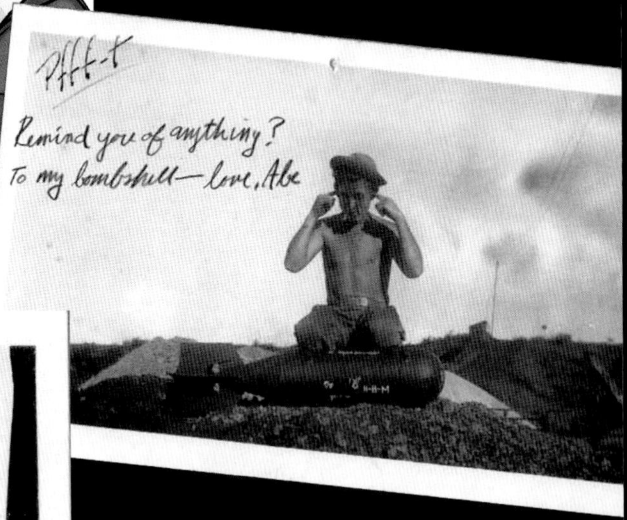
Pfff-t
Remind you of anything?
To my bombshell—love, Abe

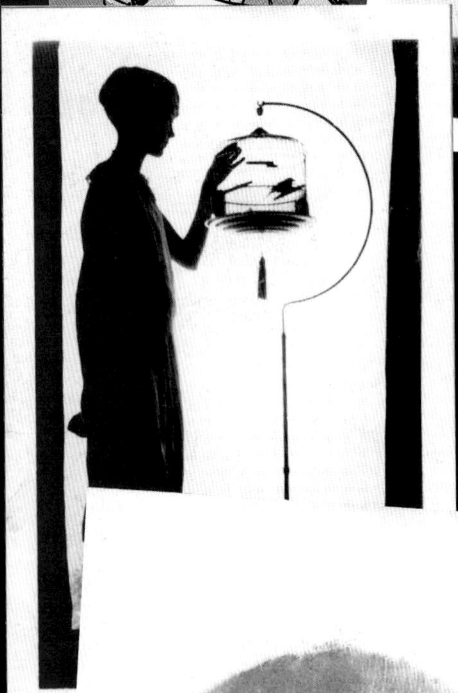

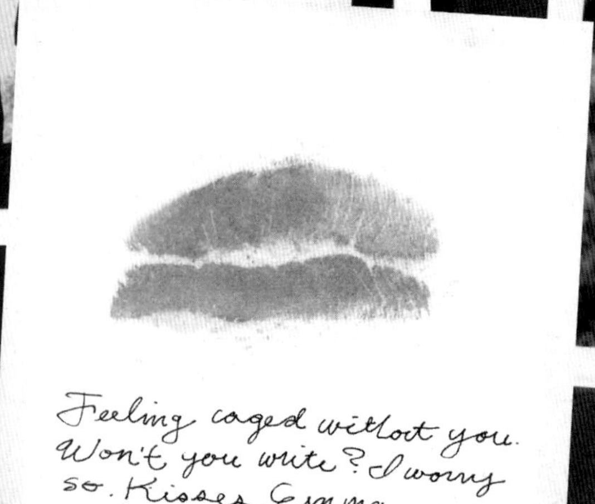
Feeling caged without you.
Won't you write? I worry
so. Kisses, Emma.

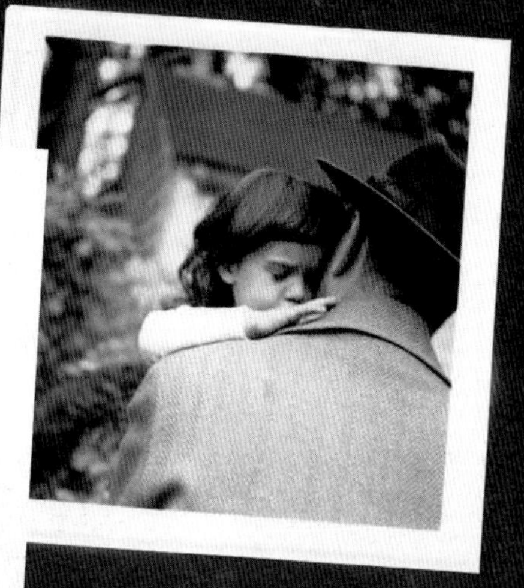

THIS IS WHY

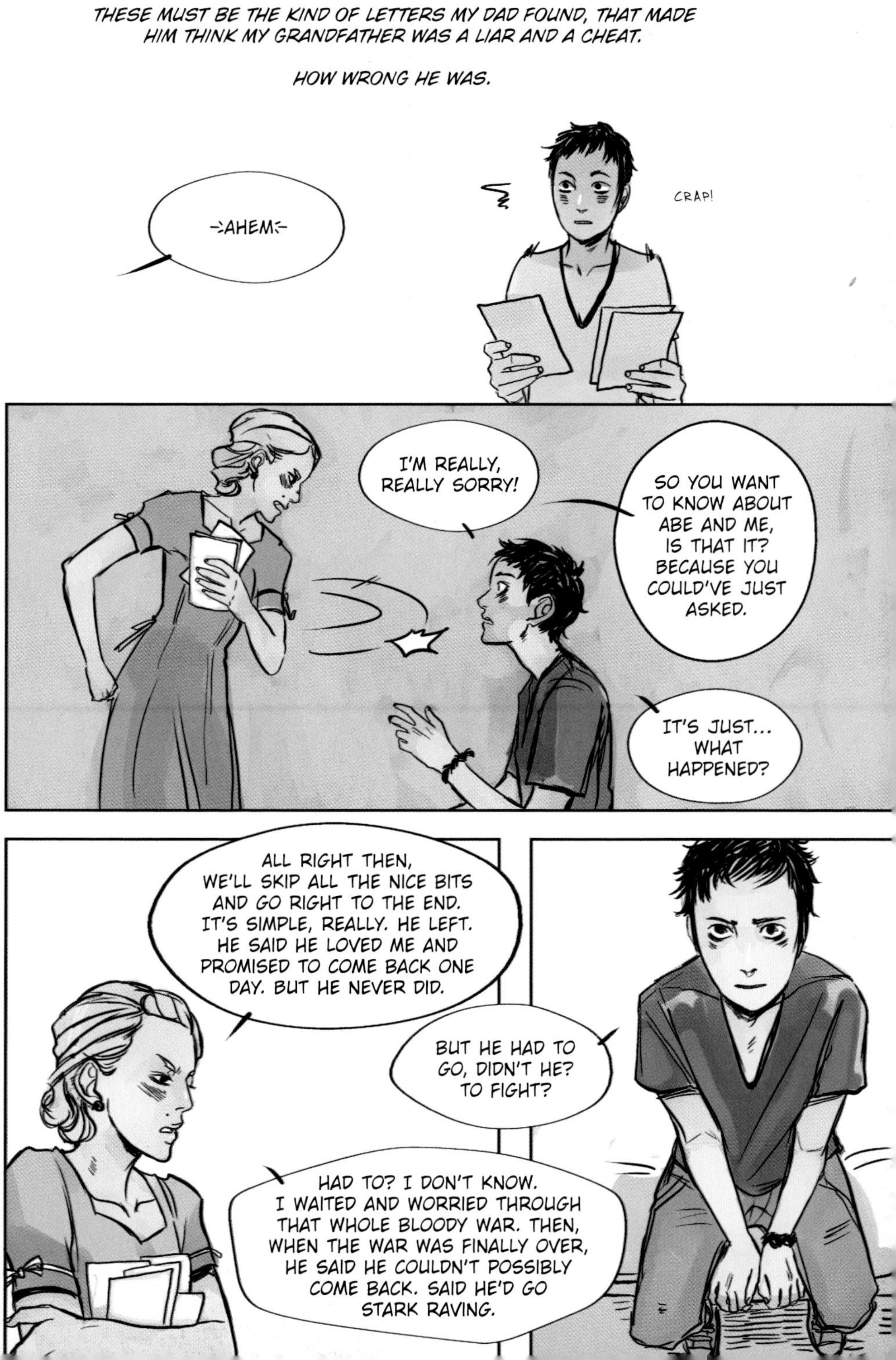
THESE MUST BE THE KIND OF LETTERS MY DAD FOUND, THAT MADE HIM THINK MY GRANDFATHER WAS A LIAR AND A CHEAT.
HOW WRONG HE WAS.
-AHEM-
CRAP!
I'M REALLY, REALLY SORRY!
SO YOU WANT TO KNOW ABOUT ABE AND ME, IS THAT IT? BECAUSE YOU COULD'VE JUST ASKED.
IT'S JUST... WHAT HAPPENED?
ALL RIGHT THEN, WE'LL SKIP ALL THE NICE BITS AND GO RIGHT TO THE END. IT'S SIMPLE, REALLY. HE LEFT. HE SAID HE LOVED ME AND PROMISED TO COME BACK ONE DAY. BUT HE NEVER DID.
BUT HE HAD TO GO, DIDN'T HE? TO FIGHT?
HAD TO? I DON'T KNOW. I WAITED AND WORRIED THROUGH THAT WHOLE BLOODY WAR. THEN, WHEN THE WAR WAS FINALLY OVER, HE SAID HE COULDN'T POSSIBLY COME BACK. SAID HE'D GO STARK RAVING.

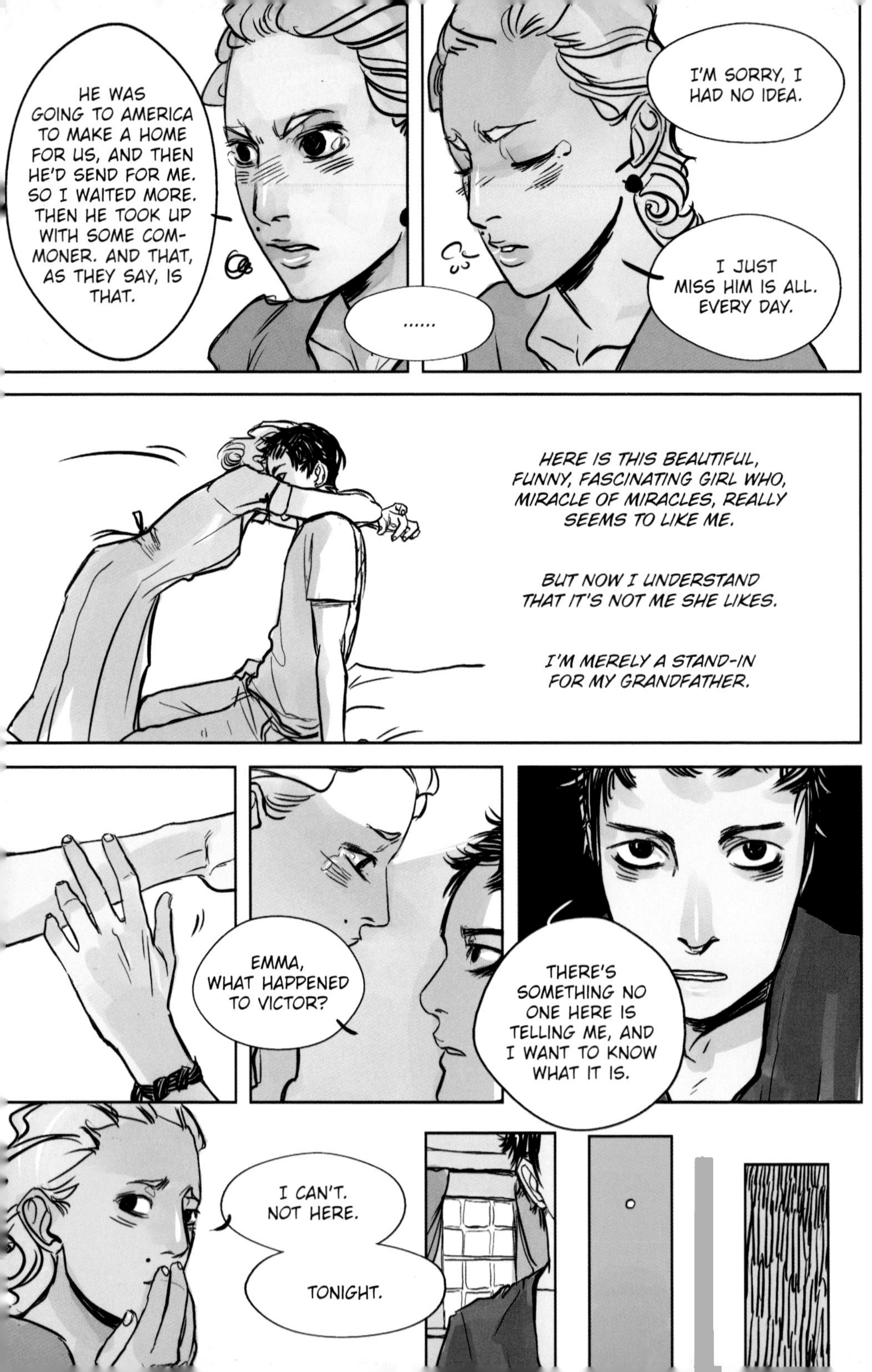
HE WAS GOING TO AMERICA TO MAKE A HOME FOR US, AND THEN HE'D SEND FOR ME. SO I WAITED MORE. THEN HE TOOK UP WITH SOME COM-MONER. AND THAT, AS THEY SAY, IS THAT.
......
I'M SORRY, I HAD NO IDEA.
I JUST MISS HIM IS ALL. EVERY DAY.
HERE IS THIS BEAUTIFUL, FUNNY, FASCINATING GIRL WHO, MIRACLE OF MIRACLES, REALLY SEEMS TO LIKE ME.
BUT NOW I UNDERSTAND THAT IT'S NOT ME SHE LIKES.
I'M MERELY A STAND-IN FOR MY GRANDFATHER.
EMMA, WHAT HAPPENED TO VICTOR?
THERE'S SOMETHING NO ONE HERE IS TELLING ME, AND I WANT TO KNOW WHAT IT IS.
I CAN'T. NOT HERE.
TONIGHT.

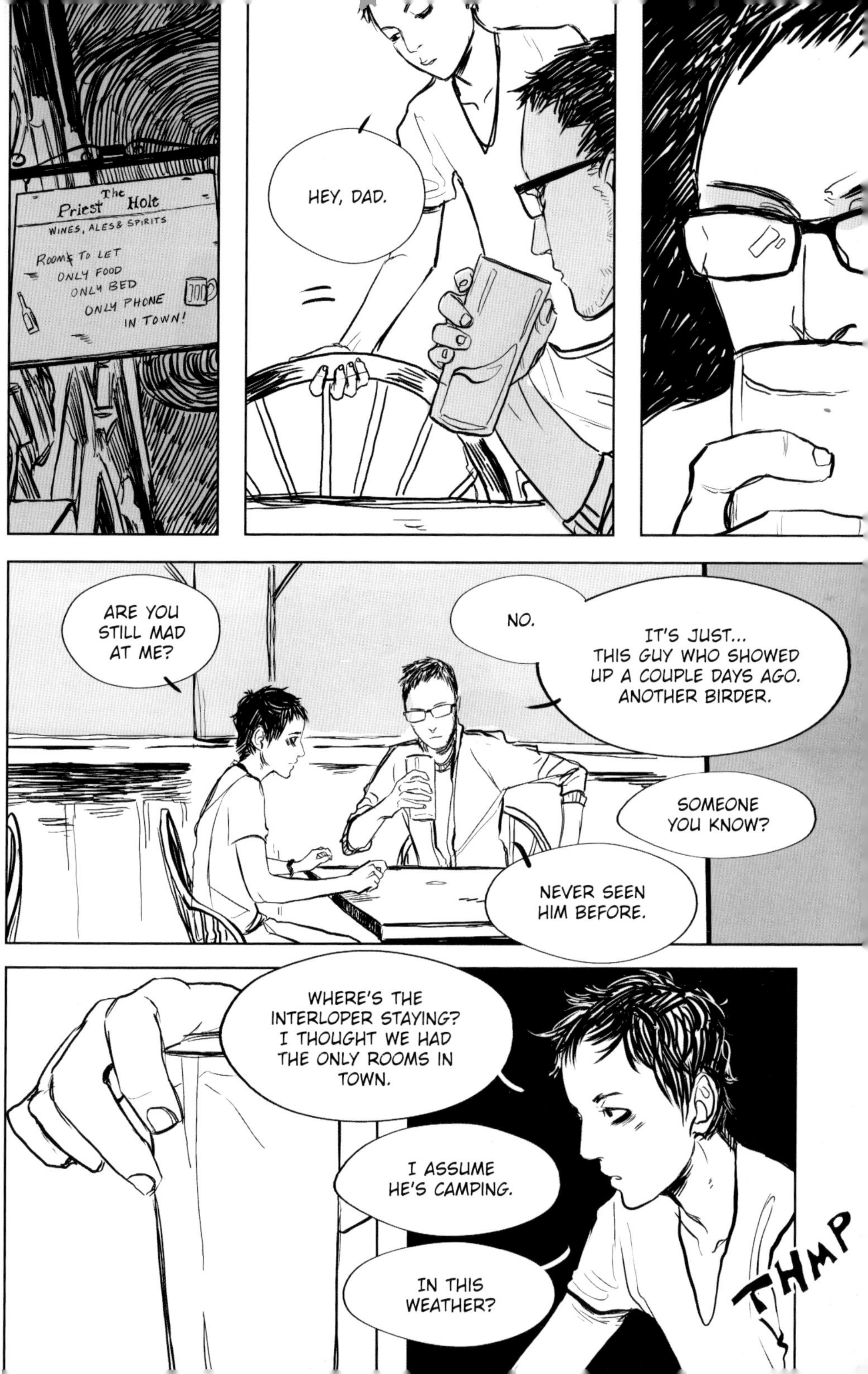

The Priest Hole
WINES, ALES & SPIRITS
Rooms To LET
ONLY FOOD
ONLY BED
ONLY PHONE
IN TOWN!
HEY, DAD.
ARE YOU STILL MAD AT ME?
NO.
IT'S JUST... THIS GUY WHO SHOWED UP A COUPLE DAYS AGO. ANOTHER BIRDER.
SOMEONE YOU KNOW?
NEVER SEEN HIM BEFORE.
WHERE'S THE INTERLOPER STAYING? I THOUGHT WE HAD THE ONLY ROOMS IN TOWN.
I ASSUME HE'S CAMPING.
IN THIS WEATHER?
THMP

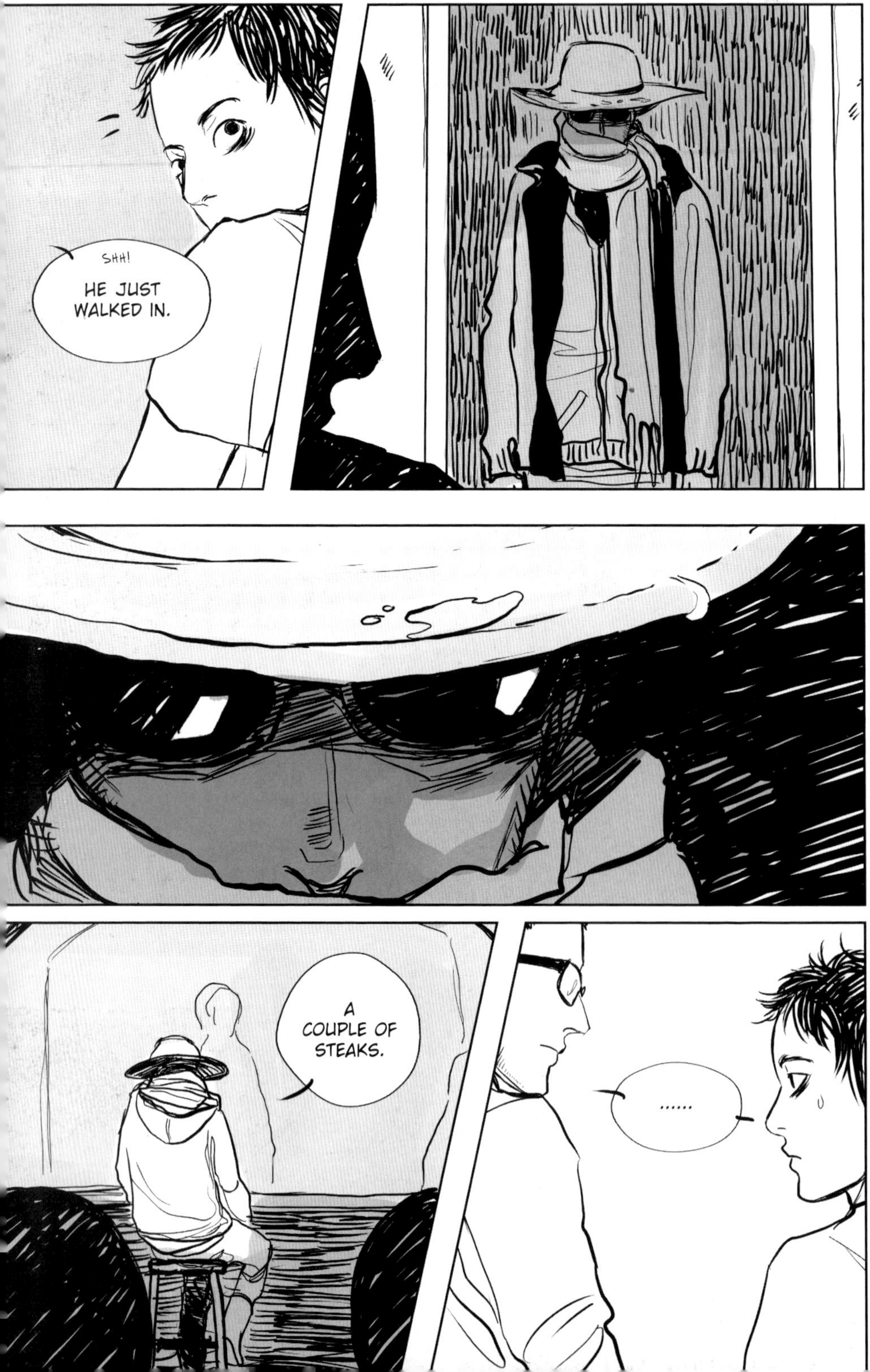
SHH!
HE JUST WALKED IN.
A COUPLE OF STEAKS.
......

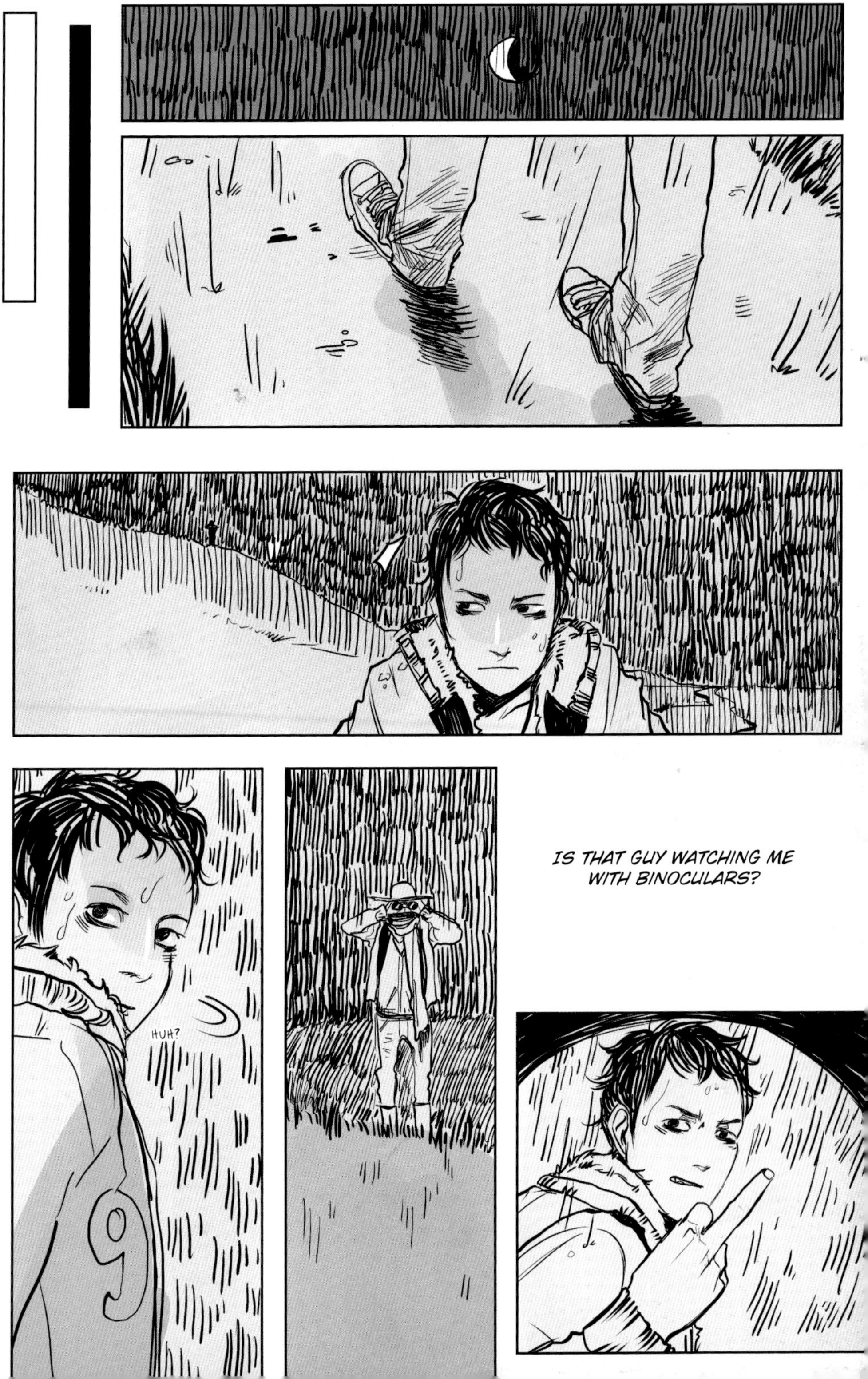
HUH?
IS THAT GUY WATCHING ME WITH BINOCULARS?

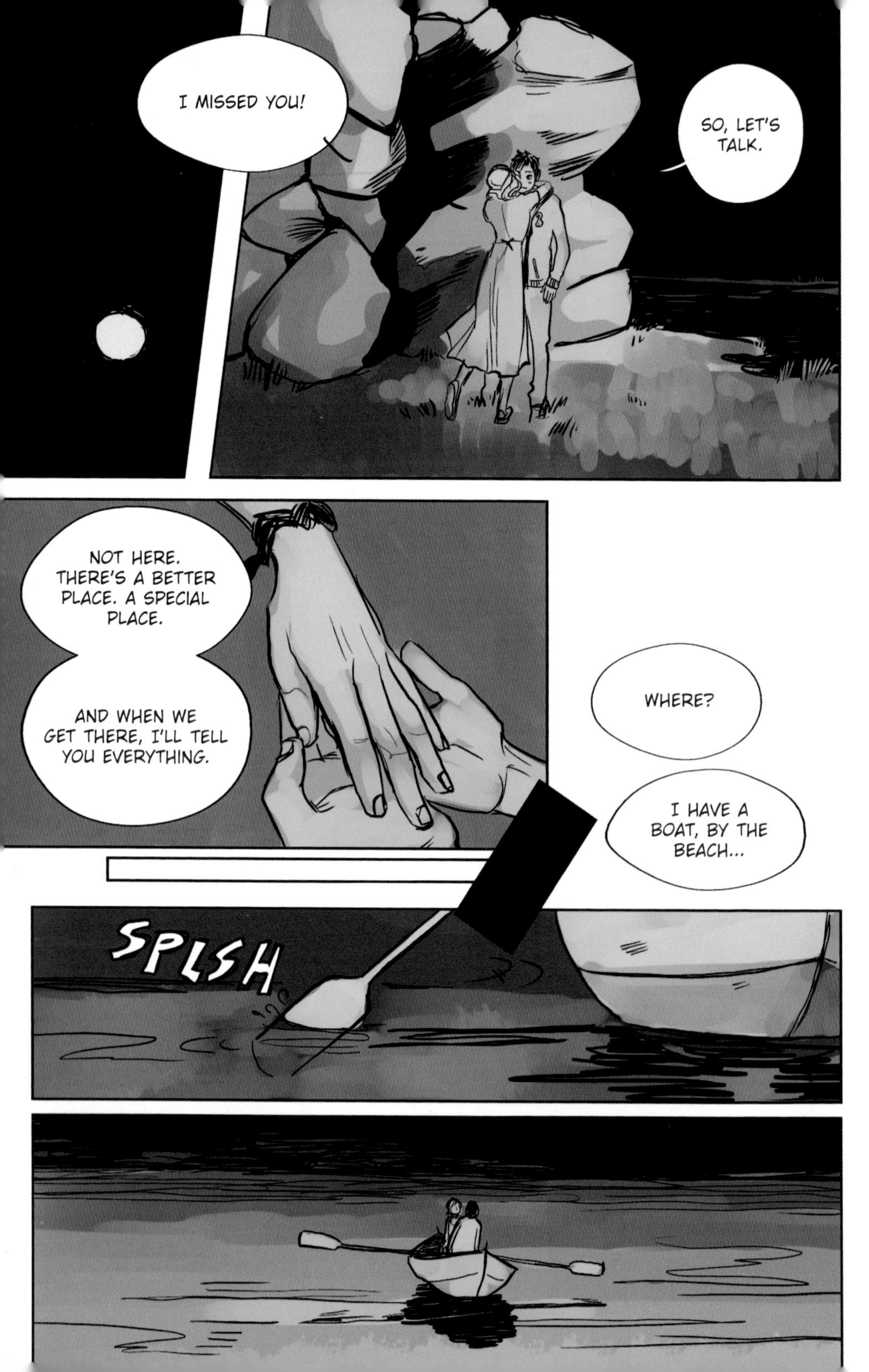
I MISSED YOU!
SO, LET'S TALK.
NOT HERE. THERE'S A BETTER PLACE. A SPECIAL PLACE.
AND WHEN WE GET THERE, I'LL TELL YOU EVERYTHING.
WHERE?
I HAVE A BOAT, BY THE BEACH...
SPLSH

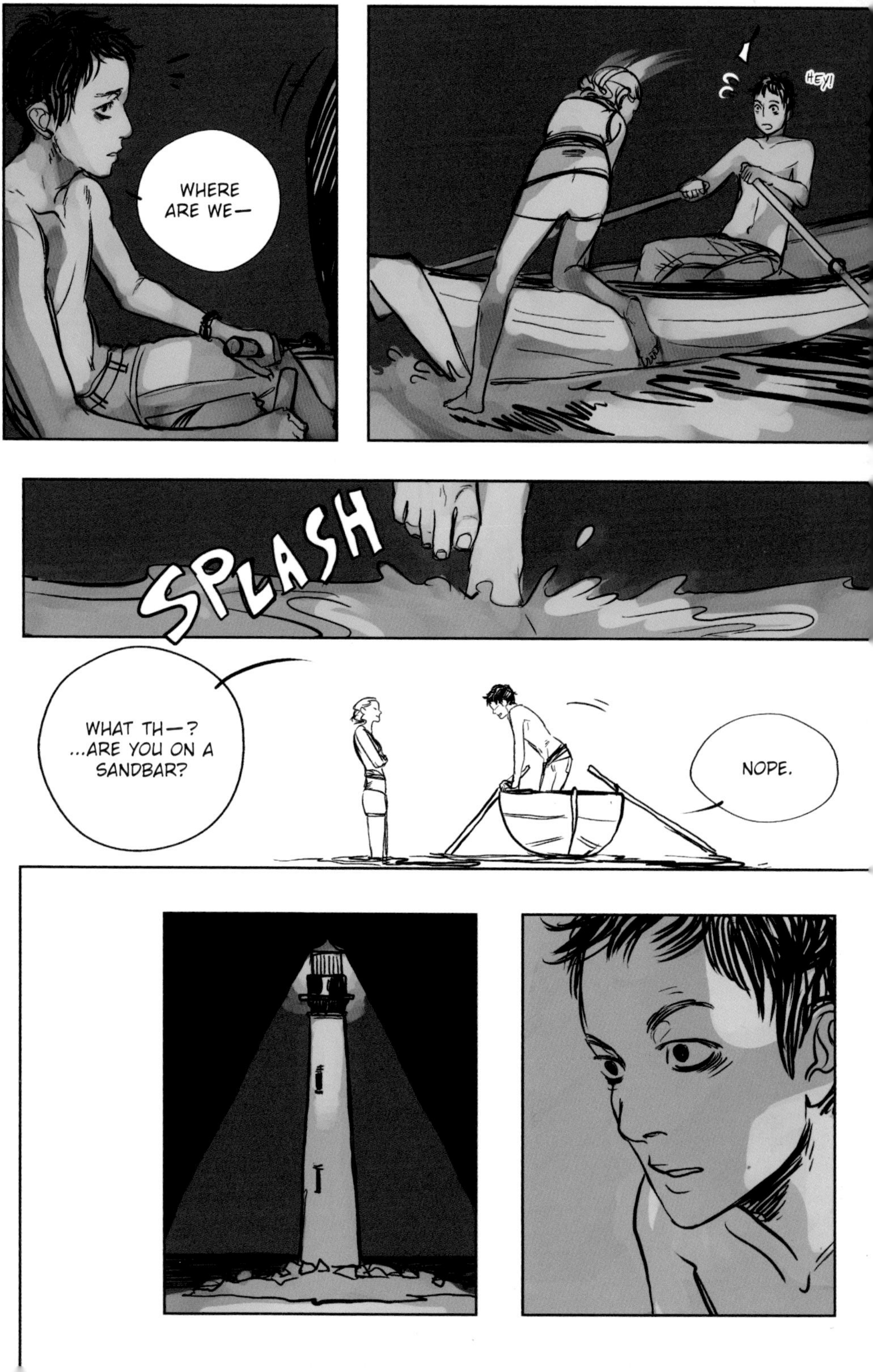
WHERE ARE WE—
HEY!
SPLASH
WHAT TH—? ...ARE YOU ON A SANDBAR?
NOPE.

A SHIPWRECK!

GRAB

WHAT?!

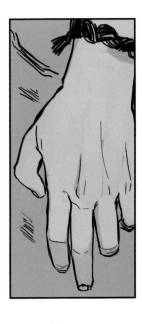

DON'T KISS HER.

SHE LOVED YOUR GRANDFATHER.

DON'T KISS HER.

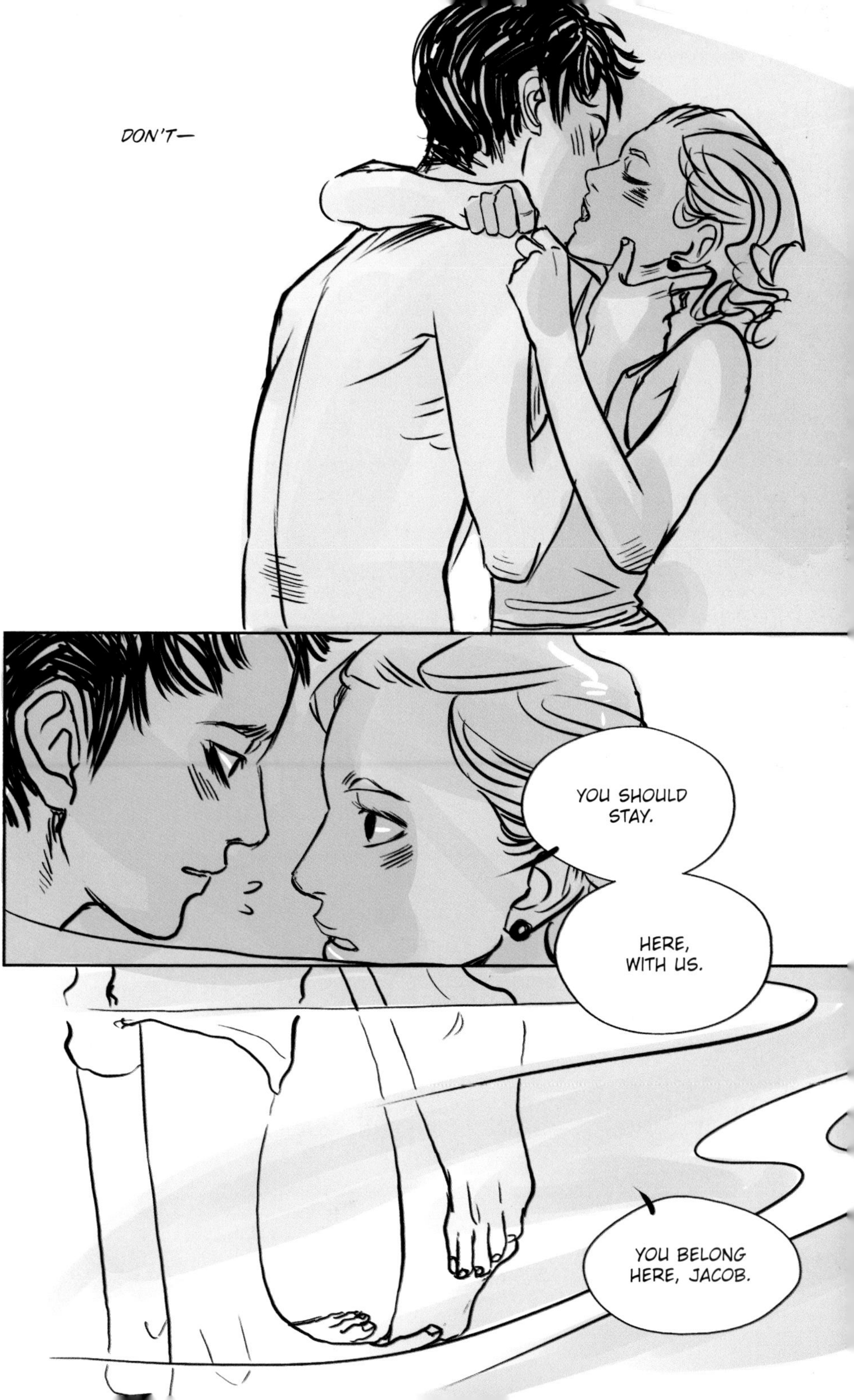
DON'T—
YOU SHOULD STAY.
HERE, WITH US.
YOU BELONG HERE, JACOB.

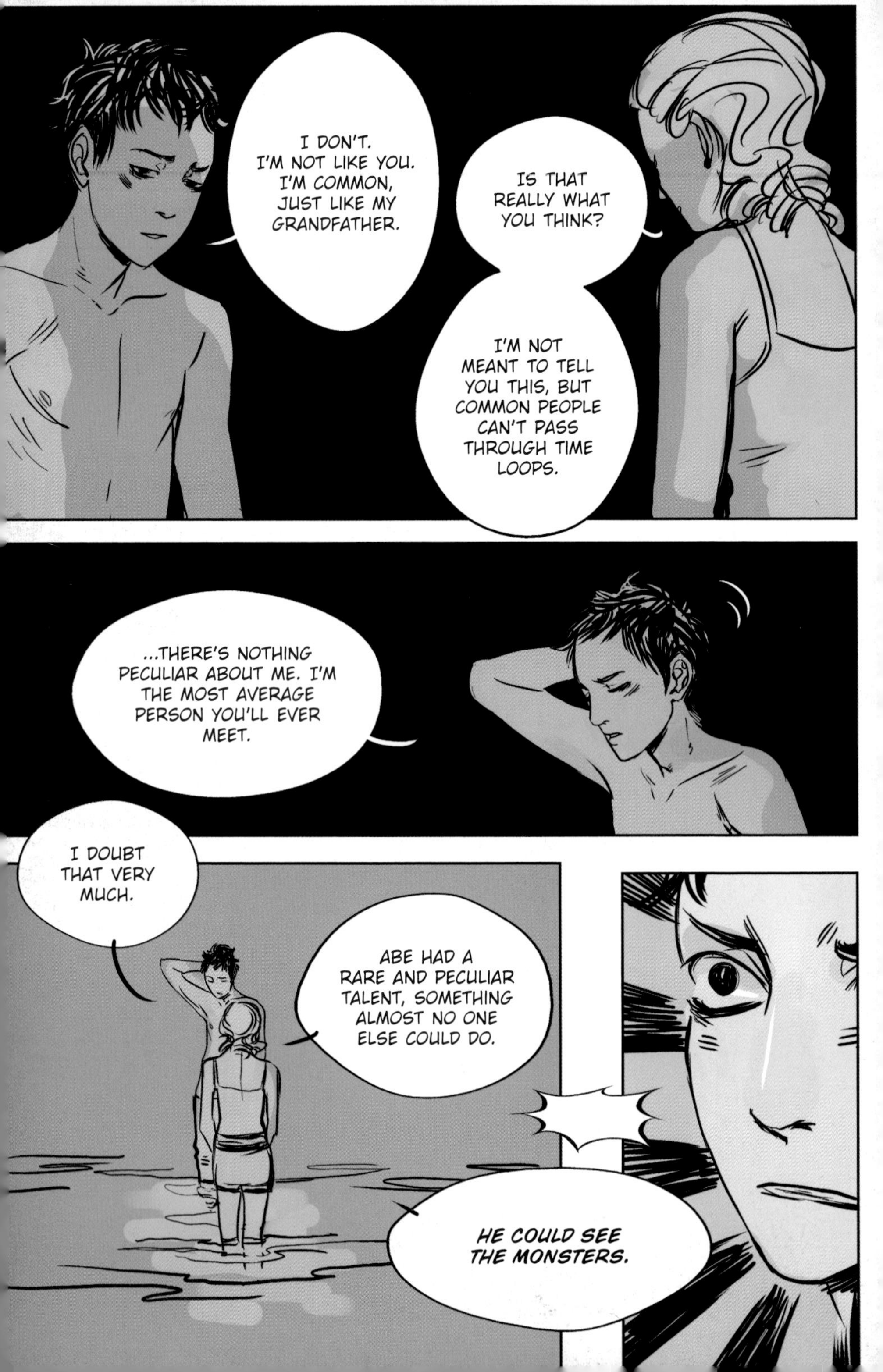
I DON'T. I'M NOT LIKE YOU. I'M COMMON, JUST LIKE MY GRANDFATHER.
IS THAT REALLY WHAT YOU THINK?
I'M NOT MEANT TO TELL YOU THIS, BUT COMMON PEOPLE CAN'T PASS THROUGH TIME LOOPS.
...THERE'S NOTHING PECULIAR ABOUT ME. I'M THE MOST AVERAGE PERSON YOU'LL EVER MEET.
I DOUBT THAT VERY MUCH.
ABE HAD A RARE AND PECULIAR TALENT, SOMETHING ALMOST NO ONE ELSE COULD DO.
HE COULD SEE THE MONSTERS.

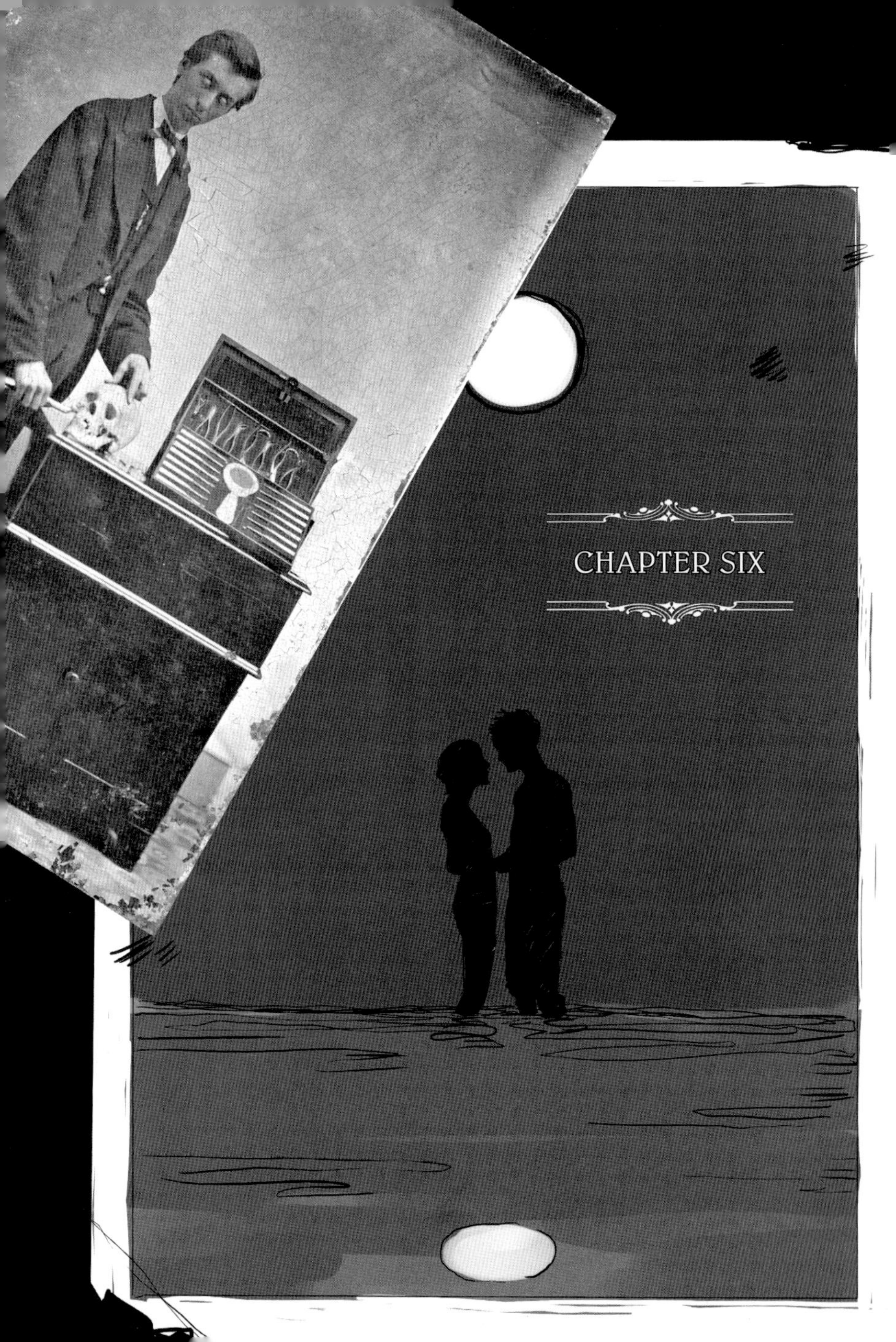

CHAPTER SIX

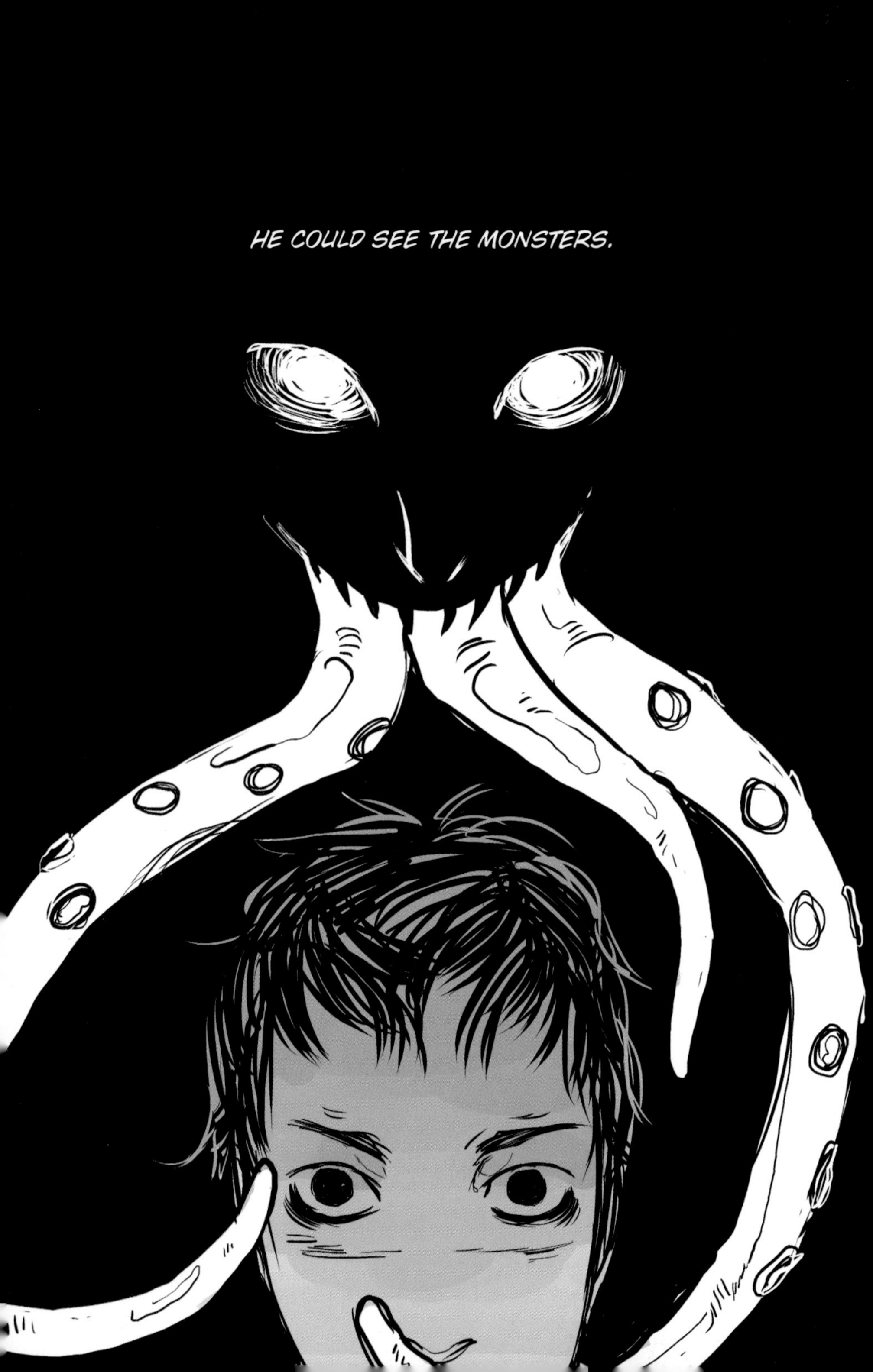
HE COULD SEE THE MONSTERS.

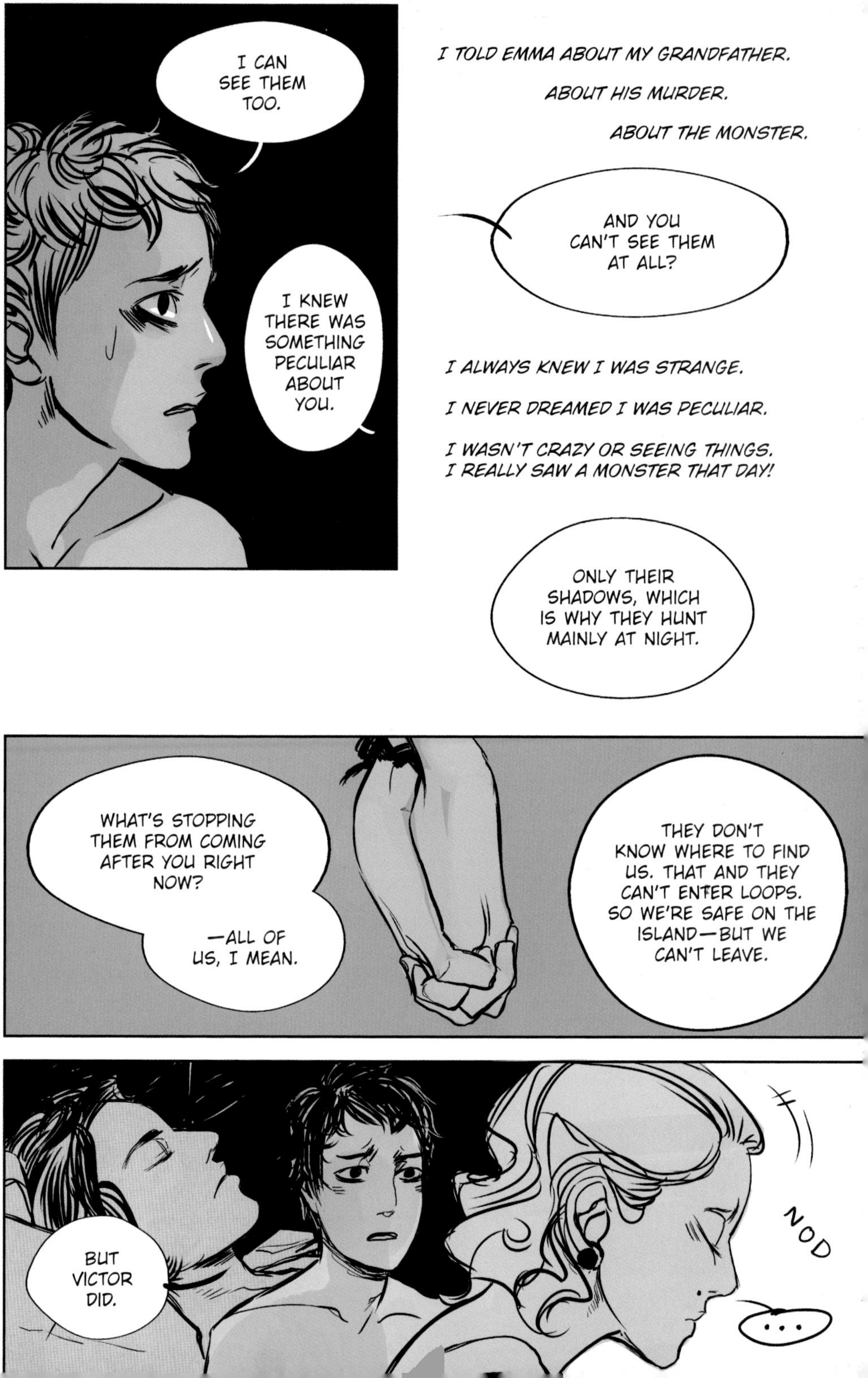
I CAN SEE THEM TOO.
I KNEW THERE WAS SOMETHING PECULIAR ABOUT YOU.
I TOLD EMMA ABOUT MY GRANDFATHER.
ABOUT HIS MURDER.
ABOUT THE MONSTER.
AND YOU CAN'T SEE THEM AT ALL?
I ALWAYS KNEW I WAS STRANGE.
I NEVER DREAMED I WAS PECULIAR.
I WASN'T CRAZY OR SEEING THINGS. I REALLY SAW A MONSTER THAT DAY!
ONLY THEIR SHADOWS, WHICH IS WHY THEY HUNT MAINLY AT NIGHT.
WHAT'S STOPPING THEM FROM COMING AFTER YOU RIGHT NOW?
—ALL OF US, I MEAN.
THEY DON'T KNOW WHERE TO FIND US. THAT AND THEY CAN'T ENTER LOOPS. SO WE'RE SAFE ON THE ISLAND—BUT WE CAN'T LEAVE.
BUT VICTOR DID.
NOD
...

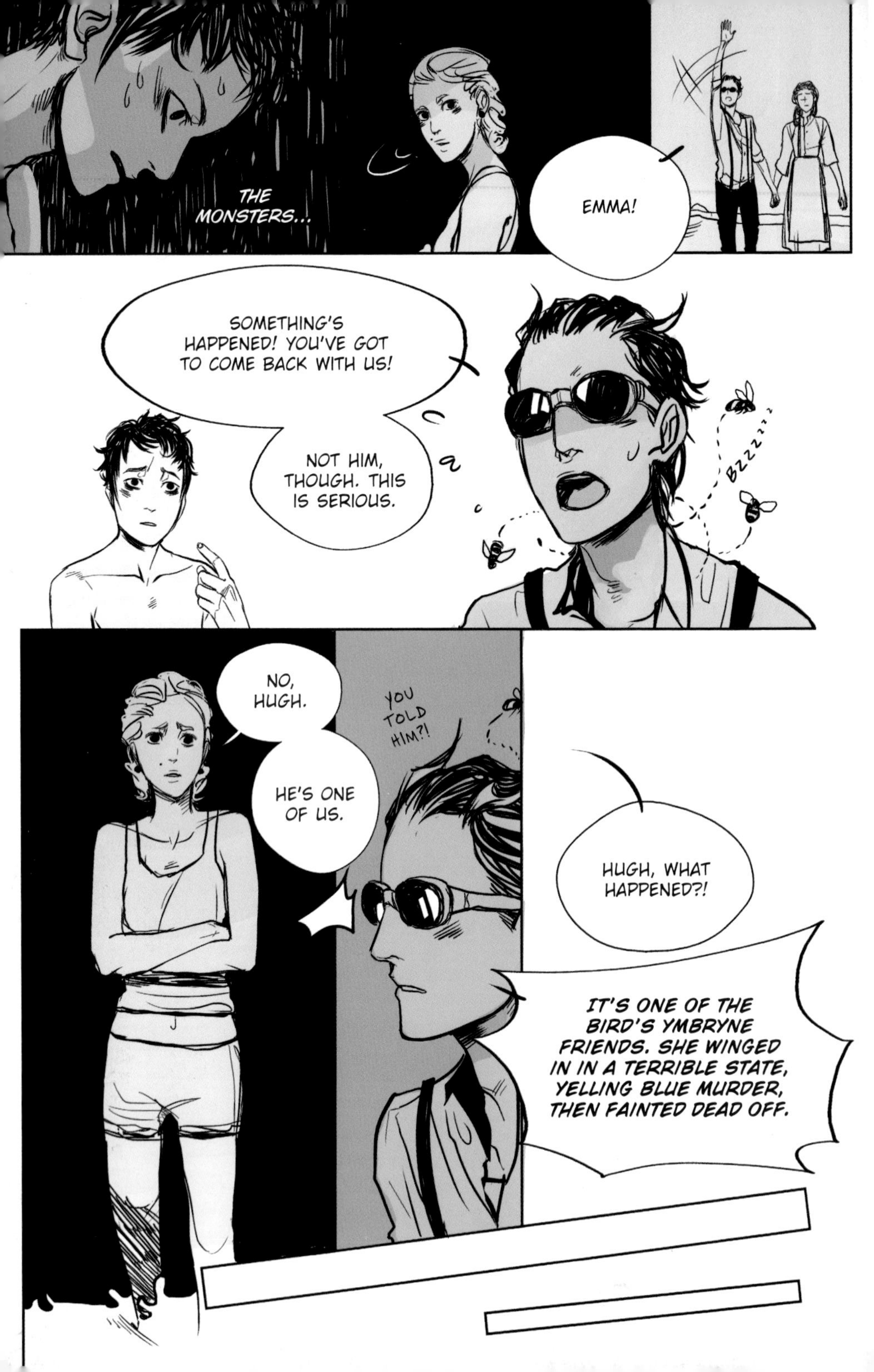
THE MONSTERS...
EMMA!
SOMETHING'S HAPPENED! YOU'VE GOT TO COME BACK WITH US!
NOT HIM, THOUGH. THIS IS SERIOUS.
BZZZZZZ
NO, HUGH.
HE'S ONE OF US.
YOU TOLD HIM?!
HUGH, WHAT HAPPENED?!
IT'S ONE OF THE BIRD'S YMBRYNE FRIENDS. SHE WINGED IN IN A TERRIBLE STATE, YELLING BLUE MURDER, THEN FAINTED DEAD OFF.

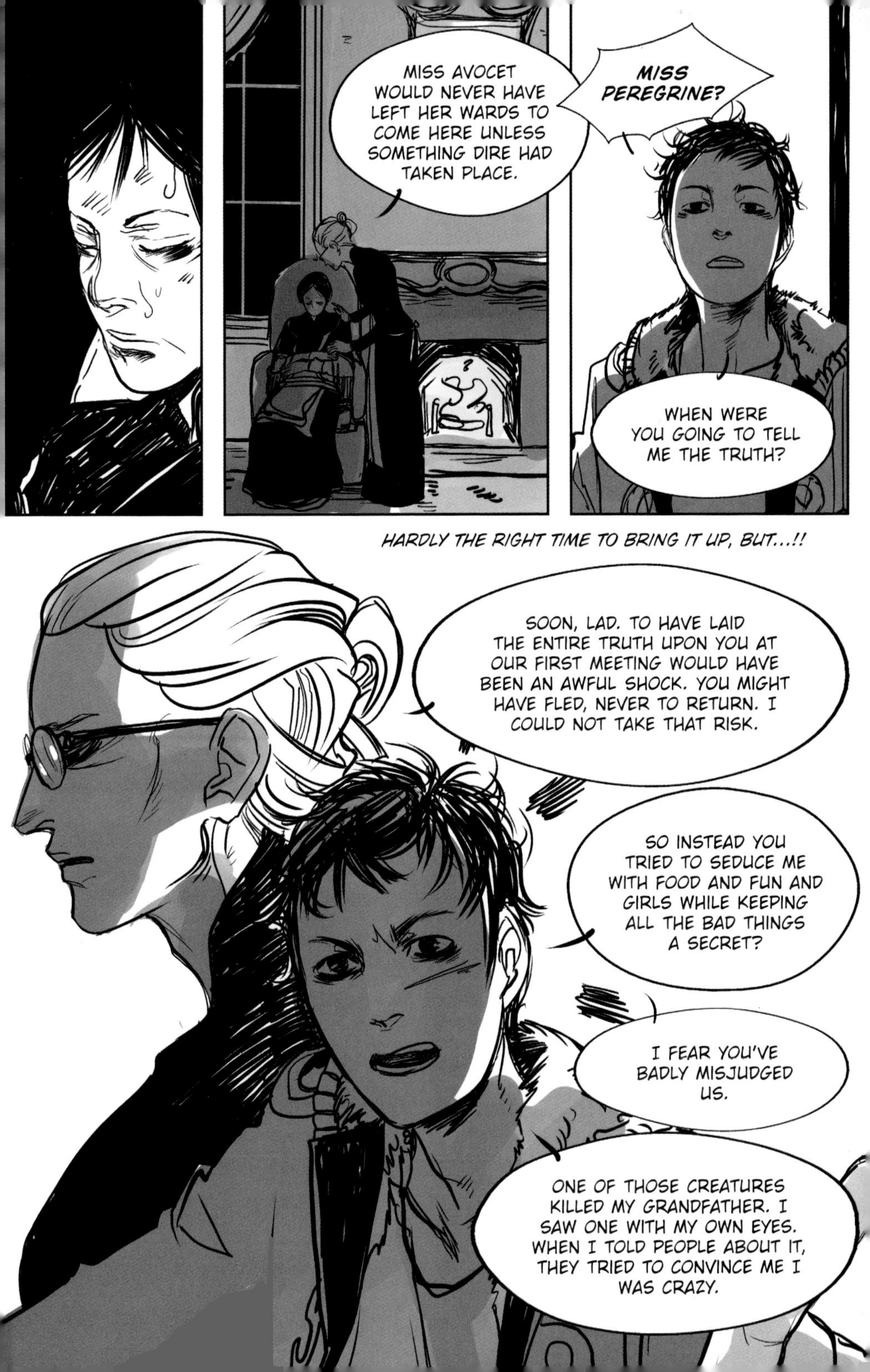
MISS AVOCET WOULD NEVER HAVE LEFT HER WARDS TO COME HERE UNLESS SOMETHING DIRE HAD TAKEN PLACE.
MISS PEREGRINE?
WHEN WERE YOU GOING TO TELL ME THE TRUTH?
HARDLY THE RIGHT TIME TO BRING IT UP, BUT...!!
SOON, LAD. TO HAVE LAID THE ENTIRE TRUTH UPON YOU AT OUR FIRST MEETING WOULD HAVE BEEN AN AWFUL SHOCK. YOU MIGHT HAVE FLED, NEVER TO RETURN. I COULD NOT TAKE THAT RISK.
SO INSTEAD YOU TRIED TO SEDUCE ME WITH FOOD AND FUN AND GIRLS WHILE KEEPING ALL THE BAD THINGS A SECRET?
I FEAR YOU'VE BADLY MISJUDGED US.
ONE OF THOSE CREATURES KILLED MY GRANDFATHER. I SAW ONE WITH MY OWN EYES. WHEN I TOLD PEOPLE ABOUT IT, THEY TRIED TO CONVINCE ME I WAS CRAZY.

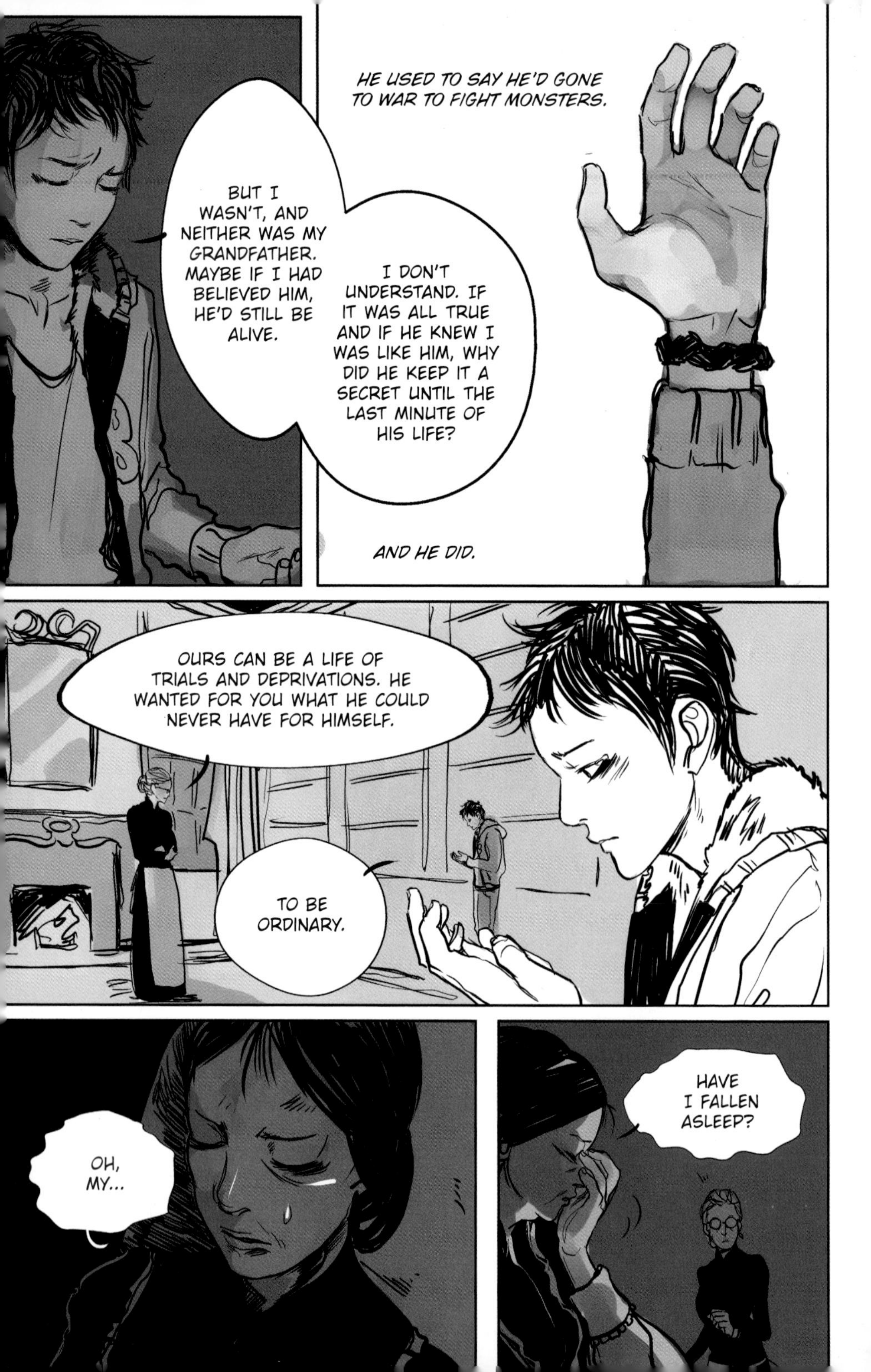
BUT I WASN'T, AND NEITHER WAS MY GRANDFATHER. MAYBE IF I HAD BELIEVED HIM, HE'D STILL BE ALIVE.
I DON'T UNDERSTAND. IF IT WAS ALL TRUE AND IF HE KNEW I WAS LIKE HIM, WHY DID HE KEEP IT A SECRET UNTIL THE LAST MINUTE OF HIS LIFE?
HE USED TO SAY HE'D GONE TO WAR TO FIGHT MONSTERS.
AND HE DID.
OURS CAN BE A LIFE OF TRIALS AND DEPRIVATIONS. HE WANTED FOR YOU WHAT HE COULD NEVER HAVE FOR HIMSELF.
TO BE ORDINARY.
OH, MY...
HAVE I FALLEN ASLEEP?

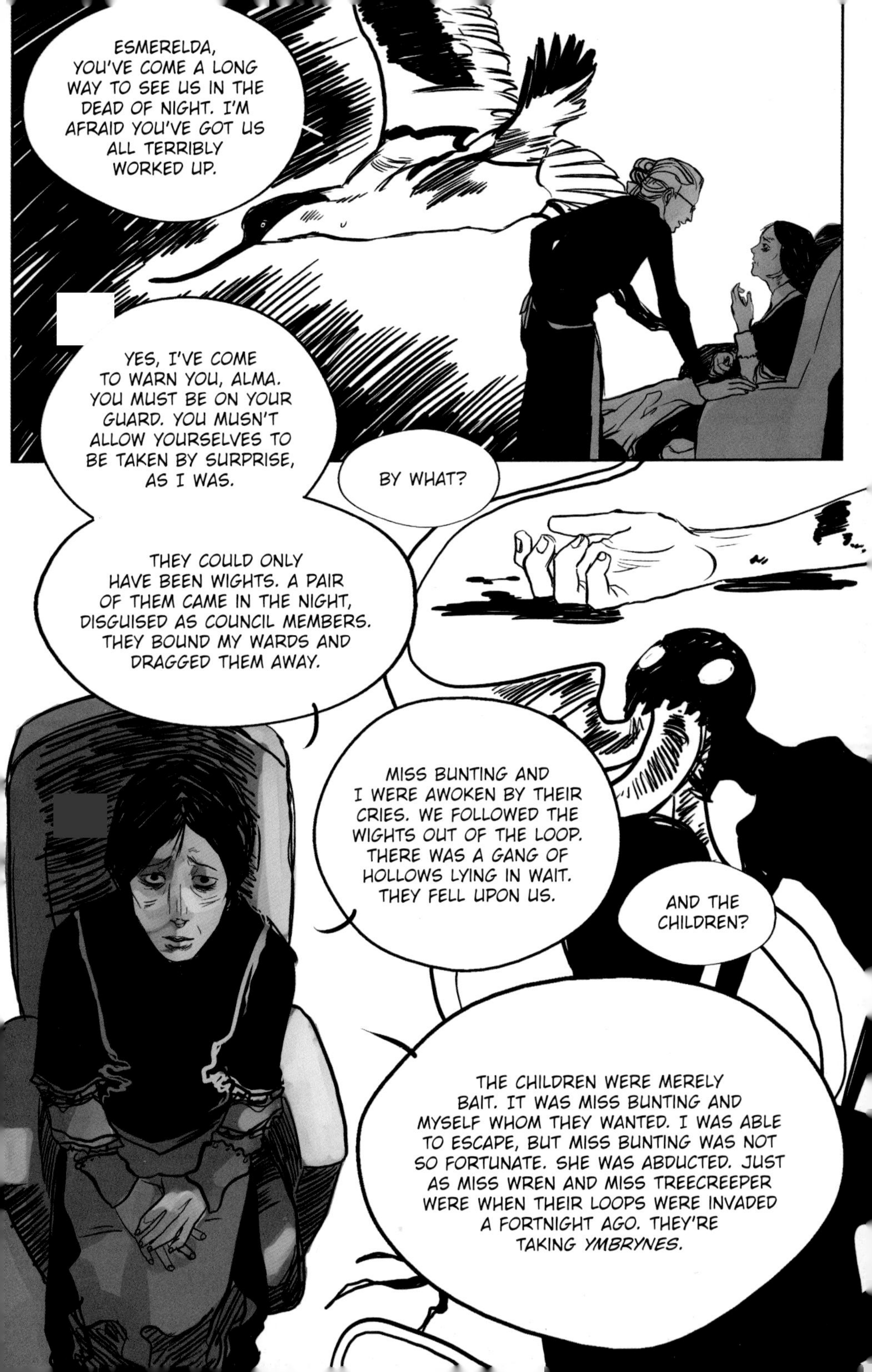
ESMERELDA, YOU'VE COME A LONG WAY TO SEE US IN THE DEAD OF NIGHT. I'M AFRAID YOU'VE GOT US ALL TERRIBLY WORKED UP.
YES, I'VE COME TO WARN YOU, ALMA. YOU MUST BE ON YOUR GUARD. YOU MUSN'T ALLOW YOURSELVES TO BE TAKEN BY SURPRISE, AS I WAS.
BY WHAT?
THEY COULD ONLY HAVE BEEN WIGHTS. A PAIR OF THEM CAME IN THE NIGHT, DISGUISED AS COUNCIL MEMBERS. THEY BOUND MY WARDS AND DRAGGED THEM AWAY.
MISS BUNTING AND I WERE AWOKEN BY THEIR CRIES. WE FOLLOWED THE WIGHTS OUT OF THE LOOP. THERE WAS A GANG OF HOLLOWS LYING IN WAIT. THEY FELL UPON US.
AND THE CHILDREN?
THE CHILDREN WERE MERELY BAIT. IT WAS MISS BUNTING AND MYSELF WHOM THEY WANTED. I WAS ABLE TO ESCAPE, BUT MISS BUNTING WAS NOT SO FORTUNATE. SHE WAS ABDUCTED. JUST AS MISS WREN AND MISS TREECREEPER WERE WHEN THEIR LOOPS WERE INVADED A FORTNIGHT AGO. THEY'RE TAKING *YMBRYNES.*

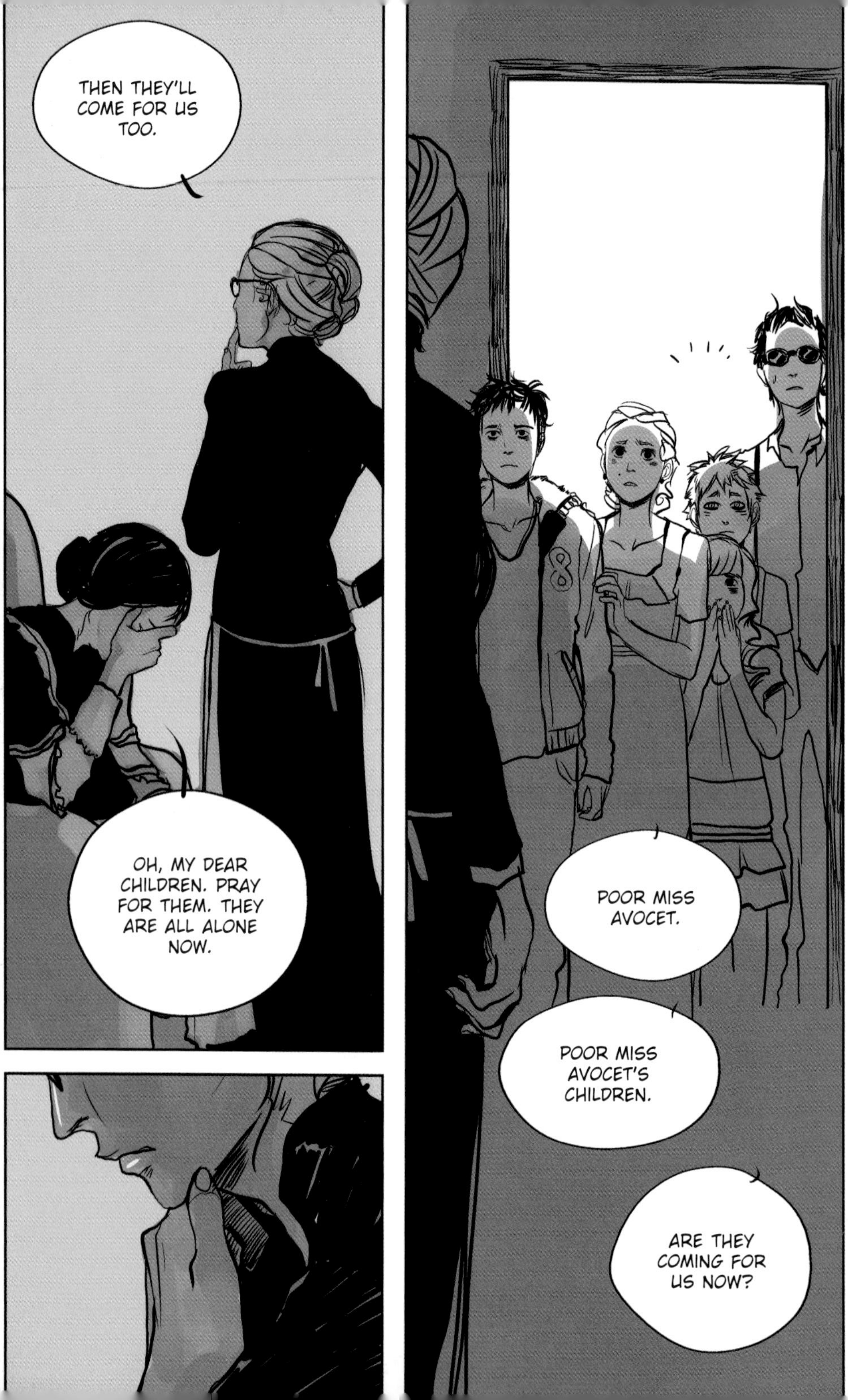
THEN THEY'LL COME FOR US TOO.
OH, MY DEAR CHILDREN. PRAY FOR THEM. THEY ARE ALL ALONE NOW.
POOR MISS AVOCET.
POOR MISS AVOCET'S CHILDREN.
ARE THEY COMING FOR US NOW?

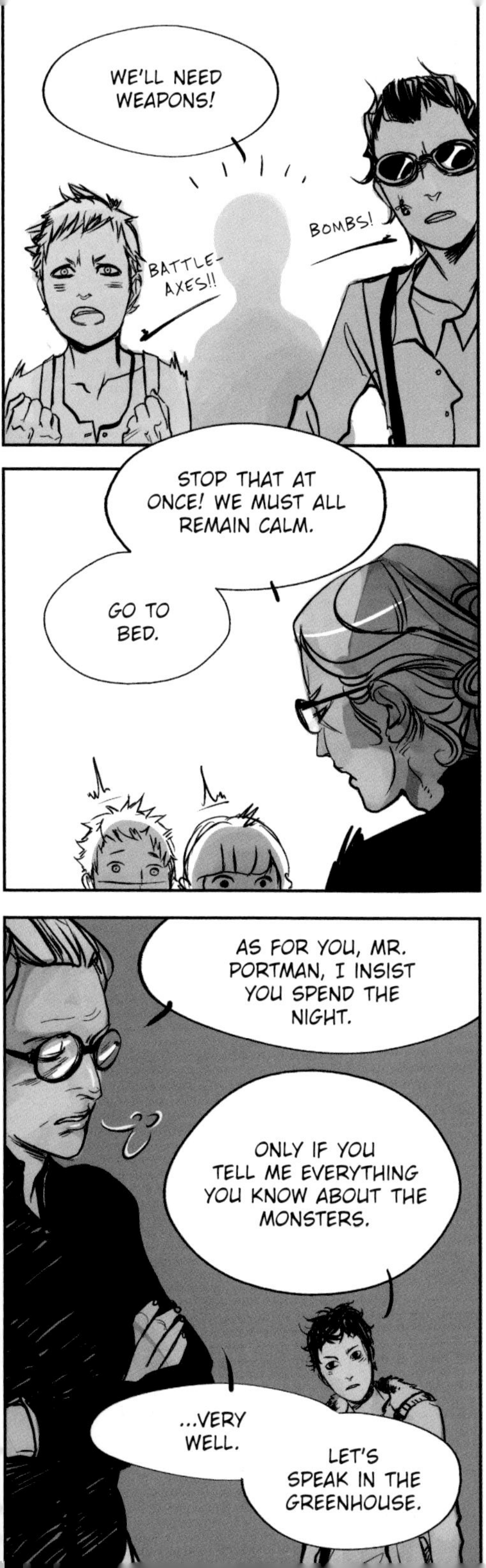
WE'LL NEED WEAPONS!
BATTLE-AXES!!
BOMBS!
STOP THAT AT ONCE! WE MUST ALL REMAIN CALM.
GO TO BED.
AS FOR YOU, MR. PORTMAN, I INSIST YOU SPEND THE NIGHT.
ONLY IF YOU TELL ME EVERYTHING YOU KNOW ABOUT THE MONSTERS.
...VERY WELL.
LET'S SPEAK IN THE GREENHOUSE.
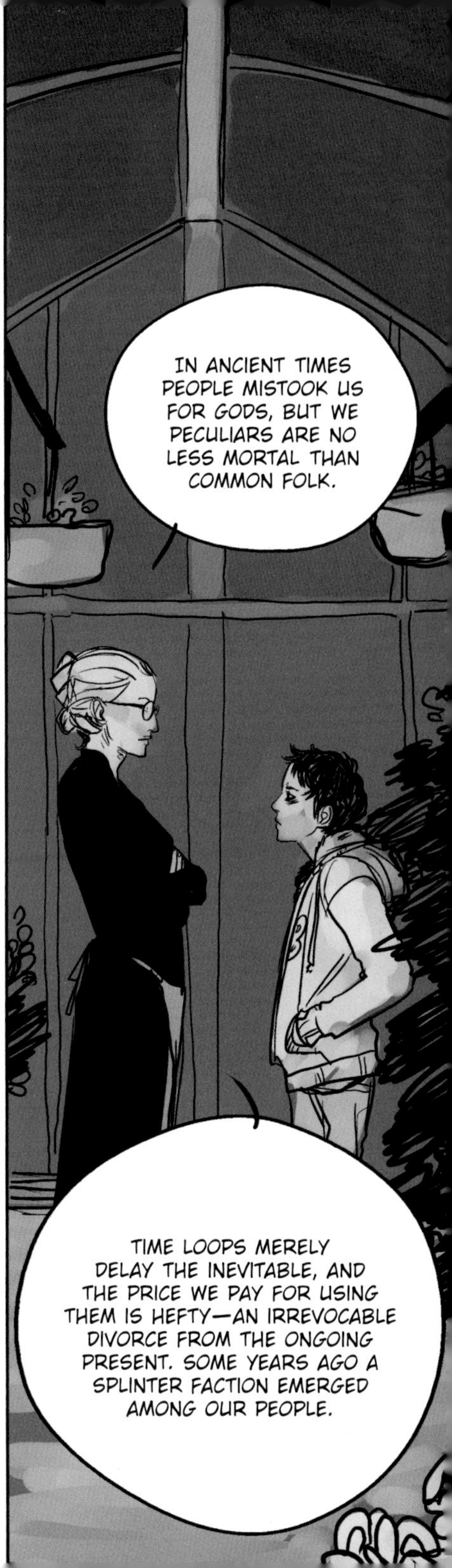
IN ANCIENT TIMES PEOPLE MISTOOK US FOR GODS, BUT WE PECULIARS ARE NO LESS MORTAL THAN COMMON FOLK.
TIME LOOPS MERELY DELAY THE INEVITABLE, AND THE PRICE WE PAY FOR USING THEM IS HEFTY—AN IRREVOCABLE DIVORCE FROM THE ONGOING PRESENT. SOME YEARS AGO A SPLINTER FACTION EMERGED AMONG OUR PEOPLE.

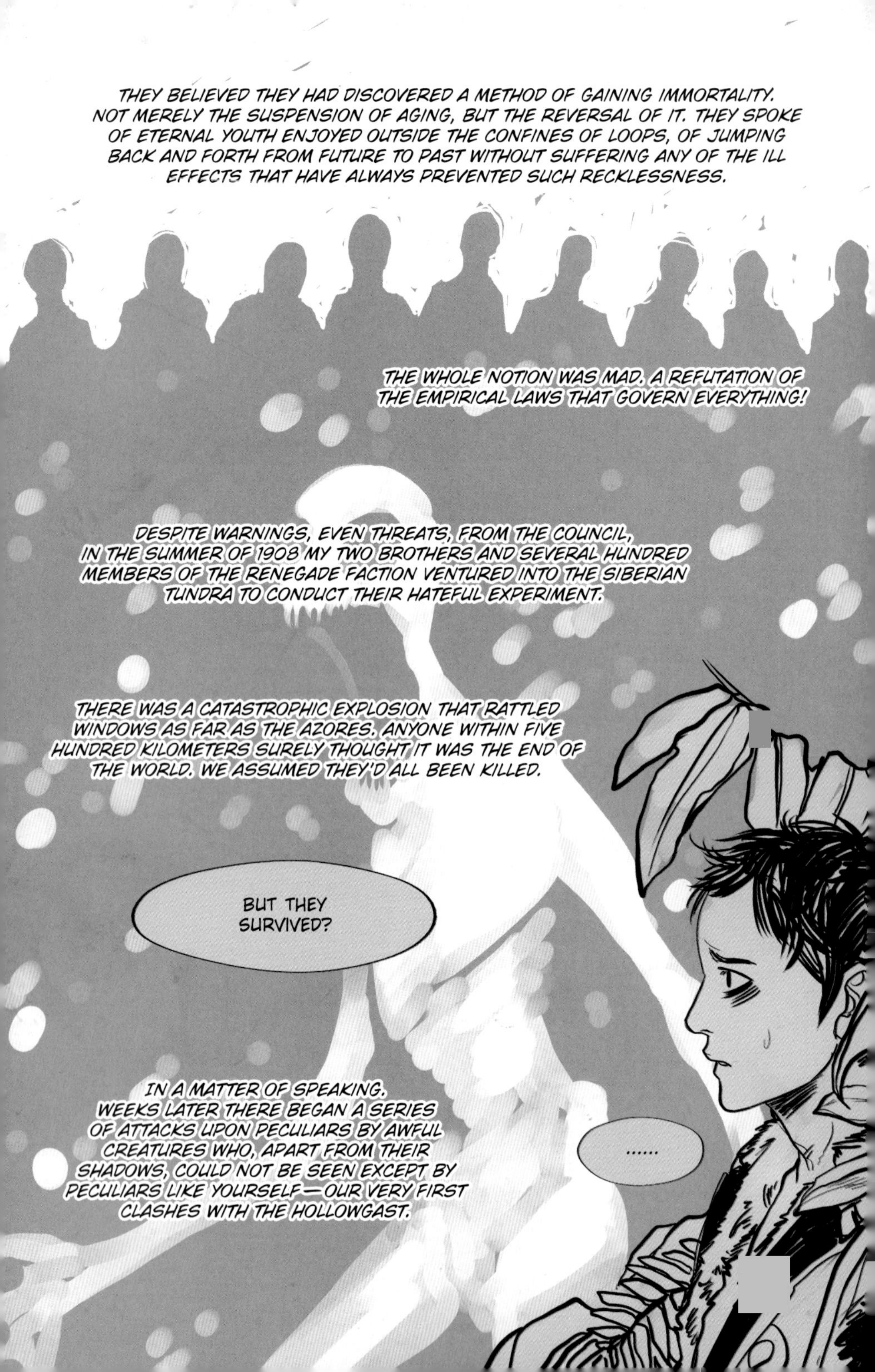
THEY BELIEVED THEY HAD DISCOVERED A METHOD OF GAINING IMMORTALITY. NOT MERELY THE SUSPENSION OF AGING, BUT THE REVERSAL OF IT. THEY SPOKE OF ETERNAL YOUTH ENJOYED OUTSIDE THE CONFINES OF LOOPS, OF JUMPING BACK AND FORTH FROM FUTURE TO PAST WITHOUT SUFFERING ANY OF THE ILL EFFECTS THAT HAVE ALWAYS PREVENTED SUCH RECKLESSNESS.
THE WHOLE NOTION WAS MAD. A REFUTATION OF THE EMPIRICAL LAWS THAT GOVERN EVERYTHING!
DESPITE WARNINGS, EVEN THREATS, FROM THE COUNCIL, IN THE SUMMER OF 1908 MY TWO BROTHERS AND SEVERAL HUNDRED MEMBERS OF THE RENEGADE FACTION VENTURED INTO THE SIBERIAN TUNDRA TO CONDUCT THEIR HATEFUL EXPERIMENT.
THERE WAS A CATASTROPHIC EXPLOSION THAT RATTLED WINDOWS AS FAR AS THE AZORES. ANYONE WITHIN FIVE HUNDRED KILOMETERS SURELY THOUGHT IT WAS THE END OF THE WORLD. WE ASSUMED THEY'D ALL BEEN KILLED.
BUT THEY SURVIVED?
IN A MATTER OF SPEAKING. WEEKS LATER THERE BEGAN A SERIES OF ATTACKS UPON PECULIARS BY AWFUL CREATURES WHO, APART FROM THEIR SHADOWS, COULD NOT BE SEEN EXCEPT BY PECULIARS LIKE YOURSELF—OUR VERY FIRST CLASHES WITH THE HOLLOWGAST.
......

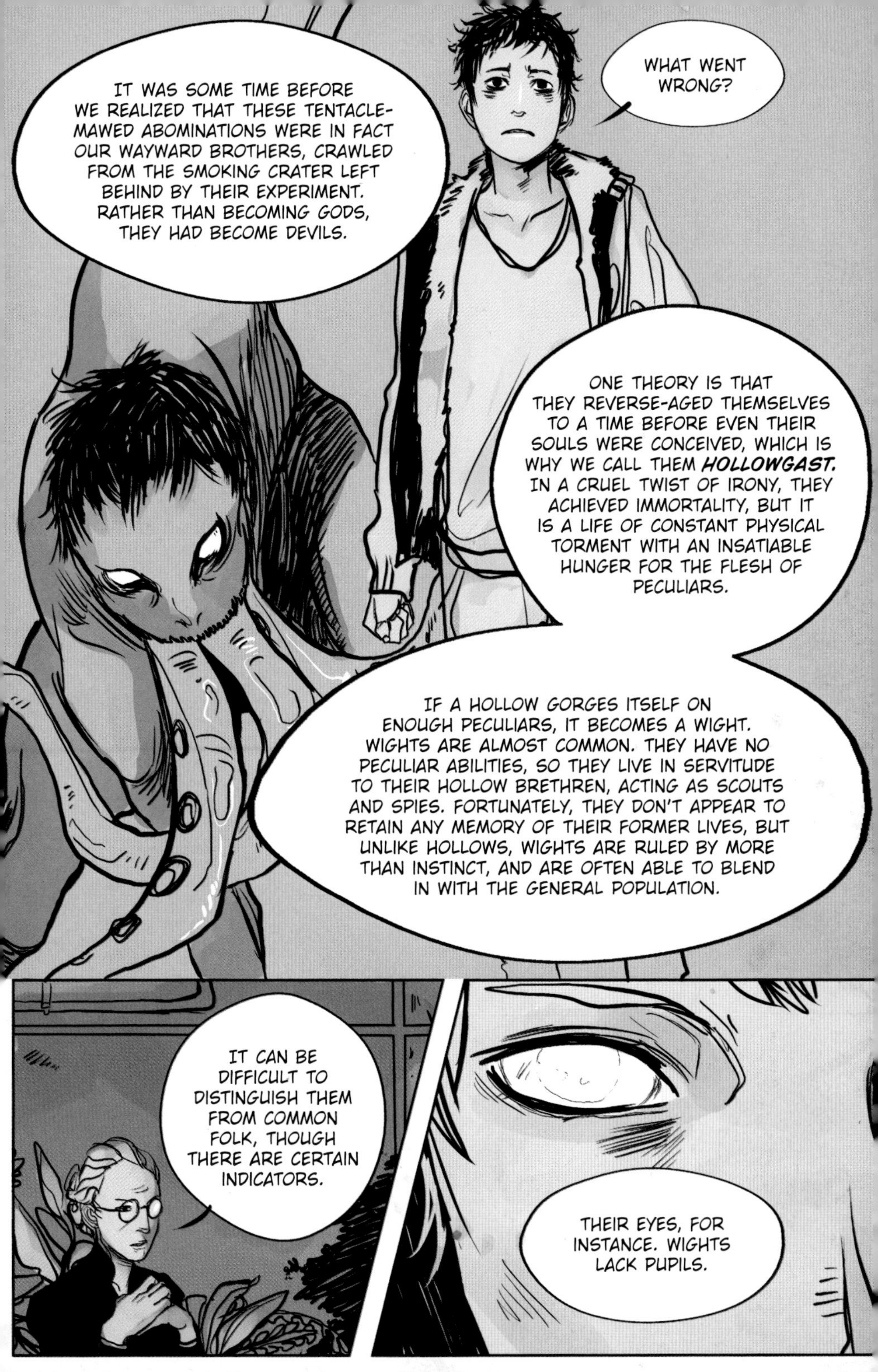
IT WAS SOME TIME BEFORE WE REALIZED THAT THESE TENTACLE-MAWED ABOMINATIONS WERE IN FACT OUR WAYWARD BROTHERS, CRAWLED FROM THE SMOKING CRATER LEFT BEHIND BY THEIR EXPERIMENT. RATHER THAN BECOMING GODS, THEY HAD BECOME DEVILS.
WHAT WENT WRONG?
ONE THEORY IS THAT THEY REVERSE-AGED THEMSELVES TO A TIME BEFORE EVEN THEIR SOULS WERE CONCEIVED, WHICH IS WHY WE CALL THEM ***HOLLOWGAST.*** IN A CRUEL TWIST OF IRONY, THEY ACHIEVED IMMORTALITY, BUT IT IS A LIFE OF CONSTANT PHYSICAL TORMENT WITH AN INSATIABLE HUNGER FOR THE FLESH OF PECULIARS.
IF A HOLLOW GORGES ITSELF ON ENOUGH PECULIARS, IT BECOMES A WIGHT. WIGHTS ARE ALMOST COMMON. THEY HAVE NO PECULIAR ABILITIES, SO THEY LIVE IN SERVITUDE TO THEIR HOLLOW BRETHREN, ACTING AS SCOUTS AND SPIES. FORTUNATELY, THEY DON'T APPEAR TO RETAIN ANY MEMORY OF THEIR FORMER LIVES, BUT UNLIKE HOLLOWS, WIGHTS ARE RULED BY MORE THAN INSTINCT, AND ARE OFTEN ABLE TO BLEND IN WITH THE GENERAL POPULATION.
IT CAN BE DIFFICULT TO DISTINGUISH THEM FROM COMMON FOLK, THOUGH THERE ARE CERTAIN INDICATORS.
THEIR EYES, FOR INSTANCE. WIGHTS LACK PUPILS.

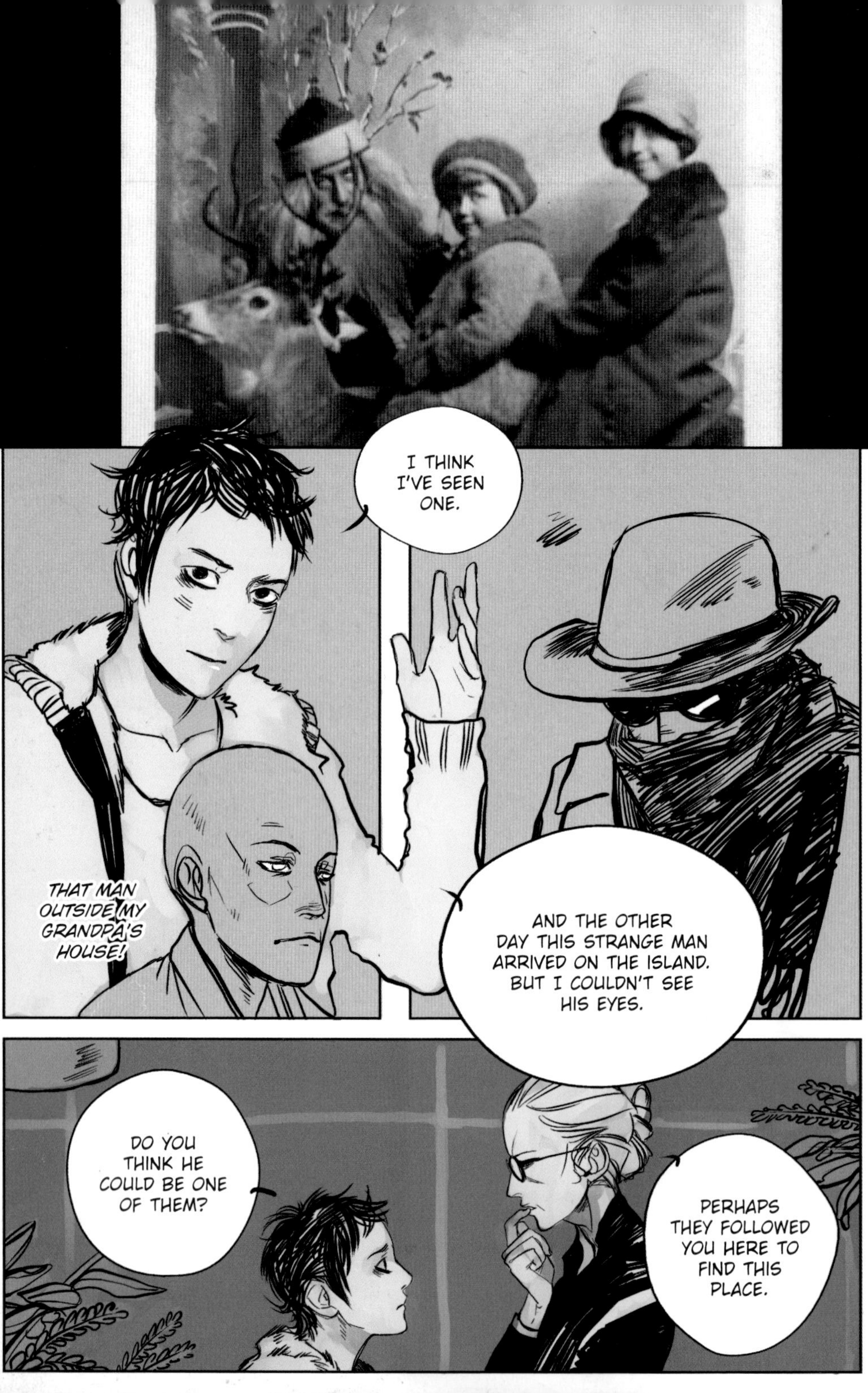
I THINK I'VE SEEN ONE.
THAT MAN OUTSIDE MY GRANDPA'S HOUSE!
AND THE OTHER DAY THIS STRANGE MAN ARRIVED ON THE ISLAND. BUT I COULDN'T SEE HIS EYES.
DO YOU THINK HE COULD BE ONE OF THEM?
PERHAPS THEY FOLLOWED YOU HERE TO FIND THIS PLACE.

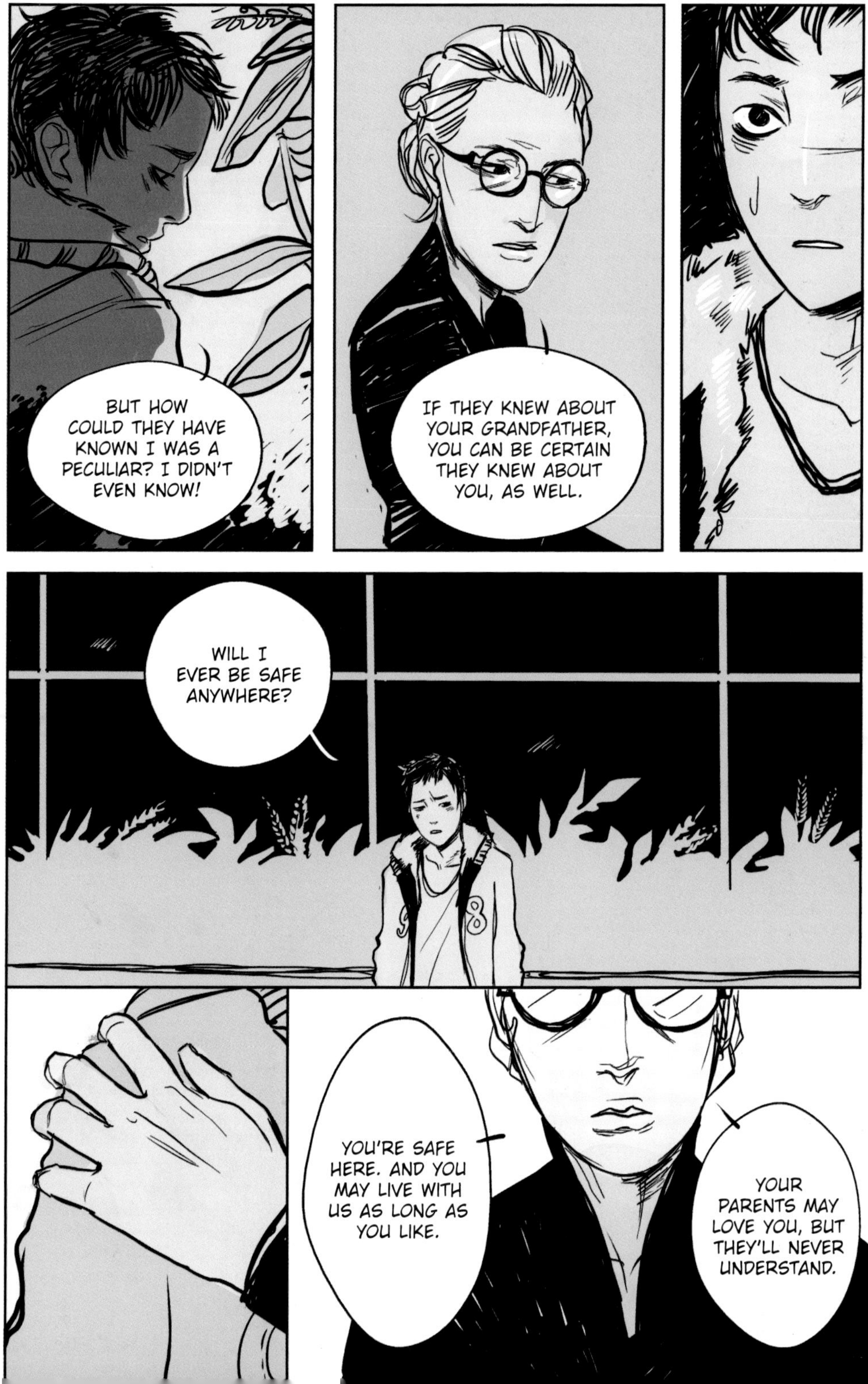
BUT HOW COULD THEY HAVE KNOWN I WAS A PECULIAR? I DIDN'T EVEN KNOW!
IF THEY KNEW ABOUT YOUR GRANDFATHER, YOU CAN BE CERTAIN THEY KNEW ABOUT YOU, AS WELL.
WILL I EVER BE SAFE ANYWHERE?
YOU'RE SAFE HERE. AND YOU MAY LIVE WITH US AS LONG AS YOU LIKE.
YOUR PARENTS MAY LOVE YOU, BUT THEY'LL NEVER UNDERSTAND.

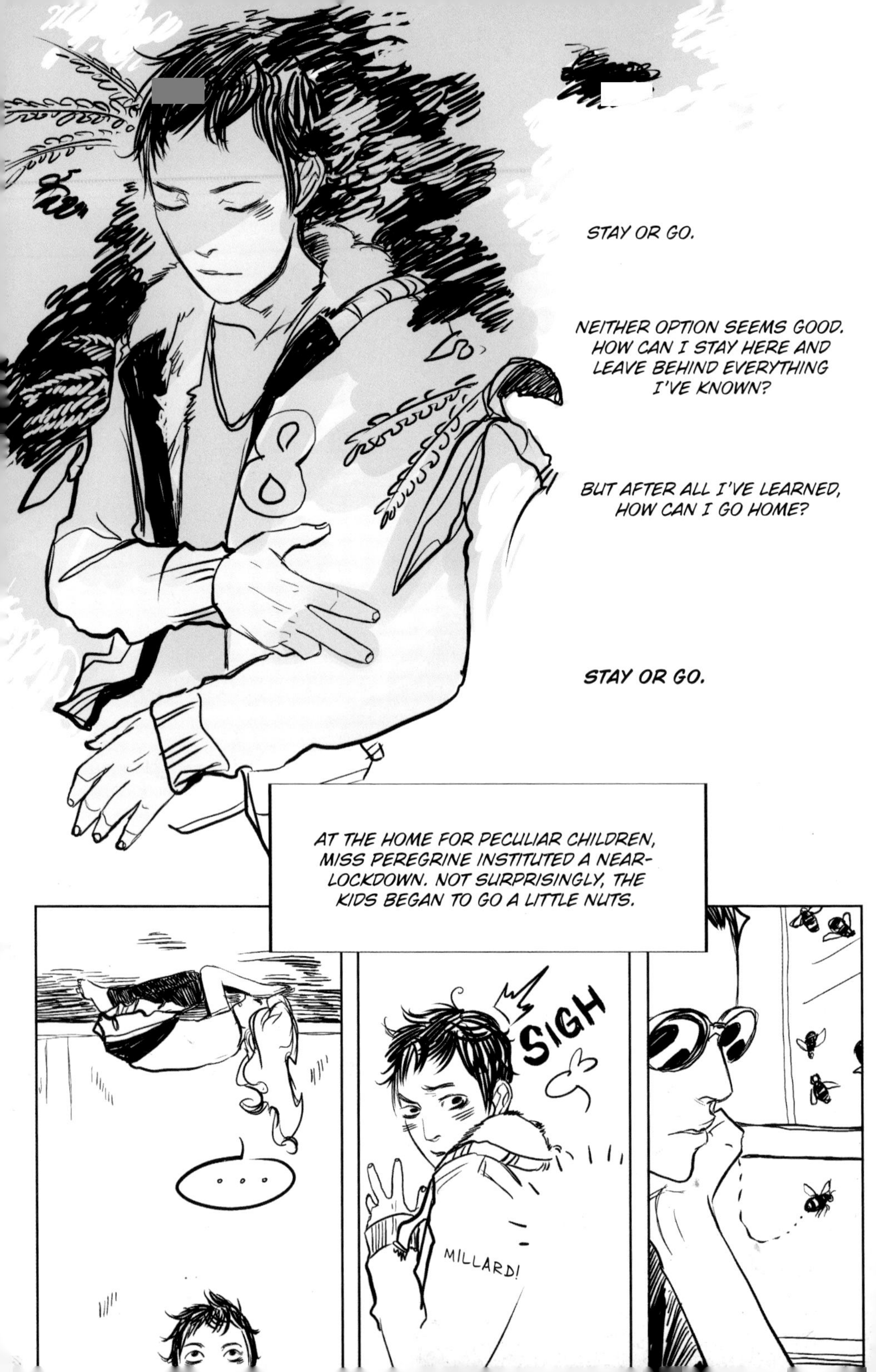
STAY OR GO.
NEITHER OPTION SEEMS GOOD. HOW CAN I STAY HERE AND LEAVE BEHIND EVERYTHING I'VE KNOWN?
BUT AFTER ALL I'VE LEARNED, HOW CAN I GO HOME?
STAY OR GO.
AT THE HOME FOR PECULIAR CHILDREN, MISS PEREGRINE INSTITUTED A NEAR-LOCKDOWN. NOT SURPRISINGLY, THE KIDS BEGAN TO GO A LITTLE NUTS.
...
SIGH
MILLARD!

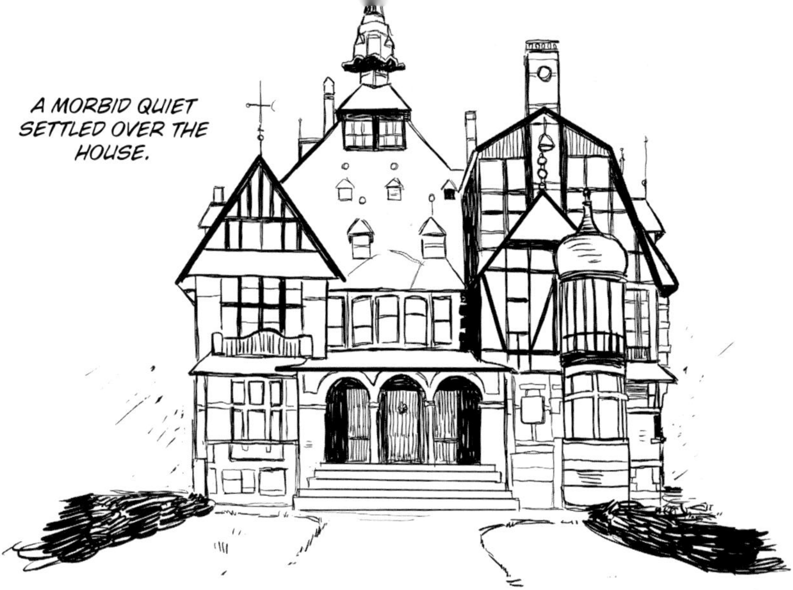
A MORBID QUIET SETTLED OVER THE HOUSE.

EMMA KEPT PUSHING FOR ME TO STAY.

MISS PEREGRINE WOULDN'T DISCUSS IT.

AND I WAS RUNNING OUT OF TIME TO DECIDE.

SOON OUR TRIP WOULD END.

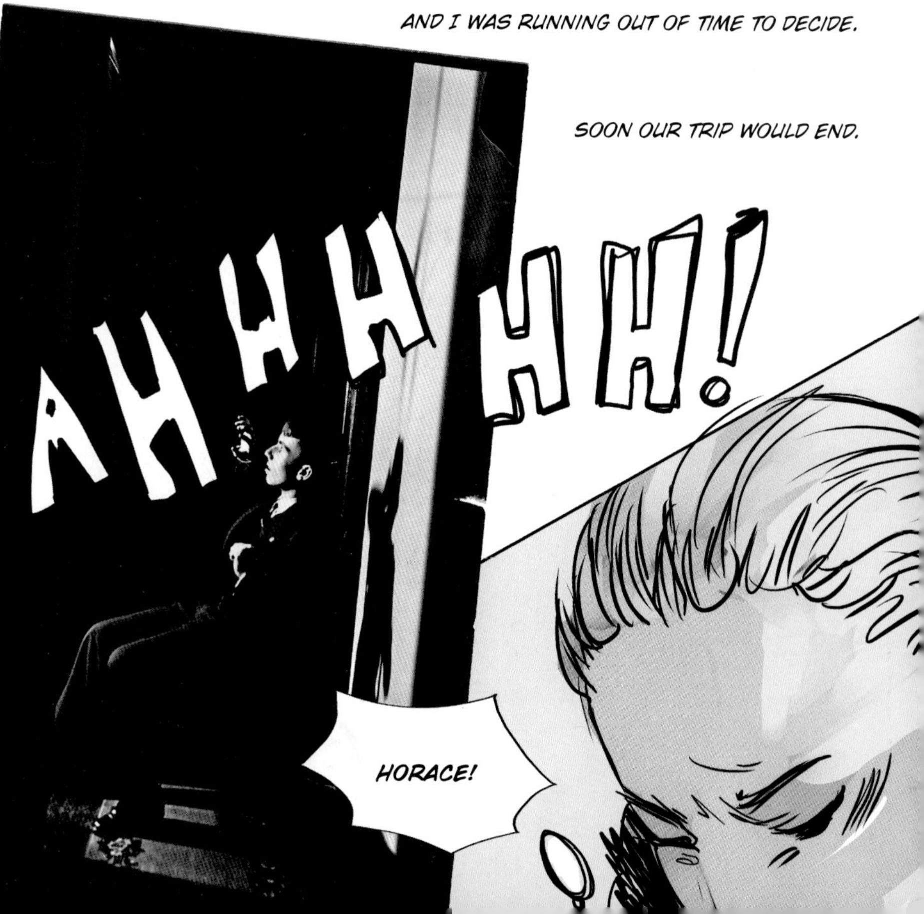
AHHHHHH!
HORACE!

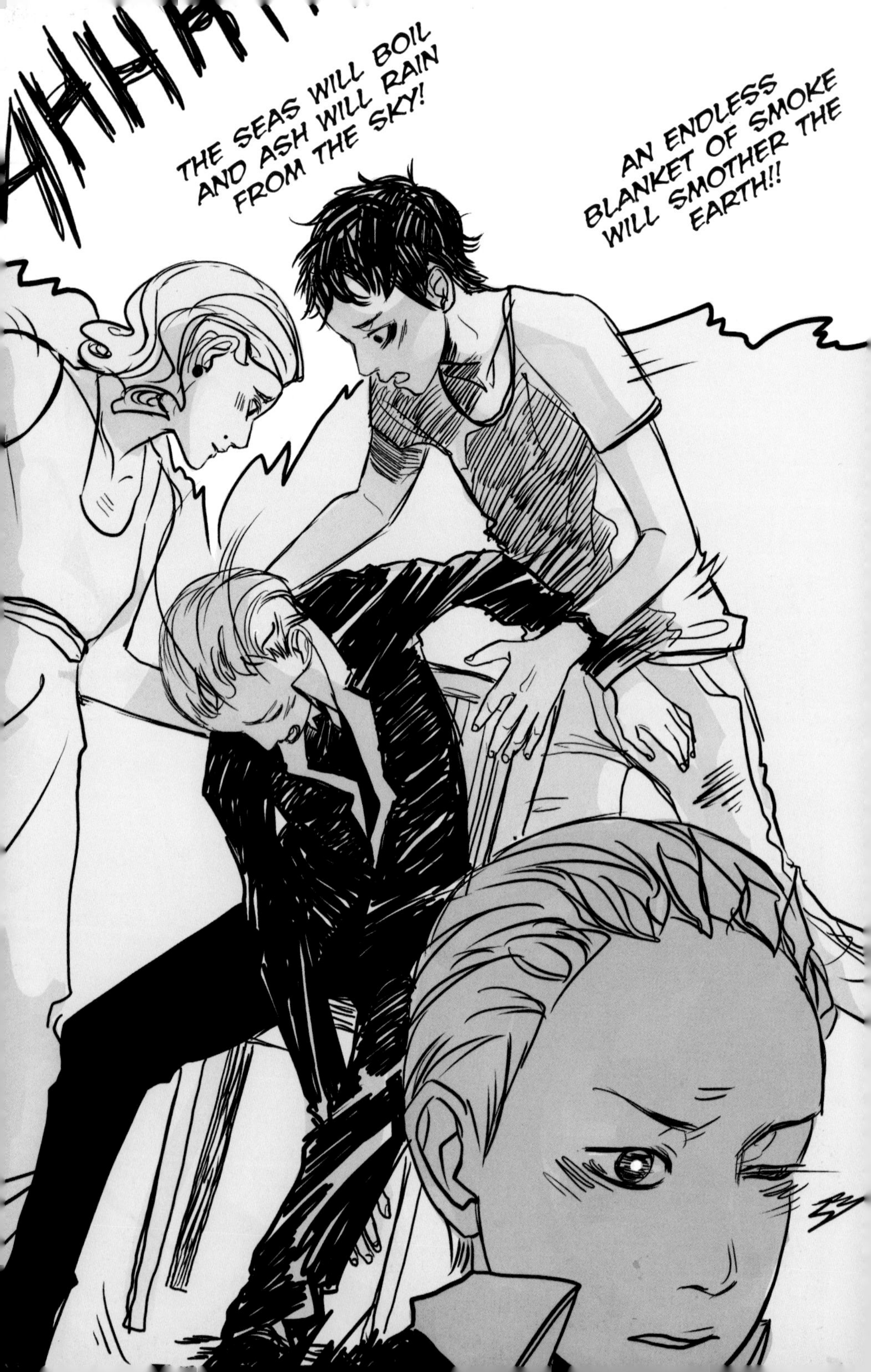
AHHH!!
THE SEAS WILL BOIL AND ASH WILL RAIN FROM THE SKY!
AN ENDLESS BLANKET OF SMOKE WILL SMOTHER THE EARTH!!

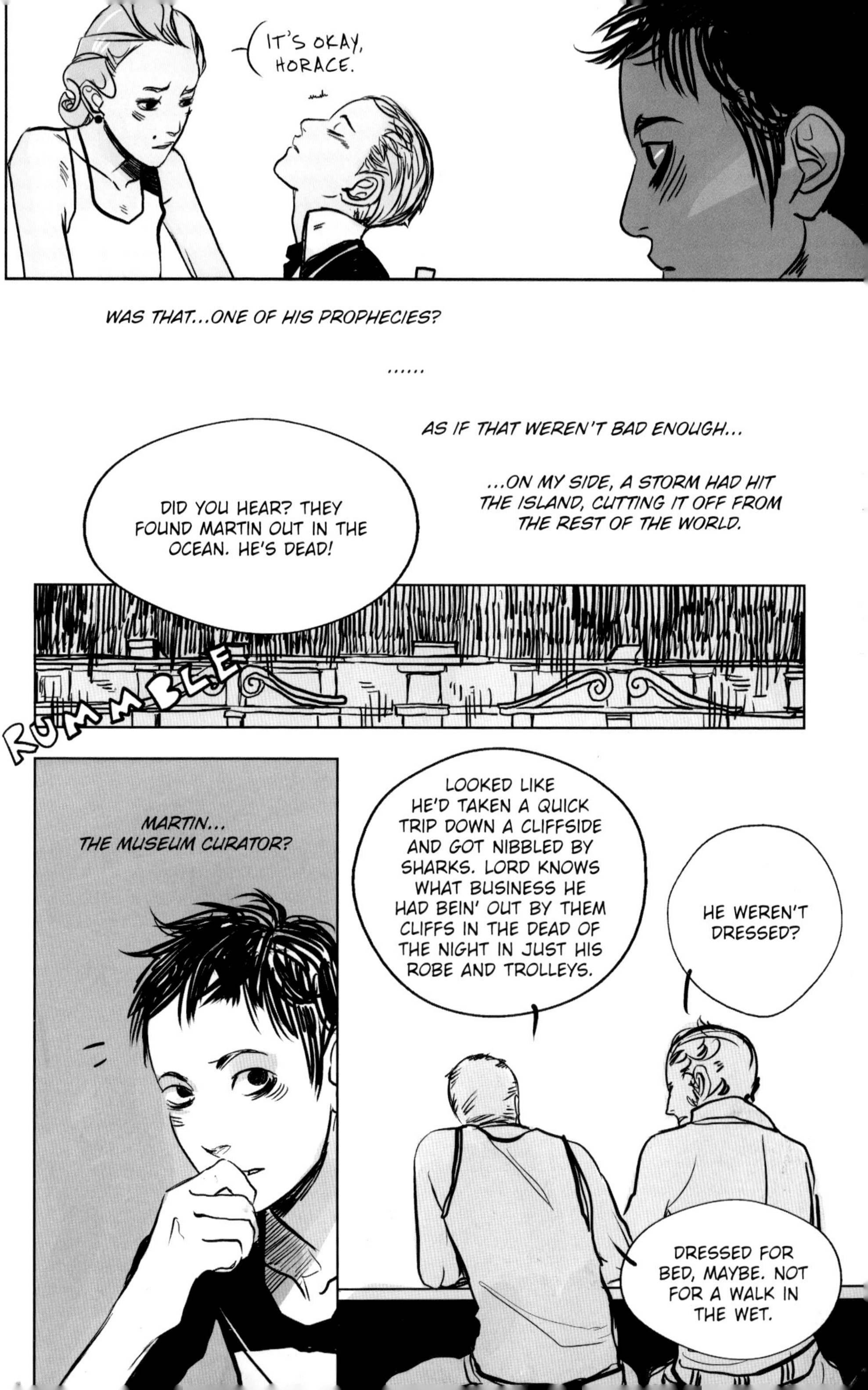
IT'S OKAY, HORACE.
WAS THAT...ONE OF HIS PROPHECIES?
......
AS IF THAT WEREN'T BAD ENOUGH...
...ON MY SIDE, A STORM HAD HIT THE ISLAND, CUTTING IT OFF FROM THE REST OF THE WORLD.
DID YOU HEAR? THEY FOUND MARTIN OUT IN THE OCEAN. HE'S DEAD!
RUMMBLE
MARTIN... THE MUSEUM CURATOR?
LOOKED LIKE HE'D TAKEN A QUICK TRIP DOWN A CLIFFSIDE AND GOT NIBBLED BY SHARKS. LORD KNOWS WHAT BUSINESS HE HAD BEIN' OUT BY THEM CLIFFS IN THE DEAD OF THE NIGHT IN JUST HIS ROBE AND TROLLEYS.
HE WEREN'T DRESSED?
DRESSED FOR BED, MAYBE. NOT FOR A WALK IN THE WET.

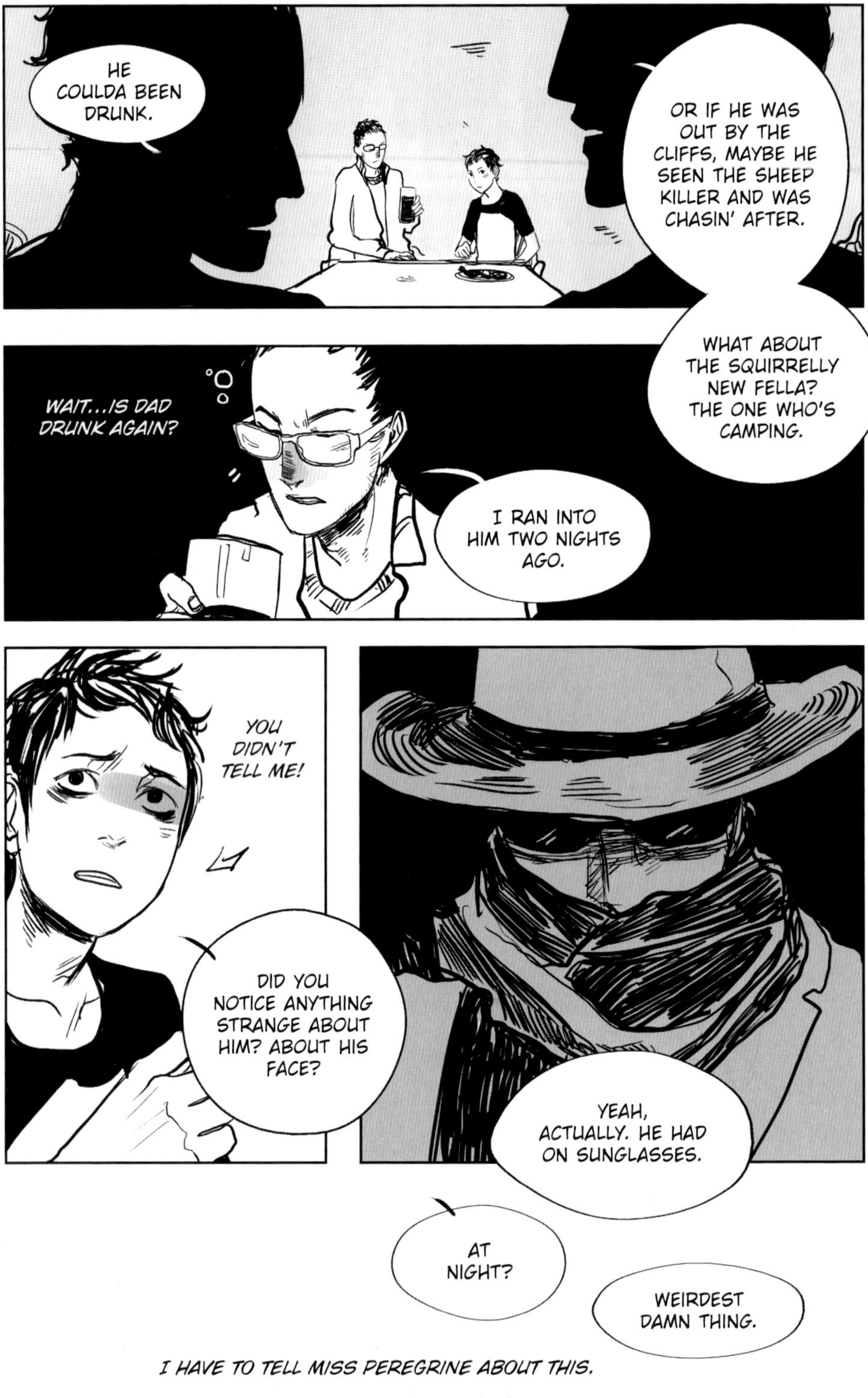
HE COULDA BEEN DRUNK.
OR IF HE WAS OUT BY THE CLIFFS, MAYBE HE SEEN THE SHEEP KILLER AND WAS CHASIN' AFTER.
WHAT ABOUT THE SQUIRRELLY NEW FELLA? THE ONE WHO'S CAMPING.
WAIT...IS DAD DRUNK AGAIN?
I RAN INTO HIM TWO NIGHTS AGO.
YOU DIDN'T TELL ME!
DID YOU NOTICE ANYTHING STRANGE ABOUT HIM? ABOUT HIS FACE?
YEAH, ACTUALLY. HE HAD ON SUNGLASSES.
AT NIGHT?
WEIRDEST DAMN THING.
I HAVE TO TELL MISS PEREGRINE ABOUT THIS.

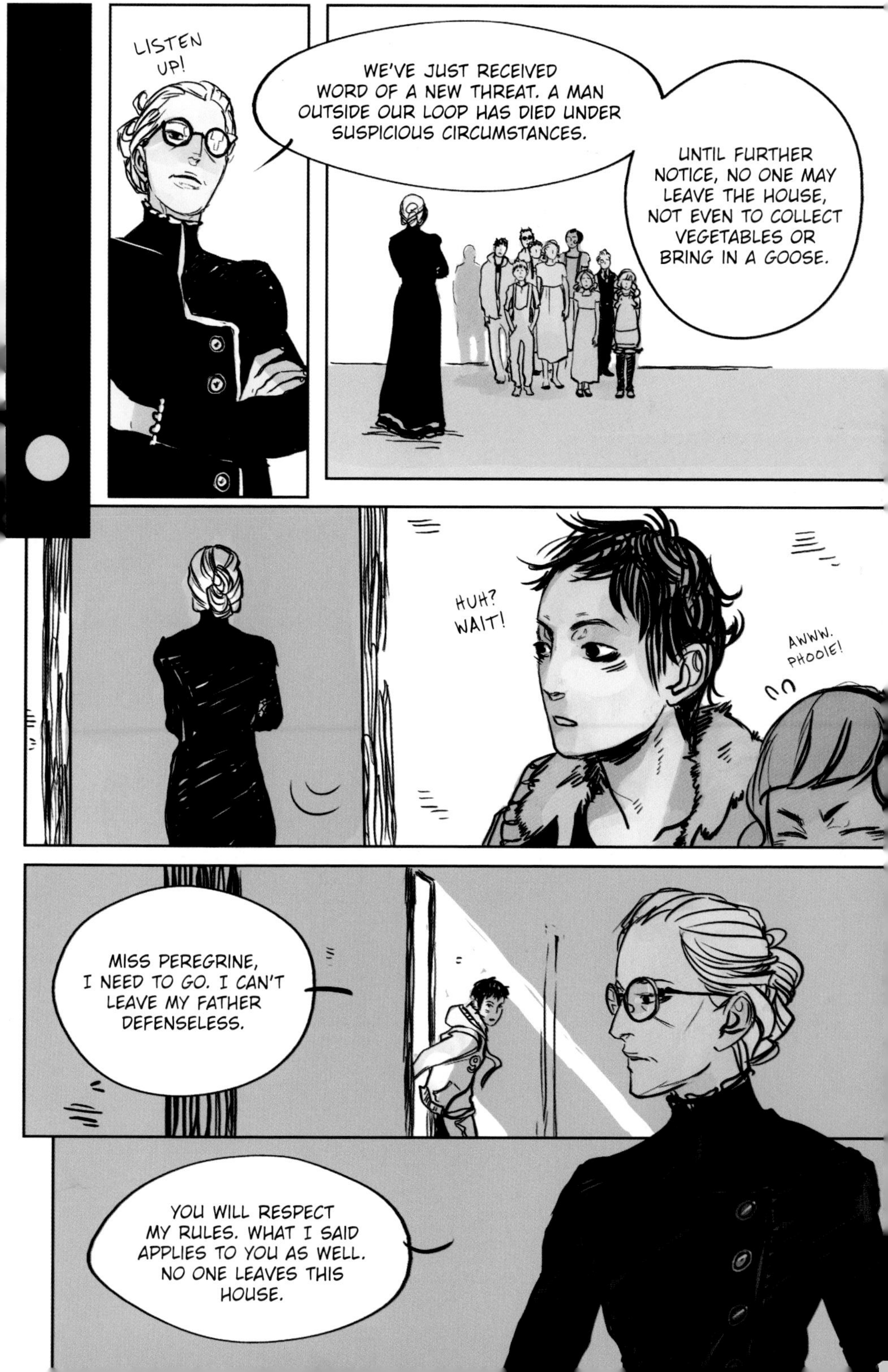
LISTEN UP!
WE'VE JUST RECEIVED WORD OF A NEW THREAT. A MAN OUTSIDE OUR LOOP HAS DIED UNDER SUSPICIOUS CIRCUMSTANCES.
UNTIL FURTHER NOTICE, NO ONE MAY LEAVE THE HOUSE, NOT EVEN TO COLLECT VEGETABLES OR BRING IN A GOOSE.
HUH? WAIT!
AWWW. PHOOIE!
MISS PEREGRINE, I NEED TO GO. I CAN'T LEAVE MY FATHER DEFENSELESS.
YOU WILL RESPECT MY RULES. WHAT I SAID APPLIES TO YOU AS WELL. NO ONE LEAVES THIS HOUSE.

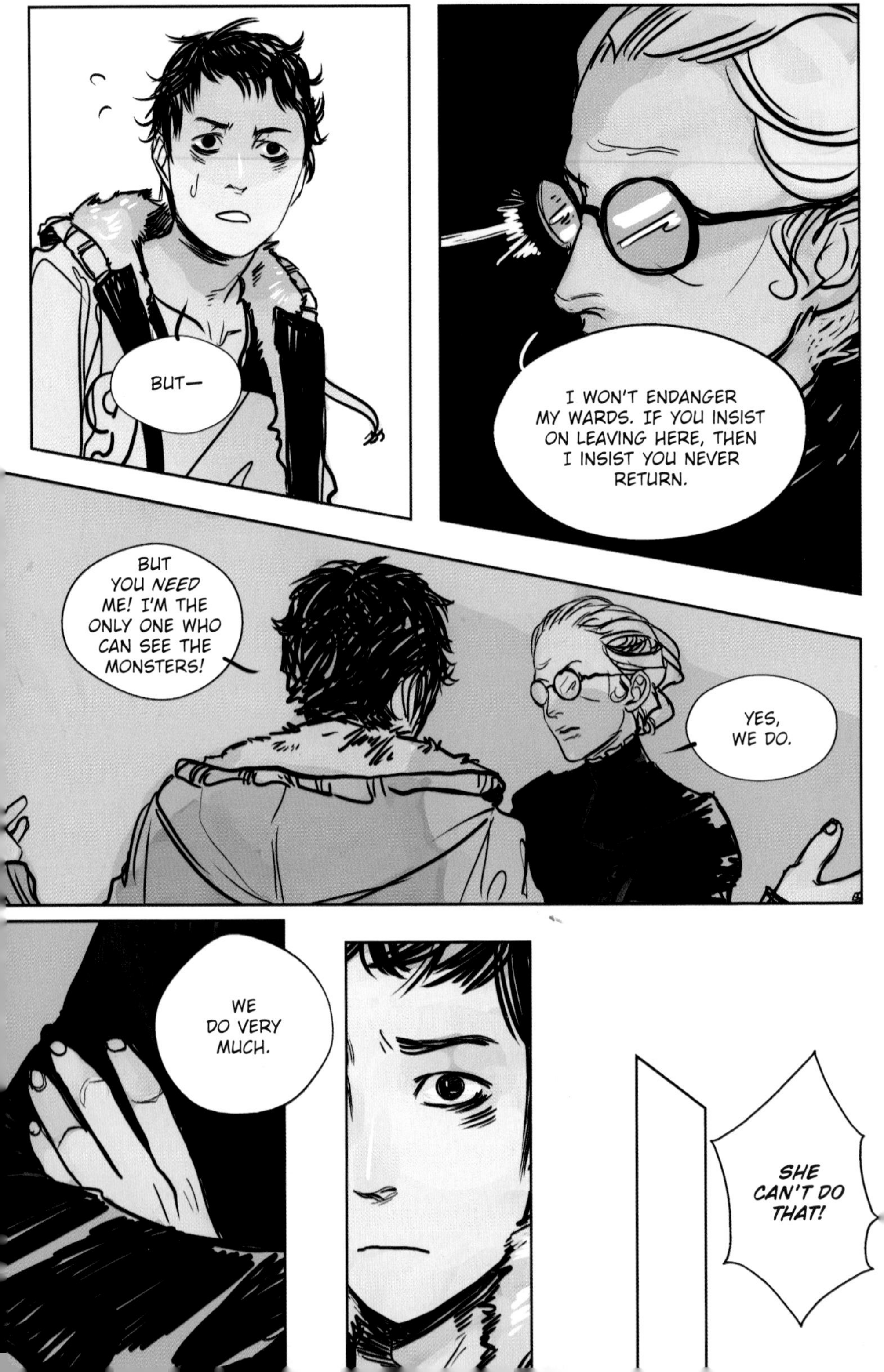
BUT—
I WON'T ENDANGER MY WARDS. IF YOU INSIST ON LEAVING HERE, THEN I INSIST YOU NEVER RETURN.
BUT YOU *NEED* ME! I'M THE ONLY ONE WHO CAN SEE THE MONSTERS!
YES, WE DO.
WE DO VERY MUCH.
SHE CAN'T DO THAT!

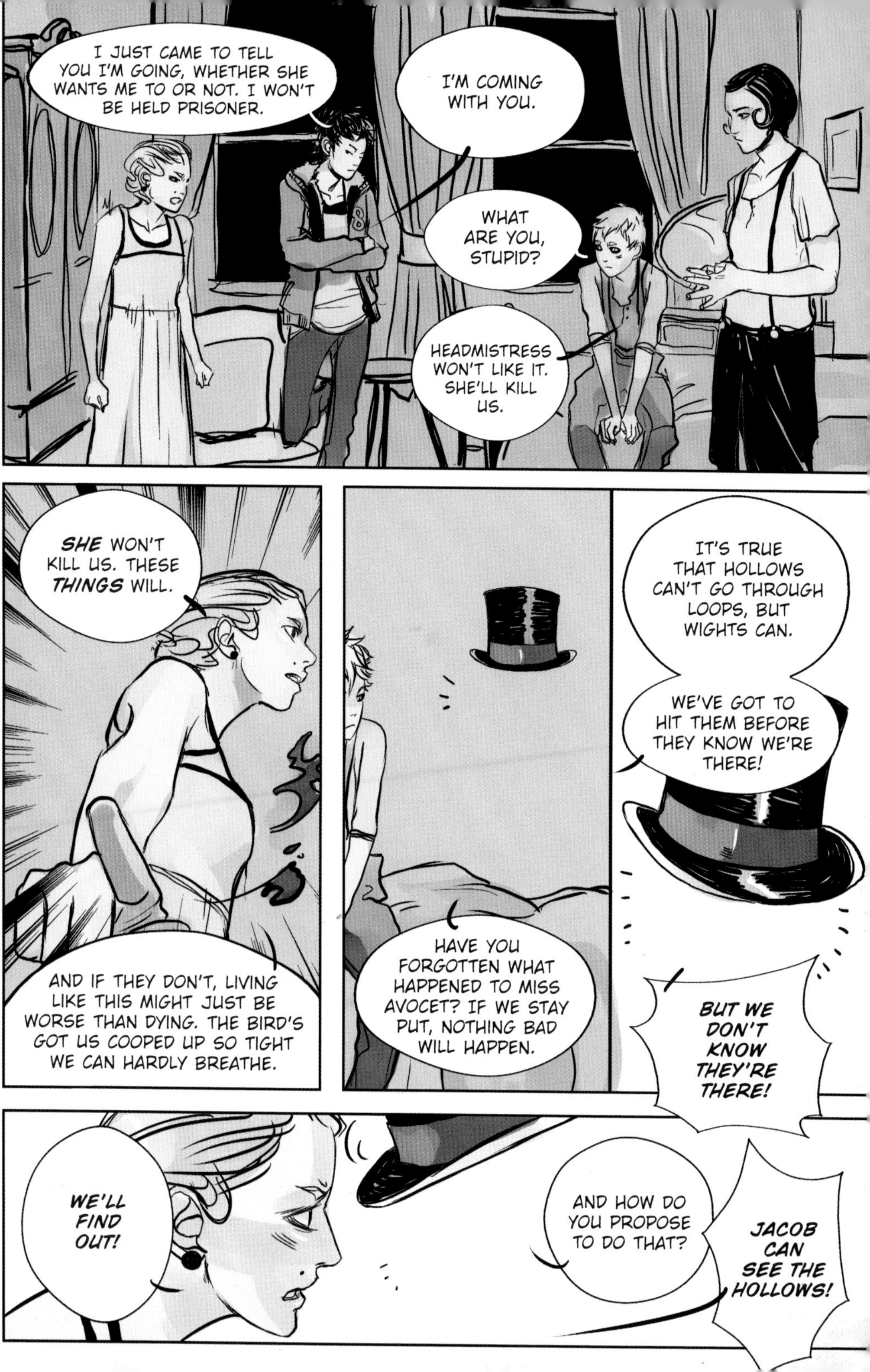
I JUST CAME TO TELL YOU I'M GOING, WHETHER SHE WANTS ME TO OR NOT. I WON'T BE HELD PRISONER.
I'M COMING WITH YOU.
WHAT ARE YOU, STUPID?
HEADMISTRESS WON'T LIKE IT. SHE'LL KILL US.
SHE WON'T KILL US. THESE THINGS WILL.
AND IF THEY DON'T, LIVING LIKE THIS MIGHT JUST BE WORSE THAN DYING. THE BIRD'S GOT US COOPED UP SO TIGHT WE CAN HARDLY BREATHE.
HAVE YOU FORGOTTEN WHAT HAPPENED TO MISS AVOCET? IF WE STAY PUT, NOTHING BAD WILL HAPPEN.
IT'S TRUE THAT HOLLOWS CAN'T GO THROUGH LOOPS, BUT WIGHTS CAN.
WE'VE GOT TO HIT THEM BEFORE THEY KNOW WE'RE THERE!
BUT WE DON'T KNOW THEY'RE THERE!
WE'LL FIND OUT!
AND HOW DO YOU PROPOSE TO DO THAT?
JACOB CAN SEE THE HOLLOWS!

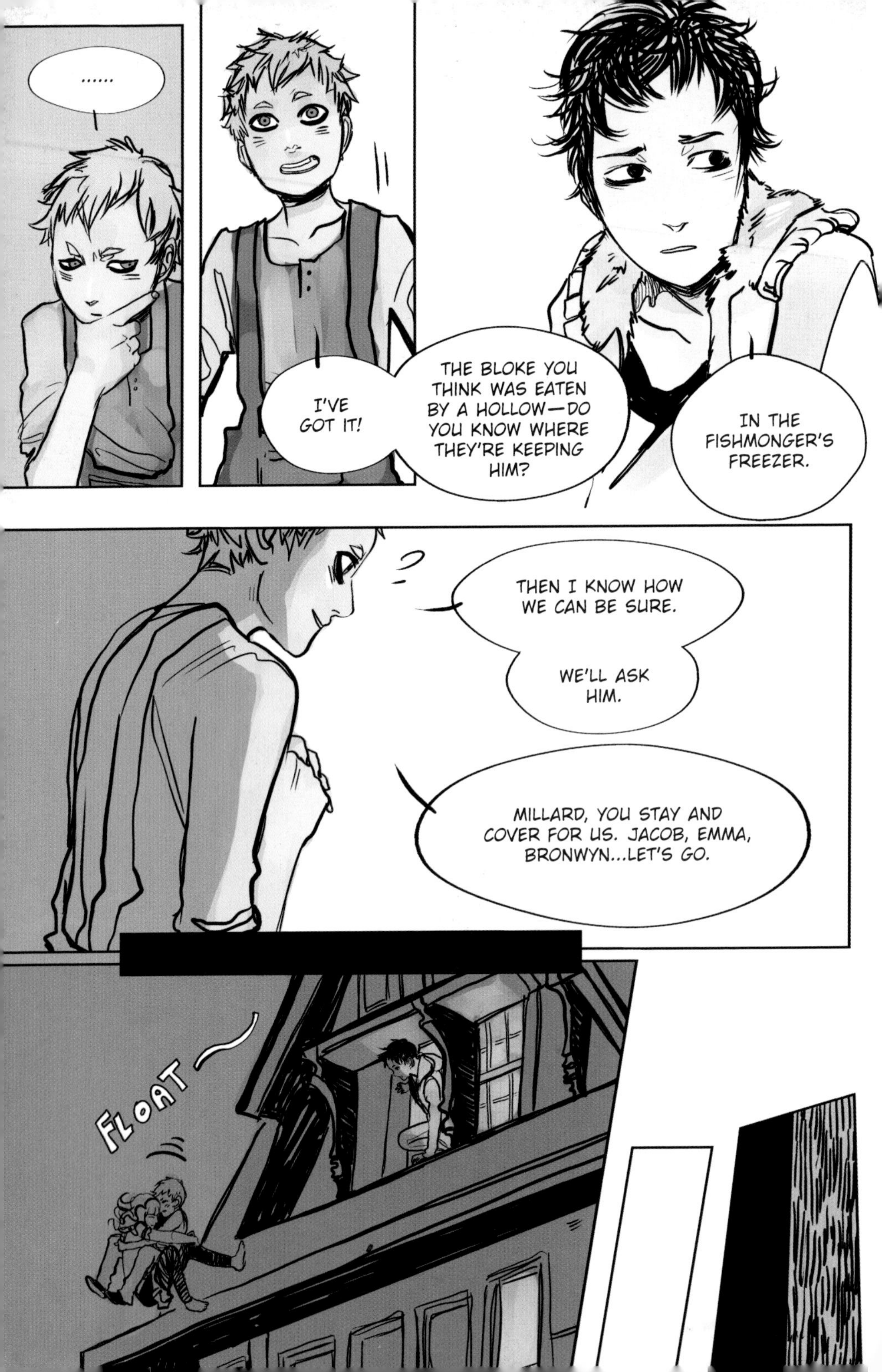
......
I'VE GOT IT!
THE BLOKE YOU THINK WAS EATEN BY A HOLLOW—DO YOU KNOW WHERE THEY'RE KEEPING HIM?
IN THE FISHMONGER'S FREEZER.
THEN I KNOW HOW WE CAN BE SURE.
WE'LL ASK HIM.
MILLARD, YOU STAY AND COVER FOR US. JACOB, EMMA, BRONWYN...LET'S GO.
[redacted]
FLOAT

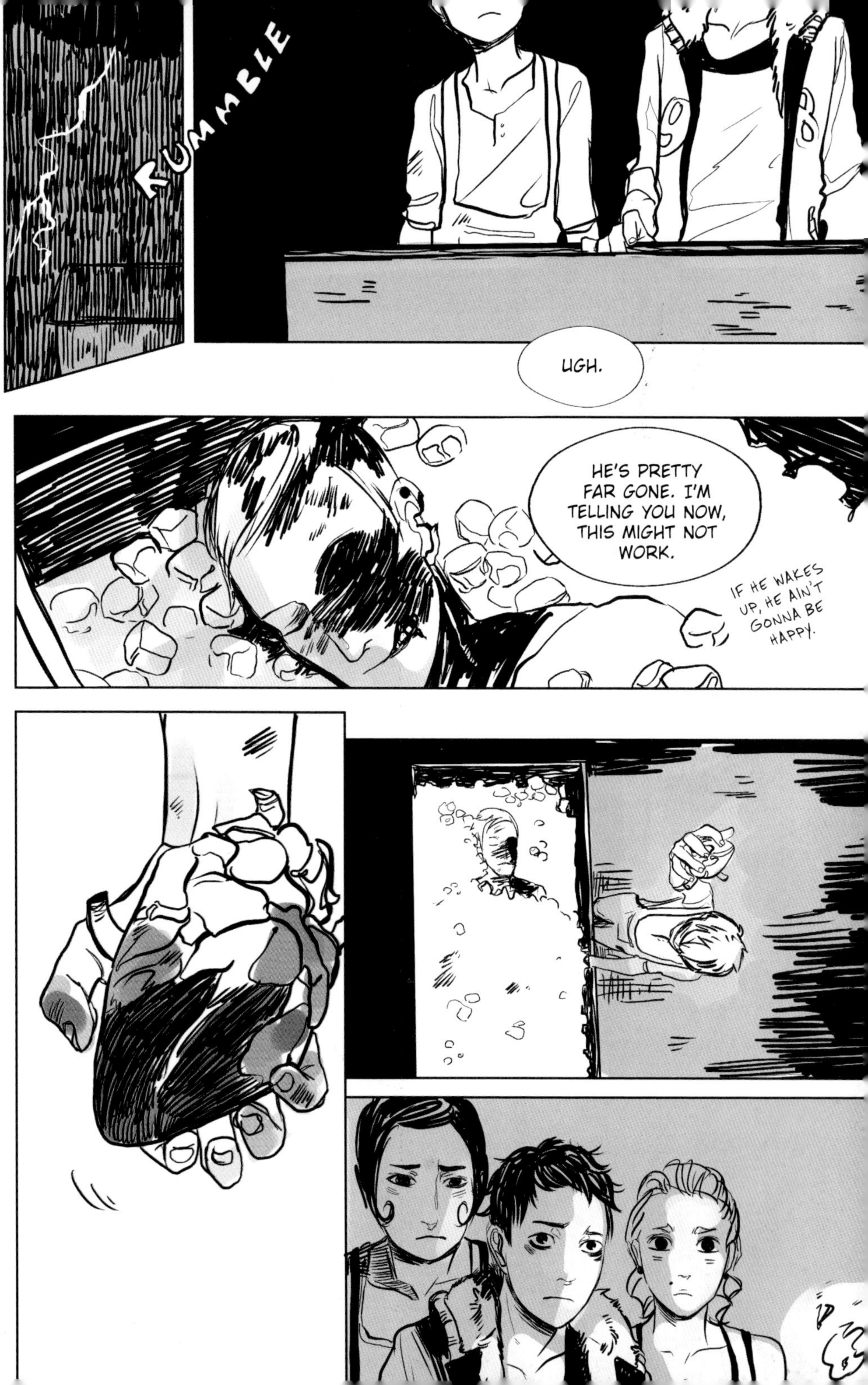
RUMMBLE
UGH.
HE'S PRETTY FAR GONE. I'M TELLING YOU NOW, THIS MIGHT NOT WORK.
IF HE WAKES UP, HE AIN'T GONNA BE HAPPY.

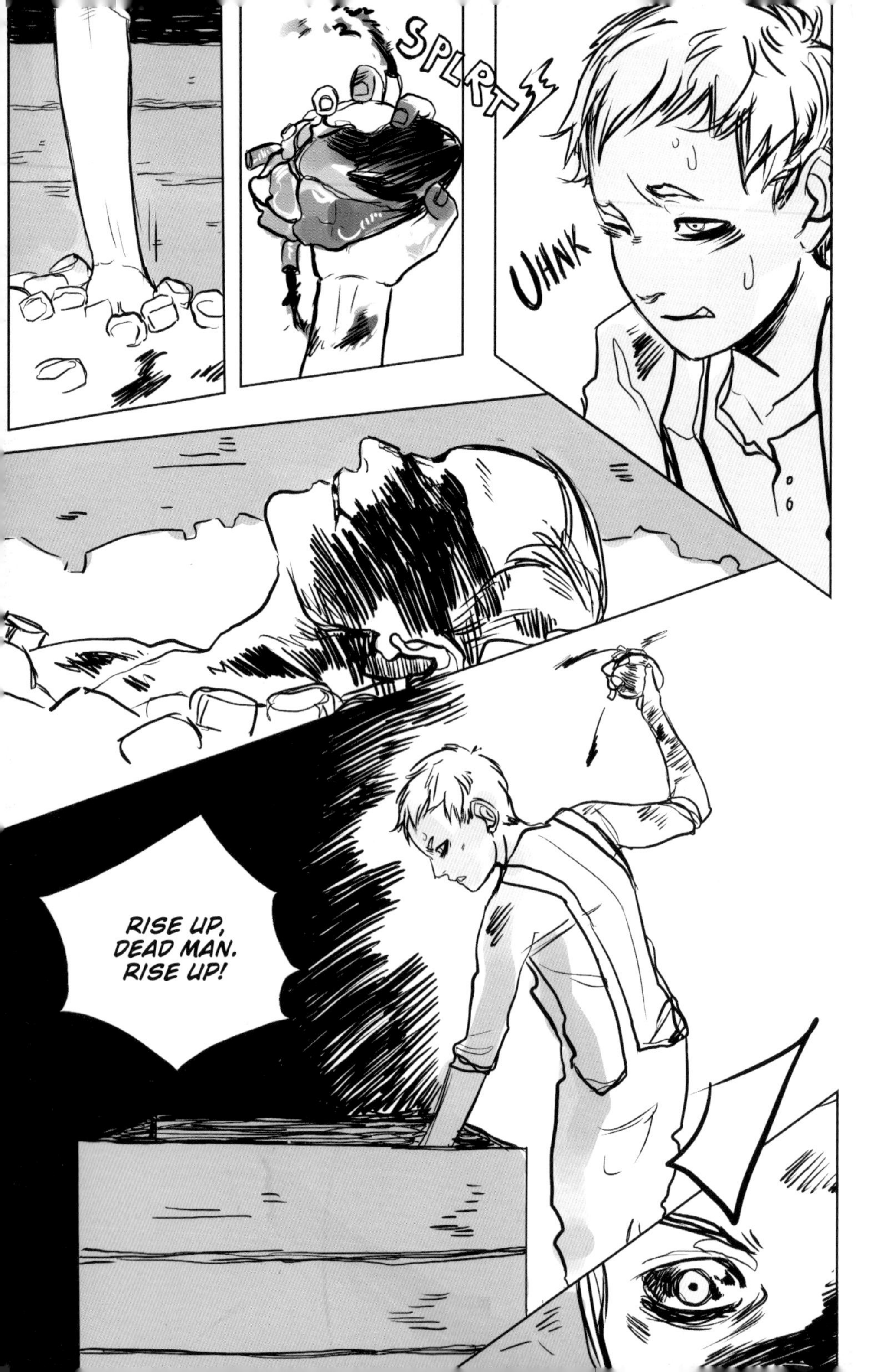
SPLRT
UHNK
RISE UP, DEAD MAN. RISE UP!

IT HURTS...!

MARTIN!

WHO KILLED YOU? CAN YOU REMEMBER?

I WAS DEAD...

...AM DEAD.

MY OLD MAN.

OH JACOB, I TOOK SUCH GOOD CARE OF HIM. DUSTED THE GLASS AND MADE HIM A HOME. I TOOK SUCH CAREFUL CARE, BUT— HE KILLED ME.

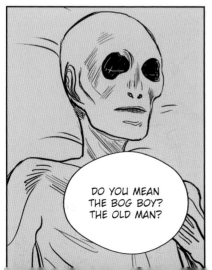

DO YOU MEAN THE BOG BOY? THE OLD MAN?

WAIT. MISS PEREGRINE TOLD ME...

"THEY ONLY BECOME VISIBLE TO THE REST OF US WHEN THEY'RE EATING."

MARTIN SAW A HOLLOWGAST—AT NIGHT, IN THE RAIN, AS IT WAS TEARING HIM TO SHREDS—AND MISTOOK IT FOR HIS MOST PRIZED EXHIBIT.

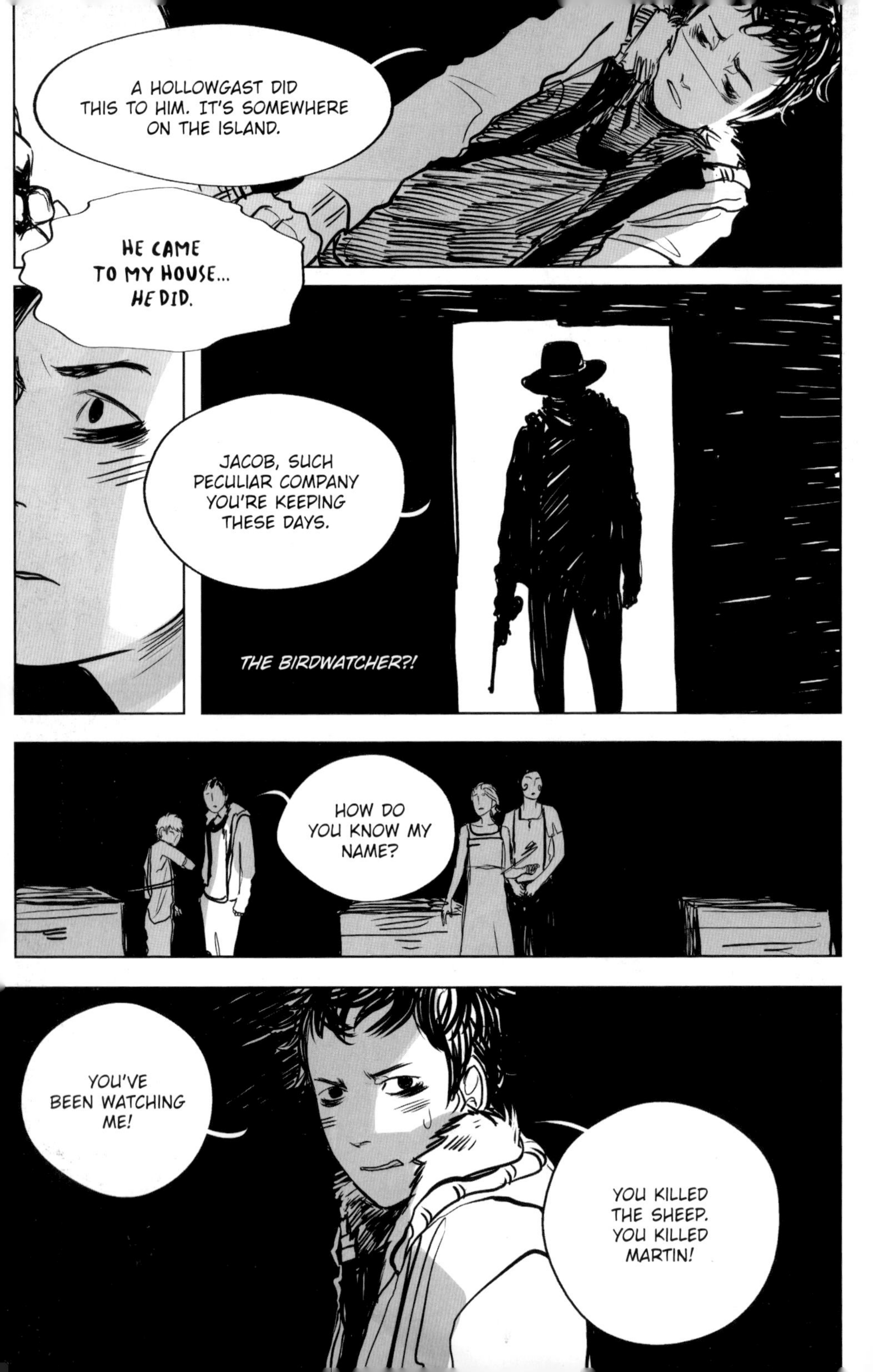
A HOLLOWGAST DID THIS TO HIM. IT'S SOMEWHERE ON THE ISLAND.
HE CAME TO MY HOUSE... HE DID.
JACOB, SUCH PECULIAR COMPANY YOU'RE KEEPING THESE DAYS.
THE BIRDWATCHER?!
HOW DO YOU KNOW MY NAME?
YOU'VE BEEN WATCHING ME!
YOU KILLED THE SHEEP. YOU KILLED MARTIN!

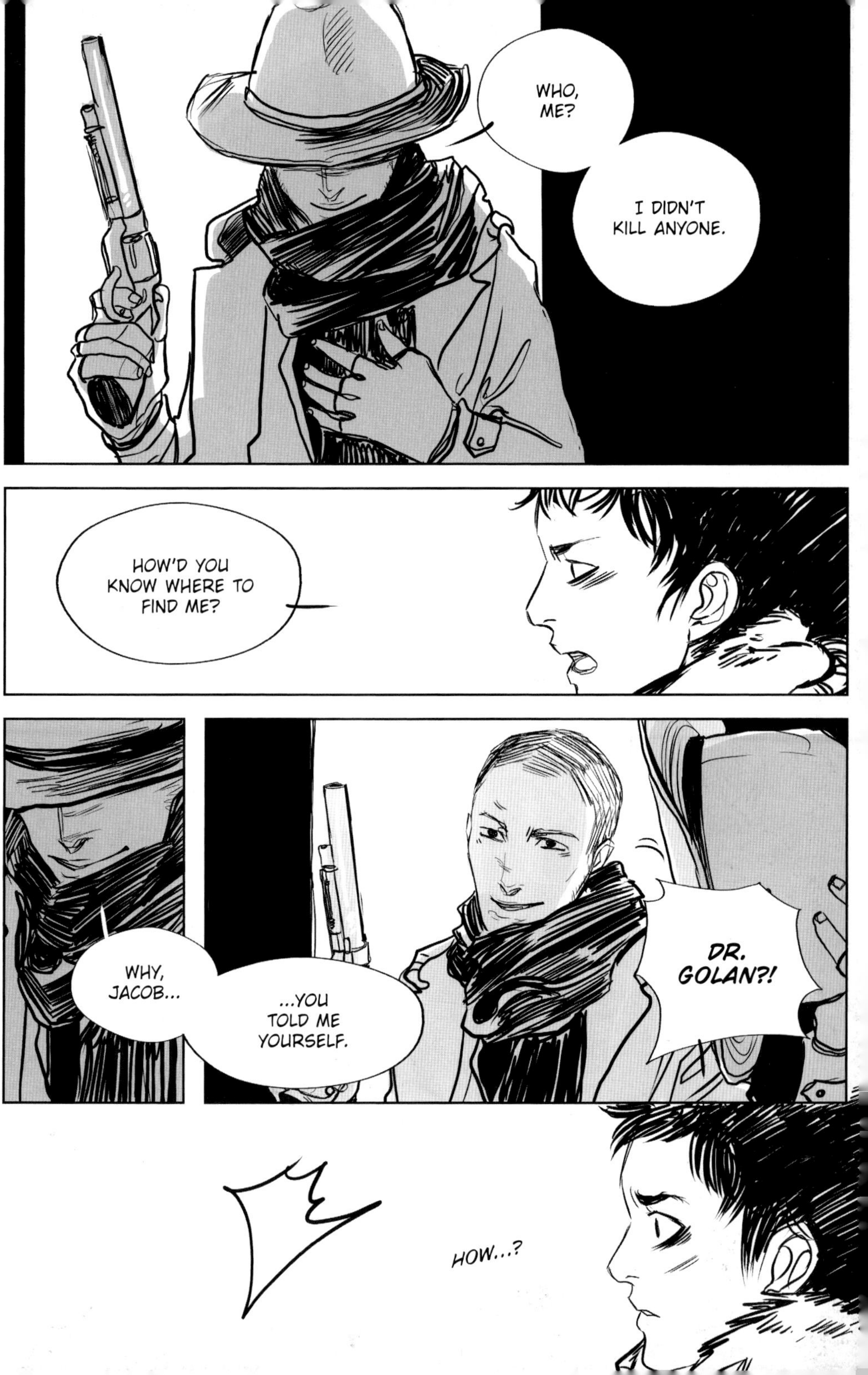
WHO, ME?
I DIDN'T KILL ANYONE.
HOW'D YOU KNOW WHERE TO FIND ME?
WHY, JACOB...
...YOU TOLD ME YOURSELF.
DR. GOLAN?!
HOW...?

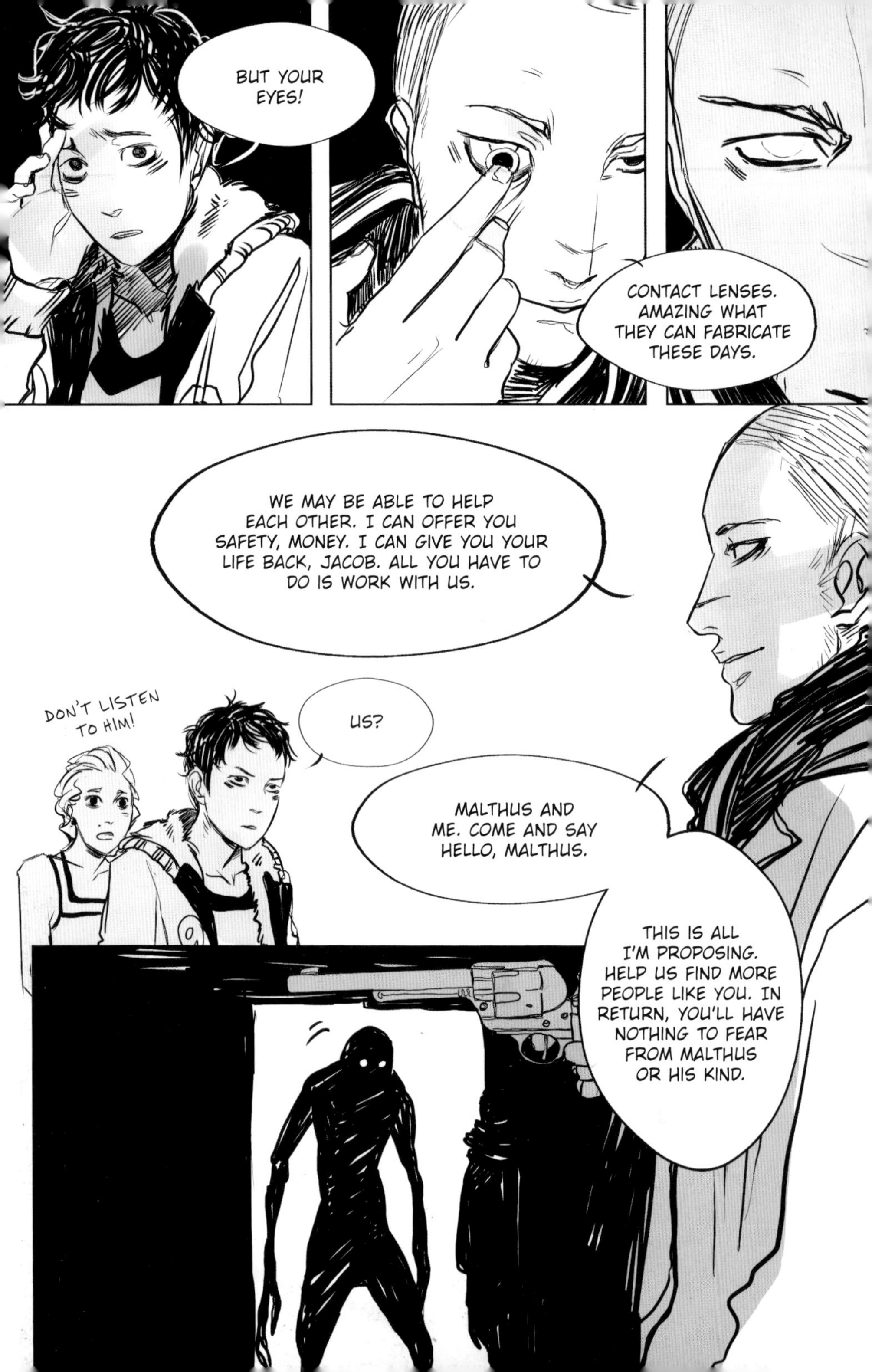

BUT YOUR EYES!
CONTACT LENSES. AMAZING WHAT THEY CAN FABRICATE THESE DAYS.
WE MAY BE ABLE TO HELP EACH OTHER. I CAN OFFER YOU SAFETY, MONEY. I CAN GIVE YOU YOUR LIFE BACK, JACOB. ALL YOU HAVE TO DO IS WORK WITH US.
DON'T LISTEN TO HIM!
US?
MALTHUS AND ME. COME AND SAY HELLO, MALTHUS.
THIS IS ALL I'M PROPOSING. HELP US FIND MORE PEOPLE LIKE YOU. IN RETURN, YOU'LL HAVE NOTHING TO FEAR FROM MALTHUS OR HIS KIND.

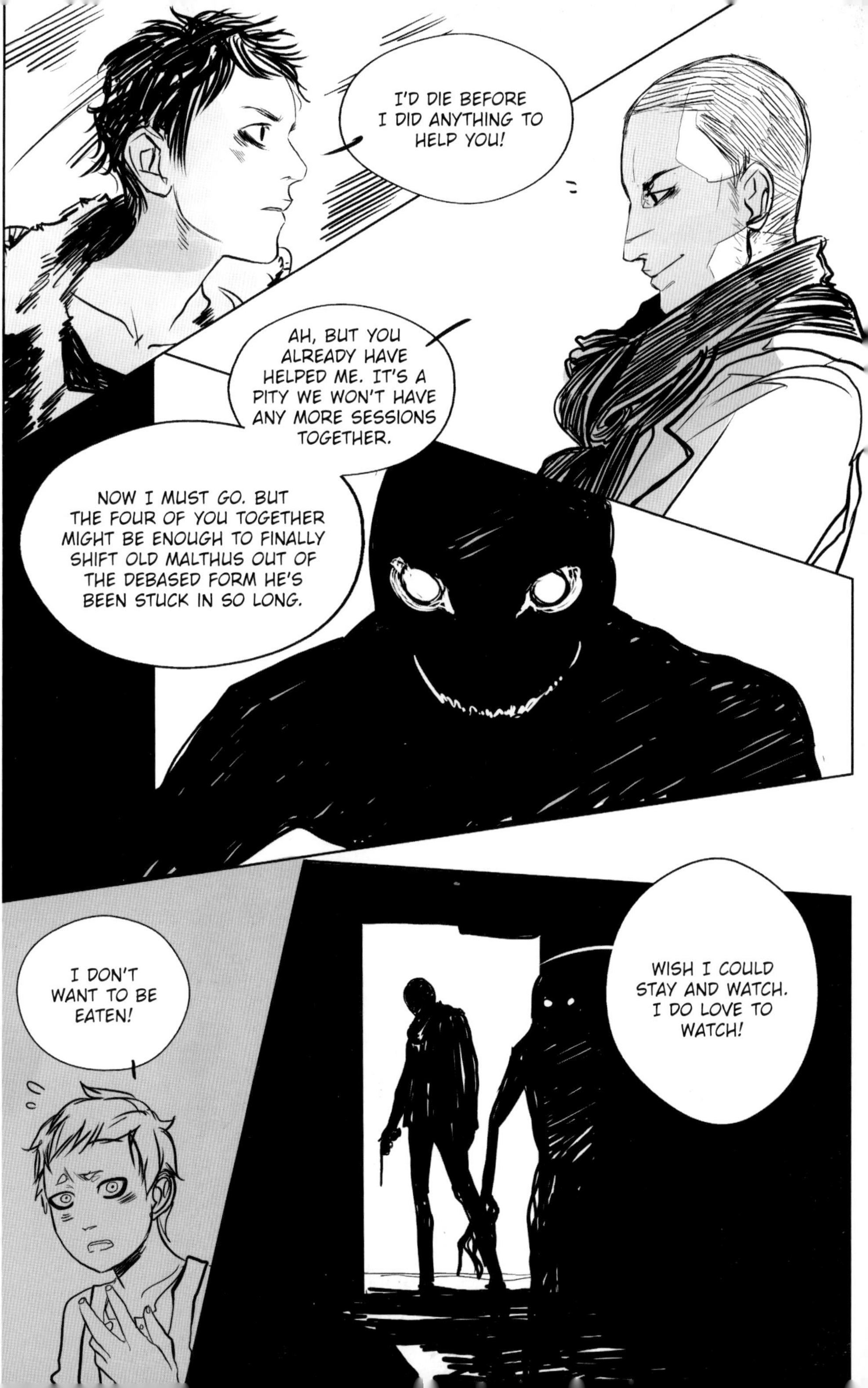
I'D DIE BEFORE I DID ANYTHING TO HELP YOU!
AH, BUT YOU ALREADY HAVE HELPED ME. IT'S A PITY WE WON'T HAVE ANY MORE SESSIONS TOGETHER.
NOW I MUST GO. BUT THE FOUR OF YOU TOGETHER MIGHT BE ENOUGH TO FINALLY SHIFT OLD MALTHUS OUT OF THE DEBASED FORM HE'S BEEN STUCK IN SO LONG.
I DON'T WANT TO BE EATEN!
WISH I COULD STAY AND WATCH. I DO LOVE TO WATCH!

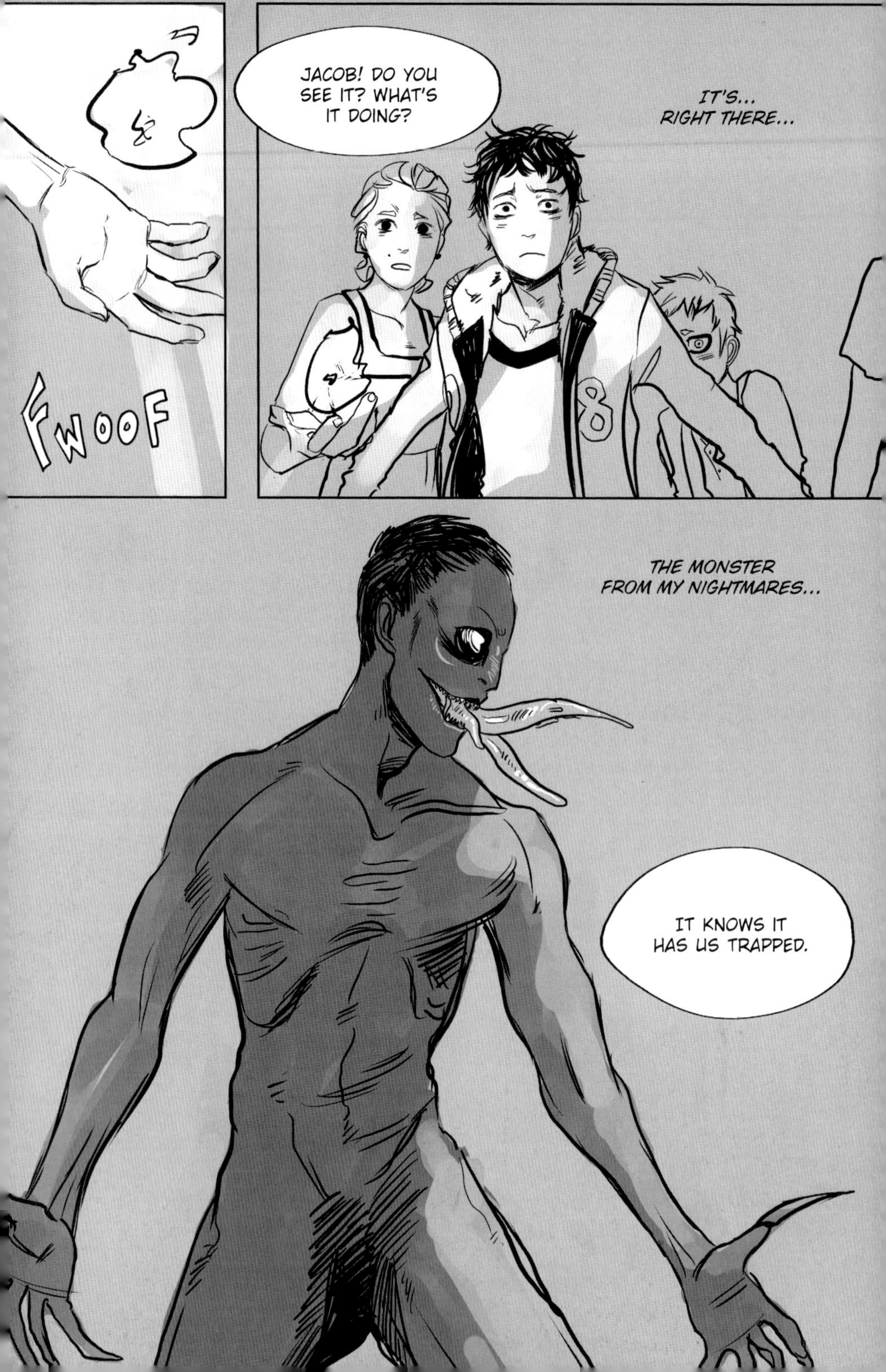
FWOOF
JACOB! DO YOU SEE IT? WHAT'S IT DOING?
IT'S... RIGHT THERE...
THE MONSTER FROM MY NIGHTMARES...
IT KNOWS IT HAS US TRAPPED.

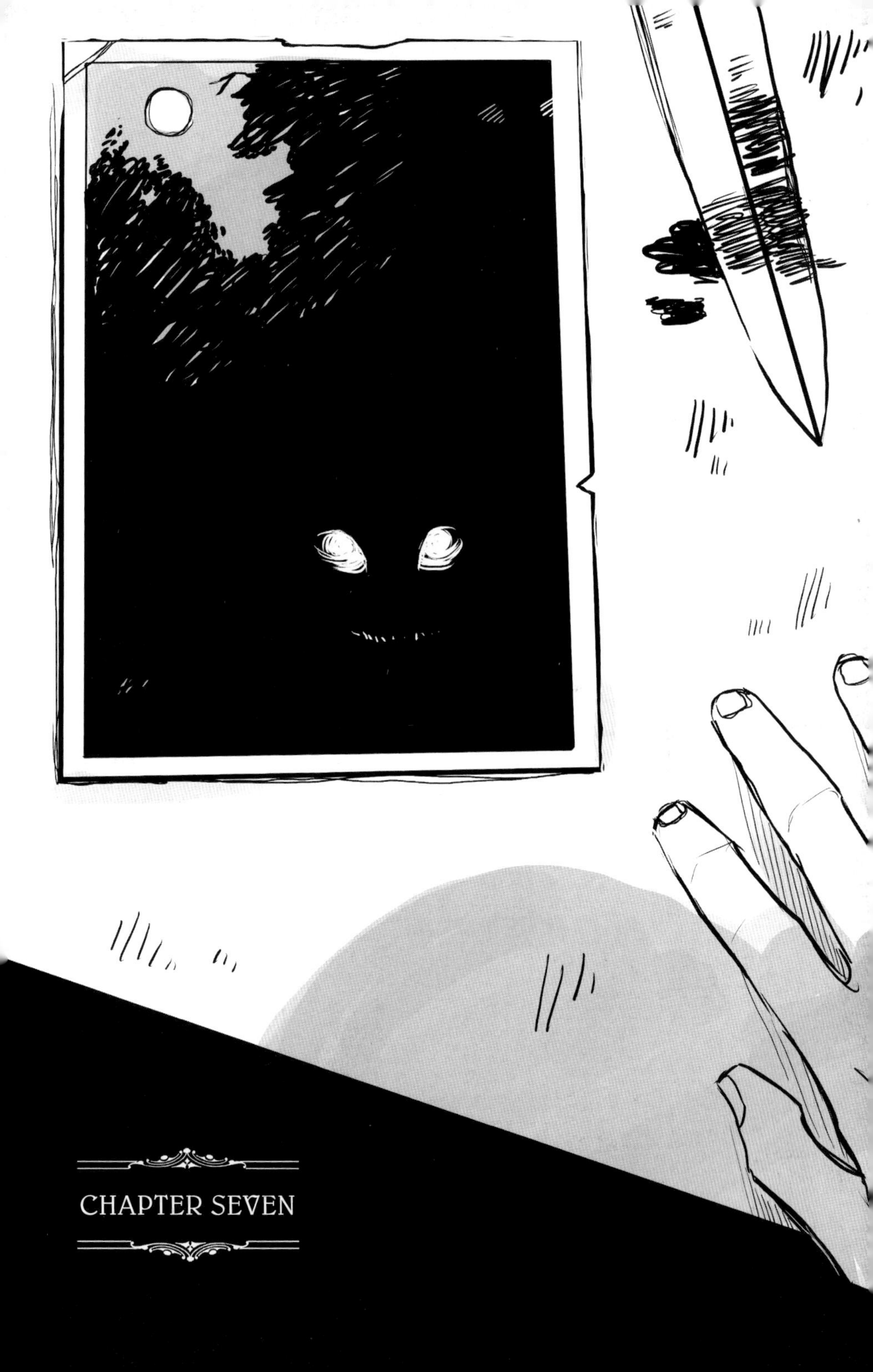

CHAPTER SEVEN

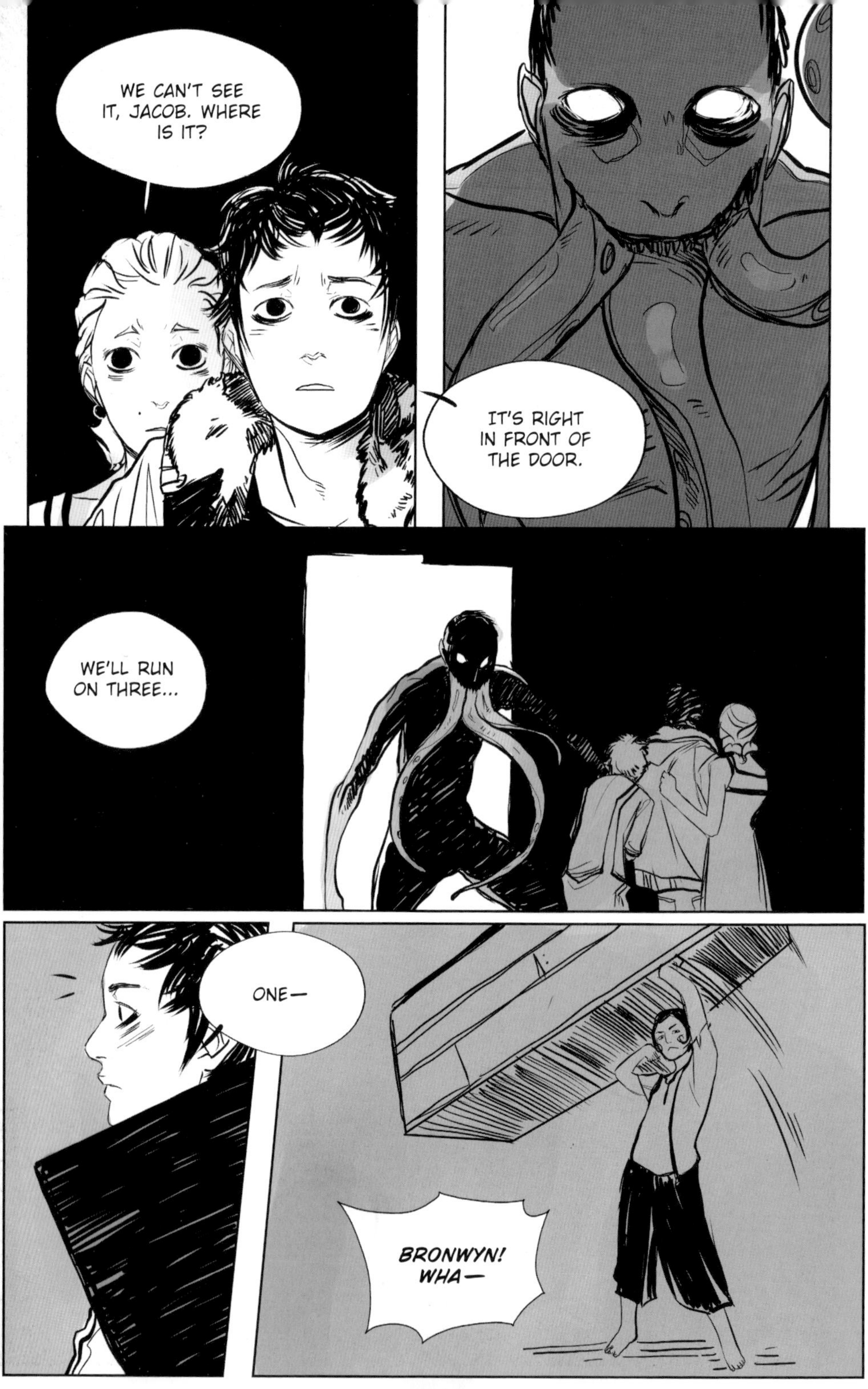
WE CAN'T SEE IT, JACOB. WHERE IS IT?
IT'S RIGHT IN FRONT OF THE DOOR.
WE'LL RUN ON THREE...
ONE—
BRONWYN! WHA—

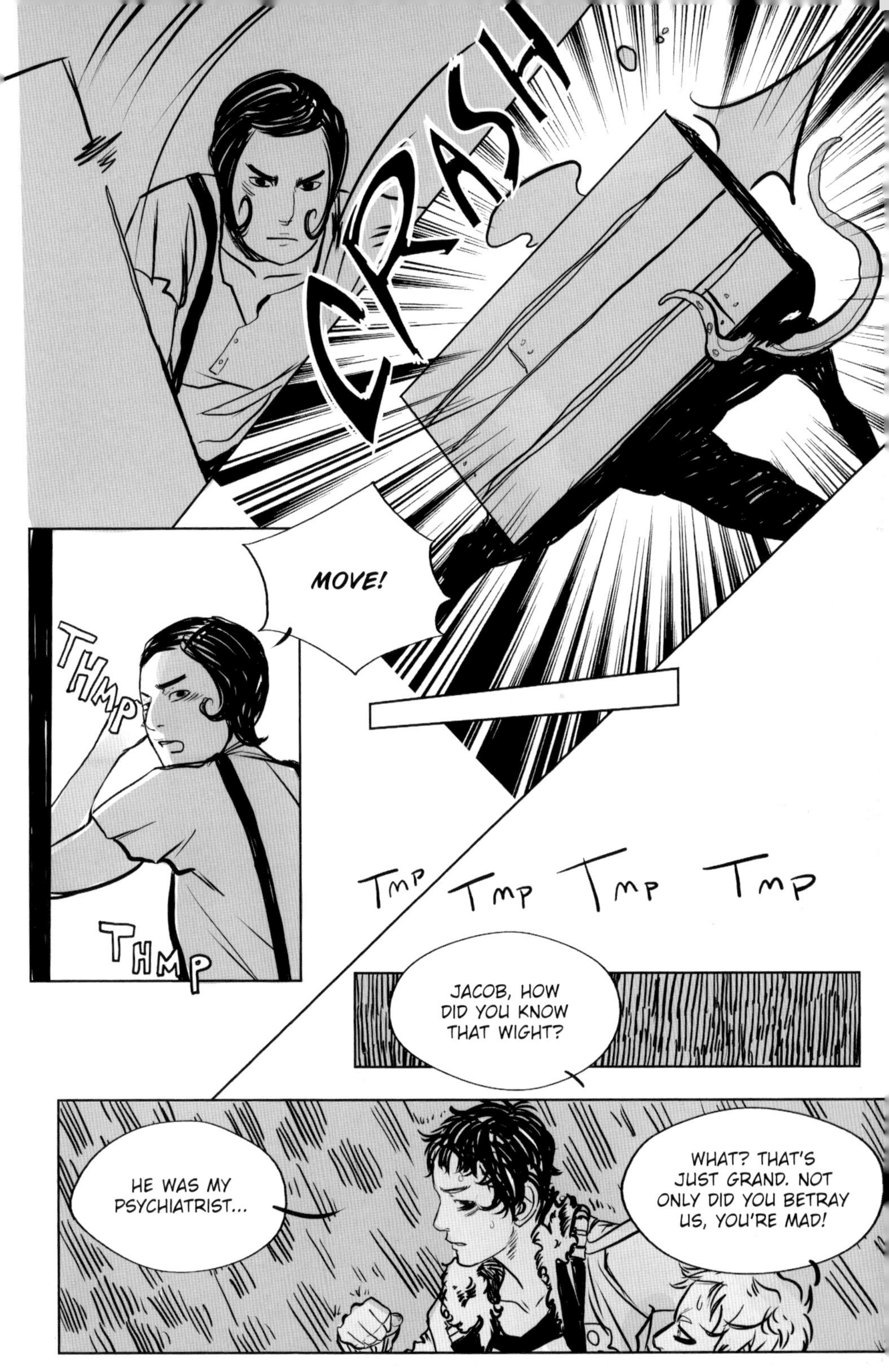
CRASH
MOVE!
THMP
THMP
TMP TMP TMP TMP
JACOB, HOW DID YOU KNOW THAT WIGHT?
HE WAS MY PSYCHIATRIST...
WHAT? THAT'S JUST GRAND. NOT ONLY DID YOU BETRAY US, YOU'RE MAD!

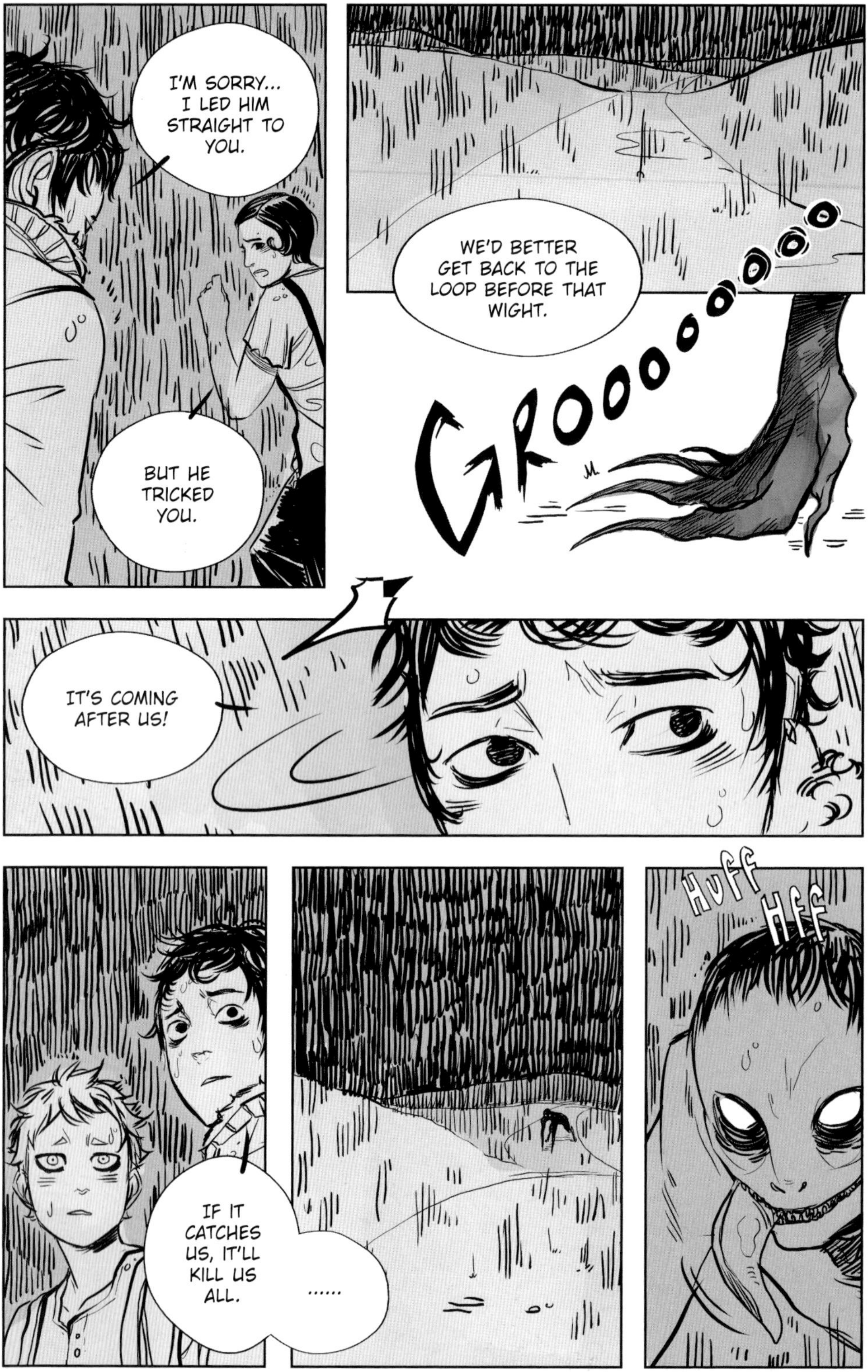
I'M SORRY... I LED HIM STRAIGHT TO YOU.
BUT HE TRICKED YOU.
WE'D BETTER GET BACK TO THE LOOP BEFORE THAT WIGHT.
GROOOOOOOOOOO
IT'S COMING AFTER US!
IF IT CATCHES US, IT'LL KILL US ALL.
......
HUFF
HFF

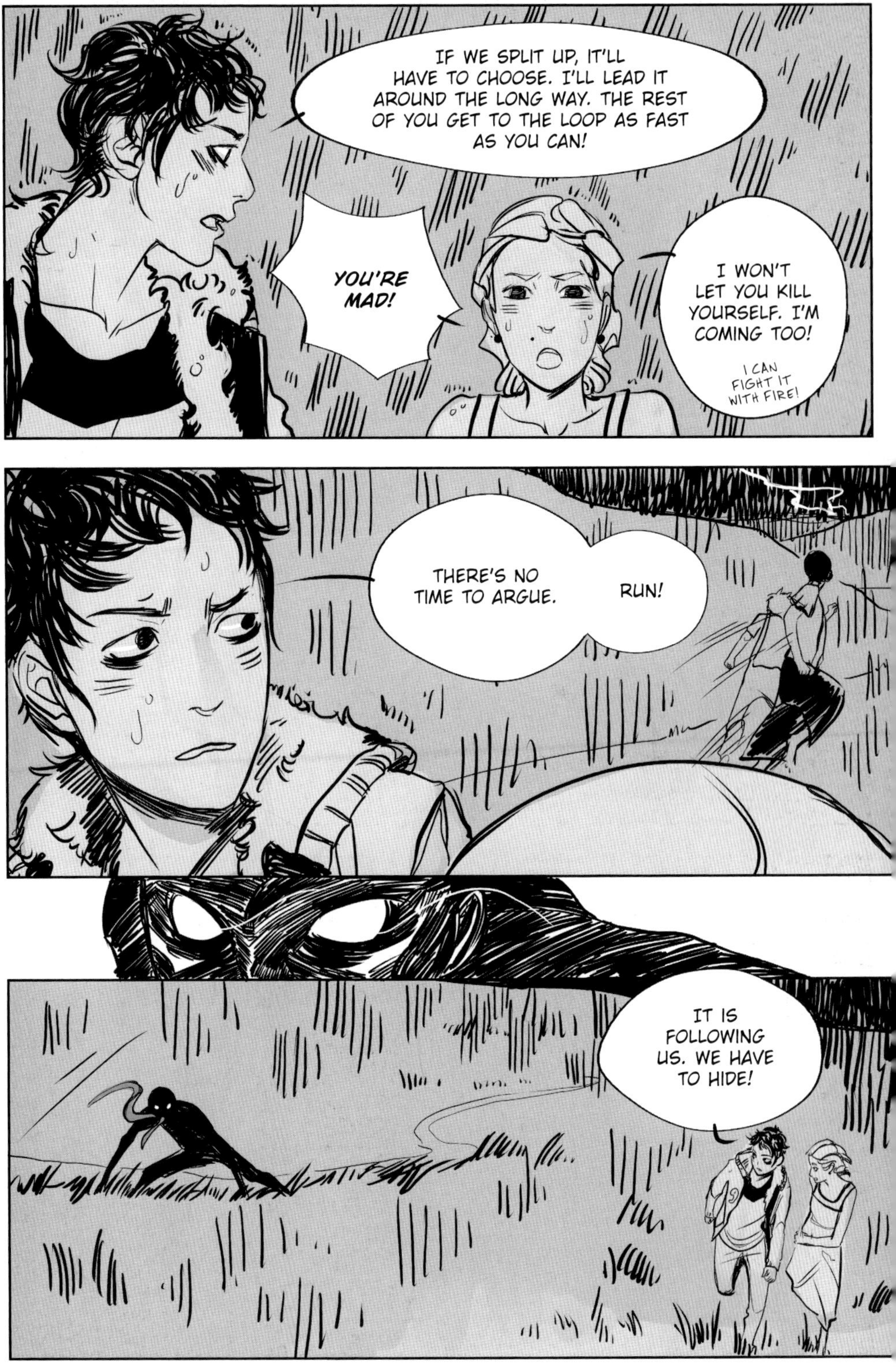
IF WE SPLIT UP, IT'LL HAVE TO CHOOSE. I'LL LEAD IT AROUND THE LONG WAY. THE REST OF YOU GET TO THE LOOP AS FAST AS YOU CAN!
YOU'RE MAD!
I WON'T LET YOU KILL YOURSELF. I'M COMING TOO!
I CAN FIGHT IT WITH FIRE!
THERE'S NO TIME TO ARGUE.
RUN!
IT IS FOLLOWING US. WE HAVE TO HIDE!

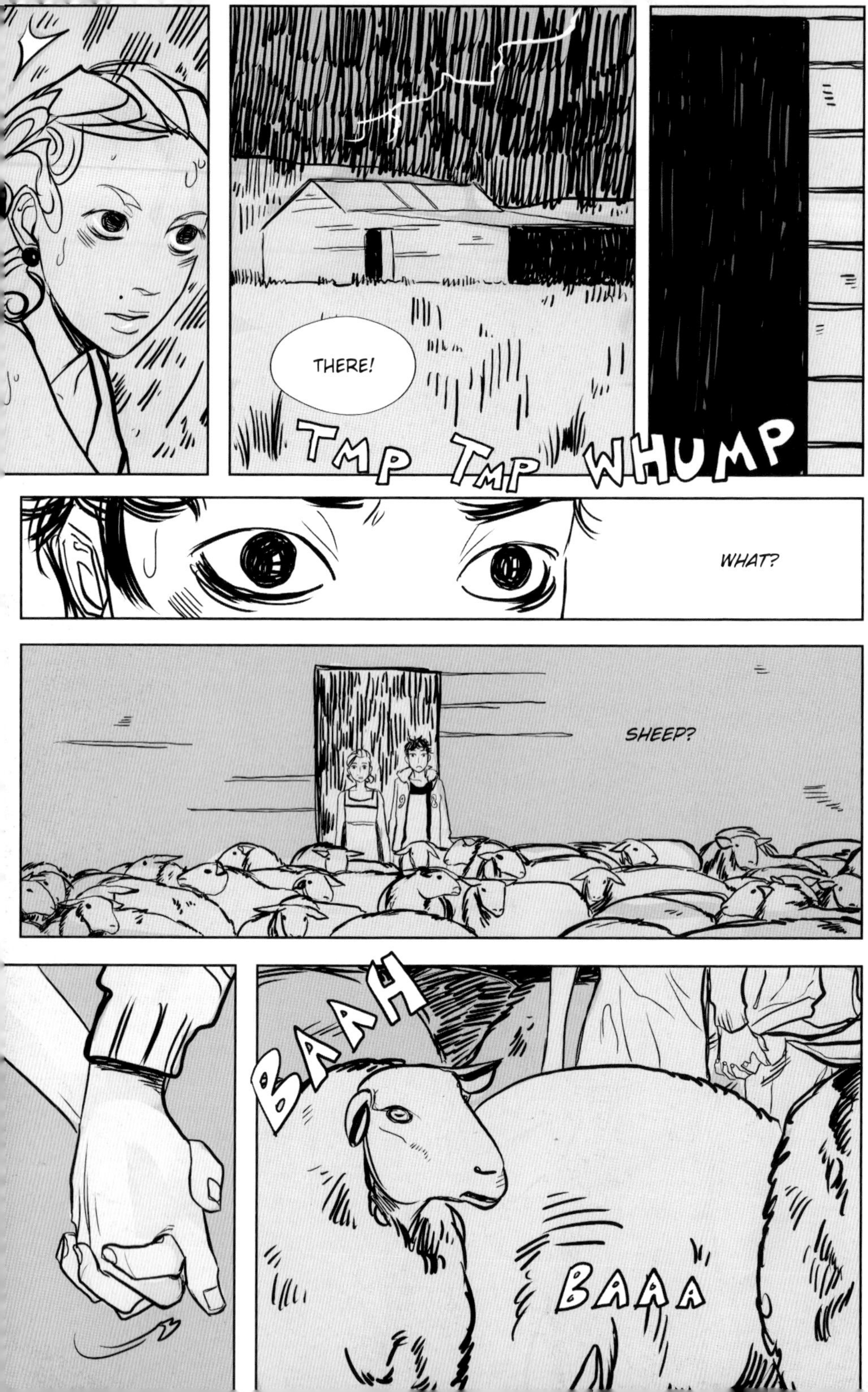
THERE!
TMP TMP
WHUMP
WHAT?
SHEEP?
BAAAH
BAAA

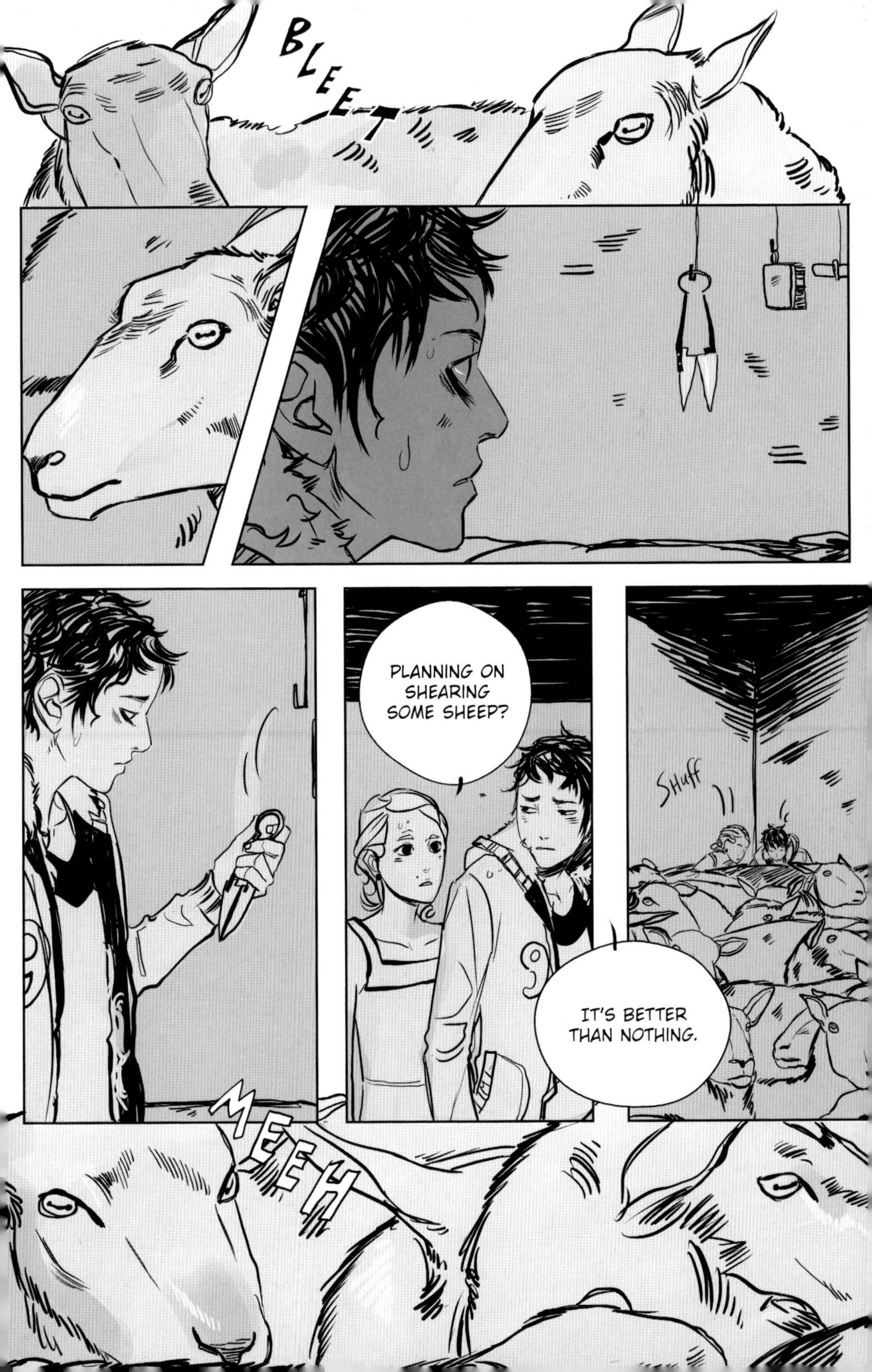
BLEET
PLANNING ON SHEARING SOME SHEEP?
SHUFF
IT'S BETTER THAN NOTHING.
MEEH

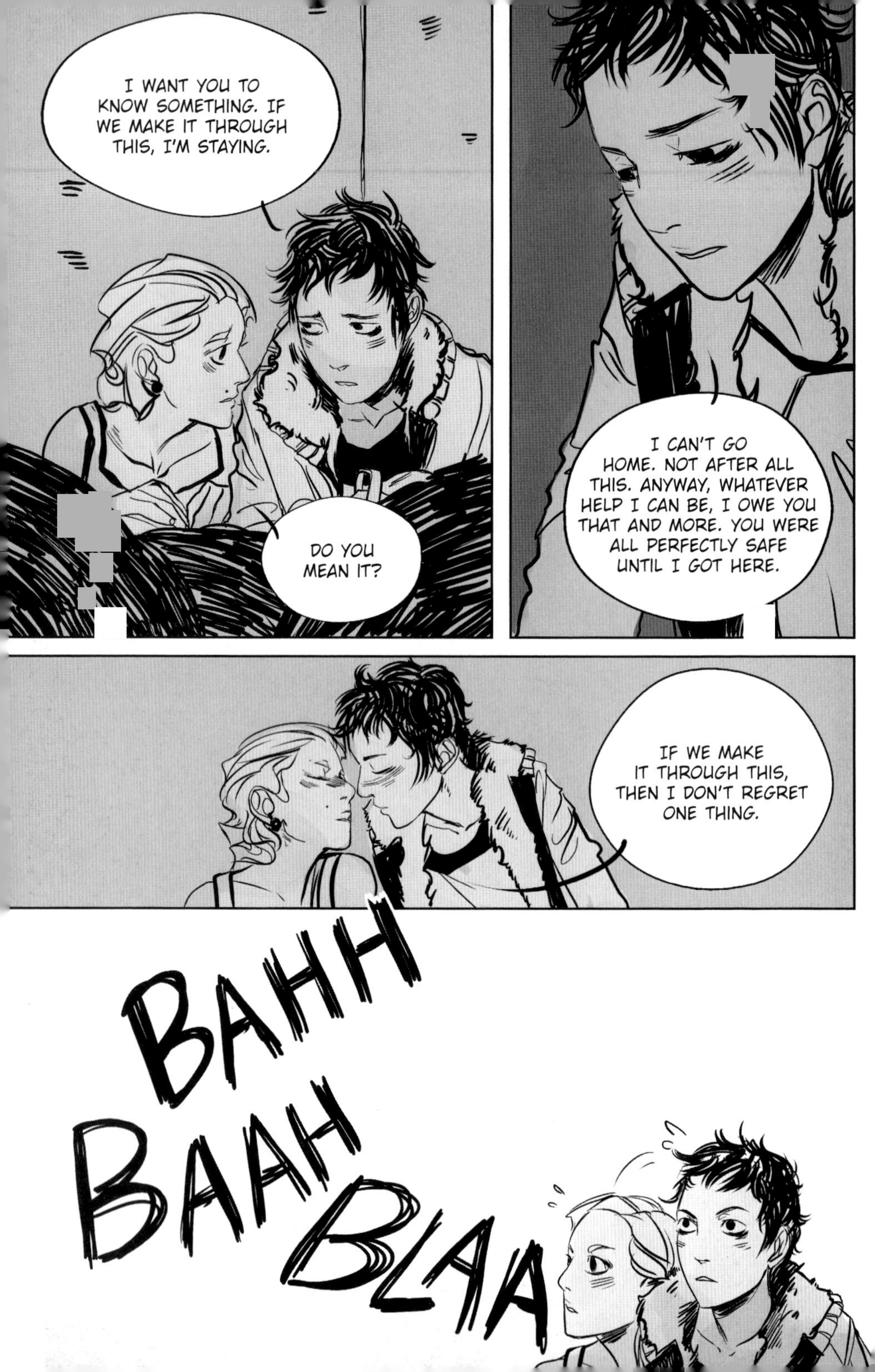
I WANT YOU TO KNOW SOMETHING. IF WE MAKE IT THROUGH THIS, I'M STAYING.
DO YOU MEAN IT?
I CAN'T GO HOME. NOT AFTER ALL THIS. ANYWAY, WHATEVER HELP I CAN BE, I OWE YOU THAT AND MORE. YOU WERE ALL PERFECTLY SAFE UNTIL I GOT HERE.
IF WE MAKE IT THROUGH THIS, THEN I DON'T REGRET ONE THING.
BAHH
BAAH
BLAA

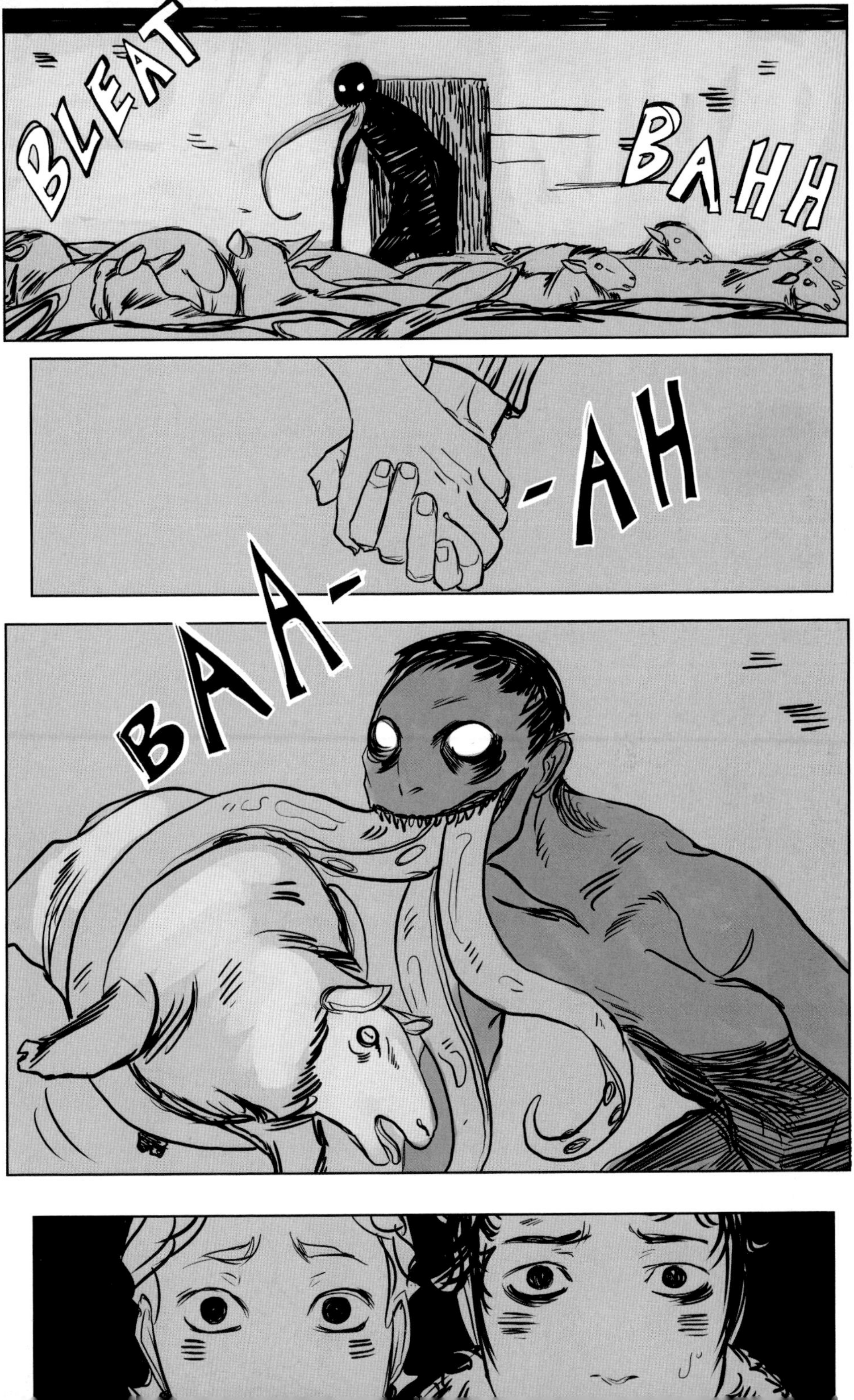
BLEAT
BAHH
BAA-
-AH

IT'S COMING RIGHT TOWARD US.

I WON'T LET US DIE HERE.

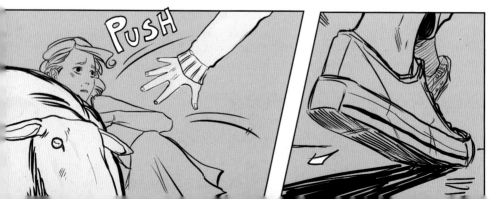

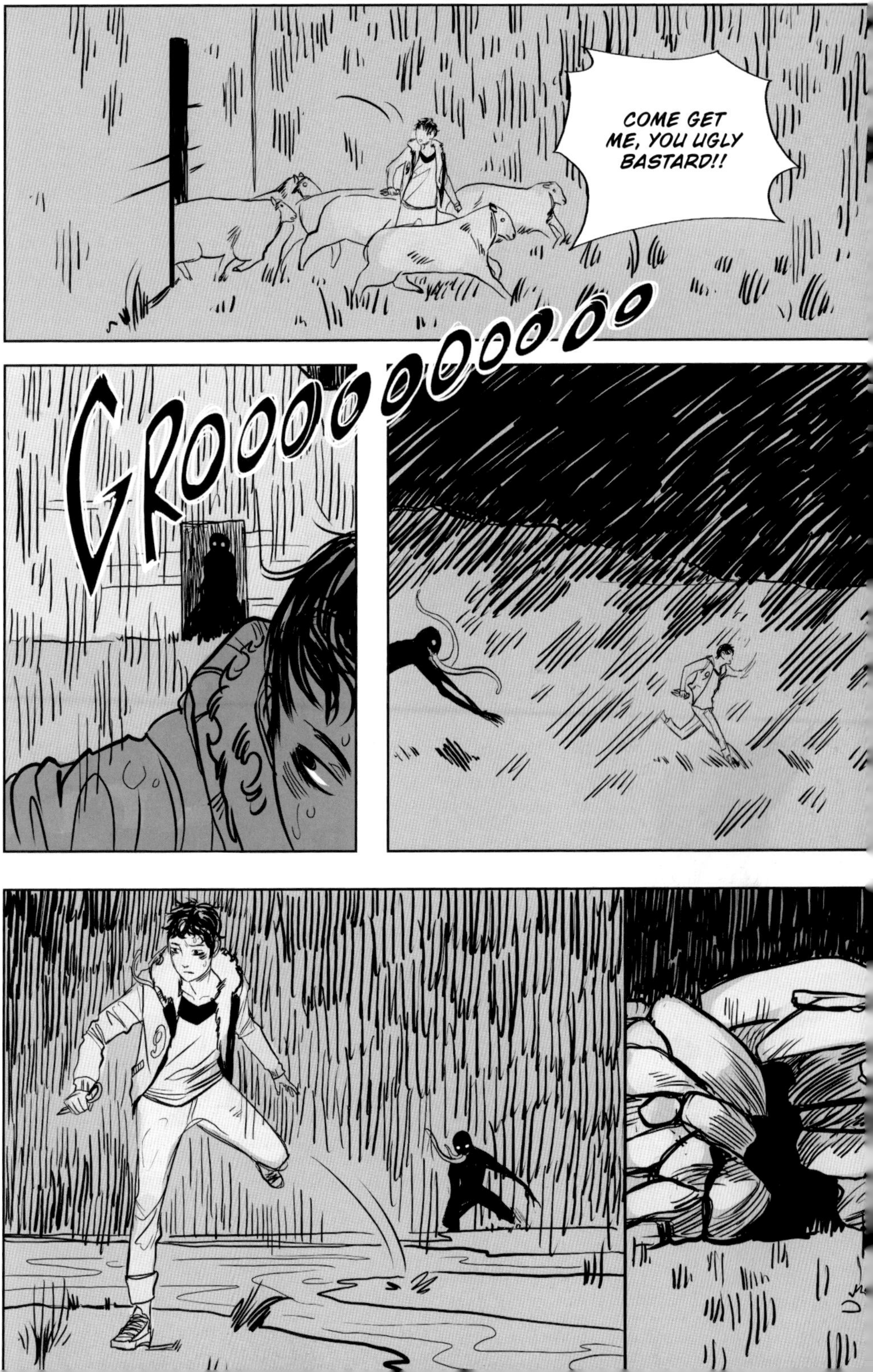
COME GET ME, YOU UGLY BASTARD!!
GROOOOOOOOOOOO

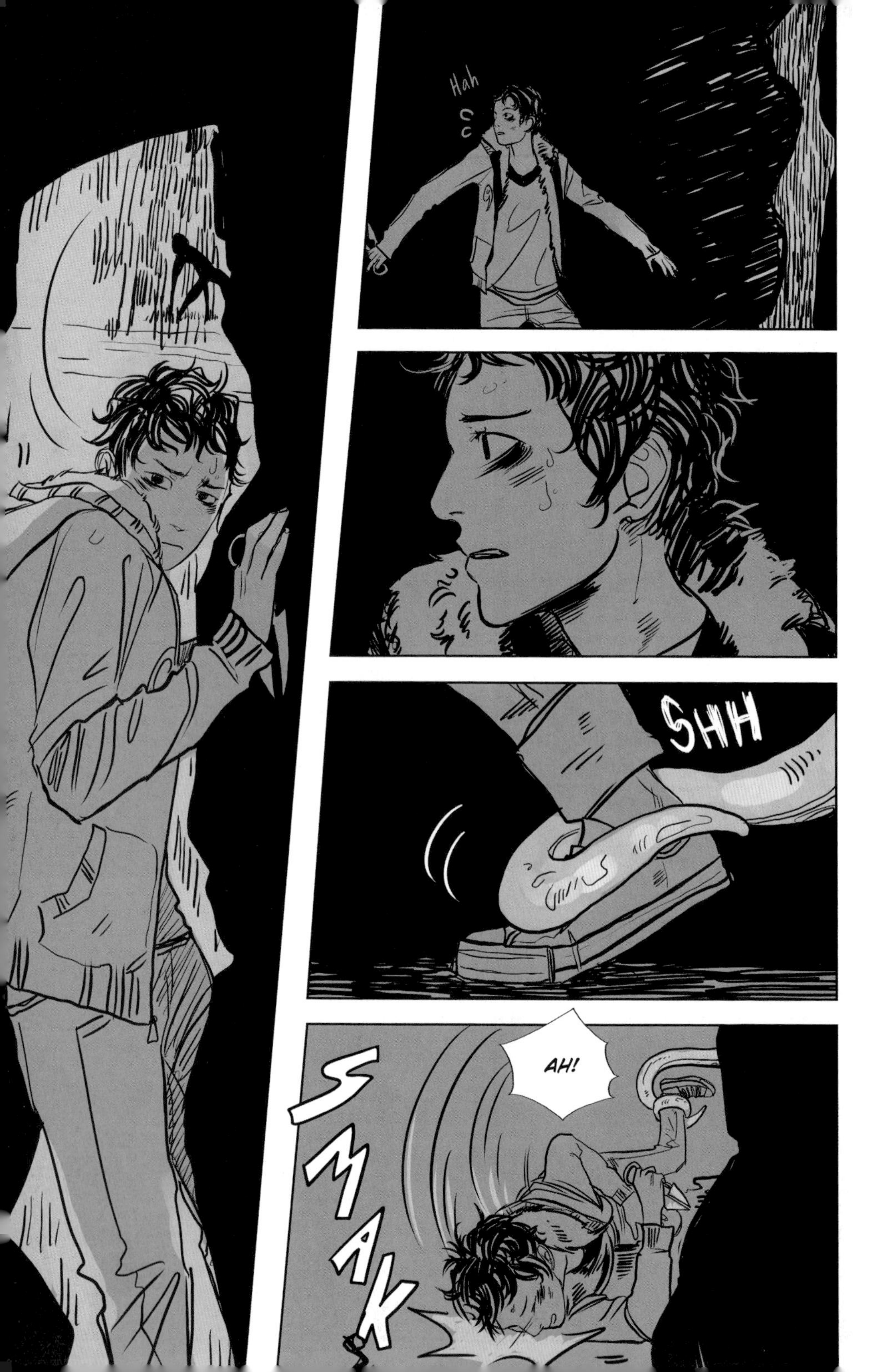
Hah
SHH
SMAK
AH!

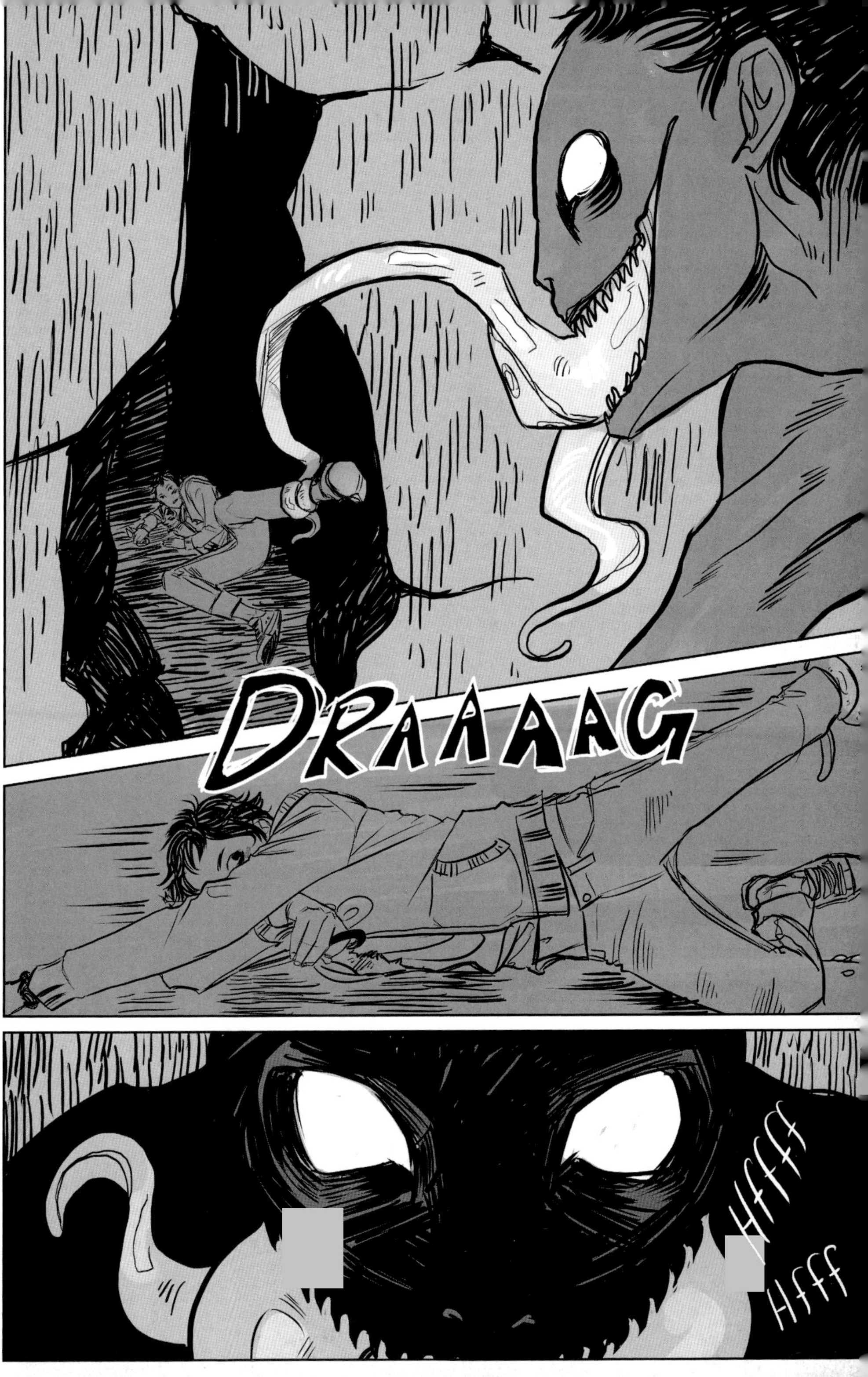
DRAAAAG
Hffff
Hffff

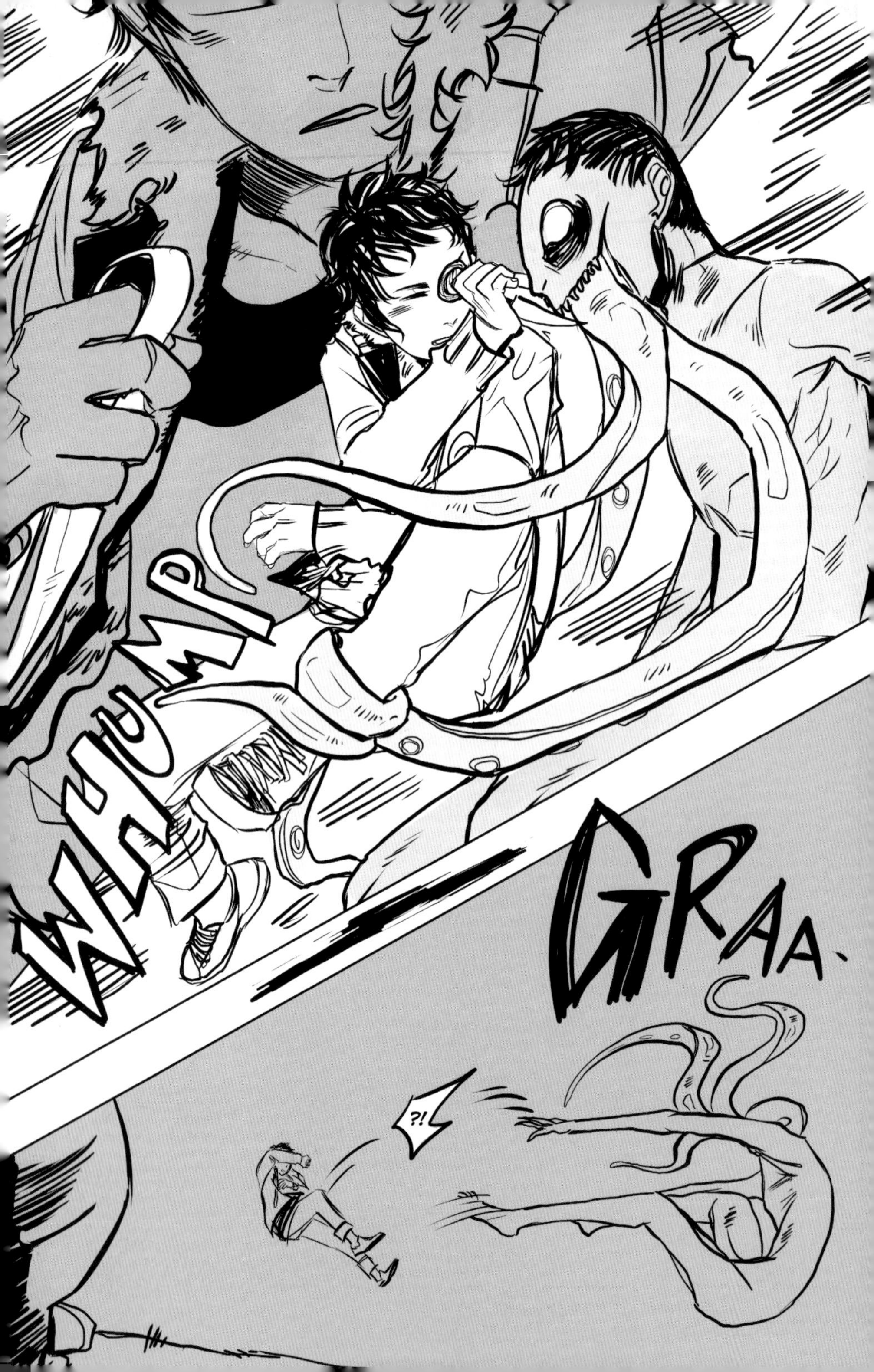
WHUMP
GRAA.
?!

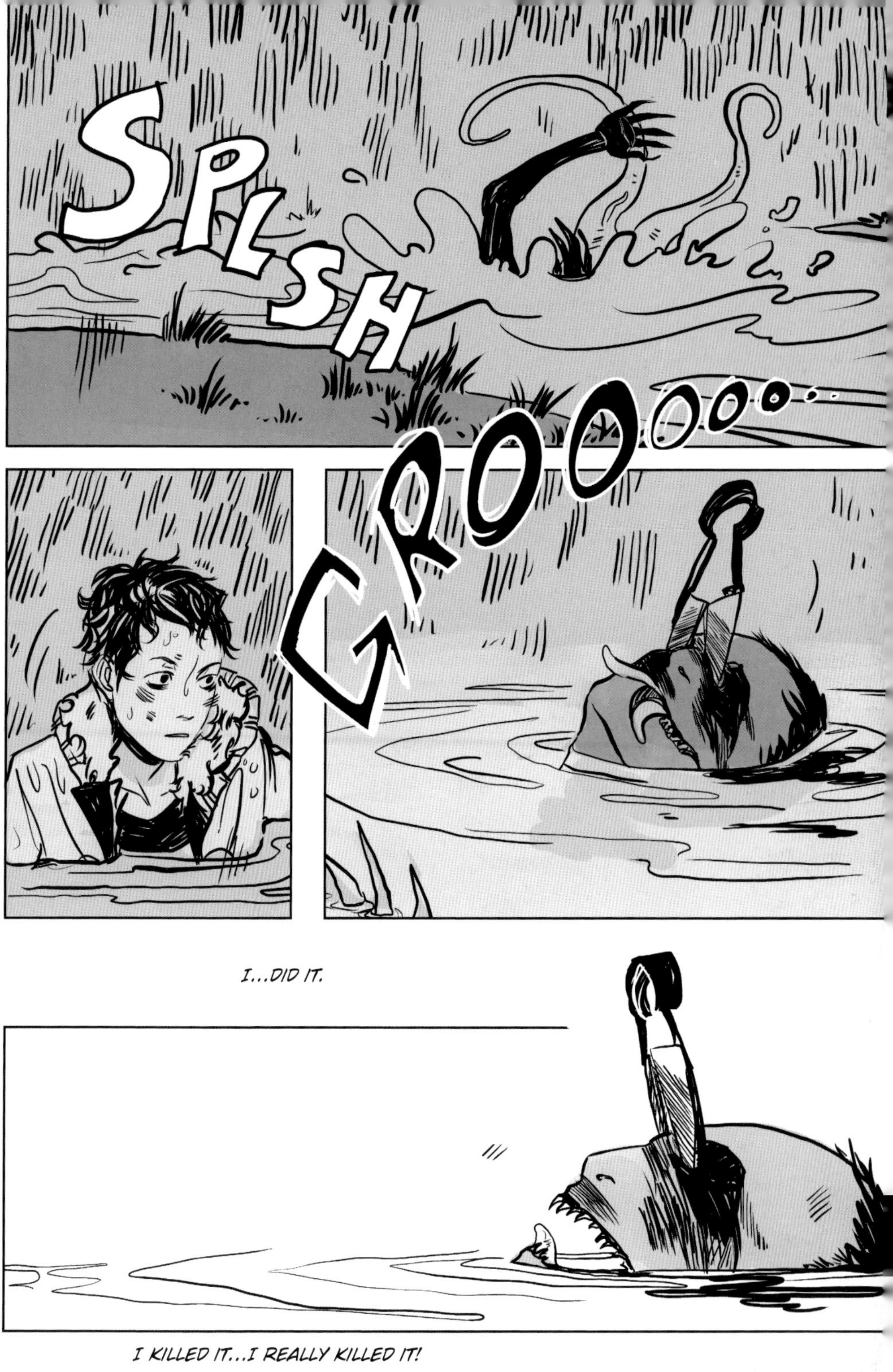
SPLSH
GROOOOOO...
I...DID IT.
I KILLED IT...I REALLY KILLED IT!

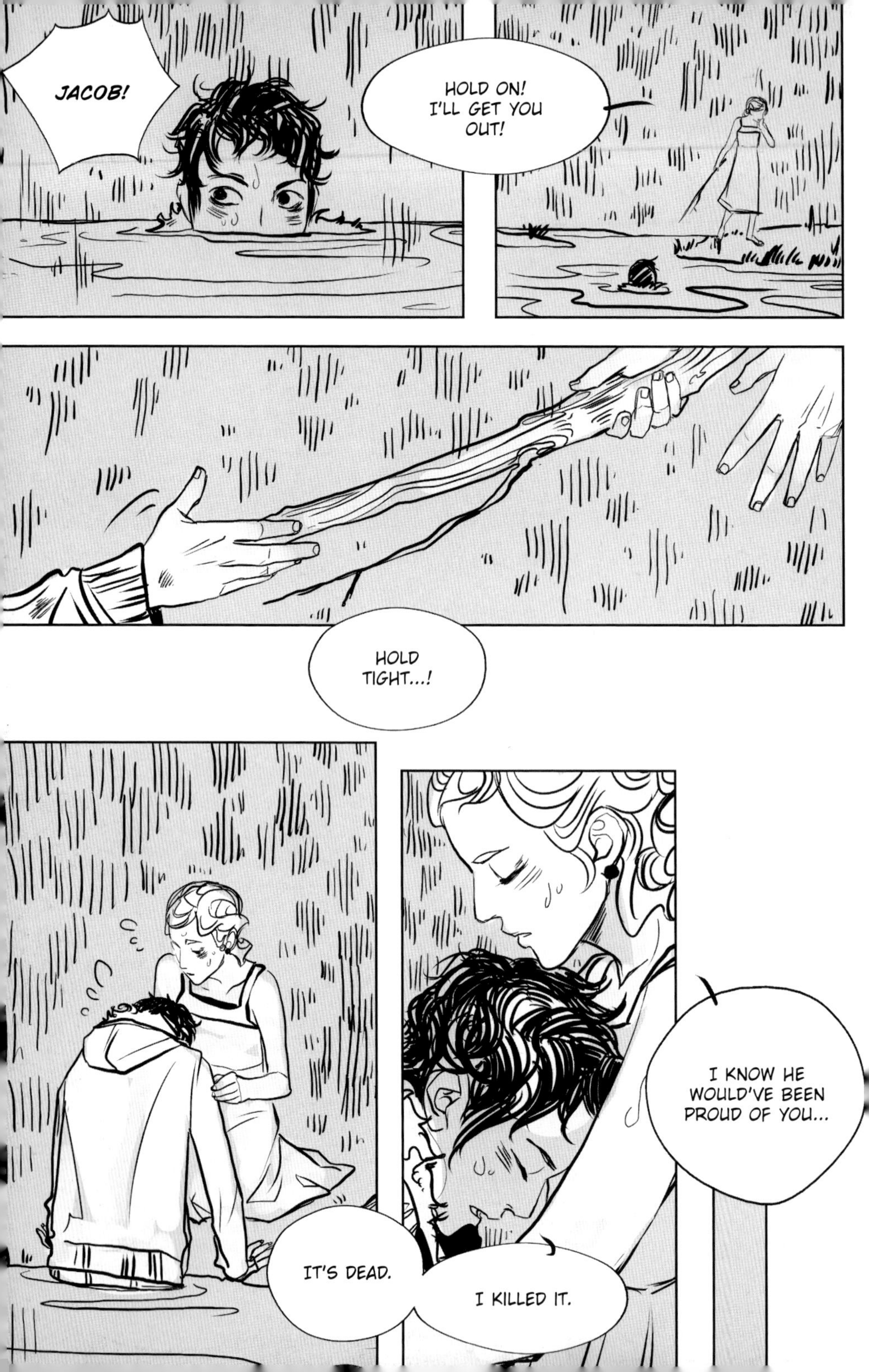
JACOB!
HOLD ON! I'LL GET YOU OUT!
HOLD TIGHT...!
IT'S DEAD.
I KILLED IT.
I KNOW HE WOULD'VE BEEN PROUD OF YOU...

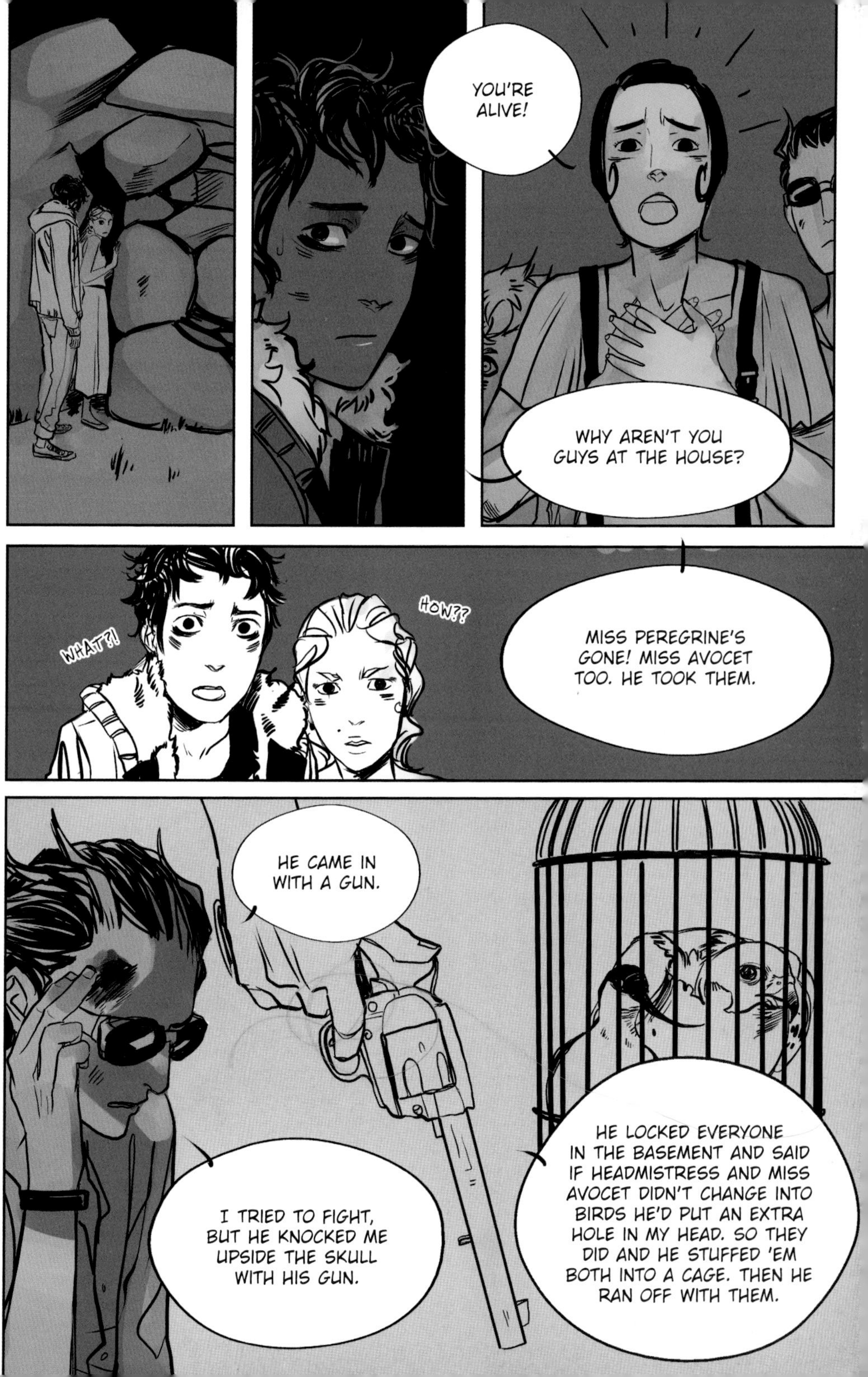
YOU'RE ALIVE!
WHY AREN'T YOU GUYS AT THE HOUSE?
WHAT?!
HOW??
MISS PEREGRINE'S GONE! MISS AVOCET TOO. HE TOOK THEM.
HE CAME IN WITH A GUN.
I TRIED TO FIGHT, BUT HE KNOCKED ME UPSIDE THE SKULL WITH HIS GUN.
HE LOCKED EVERYONE IN THE BASEMENT AND SAID IF HEADMISTRESS AND MISS AVOCET DIDN'T CHANGE INTO BIRDS HE'D PUT AN EXTRA HOLE IN MY HEAD. SO THEY DID AND HE STUFFED 'EM BOTH INTO A CAGE. THEN HE RAN OFF WITH THEM.

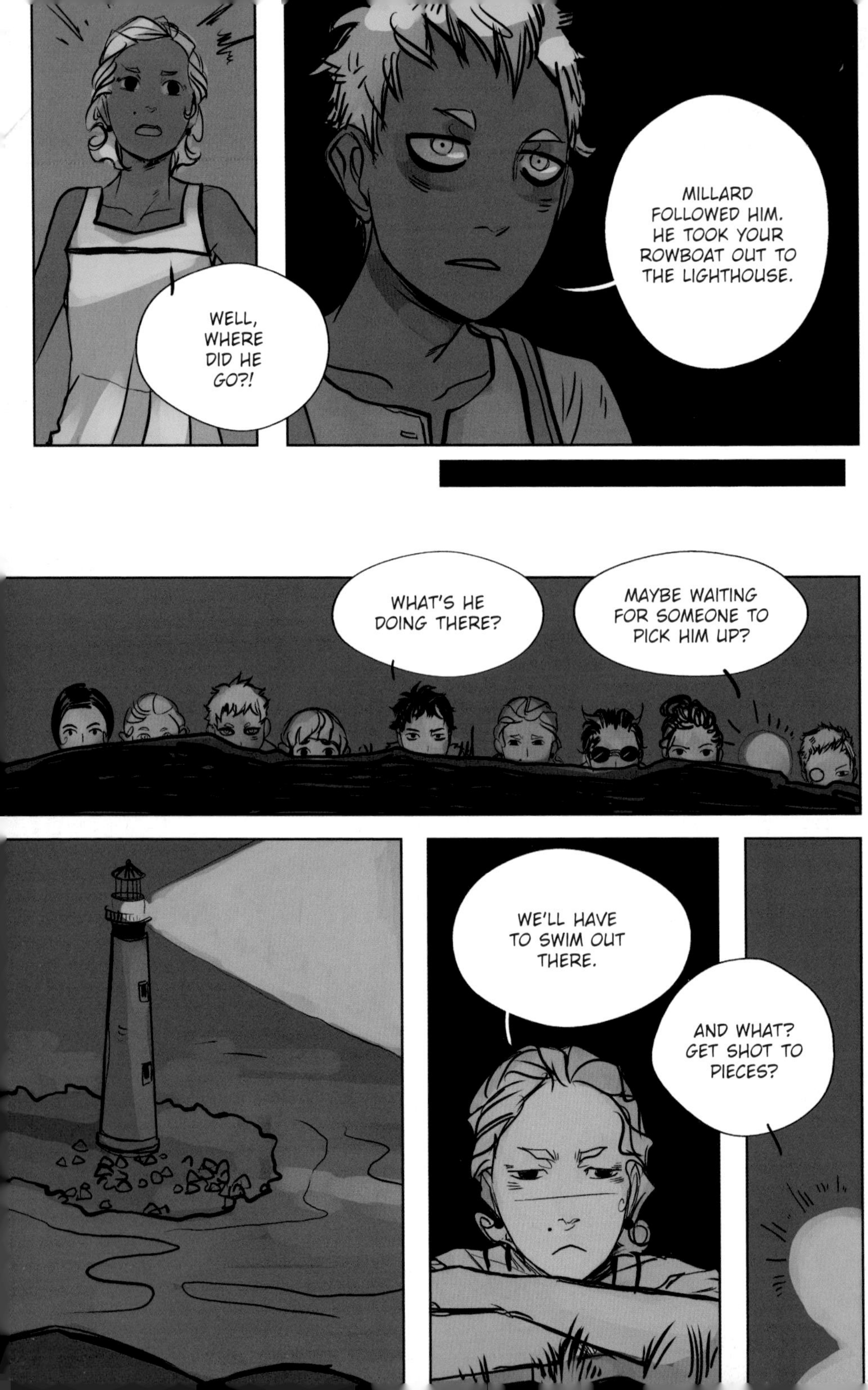
WELL, WHERE DID HE GO?!
MILLARD FOLLOWED HIM. HE TOOK YOUR ROWBOAT OUT TO THE LIGHTHOUSE.
WHAT'S HE DOING THERE?
MAYBE WAITING FOR SOMEONE TO PICK HIM UP?
WE'LL HAVE TO SWIM OUT THERE.
AND WHAT? GET SHOT TO PIECES?

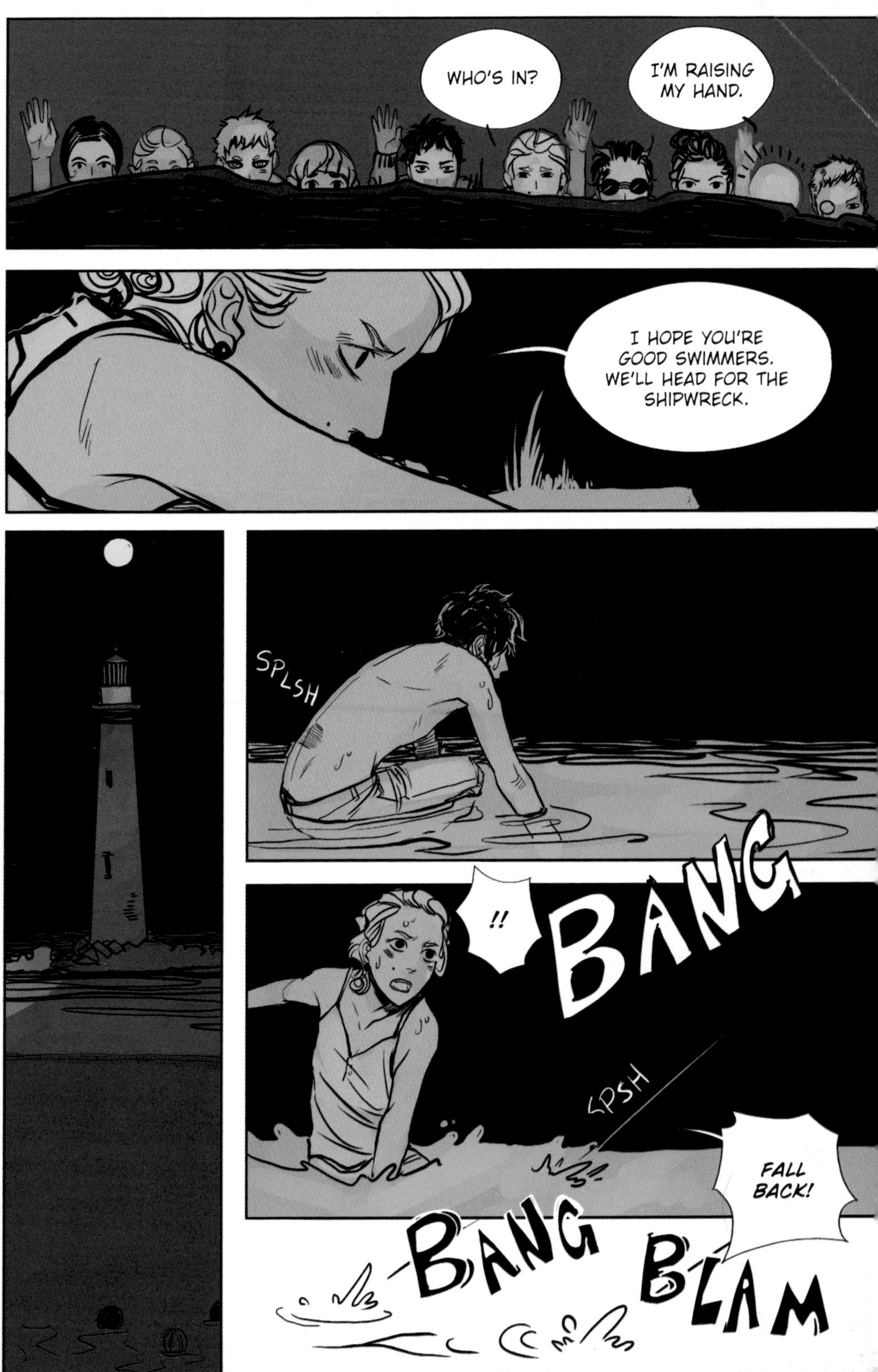
WHO'S IN?
I'M RAISING MY HAND.
I HOPE YOU'RE GOOD SWIMMERS. WE'LL HEAD FOR THE SHIPWRECK.
SPLSH
!!
BANG
SPSH
FALL BACK!
BANG
BLAM

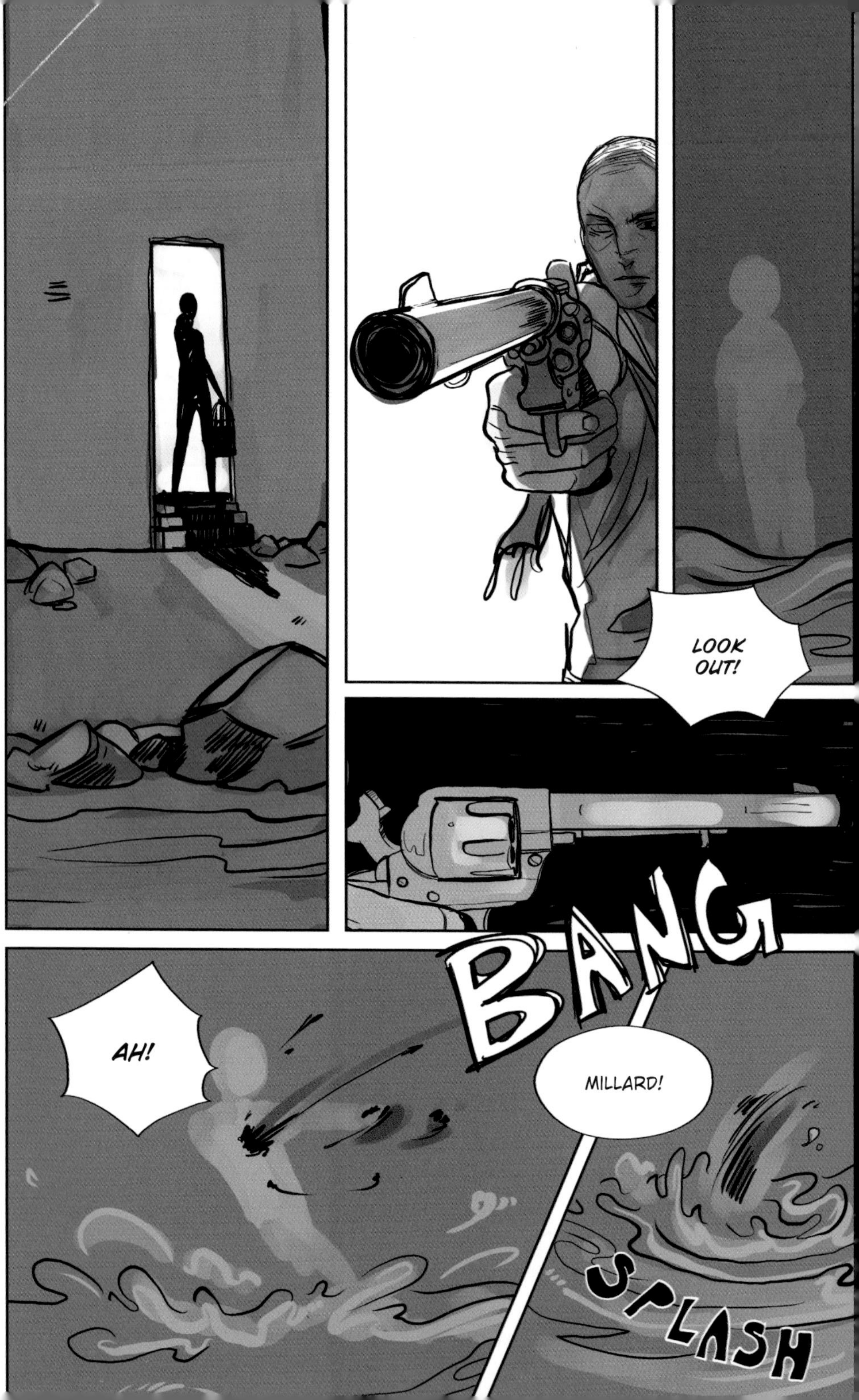
LOOK OUT!
BANG
AH!
MILLARD!
SPLASH

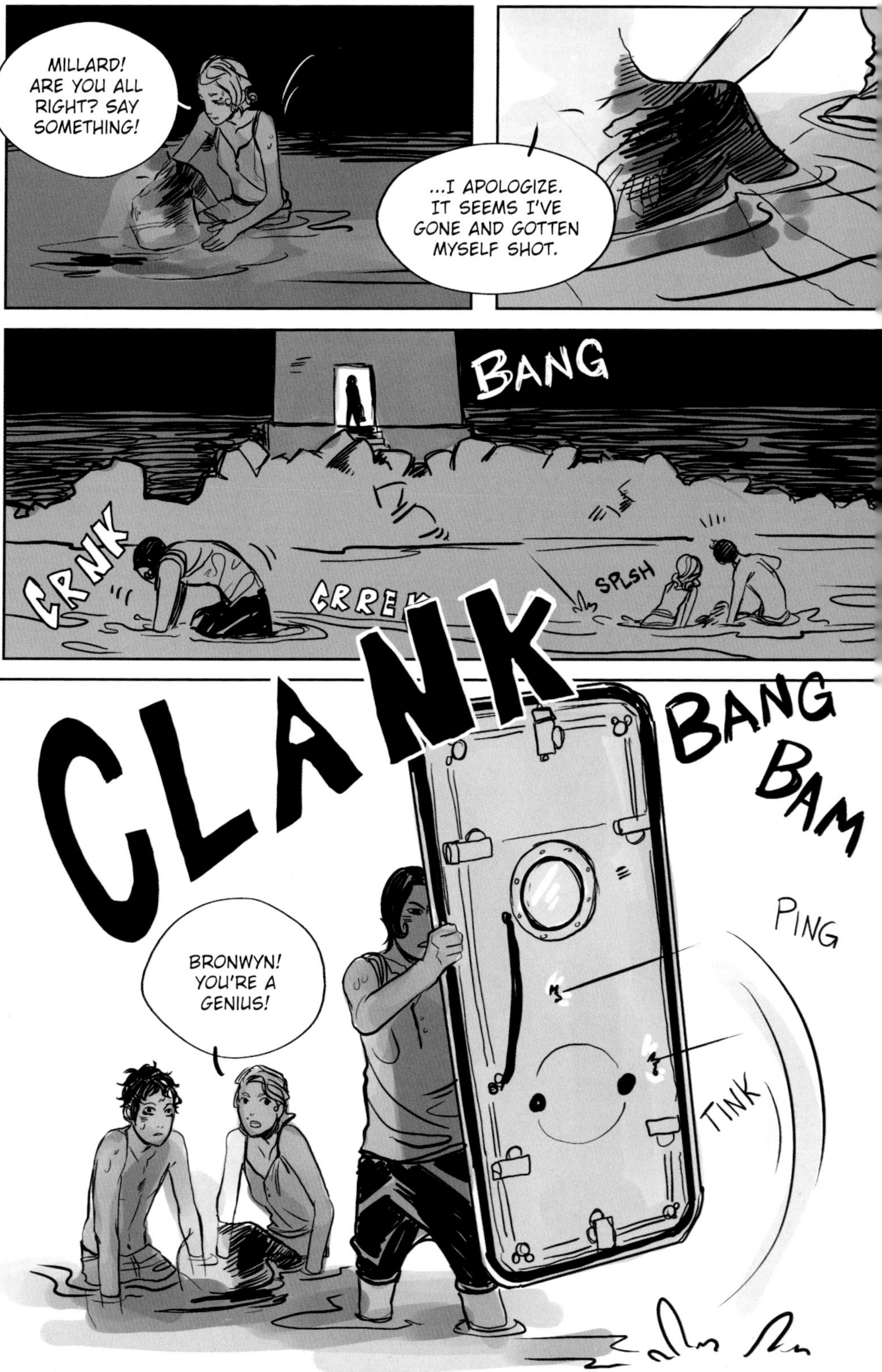
MILLARD! ARE YOU ALL RIGHT? SAY SOMETHING!
...I APOLOGIZE. IT SEEMS I'VE GONE AND GOTTEN MYSELF SHOT.
BANG
CRNK
CRREK
SPLSH
CLANK
BANG
BAM
PING
BRONWYN! YOU'RE A GENIUS!
TINK

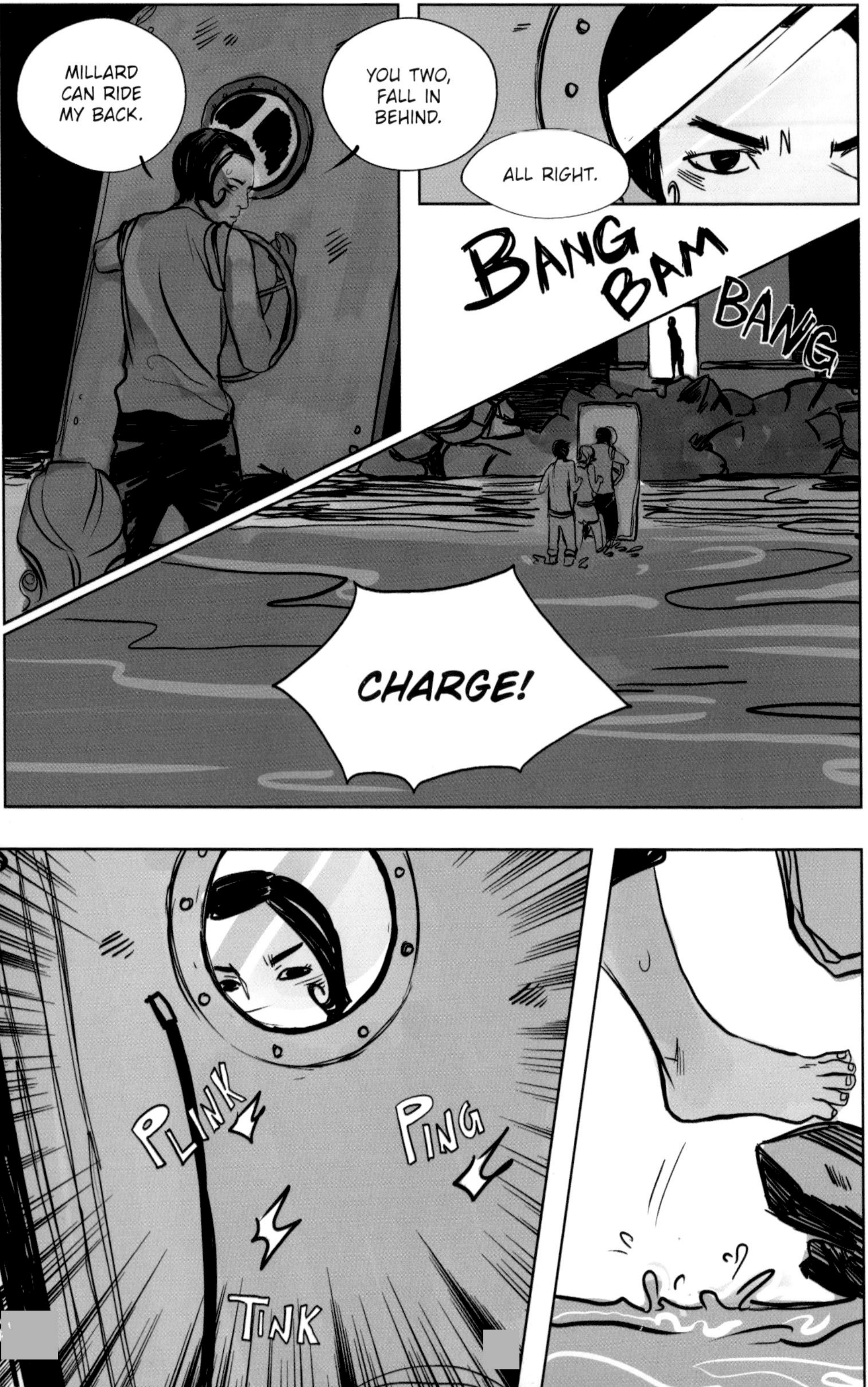
MILLARD CAN RIDE MY BACK.
YOU TWO, FALL IN BEHIND.
ALL RIGHT.
BANG
BAM
BANG
CHARGE!
PLINK
PING
TINK

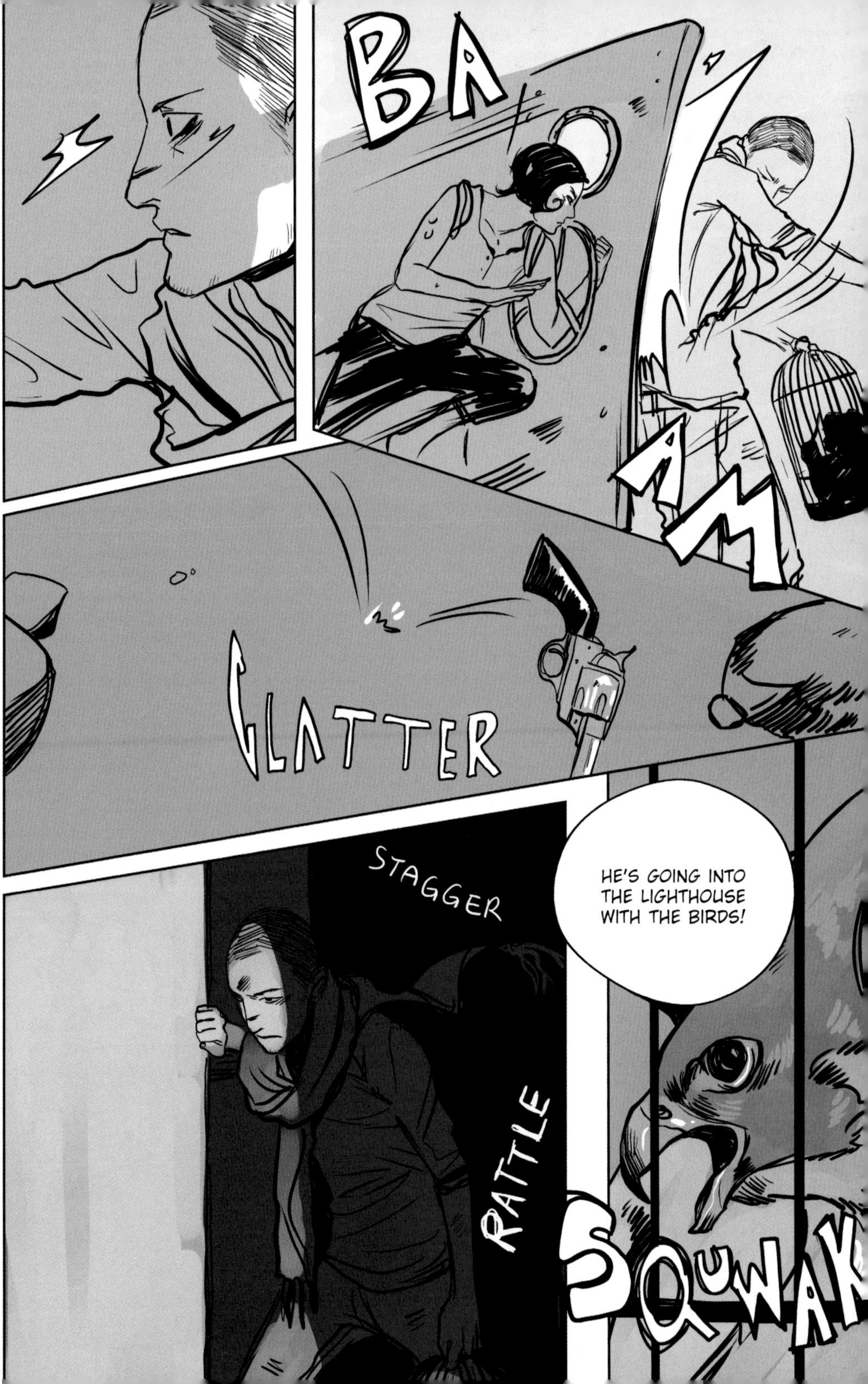

BAM
CLATTER
STAGGER
RATTLE
HE'S GOING INTO THE LIGHTHOUSE WITH THE BIRDS!
SQUWAK

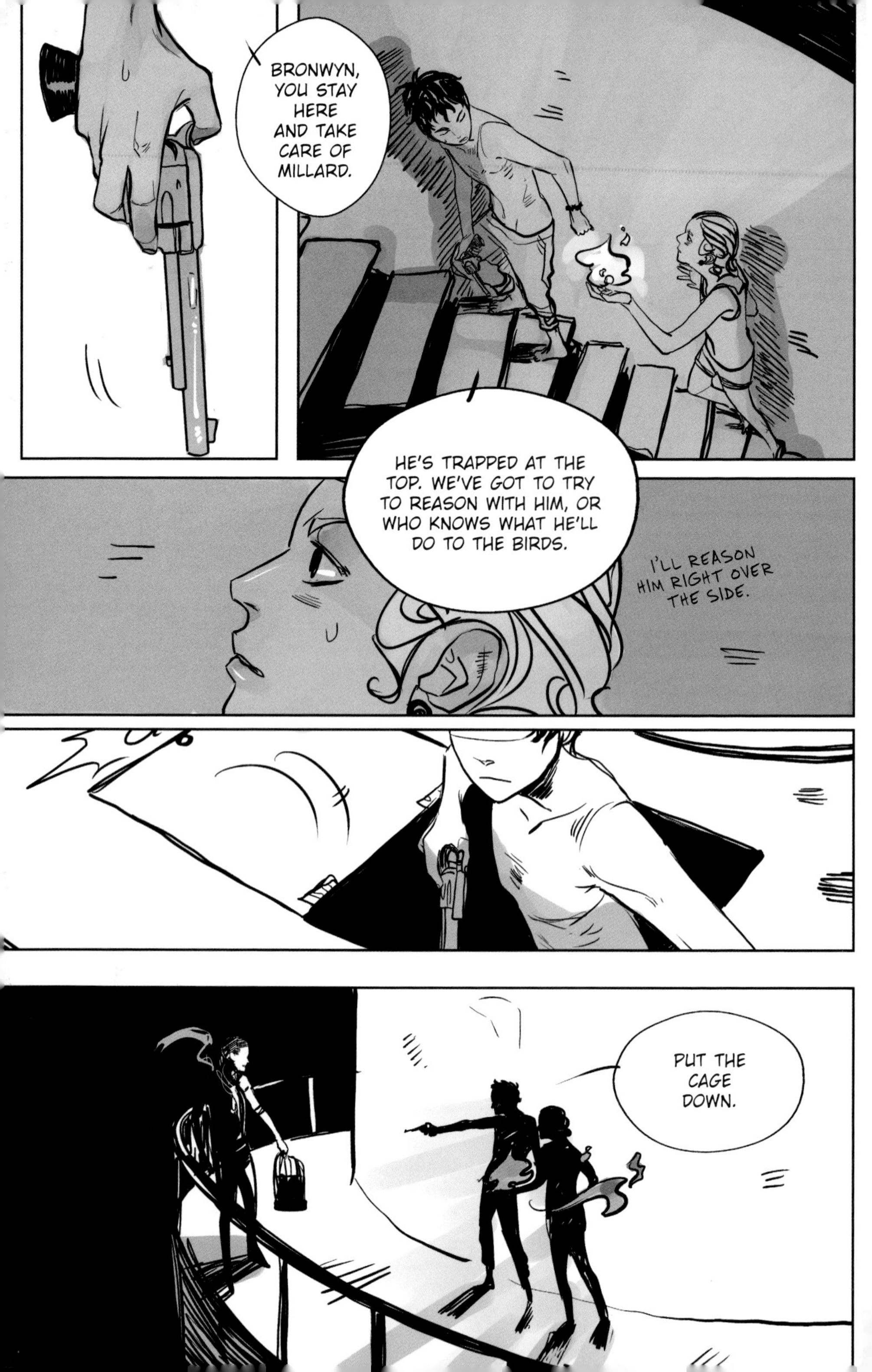
BRONWYN, YOU STAY HERE AND TAKE CARE OF MILLARD.
HE'S TRAPPED AT THE TOP. WE'VE GOT TO TRY TO REASON WITH HIM, OR WHO KNOWS WHAT HE'LL DO TO THE BIRDS.
I'LL REASON HIM RIGHT OVER THE SIDE.
PUT THE CAGE DOWN.

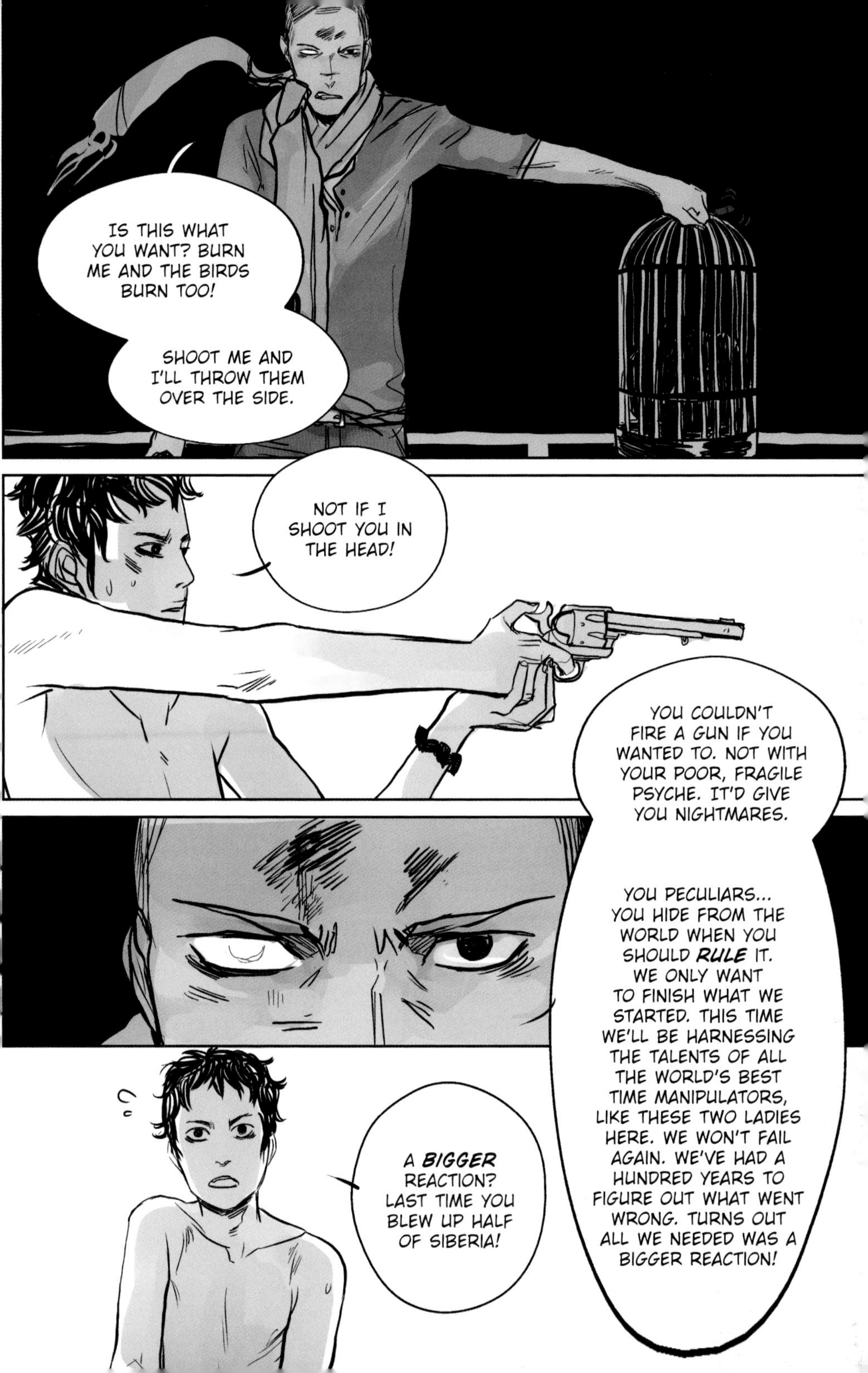
IS THIS WHAT YOU WANT? BURN ME AND THE BIRDS BURN TOO!
SHOOT ME AND I'LL THROW THEM OVER THE SIDE.
NOT IF I SHOOT YOU IN THE HEAD!
YOU COULDN'T FIRE A GUN IF YOU WANTED TO. NOT WITH YOUR POOR, FRAGILE PSYCHE. IT'D GIVE YOU NIGHTMARES.
YOU PECULIARS... YOU HIDE FROM THE WORLD WHEN YOU SHOULD RULE IT. WE ONLY WANT TO FINISH WHAT WE STARTED. THIS TIME WE'LL BE HARNESSING THE TALENTS OF ALL THE WORLD'S BEST TIME MANIPULATORS, LIKE THESE TWO LADIES HERE. WE WON'T FAIL AGAIN. WE'VE HAD A HUNDRED YEARS TO FIGURE OUT WHAT WENT WRONG. TURNS OUT ALL WE NEEDED WAS A BIGGER REACTION!
A BIGGER REACTION? LAST TIME YOU BLEW UP HALF OF SIBERIA!

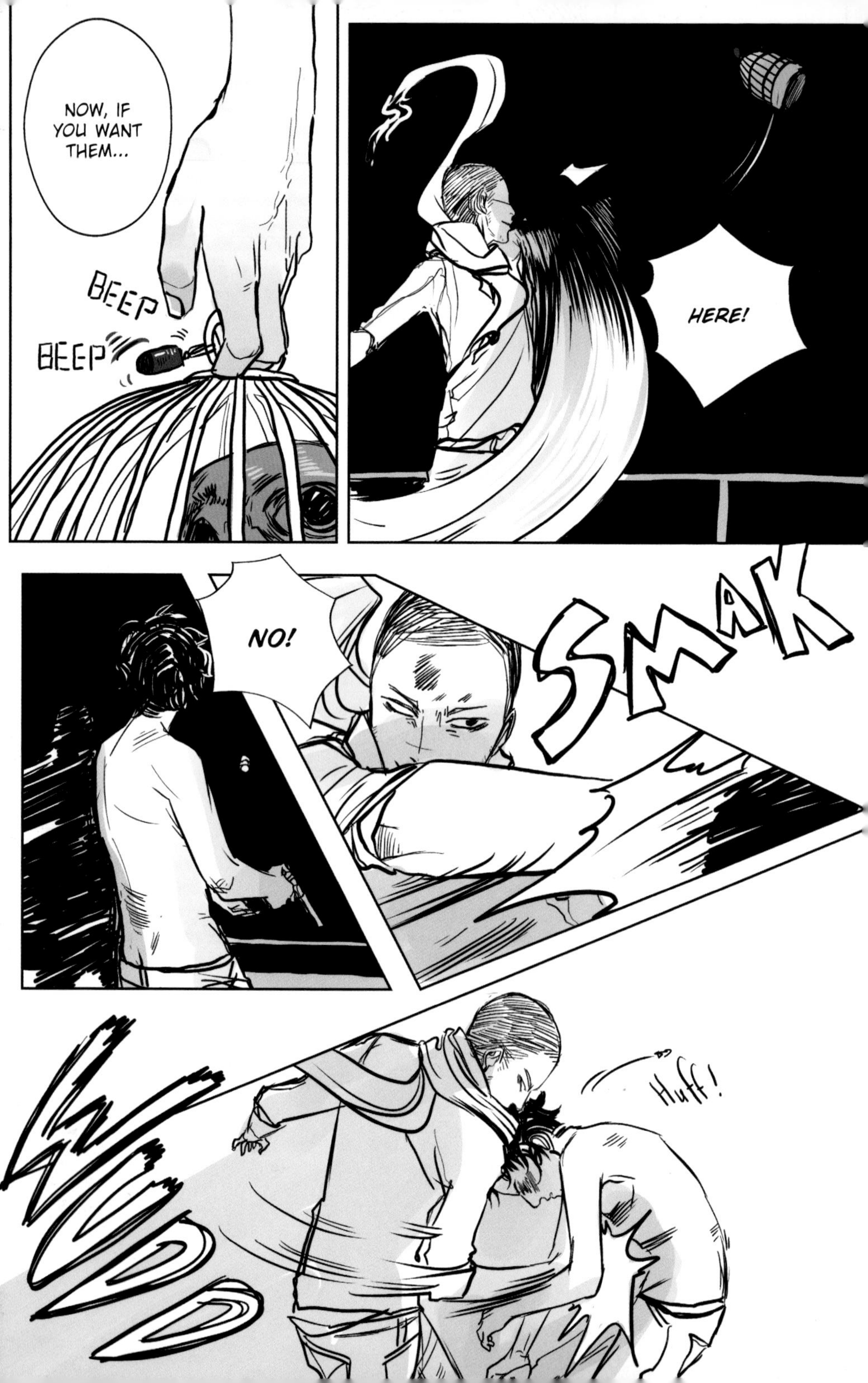
NOW, IF YOU WANT THEM...
BEEP
BEEP
HERE!
NO!
SMAK
WHOOD
Huff!

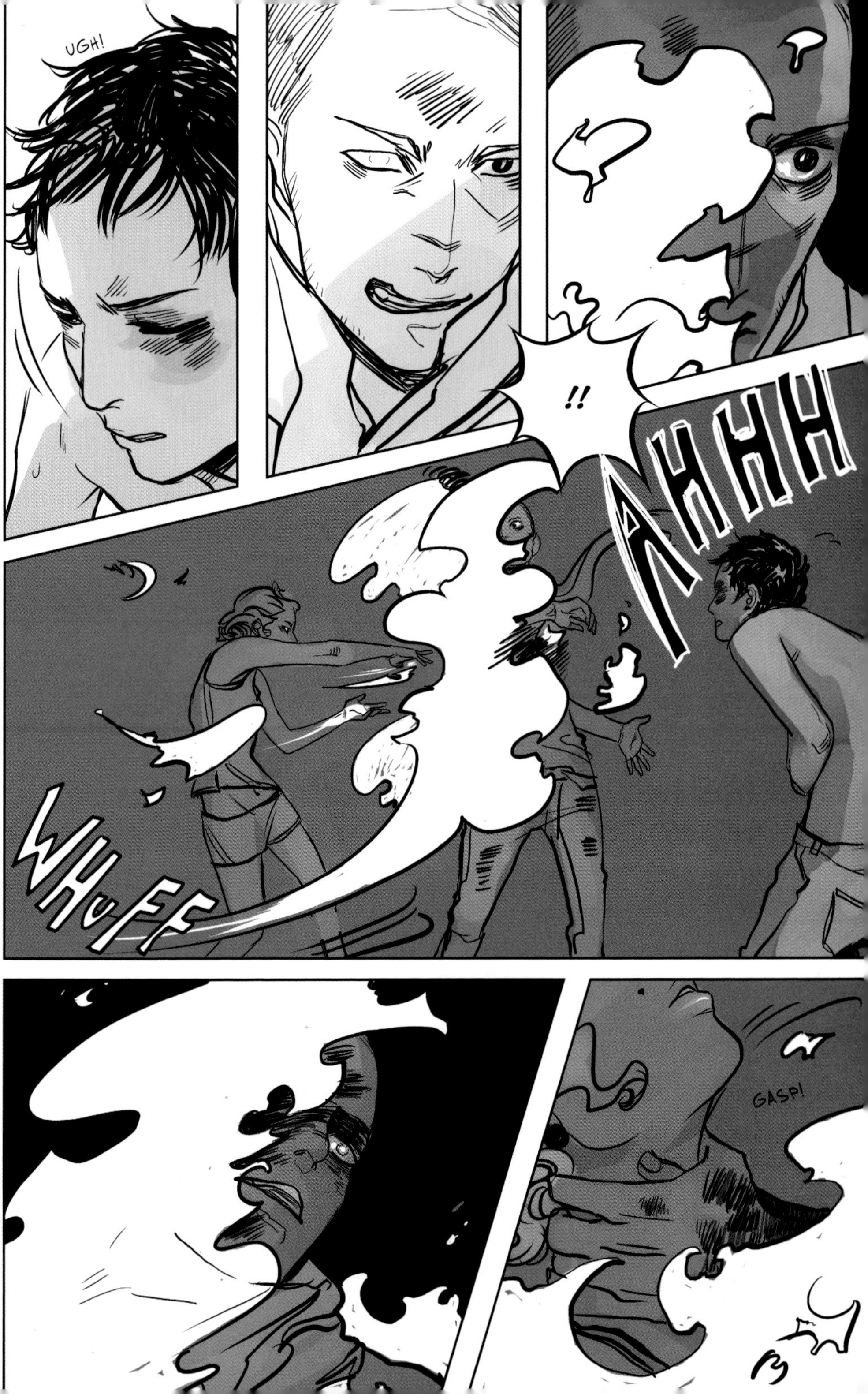
UGH!
!!
AHHH
WHUFF
GASP!

GRRIP

HNNK!

EMMA!

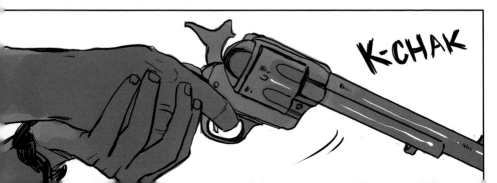

K-CHAK

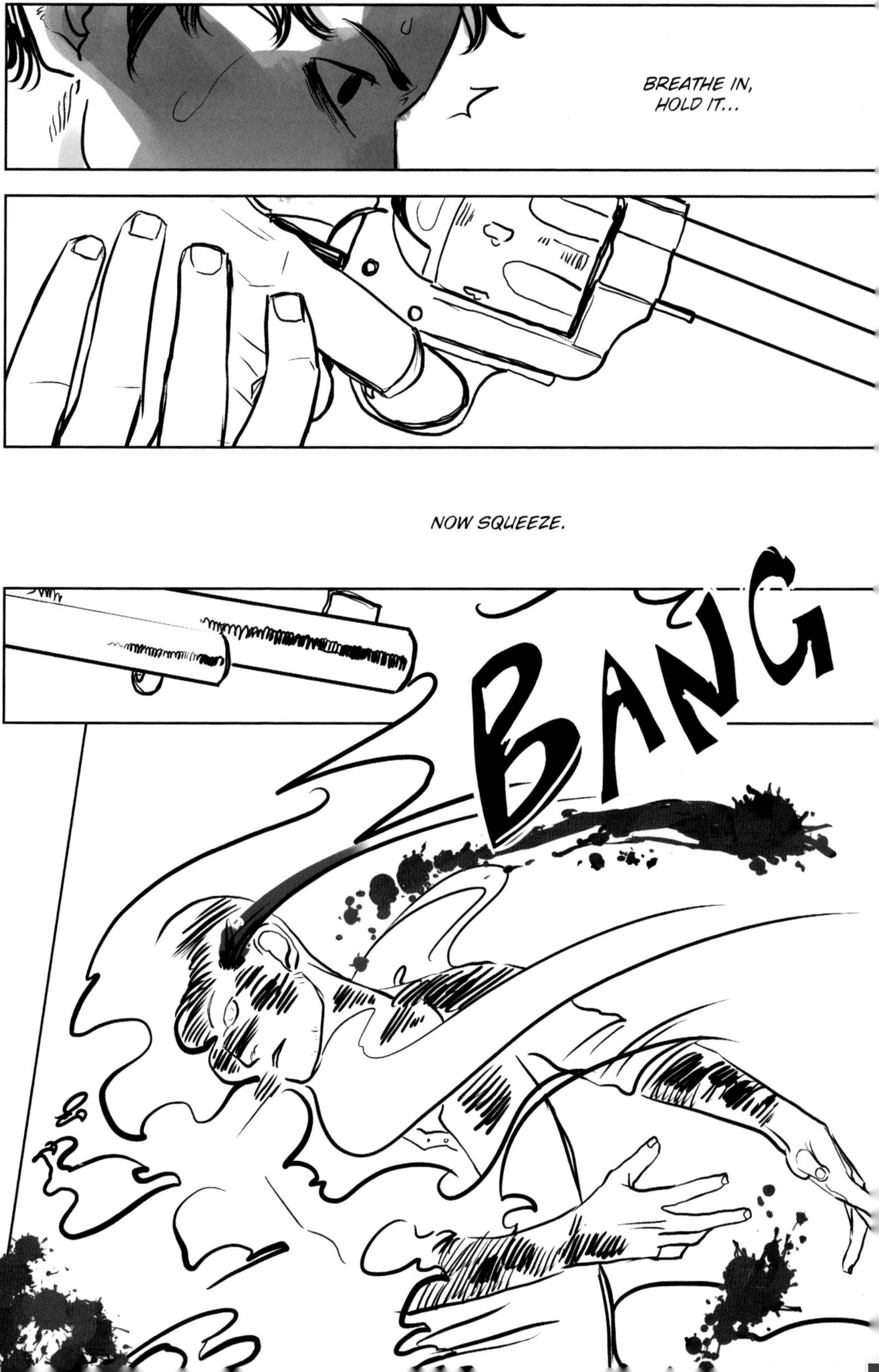
BREATHE IN,
HOLD IT...
NOW SQUEEZE.
BANG

CHAPTER EIGHT

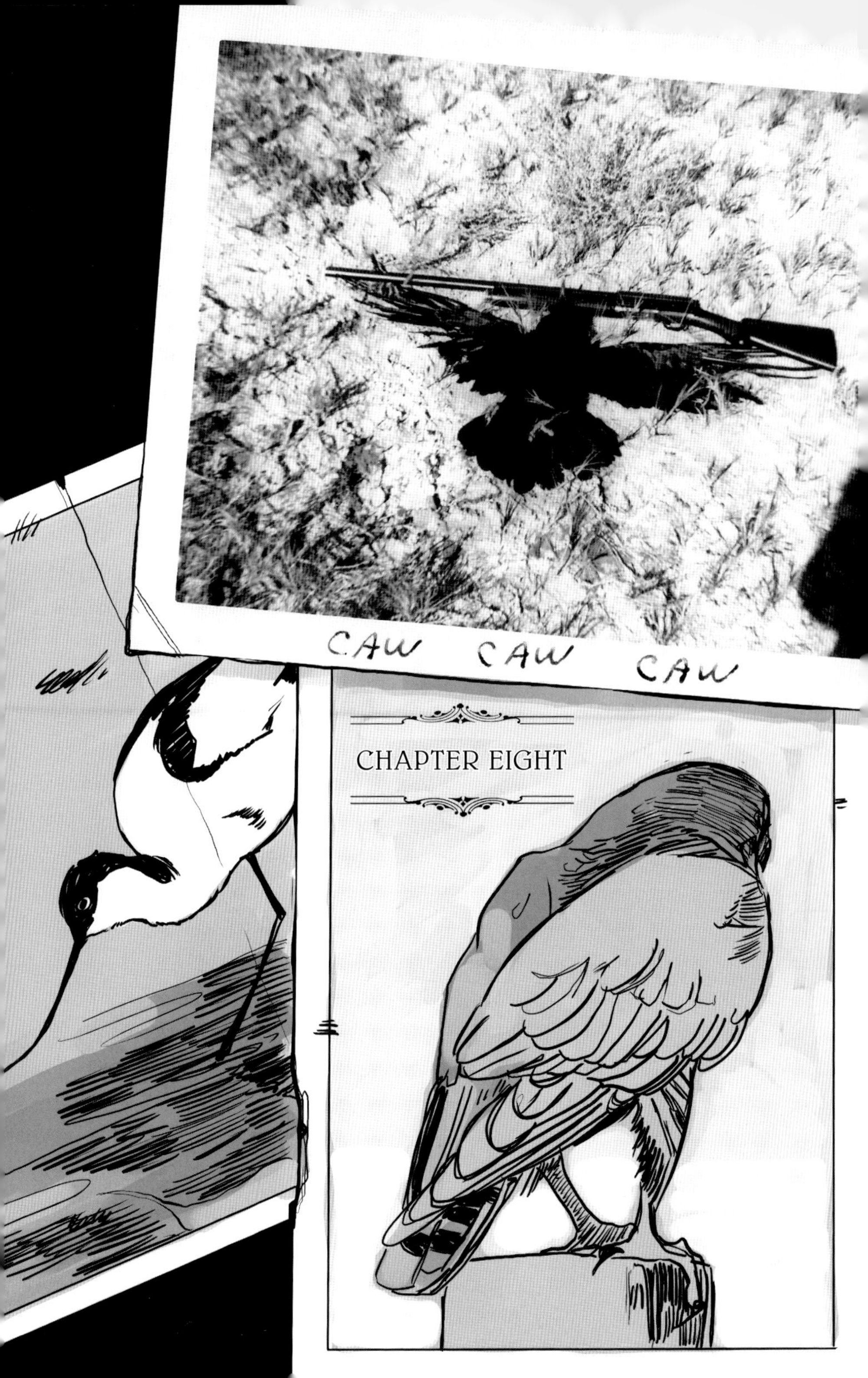
CAW CAW CAW

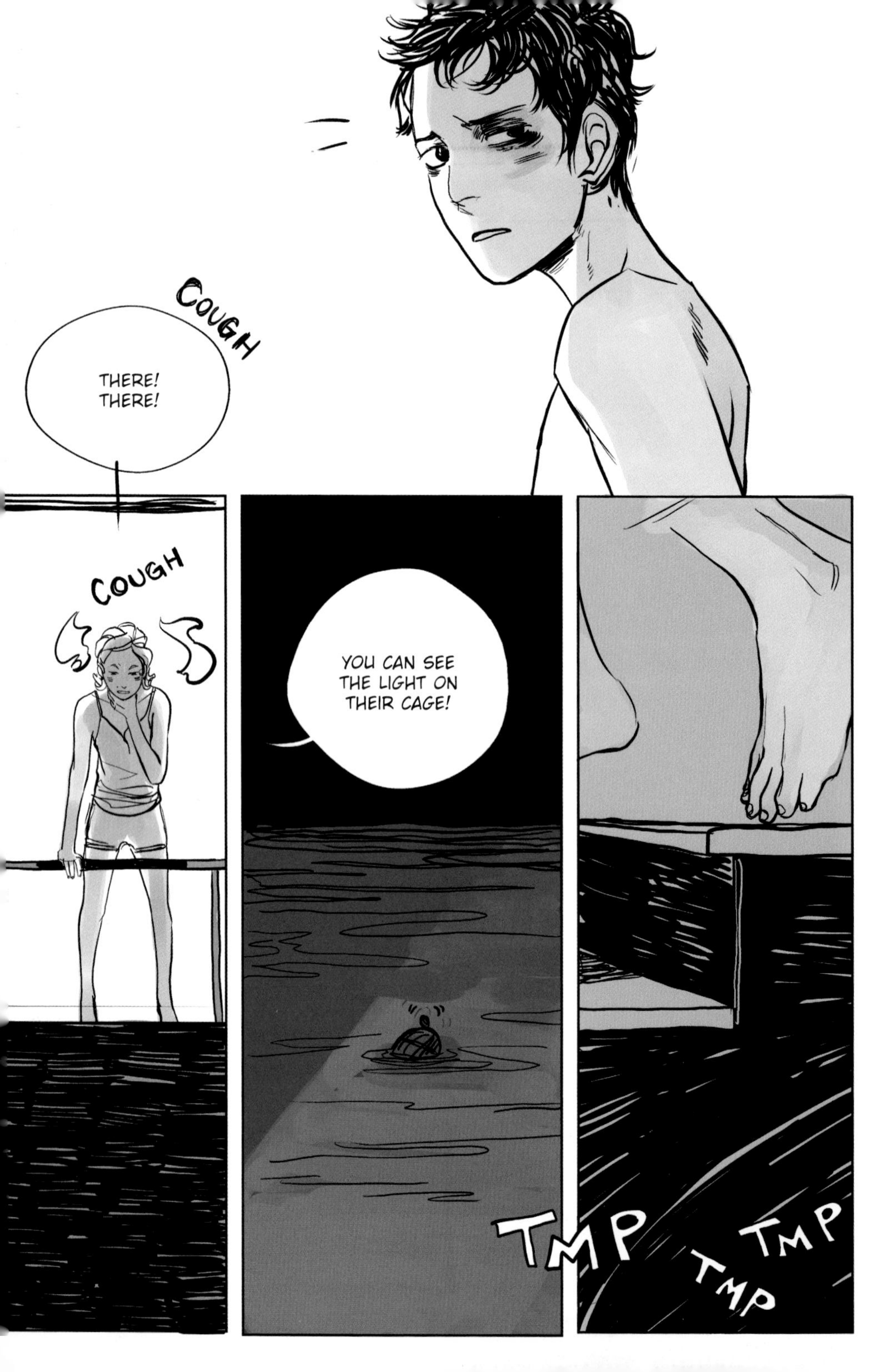
COUGH
THERE! THERE!
COUGH
YOU CAN SEE THE LIGHT ON THEIR CAGE!
TMP
TMP
TMP

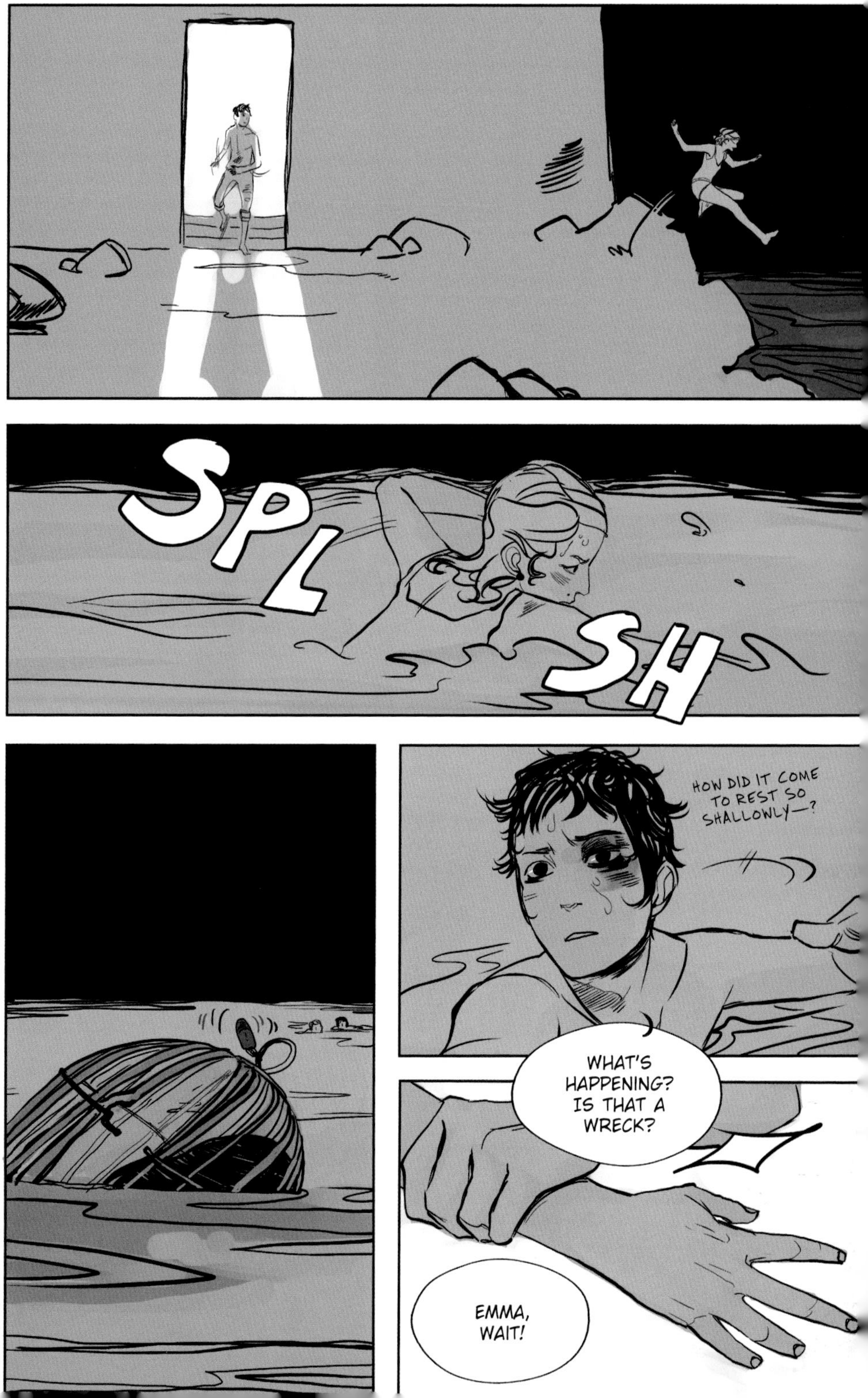
SPLSH
HOW DID IT COME TO REST SO SHALLOWLY—?
WHAT'S HAPPENING? IS THAT A WRECK?
EMMA, WAIT!

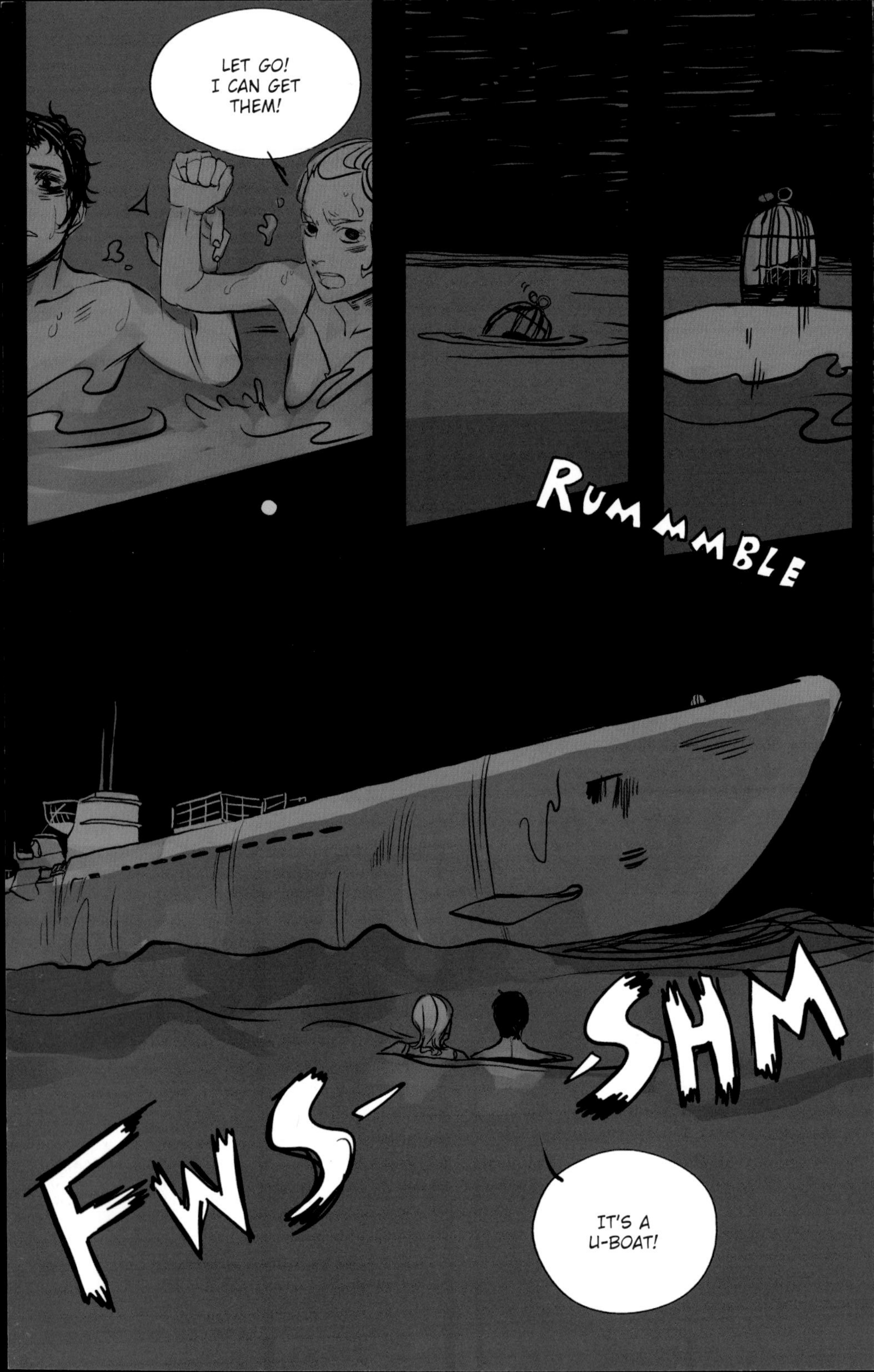
LET GO! I CAN GET THEM!
RUMMMBLE
FWS-SHM
IT'S A U-BOAT!

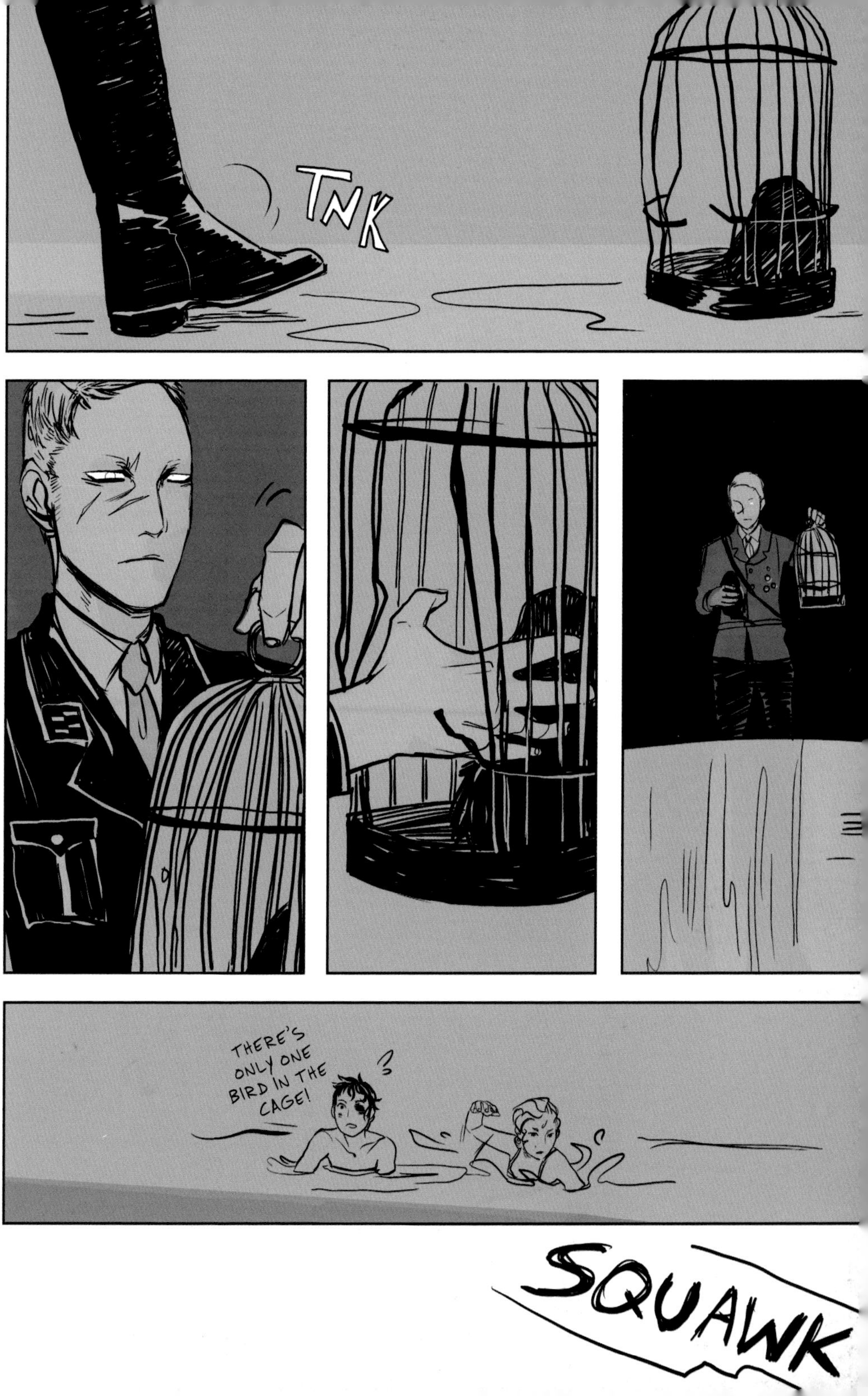
TNK
THERE'S ONLY ONE BIRD IN THE CAGE!
?
SQUAWK

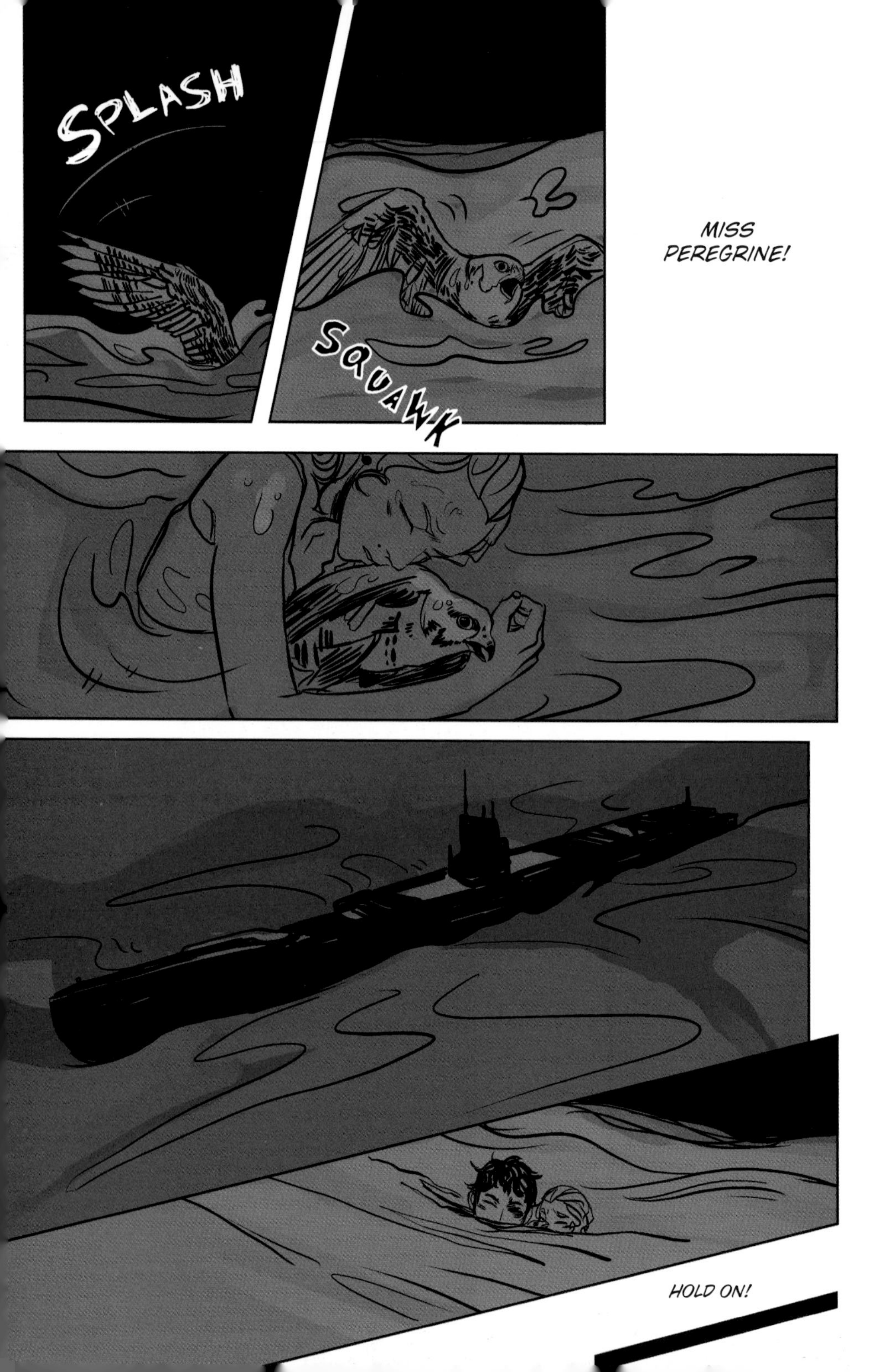
SPLASH
SQUAWK
MISS PEREGRINE!
HOLD ON!

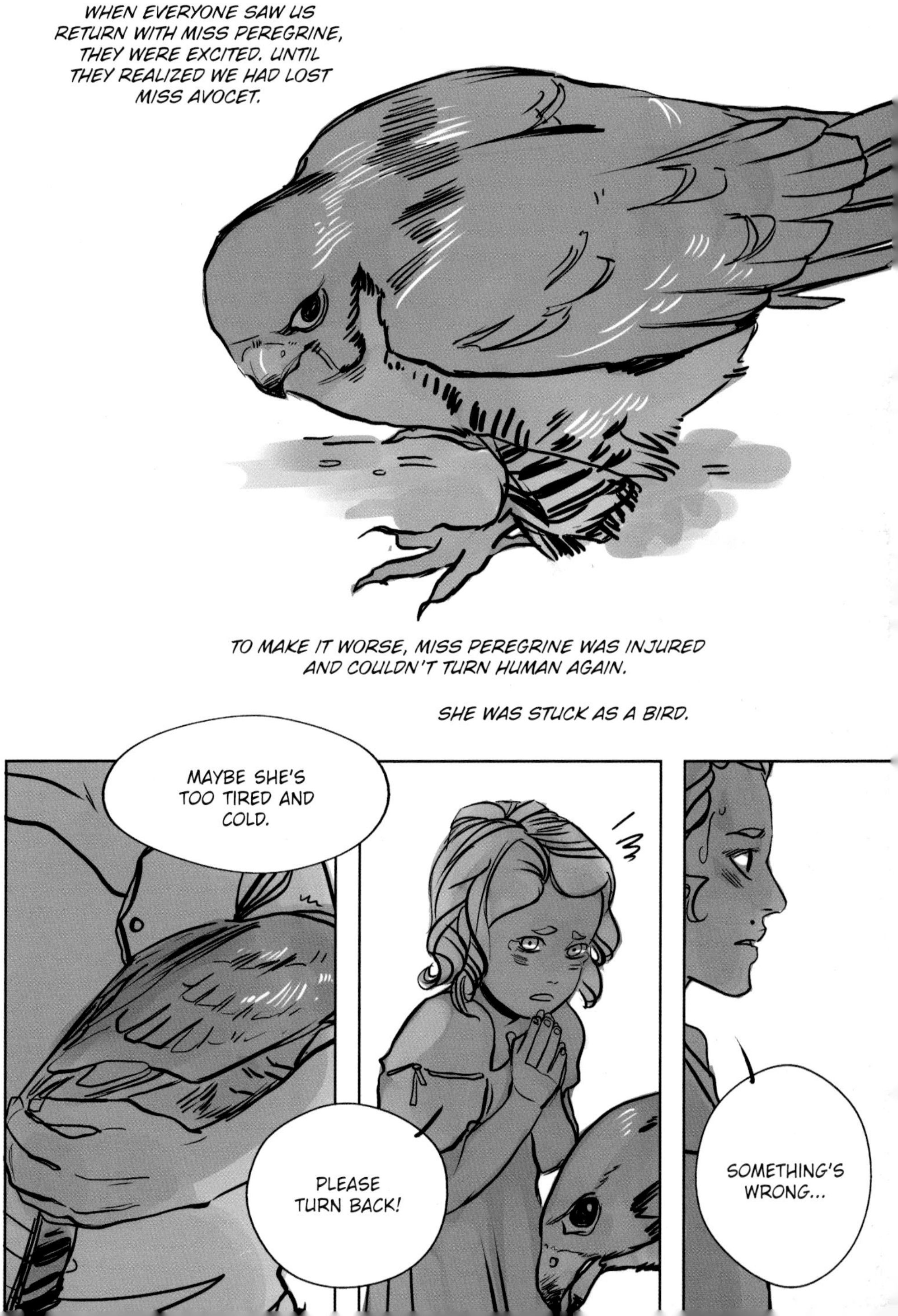
WHEN EVERYONE SAW US RETURN WITH MISS PEREGRINE, THEY WERE EXCITED. UNTIL THEY REALIZED WE HAD LOST MISS AVOCET.
TO MAKE IT WORSE, MISS PEREGRINE WAS INJURED AND COULDN'T TURN HUMAN AGAIN.
SHE WAS STUCK AS A BIRD.
MAYBE SHE'S TOO TIRED AND COLD.
PLEASE TURN BACK!
SOMETHING'S WRONG...

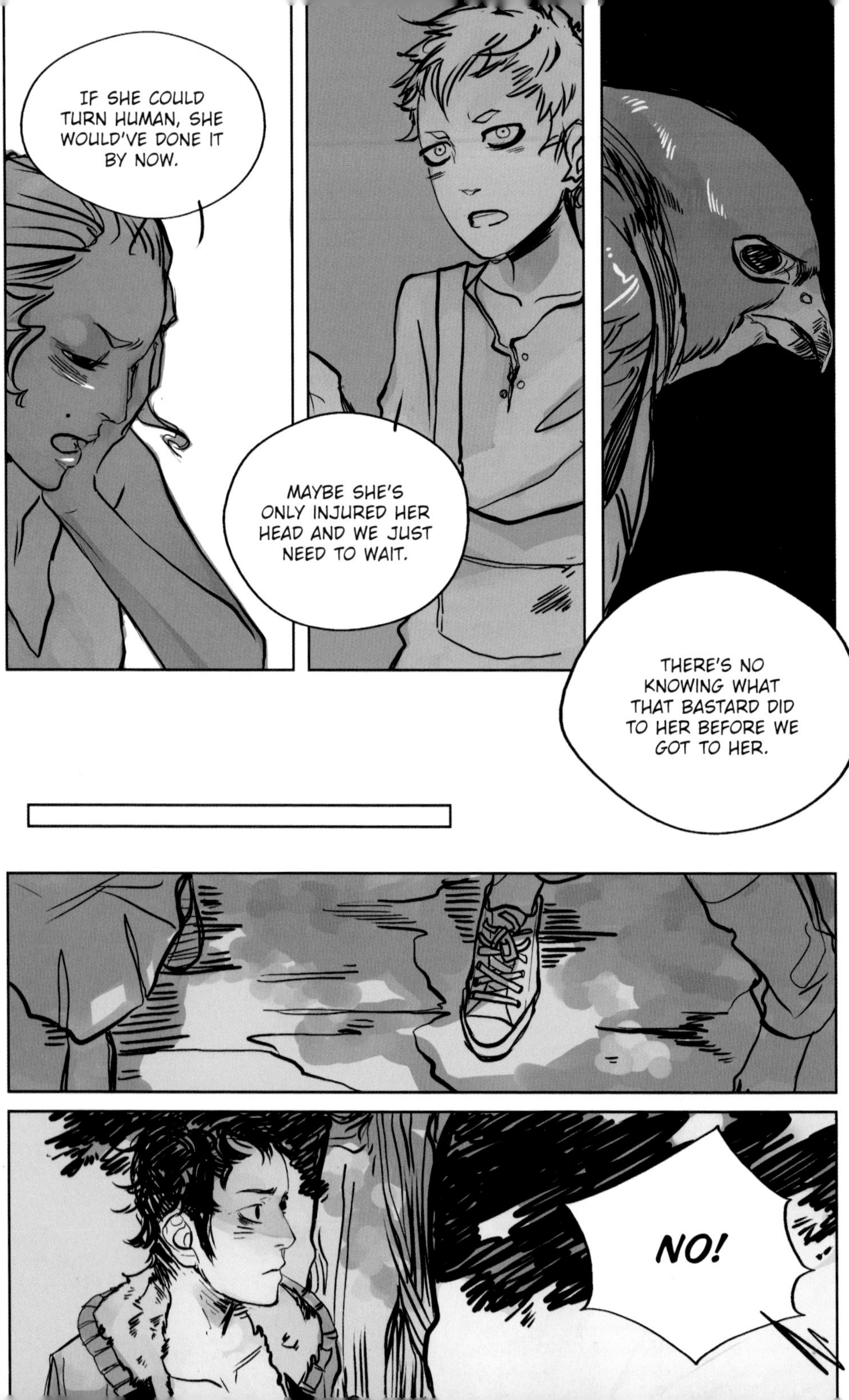
IF SHE COULD TURN HUMAN, SHE WOULD'VE DONE IT BY NOW.
MAYBE SHE'S ONLY INJURED HER HEAD AND WE JUST NEED TO WAIT.
THERE'S NO KNOWING WHAT THAT BASTARD DID TO HER BEFORE WE GOT TO HER.
NO!

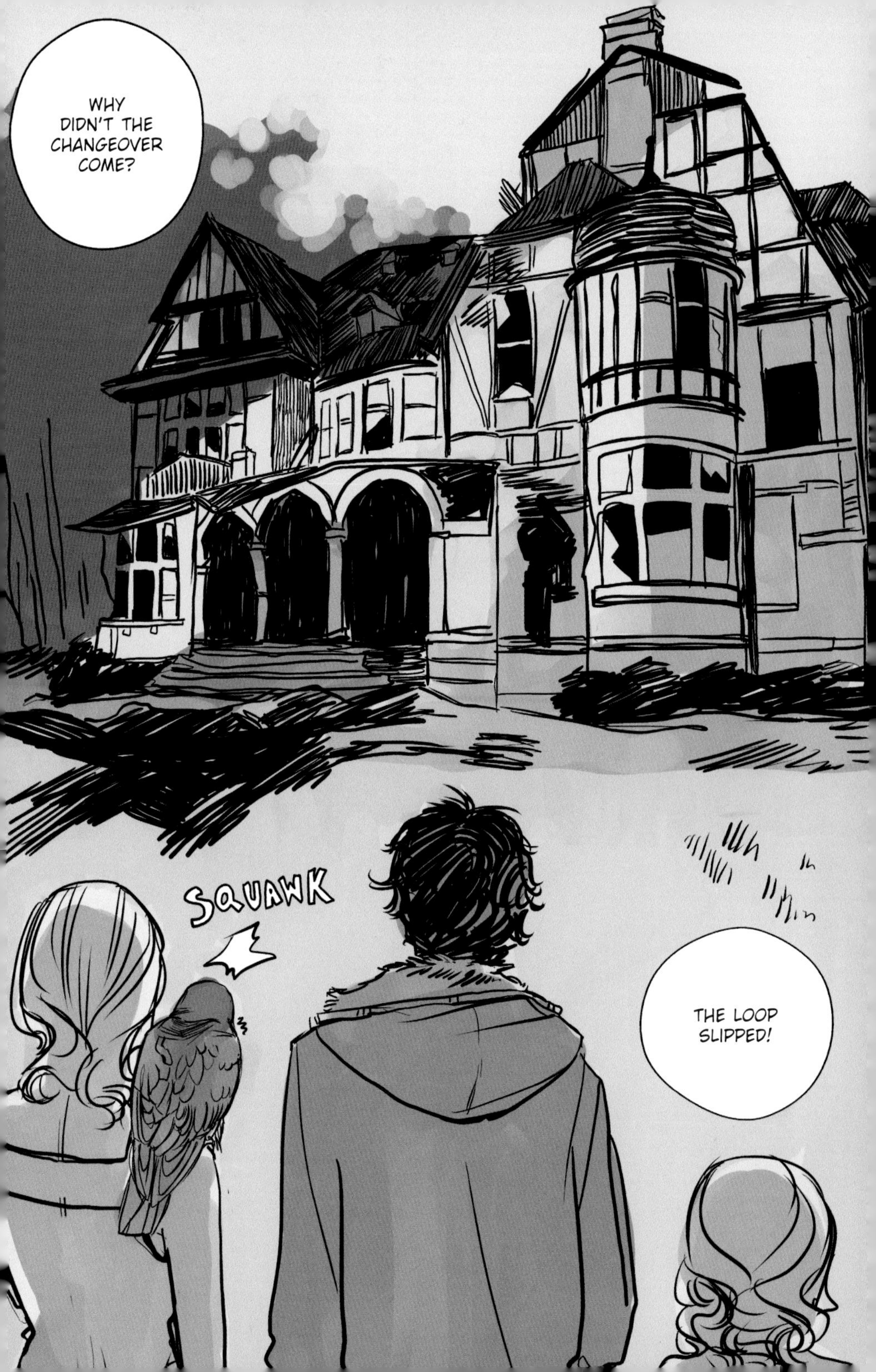
WHY DIDN'T THE CHANGEOVER COME?
SQUAWK
THE LOOP SLIPPED!

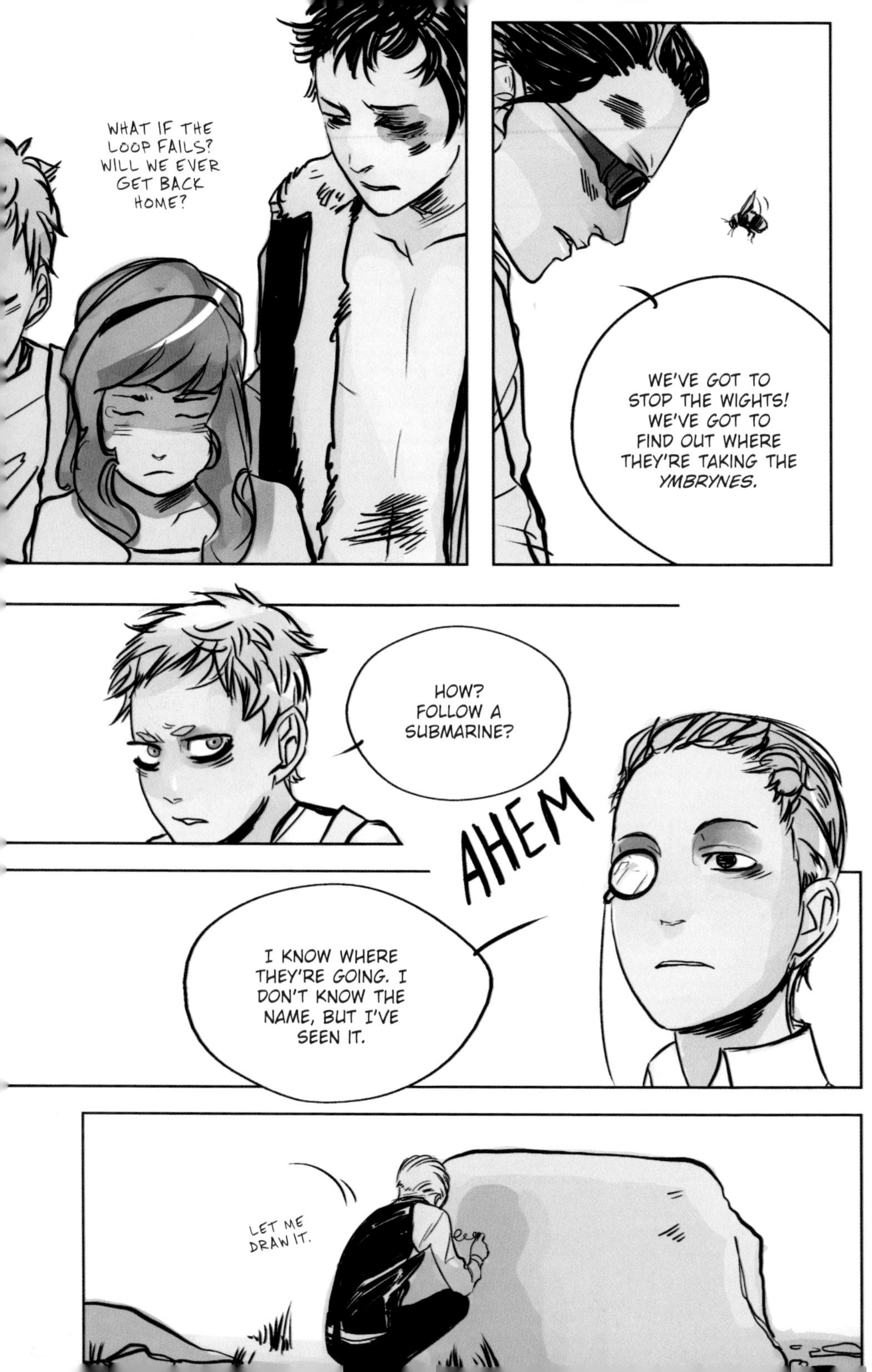
WHAT IF THE LOOP FAILS? WILL WE EVER GET BACK HOME?
WE'VE GOT TO STOP THE WIGHTS! WE'VE GOT TO FIND OUT WHERE THEY'RE TAKING THE *YMBRYNES.*
HOW? FOLLOW A SUBMARINE?
AHEM
I KNOW WHERE THEY'RE GOING. I DON'T KNOW THE NAME, BUT I'VE SEEN IT.
LET ME DRAW IT.

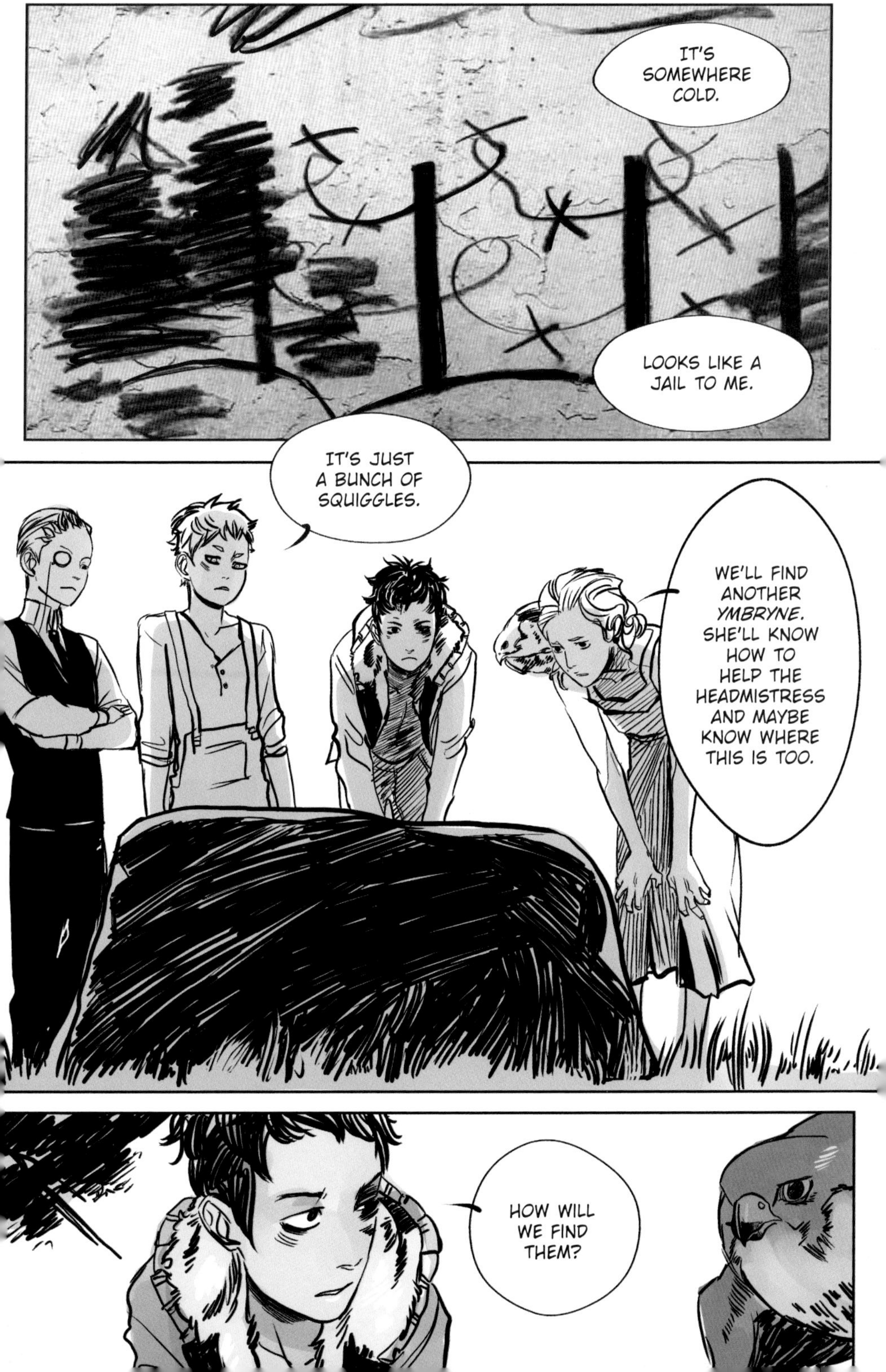
IT'S SOMEWHERE COLD.
LOOKS LIKE A JAIL TO ME.
IT'S JUST A BUNCH OF SQUIGGLES.
WE'LL FIND ANOTHER *YMBRYNE*. SHE'LL KNOW HOW TO HELP THE HEADMISTRESS AND MAYBE KNOW WHERE THIS IS TOO.
HOW WILL WE FIND THEM?

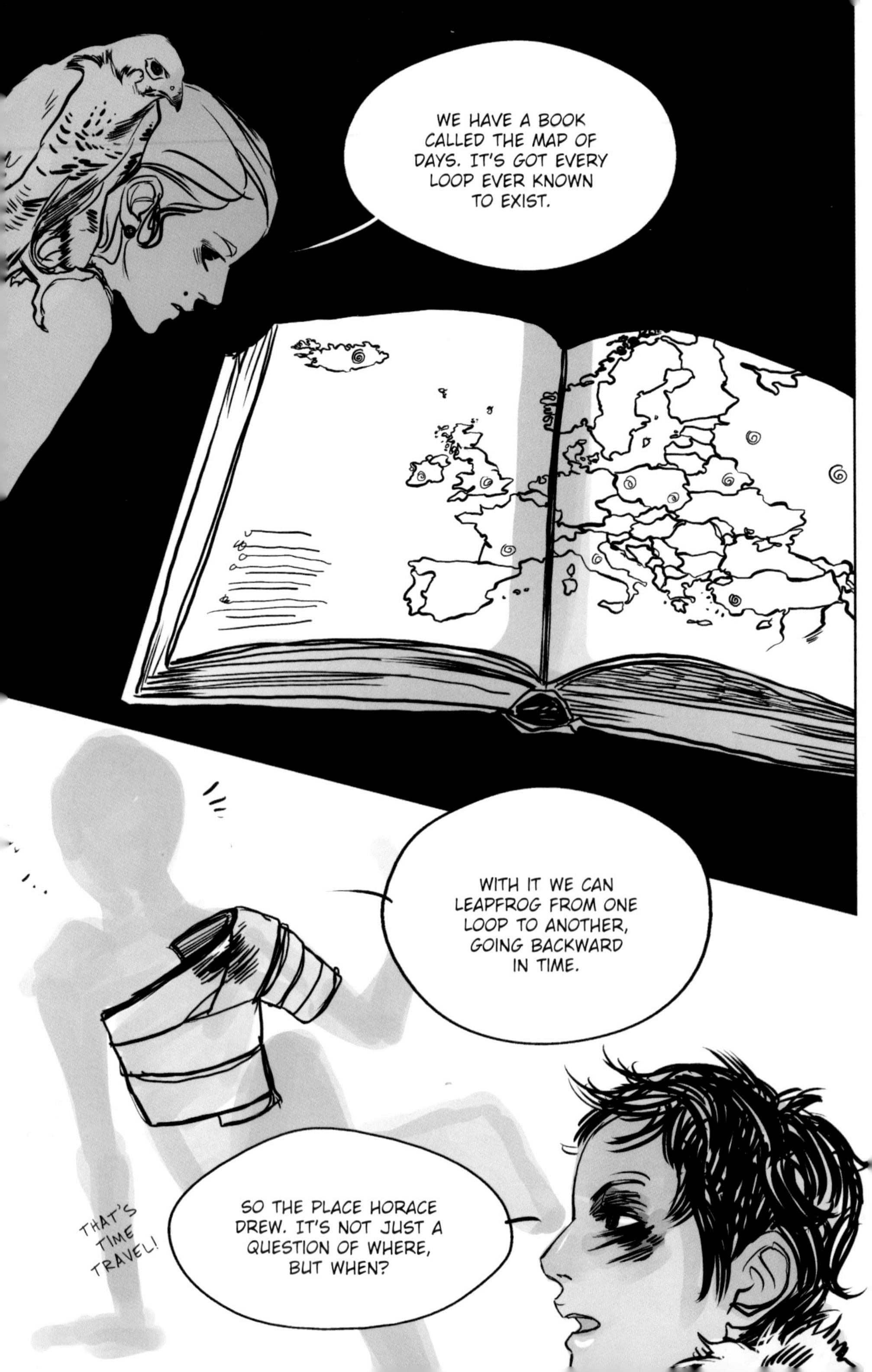
WE HAVE A BOOK CALLED THE MAP OF DAYS. IT'S GOT EVERY LOOP EVER KNOWN TO EXIST.
WITH IT WE CAN LEAPFROG FROM ONE LOOP TO ANOTHER, GOING BACKWARD IN TIME.
...
SO THE PLACE HORACE DREW. IT'S NOT JUST A QUESTION OF WHERE, BUT WHEN?
THAT'S TIME TRAVEL!

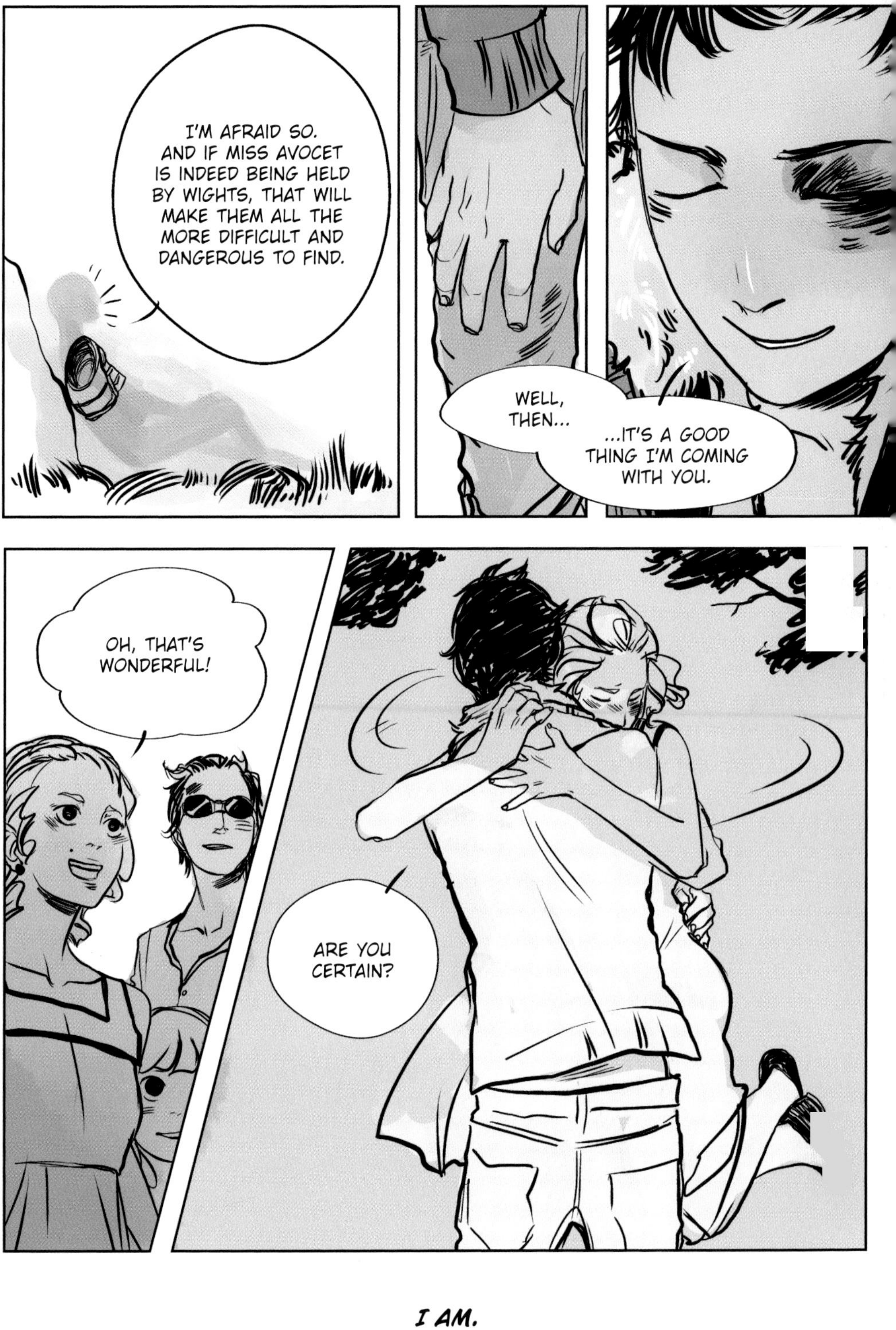
I'M AFRAID SO. AND IF MISS AVOCET IS INDEED BEING HELD BY WIGHTS, THAT WILL MAKE THEM ALL THE MORE DIFFICULT AND DANGEROUS TO FIND.
WELL, THEN...
...IT'S A GOOD THING I'M COMING WITH YOU.
OH, THAT'S WONDERFUL!
ARE YOU CERTAIN?

I AM.

THERE'S JUST ONE THING I HAVE TO DO FIRST.

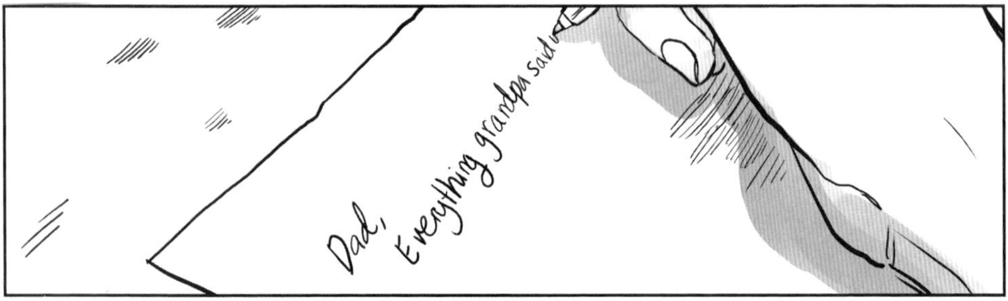
Dad,
Everything grandpa said

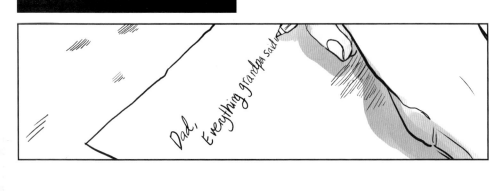

A LETTER EXPLAINING THE PECULIARS, THE HOLLOWS, AND HOW ALL OF GRANDPA PORTMAN'S STORIES WERE TRUE.

HE'S GOING TO THINK I'VE LOST MY MIND.

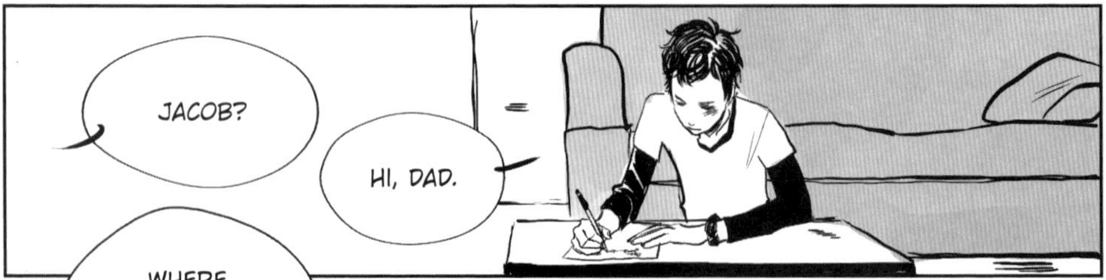
JACOB?
HI, DAD.

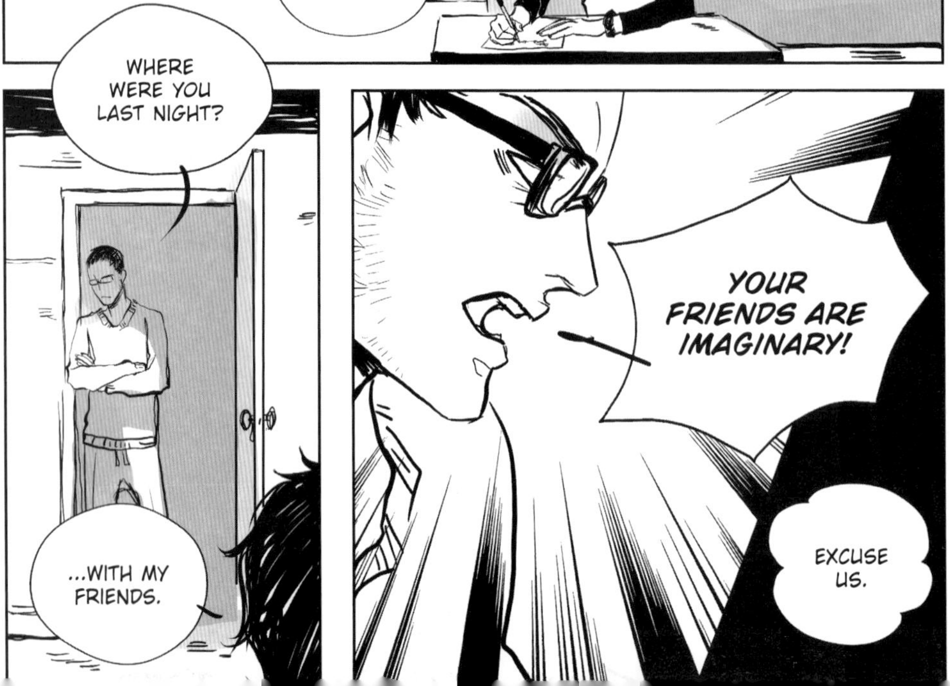
WHERE WERE YOU LAST NIGHT?
...WITH MY FRIENDS.
YOUR FRIENDS ARE IMAGINARY!
EXCUSE US.

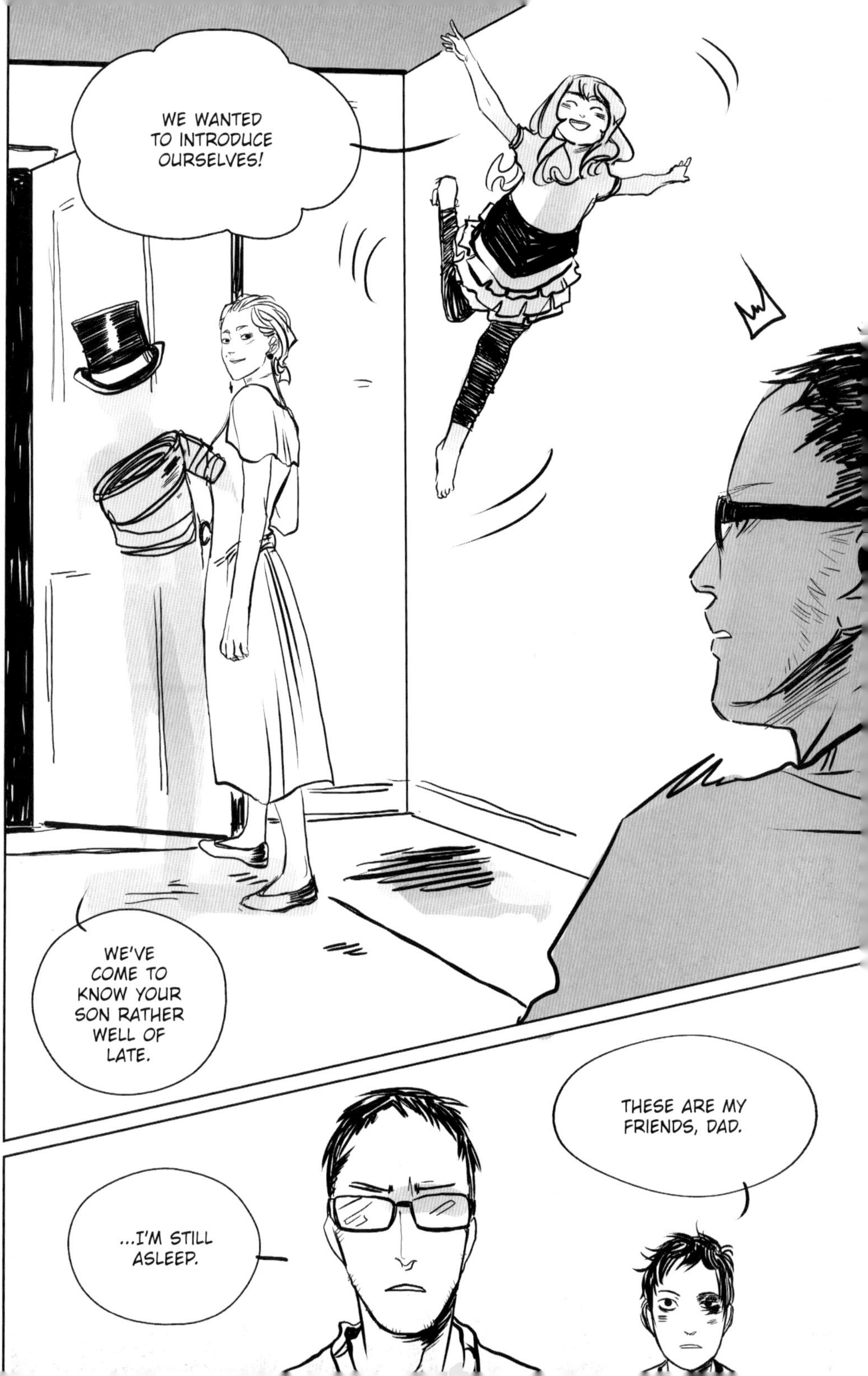
WE WANTED TO INTRODUCE OURSELVES!
WE'VE COME TO KNOW YOUR SON RATHER WELL OF LATE.
...I'M STILL ASLEEP.
THESE ARE MY FRIENDS, DAD.

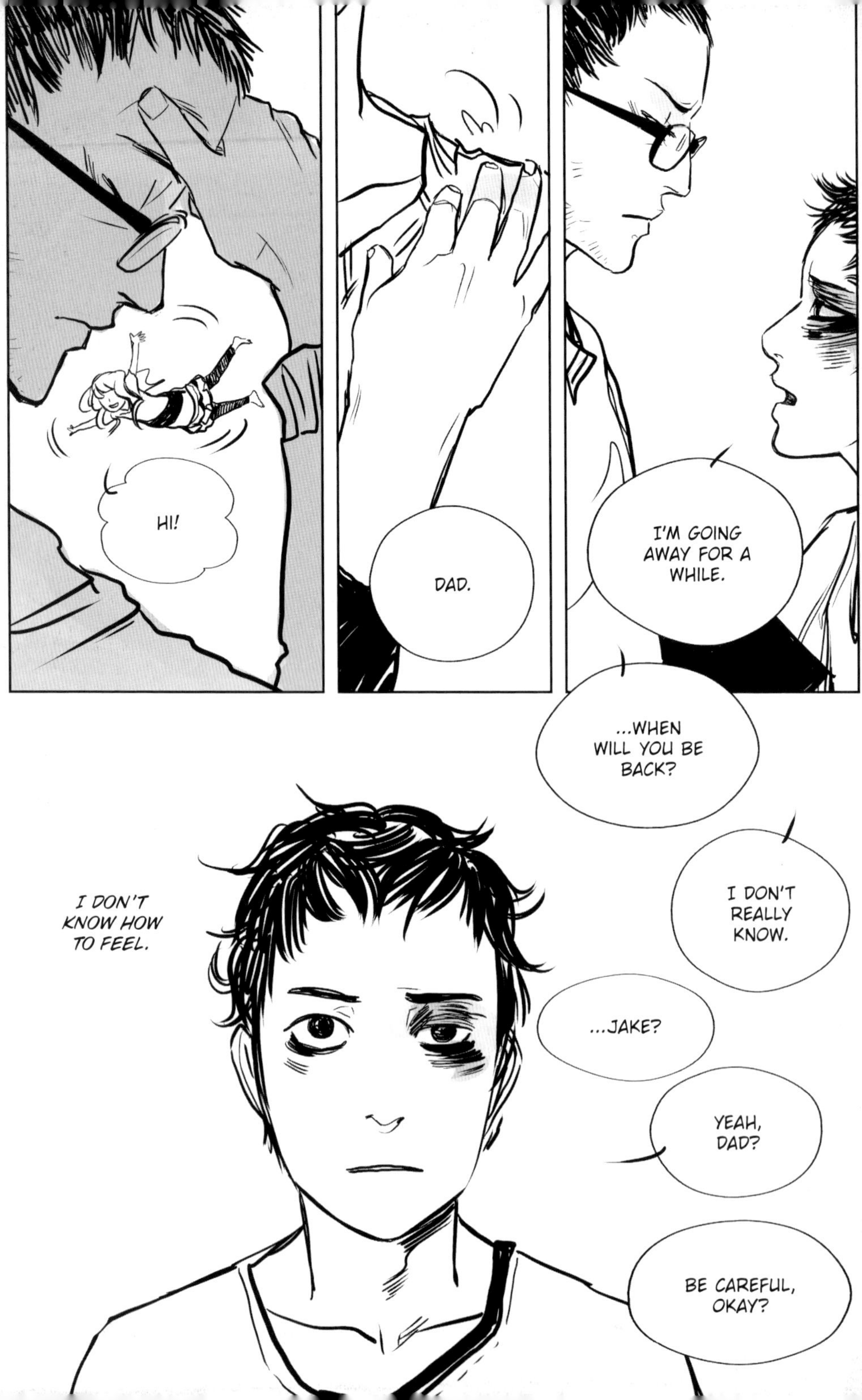
HI!
DAD.
I'M GOING AWAY FOR A WHILE.
...WHEN WILL YOU BE BACK?
I DON'T REALLY KNOW.
I DON'T KNOW HOW TO FEEL.
...JAKE?
YEAH, DAD?
BE CAREFUL, OKAY?

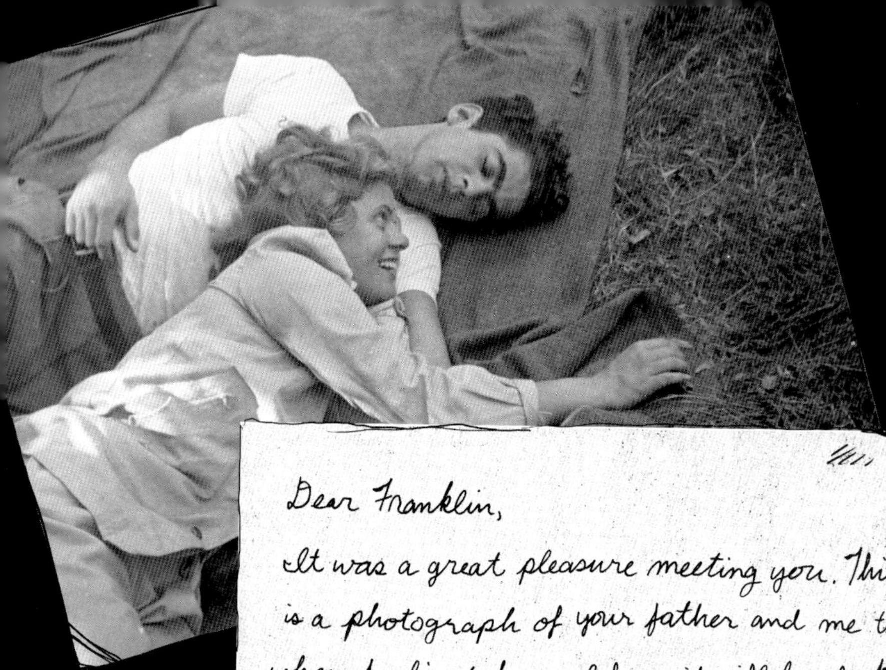

I WORRIED THAT DAD WILL JUST THINK OF IT AS A DREAM, SO EMMA WROTE HIM A LETTER TOO, AS PROOF...

...AND LEFT IT WITH A PHOTOGRAPH OF HER AND GRANDPA PORTMAN.

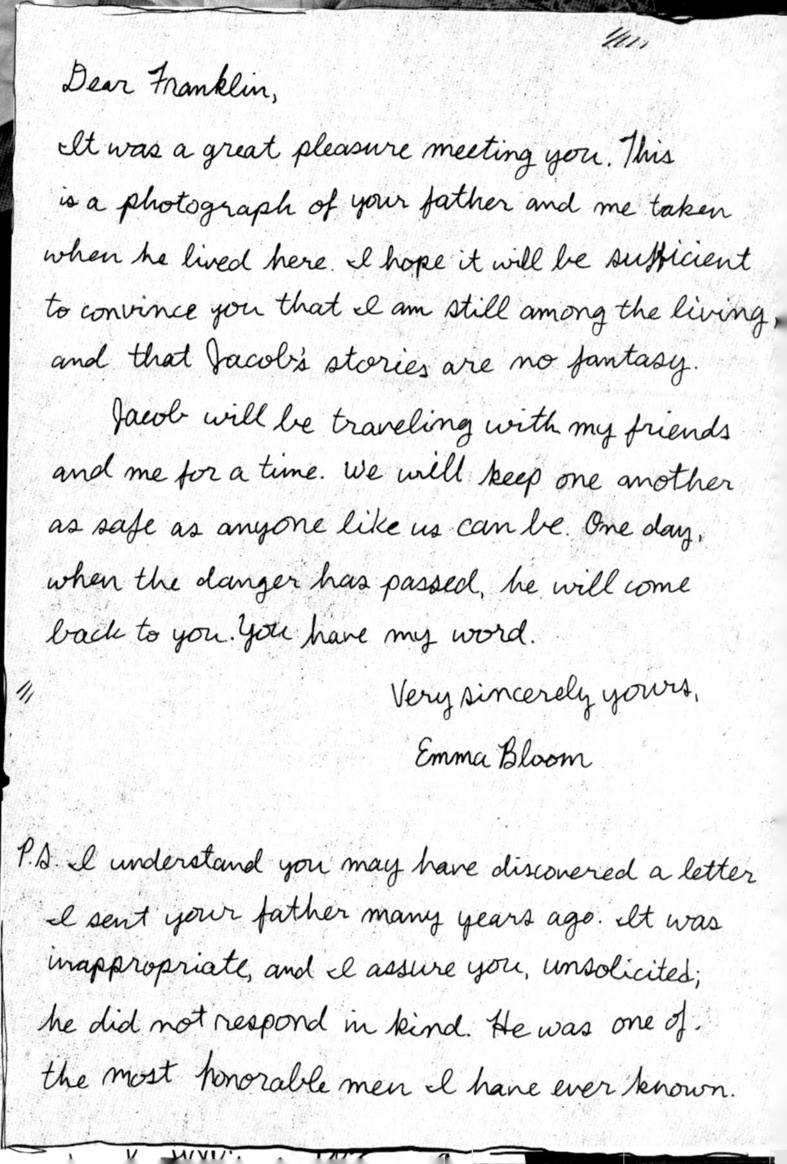

Dear Franklin,

It was a great pleasure meeting you. This is a photograph of your father and me taken when he lived here. I hope it will be sufficient to convince you that I am still among the living, and that Jacob's stories are no fantasy.

Jacob will be traveling with my friends and me for a time. We will keep one another as safe as anyone like us can be. One day, when the danger has passed, he will come back to you. You have my word.

Very sincerely yours,

Emma Bloom

P.S. I understand you may have discovered a letter I sent your father many years ago. It was inappropriate, and I assure you, unsolicited; he did not respond in kind. He was one of the most honorable men I have ever known.

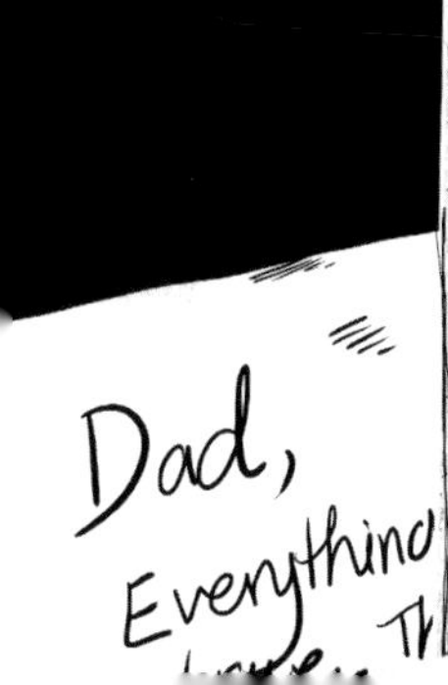
Dad,

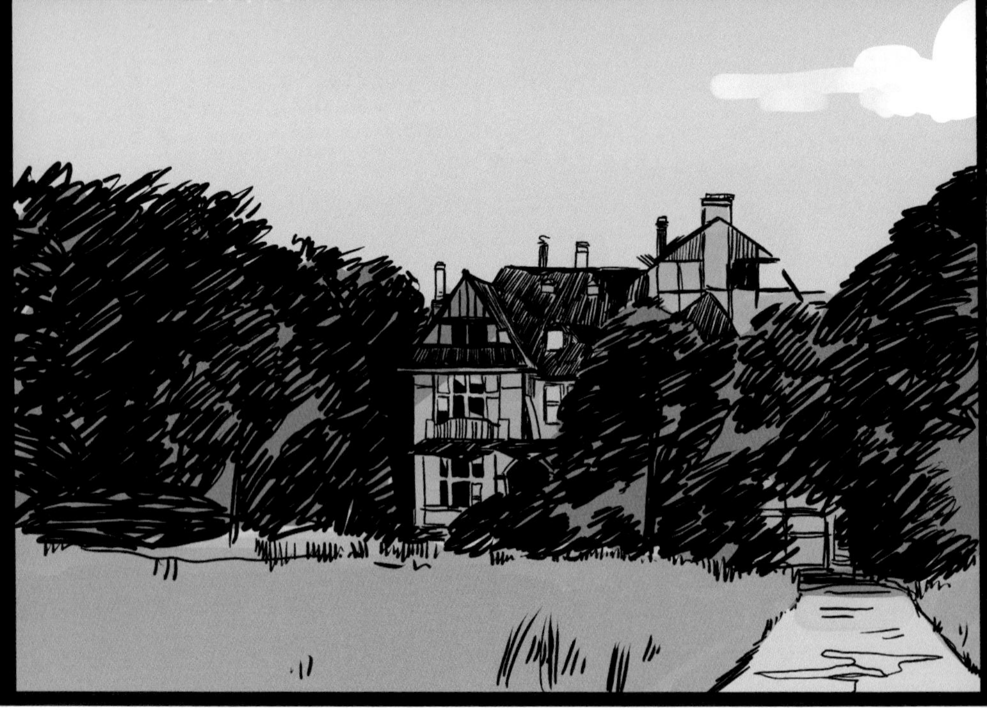

LOOKING AT IT NOW, I CAN SEE HOW IT WILL ONE DAY BECOME THE NIGHTMARE HOUSE I HAD FIRST SEEN.

I USED TO DREAM ABOUT ESCAPING MY ORDINARY LIFE, BUT MY LIFE WAS NEVER ORDINARY. I HAD SIMPLY FAILED TO NOTICE HOW EXTRAORDINARY IT WAS. LIKEWISE, I NEVER IMAGINED THAT HOME MIGHT BE SOMETHING I'D MISS.

YET AS WE STOOD LOADING OUR BOATS IN THE BREAKING DAWN, ON A BRAND-NEW PRECIPICE OF BEFORE AND AFTER, I REALIZED THAT LEAVING WOULDN'T BE LIKE I HAD IMAGINED.

AND YET MY OLD LIFE WAS AS IMPOSSIBLE TO RETURN TO AS THE CHILDREN'S BOMBED HOUSE. TEN PECULIAR CHILDREN AND ONE PECULIAR BIRD WERE MADE TO FIT IN JUST THREE ROWBOATS.

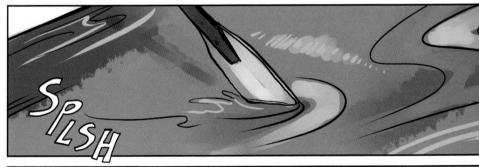

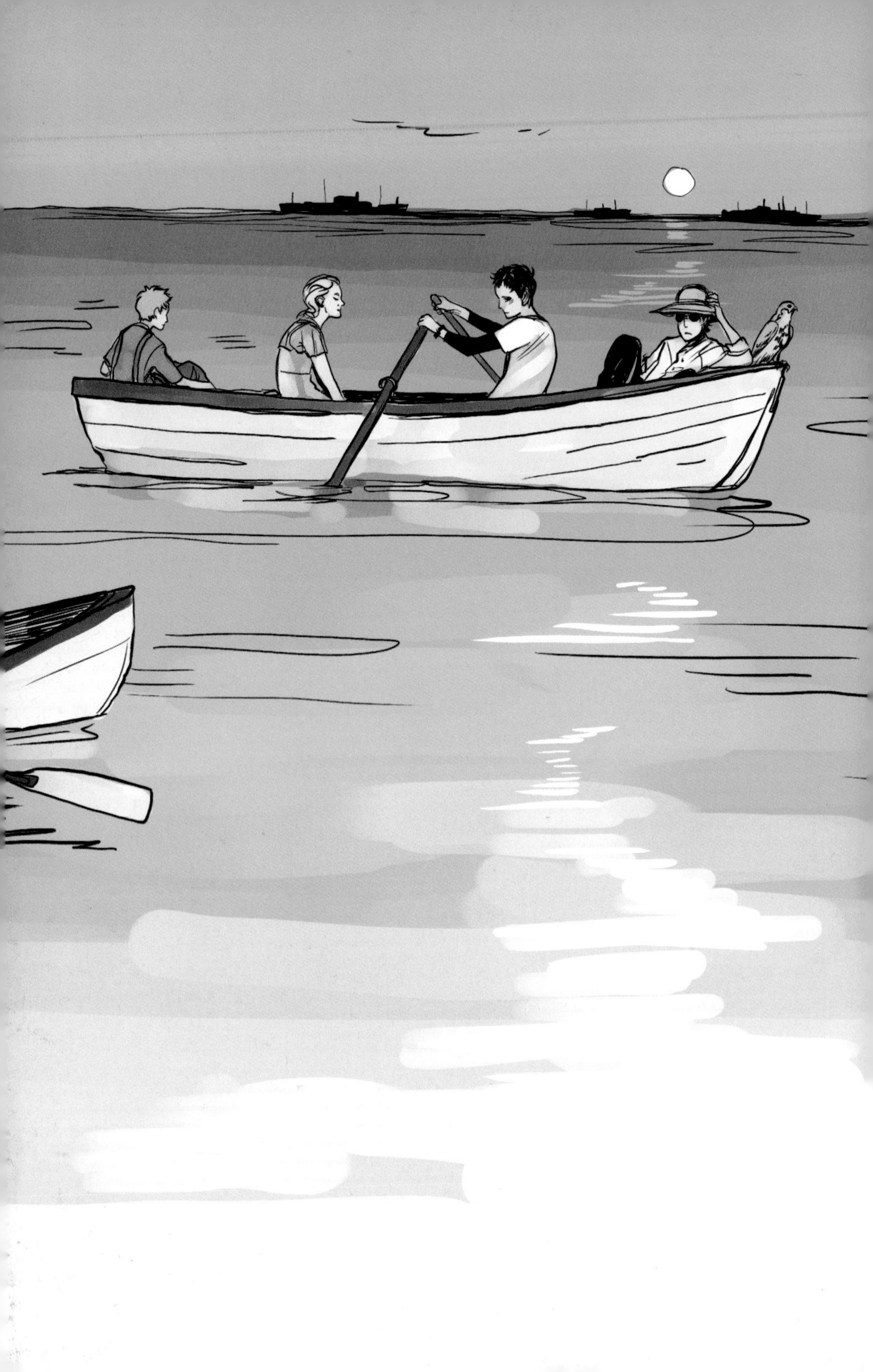

READ ON TO ENJOY
A SPECIAL PREVIEW OF

HOLLOW CITY

THE SECOND NOVEL OF
MISS PEREGRINE'S
PECULIAR CHILDREN

THE GRAPHIC NOVEL

COMING OCTOBER 25, 2016
FROM YEN PRESS

WE WERE TEN CHILDREN AND ONE BIRD IN THREE
SMALL AND UNSTEADY BOATS, ROWING WITH QUIET
INTENSITY STRAIGHT OUT TO SEA.

WE ROWED OUT THROUGH THE HARBOR, PAST
BOBBING BOATS WEEPING RUST FROM THEIR SEAMS,
PAST THE OLD LIGHTHOUSE WHICH ONLY LAST NIGHT
HAD BEEN THE SCENE OF SO MANY TRAUMAS.

OUR GOAL, THE RUTTED COAST OF MAINLAND
WALES, WAS SOMEWHERE BEFORE US BUT ONLY
DIMLY VISIBLE, AN INKY SMUDGE SQUATTING
ALONG THE FAR HORIZON.

WE ROWED IN SHIFTS, THOUGH I FELT SO STRONG THAT FOR NEARLY AN HOUR I REFUSED TO GIVE THE OARS UP.

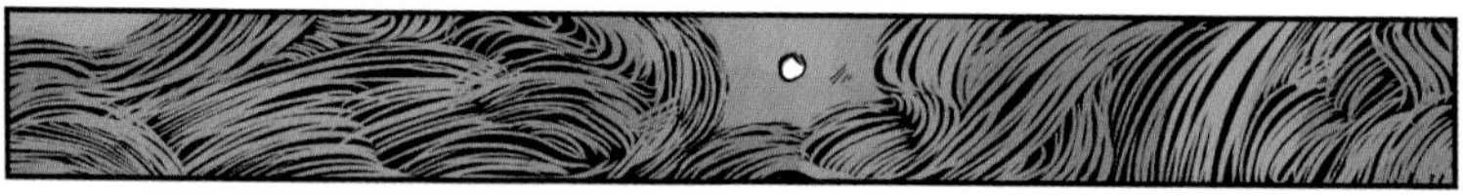

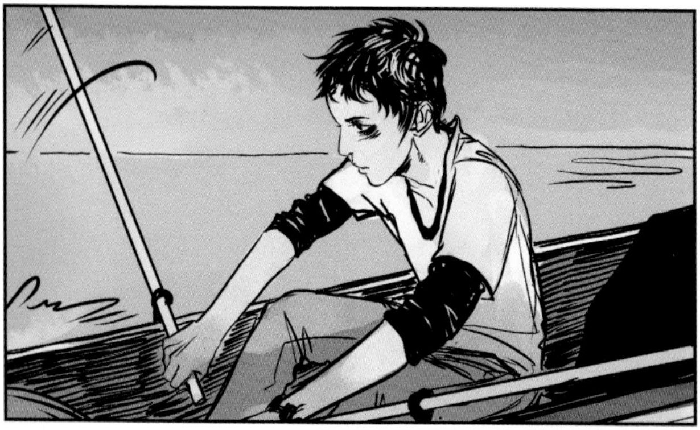

THOSE OF US WHO WORRIED ABOUT SUCH THINGS ASSUMED THE WIGHTS WERE NEARBY, SOMEWHERE BELOW US IN THAT SUBMARINE. IF THEY HADN'T ALREADY KNOWN WE'D FLED THE ISLAND, THEY'D FIND OUT SOON ENOUGH.

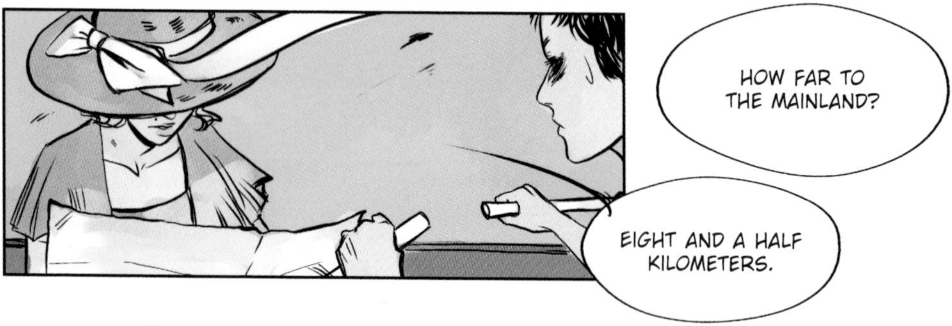
HOW FAR TO THE MAINLAND?
EIGHT AND A HALF KILOMETERS.

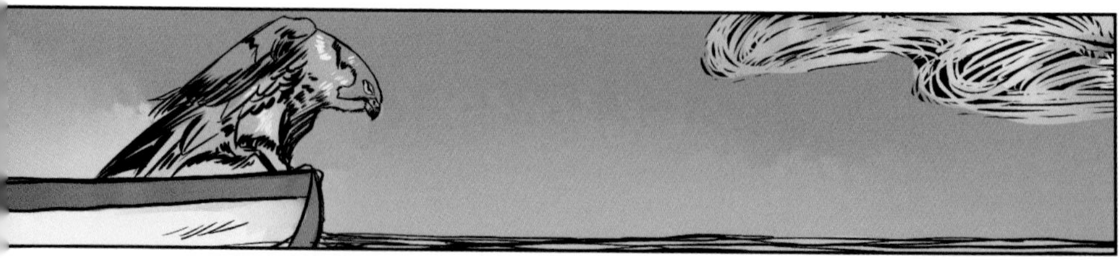

THEY HADN'T GONE TO SUCH LENGTHS TO KIDNAP MISS PEREGRINE ONLY TO GIVE UP AFTER ONE FAILED ATTEMPT. IT MIGHT HAVE BEEN TOO DANGEROUS FOR THE SUBMARINE TO SURFACE IN BROAD DAYLIGHT, BUT COME NIGHTFALL, WE'D BE EASY PREY.

SO WE ROWED, OUR ONLY HOPE THAT WE COULD REACH THE MAINLAND BEFORE NIGHTFALL REACHED US.

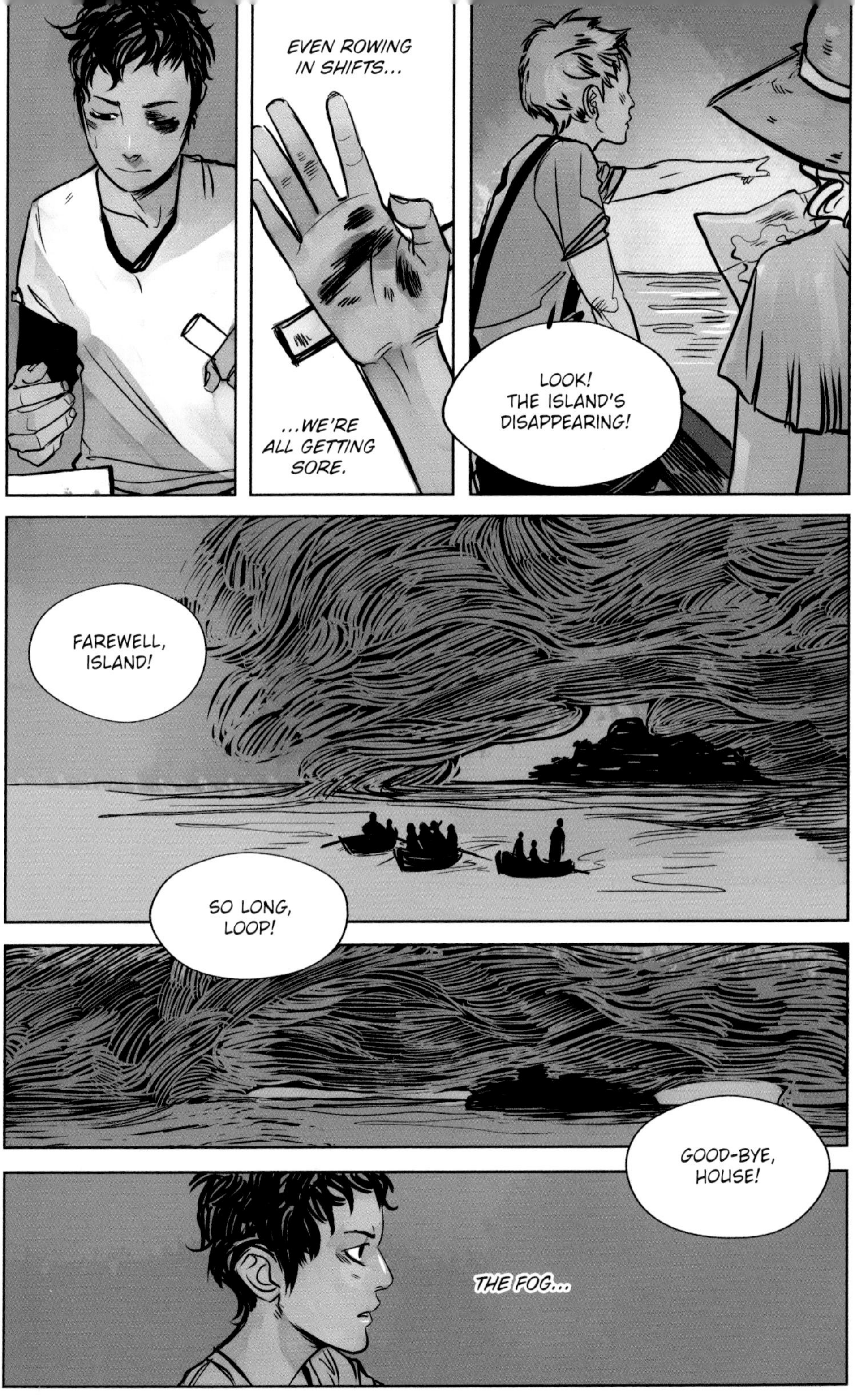
EVEN ROWING IN SHIFTS...
...WE'RE ALL GETTING SORE.
LOOK! THE ISLAND'S DISAPPEARING!
FAREWELL, ISLAND!
SO LONG, LOOP!
GOOD-BYE, HOUSE!
THE FOG...

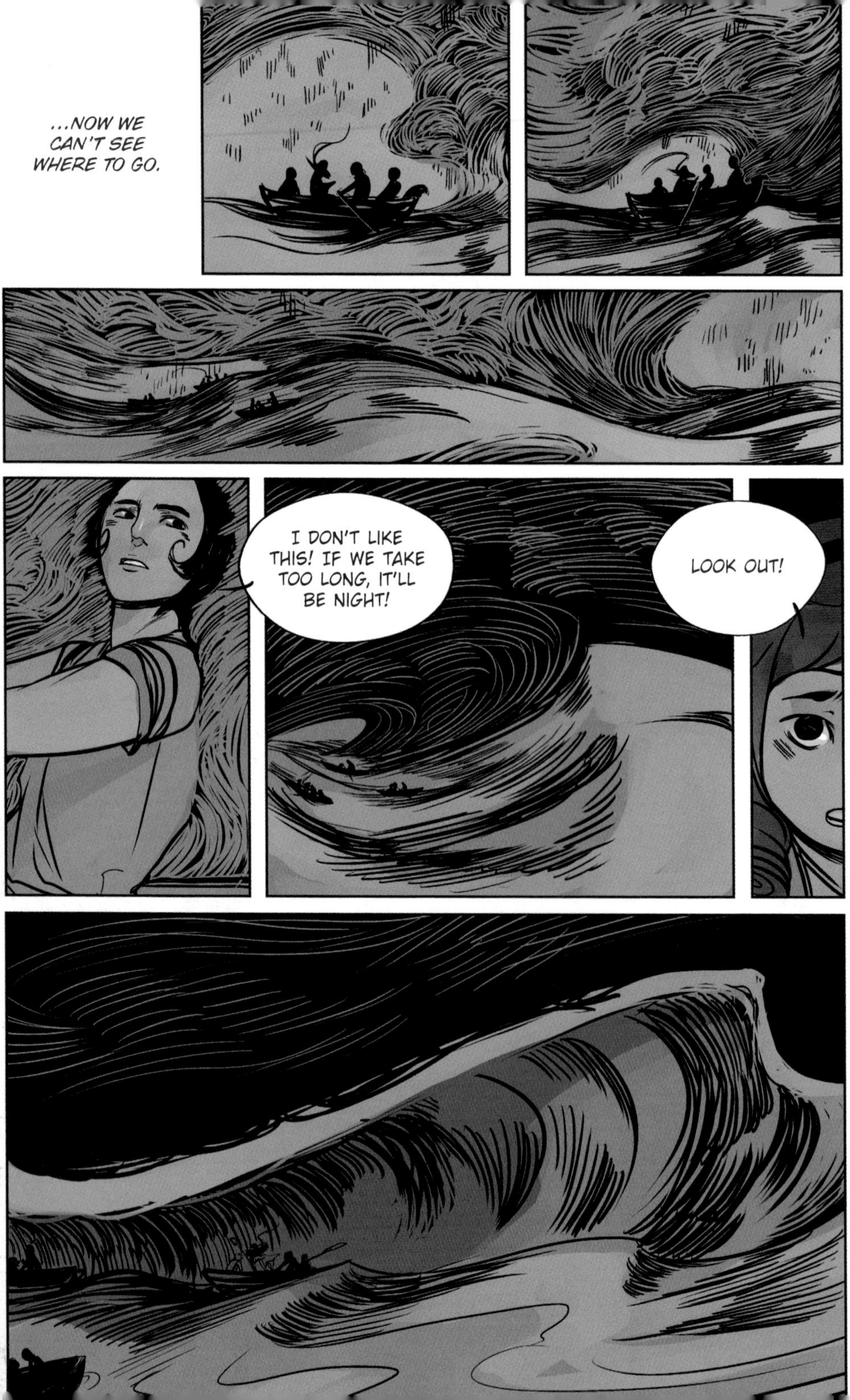
...NOW WE CAN'T SEE WHERE TO GO.
I DON'T LIKE THIS! IF WE TAKE TOO LONG, IT'LL BE NIGHT!
LOOK OUT!

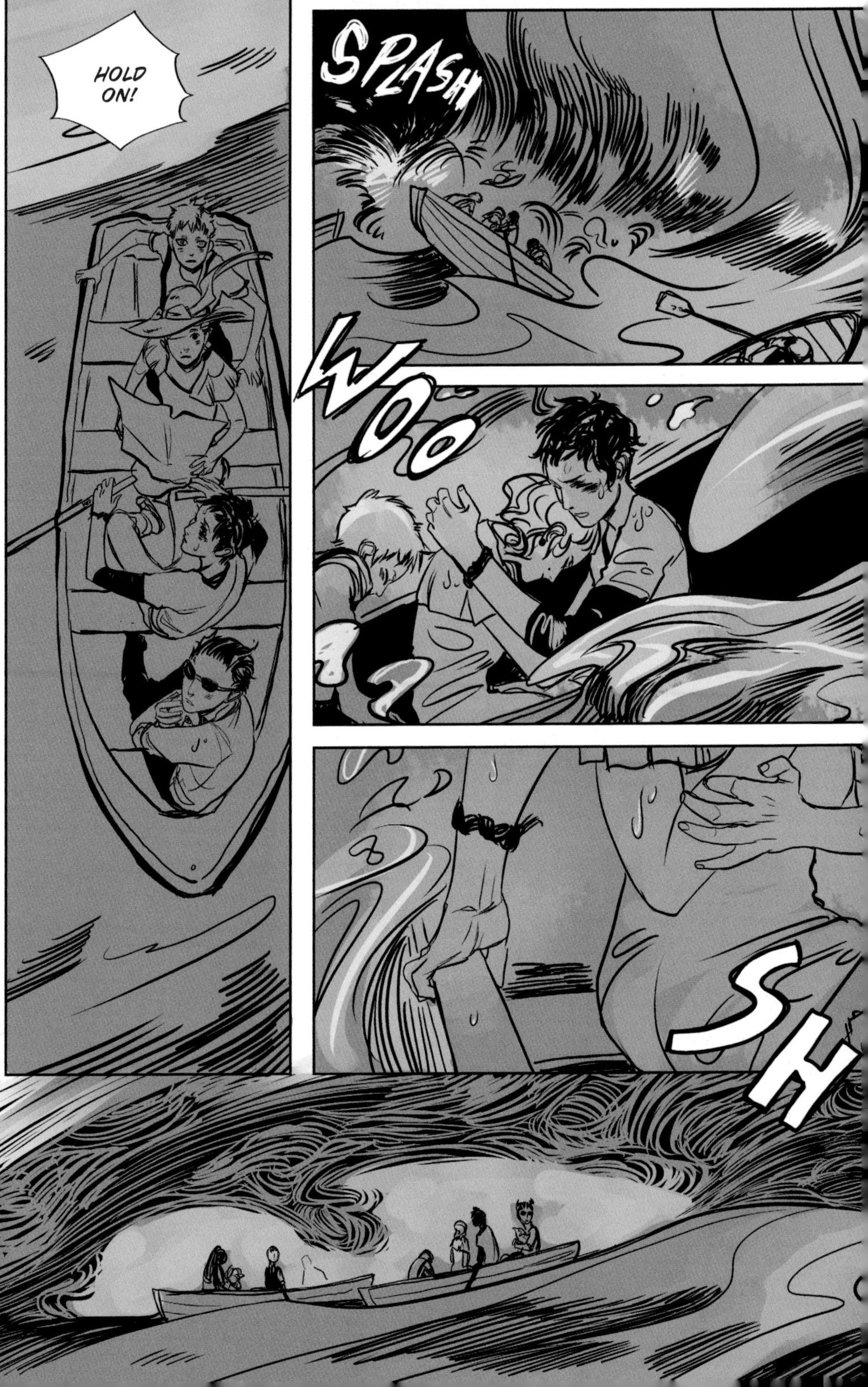
HOLD ON!
SPLASH
WOOO
SH

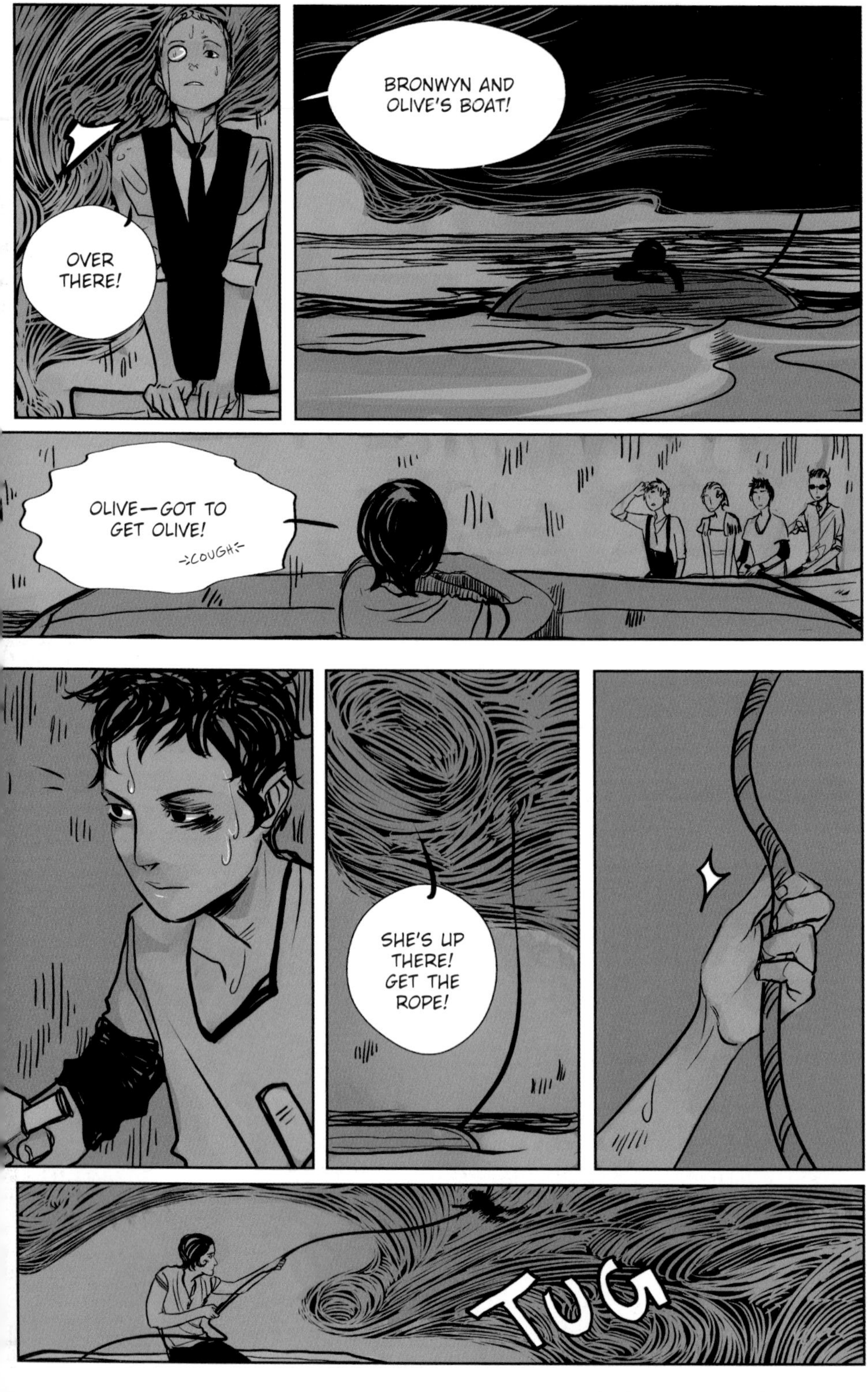
OVER THERE!
BRONWYN AND OLIVE'S BOAT!
OLIVE—GOT TO GET OLIVE!
COUGH
SHE'S UP THERE! GET THE ROPE!
TUG

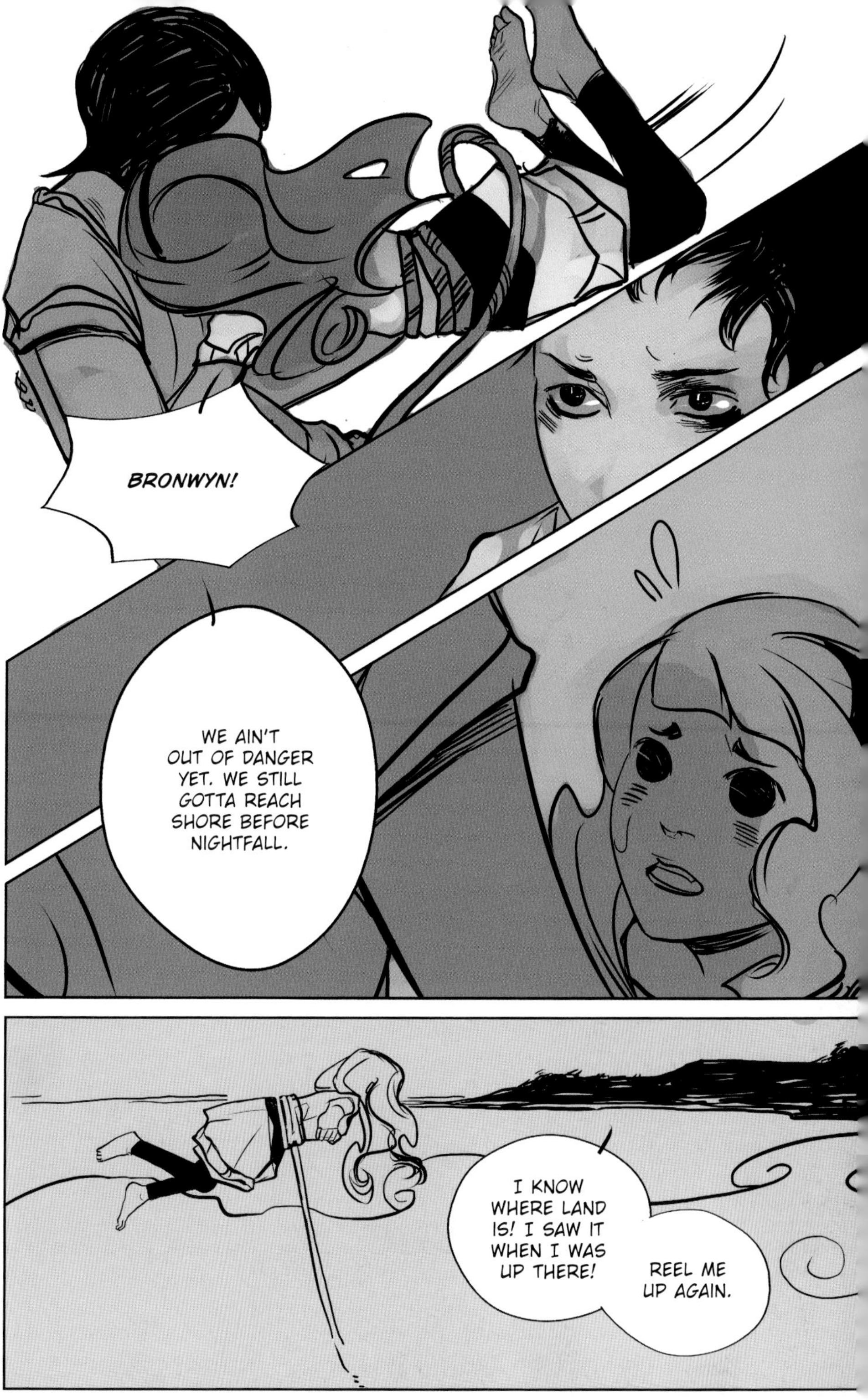
BRONWYN!
WE AIN'T OUT OF DANGER YET. WE STILL GOTTA REACH SHORE BEFORE NIGHTFALL.
I KNOW WHERE LAND IS! I SAW IT WHEN I WAS UP THERE!
REEL ME UP AGAIN.

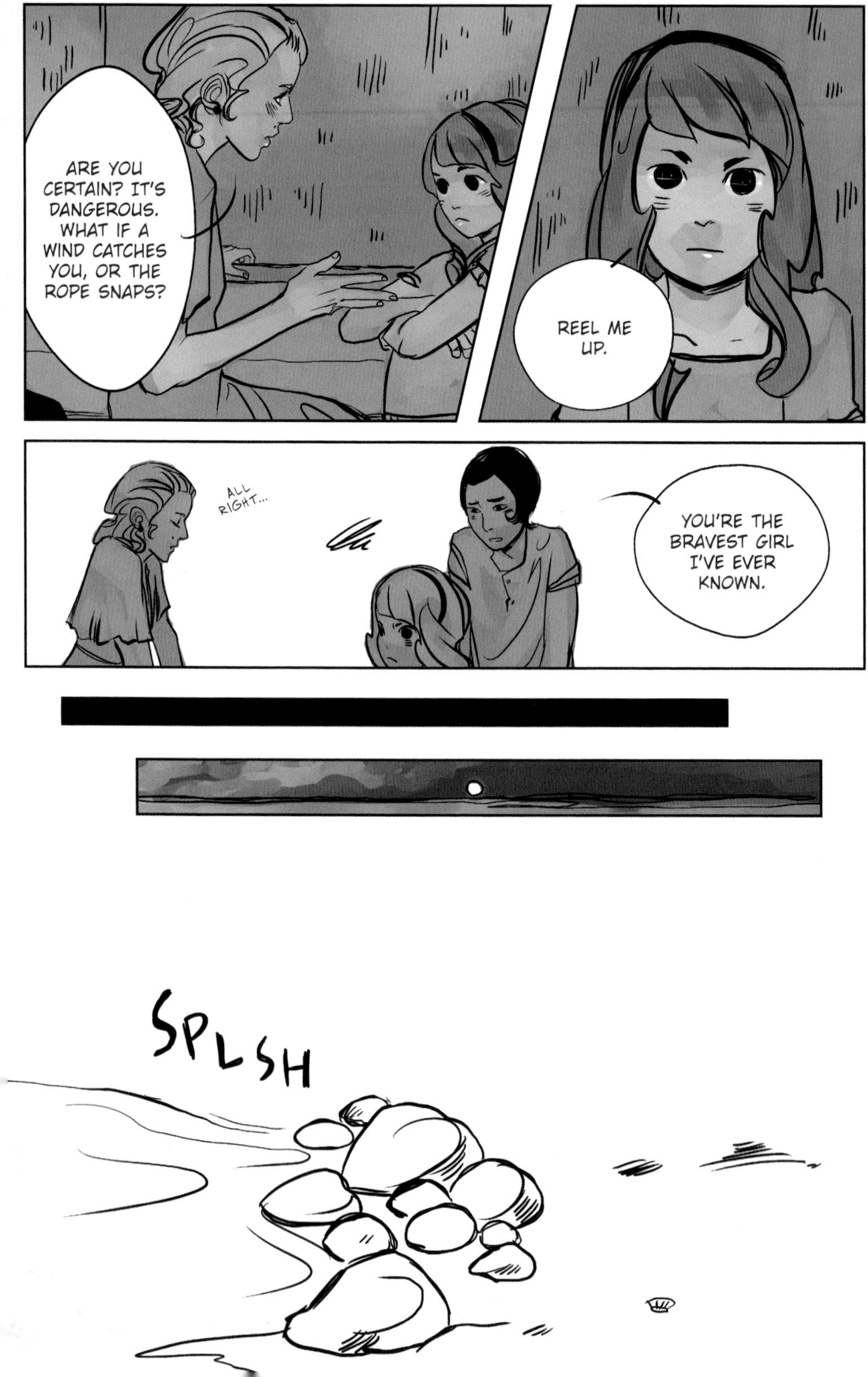
ARE YOU CERTAIN? IT'S DANGEROUS. WHAT IF A WIND CATCHES YOU, OR THE ROPE SNAPS?
REEL ME UP.
ALL RIGHT...
YOU'RE THE BRAVEST GIRL I'VE EVER KNOWN.
SPLSH

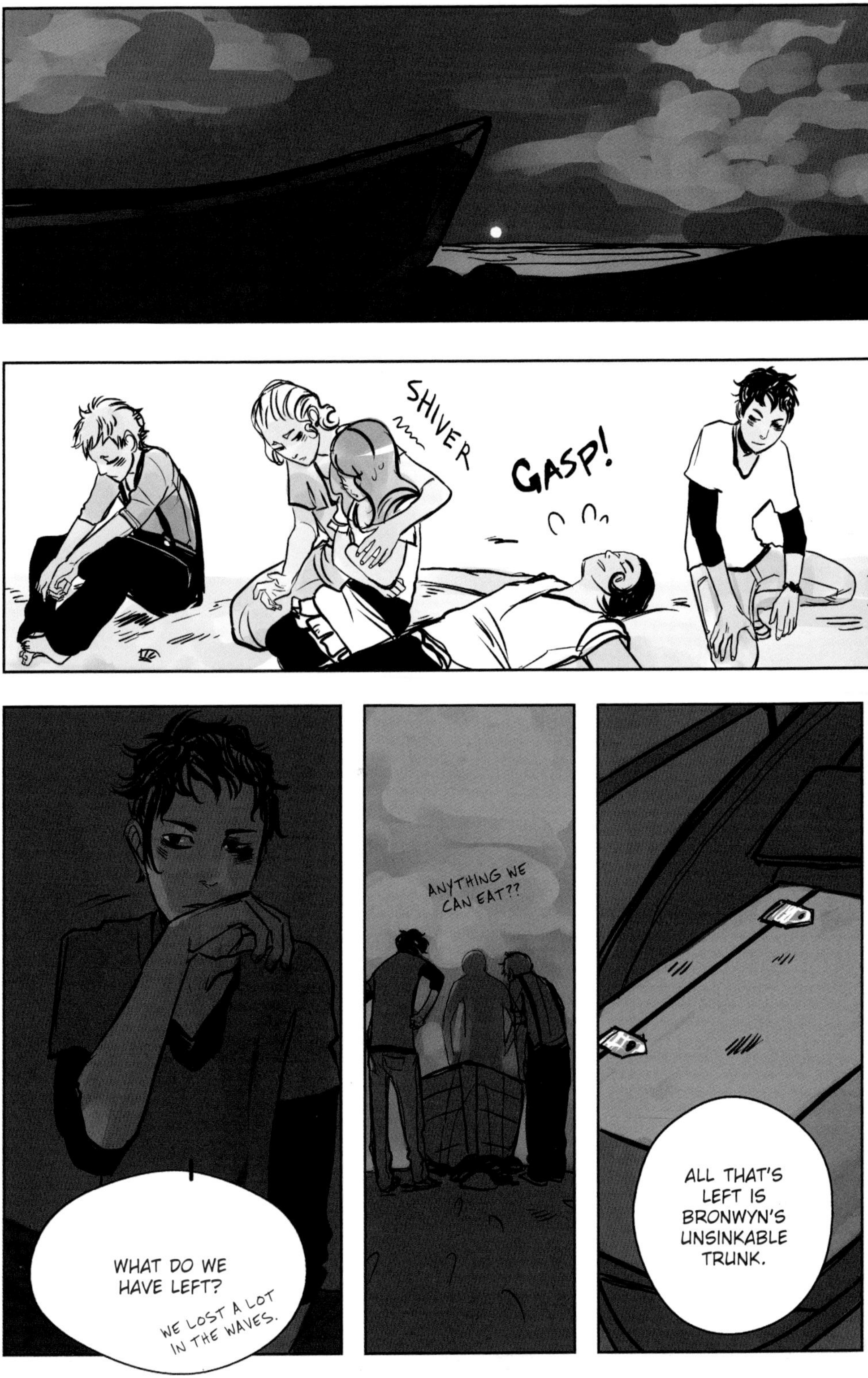
SHIVER
GASP!
WHAT DO WE HAVE LEFT?
WE LOST A LOT IN THE WAVES.
ANYTHING WE CAN EAT??
ALL THAT'S LEFT IS BRONWYN'S UNSINKABLE TRUNK.

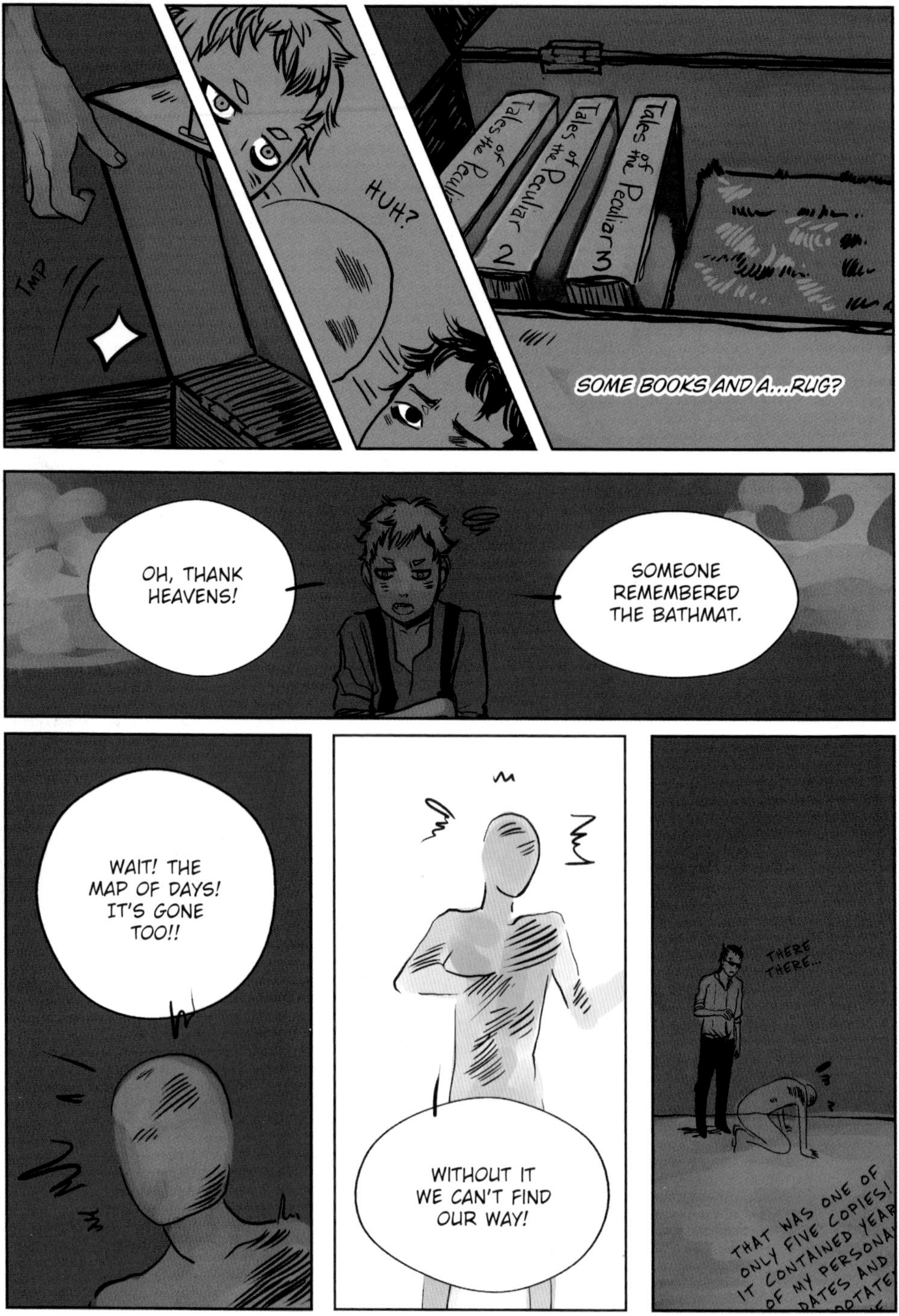
TMP
HUH?
Tales of the Peculiar
Tales of the Peculiar 2
Tales of the Peculiar 3
SOME BOOKS AND A...RUG?
OH, THANK HEAVENS!
SOMEONE REMEMBERED THE BATHMAT.
WAIT! THE MAP OF DAYS! IT'S GONE TOO!!
WITHOUT IT WE CAN'T FIND OUR WAY!
THERE THERE...
THAT WAS ONE OF ONLY FIVE COPIES! IT CONTAINED

FIND OUR WAY TO WHERE? I REALIZED THAT I HAD HEARD THE CHILDREN TALK ABOUT REACHING THE MAINLAND, BUT WE NEVER DISCUSSED WHAT TO DO ONCE WE GOT THERE.

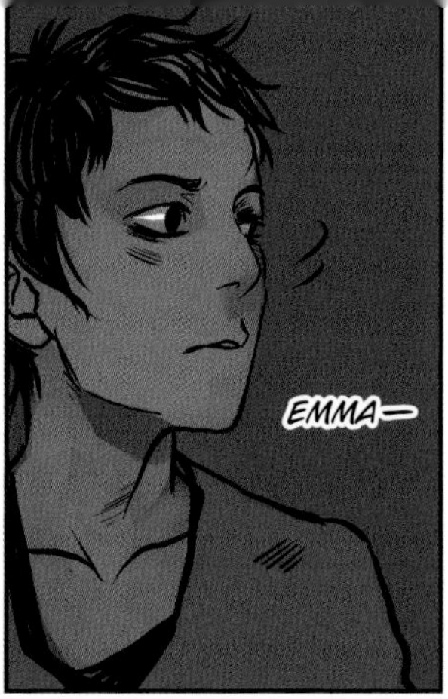
EMMA—

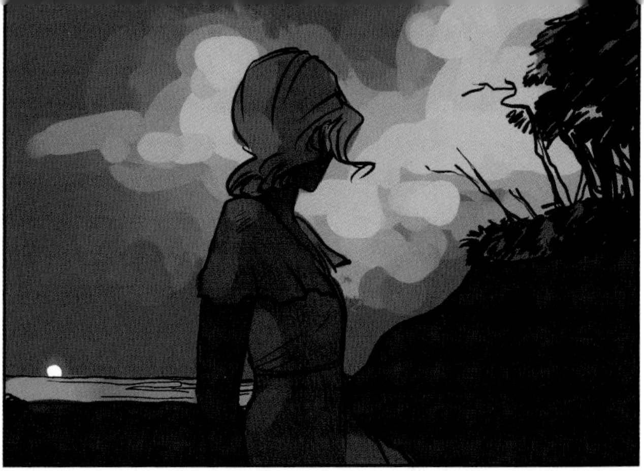

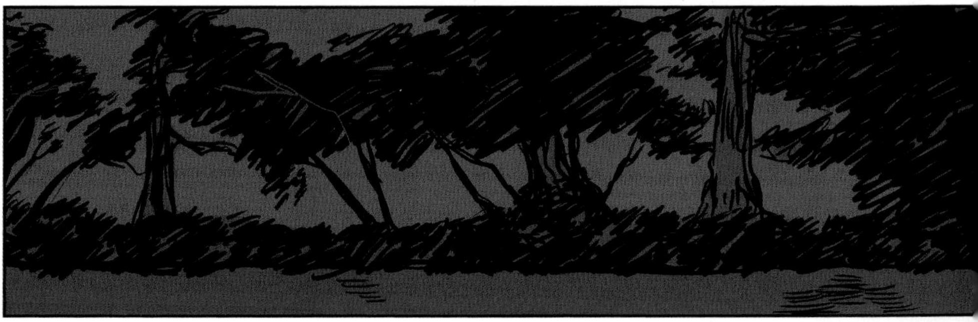

NOTHING BUT WILDERNESS. THERE'S NO TELLING HOW FAR WE'VE STRAYED OFF COURSE.

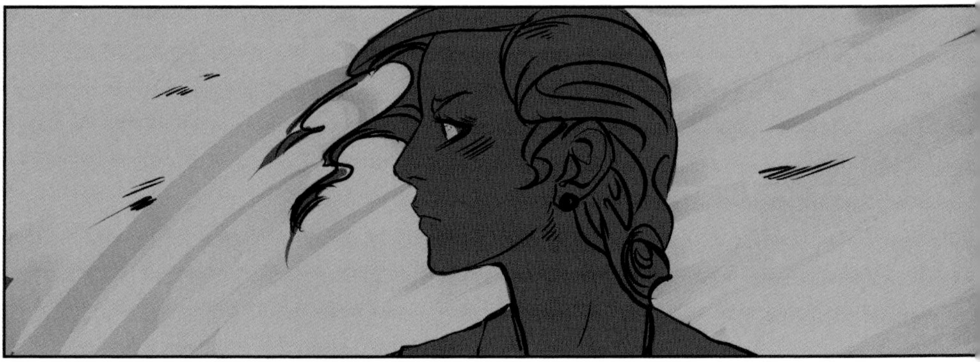

BUT...WE DON'T REALLY NEED A MAP.

OR A SIGNPOST.

OR ANYTHING ELSE.

WE NEED MISS PEREGRINE. WHOLE AND HEALTHY.

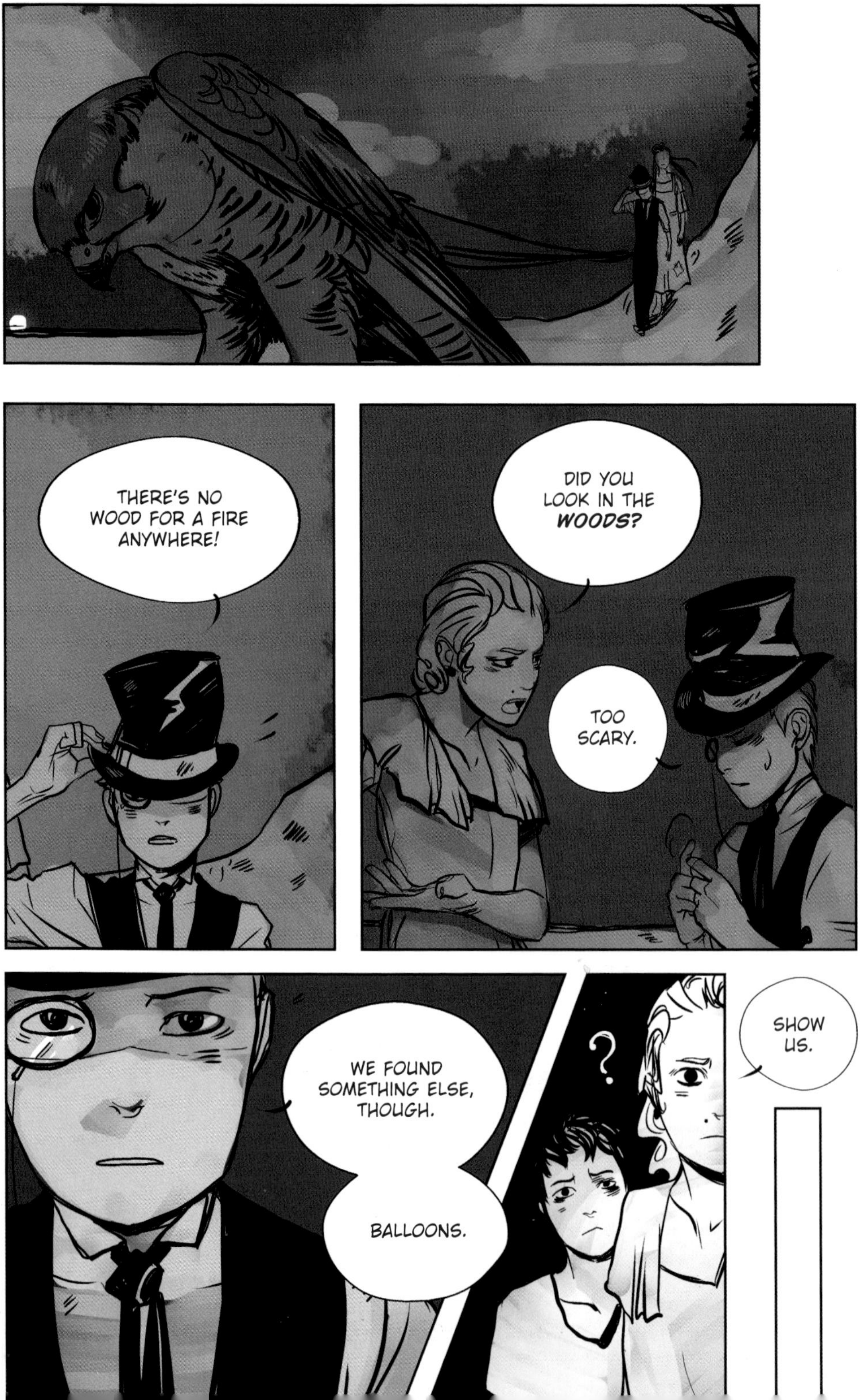
THERE'S NO WOOD FOR A FIRE ANYWHERE!
DID YOU LOOK IN THE **WOODS?**
TOO SCARY.
WE FOUND SOMETHING ELSE, THOUGH.
BALLOONS.
SHOW US.

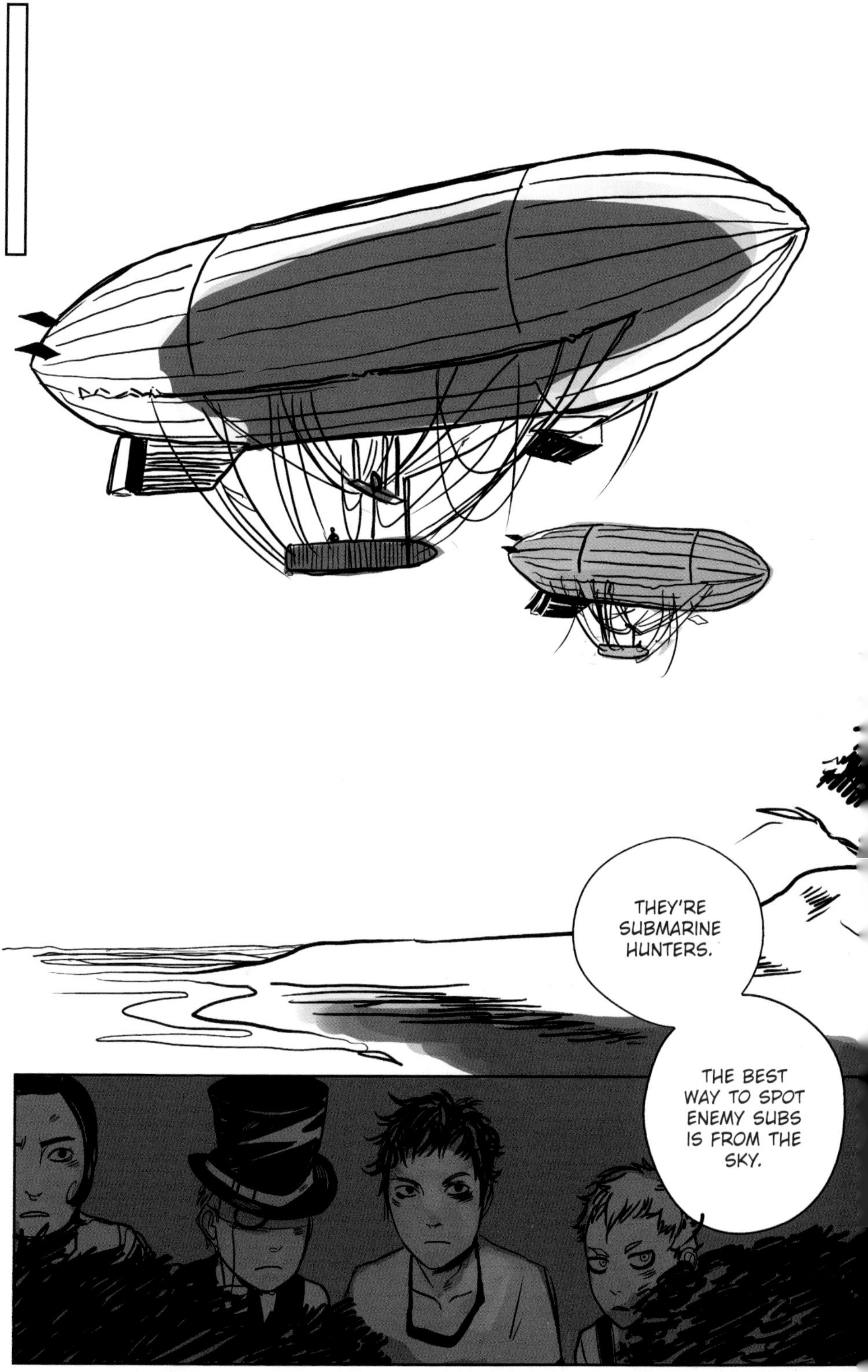
THEY'RE SUBMARINE HUNTERS.
THE BEST WAY TO SPOT ENEMY SUBS IS FROM THE SKY.

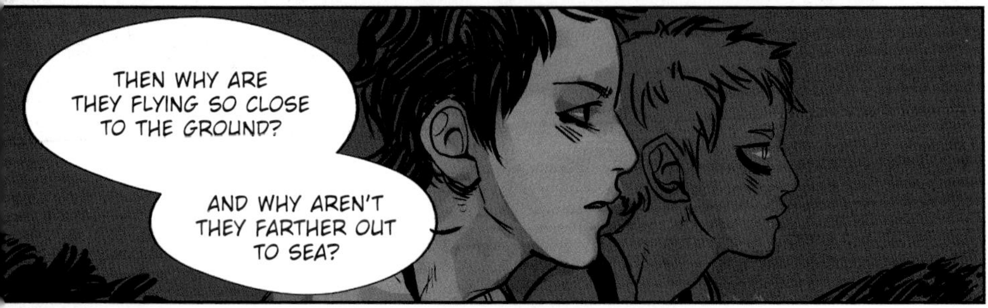
THEN WHY ARE THEY FLYING SO CLOSE TO THE GROUND?
AND WHY AREN'T THEY FARTHER OUT TO SEA?

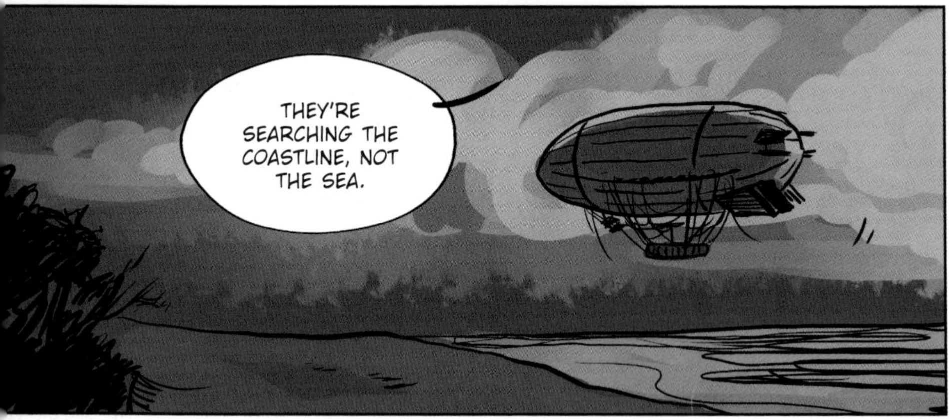
THEY'RE SEARCHING THE COASTLINE, NOT THE SEA.

WIGHTS.

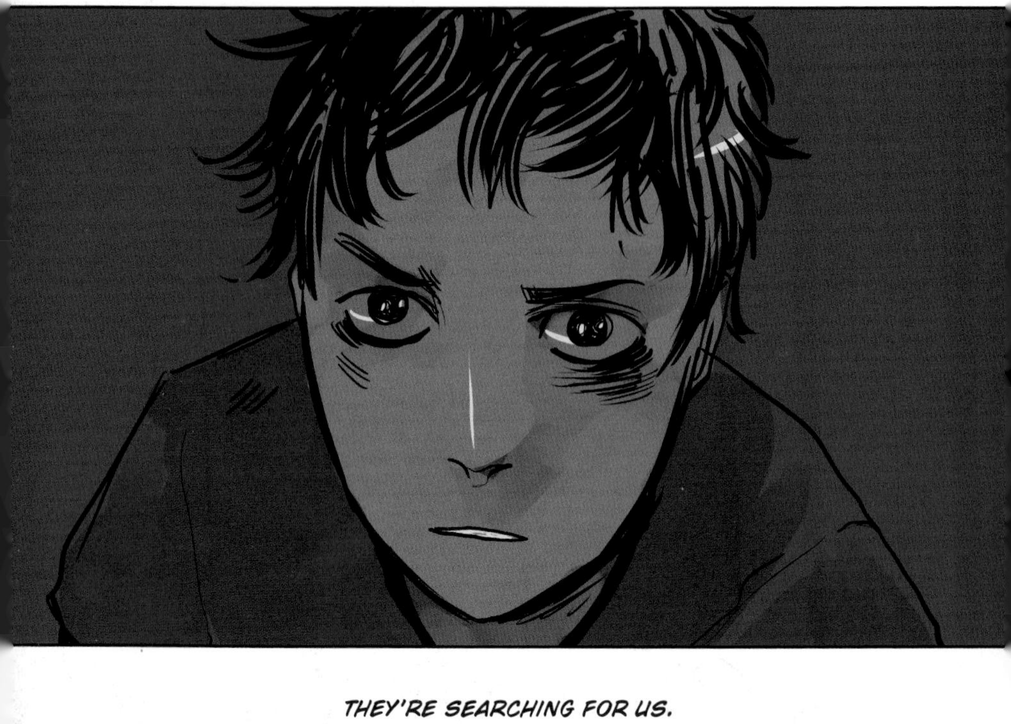

THEY'RE SEARCHING FOR US.